PATERNOSTER BIBLICAL MONOGRAPHS

PAUL AS APOSTLE TO THE GENTILES

'I like this book because, amidst the heat over current debates about the meaning of Romans, it raises questions very few people are asking—and then, in answering them, competently engages with the most important secondary literature as well. This is an important book, simply written, despite the complexity of the issues, and deserves a wide reading.'

D. A. Carson

Further comments on
Paul as Apostle to the Gentiles

'A very well written work containing a sound argument. ... This study, lucidly written, is the fruit of careful and insightful research, and will illumine for its readers what Bornkamm justly called Paul's Last Will and Testament.'
George R. Beasley-Murray

'Dr Chae's exegesis is characterised by enthusiasm, vigour and commonsense. Not everybody will agree with his conclusions or sometimes even with the process of arriving at them. However, his sober and engaging argumentation will not fail to command the respect even of those who disagree. One particular strength of this book is that in the face of so much misguided exegesis of Paul today inspired by the tragedy of the Holocaust, Dr Chae boldly and quite rightly shows that the interpretation of Paul – and of the NT in general – cannot be conditioned by the horrors of that untoward event.'
Chrys C. Caragounis

'A very well informed and argued exposition of an important dimension of Paul's letter to the Romans, where in the past the balance Paul sought for has been often misapprehended.'
James D.G. Dunn

'The book of Dr. Chae is very interesting not only because of its high scholarly quality and his deep understanding of Paul's mission and theology but also because of its insights in the foundation of Pauline mission through Old Testament texts..... This thoroughly biblical study written by a Christian of the "Two-Thirds World" has great importance for a modern missionary argumentation.'
Martin Hengel

Daniel Chae's 'treatment of Paul in his apostolic ministry is fresh and creative, and it also makes a distinctive contribution to our understanding of Paul's premier epistle, that to the Romans. An Asian contribution to Paul is an added bonus'.
Ralph P. Martin

PATERNOSTER BIBLICAL MONOGRAPHS

PAUL AS APOSTLE TO THE GENTILES

His Apostolic Self-Awareness and its Influence
on the Soteriological Argument in Romans

Daniel Jong-Sang Chae
(최 종 상)

Copyright © Daniel Jong-Sang Chae 1997

Published by Paternoster

Paternoster is an imprint of Authentic Media,
PO Box 6326, Bletchley, Milton Keynes, MK1 9GG

The right of Daniel J.-S. Chae to be identified as the Author of
this Work has been asserted by him in accordance with the
Copyright, Designs and Patents Act 1988.

*All rights reserved. No part of this publication may be
reproduced, stored in a retrieval system, or transmitted in any form
or by any means, electronic, mechanical, photocopying, recording or
otherwise, without the prior permission of the publisher or a license
permitting restricted copying. In the U.K. such licenses are issued by
the Copyright Licensing Agency,
Barnard's Inn, 86 Fetter Lane, London, EC4A 1EN*

British Library Cataloguing in Publication Data

A catalogue record for this book is available from the British Library.

ISBN-13: 978-0-85364-829-1

Scripture quotations (unless otherwise noted)
are taken from the HOLY BIBLE,
NEW INTERNATIONAL VERSION.
Copyright © 1973, 1978, 1984, by International Bible Society. Used
by permission of Hodder & Stoughton Limited.
All rights reserved.

'NIV' is a registered trademark of International Bible Society.
UK trademark number 1448790

Typeset by Daniel Chae, with the assistance of D.H. Shin,
using *Microsoft Word* 7.0 software.

Printed and bound by Lightning Source

To

Our Supporting Churches

and

Prayer Partners

PATERNOSTER BIBLICAL MONOGRAPHS

Series Preface

One of the major objectives of Paternoster is to serve biblical scholarship by providing a channel for the publication of theses and other monographs of high quality at affordable prices. Paternoster stands within the broad evangelical tradition of Christianity. Our authors would describe themselves as Christians who recognise the authority of the Bible, maintain the centrality of the gospel message and assent to the classical credal statements of Christian belief. There is diversity within this constituency; advances in scholarship are possible only if there is freedom for frank debate on controversial issues and for the publication of new and sometimes provocative proposals. What is offered in this series is the best of writing by committed Christians who are concerned to develop well-founded biblical scholarship in a spirit of loyalty to the historic faith.

Series Editors

I. Howard Marshall, Honorary Research Professor of New Testament, University of Aberdeen, Scotland, UK

Richard J. Bauckham, Professor of New Testament Studies and Bishop Wardlaw Professor, University of St Andrews, Scotland, UK

Craig Blomberg, Distinguished Professor of New Testament, Denver Seminary, Colorado, USA

Robert P. Gordon, Regius Professor of Hebrew, University of Cambridge, UK

Tremper Longman III, Robert H. Gundry Professor and Chair of the Department of Biblical Studies, Westmont College, Santa Barbara, California, USA

Contents

Preface xiii

INTRODUCTION 1
  1. THE PROBLEM 1
  2. TOWARDS AN ADEQUATE INTERPRETATION 13
  3. THE OCCASION AND THE PURPOSE OF ROMANS 14

Chapter 1
ROMANS 15:14-21: AN INTERPRETATIVE KEY FOR THE LETTER? 18

  1. ROMANS, WRITTEN UNDER PAUL'S APOSTOLIC SELF-AWARENESS: 15:14-21 21

    A. Romans as a Bold Letter: 15:14-15a 21
    B. The Basis of Paul's Boldness: 15:15b-21 25
      (a) Paul's Self-Awareness of his Role: 15:15b-16 26
      (b) The Fruit of Paul's Apostolic Ministry: 15:17-20 28
      (c) Paul's Evangelistic Principle Based on OT Prophecy: 15:21 30
    C. The Content of Paul's Boldness 32
      (a) 'Isaiah Very Boldly Says,': 10:20-21 33
      (b) 'I am not Ashamed of the Gospel.': 1:16-17 35
    D. Summary 37

  2. ROMANS SPRINGS FROM PAUL'S APOSTOLIC SELF-AWARENESS: 1:1-15 38

    A. Paul's Self-Introduction concerning his Apostleship to the Gentiles: 1:1-7 39
    B. Paul's Apostolic Obligation to the Gentiles: 1:8-15 44

3. THE EQUAL INCLUSION OF GENTILES IN GOD'S SALVATION:
   1:16-17 46

   A. ''Ιουδαίῳ ... πρῶτον': the Priority of Jews? 46
   B. ''Ιουδαίῳ τε πρῶτον καὶ ῞Ελληνι': the Inclusion of
      the Gentiles. 49

4. CHRIST'S SERVICE FOR BOTH JEWS AND GENTILES: 15:8-9A 51

   A. 15:8-9a within the Context 52
   B. The Syntax of 15:8-9a 53

5. THE OT PREDICTIONS CONCERNING THE GENTILES:
   15:9B-12 58

   A. Rom 15:9b (=LXX Ps 17:50=LXX 2 Kgdms 22:50) 59
   B. Rom 15:10 (=LXX Deut 32:43) 61
   C. Rom 15:11 (=LXX Ps 116:1) 62
   D. Rom 15:12 (=LXX Isa 11:10) 64
   E. Conclusion 66

6. CONCLUSION 68

Chapter 2
THE EQUALITY OF JEW AND GENTILE IN SINFULNESS:
1:18-3:20 72

1. AN ACCUSATION OF HUMAN SINFULNESS REFLECTING
   ISRAEL'S HISTORY: 1:18-32 73

   A. Is Jewish Idolatry Accused on the Basis of the Genesis
      Narratives? 75
   B. Is the Charge of Sexual Immorality Levelled at the
      Gentiles Alone? 83
   C. Should not Jews be Condemned More for their Refusal
      to Retain the Knowledge of God? 86
   D. Did God Give Israel over to Sinfulness? 89
   E. Conclusion 92

2. A More Direct Indictment of Jewish Complacency:
    2:1-29..94

    A. The διό of 2:1 and its Implication for the 'Argument'
       of 1:18-2:5..95
    B. The Argument Concerning Divine Impartiality: but in
       Favour of Gentiles?: 2:6-11...103
    C. Critical Arguments about Jews and Affirmative
       Statements about Gentiles: 2:12-29......................................109
       *(a) An Affirmative Statement—'Gentiles Do the Law':
       2:12-16*..110
       *(b) A Critical Argument—'Jews Break the Law':
       2:17-24*..115
       *(c) The Physical Circumcision of the Jews and the
       Spiritual Circumcision of the Gentiles: 2:25-29*.................123
       (d) Summary..127

3. A Further Scriptural Argument against Jewish
   Complacency: 3:1-20 129

   A. Scripture Affirms God's Judgement upon Unbelieving
      Jews as Legitimate: 3:1-8...130
   B. Jewish Depravity as the Focus of Paul's Argument in
      3:1-20..133
   C. Scripture Affirms Jewish Depravity as Equal to Gentile
      Sinfulness: 3:9-18..141
   D. Summary..149

4. Conclusion.. 150

Chapter 3
THE EQUALITY OF JEW AND GENTILE IN JUSTIFICATION:
3:21-4:25..153

1. The Equality in Justification by Faith: 3:21-26.................156

   A. The Righteousness of God apart from the Law......................157
   B. Justification by God's Grace and by Human Faith in
      Christ..159

2. JEWISH BOASTING IS EXCLUDED: 3:27-4:25 164
   A. Human Boasting or Jewish Boasting? 164
   B. The Jewish Boasting in the Law 169
   C. The Jewish Boasting in God 171
   D. The Jewish Boasting in Abraham 179
3. ABRAHAM THE FATHER OF MANY NATIONS / GENTILES:
   4:1-25 181
   A. Abraham's Justification and the Blessing of 'the
      Ungodly': 4:1-8 183
   B. Abraham's Faith and his Fatherhood: 4:9-12 187
   C. The Promise and Abraham's Fatherhood of Many
      Nations / Gentiles: 4:13-25 195
4. CONCLUSIONS 202

Chapter 4
THE EQUALITY OF JEW AND GENTILE IN THE NEW STATUS:
5:1-8:39 206

Chapter 5
THE EQUALITY OF JEW AND GENTILE IN THE PLAN OF GOD:
9:1-11:36 215

1. THE CONNECTION BETWEEN ROMANS 1-8 AND 9-11 221

2. GOD'S FREEDOM IN HARDENING JEWS AND ELECTING
   GENTILES: 9:1-29 224
   A. The Jewish Privileges (Shared by Gentiles): 9:1-5 225
   B. God's Freedom of Election: 9:6-23 227
   C. God's Election and its Application to Jews and
      Gentiles: 9:24-29 234
   D. Summary 238

3. THE UNIVERSAL SALVIFIC PRINCIPLES AND ISRAEL'S
   UNBELIEF: 9:30-10:21 239
   A. Faith in Christ, the Means for Salvation: 9:30-10:13 241

B. The Missionary Principle and Israel's Unbelief:
  10:14-21 244
C. Summary 248

4. THE MESSIAH'S REJECTION: A REVERSAL OF PRIORITY IN
   MISSION: 11:1-36 250

   A. Israel's Hardening: 11:1-10 253
   B. God's Outworking of the Salvation for Gentiles and
      Jews: 11:11-16 259
      (a) Is Israel's Stumbling a Necessary Part in
          God's Plan? 260
      (b) Israel's Loss and the Gentiles' Riches 262
   C. An Admonition to Gentile Believers: 11:17-24 270
   D. The Mystery of the Interdependence and Equality
      of Jew and Gentile: 11:25-32 272
      (a) The Possible Gentile Arrogance and the Mystery 273
      (b) Paul's Restraint from Advocating the Jewish
          Primacy 276
      (c) Salvation by Faith in Christ, not by a *Sonderweg* ... 280
   E. Summary 282

5. CONCLUSION 285

CONCLUSIONS 289

Appendix
FURTHER NOTES ON PAUL'S APOSTOLIC SELF-AWARENESS AND HIS
'MY GOSPEL' 302

Abbreviations 308

Bibliography 312

Index of Passages 339

Index of Authors 360

Index of Subjects 367

Preface

I started my research to investigate the correlation between Paul's mission and his theology (especially, soteriology). Soon it has become apparent that this task was too broad to be dealt with in a PhD dissertation. Considering Romans 15:14-21 as a clear evidence for a presupposition that Paul's theology has been influenced by his self-awareness of being apostle to the Gentiles, I was content to confine the scope of my work to Romans alone. I have proposed that this is the passage in which Paul himself indicates why and how he has written the letter, and so with which we can enter into its meaning.

This research was a part of our on-going service for mission. My wife and I had privilege to preach the gospel around the world with the members of M/V Logos (1979-84) and M/V Doulos (1987-88), the missionary ships of Operation Mobilisation. The perspective gained from our missionary experience has helped me understand better Paul the missionary theologian and this letter.

Apart from some revisions, this book contains the investigation undertaken at London Bible College (LBC), and awarded a PhD degree by Brunel University in June, 1995. I would like to thank many of those who have helped me for this research and publication. My most sincere thanks are due to my supervisor, Dr Max M. B. Turner, now Vice Principal of LBC, for his careful guidance and unfailing support. I would also like to thank my second supervisor, Prof Ralph P. Martin for his constructive criticisms and consistent encouragement and interest in my work, and also for introducing me to Prof Martin Hengel. I am indebted to Prof Hengel and Prof Otto Betz of Tübingen University for their sincere interest in my subject and for their generous time in discussion. Their kindness helped my family to spend six very useful months in Tübingen.

My thanks are also due to Dr F. Peter Cotterell, the then Principal of LBC, for his guidance and encouragement as my supervisor at the early stage of my research on Paul. I am also very grateful to my examiners, Prof George R. Beasley-Murray and Dr Stephen Motyer for their valuable comments and criticism. I am very appreciative of Dr Chrys C. Caragounis of Lund University, Sweden, not only for his stimulating lectures on Romans during my undergraduate course at LBC, and for his 'tutorial' during our stay in Tübingen (he came there too!), but also for his comments and corrections which were very helpful in revising this work for publication.

I am grateful to Prof I. Howard Marshall for his ready acceptance of this work as a *Paternoster Biblical and Theological Monograph*. My appreciation also goes the editorial team of the Paternoster Press, and especially to Mr Jeremy Mudditt who has overseen the publication with efficiency and kindness.

I wish to acknowledge with gratitude the support of my fellow Koreans. I am grateful to both Dr David Tae-Woong Lee, Director of Global Missionary Fellowship, and its Board members for granting me study leave to make this research possible. I owe a considerable debt of gratitude to our supporting churches and prayer partners for their financial and prayer support. So it is my joyful duty to dedicate this book to them. Among them, I am especially indebted to the Revd Jung-Gil Hong and the Revd Han-Heum Ok for their constant love and care. Special thanks are also due to the Torch Scholarship Fund, Seoul, who generously supported me for four years.

I am thankful to Mr Dae-Hyun Shin for his willing assistance to prepare camera-ready copy of this book. My deepest appreciation is of course due to my wife, Helen, for her enormous support and willing sacrifice, and I have duly dedicated the thesis version of this book to her. I must also thank our lovely girls, Juhae, Dah-Eun and Eunjee for their patience and love.

Soli Deo gloria

September, 1996　　　　　　　　　　　　　　　　　　Daniel J-S Chae

Introduction

1. The Problem

Paul is (perhaps) best known to us as 'apostle to the Gentiles' (11:13; 15:16; Gal 2:7-9; cf. Col 1:25-27; Eph 3:1-13). Although Paul never calls himself 'the sole apostle to the Gentiles',[1] he is everywhere conscious of fulfilling that role.[2] He has preached the gospel to Jews and Gentiles (15:19; 1 Cor 9:19-23), but he realises keenly that he is an apostle to the *Gentiles*, called specifically to work among them (1:5; 11:13; 15:16-21; Gal 1:16; 2:8-9; cf. Acts 9:15; 26:16-20; 1 Tim 2:7). Since the Christophany near Damascus was such a personal call-experience,[3] he could not provide objective evidence for his apostleship. His own hard work (15:19-21; 1 Cor 15:10; 2 Cor 11:23), its fruits (1 Cor 9:2) and even other apostles' 'approval' (cf. Gal 2:7-9) were not enough to secure his apostolic recognition in some Christian circles.[4]

Thus Paul insistently claims the title for himself, knowing that 'he has been appointed by God to fill the key position in the last

---

[1] Dunn, *Romans* 1, 16; de Lacey, 'Gentiles', 337; Beardslee, *Human Achievement*, 92. Cf. Meyer, *Romans* 1, 51.

[2] Cf. Best, 'Revelation', 19-20, who argues that Paul is the only apostle to the Gentiles 'in the full sense', with which phrase Best means Paul's capacity to be equal with Peter as an apostle.

[3] Kim, *Origin*, 56-66, is certainly right to assert that Paul was called to be an apostle at the time of the Christophany on the way to Damascus. Cf. also Dunn, 'Light', 259.

[4] See Best, 'Paul's Apostolic Authority', 3-25.

great drama of salvation'.[5] Paul defends his *apostleship* in the Corinthian letters,[6] but it is his *Gentile* apostleship that he stresses in Galatians and Romans. If this is so, then an important question must be raised: if Paul is so conscious of having been chosen by God to be apostle to the Gentiles, how did that self-awareness relate to his theology? Our particular concern in the present study is to show how that consciousness has influenced the content and the structure of his soteriological argument in his letter to the Romans. We will emphasise that the subject matter of Paul's soteriological argument is the equality of Jew and Gentile as we investigate the way Paul structures his argument, and we will propose that Paul's self-awareness of being apostle to the *Gentiles* functions as the controlling factor for the shape of his argument. We now turn to indicate the general direction of our investigation and the need of our present study within the current state of research.[7]

In order to determine the subject matter, scholars tend usually to designate a unit as a central theme for the letter, either Romans 1-4, or 5-8, or 9-11, or 12-16,[8] and use their choice of the central theme as the interpretative key for the entire letter.[9] Especially since the Reformation, Romans has largely been seen as expounding the righteousness of God or justification by faith,[10] but

---

5   Munck, *Paul*, 43, 49. See Sandnes, *Paul, passim*, for Paul's self-awareness of being a special prophet in the last days.

6   See Barnett, 'Apostle', 49-50.

7   Due to the limit of the space, we are not able to examine the history of the interpretation of Romans, but content ourselves with referring to some previous works on this topic: Godsey, 'Interpretation', 3-16; Jewett, 'Impulses', 17-31; Deidun, 'Romans', 601-604.

8   This division is adopted by, e.g. Cranfield, *Romans* 1, 28-29; Fitzmyer, *Romans*, viii-xii; Moo, *Romans 1-8*, 29-31. But Dunn, *Romans* 1, vii-xi; idem, 'Romans:Analysis', 2842-2843, divides the sections into Rom 1-5; 6-8; 9-11; 12-16, whilst Stuhlmacher, *Romans*, vii, does as Rom 1-8; 9-11; 12-16.

9   Käsemann, *Perspectives*, 76, asserts 'justification by faith' as expounded in Rom 1-4 as the central theme; also Seifrid, *Justification, passim*, especially 255-270. For Schweitzer, *Mysticism*, 224-225, Rom 5-8 is the central unit. For Baur, *Paul* 1, 315, and Stendahl, *Paul, passim*, Rom 9-11 is the centre and climax. For Minear, *Obedience*, 7-12, and Watson, *Paul*, 88-105, the situation described in Rom 14-16 is the interpretative key for the entire letter. See also below pp. 18-19 n.3.

10   A more recent advocate of this view is Kim, *Origin*, 357:

this position has been vigorously opposed by Stendahl (in our view, to a large extent correctly).[11] However, many post-Holocaust interpreters, including Stendahl himself, find Romans 9-11 to be the centre, and claim that Romans was written to prevent Christianity from turning into an anti-Jewish movement.[12] According to them the fundamental theological principle of Romans 9-11 is an affirmative exposition of God's faithfulness to his promises to Israel despite her failure to respond to the gospel. Since Romans 9-11 is the climax of the letter, they contend, the entire letter must be read from this perspective.[13] They assert that Paul's 'entire mission to the Gentiles is *only a roundabout way of saving all Israel*';[14] thus he establishes the priority of the *Jews* in Romans,[15] because he perceived himself to be the 'apostle to the Gentiles *for Israel's sake*'.[16]

However, we question this prevailing view, because it does not take adequate notice of one crucial point: Paul constantly makes affirmative statements about and on behalf of the Gentiles, and, conversely, makes critical statements in most cases concerning the Jews throughout Romans 1-11, *including* 9-11 (as we shall

---

In Gal 2-3; Rom 3-4; 9-10 Paul's most important concern is not to argue for the inclusion of the Gentiles, but to expound the gospel in Jesus Christ by grace and through faith; only as a consequence of this gospel does Paul refer to the salvation of the Gentiles on the same basis as that of the Jews and to the problem of the Jews' refusal to avail themselves of this salvation.

Our study will attempt to demonstrate that the case is quite the reverse: in Romans (and similarly in Galatians) Paul's most important concern is to argue for the equal inclusion of the Gentiles; mainly in the course of establishing this argument does Paul refer to the justification by faith apart from the law. Cf. for an opposite view, see Bornkamm, *Paul*, 116. For further interaction with Kim, see our Appendix in pp. 302-307.

11 Stendahl, *Paul*, 2, 26-27, 129-133. See *infra* pp. 153-156.
12 E.g. Wiefel, 'Jewish Community', 100f; Wright, *Messiah*, 232.
13 Notably, e.g. Noack, 'Current', 164.
14 Lapide, in Lapide and Stuhlmacher, *Paul*, 44, with added emphasis.
15 E.g. Noack, 'Current', 163-164: together with other materials in Gal and Phil, Rom 9-11 serves 'one definite purpose, namely that of the priority of the Jews and the demand of Jerusalem on Paul' (p. 164).
16 Stuhlmacher, in Lapide and Stuhlmacher, *Paul*, 26 (emphasis added); so similarly, Sinclair, *Jesus*, 40: 'Despite the fact that he opens the letter by identifying himself as an apostle to all nations (1:5), he repeatedly suggests that his first and foremost goal is to help the Jews.'

see). It is true that, more often in Romans than in any other of his letters, Paul speaks of Jewish privileges (1:16; 3:1-2; 9:4-5; 11:26-29; cf. Gal 3:13; Phil 3:4b-8; 1 Thess 2:15) and of Jesus' special relationship to the Jews (1:2-3; 9:5; 15:8). It is essential, however, to note that Paul hardly expounds them to establish Jewish primacy; rather, what he *argues for*, as we will show, is the equality of Jew and Gentile.[17] An investigation of this aspect will constitute the heart of our present study, but, for the present, a brief survey of the character of Paul's argument in Romans will be made to justify our questioning of the above-mentioned pro-Jewish interpretation of Paul and Romans.

Paul's assertion of the theological axiom of divine impartiality (2:6-11) is intended to indicate that (self-righteous) Jews are also subject to God's wrath and judgement, whilst (believing) Gentiles are also included in God's favour of salvation, glory, honour and peace. He declares that whilst 'Gentiles ... do by nature the things required by the law' (2:14), Jews 'dishonour God by breaking the law' (2:23). Paul excludes Jewish boasting in the law, their exclusive relationship with God and having Abraham as their forefather (2:17, 23; 3:27; 4:1-25). He argues that the God of the Jews is the God of the Gentiles too (3:29-30). A surprising retelling of the Abraham story is rhetorically presented in order to maximise Paul's argument that Abraham is also the father of many nations (=Gentiles). Both Jews and Gentiles are equal in Adam and in Christ. Israel's unbelief (9:27-29, 31-33; 10:18-19, 21; 11:7-10, 20, 28a) and the Gentiles' belief (9:25-26, 30; 10:20; 11:11, 17, 19-20a, 22) are confirmed as a *fait accompli* in Romans 9-11. Paul establishes his argument with numerous OT quotations, especially in Romans 1-4 and 9-11. It is striking to note that when he cites OT passages concerning Jews, he chooses some of the most severely critical. On the other hand, he applies to *Gentiles* some of the most affirmative passages. What is more, he never uses the OT to accuse Gentiles, but rather to explain *Israel's* unbelief and also the Gentiles' faith and their inclusion in the true people of God. It is also surprising to note that when Paul makes some affirmative remarks about Jews (3:1-2; 9:3-5; 11:1, 26-32), he does not expound them as arguments, but simply mentions

---

17 See *infra* pp. 46-49; Chae, 'Paul's Apostolic Self-Awareness', 124-125.

them. Each of these observations awaits our careful substantiation in the following chapters.

Paul the Jew would have required much courage to present affirmative arguments for the Gentiles and arguments critical of the Jews. This is probably why he admits that he has written the letter rather boldly (15:15). We suggest that Paul's affirmative argument for the Gentiles is to affirm or even to defend the legitimacy of the salvation of the Gentiles by providing the theological basis for their inclusion in the true people of God. On the other hand, Paul's critical judgement of the Jews is to indict their complacency and unbelief. Of course, Paul's intent is not to put one ethnic group above another. But by employing this 'biassed' line of argument he intends to establish the equality of the Gentile with the Jew. This perception is supported by the numerous occurrences of the term πᾶς throughout Romans 1-11, and the more specific declaration, 'There is no difference [between Jew and Gentile]' (3:22; 10:12; cf. 1:16-17; 2:9-11; 3:9, 29-30; 4:16; 5:12-21; 10:11-13; 11:30-32; 15:7-12; Gal 3:28; Col 3:11).

We will attempt to demonstrate, therefore, that *Paul's subject matter in Romans is the equality of Jew and Gentile*. Stendahl has contended that Paul's primary concern is to explain 'the relation between Jews and Gentiles',[18] but he does not specify the *nature* of that relation. He does not say, and even does not seem to mean, their *equality*. In his *Paul, the Law, and Jewish People* (1983), however, E.P. Sanders repeatedly stresses the theme of the *equality of Jew and Gentile*, which he had asserted (briefly) in his former work, *Paul and Palestinian Judaism* (1977).[19] According to Sanders, what is stressed in the thematic statement in 1:16 is its second part: 'to all who believe, to the Jew first and also equally to the Greek', and Paul's arguments in Romans 1-4 are presented 'in favor of the equality of Gentiles and against the assumption of Jewish privilege'.[20] He is also correct to emphasise that Paul's argument is that 'salvation for both Jews and Gentiles must be based on the same ground', and that Paul's main device for achieving this equality is to stress 'the equal opportunity of access

---

18 Stendahl, *Paul*, 1, 3; so also Sinclair, *Jesus*, 25.
19 Sanders, *Palestinian Judaism*, 488-491, 499.
20 Sanders, *Jewish People*, 30, 33. Earlier, in *Palestinian Judaism*, 490-491.

on the part of the Gentiles'.[21] 'Paul is, in effect, arguing for the equality of the Gentile.'[22] Sanders thus repeatedly stresses that Paul argues for the equality of Jew and Gentile.[23]

However, Sanders does not perceive this theme of equality outside Romans 1-4, except in the repeated πᾶς in 10:9-13 and in the especially clear declaration, 'There is no difference between Jew and Gentile' (10:12).[24] He simply highlights some obvious statements (1:16; 2:11; 3:9, 22; 4:16; 10:9-13), but unfortunately he does not explain *how* Paul establishes this fundamental equality as an *argument*. Furthermore, he does not relate the emphasis on their equality with Paul's self-awareness of being apostle to the *Gentiles*.[25] Sanders's emphasis on the equality of Jew and Gentile thus still awaits a recasting and an adequate substantiation.[26] We shall therefore attempt to show not only that Paul's insistence on the equality of Jew and Gentile is evident throughout the letter (including Romans 9-11), but also, and more importantly, the way he structures the entire argument to establish this theme. For the last fifty years or so, the majority of post-Holocaust NT scholars have asserted that Paul's overriding concern in Romans was to affirm the primacy of the Jews. Our investigation, however, will expose the inappropriateness of this prevailing view today. What Paul argues for is neither anti-semitism nor Jewish primacy but the *equality* of Jew and Gentile.

We will further argue that Paul affirms the equality of Jew and Gentile *for the sake of the Gentiles*, because he presents his argument *as* apostle to the *Gentiles*. We find at least three passages in Romans where Paul indicates an undeniable connection between what he has written here and his self-awareness of being

---

21 Sanders, *Jewish People*, 123, 131.
22 Sanders, *Palestinian Judaism*, 488-489.
23 Sanders, *Jewish People*, 5, 30, 33, 40-41, 47, 123, 131, 147, 153, 208.
24 Sanders, *Jewish People*, 40-41.
25 Sanders, *Jewish People*, 153: 'a main theme [in Romans 1-4?] [is] that Jew and Gentile are on equal footing. .... It may be that this reflects a conscious or unconscious concern with the situation of the Gentiles which antedates his conviction that his mission was to bring them into the eschatological people of God.' He then adds, 'This ... is *entirely speculative*' (emphasis added). Sanders is not certain, then, what made Paul affirm equality in the way it is expressed in Romans.
26 Kaylor, *Covenant Community*, 19, 61, may be considered a notable exception, but he does not go much further than what Sanders has already said.

apostle to the Gentiles. The most explicit one is 15:15-16: 'I have written rather boldly on some points on the basis of the grace (διὰ τὴν χάριν; i.e. apostleship) God gave me *in order to be* a (true) minister of Christ Jesus to the Gentiles (εἰς τὸ εἶναί με λειτουργὸν Χριστοῦ Ἰησοῦ εἰς τὰ ἔθνη) with the priestly duty of proclaiming the gospel of God, so that Gentiles might become an offering acceptable to God, sanctified by the Holy Spirit' (15:15-16).[27] A similar indication of apostolic status and obligation has already been made in 1:1-15.[28] Paul also clearly says that he writes the section 11:13-32[29] specifically to Gentile believers as their apostle. Since he expresses his apostolic self-awareness in the introductory remarks (1:1-15), in the middle part (11:13-32; 12:3) and in the concluding section (15:14-33), one may legitimately assume that his argument in the entire letter is influenced by it. Thus the aim of this study is to investigate the hypothesis that Paul's self-awareness of being apostle to the Gentiles has controlled both the content and the structure of his inclusive soteriological argument in Romans,[30] which affirms the equality of Jew and Gentile.

The study of the place of Paul's apostolic self-awareness in his theology remains substantially underdeveloped. Its importance was first asserted by A. Deissmann, and was formulated by A. Schweitzer in modern times,[31] but it is O. Cullmann's 1936 arti-

---

27 My translation. See *infra* pp. 21-28.
28 Jervis, *Purpose*, 75-78, 158.
29 This passage forms a unit of address to Gentile believers with the pronouns 'ὑμεῖς' and 'σύ'.
30 What Paul mainly *argues* in the presentation of his soteriology in Romans is *inclusive* soteriology. He argues that *Gentiles are included* in the salvific blessing of God promised to Israel on equal terms, i.e. by faith apart from the law. See Tidball, 'Social Setting', 890. This inclusive soteriology deals with 'justification', 'faith', 'law', 'Jews' and 'Gentiles'. Paul does not really argue concerning other soteriological themes, e.g. the cross, atonement or resurrection (cf. 1 Cor 15:3-8), but simply states them (3:21-26; 4:24-25; 5:8; 6:4; 8:34). The primary focus of our study is, therefore, on the former subjects.
31 Deissmann, *Paul*, 231-233. For Schweitzer, *Mysticism*, 177-187, Paul had a theological conviction that the salvation of the full number of the Gentiles anticipated the Parousia; being fully aware that he was specifically appointed for this task of bringing in the Gentiles, Paul carried out the most extensive missionary work; his insistence on the law-free gospel was applied

cle that has been more influential.³² Although Cullmann's assertion that ὁ κατέχων in 2 Thess 2:6-7 is the apostle himself, has made his article less acceptable, he pointed out that Paul thought that the arrival of the parousia depended on his own missionary endeavours. So much so has Paul's apostolic self-awareness taken the central place in his ministry and theology.³³ J. Munck has developed Cullmann's insight and expressed it more precisely, especially in connection with Romans:

> It is therefore very important that in the chapter in which he reveals to the Romans the mystery of the divine plan, he reminds them of his own service as apostle to the Gentiles (Rom. 11.13). .... Paul's apostolic consciousness in its eschatological form stands in the centre of his personality and theology in quite a different way from that usually supposed.³⁴

Munck's fundamental insight, however, has been overshadowed by the subsequent intensive interaction of scholars with his criticism of the Tübingen school. The assumptions of Schweitzer, Cullmann and Munck are based on 'a uniformly future orientation for the eschatological dimension of Paul's missionary understanding', and such an eschatological perception has made their insight concerning Paul's self-awareness less convincing.³⁵ Perhaps this is why Munck's claim did not generate significant studies on the role of Paul's self-understanding in his theology.

Writing in 1991, K.O. Sandnes observed that no-one had undertaken a monographic study on Paul's apostolic self-consciousness.³⁶ His own monograph itself is an investigation of Paul's self-understanding as a prophet. However, as Sandnes admits, 'Paul never calls himself a prophet', and, if Paul claims to be a prophet, he does so only indirectly (Acts 21; 1 Cor 14:6).³⁷ If

---

only to the Gentiles so as the Gentile converts to be counted into that 'full number' as Gentiles; see also his *Paul*, 246-247.

32 Cullmann, 'Le caractère eschatologique', 210-245; cf. the German translation of this article, 'Der eschatologische Charakter', 305-336.

33 So maintains Cullmann, *Salvation*, 120, 250.

34 Munck, *Paul*, 41-42.

35 Bowers 'Mission', 617; see pp. 616-618, for an excellent treatment on this topic.

36 Sandnes, *Paul*, 4.

37 Sandnes, *Paul*, 2-4, 243; Sandnes's thesis: 'Paul really did conceive of his apostolate and his commission to preach the gospel to the Gentiles in prophetic terms' (p. 240). There are certainly some associations between the

Sandnes' monograph on Paul's *indirect* self-affirmation claims to be the first one of that kind, how surprising that there is none, to our knowledge, on his *explicit* claim to being *apostle to the Gentiles*! Some scholars have duly stressed Paul's call to the apostolate or his self-awareness of it.[38] However, the question as to what extent or in what way his apostolic self-awareness is reflected in his theology, and in particular his soteriology, still requires a fresh and substantial investigation. Due to the complexity of this question, however, we will confine ourselves to investigating the argument on the basis of one (albeit vitally important) part of the total evidence (i.e. Romans), and will propose that Paul's apostolic self-awareness has influenced him to affirm the equality of Jew and Gentile in his soteriological argument in Romans. Our primary focus will also be how his self-understanding affects the *rhetoric* of his argument – not the *fact* of his Gentile mission.

Broadly speaking, our study also concerns the correlation between Paul's Gentile mission and his theology. That Paul's mission is fundamental for understanding the apostle and his theology is one of the very few points upon which Pauline scholars have reached a consensus in recent years.[39] This correlation had already been contended by, for example, G. B. Stevens (1892) and M. Kähler (1908).[40] It was J. Munck (1954), however, who emphasised it

---

terms ἀπόστολος and προφήτης in the LXX and the NT, and the linguistic correspondence between Paul's call to apostleship (Gal 1:15-16a) and the call of the OT prophets. Sandnes notes that earlier Hall, *Paul*, 157-202, devoted a quarter of his monograph to examining Paul as a Christian prophet with special reference to Paul's interpretation of the OT in Rom 9-11.

38 E.g. Munck, *Paul*, 11-68; Stendahl, *Paul*, 7-23; Kim, *Origin*, 56-66; Sandnes, *Paul*, 48-76; Becker, *Paul*, 57-81. See particularly Kennedy, 'St. Paul's Apostolic Consciousness', 8-13; Fridrichen, 'Apostle', 1-23; Holtz, 'Selbstverständnis', 321-330. Especially on Paul's consciousness of his role in God's plan with particular emphasis on the Gentiles, see Caragounis, *Mysterion*, 142-143.

39 The editors of the *Dictionary of Paul and his Letters* (1993) state in the Preface that there has been 'no resolving of the matter and very few points of consensus' since W.D. Davies' remark made in 1948: '"It has been a matter of controversy among New Testament scholars how best we should interpret the theology of Paul"'.

40 Stevens, *Pauline Theology*, 25:
   The mission and theology of Paul are involved in each other, and cannot be separated. His theology— his "gospel" (Rom 2:16;

most by asserting, '[A]ll Paul's work as a thinker arises from his missionary activity, and its object is missionary work. .... His theology arises from his work as apostle and directly serves that work.'[41] Munck's insight has greatly influenced both K. Stendahl and E. P. Sanders, who have set a new direction in Pauline studies, especially concerning the correlation of Paul's mission and his theology. In his penetrating article, 'The Apostle Paul and the Introspective Conscience of the West' (1963), Stendahl asserted that Paul's view of the law was the result of 'his grappling with the question about the place of the Gentiles in the Church and in the plan of God, with the problem Jews/Gentiles or Jewish Christians/Gentile Christians'.[42] Later he reasserts that Paul's doctrine of justification by faith has grown 'as he defends the right of Gentile converts to be full members of the people of God'.[43]

Sanders expresses the connection even more precisely and convincingly. He suggests that there are two fundamental convictions which shaped Paul's theological thinking and apostolic career, namely,

(1) that Jesus Christ is Lord, that in him God has provided for the salvation of all who believe ...., and that he will soon return to bring all things to an end; (2) that he, Paul, was called to be the apostle to the Gentiles. .... It is on the basis of these two *convictions* that we can express Paul's theology .....[44]

On the second conviction, he explains,

16:25; Gal 1:6, *sq.*)— was simply an exposition and justification of those truths which were involved in the Messiahship of Jesus, and which it was his work to proclaim to the Gentile world. His epistles, in their original intention, were but a means of enlarging his work and influence as a preacher to the nations; they were written to assist and supplement his missionary labours.
For Kähler, *Schriften*, 190, mission is the mother of theology.
41   Munck, *Paul*, 67; cf. Barrett, 'Paulus', 3-4, 14.
42   Stendahl, 'Introspective Conscience', now reprinted in *Paul*, 84; cf. Henry, *New Directions*, 175-177. Earlier (in 1959) W. Manson, 'Notes', 64, made a very brief remark in passing: '[Romans] represents the mature product of years of earlier debate with Jews and Gentiles throughout the world'.
43   Stendahl, *Paul*, 130.
44   Sanders, *Palestinian Judaism*, 441-442. He notes that determining accurately the starting point and the centre of Paul's religious thought is one of the most difficult areas in Pauline studies (p. 433).

Christ saves Gentiles as well as Jews. This was not only a theological view, but it was bound up with Paul's most profound conviction about himself, a conviction on which he staked his career and his life: he was the apostle to the Gentiles. The salvation of the Gentiles is essential to Paul's preaching; and with it falls the law; for, as Paul says simply, Gentiles cannot live by the law (Gal. 2.14).[45]

What Sanders asserts then is that Paul's self-awareness of being apostle to the Gentiles was the controlling factor for his life and theology, and it led him to affirm the salvation of the *Gentiles*. However, Sanders does not develop this insight in his monograph, *Paul and Palestinian Judaism*, nor in his succeeding volume, *Paul, the Law, and Jewish People*, since his more immediate concern was Paul's attitude towards Judaism and the law,[46] a concern which has produced lively debate among NT scholars.

Thus the emphasis on the place of Paul's Gentile mission in his theology is nothing new.[47] Some have asserted this element with special reference to Romans.[48] No one doubts that Paul's Gentile

---

45 Sanders, *Palestinian Judaism*, 496. He continues:
Further, it was a matter of common Christian experience that the Spirit and faith come by hearing the gospel, not by obeying the law (Gal. 3.1-5). More important, they come *only* this way. *It is the Gentile question and the exclusivism of Paul's soteriology which dethrone the law* (pp. 496-497: his emphasis).

46 Sanders, *Jewish People*, ix, 207-210.

47 Cullmann, 'Eschatology and Missions', 50: 'In Pauline thought the missionary motive, ... , permeates the whole theology of the apostle, and is intimately connected with his sense of missionary vocation.' Others who emphasise this include W.G. Kümmel, *Theology*, 138-139:
Paul was *the* missionary of primitive Christianity who with a definite decision brought the gospel to non-Jews and drew the theological and practical inferences from this task. ... Paul was a theologian, but he was theologian as missionary, and therefore his theological thinking is to a large extent determined by the *discussion with his communities*....

Hengel, *Jesus*, 50-53, puts it more precisely:
In them [the epistles] Paul develops his theological ideas as a *missionary*; i.e. the *Sitz im Leben* of Pauline theology is the apostle's mission. .... Paul ... becomes the first Christian "theologian" because he is a missionary; that is, his theology is "mission theology" in the comprehensive sense.

48 Dahl, 'Missionary Theology' in *Studies*, 70-94: 'The theology of Romans is closely tied to the Pauline mission with its historical and eschatological

mission perspective, his practical experience among Gentiles and his self-awareness of his apostolic obligation, have all affected his theological thinking. It is how this is spelled out that will be the issue of contention here. We will show that Paul's consciousness of his call to the Gentile mission has affected the *content* and the *structure* of his soteriological argument in (especially) Romans 1-11; he affirms the equality of Jew and Gentile by drawing a critical picture of the Jews and by making affirmative arguments for the Gentiles. Paul constantly defends the legitimacy and the sufficiency of Gentile salvation apart from the law. But modern scholarly study has paid relatively meagre attention to this vital subject, as W.P. Bowers has observed recently (1993):

> .... with notable exceptions, the apprehension of Paul's mission within his theological reflection, as one of its integral and even generative features, can only be found at the margins of the scholarly discussion or in some underlying assumptions. This deficiency is yet to be addressed adequately even within contemporary Pauline research.[49]

Our engagement with these issues in the present study finds justification in just such a current state of research. Sanders' insight that Paul affirms the equality of Jew and Gentile still awaits substantiation of *how* Paul establishes it as an *argument*. The question as to what extent or in what way Paul's apostolic consciousness of Gentile mission is reflected in his theology, still requires a fresh investigation.

---

perspectives' (p. 88); and for the wider context of Paul and his theology: 'His theology and his missionary activity were inseparable from one another' (p. 70). Jewett, 'Ecumenical Theology', 598: 'the theology of Romans should be understood in the light of Paul's missional purpose.' Cf. Schrenk, *Studien*, 81ff: 'Der Römerbrief als Missionsdokument' as the title of a chapter.

49 Bowers, 'Mission', 613, 608. Bowers himself acutely stresses the need to understand Paul and his theology from his Gentile mission perspective:
> Yet given Paul's evident preoccupation with his vocational mission, we may rightly suppose that no adequate understanding of Pauline theology will be achieved until his perspective on mission has been integrated into the larger interpretation of his theology, showing the place and relationships of the Gentile mission within his theological reflection. Without such an achievement, we will not have an adequate understanding either of Paul's mission or of his theology (p. 613).

Introduction

2. Towards an Adequate Interpretation

We will attempt to address these issues by pursuing this research mainly on exegetical grounds. This will allow us to discern what the *text* says, and thus to yield ourselves presuppositionlessly to the perspective which the text itself may offer and to grasp Paul's argument as adequately as possible. We will, first, investigate 1:1-15 and 15:14-21, passages in which Paul indicates his reasons for and approach in writing this letter. Since the latter passage contains a clearer indication than the former, we will examine Romans 15 first. If we find thematic coherence between 15:14-21 and 1:1-15, we may assume that the entire letter is thematically coherent. We will show that the coherent theme is *Paul's consciousness of his apostleship to the Gentiles*. In order to test our case, we will examine whether this theme concerning 'Gentiles' also coheres more specifically with the thematic opening statement (1:16-17) and the thematic conclusion (15:7-13). We will discover that these four passages that contain the indication of the character of Romans are woven together with the key term 'ἔθνη'. Thus we will be allowed to interpret Romans from the Gentile mission perspective. This issue will be investigated in Chapter 1, mainly from these passages.

Secondly, Paul's extensive use of the OT in this letter is evidently characteristic. That the gospel which he expounds in Romans was promised in the OT is clearly indicated at the beginning and at the end of the letter, and also elsewhere (1:2; 3:21; 9:6a; 16:25-26). Thus we will adopt Paul's use of the OT as a crucial interpretative key for his argument in the letter. Since he modifies the texts and the contexts of the original to suit his own argument (as we will show),[50] we will compare the original texts/contexts

---

50 Schlatter, *Church*, 65; Hunter, *Paul*, 64; Ellis, *OT in Early Christianity*, 74, concludes, after a historical survey of research on the subject, that
> in recent decades the research has shown that, in part, the textual question is itself a hermeneutical question and that textual variations are sometimes deliberate alterations, a kind of implicit midrash adapting the text more clearly to its present application.

Gardiner, *Old and New Testaments*, 317-318 (as cited in Kaiser, *Uses*, 9-10), also contended in 1885 that,
> in all quotations which are used argumentatively, or to establish any fact or doctrine, it is obviously necessary that the passage in

and Paul's modifications in order to grasp his intent for appealing to and modifying these OT passages. C.D. Stanley's *Paul and the Language of Scripture* (1992) offers an excellent comparative study on the *textual* variations, but since it rules out a consideration of *contextual* modifications almost entirely, it hardly helps us understand Paul's intention in using these modified quotations for his argument.[51] We will pay careful attention to Paul's modifications of the text and the context (with more treatment on the latter, since Stanley covers the former).

Thirdly, we will also attempt to interpret the letter against its historical background. In order to grasp the author's intention and the readers'/listeners' response,[52] we will pay attention to the thinking and theological understanding of Paul's own day. We will thus examine apocryphal, pseudepigraphical and rabbinic literature whenever appropriate, so as to highlight the points of Paul's argument and his possible intention in departing from the traditional Judaism of his day. Of course, other 'authentic' Pauline letters (and other NT writings) will be referred to so as to understand Paul's language and theology in a wider context.[53]

3. The Occasion and the Purpose of Romans[54]

For the more immediate historical background, we will briefly consider the occasion and the purpose of the letter. An adequate

---

question should be fairly cited according to its intent and meaning,
in order that the argument drawn from it may be valid.

51 Stanley, *Language*, 359, maintains that textual modification is not made to support NT authors' arguments. Thus his study does not examine '"Paul the rhetor"' (p. 360 n. 50).

52 Most of the first recipients of this letter (i.e. the believers in Rome) were *listeners to* rather than *readers of* the letter. Throughout this study hereafter, however, we will designate them as '*readers*' for the sake of convenience, and for the reason that *we* interpret the letter as 'readers'.

53 We take Romans, 1 & 2 Corinthians, Galatians, Philippians, Colossians, 1 & 2 Thessalonians and Philemon to be authentic Pauline letters. Ephesians, 1 & 2 Timothy and Titus will be regarded as deutero-Pauline. Although we regard the Book of Acts as largely historical (following Marshall, Cremer, Thornton and Hengel), we will not use it as a source to interpret Paul.

54 The issues addressed here are dealt with in my article, 'Paul's Apostolic Self-Awareness and the Occasion and Purpose of Romans', in A. Billington, T. Lane and M. Turner (eds.), *Mission and Meaning: Essays Presented to Peter Cotterell* (Carlisle: Paternoster, 1995), 116-137.

understanding of the situations of the churches in Rome and in Jerusalem, and of Paul's own personal circumstances, will certainly help us comprehend Paul's argument better. It seems most probable that the occasion of the letter maximised Paul's self-awareness of being apostle to the Gentiles. He had planned many times to visit the Roman believers in order to strengthen them by imparting to them some teaching and instructions (1:8-13). He had always been conscious of his apostolic obligation to 'preach the gospel' to them (1:14-15). However, he has now made a critical decision to go to Jerusalem, not to Rome. So he writes a letter as a substitute for his personal visit, and with it (we argue) he wishes to accomplish what he wanted to do through his intended visit. His decision to go to Jerusalem also reflects his apostolic self-understanding. He does not go there merely to deliver the collection. Rather, he desires to use the occasion to explain the legitimacy of the salvation of the Gentiles to the believers in Jerusalem, and hopes to get the 'receipt' of their recognition of this legitimacy in response to that gift from the Gentiles. Realising that his missionary work everywhere has been devastated by judaisers, Paul attempts to influence the 'roots' in Jerusalem from which his opponents draw their support directly or indirectly (cf. Gal 2:1-12; Acts 15: 1-5; 21:20-26).

The present situation in Jerusalem seems more serious than that described in Gal 2:1-5.[55] At that time he went to Jerusalem not only in response to a revelation but also with a strong conviction of his apostleship to the Gentiles so as to defend 'the gospel that I [Paul] preach among the Gentiles' 'so that the truth of the gospel might remain with [them]' (Gal 2:2-5). He goes there yet again under an even greater apostolic consciousness of his obligation to defend and secure the legitimacy of the salvation of the Gentiles and the mission to them. Going to Jerusalem involves another risk. He could foresee the possibility of his long imprisonment or even martyrdom at the hands of unbelieving Jews (15:31a; cf. Acts 19:21; 20:22-25; 21:4-14). Yet the apostle is determined to go to Jerusalem. Therefore the letter is intended to serve as a

---

55 Despite his previous success on a similar occasion (cf. Gal 2:7-10; Acts 15:1-31) he now fears possible rejection and trouble from the believers and the unbelievers in Jerusalem (Rom 15:31).

permanent substitute for his desired visit because he feared he might not ever arrive at Rome.[56]

At the same time he is aware of the need to help the Roman church to solve the internal dispute between the 'strong' and the 'weak', and also to equip them against foreseeable trouble by (judaising) agitators (16:17-20), so that what happened in Galatia might not be repeated in Rome. Considering the seriousness of those internal and external problems, the slender possibility of his visit to Rome and the strategic importance of the Roman church in mission, the apostle puts all his own being and strength into this letter. The length and the theological depth are to be understood from this perspective. In other words, he is fully conscious of himself as apostle to the Gentiles whose obligation is not only to preach the gospel to them but also to equip them against and defend them from any attack which might undermine their legitimacy of salvation gained by believing in the death and the resurrection of Christ. What drives him to go to Jerusalem at the risk of his own life is his self-awareness of being the apostle to the Gentiles; so he goes there as the one who must defend the law-free gospel and get the 'receipt' of recognition for the sake of the Gentiles. With the same sense of apostolic obligation Paul desires to carry out his 'priestly duty' towards the Romans by means of writing them this letter. The content and the structure of Paul's argument (as we will show) expose the weakness of the prevailing post-Holocaust view that Paul writes Romans in order to correct an 'anti-semitism' among the Roman Gentile believers.[57] We will show rather that he writes it to secure the legitimacy of Gentile salvation by affirming the equality of Jew and Gentile.

This leads us to examine the texts of Romans. In Chapter 1 we will investigate 15:14-21 as the interpretative key to the meaning of the letter. The section 1:1-15 will then be examined so as to determine the extent of coherence between the introductory and the concluding sections, and to identify the nature of the theme in these important parts of the letter. The thematic introductory

---

56 *Pace* Seifrid, *Justification*, 190, 209, for asserting the letter to be a *temporary* substitute; Bornkamm, 'Last Will', 16-28, for clearly excluding the possibility of Paul's death in Jerusalem.

57 E.g. Wiefel, 'Jewish Community', 100-101; Lapide and Stuhlmacher, *Paul*, 25-30, 32, 44; similarly Munck, *Paul*, 42-49. Cf. Stendahl, *Paul*, 3, 132.

statement of 1:16-17 will be studied in the light of the two earlier passages, then it will be compared with the thematic conclusion in 15:7-13. We will show that both 1:1-15 and 15:14-21 highlight Paul's apostolic self-awareness especially in connection with the Gentiles, and that both 1:16-17 and 15:7-13 are coherent with the theme of the equality of Jew and Gentile. This Chapter will thus enable us to establish the grounds for viewing Paul's self-awareness of being apostle to the Gentiles as the controlling factor in his inclusive soteriological argument.

With the results from these preliminary investigations, Chapters 2-5 will examine the content of this argument as being the equality of Jew and Gentile, and how Paul shapes his argument to establish this equality. More specifically, Chapter 2 (on 1:18-3:20) will examine Paul's argument concerning the equality of Jew and Gentile in sinfulness (in which *Jewish* sinfulness is more stressed). Chapter 3 (on 3:21-4:25) will focus on the equality of Jew and Gentile in justification (in which *Gentile* justification is further affirmed). Since Romans 5-8 does not deal with Jew–Gentile issues directly, it will be less extensively treated in Chapter 4. We will note that in this section Paul explains the equal status of Jew and Gentile on the basis of what he has argued in Romans 1-4. The final Chapter will be on Romans 9-11, where the apostle argues for the equality of Jew and Gentile in the salvific plan of God. Although we do not examine Romans 12:1-15:7, we affirm that the practical exhortation given there is made on the basis of the theological foundations established in Romans 1-11 and on the basis of God's grace given to Paul in the form of his apostleship to the Gentiles (12:1-3; 15:15-16).

Chapter 1

Romans 15:14-21:
An Interpretative Key for the Letter?

It is often said that in order to gain a proper understanding of Romans it is vital to consider the primary subject matter for which Paul is actually arguing.[1] '*How* do we determine it?' is then a crucial issue. Even though one may interpret the whole letter in a critically sensitive and responsible manner, one must be careful to establish that the subject matter is really what Paul himself is arguing about. For a long time it has been considered that the theme of the 'righteousness of God' or 'justification by faith' is Paul's main point of argument in Romans. However, the facts that the term δικαιο- completely disappears after 10:10 (except 14:17), and that the theme is not mentioned in Paul's conclusion (15:7-21), and that the 'works' and the 'law' are often positively portrayed in Romans (cf. 2:6, 13; 3:31; 7:12, 14, 16), lead us to question with K. Stendahl whether it is actually Paul's main subject matter. Rather it seems employed to establish his more fundamental theme, which is, for Stendahl, the relation between Jew and Gentile.[2] Furthermore, some interpreters of Romans often designate certain passages or sections of the letter as their interpretative key.[3] Plausible though such suggestions

---

1 Wright, 'Romans', 187.
2 Stendahl, *Paul*, 1, 3, 4.
3 E.g. for Baur, *Paul* 1, 315, Rom 9-11 is the interpretative key to the whole letter, thus he interprets Rom 9-11 before he does Rom 1-8; Watson, *Paul*, 98, designates 14:1-15:13; Campbell, 'Romans III', 25-42, titles his

Romans 15:14-21: An Interpretative Key?

may be, there is still a danger of locating this key according to one's own presuppositions, or of misinterpreting the key. Typical is the recent case of F. Watson. He designates 14:1-15:13 to be such a key passage, and argues that since the Roman Christian community is so severely divided into two congregations, Paul encourages Roman Jewish believers to separate from the Jewish community in Rome and to join the Paulinists as one congregation in worship. Watson interprets the entire letter from this perspective,[4] and yet overlooks the fact that 'Paul's *theology* does not provide a rationale for separation but on the contrary seeks a resolution of the key to how Paul deals with the problem of division between Jew and Gentile in Rome'.[5]

We propose, therefore, to begin with locating a passage in which *Paul himself indicates why and how he has written the letter*, and through which we can enter into the meaning of the letter. We find the best possible indication in 15:14-21:

> But I have written very boldly to you on some points, so as to remind you again, because of the grace that was given me from God, to be a minister of Christ Jesus to the Gentiles, ministering as a priest the gospel of God, that *my* offering of the Gentiles might become acceptable, sanctified by the Holy Spirit (15:15-16; NASB).

Some scholars have deduced the purposes of the letter from 15:14-33.[6] But hardly anyone has paid adequate attention to 15:14-21[7] in order to investigate the possibility of it being the

---

article, 'Romans III as a Key to the Structure and Thought of the Letter'. Similarly, for Pauline theology in general, a major concern has long been the isolation of an interpretative key which would unlock the whole of his theology with coherence and explain the particular shape of that theology. While some have paid special attention to the background of Paul, such as Judaism or Hellenism, others have focused on the conversion-call experience as the explanatory key to Paul's theology. However, the result of this long researched subject is confusion rather than consensus (cf. Martin, *Reconciliation*, 16-31; Plevnik, 'Center', 461-478; Hafemann, 'Paul', 674-77; *DPL*, ix).

4   Watson, *Paul, passim*.
5   So correctly Campbell, 'Separation', 130.
6   E.g. Kettunen, *Abfassungszweck*, 146ff; Wedderburn, *Reasons*, 97-102; perhaps the most thorough treatment from this perspective is offered by Elliott, *Rhetoric*, 69-104; cf. Klein, 'Purpose', 32-34.
7   So Hahn, *Mission*, 107, laments that too little attention has been paid to this section, even if it contains a 'great summary, the basic ideas of the Pauline view of the mission'. Cf. Müller, 'Grundlinien', 212-235.

interpretative key for the whole letter. On the basis of 15:15-16, we have suggested in the Introduction that Paul's self-consciousness of being apostle to the Gentiles might have shaped the content and the structure of his soteriological argument in the letter. The aims of this chapter are to examine 15:14-21 as the interpretative key to the meaning of the letter, to establish that the subject matter of the letter is related to the issues of the Gentiles, and to demonstrate the extent of the role of Paul's apostolic self-consciousness in writing this letter to the Roman Christians.

We shall begin by examining 15:14-21, because here Paul indicates not only the character of the letter but also his approach in writing. Here we shall attempt to establish the hypothesis that Paul has written this letter from his particular apostolic perspective to affirm the legitimacy of Gentile salvation gained by faith alone, and we will propose that his affirmation of the legitimate inclusion of the Gentiles in God's salvific blessing is fundamentally related to his apostolic self-understanding. Admittedly 15:14-21 is a passage late in the letter. One may thus argue that it cannot be the *starting* point for the interpretation of the letter but only a *post hoc* rationalisation that puts Paul's self-consciousness of being the apostle to the Gentiles in primary place. We accept this objection. But *if* this late passage does thematically cohere with the introduction of the letter (1:1-15), our methodology of starting from 15:14-21 can be justified. The reason why we start from 15:14-21 is simply because here Paul makes a much clearer indication than anywhere else in the letter. Thus we will compare 15:14-21 with 1:1-15 so as to establish their thematic correspondence. Our investigation will show that the introductory and the concluding sections thematically cohere with the key theme 'ἔθνη'.

The examination of 1:1-15 will lead us to pay more specific attention to 1:16-17, where the thematic statement for the entire letter is clearly expressed. We will aim to discover whether the theme we have found in 15:14-21 (i.e. the affirmation of the legitimacy of the salvation of the Gentiles) is also shown in the thematic statement. Here we will show that the equal inclusion of the Gentiles in God's salvific blessing is indeed clearly intended. We will find a thematic parallel in these passages (15:14-21; 1:1-15; 1:16-17). However, to establish our hypothesis firmly, we must turn to the thematic conclusion of the letter in 15:7-13; thus we will consider whether it too coheres with the thematic introduction of 1:16-17. We will examine 15:7-13 in two parts: 15:8-9a and 15:9b-12.[8] We will study 15:8-9a, where Paul structures the argument to relate Christ's service for both Jews and Gentiles, and yet more specifically to the salvation of the Gentiles. The catena of OT quotations in 15:9b-12 will be then analysed. Here we will show how Paul links the catena with the key theme 'ἔθνη' and stresses that the legitimate and equal inclusion of the Gentiles into the true people of God is clearly predicted in the OT. What we will study in this chapter can be diagrammatically portrayed as follows.

```
1:1-15          Personal Introductory Remarks
1:16-17         Thematic Introduction to the main body of Romans

15:7-13         Thematic Conclusion of the main body of Romans
15:14-21(33)    Personal Concluding Remarks
```

In short, we will examine the passages mentioned above, and how they cohere with one other, especially with 15:14-21, so as to determine whether 15:14-21 can be regarded as a significant interpretative key to the meaning of the letter. The sections 1:16-17 and 15:7-13 indicate the subject matter of the letter; furthermore, 15:14-21 and 1:1-15 reveal not merely the subject matter but also significantly, Paul's apostolic self-consciousness in writing the letter to the Romans.

1. Romans, Written under Paul's Apostolic Self-Awareness: 15:14-21

A. *Romans as a Bold Letter: 15:14-15a*

Paul indicates his approach to the letter in 15:14-21, which contains a rhetorical acknowledgement that his addressees are already 'full of goodness, complete in knowledge and competent to in-

---

8 We will examine 15:7 and 15:13, but our division of the sections as 15:8-9a and 15:9b-12 is due to our more particular emphases on Christ's service and on the OT catena.

struct one another' (15:14). He has often expressed his confidence in them (1:8; 6:17; 16:19),[9] and his initial approach in writing is 'to remind' them of the things which they have believed and exercised in their Christian life. However, this does not mean they have no need of further instruction,[10] despite the expression πεπληρωμένοι πάσης [τῆς] γνώσεως.[11] Rather the emphatic addition καὶ αὐτὸς ἐγώ ('I myself too [no less than others]': 15:14),[12] and the perfect passive πέπεισμαι, seem to indicate Paul's sincerity in what he subsequently says.[13]

Paul says he has written this critical letter rather boldly.[14] The emphasised τολμηρότερον indicates not only that Paul has written more profoundly than anything the Roman believers already know,[15] but also that Paul is conscious that some of what he has written would be hard for the readers to accept, because it

---

9   Thus, Watson's assertion in *Paul*, 96-97, that the church in Rome exhibited marked division between the Jewish and the Gentile believers, even to the point of two congregations, is certainly exaggerated. Cf. Cranfield, *Romans* 2, 752.

10   The conjunction δέ in v. 15 is to be taken as 'in some *contrast* to what has preceded.' (Monro, *Homeric Grammar* (1882), 245, as cited in Robertson, *Grammar*, 1183; similarly Zerwick, *Greek*, 157. So render Gifford, *Romans*, 225, as 'nevertheless'; Shedd, *Romans*, 412, as 'however'; NASB as 'but'.

11   One should not take such assurance as expressed in 15:14 at face value. *Pace* Sanday and Headlam, *Romans*, 403, for asserting that the Romans have 'a deep and comprehensive grasp of the real principles of Christianity' in its entirety. Compare, for example, 1 Cor 1:5-7 with 1 Cor 12-14. For the rhetorical function of such assurance, see O'Brien, *Thanksgiving*. Even though the Roman believers may have such a complete knowledge, they still need to be exhorted to exercise brotherly love, as is emphasised throughout 12:9-15:13 (cf. 1 Cor 13:2: καὶ εἰδῶ τὰ μυστήρια πάντα καὶ πᾶσαν τὴν γνῶσιν).

12   Cranfield, *Romans* 2, 752.

13   Paul does not use the expression as flattery to avoid offence (*pace* Black, *Romans*, 174; Käsemann, *Romans*, 392); furthermore, it seems more than Christian courtesy (Cranfield, *Romans* 2, 752). And there seems to be no reason to doubt Paul's genuineness, for he does not directly confront his readers despite his determination to be bold in writing this letter (15:15).

14   The rendering of the comparative τολμηρότερον is varied: e.g. 'quite bold(ly)' (NIV, TEV); 'somewhat boldly' (NEB); 'more boldly' (KJV); 'rather boldly' (NRSV); 'somewhat or rather boldly' (Murray, *Romans* 2, 209). The stronger sense, 'very boldly' is found in RSV, NASB, BAGD, 506; cf. 'much too boldly' (Black, *Romans*, 174). Dunn, *Romans* 2, 859, is probably correct to say that the latter (i.e. 'very boldly') is too strong.

15   *Pace* Black, *Romans*, 174-175.

touched on some very sensitive subjects.[16] With τολμηρότερον Paul does not mean 'bluntly', denoting 'insensitively' or 'presumptuously confident', because he shows a great sensitivity in his presentation of argument. Rather he seems to mean 'boldly', connoting 'courageously or confidently daring towards or against someone or a view' (cf. 2 Cor 11:21), because he writes with the strong intention of establishing his readers in what he regards as absolutely vital truth (1:11), whose content we shall examine below.

The epistolary aorist ἔγραψα may refer to any particular portion or to the entire epistle,[17] but it seems more probable that it relates to the whole letter.[18] G. Klein is right to say, 'It is from the preaching responsibilities outlined here (15:15-16) that Paul derives the preceding contents of the [entire] letter'.[19] Then, in the present passage, 'Paul offers the recapitulation, the full statement of the thesis [of Romans]'.[20] K. Barth also notes that the principle in 15:15-16 turns out to be the spirit fundamental throughout the letter, and that boldness is the mark of Romans as a whole.[21] Paul is concerned that his readers might be confused by the revolutionary perspective from which he addresses the issues, or, in fact, by

---

16 Wedderburn, *Reasons*, 100: but he identifies that the contents of the 'some points' are the collection journey to Jerusalem, the advice to the weak and the strong (14:1-15:13) and 'the righteousness of God' as the 'raw nerves' (pp. 108-123).

17 Cf. Robertson, *Grammar*, 846; Moulton and Turner, *Grammar* 3, 73.

18 Our presupposition denies Schmithals' hypothesis that Romans is a composite letter made up of at least two letters (Letter A, containing 1:1-4:25; 5:12-11:36; 15:8-13; Letter B, 12:1-21; 13:8-10; 14:1-15:4a, 5-7, 14-32; 16:21-23; 15:33). See Wedderburn, 'Purpose', 197-200, for excellent criticism of Schmithals' thesis.

The ἔγραψα usually refers to a letter just finished (cf. John 20:31; Phlm 19; 1 Pet 5:12; 1 John 5:13), or to a previous letter (1 Cor 5:9, 11, and most probably 2 Cor 2:3, 4, 9; 7:8-12; cf. 3 John 9). The verb ἔγραψα in Gal 6:11 may refer to Gal 6:11-18, which Paul writes in his own hand, but the reason why he writes so emphatically with big letters in his own hand is not merely because of the content in Gal 6:11-18, but surely because of the content of the entire letter. So rightly Käsemann, *Romans*, 391; Klein, 'Purpose', 34 n. 23, who rightly insist that the reference in 15:15 is not to be confined to 14:1-15:13.

19 Klein, 'Purpose', 34.
20 Wuellner, 'Paul's Rhetoric', 136.
21 Barth, *Romans*, 528-530.

the presentation of his theology, and hence he makes it explicit that he has written in this way *deliberately*.[22] In fact, these verses indicate that 'the matters Paul writes about spring from the nature of his special apostleship to the Gentiles'.[23]

Before we examine the basis and the content of his daring writing, one more point in our section deserves special attention in this context. Paul says he has written somewhat boldly, 'ἀπὸ μέρους'. J. Murray particularly rejects the quantitative rendering of this Greek phrase ('in some parts' or 'on some points')[24] as 'scarcely warranted'.[25] The qualitative interpretation ('in some measure'), however, does not seem to match Paul's emphatic expression of his boldness. Paul's use of ἀπὸ μέρους elsewhere in Romans seems to suggest the quantitative rendering. Firstly, the phrase πώρωσις ἀπὸ μέρους in 11:25 denotes 'a partial hardening' of the Jews, and this does not mean that unbelieving Jews have hardened their hearts 'in some measure' but rather that a large proportion of Jews do not believe at all whilst others do wholeheartedly. Secondly, ἀπὸ μέρους ἐμπλησθῶ in 15:24 also indicates that Paul desires to enjoy the company of the Roman believers for a while, that is, for a certain period of time, rather than to a certain degree or quality of their company. Thus it seems most probable that with the phrase ἀπὸ μέρους in 15:15 Paul indicates that he has been rather bold *on some points* or *on certain subjects*.[26]

Scholars have attempted to identify those 'parts' on which Paul has written with boldness. While C.E.B. Cranfield, U. Wilckens and M.A. Seifrid choose 12:1-15:13, W. Sanday and A.C. Headlam offer more specific locations: 4:12ff, 19; 8:9; 11:17ff; 12:3; 13:3ff; 14:; 15:1.[27] J.D.G. Dunn also maintains that the phrase

---

22 Paul often checks the readers' response: 'I see that my letter hurt you, but only for a little while' (2 Cor 7:8-12), but he notes that he had done deliberately.

23 So correctly, Robinson, 'Priesthood', 231.

24 For example, RSV, NIV, Phillips; similarly NEB, TEV, Käsemann, *Romans*, 391; Cranfield, *Romans* 2, 750, 753; Sanday and Headlam, *Romans*, 404; Dunn, *Romans* 2, 858-59; BAGD, 506; Newman and Nida, *Romans*, 279.

25 Murray, *Romans* 2, 209, n. 19, but he does not provide evidence for his strong assertion.

26 Newman and Nida, *Romans*, 279.

27 Cranfield, *Romans* 2, 750, 753; Seifrid, *Justification*, 193; Sanday and Headlam, *Romans*, 404.

means 'in part', referring to 'part of the letter, that is, presumably 12:1-15:13', where Paul deals with specific situations in Rome itself. However, Dunn plausibly adds, 'since he [Paul] is linking back in mood and theme to 1:8-15, it may be better to take the ἀπὸ μέρους as a polite self-deprecatory reference to *the whole of the letter* which came between these two sections (1:16-15:13)'.[28]

There are further reasons why we believe that ἀπὸ μέρους refers to more than 12:1-15:13. First, one must wonder why Paul would need to write 'rather boldly' when his injunctions deal only with common and general issues about brotherly love. Especially in 12:1-15:13, Paul seems very careful and balanced. He does not seem to touch raw nerves by demanding any actions that would not be acceptable. Second, putting the issue of the practical injunctions above nomism may constitute such boldness, but it is important to note that Paul's boldness even on the practical issues (12:1-15:13) is, in fact, based on his theological teaching in the previous section of 1:18-11:36,[29] as the conjunction οὖν in 12:1 indicates.[30] Third, Paul's intrepidity is certainly related to his self-consciousness when he mentions his priestly duty in 15:16 (λειτουργός), and he urges (the Roman) believers to offer their bodies as a living sacrifice (12:1). But it is to be noted that Paul's sacred service is already mentioned in 1:9 (λατρεύω). Furthermore, his apostleship given by grace (15:16) not only extends back to 12:3 but much further back to the beginning of the letter (1:5).[31] Therefore, the 'some points' mentioned out of his priestly duty are not limited to 12:1-15:13, but include the whole of 1:18-15:13. Our present study will reveal the subjects related to the 'some points'.

B. *The Basis of Paul's Boldness: 15:15b-21*

Paul, then, makes clear what caused him to write such a bold letter to the church which he had neither founded nor yet visited.

---

28 Dunn, *Romans 2*, 858-859, with added emphasis; and thus Seifrid, *Justification*, 193, seems to have misunderstood Dunn. Käsemann, *Romans*, 391-392, also takes the phrase to refer to 'some places' wider than the exhortation section.
29 Wright, *Messiah*, 227.
30 Cotterell and Turner, *Linguistics*, 190.
31 *Pace* Seifrid, *Justification*, 193.

He says he could be bold διὰ τὴν χάριν τὴν δοθεῖσάν μοι ὑπὸ τοῦ θεοῦ, and this grace is expressly related to his apostleship to the Gentiles (15:15b-16; cf. Gal 1:15-16). Moreover, Paul's boldness is also based on his 'boasting' that comes from his personal missionary experience among the Gentiles (15:17-21). What Paul has written to the Romans are not mere abstract theological assertions, but insights proven through his missionary experience (among both Jews and Gentiles) and accompanied by the endorsement of the Holy Spirit (cf. Gal 3:1-5).

(a) Paul's Self-Awareness of his Role: 15:15b-16
Paul makes it clear that he received grace from God to become a minister (λειτουργός)[32] to the Gentiles with the priestly duty of proclaiming the gospel (15:15-16; Gal 1:15f; 2:9; cf. Acts 9:15; 22:17-21; 26:16f). The composition of διά with an accusative[33] is probably best understood by taking τὴν χάριν as the accusative of τὴν δοθεῖσάν μοι ὑπὸ τοῦ θεοῦ.[34] So even though διά is followed by an accusative it is to be taken as genitive meaning 'on the basis of', 'on account of' or even 'because of' without strong causal sense.[35] Paul has written a bold letter *by* (in the sense of a basis), or *because of* (in the sense of an obligation; cf. 1:14) the grace given by God. In other words, his boldness is

---

32 Paul does not call himself an 'ἀπόστολος' *here*, but a λειτουργὸς Χριστοῦ Ἰησοῦ εἰς τὰ ἔθνη, most probably to match the cultic language in the immediate context. The combination of the term λειτουργός with the subsequent cultic language, ἱερουγεῖν and προσφορά, suggests that most probably it means 'priest'. The language is strongly related to the Temple (Cranfield, *Romans* 2, 755-756; Wilckens, *Römer* 3, 118; Ziesler, *Romans*, 341; Dunn, *Romans* 2, 860), and thus it seems better to translate 'priest' (e.g. Barrett; Wilckens; Dunn) than 'levite' (Cranfield, *Romans* 2, 755; Sanday and Headlam, *Romans*, 405).

33 Διά with a single accusative usually implies causal sense: *on account of* (e.g. Mark 6:26; Acts 18:2; 28:2; Rev 12:11; 13:14), or final sense, *for* (Matt 24:22; Mark 2:27; John 11:42; 12:30), or *with a view to* (Rom 3:25; 4:25; 11:28, etc.): Moulton and Turner, *Grammar* 3, 267-268.

34 The phrase ultimately points back to Paul's Damascus road experience, without which Paul's apostleship and subsequent missionary work cannot be correctly understood (cf. Gal 1:15-16; 1 Cor 9:1-2; 15:8-9); see Kim, *Origin, passim*; Müller, 'Grundlinien', 228.

35 Cf. Robertson, *Grammar*, 583, who lists διὰ τὴν χάριν of 15:15 and 12:3 with the examples of διά+ genitive, connoting '*through*' or '*by*'.

based on the grace given to him to be a minister of Christ.[36] Furthermore, this clause is closely connected with 1:5 and 1 Cor 3:10, where Paul also assumes his apostleship to the Gentiles (cf. 12:3).[37] His doctrinal teaching and practical exhortation are, then, based on the apostolic grace given to him.

Nevertheless, the above understanding does not sufficiently convey Paul's point when the phrase διὰ τὴν χάριν τὴν δοθεῖσάν μοι is to be understood together with εἰς τὸ εἶναί.[38] Syntactically the latter phrase can qualify either 'ἡ χάρις δοθεῖσάν μοι' or 'ἔγραψα'. Some commentators connect it with the former: 'It is only because of the grace given him of God that he could dare to write as he did.'[39] This understanding suits the context. But if Paul's bold writing is based only on apostolic grace,[40] he might have written something like this: 'because of the grace given to me by God *through which I became*[41] a minister of Christ Jesus to the Gentiles', or, 'because of the grace given to me by God *as* a minister of Christ Jesus to the Gentiles', because he has been already made a minister of Christ.

However, the fact that the phrase εἰς τὸ εἶναί 'expresses hardly anything but purpose'[42] indicates that he expresses more than the notion that his apostolic grace prompted him to write this letter.[43] If this phrase is subordinated to the main verb ἔγραψα, the verse would mean, 'I have written rather boldly on the basis of the grace God gave me (i.e. apostleship to the Gentiles)... *in order* for me *to be* a (*true*) minister of Christ Jesus'. Then what

---

36 BAGD, 181; Dunn, *Romans* 2, 859.
37 So also in 1 Cor 15:10; Gal 2:9; cf. Eph 3:8. See Munck, *Paul*, 49, for the relation between Paul's apostleship and God's grace.
38 The εἰς τὸ εἶναί has seldom received proper attention as to its full implication: even some of most detailed commentaries, such as those by Cranfield, Dunn and Käsemann, hardly make any comment on it.
39 Murray, *Romans* 2, 210.
40 E.g. Morris, *Romans*, 510-11; Murray, *Romans* 2, 210.
41 The verb γίνομαι is rather common in Paul: 1 Cor 9:20, 22; 13:1; cf. Rom 2:25; 6:5; 7:13; 1 Cor 1:30; 8:9; 15:37; 2 Cor 5:21; 6:14; Gal 3:13.
42 Moulton and Turner, *Grammar* 3, 143. Cf. Paul's use of εἶναί without εἰς τό in Romans (1:22; 9:3).
43 The phrase εἰς τὸ εἶναί with an accusative is peculiar to Paul (1:20; 3:26; 4:11, 16; 8:29; 15:16; 1 Cor 10:6, cf. Phil 1:23; Eph 1:12); Εἰς τό with infinitive occurs 72 times in the NT, of which 50 are found in Paul; Robertson, *Grammar*, 1071.

has been written in the letter could determine whether Paul is a true apostle to the Gentiles or not. Paul indeed has a strong sense of obligation (ὀφειλέτης: RSV) to be a servant apostle to the Gentiles (1:14-15). In short, what Paul has written in this letter proves his true apostleship to the Gentiles.

Paul is apostle to the Gentiles because that is what he is called to be; but more importantly, in his life and ministry that call must be constantly proved by fulfilling his duty as their apostle.[44] That God has indeed called him to be apostle to Gentiles can gain objective recognition only when it is proven by his life and work (cf. 1 Cor 3:6; 4:5; 9:1-18; 15:10; 2 Cor 11:23; Gal 2:7-9; 3:1-5; Col 1:24-29). Therefore, he attempts to prove his apostleship through the fruit (i.e. the converts and their godly lifestyle) of his work (cf. 1 Cor 9:2; Gal 3:1-5). However, Paul the writer/dictator of the letter achieves a more permanent and vital role as apostle to the Gentiles than Paul the missionary ever could through his hard work among the Gentiles during his lifetime. What he has written, for example, in Romans consequently fulfils a permanent apostolate since it provides the fundamental theological rationale for the legitimacy of Gentile salvation and the mission to them. Then Paul's bold writing in Romans is not only the *result* of his apostleship, but also the *means* by which he proves and expresses his apostleship to the Gentiles. He declares, therefore, in the extremely emphatic structure of 11:13, that ἐφ' ὅσον μὲν οὖν εἰμι ἐγὼ ἐθνῶν ἀπόστολος: 'Since therefore I myself am indeed an apostle of the Gentiles.'[45]

(b) The Fruit of Paul's Apostolic Ministry: 15:17-20

Paul has further grounds for his boldness in writing Romans, namely, his missionary accomplishment in Christ among the Gentiles.[46] Both the οὖν and the definite article τήν[47] before

---

44 So similarly Bultmann, *Theology* 1, 291. In this respect Jervell's observation in 'Jerusalem', 54, seems correct: as much as the churches need Paul, Paul needs them, for his further life and work as the missionary apostle is dependent on his converts' proper Christian living as believers (2 Cor 10:15-17; Phil 1:5-19; 1 Thess 2:19-20; 3:6-9).

45 See *infra* pp. 262-266 for fuller treatment of this verse.

46 The accomplished result of work from Jerusalem to Illyricum is the basis of his boasting (see Bowers, 'Fulfilling the Gospel', 185-198). Within the context of 15:18b-19, the ὥστε with the perfect infinitive πεπληρωκέναι can hardly denote a purpose, but a result. So Barth, Cranfield, Käsemann,

καύχησιν indicate that 15:17 is related to 15:16. Paul's boast in Christ for his service to God[48] is further explained by 15:18 (γάρ); and indeed καύχησιν and τολμήσω τι λαλεῖν provide a similar nuance.[49] Thus the basis for the boast Paul dares to make is Christ's accomplishment through him 'in leading the *Gentiles* to obey God by what [he has] said and done' (15:18; cf. 2 Cor 1:12-14).

Furthermore, the infinitive λαλεῖν is equivalent to γράφειν here: the work of Christ through him among the Gentiles which he dares to speak of is related to what he has written in Romans. His speeches and writings (i.e. his theology) are deeply rooted in his personal experience of the Spirit within the context of mission among Jews and Gentiles, but his emphasis is placed on the latter. He sets out on missionary work because he was called to preach the gospel. But now he proves his calling by the fruit of his successful work, and he declares that his success as an apostle lies in bringing *Gentiles* to obey the gospel of Christ in faith (cf. 2 Cor 10:15).[50] Paul does not mention 'Jews' here, but makes it clear that 'the single comprehensive drive of his apostolic work had been "to win obedience from the Gentiles" (15:18)',[51] because he had 'received grace and apostleship to call people from all the *Gentiles* to the obedience that comes from faith' (1:5). It is significant to note that Paul openly and specifically declares his apostleship to the Gentiles (1:5-6; 11:13; 15:16; Gal 1:15-16; 2:7-

---

Wilckens, Dunn in their commentaries. Although the combination in classical Greek often indicates purpose (see Liddell and Scott, *Lexicon*, 909), its use for purpose is rare in the NT: Robertson, *Grammar*, 990, gives ὥστε ἐκβάλλειν (Matt 10:1) as the only solid example of 'pure' purpose.

47 See the discussion in favour of the presence of the article in Cranfield, *Romans* 2, 757 (cf. Käsemann, *Romans*, 393; Dunn, *Romans* 2, 861); for the opposite view see Sanday and Headlam, *Romans*, 405-406.

48 Cf. Paul's similar composition: 'καυχώμενοι ἐν τῷ θεῷ διὰ τοῦ κυρίου ἡμῶν Ἰησοῦ Χριστοῦ' (5:11).

49 This is also the case in 2 Cor 11:21 (τολμαῷ), 30 (καυχήσομαι), where Paul's boast is based on his hard work among the Jews and Gentiles (2 Cor 11:23-33; so also 1 Cor 15:10; 2 Cor 11:23; Col 1:29). Paul's claim of his 'harder work' seems to be measured in the context of mission.

50 Bultmann, *Theology* 1, 291, correctly relates 15:18 to 15:15-16; Ziesler, *Romans*, 342.

51 Minear, *Obedience*, 1. Cf. Black, *Romans*, 175, who assert that 'to win obedience from the Gentiles [is] the main purpose of the Epistle to the Romans'.

9),[52] despite the presence of strong Jewish elements in the Roman church.[53] Paul is fully conscious of his role and obligation towards the Gentiles, and so he laboured among them harder than other apostles (cf. 15:19-20; 1 Cor 15:10).

(c) Paul's Evangelistic Principle Based on OT Prophecy: 15:21

The quotation from LXX Isa 52:15 provides the background not only of Paul's apostolic self-understanding (cf. Jer 1:5; Isa 49:5; Gal 1:15) and evangelistic principle in 15:20 but also of his missionary practice in 15:19. Paul's 'service to God' has been carried out according to a specific principle (15:20) based on the prophecy (15:21) whose specific goal is to lead Gentiles to obey God (15:18). Thus Paul's theology seems to be best understood as mission theology.[54] The quotation in 15:21 is selected to support his vocation as a pioneer preacher[55] or to emphasise his policy of not entering the 'territory' of others.[56] But it is important to note that Paul turns to virgin territories because of the *Gentile people* rather than because of the policy. Thus he legitimises, from the OT passage, his missionary work among the Gentiles.

MT Isa 52:15b כִּי אֲשֶׁר לֹא־סֻפַּר לָהֶם רָאוּ וַאֲשֶׁר לֹא־שָׁמְעוּ הִתְבּוֹנָנוּ

LXX Isa 52:15b (=Rom 15:21) οἷς οὐκ ἀνηγγέλη περὶ αὐτοῦ
ὄψονται καὶ οἳ οὐκ ἀκηκόασιν συνήσουσιν

The LXX translation has modified the emphasis from the message ('what') to the people ('those who'). Although the quotation is taken verbatim from the LXX, the context is considerably altered in Romans. According to the context in Isaiah, the nations

---

52   See Paul's other various descriptions of his own role: God's servant (1 Cor 3:5; Col 1:23), 'God's fellow worker' (1 Cor 3:9; 2 Cor 6:1), 'the aroma of Christ to God' (2 Cor 2:14-16), 'minister of a new covenant' (2 Cor 3:6), 'Christ's ambassador' (2 Cor 5:20).

53   This is an *assumption* according to Stowers, *Rereading, passim*, but the content of Paul's argument throughout the letter (as we will show) suggests that his view is highly questionable.

54   Hengel, *Jesus*, 50; Müller, 'Grundlinien', 220.

55   Ziesler, *Romans*, 343.

56   Black, *Romans*, 176.

and kings will be appalled or awe-struck[57] in the presence of the Servant of Yahweh. The appearance of the Servant is *not* good news for these Gentiles, and what they see reduces them to speechlessness, because they had not heard and thus prepared themselves for the surprising appearance of the Servant.[58] Paul uses the same passage, however, to insist that hearing his message is a *blessing* for the Gentiles by changing the negative context into a positive one.[59] He wants to convey the impression that his coming to preach to the Gentiles who have never heard the gospel, brings joy and salvation to those who had no hope but could have expected only judgement at the awesome appearance of the Servant.[60]

This quotation effectively combines Paul's own conviction of his call to the Gentiles (1:1, 5) with his theological argument about the universality of the gospel.[61] If 'Deutero-Isaiah is thinking of the widespread publicity to be given to the work, but not of heathen spheres outside Israel', as Westermann suggests,[62] to that extent Paul's application from this quotation of a world-wide proclamation is significant. This final quotation from the OT in this letter seems to have been carefully chosen to affirm the blessing of the salvation of the Gentiles, and thus of his own missionary work among them. It appears that Paul is conscious of his function as the priestly minister of Christ, fulfilling this Isaianic prophecy. Indeed Isaiah seems to be Paul's favourite prophet, and his apostolic consciousness seems to have been deeply influenced by the prophetic promises (and of Isaiah in particular).[63] Thus R.B. Hays is right to observe,

---

57 North, *Isaiah 40-55*, 131; Westermann, *Isaiah 40-66*, 259.
58 Delitzsch, *Prophecies* 2, 285.
59 Cf. Liddon, *Romans*, 287.
60 Paul may perceive himself to be the one who introduces the eschatological Servant to the Gentiles so that they may see and understand who the Servant really is. So plausibly Käsemann, *Romans*, 395; Dunn, *Romans* 2, 866; idem, *Jesus and the Spirit*, 113, 389, n. 70; but rejected by Cranfield, *Romans* 2, 765 n. 2.
61 Dunn, *Romans* 2, 869; Allen, 'Old Testament', 23.
62 Westermann, *Isaiah 40-66*, 259.
63 According to Hays, *Echoes*, 162, Paul cites most frequently from Isaiah (28 citations), while Psalms (20), Deuteronomy (15) and Genesis (15) are also often cited. Ellis, *Paul's Use*, 150f, lists 18 citations from Isaiah in Romans alone (13 from Psalms, 7 from Genesis and 6 from Deuteronomy).

Isaiah offers the clearest expressions in the Old Testament of a universalistic, eschatological vision in which the restoration of Israel in Zion is accompanied by an ingathering of Gentiles to worship the Lord; that is why this book is both statistically and substantively the most important scriptural source for Paul.[64]

However, it is also important to note that Paul uses the texts from Isaiah for his own particular purposes in Romans; thus he substantially modifies the contexts and even the text of the quotations (as we have seen above, and will see in subsequent chapters).[65]

C. *The Content of Paul's Boldness*

In the above section we have tried to show that Romans is a daring letter written under Paul's self-awareness of being apostle to the Gentiles. To establish our hypothesis further we need to provide the evidence that the *content* of Paul's boldness is indeed related to the Gentiles. In other words, we must show that what Paul boldly argues for in Romans is the affirmation of the legitimacy of the salvation of the Gentiles. He declares that the only thing that he will dare (τολμήσω) to speak (or write) about is the obedience (i.e. salvation) of the Gentiles (15:18). Thus he specifies his boldness as gained from his apostolic work among the Gentiles, as we have suggested above. We shall examine at least two more places (10:20 and 1:16) to substantiate our contention that the content of Paul's boldness is the equal inclusion of the Gentiles in God's salvific blessing.

---

64 Hays, *Echoes*, 162. See Oss, 'Note', 105-112, notes that Paul distinctively uses texts from Isaiah for his argument; cf. Dinter, 'Prophet Isaiah', 48-52.

65 At least three further observations can be made. First, Paul often appeals to the name 'Isaiah' as an authority: '*Isaiah* says...' (9:27-28, 29; 10:16, 20, 21; 15:12). Second, Paul adds his interpretation as he appeals to the texts: 'Isaiah *cries out*' or 'Isaiah *very boldly* said' (9:27-28, 29; 10:20), while he makes no such additions to Moses (9:15; 10:5, 19) or to David (4:7-8; 11:19). Third, and most importantly, all quotations from Isaiah in Romans (with only one exception: 3:15-17) are cited to elucidate his argument about issues relating to Jews and Gentiles. To be more specific, they are employed to affirm the *unbelief* of the Jews (2:24; 9:27-28, 29, 33; 10:16, 21; 11:8; cf. 11:26-27b), the *inclusion* of the Gentiles (10:20; 15:12, 21), and the *universality* of salvation (9:33; 10:11, 15; 11:34-35; 14:11).

(a) 'Isaiah Very Boldly Says,': 10:20-21

LXX Isa 65:1a	ἐμφανὴς ἐγενόμην τοῖς ἐμὲ μὴ ζητοῦσιν
	εὑρέθην τοῖς ἐμὲ μὴ ἐπερωτῶσιν
2a	ἐξεπέτασα τὰς χεῖράς μου ὅλην τὴν ἡμέραν
	πρὸς λαὸν ἀπειθοῦντα καὶ ἀντιλέγοντα

Rom 10:20a	Ἡσαΐας δὲ <u>ἀποτολμᾶ</u> καὶ λέγει,
20b	Εὑρέθην [ἐν] τοῖς ἐμὲ μὴ ζητοῦσιν,
20c	ἐμφανὴς ἐγενόμην τοῖς ἐμὲ μὴ ἐπερωτῶσιν.
21a	πρὸς δὲ τὸν Ἰσραὴλ λέγει,
21b	Ὅλην τὴν ἡμέραν ἐξεπέτασα τὰς χεῖράς μου
	πρὸς λαὸν ἀπειθοῦντα καὶ ἀντιλέγοντα.

In the course of substantiating his argument concerning the unbelief of the Jews towards the end of Romans 10, Paul quotes LXX Isaiah 65:1a and 2a in 10:20-21. Here he introduces the citation by using a similar language of boldness (τολμα-). The quotation is taken verbatim from the LXX except for a few transpositions.[66] He remarks that 'Isaiah very boldly says' (Ἡσαΐας δὲ ἀποτολμᾶ καὶ λέγει) in making such a statement (10:20-21).[67] According to the contexts in both MT and LXX, Isa 65:1-2 is a prophecy about the *salvation* of rebellious Israel who did not seek God. But such a context has been remarkably altered in the course of Paul's own argument in 10:20-21. Isa 65:1 and 2 originally refer to the same people, the Israelites. But seeing a minor contrast between Isa 65:1 and 2,[68] Paul takes the words of the former verse (which are clearly intended for Israel) and strikingly reapplies them to the Gentiles,[69] with only Isa 65:2 applied to the Jews.[70]

---

66 See Stanley, *Language*, 144-147. We will leave a fuller examination of this passage to Chapter 5 (see *infra* pp. 246-248).

67 The compound verb ἀποτολμάω with the perfective ἀπο connotes to 'carry daring to its limit' (Moulton and Howard, *Grammar* 2, 298, as cited in Rienecker and Rogers, *Linguistic Key*, 371).

68 The contrast is only related to the emphasis of each verse; Isa 65:1 is about *God's revelation* to the obstinate nation (i.e. Israel) and 65:2 is about *Israel's obstinacy*.

69 Paul does not explicitly mention 'Gentiles' in his introductory comment in 10:20a, but his allocation of 10:21 specifically to 'Israel' makes it

Moreover, to the Gentiles Paul applies the phrase ἐμφανὴς ἐγενόμην, which referred to God's self-revelation to Israel and to Moses (Exod 3:14).[71] However, by transposing the verbs in 65:1, he stresses the fact that God was found by 'those [Gentiles] who did not seek me' (cf. 9:30), though for Isaiah it was 'those [Israelites] who did not seek me'. Such an emphasis should not be overlooked, since the interpretation is expressed in a way that would be most offensive to many Jews, who maintained a prevalent hatred towards Gentiles (e.g. especially *Jub.* 22:16, 20-21; 32:19; 35:14; cf. Sir 36:1-17). In fact, Jews did not apply the prophecy of Isa 65:1-2 to Gentiles except to Rahab and Ruth.[72] Paul's assertion in 10:20-21 has been made in such a historical context.[73] Paul's boldness goes even further. In contrast to the affirmative remarks about the Gentiles' *faith* in 10:20, he applies Isa 65:2 to make a sharply critical statement about the *unbelief* of the Jews in the very next verse. What Paul stresses is not hope for Israel in the light of the divine grace and patience (unlike in the Isaianic context), but Israel's obstinate rejection of God's grace despite his endless patience (cf. the emphatic position of ὅλην τὴν ἡμέραν).[74]

Saying to the (exclusivist) Jews that God has been found by Gentiles, or that he has accepted them, is a courageous statement for a Jew to make. Announcing to the (self-complacent) Jews that they themselves are a disobedient and obstinate people, is another brave assertion. But to say, as a Jew, to fellow Jews, that the blessing of finding God has been granted to the Gentiles whilst the Jews themselves remain disobedient, and thus that *they* have not found God, demands even greater boldness. With his inter-

---

abundantly clear that he is talking about the salvific blessing of the Gentiles in 10:20: so also Dunn, *Romans* 2, 626.

70   Cranfield, *Romans* 2, 540.
71   Dunn, *Romans* 2, 626.
72   See Str-B 3, 285.
73   See further Dodd's comment, *Romans*, 181-182:
     .... the magnificent promises of the Second Isaiah .... were associated with a call to Israel, as the Servant of Jehovah, to accept a mission to the Gentiles. The Jews preferred to follow Ezekiel, Ezra, and the exclusivist party, and to foster a fantastic national pride upon a narrowing religion which canonized envy, hatred, malice, and all uncharitableness against the Gentile.
74   *Pace* Cranfield, *Romans* 2, 541-42. Cf. Dunn, *Romans* 2, 627.

pretative comment, 'Isaiah was very bold', Paul implies that Isaiah had to be very intrepid because his message was about the *faith* of the Gentiles and the *unbelief* of the Jews. But in fact it was *not* Isaiah's message. He announced the *blessed salvation* of the (rebellious) Jews, and thus he did not need such courage to announce the good news to his contemporary audience.

The 'boldness' in 10:20 is, therefore, to be attributed neither to Isaiah (Cranfield) nor to Isaiah's prediction (Dunn), but to Paul himself. It is Paul who makes an assertion offensive to Jews by strikingly modifying the context of the quotation for his own argument. Paul portrays Isaiah as though the prophet himself maintained the same position as he himself does about the salvation of the Gentiles and the rejection of the Jews. But it is Paul who stresses that in taking this stance, Isaiah spoke very dauntlessly; so he is conscious that he too is writing with similar prophetic courage when he treats the theme in the same way. That is, *here Paul indicates that he has also been very bold to write about the salvific blessing of the Gentiles and the disobedience of the Jews.* Then it is clear that Paul uses the τολμα- language in Romans (ἀποτολμάω in 10:20; τολμηροτέρως in 15:15; and τολμάω in 15:18) primarily in connection with affirmation of the salvific blessing of the *Gentiles*.

(b) 'I am not Ashamed of the Gospel.': 1:16-17

Paul does not express his boldness only towards the end of this letter; he sets the course of his bold argument right at the beginning of the letter.[75] He says that he is not ashamed of the gospel in 1:16a,[76] because it is the very revelation of God's righteousness, the dynamic power of God for salvation. Furthermore, he is confident in the gospel because it brings salvation to *everyone* who believes without ethnic distinction. Despite the presence of the πρῶτον in 1:16, Paul's main reason in emphasising the παντί is to indicate the inclusion of the Gentiles in the salvific blessing of God. This also becomes clear in 10:11-12, where Paul makes a similar declaration: 'Anyone who trusts in him will *never put to shame*. For there is no difference between Jew and Gentile'. Here

---

75 Seifrid, *Justification*, 211. See Grayston, '"Not Ashamed"', 569-573, for a discussion of various interpretations of Paul's unashamedness.

76 Dahl, *Studies*, 78, plausibly connects the concept of 'οὐ ἐπαισχύνομαι' of 1:16 with 'boldness', but fails to do so with that of 15:15.

the unashamedness is based on faith in Christ and on the abolition of soteriological distinction between Jew and Gentile. The declaration in 10:11-13 is made to affirm the equality of Jew and Gentile with respect to the means of salvation, namely, faith (see Chapter 5). This passage closely parallels 1:16. Here again Paul stresses the equality of Jew and Gentile. The reason why Paul has been eager to preach the gospel in Rome (1:15) is because (γάρ) he is not ashamed of the salvation message of the gospel as applicable equally to Jew and Gentile. Believers can be strengthened and united when they understand this implication of the gospel.[77]

Together with his apostolic calling, Paul received a special divine communication (Gal 1:12). The same gospel of God through which salvation can be granted to everyone who believes is given to the other apostles to preach (1 Cor 15:3-11); but the gospel truth 'that a man is justified by faith apart from observing the law' (3:28) is particularly committed to Paul.[78] He would have needed much courage if he was to preach the 'good news' which he has presented in this letter. It is because (as we shall show in the following chapters) he often makes argument on behalf of believing Gentiles and portrays a critical picture of unbelieving Jews, especially in Romans 1-4 and 9-11.

---

[77] In his letter to the Corinthians (2 Cor 10:8-10), Paul has already declared that he is not ashamed (a similar verb, future passive αἰσχυνθήσομαι) of his apostolic authority the Lord gave him. This passage is directly related to Rom 1:1-5, 16 in both language and ideas. But furthermore, it significantly parallels our present interest in Romans: in 2 Cor 10:10 Paul accepts his opponents' remarks that his letters are 'weighty and forceful', which clearly means that Paul has written very bold letters. Paul takes up his opponents' comment, and declares that he has done so because of the God-given authority to build up the believers in Corinth (2 Cor 10:8; 1 Cor 13:10). To the Corinthians he wrote the forceful and weighty letters to build them up (οἰκοδομή; 1 Cor 14:3, 5, 12, 26; 2 Cor 10:8; 12:19; 13:10), by giving blunt advice on praxis according to his apostolic authority. Very similarly, to the Romans he writes a bold letter to strengthen them (στηριχθῆναι; 1:11; 15:15; 16:25), not only by giving them some practical exhortations about Christian praxis, but also by explaining the implication and the significance of the salvation they have received by faith in Christ. Thus he demonstrates that he is indeed a true minister of Christ for the Gentiles.

[78] This is perhaps what Paul means when he claims that this gospel is '*my* gospel' (2:16; 16:25; cf. 2 Tim 2:8); see *infra*, 297-299; Appendix, pp. 302-307.

D. Summary

In 15:14-21 Paul indicates more clearly than anywhere else in the letter how and why he has written. He admits that he has been bold on some points on the basis of his apostleship to the Gentiles. He says that he has taken a courageous stand on theological issues in order to prove himself a true apostle to the Gentiles. Paul often tried to prove his apostleship by his hard work and its fruits (1 Cor 9:2). He has been eager 'to preach the gospel' to the Roman believers because of his sense of apostolic obligation towards the Gentiles (cf. 1:14-15). Circumstances allow him to do so only in writing, and he has taken a rather fearless and audacious approach as he writes about the implications of the gospel. He has written as their apostle, and expects that what he has written will demonstrate his true apostleship to the Gentiles.

His personal experience of the Holy Spirit during his evangelistic ministry, especially among the Gentiles, has provided further ground for prophetic boldness (15:17-18). The content of his boldness is derived from the explanation of the deeper implication of the gospel with regard to the legitimacy of the salvation of the Gentiles, which became available to them by faith apart from observing the law. Paul identifies his boldness with that of Isaiah (65:1-2), who, according to Paul, prophesied the blessing of the Gentiles in finding God, and, at the same time, the unbelief and rejection of the Jews. The fact that he relates his ministry solely to the Gentiles seems significant. The last quotation in the letter (15:21) also indicates that 'a ... theme of primary importance in Pauline exegesis concerns the *rejection* of the Jews and the *"calling"* of the Gentiles',[79] and this theme is abundantly evident, as we will show in the following chapters. His close dependence upon the texts of Isaiah throughout the letter is most probably due to the common denominator of the universalistic and eschatological perspective shared by Isaiah and Paul.

Paul's daring approach in writing Romans is, in fact, indicated at the beginning of the letter where he declares that he is not ashamed of the gospel (1:16), emphasised by Paul's, 'to *everyone* who believes, to Jew first and also [equally] to Gentile'. Paul adds the explanatory phrase 'and also [equally] to Gentile', and uses the recurrent terminology of πίστις/πιστεύω in 1:16-17.

---

[79] Correctly Ellis, *Paul's Use*, 121; cf. Hays, *Echoes*, 162-163.

Thus Paul not only indicates the universality of salvation now available in Christ, but also shows us his deeper concern, that is, the faith of the Gentiles (cf. 9:30; 10:20; 15:17-18) and the unbelief of the Jews (cf. 9:31-33; 10:21; 11:7-10, 20). Thus the centre of gravity in Romans is the affirmation or the defence of the legitimacy of Gentile salvation, granted by divine grace and gained by human faith apart from the law. Paul maintains that for the Gentiles salvation is available on equal terms with Jews (i.e. by faith; 3:28, 30). This equality is in terms of their opportunity to become God's people, and not in terms of the Jewish way of salvation (i.e. by keeping the law; 9:32). The Jews are rather to follow the example of the Gentiles who solely exercised faith to be saved, which (as we will show in subsequent chapters) is an important argument throughout the letter (1:18-15:13).

As we admitted earlier 15:14-21 is a late passage. Our proposal to take Romans 15:14-21 as the interpretative key to the meaning of the letter can stand, if this concluding section (15:14-21) thematically corresponds to the introductory passage (1:1-15). Then we may be justified in reading the entire letter from the particular perspective gained from our investigation; and the contention that we will attempt to establish further is that *the explicit theme in both sections is Paul's apostolic self-awareness of his being the apostle to the Gentiles in writing this letter*. Our next task is then to examine 1:1-15 in order to determine its thematic correspondence with 15:14-21, and if we find coherence there it will allow us to interpret the main body (1:16-15:13) from the perspective of Paul's apostolic self-awareness.[80]

2. Romans Springs from Paul's Apostolic Self-Awareness: 1:1-15

The aim of this section is to investigate to what extent 1:1-15 corresponds to 15:14-21(33), and thus whether this introduction also suggests the same or a similar interpretative approach to the letter as we have proposed for 15:14-21. The summary analysis below clearly indicates that both passages are in close thematic parallelism:[81]

---

[80] Klein, 'Purpose', 34, n. 22.
[81] A parallel between 1:1-17 and 15:13-33, though different from our analysis, is also observed by Minear, *Obedience*, 37.

1:1-7   Personal prospect of the approach to Romans
=15:14-21   Personal retrospect of the approach to Romans
            theme: *Paul's apostleship to Gentiles in harmony with the OT*

1:8-15   Earlier plan to visit Rome
=15:22-33   Future plan to visit Rome
            theme: *A strong desire for the apostolic visit*

1:16-17   Thematic introduction to the main body of Romans
=15:7-13   Thematic conclusion of the main body of Romans
            theme: *The inclusion of the Gentiles in God's salvation*

We will examine Paul's indication concerning his initial approach to the letter in 1:1-7, and whether such a hint coheres with his retrospective explanation given in 15:14-21, and thus supports our earlier hypothesis that the latter passage is the interpretative key to the meaning of the letter. In 1:8-15 Paul tells the Romans about his great desire to visit them, and we will briefly consider any indication that what he writes in the letter is largely what he wished to communicate during his intended apostolic visit. If our findings cohere with what we have already found in 15:14-21, we may embark on the interpretation of the main body of the letter (1:16-15:13) from the perspective gained in this chapter.

A. *Paul's Self-Introduction concerning his Apostleship to the Gentiles: 1:1-7*

Paul introduces himself as δοῦλος and ἀπόστολος. The term ἀπόστολος is qualified by κλητός and ἀφωρισμένος, which stress the element of being specially chosen for a specific task. These terms of commission not only correspond to those of Gal 1:15-16, where Paul's apostleship to the Gentiles is most emphasised, but are also closely linked with the theme of Isa 49:1-8. Paul quotes from the Book of Isaiah more than any other OT book, and thus most probably he has an Isaianic theme in mind.[82]

---

82 Dunn, *Romans 1*, 8-9. See above pp. 31-32, nn. 63, 65.

He seems to assume that his role is that of fulfilling the prophecy given to Isaiah, in which God calls his servant to a greater ministry to the Gentiles than to 'the tribes of Jacob' (Isa 49:6; cf. Acts 13:47). He indeed specifies his apostleship as being *to the Gentiles* (1:5; 11:13; 15:16; Gal 1:15-16; 2:7-9).[83] Thus, when he says that he is 'set apart for the gospel of God', he is fully conscious of his call being the reversal of the prevailing Jewish idea: 'the ideal of separation *from* the Gentiles now became for Paul separation *for the sake of* the Gentiles.'[84] This is the fundamental structure of Pauline thinking.[85] Thus the self-introduction seems to have been expanded to give a better understanding of the direction of Paul's argument: 'Paul, ...called to be an apostle [to the Gentiles] and set apart for the gospel of God [which extends even to the Gentiles]' (1:1). For Paul the grace and apostleship[86] he has received for the Gentiles are fundamental to his self-understanding, and are intended to serve God's saving plan, a plan which had always included the Gentiles.[87]

Paul's task is to bring the obedience of faith among all Gentiles (εἰς ὑπακοὴν πίστεως ἐν πᾶσιν τοῖς ἔθνεσιν) by proclaiming the gospel of God, which had been promised beforehand (προεπηγγείλατο)[88] on God's own behalf through the prophets (i.e. the entire OT: 'in the holy Scriptures').[89] Right at the beginning of the letter, he indicates that his exposition of the gospel will be much dependent on the foretold promises of the OT (1:1-

---

83 Munck, *Christ*, 122.

84 Dunn, *Romans* 1, 9. In his pre-Christian days, Paul was a 'separated one', i.e. a Pharisee devoted to maintaining the law and traditions of the fathers (Gal 1:13-14; Phil 3:4-6; cf. Acts 22:3; 23:6; 26:5): see Hengel, *Pre-Christian Paul*, 40-53.

85 Müller, 'Grundlinien', 232.

86 Paul often combines 'grace and apostleship', e.g. 12:3; 15:15-16; 1 Cor 3:10; Gal 1:15-16; 2:9. See Cranfield, *Romans* 1, 65-66, who takes the phrase as 'grace of apostleship'; Lightfoot, *Notes*, 246, '"the gracious privilege of the Apostleship", or "the grace which fits for the Apostleship", [because] the Apostleship is itself the χάρις', and Newman and Nida render it, 'the privilege of being an apostle' (*Romans*, 11-12).

87 Dunn, *Romans* 1, 18; Jervis, *Purpose*, 158.

88 The only other usage in the NT is 2 Cor 9:5, but this is about the preparation of the offering for Jerusalem believers.

89 Meyer, *Romans* 1, 42: the phrase is 'a reference to *all who in the OT have prophesied the gospel* (even Moses, David and others not excluded)'. Cf. Cranfield, *Romans* 1, 56 n. 4; Ziesler, *Romans*, 60.

2).⁹⁰ For Paul, the gospel is the goal of the promises in the OT, and now he announces Jesus' fulfilment of these promises as the Messiah.⁹¹

The 'obedience of faith' is a central theme in the letter.⁹² It is often considered that the term 'obedience' is specifically connected with the Jews, for it is 'Israel's proper response to God's covenant grace (Deut 26:17; 30:2)'.⁹³ But it is also important to note that Paul relates this term to the faith of the Gentiles. Thus Dunn is certainly right to state: 'Paul intends his readers to understand the faith response of the Gentiles to the gospel as the fulfilment of God's covenant purpose through Israel.'⁹⁴ The obedience of faith from the Gentiles brings honour to God (1:5; 9:17; 10:11-13; 15:9, 18; 16:26; cf. Acts 14:27; 15:3-4, 12; 21:19-20), whilst the unbelief and disobedience of the Jews bring dishonour to God among the Gentiles (2:24). For Paul salvation from God is by faith, and it is Gentiles who have exercised this faith (9:30).

God has foretold his good news in the Holy Scriptures about his Son who would fulfil the content of the εὐαγγέλιον through his death and resurrection, and so '[Christ] is its decisive content'.⁹⁵ But Paul's explanation of the gospel is more than this; he goes on to assert that this gospel was intended for the *Gentiles* as well, although it was promised in the *Jewish* Scriptures. For Paul 'the gospel of God' and 'the apostleship from God' are inseparable. As the former was promised in the Scriptures, so also was the latter. The gospel of God should be proclaimed among the Gentiles, too, as was originally intended.⁹⁶ Paul shows the direction of his argument: the gospel of God is concerned with both Jew and

---

90 See Giblin, 'As It Is Written', 477-489, who argues that the phrase 'εὐαγγέλιον ὃ προεπηγγείλατο, rather than 1:16-17, contains the thematic idea of the letter. However, the facts that 1:16-17 has the word 'gospel', and that Hab 2:4 is quoted, suggest that 1:16-17 is in harmony with 1:2, and is the clearer statement of the theme.
91 Cf. Lightfoot, *Notes*, 244-245.
92 See Davies, *Faith, passim,* concerning this theme in reference to Rom 1-4.
93 Dunn, *Romans* 1, 18.
94 Dunn, *Romans* 1, 18.
95 Käsemann, *Romans*, 10.
96 More than a half of the 53 OT quotations in Romans are cited to substantiate the legitimacy of the salvation of the Gentiles, as we will show in the following chapters.

Gentile equally,[97] and yet with a greater emphasis on the latter, as we shall see.[98] With the expression εἰς εὐαγγέλιον θεοῦ, ὃ προεπηγγείλατο διὰ τῶν προφητῶν αὐτοῦ ἐν γραφαῖς ἁγίαις, Paul indicates that he will explain the εὐαγγέλιον as the fulfilment of God's promise, and that his claim with respect to the gospel will be justified on the basis of the word of God spoken through the prophets. For this reason he quotes the OT Scriptures in Romans more than in any other of his epistles, and thus substantiates his argument.[99]

Paul's subject in this letter is the gospel in fulfilment of the promise shown in the OT,[100] and the gospel which God promised beforehand through the prophets in the OT is *not only* περὶ τοῦ υἱοῦ αὐτοῦ *but also* God's promise that through him the obedience of faith will be proclaimed among the Gentiles for his name's sake (1:2-5).[101] It is to be noted that in Romans Paul does not use the OT Scriptures to establish the Messiahship of Jesus nor to prove his death and resurrection,[102] but predominantly to establish the universality of sin and justification (Rom 3-4), and the unbelief of Israel and the faith of the Gentiles (Rom 9-11). Paul's use of the OT in favour of the Gentiles is already clear in Galatians: 'The Scripture foresaw that God would justify the Gentiles by faith, and announced the gospel in advance to Abraham: "All nations will be blessed through you"' (Gal 3:8). Also he makes it clear in Romans that the Law and the Prophets have testified that a righteousness from God would be made known apart from the law, available through faith in Jesus Christ for all

---

97 Cf. Ziesler, *Romans*, 64.

98 *Infra* pp. 46-51.

99 Paul cites no less than fifty-three quotations (and twenty-seven allusions) in Romans to establish his argument (Ellis, *Paul's Use*, 150-154). It means over 60% of OT quotations in the Pauline letters appear in Romans.

100 Murray, *Romans* 1, 4.

101 1:1-7 is one sentence in Greek, and v. 5 is connected to v. 2; thus what is promised in the OT is both 'about his Son' and the proclamation of his Messiahship to the entire world. An almost exact parallel can be found in Luke 24:27, 44-46 *and* 47, where both Christ's suffering/resurrection *and* the proclamation of his name to the world, are assumed as having been written beforehand in the OT.

102 Probably Paul does not see the need to elaborate this aspect because his readers have already believed in the gospel concerning Jesus' death and resurrection.

who believe without any ethnic distinction (Rom 3:21-22). The entire argument in appealing to Abraham and David in Romans 4 is to establish that the blessedness which David mentions is not only for the circumcised but also for the uncircumcised (4:9). Paul emphasises that the Gentiles who are of the *faith* of Abraham can also legitimately lay claim to his ancestry (4:16-22).[103] Paul's use of the OT, therefore, seems to have been fundamentally based on his view that the OT prophecies and promises support his apostleship to the Gentiles and his missionary work among them.

Paul directs his letter 'to all (πᾶσιν) in Rome'. The use of the πᾶσιν is not necessarily to indicate that the Roman believers are disqualified from being called an ἐκκλησία,[104] but is used rather to embrace both the Jewish and the Gentile believers.[105] In the introductory section, Paul indicates that this letter is written for *all* the 'saints' in Rome individually and ethnically. In the opening section, Paul hints at the new status of the believers, including *Gentile* ones, of which he will say more in Romans 5-8 and 9-11. We may now summarise the significance of what he says in 1:7 as follows:

The phrase κλητοί ἅγιοι (1:7) is connected with the expression ἡγιασμένη ἐν πνεύματι ἁγίῳ at the conclusion of the letter, especially with reference to the Gentiles.[106] The verb ἁγιάζεσθαι also belongs to the notions of calling, election and sanctification (8:33; 15:16). Thus Paul's description of his work (involving calling, obedience and sanctification) as a λειτουργός for the Gentiles (1:9; 15:15-16) is significant. Being loved by God is something commonly applied to the Jews in the OT (Ps 60:1-12, esp. v. 5; 108:1-13), but for Paul God's love is now also extended to the Gentiles. Again, the term 'saints' expresses Israel's special sense of being chosen by God as his people

---

103 See Chapter 3 for further discussion.

104 *Pace* Klein, 'Purpose', 41-42; Bartsch, 'Empfänger', 86; cf. Watson, *Paul*, 104. Paul's description of the Roman believers as ἀγαπητοῖς θεοῦ, κλητοῖς ἁγίοις (1:7b), and of their spiritual quality (6:17; 12:5; 15:14-15; 16:19), clearly indicates that the Roman congregation *is* a church (cf. Phil 1:1). But see Cranfield, *Romans* 1, 22, n. 2, 70-71.

105 Käsemann, *Romans*, 15: the stressed term πᾶσιν 'embraces all the members of the community'. Lightfoot's perception, *Notes*, 246, seems most plausible: 'an endeavour to bind together two sections of that Church...: "to all, whether Jews or Gentiles; I make no difference".'

106 Cf. Sir 36:12; *Jub.* 2:20; *Ps. Sol.* 18:4; *2 Apoc. Bar.* 78:3, where God's love/call is exclusively claimed for Jews.

(e.g. Deut 7:6; Ps 16:3; Isa 4:3; Dan 7:18; Wis 18:9, etc.), but now Paul applies this expression to Gentiles as well (cf. Col 1:2).

The term 'holy' is chiefly applied to God, and also to Israel as the people of God;[107] and so in Judaism it is never applied to the Gentiles. Paul's application of this term to Gentile believers too is thus striking (so also in Col 1:2, 12, 22: 'holy .... brothers in Christ at Colossae'). Since the 'holiness' of Israel is derived from God's gracious election, the Gentile believers are 'holy' on the same basis, although for Paul the basis of election or holiness is through incorporation in Christ (1 Cor 1:2).[108] According to this grace of God the Gentile believers have become ἀγαπητοί, κλητοί and ἅγιοι. To make such a declaration to those who (used to) maintain superiority over Gentiles needs much courage and boldness.

B. Paul's Apostolic Obligation to the Gentiles: 1:8-15

We have mentioned this passage very briefly in the Introduction with respect to the purposes of the letter. Again only brief comment will be made here.[109] First, Paul describes his service to the gospel with the verb λατρεύω (1:9), which clearly indicates a cultic character. Paul has been commissioned with the priestly duty of preaching the gospel to the Gentiles, thus offering them to God as a pleasing sacrifice. This closely parallels 15:15-16 (λειτουργός). The meanings of λειτουργέω and λατρεύω are fundamentally the same and relate to 'the sacred ministering and priestly service that every believer can offer to God through prayer and personal adoration'.[110] At the beginning of the letter, Paul indicates that his ministry is related to the sacred service (so also 12:1), but at the end of the letter, he explicitly mentions that his priestly service is specifically conducted among the Gentiles, with the result that they are his offering to God.

Second, Paul's commitment to preach to the Gentiles is spelled out in 1:14: Ἕλλησίν τε καὶ βαρβάροις, σοφοῖς τε καὶ ἀνοήτοις ὀφειλέτης εἰμί. Most scholars are in general agreement that 'both pairs denote the whole of Gentile humanity, but

---

107 Cf. Cranfield, *Romans* 1, 70.
108 Cf. Dunn, *Romans* 1, 19-20; Cranfield, *Romans* 1, 70.
109 For a fuller treatment, see my article, 'Paul's Apostolic Self-Awareness and the Occasion and Purpose of Romans', 116-137.
110 Hill, *Discovery Bible*, 543; Thayer, *Lexicon*, 372-373, 375; BAGD, 467, 470; also Müller, 'Grundlinien', 225-226.

they represent different groupings of the same totality'.[111] It is also striking to see that the combination of the pairs is other than 'the perhaps more expected contrast of Jew and Greek'.[112] Indeed Paul has not yet mentioned the Jew.[113] On the contrary, he confirms that he 'received grace and apostleship to call people from among all the *Gentiles*' (1:5). Thus 1:8-15 also indicates that Paul's primary apostolic concern is related to the Gentiles.

He expresses his consciousness of being a debtor to these various groupings of Gentiles, not only because God laid upon him a duty toward them but also because, as F. Godet puts it, 'All those individuals, of whatever category, Paul regards as *his creditors*. He owes them his life, his person, in virtue of the grace bestowed on him and of the office which he has received'.[114] So P.S. Minear aptly observes: 'To the extent that Paul was indebted to God for his call, to that very extent he was indebted to those Gentiles for whose sake God had called him.'[115] Paul seems to have had a sense of appreciation of the Gentiles as well as a sense of voluntary obligation to preach to them, for whose sake he has been called. That is why he expresses his great desire to visit Rome and to preach the gospel to them. Now he attempts to fulfil his apostolic obligation by preaching *in writing* the gospel.

To sum up: Paul specifies his apostleship to the Gentiles right at the beginning of the letter (1:1, 5, 14-15). He is conscious that he was called and set apart to be an apostle who was to preach the gospel of God as the fulfilment of what God had promised beforehand in Scripture. He is fully aware that his apostleship is to bring about the obedience of faith from the Gentiles, and this

---

111 Cranfield, *Romans* 1, 83-85; so also Knox, 'Romans', 389; Dunn, *Romans* 1, 33; Ziesler, *Romans*, 66; Morris, *Romans*, 63. Cosgrove, 'Rom 1:18-4:25', 623. Cf. Bartsch, 'Empfänger', 83, who asserts that Paul refers to Jews with the term 'barbarians'.

112 Dunn, *Romans* 1, 35.

113 Thus, NIV's rendering, 'Greeks and *non-Greeks*' is misleading, because the latter can denote Jews, which here is not meant. Jewett's view in 'Ecumenical Theology', 603, is even more implausible: 'Those Jewish Christians whose Jewish accent remained prominent and who did not have enough education to be fully conversant with Greco-Roman culture would fall under this category [i.e. 'βάρβαροι'].'

114 Godet, *Romans*, 89; also affirmatively cited by Murray, *Romans* 1, 24 n. 18. Cf. Gager, *Origins*, 253.

115 Minear, *Obedience*, 104-105.

certainly coheres with what he writes in 15:14-21. In 1:1-15 Paul embraces believing Jews and Gentiles together, and treats them as one equal group (πάντες), who are described as ἀγαπητοί and κλητοὶ ἅγιοι (1:7). He also says that he has prayed and planned to visit the believers in Rome in view of his apostolic obligation to strengthen them by 'preaching the gospel' to them. Just as he had planned the visit under the strong sense of his apostolic self-consciousness, so now he writes this letter under the same mandate in order to fulfil his 'priestly duty' mentioned in 15:16.

3. The Equal Inclusion of Gentiles in God's Salvation: 1:16-17

We have shown that the beginning of the letter is shaped by Paul's apostolic self-consciousness and that this theme coheres with the clearer indication he makes in 15:14-21. The equal inclusion of the Gentiles into God's salvific blessing has already been examined from passages such as 10:20-21 and 15:21.[116] Does this theme also correspond to the thematic statement of the entire letter expressed in 1:16-17? We will investigate whether the thematic statement is made in order to affirm the priority of the Jew or to express the fundamental equality between Jew and Gentile in the gospel of God.

A. 'Ἰουδαίῳ ... πρῶτον': the Priority of Jews?

We have already noted that Paul indicates in 1:16-17 that he approaches his argument with much boldness.[117] The statement in 1:16-17 is not merely an affirmation of Paul's unshrinking proclamation of the gospel, but it is also a thematic statement[118] in which Paul reveals his approach to his argumentation in the rest

---

116 *Supra* pp. 30-35.
117 *Supra* pp. 35-36.
118 Most commentators regard 1:16-17 as containing the theme of Romans: e.g. Barth, *Romans*, 35; Meyer, *Romans* 1, 66; Nygren, *Romans*, 65; Barrett, *Romans*, 27; Käsemann, *Romans*, 21; Cranfield, *Romans* 1, 87; Black, *Romans*, 43; Wilckens, *Römer* 1, 77; Dunn, *Romans* 1, 36-37; cf. Ziesler, *Romans*, 35, 67.

Romans 15:14-21: An Interpretative Key? 47

of the letter.[119] Moreover, it conveys the apostolic purpose.[120] The reason why Paul is eager to preach the gospel to all in Rome (1:15) is because he is not ashamed of the gospel (an important 'γάρ' in 1:16a). The gospel itself is the power of God for salvation to *everyone* who believes. Then Paul adds, "Ἰουδαίῳ τε πρῶτον καὶ Ἕλληνι'.

This phrase is often taken as indicating the existence of two groups, the Jews and the Gentiles, of which the former has priority over the latter which is, however, also included. But in the Greek text Paul closely connects Jew and Gentile as a group described as παντί, by employing 'τε... καί'.[121] Just as Paul's 'πρῶτον' is not to be ignored, as we shall see below, so neither is his 'τε', because not only does it suggest 'the fundamental equality of Jew and Gentile in the face of the gospel'[122] but also sets aside the distinction between the two groups.[123] Thus N.T. Wright seems to offer the most appropriate rendering of the phrase: 'for the Jew first and also, equally, for the Greek'.[124]

The qualifier πρῶτον certainly qualifies Ἰουδαίῳ, and so it appears to denote a Jewish 'priority' in the sense of privilege or primacy.[125] The sense of privilege, however, is denied by the fact that *trouble and distress* as well as glory, honour and peace are also "Ἰουδαίῳ τε πρῶτον καὶ Ἕλληνι' (2:9-10). The immediate concluding remark is also striking: 'For God does not show fa-

---

119 Dunn, *Romans* 1, 37, 40.
120 Dahl, *Studies*, 82; Dunn, *Romans* 1, 33; Jewett, 'Ecumenical Theology', 609, but their insight has not been substantiated.
121 See BDF, 230, for the syntax of 'τε ... καί'.
122 Cranfield, *Romans* 1, 91.
123 BDF, 230: 'with τε καί [Rom 1:16] the distinction is rather set aside'.
124 Wright, 'Romans', 187f. But most of the English translations and commentators do not demonstrate the full significance of the phrase. KJV, RV, RSV and NASB render it as 'to the Jew first(,) and also to Greek'; and JB, NEB and Phillips allude to the priority of the Jews by using the conjunction 'but': '(for) (the)Jew first, *but* (the) Greek also (as well)'; it is NIV that indicates it most clearly: 'first for the Jew, *then* for the Gentile'. Some commentators also suggest such an allusion: Barrett, *Romans*, 27, 'Jew first, and then the Gentiles too'; Black, *Romans*, 44, though using RSV text, understands it as 'first to the Jew..., then to Greeks'; Kümmel, *Theology*, 193, cautiously puts 'then' in brackets: 'first to the Jews and [then] to the Greeks'. But it is significant that *Jewish New Testament* (translated by D.H. Stern) renders it, 'to the Jew especially, but equally to the Gentile'.
125 Cf. Sinclair, *Jesus*, 33.

vouritism [to Jews]' (2:11).¹²⁶ Such a sense of privilege is constantly denied or balanced by another perhaps more important claim, 'There is no difference' (3:22; 10:12; cf. Gal 3:28; Col 3:11). Furthermore, it seems evident from a wider context of Romans that Paul's primary concern was *not* to emphasise or defend the priority of the Jews as such in relation to the gospel.¹²⁷ In fact he says, 'As far as the gospel is concerned, they [the unbelieving Jews] are enemies [of God] on your account' (11:28a).

Of course, Paul claims that there is much advantage in every way in being a Jew, for to them the very words of God have been committed (3:1-2). It is striking, however, to note that Paul, a coherent writer, does not continue the list of Jewish advantages which he has started with πρῶτον ('first of all').¹²⁸ Neither does he explain it to give a logical base for Jewish advantages. In fact, he gives no support for an affirmation of Jewish advantage with 3:3-8; rather, he speaks against it. Furthermore, his immediate conclusion is, 'Are we [Jews] any better? Not at all! ... Jews and Gentiles alike are all under sin' (3:9). He then arrives at the overriding conclusion, 'There is no difference' (3:21-26). Neither does Paul expound the Jewish privileges in 9:4-5; he simply mentions them. On the contrary, he affirms the fact that Gentiles are included in those privileges throughout the letter, as we will show in Chapter 5.¹²⁹

Thus the πρῶτον in 1:16 needs to be understood in the wider context of Romans and of the other Pauline letters. The πρῶτον seems rather to indicate Jewish chronological priority in the first claim on the Messianic salvation.¹³⁰ The Jews had the privilege of

---

126 Such a note of 'no distinction thus no favouritism' frequently recurs in Romans and in other Pauline letters (1:5; 2:11; 3:9, 12, 19, 20, 22, 23, 27-31; 4:11, 12, 16; 5:12, 18; 8:32; 9:24; 10:4, 11, 12, 13; 11:32; 15:11; 1 Cor 1:22-24; 12:13; Gal 2:14-16; 3:26-29; Col 3:11; cf. Gal 5:6; 6:15).

127 *Pace* Beker, 'Faithfulness', 14. See *supra* pp. 14-16; for a fuller treatment, see Chae, 'Paul's Apostolic Self-Awareness', 123-126.

128 Dodd, *Romans*, 70f, seems distressed by the fact that Paul presents the argument in 3:1-8 in an 'obscure and feeble' way, and 'in the end dismisses the subject awkwardly'. But he wrongly expects Paul to defend the advantage of the Jews at this point.

129 *Infra* pp. 225-227.

130 Cf. Meyer, *Romans* 1, 67; Kaylor, *Covenant Community*, 34: 'That priority [i.e. "the Jew first"] is not a matter of God's partiality but due to only

preparation; salvation was of the Jews (John 4:22; Acts 2:39).[131] It is difficult, however, to maintain that the phrase Ἰουδαίῳ τε πρῶτον καὶ Ἕλληνι indicates the decisive evidence that Paul argues for the salvific advantage of the Jew,[132] because for him salvation is now open to everyone who believes without ethnic distinction.

B. *'Ἰουδαίῳ τε πρῶτον καὶ Ἕλληνι': the Inclusion of the Gentiles.*

C.K. Barrett stresses the importance of 1:16-17 by saying that it contains 'a summary of Paul's theology as a whole'.[133] If this remark sounds rather an exaggeration, Dunn represents the common view: the passage presents 'clearly the thematic statement for the entire letter'.[134] Scholars also generally agree that the major *theme* of the letter is the 'righteousness of God'. R. Bultmann, for example, puts much emphasis on 'the righteousness of God' as the theme of the entire letter, but makes no comment on 1:16b.[135] Dunn, however, provides a different emphasis. Observing that the theme is placed at the climax of the introduction, which has been deliberately built up by the usage of εὐαγγέλιον /εὐαγγελίσασθαι (1:1, 9, 15, 16) and of πίστις /πιστεύειν (1:5, 8, 12, 16, 17), he suggests that the principal emphasis in these verses should not be focused exclusively on 1:17, but on 1:16b.[136] Nevertheless, he expounds Romans largely under the theme of 'the righteousness of God', and maintains that the aim of the

---

God's historical working; however, it is finally reduced to a chronological priority and has no ultimate distinguishing force'.

131 The lines of preparation for the full revelation of the salvation of humanity were laid in Israel (Ziesler, *Romans*, 70), and so they were given the first opportunity for salvation according to their religious heritage.

132 So correctly Seifrid, *Justification*, 212; Murray, *Romans* 1, 28; Marshall, *Acts*, 230: the basis of the privilege of 'to the Jew first' is 'never made absolutely clear in the NT'. *Pace* those who assume a *Sonderweg* for the salvation of the Jews; for our critique of the views of Mussner and Stendahl, see *infra* pp. 280-282; p. 280 n. 271.

133 Barrett, *Romans*, 27; idem, 'I am not Ashamed', 19-50.

134 Dunn, *Romans* 1, 37; Cranfield, *Romans* 1, 87.

135 Bultmann, *Theology* 1, 271, 280, 286.

136 Dunn, *Romans* 1, 37-40. So also Sanders, *Jewish People*, 30; Hvalvik, '"To the Jew First"', 1-8.

whole epistle was to explain and defend the 'double emphasis' of Jewish priority and faith-alone.[137] So also Cranfield: 'The paradoxical insistence both on the fact that there is no διαστολή (3:22, 10:12) and also at the same time on the continuing validity of the Ἰουδαίῳ... πρῶτον... belongs to the substance of the epistle.'[138]

E.P. Sanders also notes a greater emphasis on the second part of 1:16 (παντὶ τῷ πιστεύοντι, Ἰουδαίῳ τε πρῶτον καὶ Ἕλληνι) than on the first part of 1:17 (δικαιοσύνη γὰρ θεοῦ ἐν αὐτῷ ἀποκαλύπτεται). He claims that the key to Paul's thought is the *equality* of both Jews and Gentiles in the matter of attaining salvation.[139] He plausibly asserts: 'The thrust of this [i.e. the phrase Ἰουδαίῳ τε πρῶτον καὶ Ἕλληνι] is not to claim superiority for the Jew: that is virtually presupposed. Paul is, in effect, arguing for the equality of the Gentile.'[140]

Sanders' interpretation seems correct for the following reasons. Firstly, as Cranfield correctly notes, 'the word τε ... is suggestive of the fundamental equality of Jew and Gentile in the face of the gospel'.[141] If the phrase Ἰουδαίῳ τε πρῶτον καὶ Ἕλληνι were not added, believing Jews would naturally assume that every (believing) Jew would be saved on the basis of OT texts such as Joel 2:32-3:21, where the salvation of *every Jew* who calls upon the name of the Lord is promised. The phrase is probably added therefore to put the Gentiles on an equal level with the Jews. Secondly, the παντί embraces both Jew and Gentile, and the only condition for salvation is 'faith' (τῷ πιστεύοντι). Paul affirms that it is Gentiles who believe rather than Jews (9:25-26, 27-29, 30, 31-33; 10:20, 21; 11:7, 20, etc.). The reason why Paul stresses 'faith' in 1:16-17 and 3:21-31 is probably because it highlights the basis of salvation which is now equally available in Christ Jesus to both Jews *and* Gentiles. This affirmation implies that he adds τε .... καὶ Ἕλληνι in 1:16-17 with the intention of establishing the theological truth that the Gentiles are equally included in God's salvific blessing. Thirdly, (as we will substantiate in the

---

137 Dunn, *Romans* 1, 37-40.
138 Cranfield, *Romans* 1, 91.
139 Sanders, *Jewish People*, 56-57 n. 63.
140 Sanders, *Palestinian Judaism*, 488-489. So also in his *Jewish People*, 30.
141 Cranfield, *Romans* 1, 91.

following chapters) Paul does not provide any argument for the primacy of the Jews in Romans. Rather he makes critical remarks about the unbelief of Jews. What he argues for in the letter is the equality of Jew and Gentile by affirming the legitimacy of the salvation of the Gentiles. Paul's stress in 1:16b is not on "Ἰουδαίῳ ... πρῶτον', but rather on 'τε ... καὶ Ἕλληνι'. This line of investigation will constitute the heart of our present study.

We have argued above that the main point of the thematic statement in 1:16-17 is not to establish the priority of the Jews but to stress the equal inclusion of the Gentiles in the salvific blessing of God. Whether our understanding is correct or not can be ascertained from the thematic conclusion of the main body of the letter (15:7-13), because we may rightly expect from Paul, a coherent thinker, that the thematic introduction to the main body of the letter (1:16-17) would agree with the thematic conclusion (15:7-13). A careful examination of 15:7-13 will reveal not only the conclusion of Paul's argument in the entire letter, but also his intention in the thematic introductory statement (1:16-17). Now we turn to examine 15:7-13 to conclude our investigation in this chapter. The section will be divided into two parts: 15:8-9a, where Paul interprets Christ's service for Jews and Gentiles, and 15:9b-12, where the structure of his argument is shown in affirming the place of the Gentiles by his striking use of OT passages.

4. Christ's Service for both Jews and Gentiles: 15:8-9a

The section 15:7-13 is often considered not only as 'the climax of the theological and ethical argument',[142] but also as 'the real summing up of the entire letter'.[143] But scholars differ in their views about the *subject matter* of, or Paul's intention concerning, the passage. F.C. Baur denies the genuineness of 15:1-13 because, for him, Paul could not possibly make the concession in 15:8 'to the Jews as to call Jesus Christ a minister of circumcision' who confirms God's promises to the Fathers, after having stressed so much the unfaithfulness and unbelief of the Jews.[144] Sanday and Headlam object to Baur by saying that 15:8 is in fact the whole

---

142 Jewett, 'Ecumenical Theology', 600.
143 Wright, 'Romans', 188; cf. Wilckens, *Römer* 3, 104-105.
144 Baur, *Paul* 1, 353-354.

point of the entire letter, which confirms the priority of the Jews (1:16; 2:9-10; 11:17-25).[145] Setting aside the correctness or otherwise of their conclusions, they all agree that 15:7-13 (or more specifically 15:8-9a) affirms Christ's service as directed primarily to the Jews. More recent scholars also maintain a similar position. J. Ziesler and H. Moxnes, for example, put more weight on Christ's service to the Jews by assigning the clause 'in order to confirm the promises' almost exclusively to the Jews.[146] We will submit two objections (contextual and syntactical) to the common view defended by Ziesler and Moxnes, and propose the hypothesis that Paul's deeper intention for mentioning Christ's service here is to stress Christ's inclusive ministry for the *Gentiles*.

A. *15:8-9a within the Context*

Our present passage appears between 15:5-7 (which is the summing-up of the exhortation for unity given in 14:1-15:4) and 15:9b-12 (which is the scriptural proof for Gentiles' glorification of God for his mercy). Although Paul does not identify the 'weak' and the 'strong' with particular ethnic groups, the 'γάρ', the 'περιτομή' and the 'ἔθνη' in vv. 8-9 indicate that the concluding exhortation is somehow related to the Jew-Gentile issue. Paul writes 15:9b-12 to substantiate his claim that 'the Gentiles may glorify God for his mercy' (15:9a), the result having been made possible through Christ's service. Thus (as we will show) assigning the phrase 'in order to confirm the promises' rather exclusively, or even primarily to the Jews, seems to miss the very point which Paul attempts to make by connecting Jesus' ministry and the OT quotations with the thematic key word, 'ἔθνη' (15:9-12).

Moreover, those who maintain that here Paul affirms the priority of the Jews seem also to have misunderstood Paul's argument so far, especially in Romans 4; 9-11.[147] Paul surely knew that Jesus' ministry was among the Jews,[148] but he does not argue for it there. Instead he has argued that the promise to Abraham is

---

145 Sanday and Headlam, *Romans*, 399.
146 Moxnes, *Theology*, 87; Ziesler, *Romans*, 339; see also Ziesler's comment elsewhere (*Pauline Christianity*, 20): 'his [Christ's] ministry was essentially to Israel (Rom 15:8)'.
147 We will attempt to demonstrate this in our Chapters 3 and 5 in detail.
148 Keck, *Paul*, 40.

Romans 15:14-21: An Interpretative Key?

effective not only for the descendants according to flesh, but also for those [Gentiles] of the same faith (4:12, 16, 22-24). In fact, an important point which Paul attempts to make in Romans 4 is that Abraham believed against all hope 'in order to become the father of many nations (=Gentiles; 4:18)'.[149] Again, in Romans 9 he has argued that the word of God that has not failed (9:6; ἀλήθεια θεοῦ: 15:8) is not to be limited to the Jews alone but includes the Gentiles also; and he elaborates this theme throughout the section Romans 9-11.[150] Thus Paul seems to say that Christ's service and the promise to the patriarchs were intended to include both Jews *and* Gentiles. R. B. Hays may be right to link the καθὼς γέγραπται to both 15:9a and 15:8a,[151] but the more emphasised theme concerning the 'ἔθνη' is to be noted. Although 15:9b and 10 contain references to the Jews ('I', and 'with his people'), the reference 'ἔθνη' is more evident and prominent in the catena.

B. *The Syntax of 15:8-9a*

That the main verb is missing in 15:9a causes difficulties in connecting the phrase τὰ δὲ ἔθνη ... δοξάσαι of 15:9a to 15:8. But the different discussions can be grouped into two categories[152] — some take 15:9a as

> (a) directly subordinate to λέγω γάρ, with εἰς τὸ βεβαιῶσαι, κτλ. as parenthetical, which would render: 'I tell you *that* Christ has become a servant of the Jews for God's truth, to confirm the promises made to the fathers, *but that* the Gentiles are glorifying God for his mercy.'[153]

Others take it as

> (b) dependent on εἰς τό and co-ordinating with βεβαιῶσαι τὰς ἐπαγγελίας τῶν πατέρων, which would render: 'I tell you that Christ has become a servant of the Jews for the sake of God's truth, in order to con-

---

149 See *infra* Chapter 3.
150 See *infra* Chapter 5.
151 Hays, 'Christ', 124.
152 See Cranfield, *Romans* 2, 742-744, for discussion of six options. See also Wilckens, *Römer* 3, 106.
153 So similarly Cranfield, *Romans* 2, 742-744; Stuart, *Romans*, 541; Godet, *Romans*, 470-471.

firm the promises made to the fathers, and the Gentiles glorify God for his mercy.'[154]

Cranfield who favours (a) argues that 15:9a is directly connected to the opening λέγω of 15:8 (rendering δέ with a strong adversative, 'but'). This view is grammatically possible and plausible, particularly as it puts the two ὑπέρ terms in parallel.[155] However, Dunn objects for at least three reasons. First, putting 15:9a as contrast (between 'the promises of the fathers' and the acceptability of the Gentiles), is not coherent with Paul's earlier argument in, e.g. 4:16; 9:8.[156] Second, since both ἀλήθεια and ἔλεος indicate God's character as portrayed in the OT, the verses are not to be taken as adversative. Third, 'Paul's whole point is that Christ became servant of the circumcised *not* with a view to their salvation alone, but to confirm *both* phases of God's saving purpose: to Jew first but also to Gentile'.[157] Thus he translates δέ as 'and' by taking Christ's service equally for the Jews and for the Gentiles. This construction makes it clear that 'the call of the Gentiles is shown to be (as it certainly was), equally with the fulfilment of the promise to the Jews, dependent on the covenant with Abraham (4:11, 12, 16, 17)'.[158]

However, Dunn does not consider Paul's intent in this construction. He plausibly juxtaposes Christ's service for the Jews and for the Gentiles. Yet this is not enough to grasp the point of the argument. First, those who contend for the option (b) see the two effects of Christ's work. C. Hodge, for example, contends: 'the one, that the truth of God has been vindicated by the fulfilment of the promises made to the Jews; and the other, that the Gentiles have been led to praise God for his mercy.'[159] They seem right to see two effects of Christ's work, but in this case καί should have been used rather than a mere consecutive δέ. Second, Paul has argued thus far that 'the promises made to the fathers' are not to be limited to the Jews alone (4:13, 16; 9:4, 8; cf. 2 Cor

---

154 Cf. Barrett, *Romans*, 249; Dunn, *Romans* 2, 846-848.
155 Cranfield, *Romans* 2, 742-744.
156 Dunn, *Romans* 2, 847-848; so also Sanday and Headlam, *Romans*, 398.
157 Dunn, *Romans* 2, 847-848; the quotation is from p. 848, with his emphases.
158 Sanday and Headlam, *Romans*, 398.
159 Hodge, *Romans*, 433.

1:20-21). Especially the phrase εἰς τὸ βεβαιῶσαι τὰς ἐπαγγελίας τῶν πατέρων is probably the recapitulation of εἰς τὸ εἶναι βεβαίαν τὴν ἐπαγγελίαν in 4:16. There Paul has already affirmed that the promises to the fathers were intended 'not only to those [Jews] who are of the law but also to those [Gentiles] who are of the faith of Abraham' (4:16), and the argument reveals that his focus is on the latter. Third, this view does not take note of the carefully constructed grammatical parallel between 15:8a and 9a, and between 15:8b and 9a. These considerations lead us to suggest a third option, (c) taking 15:9a as subordinated to εἰς τὸ βεβαιῶσαι, κτλ and as related to γεγενῆσθαι. Both 15:8a and 9a are syntactically parallel: the *accusatives* of Χριστός and of the plural τὰ ἔθνη, the two aorist infinitives, and the parallel usage of the conjunction ὑπέρ, as shown below:

15: 8a   Χριστὸν διάκονον <u>γεγενῆσθαι</u> περιτομῆς <u>ὑπέρ</u> ἀληθείας θεοῦ,
8b   εἰς τὸ <u>βεβαιῶσαι</u> τὰς ἐπαγγελίας τῶν πατέρων
9a   τὰ δὲ ἔθνη <u>ὑπέρ</u> ἐλέους <u>δοξάσαι</u> τὸν θεόν

Grammatically εἰς followed by the accusative of the articular infinitive in the aorist expresses a strong purpose, connoting 'in order to confirm' or 'with a view to the confirmation of the promises made to the fathers'. Paul's retention of the δοξάσαι in the aorist (where one could expect the present tense) does not seem to point 'to the historical fact that the Gentiles had already been received into the Church',[160] nor to express 'one comprehensive act of thanksgiving on their [the Gentiles'] admission once for all into the Church of God'.[161] Paul's use of present/future tenses in the following quotations seems to indicate that he is more concerned with the Gentiles' present/future glorification of God rather than with punctiliar or collective past acts. The unusual usage of δοξάσαι in the same aorist infinitive here seems to indicate that this δοξάσαι is parallel to the aorist βεβαι-

---

160 Liddon, *Romans*, 277.
161 Vaughan, *Romans*, 252.

ὦσαι, and thus dependent on εἰς τό,[162] which also implies a strong purpose: Christ's service specifically with the Gentiles' praise of God for his mercy in view.[163]

E.H. Gifford plausibly observes the same grammatical construction between ὑπὲρ ἀληθείας and ὑπὲρ ἐλέους. But he asserts that the main emphasis of the passage lies in 15:8b, for Paul is appealing to the 'strong', i.e. the Gentiles, to bear the 'weak' Jewish believers, by emphasising Christ being a Jew in fulfilment of the promise to the fathers.[164] At this point J. Moiser seems right to say that Paul is talking more directly to the 'strong' in 15:1-6, and to the 'weak' in 15:7-12. As the 'strong' should acknowledge the privileges of the 'weak', the 'weak' should now recognise the legitimacy of the 'strong'.[165] According to H.P. Liddon, Christ became the servant of the circumcision at his incarnation for the following reasons: (1) *generally*, to prove God's truthfulness, and (2) *specifically* to confirm the promises to the Patriarchs, and above all to make Gentiles glorify God for his mercy.[166] The positions of ὑπὲρ ἀληθείας θεοῦ right after the περιτομῆς, and ὑπὲρ ἐλέους right after the τὰ ἔθνη, suggest that Paul mentions Christ's ministry for the Jews in general terms but for the Gentiles with a specific emphasis. Furthermore, the δέ in τὰ δὲ ἔθνη is probably 'inserted for the sake of more full and entire explanation',[167] and thus it probably connotes 'add[ing] further'[168] or 'more specifically'. The Jews would glorify God for his truthfulness as he fulfilled his promises to the fathers, and the Gentiles would glorify God for his mercy as he included Gentiles also in his promises to the fathers.

The clause εἰς τὸ βεβαιῶσαι τὰς ἐπαγγελίας τῶν πατέρων (15:8b) is stressed; and it could be placed even before 15:8a. But by putting 15:8b between 15:8a and 9a, Paul seems to have two goals: (a) to ensure connections not only with Χριστός in both 15:7b and 8a, but also with the ἔθνη in 15:9a, which introduces

---

162 Barrett, *Romans*, 249, following Lietzmann.
163 Godet, *Romans*, 471, correctly rejects Hofmann's view of δοξάσαι being an optative, but he does not note the careful construction with the aorist tense of the infinitive to parallel the same aorist βεβαιῶσαι.
164 Gifford, *Romans*, 224.
165 Moiser, 'Rethinking', 580.
166 Liddon, *Romans*, 277.
167 Stuart, *Romans*, 540-541.
168 Stuart, *Romans*, 541.

the key Gentile theme of the OT quotations in 15:9b-12; and (b) to narrow down his assertion from a general fact to specific affirmations: (i) Christ is from the Jews, (ii) he confirms the promises given to the Jewish fathers, and (iii) Christ's service is more specifically related to the Gentiles. Paul structures his argument in order to bring more emphasis to the Gentile element. Then we may interpret the construction of the passage as saying:

> I tell you that Christ became a servant of the Jews for God's truth [not only] in order to confirm the promises to the fathers, but [more specifically] in order for the Gentiles to glorify God for his mercy.[169]

God's promises embraced both Jews and Gentiles, as Paul has emphatically argued in, e.g. 4:13-16. For Paul God has confirmed his promises to the fathers for both Jews and Gentiles,[170] which can be seen as 'God's truth' for the Jews and 'his mercy' for the Gentiles.[171]

However, with the emphatic and frequent ἔθνη[172] Paul not only recapitulates the earlier argument concerning the emphasis on the salvation of the Gentiles in Romans 2-4 (2:14; 3:29-30; 4:16-18) and 9-11 (9:24-26, 30; 10:20; 11:11-15, 25),[173] but also presents a decisive climax to his purpose in writing Romans with his deliberate choice of, and intensive argument from, every section of the OT, as we will show in the next section. For Paul, Christ's service for the Gentiles does not contradict the OT but, rather, fulfils it.[174] Furthermore, it is vital to note that Paul's point in 15:8-9 is not that the Gentiles' glorification of God is 'only as a secondary

---

169 Cf. NIV, RV, TEV, NEB, JB, NJB, RSV and NRSV, which connect 15:9a to 8b with similar emphasis. Our view allows a certain contrast between v. 9a and v. 8a, as expressed with δέ.

170 See *infra* Chapter 3.

171 It is noticeable that in Romans Paul mainly uses ἔλεος/ἐλεέω in relation to the Gentiles. The whole point of 9:15-23 is that God was pleased to show mercy to the Gentiles; and this is so in 11:30-32 (except 11:31b; cf. 11:32). 15:8-9 indicates that God not only showed mercy in Christ, but also that the Gentiles have responded to his mercy, whilst the Jews have not (11:30).

172 No less than six times in 15:9-12.

173 Dunn, *Romans* 2, 848.

174 Morris, *Romans*, 504-505.

result of this Messiahship',[175] but to indicate a *more specified intention* of Jesus' Messiahship.[176]

One may argue that our interpretation is not sufficiently supported by the syntax; the δέ is rather weak to convey the weight of meaning which we are attributing. Indeed, a ἵνα (as in Gal 3:14) or ὅπως (as in 9:17a, b: LXX Exod 9:16; Gal 1:4) would have been better for our position. However, we claim that the syntax still permits such a view and we have advanced reasons for thinking that this might be what Paul *meant* to say, even if he could have expressed the purpose more sharply. Paul had already connected Christ's service (solely) to the *Gentiles* in Gal 3:14: ἵνα εἰς τὰ ἔθνη ἡ εὐλογία τοῦ Ἀβραὰμ γένηται ἐν Χριστῷ Ἰησοῦ. Then it is possible that here in Romans he expresses himself rather vaguely. In Romans Paul has also already argued for applying the promise to the fathers to the believing Gentiles (4:16-17),[177] and Christ's obedience to all humanity (5:12-21).[178] The plausibility of our argument can be further demonstrated from the carefully selected OT passages in 15:9b-12, which clearly highlight Christ's ministry with respect to the Gentiles.[179]

5. The OT Predictions concerning the Gentiles: 15:9b-12

At the outset of the letter Paul has indicated that the gospel he was called to preach was 'promised beforehand through his prophets in the Holy Scriptures' (1:2). In the concluding section of the letter he sums up his argument by citing a string of OT passages. We may then construe that the main point of this catena is what Paul has been arguing for all along in the entire letter, and thus gives us a hint of how to interpret Paul's use of the OT in Romans. It is significant that Paul selects the passages containing

---

175 *Pace* Sanday and Headlam, *Romans*, 398.

176 In the Gospels, Jesus' ministry is portrayed with far more emphasis on the Jews (see Jeremias, *Nations*, 24-51; Hanson, *Paradox*, 79-97, especially p. 96), and in comparison, Paul's application of Jesus' ministry with more specific focus on the Gentiles, is significant.

177 See *infra* Chapter 3.

178 See *infra* Chapter 4.

179 Hays, *Echoes*, 72 infers that Paul's presentation of Jesus' service in relation to the Gentiles (15:9a) is influenced by his understanding of LXX Ps 17.

Romans 15:14-21: An Interpretative Key? 59

the key word 'ἔθνη',[180] and modifies the texts and contexts to establish his argument, as we shall show. C. Stanley's examination of the textual variations alone seems inadequate to help us grasp Paul's purpose in this precisely composed catena.[181] We shall show that with these OT passages Paul attempts to illustrate that the inclusion of Gentiles in the Jews' worship of God is 'the eschatological fulfillment of the scriptural vision'.[182] The fact that this catena is connected to 15:8-9a with καθὼς γέγραπται, indicates Paul's intention to emphasise Christ's service to the *Gentiles*.[183]

A. Rom 15:9b (=LXX Ps 17:50=LXX 2 Kgdms 22:50)

MT Ps 18:50   עַל־כֵּן אוֹדְךָ בַגּוֹיִם יְהוָה וּלְשִׁמְךָ אֲזַמֵּרָה

LXX Ps 17:50 διὰ τοῦτο ἐξομολογήσομαί σοι ἐν ἔθνεσιν κύριε καὶ τῷ ὀνόματί σου ψαλῶ
Rom 15:9b Διὰ τοῦτο ἐξομολογήσομαί σοι ἐν ἔθνεσιν,   καὶ τῷ ὀνόματί σου ψαλῶ.

LXX Ps 17:50 (=LXX 2 Kgdms 22:50[184]) is quoted exactly (except for the omitted vocative κύριε) in 15:9. However, it is indeed striking to note the significant change in the context:[185] in

---

180 Ellis, *Paul's Use*, 50, 102, n. 2; Hays, *Echoes*, 71. The fact that this chain of quotations is the only example in the Pauline letters where the selection is taken from every section of the OT seems to show that he is confirming his argument to safeguard Gentile salvation, a theme which has been raised from the beginning of the letter (1:2), and especially in Rom 3-4; 9-11.
181 Stanley, *Language*, 179-183, himself maintains a Pauline composition; Hays, *Echoes*, 71-73, asserts that Paul selects the passages with a precise intention.
182 Hays, *Echoes*, 71.
183 Dunn, *Romans* 2, 848: 'The following quotations (vv. 9-12) elaborate principally the latter theme of vv. 8-9a.'
184 This verse is identical with LXX Ps 17:50, except the transposition of κύριε and that the definite article τοῖς and the preposition ἐν are added (...σοι Κύριε ἐν τοῖς ἔθνεσιν καὶ ἐν τῷ ὀνόματί ...).
185 Commentators pay little attention to Paul's modification of the context; Barrett and Dunn take no note at all, while Sanday and Headlam, *Romans*, 398, and Cranfield, *Romans* 2, 744-46, offer minimum treatment.

the original context David praises God for his deliverance from the hand of his (Gentile) enemies and from the hand of Saul (LXX 2 Kgdms 22:1=LXX Ps 17:1). Apart from 'the attackers from my people' the hostile Gentile nations are seen as David's enemies,[186] foes and violent men (LXX Ps 17:49f) who are outside God's help and salvation (LXX Ps 17:42), and who are utterly destroyed by David (LXX Ps 17:38f, 45-49). The reason why David praises the Lord God is because of 'God's wonderful act of rescue of his royal servant'[187] from the Gentile enemies, that is, he celebrates the *Gentiles' complete defeat*. But Paul quotes this verse as though (note 'as it is written') David praises God because the Gentiles glorify God for his mercy of granting them salvation (15:9).[188] Moreover, the fact that Paul does *not* quote the very next verse, '... he shows unfailing kindness (cf. Exod 20:6; Deut 5:10, etc.) to his anointed, *to David and his descendants for ever*' (LXX Ps 17:51), seems to suggest that Paul's primary reason for quoting only LXX Ps 17:50 and not 17:51 is due to his overall intention to secure the place of the salvation of the *Gentiles* rather than to confirm God's covenant faithfulness to Israel, David's descendants.

Furthermore, according to the context in the Psalm, the Gentiles are not at all participating with the pious Jew (David) in praise and worship, but Paul significantly includes such a notion here: the Gentiles do glorify God for his mercy (15:9a), '*Therefore*' [or '*for this reason*' (Διὰ τοῦτο)] I will praise[189] you among the Gentiles' (15:9b). The bases for 'therefore' in the Psalm and in Rom 15:9 are completely different. In this first quotation Paul finds the joint worship in the believing community of the Jews and the Gentiles,[190] and uses it as an *Überschrift* for the entire section of the quotations (15:9-12).[191] In the words of David, Paul may have seen his own role as the (Jewish) apostle to

---

186 Anderson, *Psalms 1*, 166.

187 Craus, *Psalms 1-59*, 266.

188 For Luther, *Romans*, 213, such a usage is neither an improper use of Scripture nor a contradiction to what he has argued all along.

189 The verb ἐξομολογήσομαι means to 'confess publicly' (Zerwick and Grosvenor, *Analysis*, 491), but it is used in the LXX of praising God in temple worship (Morris, *Romans*, 505 n. 50).

190 Cranfield, *Romans* 2, 745.

191 Schlier in Dunn, *Romans* 2, 849; but Dunn himself prefers to take the view that the Gentiles' joining in the praise is not envisaged in this quote.

the Gentiles.[192] Paul stresses that this prophecy provides the basis for receiving the Gentiles into the church.[193]

B. Rom 15:10 (=LXX Deut 32:43)

Paul presses his point further by quoting LXX Deut 32:43 exactly,[194] and by linking the quotations of 15:9 and 10 with καὶ πάλιν λέγει.[195] In Deut 32:43 Moses calls on the Gentiles to rejoice not because of their own salvation (32:35, 41, 43c) but because of the salvation of Israel ('[He] will make atonement for his land and his people [Israelites]': 32:43d). In fact, the Gentiles in Canaan who resisted Israel are seen as Israel's adversaries, upon whom God's vengeance will be executed.[196] The original Hebrew context of this verse is 'a strong promise of God's covenant faithfulness to his people',[197] and the summon for the Gentiles is to *'Praise his people, O you nations'* (הַרְנִינוּ גוֹיִם עַמּוֹ).[198]

LXX Deut 32:43   εὐφράνθητε ἔθνη μετὰ τοῦ λαοῦ αὐτοῦ
Rom 15:10   Εὐφράνθητε, ἔθνη, μετὰ τοῦ λαοῦ αὐτοῦ.

But in the LXX the verse is not only expanded but also significantly modified by adding μετά: 'Rejoice, O Gentiles, *with* his people.' This is probably done to lessen the offensiveness of Deuteronomy 32 to the Gentiles in a Diaspora context.[199] However, it is significant indeed to see Paul taking this short sentence out from a very long verse and using it to express his own theology, namely, that 'God's original purpose and promise of the

---

192 Käsemann, *Romans*, 386.
193 Boylan, *Romans*, 228.
194 For Calvin, Paul is quoting from Ps 67: 3, 4a, 5 (Ps 97:1 as well, for Luther, *Romans*, 213), where a similar idea is repeated: 'May the peoples praise you, O God; may all the peoples praise you.'
195 'Furthermore it says' (Dunn, Käsemann); λέγει without a subject is also found in, e.g. 9:25; 10:21; Gal 3:16; cf. Eph 4:8; 5:14.
196 Craigie, *Deuteronomy*, 389.
197 Dunn, *Romans* 2, 849.
198 RSV, so too Craigie; though the Hebrew text is uncertain: NRSV renders as 'Praise, O Heavens (שׁמים), his people'; so similarly REB, NAB, NJB.
199 Dunn, *Romans* 2, 849.

covenant made to Israel is now open to all [i.e. even for Gentiles] who believe'.[200]

Furthermore, Paul summons the Gentiles to rejoice not merely for the salvation of Israel, as in Deuteronomy, but also significantly for *their inclusion* in *her salvation* which has been made available to them because of God's mercy shown in Christ's service (15:8-9a). Thus Gentiles and Jews shall unite in the praise of God for their salvation.[201] It is more than eschatological praise to God,[202] for many believing Gentiles have already been rejoicing together with believing Jews. That Paul (probably deliberately[203]) omits the eschatological expression ἐν τῇ ἡμέρᾳ ἐκείνῃ in 15:12 warns us not to over-emphasise the eschatological interpretation, although Paul's frequent use of ἀνίστημι in connection with resurrection has led some to stress such an interpretation.[204]

C. Rom 15:11 (=LXX Ps 116:1)

This quotation from LXX Ps 116:1 is taken to provide a further proof that 'the inclusion of the Gentiles was not a divine afterthought'.[205] Only the first verse of the two in the Psalm is quoted here, but the second verse gives us a clear impression why Paul has selected this Psalm: the psalmist summons all the Gentiles to praise God for his mercy and truth,[206] which corresponds with 15:8-9a.

MT Ps 117:1   הַלְלוּ אֶת־יְהוָה כָּל־גּוֹיִם שַׁבְּחוּהוּ כָּל־הָאֻמִּים

LXX Psa 116:1 αἰνεῖτε τὸν κύριον πάντα τὰ ἔθνη ἐπαινέσατε
               αὐτόν πάντες οἱ λαοί
Rom 15:11   Αἰνεῖτε, πάντα τὰ ἔθνη, τὸν κύριον, καὶ
               ἐπαινεσάτωσαν αὐτὸν πάντες οἱ λαοί.

---

200 Dunn, *Romans* 2, 849.
201 Sanday and Headlam, *Romans*, 398.
202 Cf. Käsemann, *Romans*, 386.
203 Since this is the only change in the verbatim quotation.
204 E.g. Käsemann, Wilckens, Dunn in their commentaries; but cf. Cranfield who takes it as 'one who rises' without giving much force to resurrection.
205 Anderson, *Psalms* 2, 796.
206 Cf. Ps 22:27-29; 47; 72:11-19; 100; 113:2-3.

Paul makes two significant modification to the text. (1) Paul has moved the phrase πάντα τὰ ἔθνη forward, and thus emphatically expresses that he specifically addresses the Gentiles. For Paul it is important for 'all you Gentiles' to praise the Lord, and so he exhorts them to praise the Lord. The advanced phrase indicates that for Paul the Gentiles' praise of God was the most important reason for the citation.[207]

(2) The modification of the imperative from the second person plural (ἐπαινέσατε) to the third person plural (ἐπαινεσάτωσαν), together with 'καί' in front, seems to indicate that through the Psalm Paul primarily speaks to the Gentiles, and urges them to let πάντες οἱ λαοί praise the Lord.[208] The Gentiles should praise God for his mercy, and for his promises to the patriarchs of the Jews, but furthermore it is vital for the believers to *let* all the peoples praise him.[209] Almost Paul's entire life after his conversion was devoted to enabling the Gentiles to praise God by proclaiming the gospel of Christ to them.

Paul also makes some contextual changes. For the psalmist, the mercy is (exclusively) 'towards us [i.e. the *Israelites*]' (LXX Ps 116:2), but for Paul it is given to the *Gentiles,* though not exclusively (15:9a). According to the Psalm the reason why the nations should praise the Lord is because of God's steadfast love toward 'us', i.e. Israel, or because of 'their belonging to the realm of creation'.[210] But according to the context of Romans, they should rejoice because of God's mercy toward themselves.

Furthermore, in the Psalm πάντα τὰ ἔθνη and πάντες οἱ λαοί seem to refer to the same addressees (in contrast to 'us' in LXX Ps 116:2), yet have been variously employed to avoid literary repetition. But in Romans the phrases seem to have been used to refer to different ethnic groups. The quotation exhorts Group A (πάντα τὰ ἔθνη) to let Group B (πάντες οἱ λαοί) praise the Lord. Group A may represent the believing Gentiles, and Group B the unbelievers (either Gentiles or Jews, or both). If we are right,

---

[207] Similarly, Stanley, *Language*, 181-182.

[208] The renderings of NIV, TEV and NJB do not convey this modification, but correctly, NRSV, REB, NAB and NASB.

[209] The translation of, e.g. NIV does not convey the implications of this change; but correctly, e.g. NASB, RSV, RV.

[210] Martin-Achard, as cited in Anderson, *Psalms* 2, 796; Similarly, Craus, *Psalms 60-150*, 391.

we may infer that through the modification of the quotation, Paul implicitly encourages Group A to witness to Group B, thus enabling the latter to praise the Lord. From the phrases πάντα τὰ ἔθνη and πάντες οἱ λαοί Paul finds what he has attempted to put across emphatically concerning universality in Romans 9-11 with phrases, 'all the earth' and 'the ends of the world', and 'everyone' or 'all' (e.g. 10:11, 13; 11:32), but with a clear intention to affirm the salvific blessing of the Gentiles.

D. Rom 15:12 (=LXX Isa 11:10)

MT Isa 11:10   וְהָיָה בַּיּוֹם הַהוּא שֹׁרֶשׁ יִשַׁי אֲשֶׁר עֹמֵד לְנֵס
עַמִּים אֵלָיו גּוֹיִם יִדְרֹשׁוּ וְהָיְתָה מְנֻחָתוֹ כָּבוֹד

LXX Isa 11:10 καὶ ἔσται ἐν τῇ ἡμέρᾳ ἐκείνῃ ἡ ῥίζα τοῦ Ἰεσσαὶ καὶ ὁ ἀνιστάμενος ἄρχειν ἐθνῶν ἐπ' αὐτῷ ἔθνη ἐλπιοῦσιν καὶ ἔσται ἡ ἀνάπαυσις αὐτοῦ τιμή

Rom 15:12   Ἔσται ἡ ῥίζα τοῦ Ἰεσσαί, καὶ ὁ ἀνιστάμενος ἄρχειν ἐθνῶν· ἐπ' αὐτῷ ἔθνη ἐλπιοῦσιν.

This final quotation of the catena is taken exactly from LXX Isa 11:10 (which is considerably paraphrased from the Hebrew text), except for the omission of ἐν τῇ ἡμέρᾳ ἐκείνῃ. A further reinforcement of the argument is again indicated by καὶ πάλιν Ἡσαΐας λέγει. According to the wider context of LXX Isa 11, the author rejoices because of the salvation of the Israelites (Isa 11:11-12; 12:1-2) and the imminent arrival of the messianic kingdom. The Messiah's 'rule over the nations: ἄρχειν ἐθνῶν' means their destruction ('the enemies of Judah shall perish'; Isa 11:13); 'the Root of Jesse' will do exactly what the Lord did to the Egyptians when he delivered Israel from them (Isa 11:16). From such a context Paul selects the verse to emphasise the Gentiles' salvation and hope. The nuance of the LXX sentence 'The nations will hope in him' (ἐπ' αὐτῷ ἔθνη ἐλπιοῦσιν), conveys the Gentiles' 'hope', and it seems only natural for Paul to appeal to Isaiah, who is above all the prophet of the influx of the nations (cf. e.g. Isa 2:2-4; 40-55).

It is striking to note, however, that with this quotation Paul directly links the Gentiles with the Messiah. Paul implies that the Messiah arose to rule the Gentiles, and thus in him the Gentiles shall hope. Often the messianic promise comprises both the vindication of Israel and the *destruction of the Gentiles* (Ps. 2:8-9; 72:8-9; 110:1; *Pss. Sol.* 17:30).[211] For Paul, as for many other Jews, however, the messianic promise brings hope to the Gentiles,[212] and he could find numerous biblical and extrabiblical references as well (e.g. Ps 22:27; 86:9; Isa 9:2; 49:6; 56:6-7; 60:3; Dan 7:14; Tob 13:11; 14:6-7; *Pss. Sol.* 17:35-36). It is significant that Paul selects a positive phrase from such a 'negative' context for Gentiles, probably to correct a prevailing critical attitude on the part of Jews towards Gentiles. The selection of the verse which sums up the quotations as a whole,[213] seems to convey sufficiently clearly that Paul's intention is related to affirming or safeguarding the legitimacy of Gentile salvation as being the fulfilment of prophecy: the Gentiles shall hope in the Messiah, the Son of David.

By continuing the theme of hope in 15:13, Paul resumes the point he had stressed earlier in 8:22-25 and in 15:4-6. The benedictory prayer of 15:13 corresponds to 15:4-6 where practical unity within the community is stressed with the theme of hope that causes 'endurance and encouragement'. 'Hope' is a prominent theme in Romans,[214] and Paul sums up the argument of 12:1-15:13 with a reference to the hope which is based on 'the root of Jesse' as promised for the Gentiles (15:12), and for his readers (15:13). Joy comes from hope (12:12). 'The God of hope' originates hope[215] and gives it to those who trust in him, and strengthens their hope by the Holy Spirit (15:16; Gal 5:5; cf. 1 Thess 4:7-8; 2 Thess 2:13).

But it needs to be noted that 15:12 and 13 are more closely related by means of a key word, 'hope'. The significant double

---

[211] Dunn, *Romans* 2, 850. For Jewish view of the Gentiles see Sanders, *Jesus*, 213-218; cf. Hengel, *Judaism* 1, 176-177.

[212] See, e.g. Chance, *Jerusalem*, 12-14.

[213] Cranfield, *Romans* 2, 747; Dunn, *Romans* 2, 850.

[214] See Wedderburn, *Reasons*, 105-108, for Paul's dealing with the theme of hope in Romans as a whole.

[215] Dunn, Morris, Murray; cf. Cranfield and Wilckens in their commentaries.

reference to 'hope' in this verse seems to emphasise the cosmic goal of redemption, joy, peace, faith and hope,[216] by connecting the hope with the Gentiles, who formerly did not have hope (cf. Eph 2:12) but have now received it. Joy and peace can come to people 'in believing' (or 'because you believe').[217] Joy is the 'joy of faith' (Phil 1:25) and the fruit of the Spirit (Gal 5:22); and this phrase (ἐν τῷ πιστεύειν), being linked with 1:16f, both reminds us of and summarises Paul's whole argument in 1:18-15:13.[218]

E. Conclusion

We have tried to demonstrate that Paul has selected and constructed the catena primarily to illustrate the salvation of the Gentiles and their inclusion in the people of God, and to show that this is scripturally legitimate. To achieve this aim he often modifies the texts and/or contexts, and such alterations indicate his intention in 'reinterpreting' the quoted passages.

We have pointed out (and will do so in the following chapters) that Paul often uses the OT in different sense from the original. Since the catena we have just examined, i.e. 15:9-12 is the last quotation from the OT in Romans, we may clarify some points in this regard. Paul's such use of the OT is not to be regarded as peculiar[219] or weakening his argument; rather it is to be taken as revealing the *true* meaning which God originally intended. In fact Paul asserts that he now discloses the mystery hidden for long ages past (16:25). He declares in his letter to the Colossians, 'I have become its [church's] servant by the commission God gave me to present to you the word of God in its fulness— the mystery that has been kept hidden for ages and generations' (Col 1:25-26). The word of God which Paul presents in its fullness is defined as 'the mystery', and God has chosen to make this mystery known among the Gentiles (Col 1:27a).[220]

---

216 Käsemann, *Romans*, 387.
217 Moulton and Turner, *Grammar* 3, 145; 4, 90. Cf. Moffatt's rendering, 'with all joy and peace in your faith'.
218 Dunn, *Romans* 2, 853.
219 See *infra* p. 142 n. 262.
220 O'Brien, *Colossians, Philemon*, 81-87. The author of Ephesians says the same thing: for him, it was 'the mystery .... which God purposed in Christ' (Eph 1:9), and it is 'that through the gospel the Gentiles are heirs together with Israel, members together of one body and sharers together in the promise in

Then Paul's interpretation of the word of God in its fullness is closely connected to the inclusion of the Gentiles in the salvific blessing of God. Paul finds justification in using the OT with the textual and/or contextual modification in his attempt to explain their legitimate inclusion in this blessing. He is convinced that he exposes the true meaning of the passages which was hidden for ages even to the authors/prophets of old generations themselves. What R.T. France comments in respect to Matthew's use of the OT is also applicable to Paul: 'what may seem to us an embarrassingly obscure and even irresponsible way of handling Scripture is in fact the outworking of a careful tracing of scriptural themes, which in different ways point to Jesus as the fulfiller not only of specific predictions, but also of the broader pattern of God's Old Testament revelation'.[221]

Since the quotations (15:9b-12) are designed to support Paul's solemn declaration in 15:8-9a as a whole (καθὼς γέγραπται),[222] we may conclude that even in 15:8-9a Paul seeks to establish the salvation of the Gentiles through Christ as a fulfilment of the promises and the prophecies, rather than to affirm the priority of the Jews.[223] That Gentiles now glorify God *may be* 'a secondary result' of Jesus' Messiahship,[224] but Paul *presents it as if it were the main point he strove to establish.* The quotations are presented in such a way as to show that the Gentiles belong equally to the true people of God, and so may glorify God 'with his people' (15:10).[225] On the basis of such equality, Paul admonishes the Jewish and the Gentile believers to 'accept one another ... just as Christ accepted you' in order to bring glory to God (15:7, 9).

Moreover, the catena serves as the conclusion of his OT quotations in the entire letter, because it parallels the introductory remark that the gospel Paul is to explain was promised beforehand in the Scriptures (1:2). Thus 15:9-12 demonstrates his use of the OT in his argument, and thus suggests to us, in retrospect or on a second reading, how the OT quotations in Romans are to be

---

Christ Jesus', and it was especially to Paul the administration of this mystery was entrusted (Eph 3:6-9).

221 France, *Matthew*, 39-40; see his fuller treatment in 'Formula Quotations', 233-251.
222 Cranfield, *Romans* 2, 745.
223 *Pace* Sanday and Headlam, *Romans*, 399; see our earlier discussion *supra* pp. 51-58.
224 Sanday and Headlam, *Romans*, 399.
225 So correctly Stuart, *Romans*, 541.

interpreted. Furthermore, the section 15:7-13, being placed at the very end of the main body of the letter (1:16-15:13), also functions as 'the real summing-up of the entire letter'.[226] Dunn contends that the subject matter of the letter is 'the inclusion of the Gentiles within the promises to his people'.[227] If Wright and Dunn are correct (and in the following chapters we will attempt to show that they are), then it is clear that Paul has argued all along to promote *unity* based on the equality of the believing Jews and Gentiles by affirming the legitimacy of the salvation of the Gentiles. Paul asserts that Gentiles are equally legitimate heirs (and not usurpers) of the promises to Abraham.[228] Therefore, we suggest that Paul's self-awareness as apostle to the Gentiles has affected his understanding of Jesus' service as also embracing the Gentiles (cf. 5:12-21), and has indeed influenced the entire presentation of his argument not only here in 15:7-13 but also in the letter as a whole.

6. Conclusion

We have sought to demonstrate that in 15:14-21 Paul indicates his approach to the argument in the letter: his 'bold' approach in writing Romans is to affirm or defend Gentile salvation, which has been brought about by grace and faith, and in so doing he demonstrates his true apostleship to the Gentiles (15:15-16). In other words, he has written in the way he has in order to fulfil his apostolic calling. His inclusive soteriology in this writing flows primarily from his self-awareness as apostle to the Gentiles. Such boldness and self-understanding are based not only on his call (1:5; 15:15-16; Gal 1:15-16, etc.) but also on his personal experience of the work of the Holy Spirit in the missionary context among Gentiles (15:17-21; cf. Gal 3:1-5).

Paul's apostolic self-awareness is also clearly expressed at the beginning of the letter (1:1-17). Here he specifies his apostleship to the Gentiles. Paul's boldness in the affirmation of the salvation of the Gentiles is already indicated when he declares that he is not

---

226 Wright, 'Romans', 188; so also Dunn, *Romans* 2, 844; Hays, 'Rebound', 89; cf. Barrett, *Romans*, 250, who remarks that 15:7-13 sums up Rom 9-11 and 14.

227 Dunn, *Romans* 2, 848; also plausibly Murray, *Romans* 2, 206; Cranfield, *Romans* 2, 745.

228 Ziesler, *Romans*, 339.

Romans 15:14-21: An Interpretative Key? 69

ashamed of the gospel, and emphasises it as the power of God for the salvation of *everyone who believes: to the Jew first and also equally to the Gentile* (1:16). We have contended that the combination of τε and καί, and the addition of "Ελληνι in the phrase Ἰουδαίῳ τε πρῶτον καὶ Ἕλληνι, are Paul's initial indication of his desire to safeguard the inclusion of the Gentiles in God's salvation. Later, by presenting his boldness as if it was Isaiah's own boldness, Paul further indicates that his primary concern is to affirm Gentile salvation in contexts where Jews have rejected the gospel (10:20-21; Isa 65:1f), and where some (believing) Jews are opposing Paul's view on the equal legitimacy of Gentiles in the gospel.

We have also discovered that the thematic introduction to the main body of the letter (1:16-17) corresponds to the thematic conclusion (15:7-13), with the specific theme of 'ἔθνη' as central. Paul interprets Christ's service and the OT primarily in connection with *Gentiles* in the concluding section of the letter (15:8-12). This is another clear indication that Paul's primary focus in the letter is to affirm the legitimacy of the salvation of the Gentiles and hence of a mission to them. The quotations are employed to affirm that the furthering of the Gentile mission is indeed in line with the original intention of God as shown in the OT.

Paul says that, under apostolic self-awareness and obligation, he has written this letter rather boldly in order to fulfil his apostleship specifically to the Gentiles. This particular perspective governs the shape of the soteriological argument throughout the letter. He interprets Christ's service and OT prophecies from this point of view. What we have attempted to demonstrate can be summed up in the diagram below:

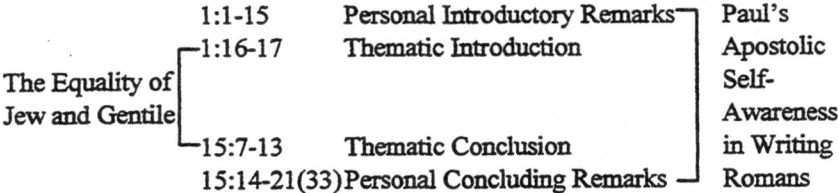

We propose therefore that Paul has written this letter under the strong self-awareness of his own apostolic call and obligation towards the Gentiles, as 15:14-21 and 1:1-17 show. The 'Gentile theme' we have highlighted is predominant not only in 1:1-15 and 15:14-21 but also especially in 1:16-17 *and* 15:7-13. Since the passage 15:14-21 contains a more specific indication of the character and intention of the letter than any other sections, we claim that 15:14-21 is the interpretative key for the meaning of the letter. We have also discovered that both 1:16-17 and 15:7-13 contain the theme of the inclusion of the Gentiles on an equal basis with Jews, and this indicates to us that the argument of the main body of the letter will be about the equality of Jew and Gentile. The fact that Paul clearly expresses his apostolic awareness towards the Gentiles in his personal introductory *and* concluding remarks (and also in 11:13 and 12:3), allows us to interpret the main body of the letter (1:16-15:13) from the perspective of his apostolic self-understanding. Also the fact that he develops the equality of Jew and Gentile in the main body of the letter (as we will show in the following chapters), suggests that it is his self-awareness of his own place as apostle to the Gentiles in God's salvific plan that has led him to assert this equality.[229]

Nevertheless, our view, that Paul's apostolic self-awareness has influenced him to affirm the legitimacy of Gentile salvation and to structure his bold soteriological argument in favour of the

---

[229] A note of clarification may be necessary at this point. What we are saying is not that Paul's theology is all the result of his own opinion of himself. Paul's theology is not incidental, nor is it conditioned by his own view of himself in a sociological context of the Roman church. Rather his self-awareness was shaped both by his theological thinking, i.e. contemplating God's salvific plan, and by his personal experiences of his call on the Damascus road and of his missionary work among Jews and Gentiles. Through them all Paul came to a deeper realisation of his own place in God's plan. This then implies that there is a reciprocal relation between Paul's theologising and his self-awareness. To the Galatians Paul stresses God's call and other apostles' approval to preach Christ among the Gentiles (Gal 1:1-2, 11-16a; 2:1-9) before he explains the implicational relation between the law and the gospel which he preached to them earlier. But to the Romans he only briefly mentions God's call (1:1-5; 12:3; 15:15-16), but concentrates on expounding another aspect of the implication of the gospel, i.e. the equality of Jew and Gentile in the salvific plan of God, especially in the light of the Christ event.

Gentiles as he attempts to establish the equality of Jew and Gentile, will be a mere hypothesis until it can be substantiated from the letter as a whole. The following chapters are oriented towards this task.

Chapter 2

The Equality of Jew and Gentile in Sinfulness: 1:18-3:20

In the previous chapter we have sought to demonstrate that Paul's self-awareness of being apostle to the Gentiles has not only prompted him to write the letter but has also set the tone of the letter. Paul's first main argument is launched in 1:18-4:25. This section forms one large part of the debate in which Paul attempts to establish the equality between Jews and Gentiles in sinfulness (1:18-3:20) and in justification (3:21-4:25). But before expounding some positive matters of justification, Paul first deals with the negative side of universal sinfulness in 1:18-3:20. Our primary focus in this chapter will be on the nature of this opening argument, underlining Paul's way of debate in which he seeks to confirm the sinfulness of humanity in general, and that of the Jews in particular. Each section of our discussion below will first expose, as its own introduction, the issues which have not been sufficiently investigated.

We will investigate some special features of human sinfulness as shown in 1:18-32. We will pay attention to the fact that in his attempt to affirm the equality of Jew and Gentile Paul attacks the unidentified 'them' *on the basis of the sinful history of Israel*. We will show that in 1:18-32 Paul indicts both ethnic groups without specifically mentioning them, and yet his argument seems to have been shaped primarily to draw Jews into his indictment so as to pave the way for the more direct attack on Judaism which he commences at 2:1. We shall show that the logical force of Paul's διό (2:1) supports our interpretation of 1:18-32. We shall also suggest that Paul's insistence on divine impartiality is in order to pronounce that Jews are also included in the divine judgement, and Gentiles in God's salvation (2:1-11). It will also be noted that, on the one hand, Paul's critical statements about Jews are made to indict Jewish complacency and, on the other, his affirmative statements about Gentiles are intended to affirm the legitimacy of Gentile salvation (2:12-29). Finally, we shall examine Paul's striking use of OT quotations (i.e. a part of the only mentioned Jewish privilege, τὰ λόγια τοῦ θεοῦ, in 3:1-2) to launch a further scriptural argument to reaffirm Jewish sinfulness (3:1-20). We suspect that not only in 2:1-3:20 but also even in 1:18-32 (where Paul is often understood to indict the Gentile sinfulness), Paul's primary intention is probably to establish *Jewish sinfulness* against their complacency based on covenantal nomism. We shall then examine the potential significance of our findings for our understanding both of Paul's argument and of the relevance to it of his self-awareness as 'apostle to the Gentiles'.

1. An Accusation of Human Sinfulness Reflecting Israel's History: 1:18-32

That in 1:18-32 'Paul wishes to establish that Gentiles are sinners'[1] has enjoyed a consensus within scholarship old[2] and new.[3]

---

1 Parker, *Commentaries*, 94.
2 Examining the Reformers' commentaries on Romans published between 1532 and 1542, Parker, *Commentaries*, 94, concludes that despite the considerable difference among the authors in details, in approach, in emphasis and in elements of the argument, this was the only general agreement among them.
3 According to Käsemann, *Romans*, 36-52, for example, this section is about 'the revelation of God's wrath on the Gentiles', whilst 2:1-3:20 concerns 'judgment on the Jews'. The commentators and other scholars who hold the same view include, Murray, *Romans* 1, 34-53; Barrett, *Romans*, 32-40; Nygren, *Romans*, 98-113; Black, *Romans*, 49-53; Sanday and Headlam, *Romans*, 39-52; Meyer, *Romans* 1, 73; Lightfoot, *Notes*, 239, 252-257; Ziesler, *Romans*, 73-79; Dodd, *Romans*, 46-55; Newman and Nida, *Romans*, 21; Boylan, *Romans*, 17-32; Gifford, *Romans*, 62; Liddon, *Romans*, 23-38; Marxsen, *Introduction*, 105; Guthrie, *Introduction*, 415; Zeller, *Juden*, 148; Bornkamm, *Paul*, 122.

Paul's condemnation of idolatry, sexual immorality (especially homosexuality), wickedness and godlessness, and the evident parallels with Wisdom 12-15, provide the basis for assuming that 1:18-32 accuses the Gentile world alone. More recently, however, it has been suggested that Paul also includes Israel in his accusation here, because the language and the theme of his indictment are rooted in the *universality* of (*inter alia*) Gen 1:26ff or Genesis 1-3.[4] We agree with this conclusion that Jews are included in Paul's indictment, but not with the argument of this hypothesis. So we will need to examine N. Hyldahl's widely accepted thesis that 1:23 depends on Gen 1:26ff (rather than Deut 4:15-18), on which such a view is largely based. We shall also examine M. Hooker's view that Jews are included here because Paul's argument is based on the wider context of Genesis 1-3. Rather, we will propose that Paul indicates the inclusion of Jews in his indictment by drawing the language and the themes from the sinful history of Israel.

That Paul also implicitly accuses Jews of sinfulness by echoing some OT passages such as LXX Ps 105:20, Deut 4:15-18 and Jer 2:11 has often been noted. But the basis of this assertion is almost exclusively the correspondence of the idolatry language in 1:23-25 with some OT passages, and we maintain that that alone cannot be sufficient to determine that Paul includes Israel in his argument in 1:18-32 as a whole. We will therefore provide more substantial evidence which will affirm that Paul indeed includes Jews not only on the basis of idolatry but also on the grounds of (homo)sexual immorality, and because of their refusal to retain the knowledge of God they had through the Law.

Furthermore, the significance and implication of Paul's use of these Jewish historical materials has hardly received adequate attention. But it is vital to consider this in order to grasp Paul's

---

For the notion that 2:1-29 is an attack on the Jews: Black, *Romans*, 54-61; Sanday and Headlam, *Romans*, 53-68: Lightfoot, *Notes*, 258-263. But some have challenged the view that Paul exclusively attacks Jews in this section; e.g. Bartsch, 'Die historische Situation', 286.

4   Most notably, Hyldahl, 'Reminiscence', 285-288; Hooker, 'Adam', 297-306. See also her 'Further Note', 181-83. Those who follow Hooker's basic thesis include Barrett, *First Adam*, 17-19; Dunn, *Christology*, 101-102; idem, *Romans* 1, 60-61; Garlington, "ΙΕΡΟΣΥΛΕΙΝ', 142-151; cf. Wedderburn, 'Adam', 413-430.

intention in this passage.[5] From the charge against Gentiles, the Jews would also readily perceive these to be their own, and in this way will be prepared for Paul's later explicit indictment against Judaism. To avoid any duplication of argument we shall not examine the generally accepted view that this sub-section is an indictment of Gentile sin; rather, our focus will be on how Paul attempts to assimilate Jews into his indictment, and the relevance of such argument for his apostleship to the Gentiles.

A. Is Jewish Idolatry Accused on the Basis of the Genesis Narratives?

There are some parallels between our present passage and typical Jewish critiques of the folly of Gentile idolatry (which was sharply developed and repeatedly intensified in the later prophets and in some intertestamental Jewish literature).[6] Some scholars thus have assumed that Paul's polemic against idolatry in Romans 1 is directed against the Gentiles, just as the author of Wisdom accuses the Gentiles of the folly of idolatry (especially Wis 14:12-31).[7] Others, however, have paid more attention to Ps 106 (LXX 105):20; Jer 2:11 and Deut 4:15-18 as a more probable background for Paul's accusation against idolatry in 1:23, even if they have not asked what Paul is doing with such material. The connection with a possible charge against *Jewish* idolatry was made only on the assumption that 1:23 echoes a Genesis background.

---

5   A typical example that does not recognise this implication is the interpretation of Fitzmyer, *Romans*, 270-290.

6   E.g. Isa 40:18-20; 41:6-7; 44:9-20; Jer 10:2-5, 14-15; Hab 2:18-19; Ps 115:4-8=135:15-18; Dan 5:4, 23. Wis 15:1-6; Jdt 8:18; *Jub.* 11:4-6, 16-17; 12:3-5; 20:8; 21:5; 22:17; *1 En.* 19:1; 46:7; *T. Naph.* 10; *Sib. Or.* 3:29-39, 279, 605-606, 722-723; 4:6-23; 5:356, 403; Josephus, *Apion* 2.33-35. *The Epistle of Jeremiah* is almost in its entirety an attack on Babylonian idolatry; see Pfeiffer, *History*, 426-432.

7   Notably Sanday and Headlam, *Romans*, 39-52. Elliott, *Rhetoric*, 173-174, most recently advocates the view that since idolatry (cf. Käsemann, *Romans*, 44) and sexual immorality (especially homosexuality) are the typical sins of the Gentiles, such sins mentioned in 1:18-32 are naturally about the Gentiles. But this view cannot be justified because throughout her history Israel was also both reminded of and warned about her falling into idolatry. In Jewish sectarianism, e.g. in the Qumran community, Israel herself was also accused of idolatry (Wright, 'Romans', 188).

This connection was first proposed by Hyldahl, who argued that the terminology in 1:23 (especially εἰκόνος, ἀνθρώπου, πετεινῶν, τετραπόδων / κτηνῶν, and ἑρπετῶν) matches and evokes Gen 1:20ff more closely than it does Deut 4:15-18 (the more commonly adduced 'background').

The linguistic basis for Hyldahl's argument is as follows: (1) 1:23 shares little of the significant Greek wording of Deut 4:15-18 (excepting ὁμοίωμα, εἰκών, and ἑρπετός; the last is plural in Romans, but singular in Deuteronomy); (2) the term ἄνθρωπος (1:23) does not occur in Deut 4:16 (but ἀρσενικός ἢ θηλυκός, 'male or female' does); (3) the order of the Romans list, man—birds—beasts—reptiles, is identical with that in Genesis, but differs from the Deuteronomic listing of male/female—beast—bird—reptile—fish. Hyldahl's hypothesis has been widely and somewhat uncritically accepted.[8] We have at least three reasons, however, for questioning his interpretation.

First, Hyldahl highlights the *differences* between the texts of Deut 4:15-18 and Rom 1:23, but ignores some important *correspondences*. For example, the phrase ἐν ὁμοιώματι εἰκόνος (1:23) corresponds on the one hand with the ποιήσωμεν ἄνθρωπον κατ' εἰκόνα ἡμετέραν καὶ καθ' ὁμοίωσιν of Gen 1:26, and on the other hand with the εἰκόνα ὁμοίωμα of Deut 4:16. It is to be noted that Paul uses the ὁμοίωμα of LXX Ps 105:20 or Deut 4:15-18 rather than the ὁμοίωσις of Genesis.[9] What Paul accuses 'them' of here is making and worshipping idols in the 'likeness' of such creatures.[10] One cannot answer

---

8 E.g. Käsemann, *Romans*, 45; Holter, 'Note', 21-23; see n. 4 above, for others who accept this hypothesis. But recently Fitzmyer, *Romans*, 282-284, has rejected it, yet without substantial argument.

9 Hyldahl correctly notes the influence of LXX Ps 105:20 on 1:23, but he is not justified in dismissing the view that Paul's use of ὁμοίωμα is taken from the Psalm, and in asserting that ὁμοίωσις and ὁμοίωμα are interchangeable. This assertion seems all the more unjustifiable because he himself is so keen to expose minor differences to disprove the connection between the Romans and Deuteronomy texts.

10 The strong warning not to make such idols is well expressed in Deuteronomy, seeing that the word ὁμοίωμα is emphatically repeated seven times in just four verses, five of them (except the first and the third occurrence) clearly connoting idols. In Genesis God created birds, beasts and reptiles, but not the 'likeness' of them; thus Romans is in this respect closer to Deuteronomy than to Genesis, as far as this important term is concerned.

either why Paul uses τετράποδα instead of the τὰ κήτη or τὰ κτήνη of Genesis (Gen 1:21, 25, 26, 28), if Paul were following the vocabulary, word order and number (whether singular or plural) of nouns exactly as they are in Genesis, as Hyldahl maintains.

Secondly, the singular ἄνθρωπος in the Genesis and Romans texts is, for Hyldahl, 'the most important term' which connects the two; by contrast, the Deuteronomy text has ἀρσενικός ἢ θηλυκός.[11] However, since the term ἄνθρωπος employed in both Gen 1:26 and Rom 1:23 is equally used in a generic sense to cover both male and female, there is 'no sure support' for Hyldahl's contention, as Käsemann rightly points out.[12] The term ἄνθρωπος of Gen 1:26 contains both 'male' and 'female', as in Gen 1:27.[13] Paul's point is the same: no image of male or female should be made as an object of worship. Therefore, the difference between the terms 'male' and 'female' in Deuteronomy and ἄνθρωπος in 1:23 cannot be as significant as Hyldahl asserts.

Thirdly, Hyldahl's assertion that Paul depends on the Genesis text rests largely on the view that the Genesis word order of animals, beasts—birds—reptiles, is repeated by Romans (1:23). But this is not entirely convincing, as this order is only one of four different lists in Genesis 1:

(1) reptiles—birds—animals—man: 1:20-26
(2) man—fish—birds—animals—reptiles: 1:26
(3) [man]—fish—birds—reptiles: 1:28
(4) [man]—beasts—birds—reptiles: 1:30.

But Hyldahl does not say which list he supposes to be identical with Paul's. In fact only the last list of man's food corresponds with Paul's 'order' of beasts—birds—reptiles (Gen 1:30), but in this instance the terminology differs considerably from Paul's. Here the Greek for 'beasts' (θηρία) is different from Paul's term (τετράποδα). It is to be noted, however, that Paul's word τετράποδα occurs in Gen 1:24. Therefore, the order and vocabulary of Paul's list corresponds, if anything, with the reversed order of the *first* list in Gen 1:20-26 (ἑρπετά—πετόμενα—τετράποδα—

---

11 Hyldahl, 'Reminiscence', 286.
12 Käsemann, *Romans*, 45.
13 Gen 1:27 also reads: καὶ ἐποίησεν ὁ θεὸς τὸν ἄνθρωπον κατ' εἰκόνα θεοῦ ἐποίησεν αὐτόν ἄρσεν καὶ θῆλυ ἐποίησεν αὐτούς.

ἄνθρωπος) rather than with the order of Gen 1:30. Thus Hyldahl's linguistic argument for a Genesis background for Paul's text from which he contends that Paul indicts Jews as well in 1:18-32, fails to convince us. Furthermore, it is not easy to see how Paul could shape a charge of idolatry from the creation narrative of Genesis. God's making of human beings in his image and their rule over the creatures seem too far removed conceptually from the making of *idolatrous* images (which is the subject of such texts as Deut 4:15-18).

While Hyldahl's own position is vulnerable, Morna D. Hooker has pursued another theory of a Genesis background (albeit on broader considerations) by noting a 'remarkable parallelism' between Romans 1 and Genesis 3, which leads her to assert that 'Paul's account of man's wickedness has been deliberately stated in terms of the biblical narrative of Adam's fall', and, specifically, that Paul portrays the figure of Adam in Rom 1:18-32, where he describes sin in terms of Adam's fall.[14] She widens the background from Hyldahl's consideration of Gen 1:20-30 to the whole of Genesis 1-3, and connects the Fall and idolatry with the common denominator 'sin'. Although there is no doubt that the wickedness detailed in 1:18-32 is the moral consequence of the Fall (e.g. 'a grain of evil seed was sown in Adam's heart from the beginning': 2 Esdr [=*4 Ezra*] 4:30: RSV; cf. also *4 Ezra* 10:14),[15] it is not clear that Paul is asserting this proposition here.[16]

A.J.M. Wedderburn rightly objects to Hooker's view by noting that, for Paul, Adam's sin was not idolatry and that the OT allusions in 1:23 are *'not of Adam's fall, but of Israel's fall into idolatry'*.[17] He then briefly mentions Ps 106:20, Jer 2:5, 11, and Deut 4:15-18, as providing a more plausible background for Paul's passage. The same point is actually anticipated in a second article by Hooker (of which Wedderburn was apparently unaware). While maintaining that Paul's thought and vocabulary are influenced by the narrative of Genesis 1-3, Hooker notes, in her succeeding article, a significant parallel not only between 1:23

---

14 Hooker, 'Adam', 297-306; the quotations are from 301. Similarly, Garlington, "ΙΕΡΟΣΥΛΕΙΝ', 145, 148; Dunn, *Romans* 1, 53; Milne, 'Genesis', 10-12.
15 Barrett, *First Adam*, 17-19.
16 See Moo, *Romans* 1, 119, for objections.
17 Wedderburn, 'Adam', 414, with his emphasis.

The Equality of Jew and Gentile in Sinfulness

and Ps 106 (LXX 105):20, but between 1:23-28 and the Psalm in general.[18] She concludes,

> It seems probable, therefore, that this section of Rom. i is influenced not only by the account of Adam's fall in Genesis, but also by Ps. cvi, and that *it is the latter passage which lies behind Paul's threefold statement of man's sin and God's punishment*.[19]

Hooker's apparent 'retreat' seems balanced and significant.[20] Her later view seems more plausible because Paul says that God's 'giving-over' of humankind to sexual immorality in 1:24 and 26 is his judgement on the idolatry of specific people (1:21-23, 25), the consequence of disregarding natural knowledge of God, and its attendant slide into 'a depraved mind'. This is not the same 'giving-over' of humanity as a general consequence of Adam's fall. If Paul had wanted to include the whole of humanity in Adam, he could have used the singular ἄνθρωπος as he does in 5:12-21, rather than ἄνθρωποι as in 1:18.

Our brief examination of the hypotheses of Hyldahl and Hooker has led us to conclude that although Paul indicts both

---

18

LXX Ps 105	Rom 1
v. 20 <u>καὶ ἠλλάξαντο τὴν δόξαν</u> αὐτῶν <u>ἐν ὁμοιώματι</u> μόσχου ἔσθοντος χόρτον	v. 23 <u>καὶ ἤλλαξαν τὴν δόξαν</u> τοῦ ἀφθάρτου θεοῦ ἐν <u>ὁμοιώματι</u> εἰκόνος φθαρτοῦ ἀνθρώπου καὶ πετεινῶν καὶ τετραπόδων καὶ ἑρπετῶν.
v. 14 <u>καὶ ἐπεθύμησαν ἐπιθυμίαν</u>	v. 24 <u>ἐν ταῖς ἐπιθυμίαις</u> τῶν καρδιῶν αὐτῶν
v. 48 <u>εὐλογητὸς</u> κύριος ὁ θεὸς Ισραηλ ἀπὸ <u>τοῦ αἰῶνος καὶ ἕως τοῦ αἰῶνος</u>	v. 25 ὅς ἐστιν <u>εὐλογητὸς εἰς τοὺς αἰῶνας</u>·
v. 41 <u>καὶ παρέδωκεν αὐτοὺς εἰς</u> χεῖρας ἐθνῶν	v. 24, 26, 28 <u>παρέδωκεν αὐτοὺς ὁ θεὸς ... εἰς ...</u>

19 Hooker, 'Further Note', 183, with added emphasis.

20 Earlier she had argued that Gen 1-3 was the primary source for Rom 1 over against the traditional view that Ps 106 was the background: 'It is clear from this comparison [of the Greek texts of Ps 106 (LXX 105):20 and Rom 1:23] that the word in our phrase which needs explanation is not ὁμοίωμα, which is taken directly from the psalm, but εἰκών [from Gen 1:26]' ('Adam', 297). In the later article, however, she makes a strong case that Ps 106 is the primary 'source' for Rom 1:23ff.

Jews and Gentiles here, the basis for his accusation is not drawn from Genesis 1-3 but shaped by *the history of Israel* as summarised, for example, in Psalm 106.[21] According to the Psalm, God's action against Israel was not the result of Adam's fall but of their own specific sinfulness (Ps 106:15; 23, 26, 40). Israel's rebellion against God and Moses, their disobedience towards God, and their idolatry with the golden calf (Ps 106:16-22), have brought God's anger and punishment upon themselves (Ps 106:23, 26-27).[22] The worship of the golden calf was one of the most notable examples of idol worship in Israel.[23] The psalmist refers to the particular incident at Horeb (Ps 106:19), but Paul may possibly be recalling such idol-worship throughout the history of Israel.

Whilst both Psalm 106 and Jeremiah 2 condemn the historical failure of the Jews, Deut 4:15-18 contains Moses's warning against idolatry. However, one very important passage has been almost completely neglected in scholarly discussion as a possible background for 1:23: namely, Exod 20:3-6.[24] A similar text reappears in Deut 4:15-18 in the form of an exhortation. The first

---

21 Fitzmyer, *Romans*, 270-283, is surely right to say that the Genesis hypothesis 'reads too much of Genesis into the text' (p. 274), and also rejects this hypothesis on the basis of the much closer parallel of Paul's themes and language to LXX Ps 105:20, Deut 4:15-18 and Jer 2:11 (pp. 274, 283). Nevertheless, his contention that Paul 'is simply extrapolating from such incidents in the history of the chosen people and applying the ideas to the pagan world' (pp. 270-271, 283), and thus that Paul does not include Jews in 1:18-32, seems highly questionable, as we will show below.

22 Cf. Kitchen, 'Calf', 225-226: The idolatrous worship of the golden calf made by Aaron after the Exodus was frequently condemned (Exod 32:4-8, 18-25, 35; Deut 9:16, 21; Neh 9:18; Ps 106:19-20; Acts 7:41). According to Webber in Sanders, *Palestinian Judaism*, 37-38, Israel's 'fall' through the golden calf incident was so serious as to be compared with Adam's fall. Although this theory has been rejected by scholars, the seriousness of Israel's idolatry is well pointed out.

23 Cf. especially the two golden calves set up at Bethel and Dan to distract the attention to the Jerusalem Temple (1 Kgs 12:26-33; 2 Kgs 17:16-20; 2 Chr 11:14-15; 13:8). Despite Jehu's reform the worship of the calves persisted in different generations (2 Kgs 10:29; cf. Hos 8:4-6; 13:2). So Oswalt, 'Golden Calves', 12, says, '.... throughout Israel's history, from exodus to exile, there was a nearly continuous worship of YHWH as a bull'.

24 See Stamm and Andrew, *Ten Commandments*, for a survey of discussion on the Decalogue.

Commandment prohibits worship of 'other gods';[25] the second refers to these 'other gods' in the form of graven images:

Exod 20:4	Rom 1	Deut 4	Gen 1
You shall not make for yourself an idol in the form (ὁμοίωμα: 'likeness') of anything			
in heaven (sky) above (birds)	birds	birds	birds
on the earth beneath (animals)	animals	animals	animals
in the waters below. (reptiles)	reptiles	reptiles	reptiles
	man	male/female	man

This second commandment is reinforced by the statement that God is a jealous God and by the pronouncement of judgement on idolatry, and these first two commandments are emphatically repeated (Exod 20:23). But the narrative goes on to relate how the Israelites so quickly turned away and made a molten calf and worshipped it. The commandment was, therefore, frequently repeated (e.g. Exod 34:14, 17; Lev 19:4; 26:1; Deut 4:15-18, 23; 7:25; 11:16; 27:15; Isa 42:8). Nevertheless, the OT tradition insists that Israel kept worshipping the images (Exod 32:1-4; Num 25:1-3; Deut 32:15-18; Judg 3:7; 1 Kgs 12:32-33; 16:31-33; 2 Kgs 17:12-17; 21:21; 2 Chr 25:14; 28:2-4; Jer 44:15-19; Ezek 8). Since they did not listen to God's warnings against idolatry (Ps 81:11-14; Ezek 20:23-26), God gave Israel over to their stubborn hearts and to their enemies. Unlike the Gentiles, Israel was warned that idolatry was the most abominable sin, the sin which she should avoid at all cost. Nevertheless, the Israelites indulged in it even to the point of sacrificing their own children to the idols (2 Kgs 16:3; Ps 106:37-39; 21:6; Jer 7:31; 19:5; Ezek 16:20-22; cf. 2 Kgs 23:10; cf. *Jub.* 1:11).[26] God's judgement was pronounced upon Israel (Isa 10:10-11; Jer 9:15-16). Since Paul's accusation of idolatry is so deeply based in the wording and ideas of the Jewish Scriptures, hardly any Jew could read 1:18-25 without sensing that Paul was including the Jews themselves in the idolatry of which they usually accused the Gentiles.

---

25 According to von Rad, this is '*the* commandment *par excellence* for Israel', as quoted in Stamm and Andrew, *Ten Commandments*, 81.

26 For the repeated warnings against child-sacrifice, see Lev 18:21; Deut 12:31; 18:10.

Furthermore, what Paul stresses in Romans 1 is the fact that 'they' exchanged the glory and the truth of God for the likeness (ὁμοίωμα) of creatures. The same condemnation had already been made by the author of Psalm 106 and by the prophet Jeremiah:

Rom 1:23 καὶ <u>ἤλλαξαν τὴν δόξαν</u> τοῦ ἀφθάρτου θεοῦ <u>ἐν ὁμοιώματι</u> εἰκόνος φθαρτοῦ ἀνθρώπου καὶ πετεινῶν καὶ τετραπόδων καὶ ἑρπετῶν.
LXX Ps 105:20 καὶ <u>ἠλλάξαντο τὴν δόξαν</u> αὐτῶν <u>ἐν ὁμοιώματι</u> μόσχου ἔσθοντος χόρτον
LXX Jer 2:11 ὁ δὲ λαός μου <u>ἠλλάξατο τὴν δόξαν</u> αὐτοῦ, ἐξ ἧς οὐκ ὠφεληθήσονται.

The last clause of Jer 2:11 clearly refers to worthless idols (cf. NIV). The verse clearly condemns the idolatry of Israel ('my people'): they forsook God (Jer 2:5, 17, 19) and followed worthless idols; thus, they themselves became worthless (Jer 2:5). Even their prophets prophesied by Baal, and followed idols (Jer 2:8). The ones who changed 'my' glory for that which does not profit are *my people, Israel*.

We have sought to demonstrate that the primary background for Paul's accusation against idolatry in Rom 1:23-25 is *the history of Israel's idolatry* rather than the creation/fall narrative of Genesis. If we are right, its implications are significant indeed. Paul's charge of idolatry is deliberately intended to encompass Jews (as well as Gentiles), even if he does not yet make that as explicit as he will in Romans 2. Furthermore, because Israelite idolatry is such a pervasive OT theme, the precise wording of Genesis 1 or Deuteronomy 4 or Psalm 106 is not as important as the influence of a fundamental theme in prophetic polemic as found (for example) in Hosea, Amos, Ezekiel and Jeremiah.

We may deduce that in 1:18-32 Paul attempts to indicate that *Jews* were as idolatrous as Gentiles. Jews have condemned Gentiles for idolatry, but they themselves have done the same thing in their own history.[27] Thus Paul reproaches Jewish hypocrisy over Gentile idolatry (cf. 2:1c, 21-22). The sin of the Jews is not merely judging others (2:1-3) but *practising the same sins* (1:32-2:3), such as idolatry, (homo)sexual immorality and the listed sins in 1:29-31, as we shall see later. It would be most natural for him

---

27 See 2 Kgs 23:13; Jer 2:28; 11:13 for the spread of idolatry in Judah.

to have the Jews in mind,[28] although he does not yet focus his argument directly towards them. Paul, the Jew, would need a certain 'boldness' to indicate such a message to fellow Jews, but he was already determined to be 'bold' in the cause of his apostolic ministry (1:16; 15:15). Thus we may initially propose that in his opening section Paul sets up a two-level argument: he undoubtedly condemns the widespread idolatry of the Gentiles. At the same time, however, he includes the Jews in his indictment, not only so as to establish universal sinfulness but also to pave the way for his more direct debate with Judaism. Similar conclusions can be drawn from Paul's accusation of sexual immorality and the knowability of God, which we shall consider next.

B. Is the Charge of Sexual Immorality Levelled at the Gentiles Alone?

Paul's condemnation of sexual immorality, especially homosexuality,[29] has led most scholars to suppose that Paul indicts *Gentile* sin here (Wis 2:16; 4:12; *T. Jud.* 14-15).[30] Homosexuality was a common practice in Greek society;[31] it was, in fact, even endorsed by some of their greatest philosophers as in some respects 'a higher form of love than heterosexuality'.[32] Moreover, the author of the Wisdom of Solomon makes a similar attack on the

---

28 See Fitzmyer, *Romans*, 274-275, who compares Paul's list with such catalogues in the OT, intertestamental writings and other Pauline letters, and concludes that Paul here displays Gentile attitudes of mind. But it is striking that only two words (φόνος, δόλος) in Wis 14:23-26 (which is a Jewish author's portrayal of Gentile immorality) appear in 1:29-31, whilst Mark 7:21-22 (which is Jesus's description of human immorality with reference to the *Jews*) contains no less than six of the same words.

29 With 'παρὰ φύσιν' (against nature), Paul may refer to homosexuality, as does Josephus, *Apion*, 2.38: 'lie with males', 'these sodomitical practices'.

30 Most notably, Fitzmyer, *Romans*, 286-287.

31 See Fitzmyer, *Romans*, 275, for works cited there in reference to homosexual practice among the ancient Greeks. See also Wright, 'Homosexuality', 413; Dover, *Greek Homosexuality*.

32 'Homosexuality', *EB* 6, 31; see also Ferguson, *Backgrounds*, 52; but in Roman society it was regarded as illegal (p. 57). See de Young, 'Meaning', 85-97, especially 89-90, and Caragounis, 'Biblical Attitude', 13-16, for a plausible treatment of the subject of homosexuality and Romans 1. Caragounis is of the opinion that homosexuality in ancient Athens was unlawful, and that Plato was against homosexuality.

Gentiles for their immoral sexual practices: 'sex perversion, disorder in marriage, adultery, and debauchery' (Wis 14:26: RSV), all of which connote sexual impurity. The phrase γενέσεως ἐναλλαγή ('sex perversion') may imply homosexuality ('changing of [sexual] kind': KJV).[33]

But does Paul have Gentile homosexuality *alone* in mind? Paul's dependence on the language and thought of LXX Psalm 105 might rather suggest that (just as he has paid special attention to the infamous incident of the 'golden calf' at Horeb[34]) he implies a reference to the Phinehas incident in the same Psalm. This recalls the indulgence in sexual immorality of the Israelites with the Moabite women, which resulted in the death of 24,000 Israelites (Ps 106:28-31; Num 25:1-13; cf. Philo, *Som.* 1.88-91).[35] If this cross-racial heterosexuality of the Jews is not a convincing parallel to Paul's charge of homosexuality in 1:26ff, we may turn to the unforgettable incident for any Jew written in the final three chapters of Judges. That incident happened during the priesthood of Phinehas the priest, Aaron's grandson (Judg 20:27-28). The reference to the same Phinehas in Ps 106:30 would unmistakably recall not only the shameful incident of Numbers 25 but also that of Judges 19-21.

The fierce battle between the tribe of Benjamin and the allies of the rest of Israel was itself a tragedy which left no less than 72,000 Israelites dead. But it is important to note that the tragedy of this fratricidal war was ignited in the first place by the homosexual lust of some of the Benjaminites (Judg 19:22ff). Their demand, 'Bring out the man ...so we can have sex with him' (Judg 19:22c; cf. Gen 19:5),[36] clearly indicates the intention of

---

33 Baab, 'Homosexuality', 639. Cf. for other renderings: 'unnatural lust' (NAB), 'sins against nature' (JB), 'confusion of sex' (RV).

34 It has been contended that the last phrase of Exod 32:6 ('...the people sat down to eat and drink, and *rose up to play*: וַיָּקֻמוּ לְצַחֵק) connotes orgiastic sexual activity (cf. Gen 26:8): see van der Toorn, 'Cultic Prostitution', 510; Davies, *Exodus*, 230-231; Cole, *Exodus*, 216.

35 In 1 Cor 10:7-8, Paul also warns the Corinthian believers from Israel's history of idolatry and sexual immorality.

36 The Hebrew word in both references is the same: וְנֵדְעֶנּוּ (Judg 19:22c) and וְנֵדְעָה אֹתָם (Gen 19:5), though the LXX renderings are different (ἵνα γνῶμεν αὐτόν and ἵνα συγγενώμεθα αὐτοῖς). According to the contexts both references clearly refer to homosexual practice; so NIV, Moffatt ('that we may rape him'); but cf. RSV, RV.

homosexual gang-rape.³⁷ Their demand even implies that homosexuality was not an unusual behaviour among themselves. Such behaviour was seen as 'a disgraceful thing' (נְבָלָה: Judg 19:23).³⁸ 'The whole shocking incident [which] made an indelible impression upon Israel'³⁹ was caused by this homosexual lust, and by the subsequent disgraceful rape of the man's concubine. Hosea refers to this immoral incident as a typical example of Israel's wickedness and sin (Hos 9:9), and for him it was the very beginning of the [(homo)sexual] sins of Israel: 'Since the days of Gibeah you have sinned, O Israel, and there you have remained' (Hos 10:9).

Moreover, Israel had often been engaged in (homo)sexual misconduct in connection with pagan cultic practices, despite the strong prohibition in the law and the concomitant death penalty (Lev 18:22; 20:13;⁴⁰ cf. *Sib. Or.* 2:73), and despite the other laws against unnatural sexual intercourse (Lev 18). The Israelites were commanded: 'There shall be no cult prostitute (קְדֵשָׁה) of the daughters of Israel, neither shall there be a cult prostitute (קָדֵשׁ) of the sons of Israel' (Deut 23:18 [MT]; 23:17 [LXX, EV]: RSV).⁴¹ But the command was frequently broken, and the continuation of cultic prostitution in ancient Israel (despite some vigorous reform movements) was a historical fact as the ample evidence shows (1 Sam 2:22; 1 Kgs 14:24; 15:12; 22:46; 2 Kgs 23:7, 14; 2 Chr 15:16; Ezek 8:14; Hos 4:13-14). Male prostitution was prevalent (1 Kgs 14:23-24), and there were special rooms for male prostitutes even in the Jerusalem Temple at times (2 Kgs

---

37 See Field, 'Homosexuality', 657, for his objection to D.S. Bailey, who asserts that the Sodom narrative does not refer to homosexual sin on the basis of the context.

38 'Rape' is the common rendering of the word elsewhere (Judg 20:6; 2 Sam 13:12; Gen 34:7).

39 Cundall, *Judges*, 198.

40 See Wright, 'Homosexuals', 125-153, for Paul's indictment (Rom 1; 1 Cor 6:9; 1 Tim 1:10) of homosexuality on the basis of the Levitical prohibitions; also briefly in, *idem*, 'Homosexuality', 414.

41 The term קְדֵשָׁה denotes a 'harlot' (Hos 4:14), and קָדֵשׁ a 'homosexual' or 'sodomite(s)', who were [homosexually] exceedingly wicked (Gen 13:13): Fitzer, 'πορνεία', *EDNT* 3, 137. See Green's translation as 'homosexual' in *Interlinear Bible: Hebrew/English* 1, 522; KJV, RV and RSV mg.: 'sodomite'. See also Craigie, *Deuteronomy*, 301f; Thompson, *Deuteronomy*, 241-242.

23:7). It is also probable that homosexual prostitution was practised in the course of idolatry,⁴² (though of course prostitution was also 'spiritualised' as a term for apostasy, as in Jeremiah).

It is possible, even probable, that Paul had this history of Jewish sexual impurity, including homosexual relations in the cultic and social life of many Jews (e.g. 2 Kgs 23:7; Exod 32:6; Judg 19:6) in mind when he wrote this letter. Then Paul's use of ἀσχημοσύνη in 1:27 may echo this (homo)sexual sin of rape, for the word is a translation of the word נְבָלָה used in Judg 19:23.⁴³ Moreover, the terminology of ἀσχημοσύνη in 1:27 could also remind Jewish readers of the Levitical prohibitions of 'abominations' (Lev 18 and 20) and of the history of Israel's failure to keep the commandments (Ezek 16:8; 23:10, 18; Hos 2:9-13). Furthermore, it is also clearly shown in *Pss. Sol.* 2:15: 'They [Jews] had defiled themselves with unnatural intercourse (ἐν φυρμῷ ἀναμίξεως)', and thus plundered the sanctuary of God (*Pss. Sol.* 8:8-12). Although Jewish readers might not fully perceive Paul's point that Jews were also guilty of disgraceful sexual immorality until 2:22, Paul is preparing the way for his more direct indictment of the Jews (2:1: 'you ... do the same thing'). In retrospect (or on a second reading/listening) his charge would perhaps have been clear enough.

C. *Should not Jews be Condemned More for their Refusal to Retain the Knowledge of God?*

Paul's attempt to include the Jews in his indictment in this subsection is also indicated in his accusation of 'their' refusal to retain the knowledge of God. For Paul a primary sin of humanity is the failure to acknowledge God (because God revealed himself plainly to humanity in creation), and to live accordingly. Because of this sin their thinking became futile and their hearts were darkened; as a consequence they fell into idolatry, which in turn led

---

42 Baab, 'Homosexuality', 639.
43 The LXX rendering of נְבָלָה in Judg 19:23 is ἀφροσύνη, but that in Gen 34:7 is ἀσχημοσύνη, and also the Greek words are interchangeable. Paul might possibly refer to homosexuality with πορνεία, just as is the case with ἐκπορνεύω in Jude 7 (cf. Gen 19:7: μὴ πονηρεύσησθε), because πορνεία is often listed next to μοιχεία (adultery) with the different connotation of sexual immorality: see Fitzer, 'πορνεία', *EDNT* 3, 137-139.

The Equality of Jew and Gentile in Sinfulness

them into sexual immorality and to moral depravity of mind. But if Paul condemns the Gentiles for not acknowledging God through the general revelation in creation, should not Jews be even more condemned for refusing to retain the knowledge of God after having received the special revelation of the 'word of God' (cf. 3:1-2)?

Paul asserts that God made what could be known of him plain, evident or clearly visible (φανερός), so that human beings can clearly know not only the existence of the God of creation but also his eternal power and deity (cf. Ps 19). They may not have saving knowledge or the whole truth, but Paul asserts that in creation they really know sufficient truth to acknowledge God the Creator.[44] The διό of 1:24 requires that the knowledge spoken of is that knowledge possible through 1:19-23. Thus Paul declares that 'they' are without excuse (1:19-20) for suppressing the truth and for not glorifying and thanking God (1:18, 21).

This is one level at which the language seems to apply to Gentiles only. But since the creation is shown to Jews as well as to Gentiles, Jews would be included in Paul's indictment here. In fact what Paul writes in 1:32 leads us to suspect that he aims at another level. There he says that 'they' know τὸ δικαίωμα τοῦ θεοῦ and yet do not practise it. The careful reader will perceive that this 'they' applies even more forcefully to (unbelieving) Jews. This is because it is to the Jews, and not to any other nation, that God's word, will and decree have been revealed (Ps 147:19-20; Jer 5:5).[45]

Jews have repeatedly heard that 'those who do such things deserve death' (1 Chr 10:13-14; Prov 10:6; 11:18-19; Ezek 18:4, 20;

---

44 At this point Emil Brunner, *Christian Doctrine*, 132, 134, seems right to say, '[T]he question of the revelation in Creation [must be distinguished from] the question of man's natural knowledge of God. The fact that sinful human beings cannot help having thoughts about God is due to the revelation in Creation. The other fact, that human beings are not able rightly to understand the nature and meaning of this revelation in Creation, is due to the fact that their vision has been distorted by sin'. See Gempf, 'Athens', 51-54, on Paul's view of natural theology with respect to the Gentiles (cf. Acts 17).

45 'He has revealed his word to Jacob, his laws and decrees (δικαιώματα: משפטם) to Israel. *He has done this for no other nation; they do not know his laws*' (Ps 147:19-20); '... surely they [i.e. the leaders of the Jews] know the way of the Lord, the requirement (κρίσις: משפט) of their God' (Jer 5:5).

33:8-9). Furthermore, they received 'τὰ δικαιώματα καὶ τὰ κρίματα καὶ τὸν νόμον καὶ τὰς ἐντολάς' (LXX 4 Kgdms [2 Kgs] 17:37), but they did not keep them (Ezek 20:24-25). In fact, later on in 7:7 Paul admits that a special revelation is necessary to know God's requirement and thus to have knowledge of sin. Since such a revelation was given to Jews, they hear and know the law (2:17-20) and approve the excellence of it and teach it to others (2:19-20). Nevertheless they break it (2:21-24). He specifically condemns unbelieving Jews because they refuse to believe God's word even though they had heard and understood it (10:18-19, 21).[46] Thus here in 1:19-21, 32 Paul probably has Jews in mind also, although he does not state this explicitly.[47]

If 'Israel alone had been privileged to be instructed in these divine precepts'[48] (cf. 3:1-2; τὰ λόγια τοῦ θεοῦ), and if both Jews and Gentiles did not acknowledge, glorify or thank God in response to God's creation, it is the Jews who should be condemned in greater measure than the Gentiles.[49] Through the special revelation of God in the law, in the Scriptures and in Christ, who had first come to the Jews (cf. 3:2; 9:4-5; 10:17-19), the Jews were in a far better position to have known God than the Gentiles were. If Paul had 2 Kgs 17:15; Jer 2:5 (cf. Wis 13:1; *Sib. Or.* 3:8-26, 763f) in his mind for the expression ἐματαιώθησαν ἐν τοῖς διαλογισμοῖς αὐτῶν (1:21), as Lightfoot suggests,[50] then such an accusation is directed towards his own people who followed the idolatry of the Gentiles. In 1:32 Paul seems to indi-

---

[46] Although this reference refers to the *gospel*, it helps us see whom Paul is accusing in 1:18-32.

[47] Nowhere does Paul say explicitly that the Gentiles have received God's decree or instructions. Rather, he says elsewhere 'the world through its wisdom did not know him' (1 Cor 1:21; cf. Eph 1:17). Gentiles certainly knew that the gods decreed death for, e.g. murder (1:29), but they knew of the universality of death only by experience. Unlike the Jews, they were not specifically told what was its cause. It was the Jews who had received God's truth through special revelation but had exchanged it for a lie (Isa 28:15; Jer 13:25; Amos 2:4-5), and who did not glorify God (1:21; cf. Isa 29:13, as quoted in Matt 15:7-9=Mark 7:69).

[48] Oesterley, *Psalms*, 581.

[49] So also Lincoln, 'Wrath', 207. Some OT prophets condemned the Jews, for not acknowledging God, and even refusing to do so (Isa 1:3; Jer 8:7; 9:3, 6; Hos 2:8; 4:1; 5:4).

[50] Lightfoot, *Notes*, 252-253.

cate the failure of the Jews who act in contrast to their knowledge of the δικαίωμα.⁵¹ That is most probably why they deserve the further indictment of the following sections (2:1-3:20).

In contrast, it is striking to see Paul the apostle to the Gentiles alluding some affirmative remarks about Gentiles in this section. By structuring the 'they' to cover both Jews and Gentiles, he not only asserts that Gentiles have real knowledge of the Creator (1:19-20) but also implies that they do know God (1:21) and his righteous decree (1:32).⁵² He actually declares that the (believing) uncircumcision keep τὰ δικαιώματα τοῦ νόμου (2:26), though without having the law (2:14). What he writes here about the knowledge that the Gentiles have about God is much more affirmative than what he writes elsewhere.⁵³

Before we conclude our investigation for this section, it is vital to understand Paul's use of the thrice-repeated clause, 'God gave them over' (παρέδωκεν αὐτοὺς ὁ θεός; 1:24, 26, 28), because it provides us with an important clue for a proper understanding of 1:18-32. This examination will allow us to strengthen our interpretation proposed in the above sub-sections.

D. Did God Give Israel over to Sinfulness?

The repeated clause, 'παρέδωκεν αὐτοὺς ὁ θεός' (1:24, 26, 28) links the three subjects we have examined above. Being intensified with διό, διὰ τοῦτο, or καὶ καθώς, it forms the core of the argument here: because 'they' refused to retain the knowledge of

---

51 Cranfield, *Romans* 1, 128: 'The compound substantive ἐπίγνωσις... must denote a knowledge which goes beyond that indicated by γνόντες τὸν θεὸν in v. 21, and which in fact includes the δοξάζειν and εὐχαριστεῖν to which that verse refers.'

52 Here Paul is different from most other Jewish writers who assert that humanity in general does not know God in full through creation (Job 5:9; 11:7-9; Eccl 3:11; cf. Exod 33:20; Deut 4:12; Sir 3:21-23; 43:31; *4 Ezra* 4:1-11; Philo, *Decal.*, 61-63; *Spec.*, 1.13-27; *Vita*, 5-10; Josephus, *War*, 7.346). Paul is close to what the author of Wisdom had said: the creation reveals sufficient knowledge about the Creator to all humanity (Wis 12-15), and so their failure to acknowledge the workmaster of the beautiful world is inexcusable (Wis 13:1-10).

53 Paul has declared that the heathen do not know 'the living and true God' (1 Thess 1:9; 4:5). To the Galatian believers he says, 'Formerly, ... you did not know God, ...but now you know [him]' (Gal 4:8-9; cf. Eph 2:12-13).

God, 'they' became idolatrous. Therefore (διό) 'παρέδωκεν αὐτοὺς ὁ θεός' to idolatry and sexual immorality, because of (διὰ τοῦτο) which 'παρέδωκεν αὐτοὺς ὁ θεός' to (homo)sexual immorality; because of their further (καὶ καθώς) refusal to retain the knowledge of God, 'παρέδωκεν αὐτοὺς ὁ θεός' to a depraved mind. God's 'giving over' is the natural consequence of 'their' refusal to retain the knowledge of God, of 'their' idolatry (1:23-25) and of 'their' immorality (1:24, 26-27). With the pronoun 'them' Paul surely refers to both Gentiles and Jews, but we will propose that the phrase 'παρέδωκεν αὐτοὺς ὁ θεός' is, from a linguistic point of view, applied more to the Jews. Thus it will support our assertion that Paul includes the Jews in his indictment in 1:18-32.

In the LXX παραδίδωμι as the translation of נָתַן or סָגַר is employed to convey mainly two ideas: (a) God hands the Gentiles over to Israel, and (b) God gives Israel over to the Gentiles. There are many references for case (a), and they are almost without exception related to God's promise to give victories in battle so as to give Israel the land which he had promised.[54] There is hardly any reference that indicates that God gave over the Gentiles because of their idolatry, sexual immorality and wickedness (cf. Gen 15:16). However, the reasons for case (b) are quite different. God gave Israelites over because of their wickedness (Judg 6:1; 13:1; LXX 3 Kgdms 14:16; LXX 4 Kgdms 21:14-15), disobedience (LXX 1 Kgdms 28:18-19; Jer 6:30; 7:29; Mic 5:3), and unfaithfulness (2 Chr 24:24; 30:7; cf. Lev 26:25). But the greatest reason which caused God to give them over to the nations was their detestable idolatry (Judg 2:10-15; 2 Chr 25:20; 28:1-5; 1 Esdr 1:53; 6:15).[55]

Moreover, the LXX translators of Psalm 106 rendered נָתַן with παραδίδωμι to describe God's reaction to Israel's association with foreign gods and their sacrifices of their own children to the idols of Canaan (Ps 106 (LXX 105):34-41; Ezek 16:18-42).

---

54 The references are numerous (see Hatch and Redpath, *Concordance*, 1058f); only to mention some: E.g., Exod 23:31; Num 21:2, 3, 34; Deut 1:8; 2:24; Jos 2:14, 24; Judg 1:4; 3:10, 28; LXX 1 Kgdms 14:10, 12; 17:47; 23:4; LXX 4 Kgdms 3:18; 18:30; 19:10; 2 Chr 16:8.

55 Some exceptions include Deut 19:12; 23:15; Jos 7:7; Judg 6:13, 16:23-24; 2 Chr 13:16.

The Equality of Jew and Gentile in Sinfulness   91

Psalm 78 expresses well that Israel's idolatry was the reason why God gave them over, and it closely parallels 1:24:

> But they put God to the test and rebelled against the Most High; they did not keep his statutes. Like their fathers they were disloyal and faithless, as unreliable as a faulty bow. They angered him with their high places; they aroused his jealousy with their idols. When God heard them, *he was very angry; he rejected Israel completely.* ... *He gave them [his people] over* (Καὶ συνέκλεισεν[56] εἰς ῥομφαίαν τὸν λαὸν αὐτοῦ: וַיַּסְגֵּר לַחֶרֶב עַמּוֹ) *to the sword* [of the Gentiles] (Ps 78 [LXX 77]:56-62).

Often Israel's idolatry is seen as 'prostitution'. In a parabolic speech to Ezekiel, the Lord says he gave up Samaria because of her detestable 'prostitution' with the Gentiles. But the lust and prostitution of Jerusalem was even greater than that of Samaria, so God turned away from Jerusalem in disgust (Ezek 23:11-21). In the allegory of unfaithful Jerusalem (Ezek 16:1-52), Ezekiel says God gave Israel over to the Gentiles (καὶ παραδώσω σε εἰς χεῖρας αὐτῶν: Ezek 16:39) because of their wickedness, idolatry and 'prostitution' with the Gentiles; Israel is also referred to as an adulterous 'prostitute' (Ezek 16:18-42). It is because of their own sinfulness that God gave Israel over to desolation and the mockery of the nations (cf. 2 Chr 30:7-8; Mic 6:16).

Such a perception is portrayed also in the literature of the intertestamental period. According to the author of 1 Esdras God gave Israel over to captivity not only because of the [past] sins of their fathers (1 Esdr 6:15-16), but because of their own [present] sins (1 Esdr 8:75-78; cf. *4 Ezra* 4:23; 5:28-30), especially idolatry (1 Esdr 1:53-57). It was so in the first century, too. According to Luke, for example, Stephen made the same accusation against the (leaders of the) Jews. Quoting Amos 5:25-27, Stephen makes it clear that Israel's idolatry caused God to give his people over ('ὁ θεὸς ... παρέδωκεν αὐτούς') to serve heavenly bodies, and this resulted in her own exile (Acts 7:42). We may contend then that

---

56 Although the LXX does not render סגר with παραδίδωμι but with συγκλείειν in Ps 77:62 (and v. 50), both Greek terms carry a similar connotation, as the same Hebrew word is translated by παραδίδωμι in 77:48. Paul employs συγκλείειν in Rom 11:32 to say that 'God has consigned [=handed over] all men to disobedience' (RSV, Moffatt), and thus uses it synonymously with παραδίδωμι in 1:24, 26, 28.

the Jews were constantly reminded of and blamed for their evil ways throughout their history.

However, Paul seems to recast the tradition somewhat significantly. For the Jews of the OT, although God handed Israel over to the Gentiles, it was for the purpose of *chastisement* and with the ultimate blessing of God's faithfulness to the covenant clearly anticipated (e.g. Ps 78:65-72; Isa 43:3ff; *Pss. Sol.* 8:32, 35; 10:3; 13:5-9). Thus it is not typical from a Jewish perspective for Paul to say that God 'handed them over' to *sinfulness* from idolatry to sexual immorality and then to a depraved mind.[57] Whilst the authors of the OT Scriptures used נָתַן or סָגַר (παραδίδωμι / συγκλείειν) to describe the consequences of sins (yet with hope), Paul uses παραδίδωμι to characterise the process of sinful degeneration rooted in a wicked attitude towards God.[58]

Our investigation, then, provides a close parallel to Romans 1, where Paul claims that the primary cause for God's giving 'them' over is their wickedness, unfaithfulness, adultery and idolatry. In the light of such a historical Jewish background and its repeated linguistic correspondences with Romans 1, the Jews of the Roman Christian community reading/listening to Paul's letter could not help being reminded of their history of being given over by God; they would then understand that Paul was speaking about the sinfulness of the Jews as well.

E. Conclusion

Paul includes the Jews in his indictment by alluding to (or even recalling) the sinful history of Israel in the areas of idolatry, (homo)sexual immorality, refusal to retain the knowledge of God and ungodliness (*4 Ezra* 4:38), rather than by appealing to the Genesis narratives, as is often insisted. Paul's indictment of idolatry, for example, is given on the basis of the principal command expressed in the first two Commandments (Exod 20:3-6). Undoubtedly Paul indicts the Gentiles in 1:18-32 (cf. 3:9), but he

---

57 Paul remarks in 11:32 that 'God has consigned [συνέκλεισεν = handed over] *all men* to disobedience,' which is for Paul the major term for sinfulness (cf. Gal 3:22-23). Dunn, *Romans* 2, 688-689, is correct to note that here Paul 'retains the emphasis on human disobedience' and yet strongly reminds Israel of her disobedience to God and disbelief in the gospel.

58 Cf. Minear, *Obedience*, 49.

does not explicitly state that he charges Gentiles in this subsection (unlike the author of Ephesians, who specifically expresses that he is writing about the spiritual problems of the *Gentiles*: Eph 4:17-19). Here Paul simply asserts *human* sinfulness. The apostle to the Gentiles treats Jews and Gentiles equally: God has revealed himself to both ethnic groups. In creation, both can clearly acknowledge the Creator and his divine power; both know God's righteous decree, but both refuse to retain the knowledge of God and have gone the way of the same sinfulness. Paul's language is mostly adopted from incidents in Israel's past (e.g. Deut 4:15-18; Ps 106, Jer 2:11), and this is evidence that he has Jews also in mind. This will become evident when he *argues* to convince his Jewish interlocutor of *Jewish* sinfulness (2:1-29).

This is why we find it difficult to agree with Fitzmyer, who asserts that a pro-Jewish reader 'loudly applauds his [Paul's] description of the pagan's moral failure'.[59] Rather, we have discovered that the Jewish readers in Rome might increasingly suspect that Paul was not only including them in his attack but may even have had them in mind as a definite target[60] (though only implicitly expressed).[61] It seems probable that Paul's self-awareness of

---

59   Fitzmyer, *Romans*, 296. Similarly Minear, *Obedience*, 48: in 1:18-32, Paul 'was conceding to his adversaries a basic justification for the rejection of fellowship with Gentiles'.

60   Cf. Beker, *Paul*, 79-80; Minear, *Obedience*, 51: God's wrath is revealed to all humanity (1:18), and 'the Jew is given priority in receiving God's wrath—"the Jew first and also the Greek" (2.10)'. Since Paul describes Gentiles as believing in and glorifying God (9:30; 10:20; 15:9-12), with his accusation that 'they' do not glorify God, he probably had Jews as a main target. See du Toit, 'Kirche', 69-77, who notes a strong correlation between 1:18-32 and 15:1-13.

61   One may then ask an obvious question: if Paul also wanted to build a case against the Jews (which he does very candidly in 2:1ff), why should he introduce the matter in such a veiled fashion? First of all, because he generally intends to indict Gentiles as well in this section; he wishes to make the charge universal, not to make the case explicitly against one or other ethnic group. Surely Gentile readers would be reminded of their own past and also see Paul describing the sinfulness of their unbelieving fellow Gentiles (because they would hardly know the connection between the Jewish historical background and Paul's use of language here).

Secondly, his ambassadorial approach in the letter (which is quite different from his authoritative rebuke and teaching to the Galatians and the Corinthians) seems to be another reason (see Best, *Converts*, 150-151). As Käsemann,

being apostle to the Gentiles has led him to affirm the equality of Jew and Gentile in sinfulness; and he would require a certain boldness to do so. By structuring the indictment in this way Paul seems to be seeking to pave the way for the more direct attack on complacent Judaism from 2:1 onwards.[62]

The readers in Rome might not have fully understood Paul's point in the 'argument' at this stage, but we propose that Paul himself has had the Jews in his mind as he indicts humanity for their sinfulness. The logical conjunction διό in 2:1 and Paul's subsequent argument seem to support our understanding, to which we now turn for a detailed examination.

2. A More Direct Indictment of Jewish Complacency: 2:1-29

In the above section we have discovered that 1:18-32 (which at first sight accused *Gentiles* of inexcusable rebellion against their knowledge of God) turned out, on more careful reading, to indict the Jews themselves at least as seriously as the Gentiles. In this

---

Romans, 390, and Jewett, 'Ambassadorial Letter', 5-20, have pointed out, Paul is writing to a church which he did not found with the task of ensuring their co-operation for a future mission to Spain (so also Lincoln, 'Abraham', 168f). By approaching the point gradually and diplomatically, he attempts to avoid any premature and unnecessary misunderstanding or rejection by Jews, for he has a lot more 'offensive' assertions to make later on (2:1-3:20; 9:1-11:16). In this connection it is illuminating to note Paul's effort to employ some 'diplomatic' expressions (such as, ὦ ἄνθρωπε, εἰ δὲ σὺ Ἰουδαῖος ἐπονομάζῃ, three occurrences of ἐάν: 2:1, 17, 25, 26) even in Rom 2, which contains 'perhaps the most extensive and direct critique of Jews and Judaism in the letters of Paul' (Carras, 'Romans 2,1-29', 185).

Thirdly, according to what Paul writes later in Romans, he might not have been able to condemn Gentiles directly or too severely in 1:18-32, for their sins were 'excusable': 'where there is no law there is no transgression' (4:15); 'but sin is not taken into account when there is no law' (5:13); 'Indeed I would not have known what sin was except through the law' (7:7); and elsewhere (3:19-20, 25; 5:20; cf. Gal 3:19; Acts 14:16; 17:30; 1 Tim 1:13b). The 'law' in the above references refers to the Mosaic law, in which the Gentiles have not been instructed (cf. 2:12, 14). This does not mean that Gentiles are not to be condemned (cf. 3:9), but it does explain why he does not charge them with the same degree of culpability as he does the Jews in 2:1-3:20.

62 Similarly Hays, *Echoes*, 93-94; *idem*, 'Relations', 194-195. Cf. Elliott, *Rhetoric*, 173-190, who argues against the view that in 2:1ff Paul indicts Jews. We will argue against Elliott's contention in the next section.

section we shall pursue our examination of Paul's more direct charge against Jewish complacency, which will affirm Jewish sinfulness more specifically. We shall begin by analysing the implications of Paul's use of the conjunction διό (2:1) for our understanding of those addressed in 2:1-16. N. Elliott has recently argued the case that the conjunction necessarily implies that the 'they' who are accused in 1:18-32 are the same as the 'you' addressed in 2:1ff, and that both must therefore be Gentiles. We shall discover that there are indeed reasons for supporting Elliott's first proposition, while doubting his second. We shall demonstrate rather that Paul's accusation is directed to a *Jewish* interlocutor, and brings to the fore the Jewish aspect of his accusation in 1:18-32. Thus this διό appears to support our understanding of 1:18-32 that Jews are also certainly targeted in Paul's accusation there.

We shall then investigate whether Paul's handling of the argument—allegedly in the interests of proving God's impartiality—does not in fact provide evidence what we may regard as further 'bias towards the Gentiles' (2:6-11). Furthermore, we shall pay attention to some possible theological reasons for Paul's critical arguments about Jews and affirmative statements about Gentiles (2:12-27). Our study will indicate that while on the one hand his critique of Judaism is more radical and strident than one would expect even from Jews with strong remnant theologies, on the other hand his argument appears to be consistently tilted (rhetorically) in favour of the Gentiles.

A. The διό of 2:1 and its Implication for the 'Argument' of 1:18-2:5

Elliott has stressed that the understanding of 2:1-16 is ultimately dependent on the interpretation of the διό in 2:1 which connects 1:18-32 and 2:1-16.[63] Various interpretations have been offered. For H. Lietzmann, for example, this διό is 'eine farblose Über-

---

63 Elliott, *Rhetoric*, 174. See Cranfield, *Romans* 1, 140-141, for a brief survey of the interpretation of this difficult διό. Cranfield himself, together with Sanday and Headlam, *Romans*, 55, and Meyer, *Romans* 1, 102, understands it to cover the whole section 1:18-32.

gangspartikel',[64] because this conjunction does not logically connect the *Gentile* 'they' of 1:18-32 with the *Jewish* 'you' ('der selbstgerechte Jude') of 2:1-16. A. Nygren accepts Lietzmann's view that 1:18-32 is a description of the sinfulness of the Gentiles and that 2:1-16 is Paul's debate with a self-righteous Jew, but criticises Lietzmann for not noting the logical force of the διό which connects 1:18-32 and 2:1-11 (or 1-16).[65] Nygren's view is supported by the observations that 'the logical connective διό in 2:1 continues the rhythm of similar constructions in 1:21, 24, 26, and 28'[66] into the immediate passage, and that elsewhere Paul hardly uses this conjunction other than to convey a logical sense (cf. 4:22; 13:5; 15:7, 22; 1 Cor 12:3; 14:13; 2 Cor 1:20; 2:8; 4:13; 5:9; 6:17; 12:7, 10; Gal 4:31; 1 Thess 5:11; Phlm 8). However, Nygren insists that the logical connective cannot directly link the *subjects* of both passages (i.e. a Gentile 'they' and a Jewish 'you'), but only the same *issue* or *ground*: namely, just as the Gentiles are sinners without excuse, so are the Jews.[67]

Elliott goes even further. He contends that the force of διό covers not only the same issue/ground (i.e. sinfulness) but also the same subject (i.e. the 'they' in 1:18-32 is to be identified with the 'you' in 2:1-16). In other words, Paul talks about the inexcusability of the Gentiles in a more distancing way by employing 'they' in 1:18-32, but addresses their Gentile guilt directly by using 'you' in 2:1-16. As far as the subject pronouns are concerned, Elliott maintains that since the 'they' in 1:18-32 undoubtedly refers to the *Gentiles*, and Paul only begins to address his Jewish interlocutor in 2:17, the loosely characterised interlocutor in 2:1

---

64 Lietzmann, *Römer*, 38-39; Käsemann, *Romans*, 54; so also Althaus, Michel, Schlier. Cf. Molland, in BDF, 235, who asserts that this is an '"illogical" διό' syntactically. Bultmann, 'Glossen', 200, takes the διό as a gloss.

65 Nygren, *Romans*, 116-117. Others who see the full logical sense include Bassler, *Impartiality*, 131, 255 n. 43; Fischer, 'Literary Forms', 214; Shedd, *Romans*, 35; Meyer, *Romans* 1, 102; Sanday and Headlam, *Romans*, 55.

66 Elliott, *Rhetoric*, 120.

67 See Elliott, *Rhetoric*, 182-184, for critical treatment of Schmeller, *Paulus*, 225-286, who has offered a substantial study of this issue similar to Nygren's.

The Equality of Jew and Gentile in Sinfulness

must also be a Gentile.[68] He devotes most of his study to arguing against Nygren (and the prevailing view[69]) that 2:1ff is not an indictment of Jews but of Gentiles. Our critical examination of Elliott's interpretation of 2:1-16 will follow later, but for the moment we may offer a piece of evidence which would support Elliott's view that both sections, 1:18-32 and 2:1-16, are directed to the *same people* (whether to Gentiles or Jews is another matter at present).

Διό occurs 22 times in the Pauline letters. All the other 21 occurrences (so also 8 in Acts) connect what follows with what precedes with self-evident conclusions.[70] In these occurrences the subjects, addressees or speakers are the same in what precedes and what follows, and there seems no reason to assume 2:1 is an exception, despite the change of pronoun.[71] Thus it seems probable that this διό indicates that Paul directs his accusation to the same people, or narrows down his argument from 2:1 onwards to either Jews or Gentiles, both of whom are included in 1:18-32.[72]

---

68 Here Elliott, *Rhetoric*, 125, follows Stowers' conclusion (*Diatribe*, 112), and cites him: 'It is anachronistic and completely unwarranted to think that Paul has only Jews in mind in 2:1-5 or that he characterizes the typical Jew.'

69 Those who contend that 2:1-11 is directed to the Jews include Käsemann, *Romans*, 53-54; Black, *Romans*, 54; Sanday and Headlam, *Romans*, 54; Cranfield, *Romans* 1, 137-139; Lightfoot, *Notes*, 258-263; Wilckens, *Römer* 1, 121; Lagrange, *Romains*, 42-43; Moxnes, *Theology*, 35; Watson, *Paul*, 109; Carras, 'Romans 2,1-29', 191-196. Cf. others who take it as directed to both Jews and Gentiles: Barrett, *Romans*, 43; Leenhardt, *Romans*, 74; Schlatter, *Gottes Gerechtigkeit*, 74-75; and most notably, Bartsch, 'Die historische Situation', 286.

70 *EDNT* 1, 336.

71 Cf. other examples in Paul with the same subject; perhaps the simplest example is, '"*I* believed; therefore (διό), *I* have spoken." With the same spirit of faith *we* also believe and therefore (διό) [*we*] speak, because *we* know that ....' (2 Cor 4:13). It is sometimes followed by imperative verbs which introduce concluding exhortations on the basis of what has been said in the preceding section (2 Cor 6:17; 1 Thess 5:11; cf. Eph 2:11; Acts 20:31; 27:25), but the exhortations are addressed to the *same people* with self-evident conclusions. Cf. the use of διό in Rom 2:1, which is very similar to 15:7-8 in its syntactical structure.

72 Cranfield, *Romans* 1, 141-42, does not see much problem with this διό, because the sins of both Gentiles and Jews are condemned in 1:18-32 (but for reasons different from ours demonstrated in the previous section, pp. 73-94).

Furthermore, if Paul was applying the same inexcusability of 'they' in 1:18-32 to the different people, 'you', in 2:1ff, then he would not have used διό but ὡσαύτως: 'likewise', 'in like manner', 'similarly', or 'in the same way'.[73] Paul does indeed use ὡσαύτως once in Romans (8:26) to say that the *same* groaning is present in *different* subjects: the whole creation (8:22), Christians (8:23-25) and the Holy Spirit (8:26-27). Without exception all 17 occurrences in the NT are employed to connect the *same* thing/manner/action that precedes the *different* people/objects that follows.[74] Elliott's view that Paul directs his accusation to the *same people* in both 1:18-32 and in 2:1-16 appears, then, to be right. However, his conclusion that the interlocutor of 2:1-16 is therefore a *Gentile* (as in 1:18-32), not a Jew, is much less secure. Now we must turn to examine Elliott's identification of the 'you' in 2:1-16 as 'Gentile'. We note at least three weaknesses in his contention.

First, Elliott builds his argument on the unexamined presuppositions that 1:18-32 represents a 'universally recognized' indictment of Gentile immorality and was 'a stock *topos* in the early church's evangelization of *the Gentiles*'.[75] According to him since 'idolatry is the root of "specially Gentile sins", which causes sexual perversions and particularly homosexuality',[76] it had been the main content of 'Christian missionary preaching in

---

73 In fact Elliott, *Rhetoric*, 184 n.3, expects the adversative connective δέ here (just as in 2:17), if Paul had turned to the different people, 'you', in 2:1ff. If Paul had wanted to use 'δέ', he would have used 'δὲ καί' rather than only 'δέ': 'But you *also* have no excuse' (2:1). In fact, Hudson, *Pauline Epistles*, 63, thus, translates 2:1 by adding, '[But the Jew has no superior standing,] and so you are without excuse'. However, if Paul speaks to different people from 2:1, the most natural connective would be 'ὡσαύτως δὲ καί' (*Likewise* you *also* have no excuse), just as in 8:26. Our interpretation can be strengthened since Paul has already spoken about the *condemnation* of the practices described in 1:28-32 by accusing them of participation in and approval for doing the wicked things in 1:32.

74 So it is elsewhere: Matt 20:5; 21:28-30, 36; 25:17; Mark 12:21=Luke 20:31; Mark 14:31; Luke 22:20; 1 Cor 11:25; 1 Tim 2:9; 3:8, 11; 5:25; Titus 2:3, 6.

75 Elliott, *Rhetoric*, 108, his emphasis.

76 Elliott, *Rhetoric*, 108, n. 3, following Käsemann, *Romans*, 44.

the Gentile world'.[77] Unfortunately he pays scant attention to the recent view that 1:18-32 also includes an indictment against *Jewish* immorality.[78] He offers minimal support (merely in a footnote) for his assertion that 1:18-32 is the description of Gentile sinfulness only.[79] He would have been much safer methodologically if he had established this assertion *before* he launched the major argument that 2:1-16 refers to Gentiles on the basis of the διό in 2:1.

Second, it is a weak point of Elliott's argument that he discounts the evidence indicating Jewish complacency over Jewish covenantal privilege as shown in, e.g. Wisdom 12-15. On the basis of the close parallels between 2:1-4 and Wisdom 11-15, Nygren has asserted that Paul turns to counter-attack this characteristically Jewish assumption in 2:1-16, which thus confronts a *Jewish* interlocutor.[80] But Elliott rejects these references as too 'selective and to a degree artificial'.[81] Although Nygren depends rather over-heavily upon some limited references, e.g. Wis 12:22 and 15:2a,[82] this cannot rule out his thesis that Wisdom portrays Jewish covenantal complacency. Our numerous additional references from Wisdom[83] surely support Nygren's view that the

---

77 Bultmann, as affirmatively cited in Elliott, *Rhetoric*, 108 n. 4. So also Michel, *Römer*, 60: Rom 1:18-32 is 'ein Beispiel der Missionspredigt des Pls [Paulus]'; Weiss, *Earliest Christianity* 1, 239-240.

78 See our study *supra* pp. 73-94. Other studies include Hyldahl, 'Reminiscence'; Hooker, 'Adam', *idem*, 'Further Note'; Barrett, *First Adam*; Wedderburn, 'Adam'; Keck, 'Romans 1:18-23', 404; Bassler, *Impartiality*, 122; Davies, *Faith*, 47-49; Cosgrove, 'Rom 1:18-4:25', 621; among the commentators, Cranfield, *Romans* 1, 119-142; Dunn, *Romans* 1, 54-76.

79 Elliott, *Rhetoric*, 119 n.1; so also Gaston, *Paul*, 119. This contention is questionable in many respects, but we need not interact with him here, since our discussion above has sufficiently dealt with it.

80 Nygren, *Romans*, 113-116.

81 Elliott, *Rhetoric*, 176.

82 Elliott's assertion that the words of Wis 12:22 'So while chastening us thou scourgest our enemies ten thousand times more' (RSV), should be understood *within the context* of God's mercy, is also correct. But his understanding of that context, that 'God has been amazingly lenient with [Gentile] sinners, and (by comparison) harsh with the faithful of Israel' (*Rhetoric*, 176-178), is not so firmly based.

83 The author of Wisdom understands that even when God judges with equity, he still governs 'us' (the Jews) with great favour in contrast to his severe punishment of Gentiles (Wis 12:18, 20-21). Jews labelled Gentiles as

Jewish complacency confronted in 2:1-5 has its background in Wisdom. Jews passed judgement on others (i.e. Gentiles) and thought that they could escape God's judgement due to his covenant faithfulness (cf. Matt 23:33). They were the ones who experienced the riches of God's kindness, tolerance and patience (2:1-4; Wis 3:9-10; 5:15-16; 11:9-10, etc.).

Furthermore, with the expression 'We are yours' (Wis 15:2), the author of Wisdom seems to share a common Jewish belief found in the OT: 'whether they are sinful or meritorious they are yours, as it is written, "Yet they are your very own people"' (Deut 9:29). And as R. Meir commented on Deut 32:5, where Moses sums up the sins of Israel, 'even when they are full of blemishes they are called children'[84] (cf. Exod 19:5; Deut 14:2; 26:19; 1 Sam 12:22; Ps 29:11; Philo, *Spec.*, 4.181). Most of all, the Jews would claim the security of being God's people, as Moses and Isaiah had proclaimed (Deut 4:6-8; Isa 60:21). Thus, as Winston puts it, the Jews would say, 'We know God will not abandon us in our sins, but this sense of confidence in God will actually prevent us from sinning in the first place.'[85]

Finally, Elliott's denial of Jewish characterisation in 2:1-5 appears unconvincing.[86] Moreover, he offers no reason to justify his claim that 2:1-5 addresses *Gentile* rather than Jewish attitudes.[87]

'lawless men' (Wis 17:2) and ungodly (Wis 3:10; 16:16), but saw themselves as God's 'sons whom thou didst love' (Wis 2:13, 16, 18; 16:26), 'the holy nation (Wis 17:2), 'thy holy ones' (Wis 3:9; 18:1, 2, 5), 'his elect' and the righteous (Wis 2:12; 3:9, 10). Thus although they knew that they also would be judged and chastened (cf. Amos 3:2: 'You only have I chosen of all the families of the earth; therefore I will punish you for your sins'), they surely believed in a divine double standard (Wis 3:9-10; 5:15-16; 11:9-10; 12:22, 27; 16:2, 4-5; 18:7-8, 25; 19:1). The last verse of Wisdom (19:22) sums up: 'For in everything, O Lord, thou hast exalted and glorified thy people [i.e. the Jews]; and thou hast not neglected to help them at all times and in all places' (RSV).

84   Cf. Winston, *Wisdom*, 281-282.

85   Winston, *Wisdom*, 282.

86   Elliott, *Rhetoric*, 176, 180-185, 190: In 2:1-16 there is no 'explicit qualification or refutation of Jewish claims'. Thus he asserts 2:1-16 must not be considered as an attack on covenantal Judaism (p. 190). Elliott's understanding seems a mere 'assumption'; see next footnote.

87   Elliott does not carry the burden to substantiate *Gentile* characterisation in this passage. His assertion could have been maintained if he had explained that *Gentiles*, rather than Jews, are the ones who pass judgement on Jews (cf. 2:2), who assume that they will escape God's judgement (cf. 2:3),

In our view, however, this passage describes *Jewish* attitudes in the light of the evidence from the OT. Paul's accusation in 2:5, for example, 'because of your stubbornness and your unrepentant heart', seems to be directed towards the Jew. Although both σκληρότης and ἀμετανόητος occur only here in the NT, the words have a rich background in the OT, where they denote the stubbornness of the Israelites[88] (Deut 1:43; 9:27; 10:16; 29:18-19[89]; 31:27; 2 Chr 36:11-14; Neh 9:16-18; Ps 78:32; Isa 28:12; 30:15; Jer 5:3, 5c; 9:13-14; 35:17; Hos 4:16; Zech 7:12; Bar 2:30, 33; cf. Ps 95:8). The Jews were constantly warned not to harden their hearts (Ps 32:8-9; 78:8; 95:8; Prov 28:14; 29:1; Isa 42:18-25; 48:4; Mal 2:2), yet they are repeatedly said to have hardened their hearts and rebelled against God (Exod 32:9; Deut 21:20; 37:27; 1 Sam 8:7, 19; 2 Chr 24:19; 30:8; Neh 9:26; Isa 1:5; 59:13; Jer 32:33; 44:16; Hos 7:14; Zech 7:11). Even within Romans, Paul, like other NT writers,[90] describes the Jews as 'a disobedient and obstinate people' (10:21), who persist in unbelief (11:23; cf. 9:31; 10:3) with hardened hearts and darkened eyes (11:7-10, 25b). The reason why God did not spare Jews even though they were the 'natural branches', was that they persisted in unbelief (11:20-21, cf. v. 23). Israel had experienced a hardening (11:25; cf. 9:18; 11:7). These descriptions seem to indicate that with such expressions as we find in 2:5 he most probably had *Jews* in mind.[91]

---

who receive God's rich kindness and yet show contempt for his kindness (cf. 2:4), and who have stubborn and unrepentant hearts (cf. 2:5).

88 Fitzmyer, *Romans*, 301: '"Stubbornness" characterised Israel of old'. We may recall that Pharaoh, the archetypal example of a hard heart, was a Gentile. But the fact that Paul does not rebuke Gentile hardness of heart elsewhere in Romans seems to indicate that here Paul focuses on Jewish hardening.

89 The Qumran community already warned the Jews (1QS 2) of their complete fall if they continued to maintain a false security, saying, '"Peace be with me, even though I walk in the stubbornness of my heart" ([cf.] Deut. xxix, 18-19)': Vermes, *Scrolls*, 63.

90 E.g. Matt 13:15; 19:8=Mark 3:5; 10:5; John 12:37-43; Acts 7:51; 19:9.

91 Rather strongly, Caragounis, 'L'univeralisme', 32-33. Our position is further strengthened by the fact that Paul's rebuke of such complacency in 2:1-4 is in line not only with the Wisdom tradition (Albright and Mann, *Matthew*, 26), but also with the OT prophetic tradition (E.g. Isa 1:2, 4, 23; 24:5, 20; 30:1, 9; 48:8; 57:4; 65:2; 66:22; Ezek 24:3; Hag 1:12; Mal 1:6; 3:5; Ps 79:6 [=Jer 10:25]; 110:5-6).

Another reason for believing that Paul has Jews rather than Gentiles in mind in 2:1-5 is that, by contrast with those he confronts there, he soon asserts that (believing) *Gentiles* have the law written on their hearts (2:15), and also circumcision of the heart (2:29). This suggests that Paul is reluctant to characterise the *Gentiles* as stubborn and disobedient. It seems probable then that Paul had Jews in mind when he speaks of, 'those who are self-seeking and who reject the truth and follow evil' (2:8, 9). The OT is full of evidence of God's mercy despite Israel's disobedience; only in the NT is such blessing also explicitly applied to Gentiles (cf. Phil 4:19; Eph 1:7; 2:7). Therefore, it seems clear that Paul directs his accusation in 2:1-5 towards 'the complacent Jew'.[92]

The NT Gospel tradition also attacks Jewish self-satisfaction. The whole question of the Gospel writers' stance in presenting the Pharisees and Sadducees in a tendentious way, is a big issue today. See Boccaccini, *Middle Judaism*, 214-216, who concludes that 'the so-called "anti-Jewish" expressions in the New Testament are in reality "anti-Pharisaic," testimony to a debate between rival groups within middle Judaism' (p. 215). But the material in the Gospels still provides evidence that the Jews, especially the Pharisees and Sadducees, were complacent. John the Baptist rebukes Jewish pride in claiming 'We have Abraham as our father' (Matt 3:9; cf. John 8:31-41), and such false security that 'the merits of Abraham were believed to guarantee God's blessing' (Matt 3:7-10) (France, *Matthew*, 92; so also Beare, *Matthew*, 92-94; Albright and Mann, *Matthew*, 26). Moreover, Jesus warns of the danger of such complacency, saying that 'the subjects of the kingdom (i.e. Jews) will be thrown outside, into darkness, whilst many from the east and the west (i.e. Gentiles) will join the feast with Abraham, Isaac and Jacob' (Matt 8:11-12). The Jews are portrayed as having indeed thought that they could escape being condemned to hell; but Jesus said they could not (Matt 23:33). The inevitability of judgement upon the 'unfruitful' Jews is solemnly declared by John the Baptist (Matt 3:10; Luke 3:9) and Jesus (Matt 7:19).

92 Cranfield, *Romans* 1, 138-139. Especially Dunn, *Romans* 1, 78, expresses this clearly:

> At the same time it is evident from the Jewish perspective of 1:19-32 that the interlocutor is envisaged as a Jew, and the centrality in the argument (v 6) of the established Jewish principle of the even-handedness of divine retribution (Ps 62:12; Prov 24:12) is calculated to win specifically Jewish assent (cf. Bassler). More subtly, the echo of Wisd Sol 15:1ff. in v 4 seems designed to undermine any Jewish assumption that God's people are free of the grosser gentile sins and that any Jewish sin is insufficient to disturb Israel's favored status as the people chosen by God.

B. The Argument Concerning Divine Impartiality: but in Favour of Gentiles?: 2:6-11

Paul's assertion that '[God] will give each person according to what he has done' (2:6) has received a great deal of scholarly attention because it appears to contradict his doctrine of justification. It must be noted, however, that here Paul is not expounding 'the doctrine of judgement or salvation' with a special reference to 'how God judges or saves', as some have assumed.[93] Rather he makes these remarks in the course of explaining the theological axiom of divine impartiality. Thus J.M. Bassler is surely correct to assert that the affirmation of God's impartiality is the climax of the section:[94] 'For he [God] will render to every man [*whether he be Jew or Greek*] according to his work[95] ..... For God shows no partiality' (2:6, 11; RSV). In this sub-section we shall investigate how and why Paul presents God's impartiality, and shall propose that his apostolic self-consciousness has influenced the shape of this argument, which suggests his further 'bias towards the Gentiles'.

Developing the insight of M. Pohlenz's *Ringkomposition* in Romans 1-2,[96] Bassler impressively demonstrates the unity of 1:16-2:11 from the syntactical and thematic points of view,[97] and comments that, although Paul changes the tone of his argument in 2:1 by changing the pronouns from the third person to the second,

---

[93] We will not, therefore, be engaged in the debate whether Paul's remarks on the 'judgement according to works' (a) are self-contradictory, or (b) merely hypothetical, or (c) refer to the 'work' of faith/repentance, or (d) mean God will indeed judge all by their works. The contenders for (a) include Sanders, *Jewish People*, 123-135; Räisänen, *Paul*, 99-108; (b) Moo, Ziesler, Lietzmann; (c) Barth; (d) Black, Cranfield, Wilckens and Dunn. (a) and (c) seem most unlikely, and between (b) and (d) the latter seems more plausible. See Cranfield, *Romans* 1, 151-153, for a survey of various interpretations, and p. 146 for the OT and NT references that God will judge according to deeds.

[94] Bassler, *Impartiality*, 123-137, and her Appendix D on p. 199; cf. Dahl, *Studies*, 80.

[95] Paul seems to remind the Jewish interlocutor of a popular OT concept (e.g. 2 Chr 6:23; Job 34:11; Ps 28:4; 62:12; Prov 24:12; Jer 17:10; Ezek 18:20; Matt 16:27), and strikingly applies it equally to Gentile and Jew as evidence for divine impartiality.

[96] Pohlenz, 'Paulus und die Stoa', especially 70-75.

[97] Bassler, *Impartiality*, 123-156.

'the basic content of the argument remains the same: God recompenses all impartially according to their actions'.[98] Bassler is surely right to note both the unity of the section 1:16-2:11 and the theme of the divine impartiality in dealing with Jews and Gentiles (cf. Acts 10:34). Such a balance or equality is indeed the underlying logic in 1:16-2:29, and further in 3:9, 22, 29-30; 4:9, 16; 10:12.[99] However, it is crucial to note that in the rhetorical argument *Paul himself does not remain impartial*[100] but rather argues *'against'* the presupposed Jewish privileges[101] and *'for'* the legitimacy of the salvation of the Gentiles.

It is important to note that although Paul stresses God's impartiality in this section, the theological axiom of divine partiality is not the *goal* towards which Paul leads the argument; it is rather a *stepping-stone* from which he develops it further. Elliott also notes this development, but his understanding of God's impartial

---

98 Bassler, *Impartiality*, 131.
99 Carras, 'Romans 2,1-29', 185. *Contra* Piper, *Justification*, 28-29, for arguing that the axiom in 2:11 does not stress the equality of Jew and Gentile. The axiom here is not directly related to the description of election but to that of salvation. Even in its relation to election Paul later asserts that God is just in granting mercy in electing Gentiles (as implied in 9:14-18: see our discussion in *infra* pp. 228-234).
100 Cf. Cosgrove, 'Rom 1:18-4:25', 621. Bassler, *Impartiality*, 155, herself also recognises that Paul's argument does not always remain impartial up until 3:9:
> the argument of 1:18-2:29 actually runs counter in one rather significant matter to the accusation of 3:9 and its supporting catena. ... It is nowhere unambiguously stated in 1:18-2:29 that all without exception have sinned... [T]he emphasis of these chapters is on the theological ground of this accusation to such an extent that the actual charge of universal sinfulness is *nowhere clearly articulated until the summary of 3:9*.

Davies, *Faith*, 52-53, also notes this, and attempts to resolve this incongruity by 'understanding 3:9ff to be a reference to the wicked only (Jew and Greek alike), and not the righteous, who live by faith' (p. 52 n. 3). He asserts:
> He [Paul] sees an impartiality of judgment which recognises the righteous (who live by faith) as distinct from the wicked. ... the chiastic structure of 2:6-11 emphasizes the impartiality of God, both in his condemnation of the evildoer, and in his blessing of the doer of righteousness.

101 Carras, 'Romans 2,1-29', 195.

judgement as the main thesis is too restrictive.[102] The theme of God's impartiality which runs through Romans 1-4[103] is not merely employed to affirm God's *judgement*, but ultimately to affirm God's *salvation* (1:16).[104] Paul explains the axiom of divine impartiality from two aspects: those of judgement and of salvation. Both judgement and salvation (blessing) will be given to Jews and Gentiles according to what they have done (2:6, 9-10). The axiom effectively serves the two grand conclusions: 'We [Jews] are not at all better [than the Gentiles]' (3:9), and 'This righteousness from God comes through faith in Jesus Christ to everyone [whether he/she be a Jew or a Gentile] who believes. For (γάρ) there is no difference' (3:22). But *rhetorically, the first aspect of judgement seems to have been stressed to affirm the sinfulness of, and thus the inevitable judgement upon the Jews, and the second one of salvation seems to have been employed to establish the equal inclusion of the Gentiles in God's salvation.* This is why we have noted that Paul's argument for God's impartiality in 1:16-2:11 serves as a stepping-stone to his affirmation of the legitimacy of Gentile salvation. We shall trace this further in our discussion of Romans 2-4 and 9-11.

Unlike earlier Jewish writers,[105] Paul emphatically adds a new dimension to this axiom by applying it to the equality of Jew and

---

102 Elliott, *Rhetoric*, 122:
> the argumentative flow is not from other premises toward 'impartiality', but *from* God's impartiality *as* an axiom ('for [γάρ] there is no impartiality[?] with God', 2.11; 'for' [γάρ] Jew and Gentile are judged alike on the principle, 'the doers of the Law are justified', 2.12-16), *toward* the main thesis, 'there is no excuse before God's judgment' (cf. 1.20; 2.1), since God judges 'what is hidden in human hearts' (2.16).

103 Bassler, *Impartiality*, 121-160.

104 *Pace* Piper, *Justification*, 29, for applying God's impartiality to the occasion 'only .... in the last judgment'.

105 In the OT God's impartiality is pronounced concerning the 'poor' and the 'rich' among the *Israelites* (Deut 1:17; 10:17; Lev 19:15; 2 Chr 19:7; Prov 28:21; cf. Exod 23:3; Job 13:8, 10; 32:20-21; 34:17-19; Ps 82:1-4; *Pss. Sol.* 2:19). Deut 10:17, 24:17 and Ps 146:9 introduce the idea that God's impartiality also extends to aliens [i.e. non-Israelites] (cf. Acts 10:34-35; 11:9). Nevertheless God's favour towards Israel is clearly expressed (Lev 26:9; Deut 7:8, 14; 10:14-22). Especially is it striking to read that 'the great God ... who shows no partiality' (Deut 10:17) is described as the God who chose Israel and favoured her above all the nations (Deut 10:15).

Gentile.[106] He emphatically asserts that God's impartiality is to be applied to both Jews and Gentiles without distinction.[107] This is indeed a somewhat bold and radical statement (cf. 15:15). Jews claimed that they would be treated differently from Gentiles,[108] but Paul declares that both Jews and Gentiles will be punished impartially. He insists that Jews will be the *first* to experience trouble and distress if they do evil (2:8-9). Jews believed that 'grace and mercy are upon his elect, and he watches over his holy ones' (Wis 3:9; 4:15), and that God's immortality, reward, glory, mercy and protection were theirs alone (Wis 5:15-16; 14:31-15:2; 16:1-2; 19:22). But now Paul overturns their pride and exclusiveness, and affirms that Gentiles too will impartially receive immortality, glory, honour and peace from God if they do good (2:7, 10), i.e. if they 'believe' (1:16; 3:22).

Bassler does not point out the reason why Paul asserts divine impartiality as a theological axiom in 1:16-2:11. We suggest that through the axiom of God's impartiality in 2:11 Paul intends to correct Jewish presuppositions and to teach two fundamental

---

The idea that God's impartiality will also bring judgement upon Israel is again reflected in the intertestamental literature (see Bassler, *Impartiality*, 18-44), but the emphasis of God's impartiality lies with Israel's hope for ultimate reconciliation with God (Wis 6:7; Sir 35:12; *Jub*, 5:15-16; 21:4; 30:16; 33:18; *Pss. Sol.* 2:18; cf. Jer 9:25; Mal 2:9). According to the author of Jubilees, 'there could be no hope for the Gentiles', as Charles says (*Apocrypha* 2, 10). In this connection Bassler's conclusion after examining divine impartiality in the OT and the deuterocanonical literature is highly illuminating:

> God's impartiality certainly concerned the relationship between Jews and Gentiles, yet it was never seen as specifically blurring the distinction between the two groups. On the contrary, impartiality promised Israel that her oppressors would not escape punishment, nor would she fail to enjoy an ultimate reward (p. 44).

106 Cosgrove, 'Rom 1:18-4:25', 621: 'This interpretation of the axiom is unprecedented within ancient Judaism.'

107 That there is no difference between Jews and Gentiles is fundamental for Paul: Rom 1:5; 2:11; 3:9, 12, 19, 20, 22, 23, 27-31; 4:11, 12, 16; 5:12, 18; 8:32; 9:24; 10:4, 11, 12, 13; 11:32; 15:11; 1 Cor 1:22-24; 10:32; 12:13; Gal 2:14-16; 3:26-29; Col 3:11; cf. Gal 5:6; 6:15. Cf. Käsemann, *Romans*, 60-61.

108 See Wis 5:15-16; 11:9-11; 12:22; *Pss. Sol.* 7:5-9; 9:18; 10:8; 11:9; 12:7. Although it was admitted that the transgressions of the Jews went beyond those of the Gentiles, Jews anticipated God's greater favour to them (*Pss. Sol.* 1:18; 8:14).

principles: (a) God's impartiality in judgement implies that (self-confident) Jews are also to be subjected to his wrath and judgement (normally thought to be reserved for the Gentiles); (b) God's impartiality in salvation and blessing indicates that Gentiles[109] (whom the Jews have considered to be outside God's blessing) are also to be included in God's favour of salvation, glory, honour and peace (promised to God's covenant people). Undoubtedly the beneficiary of the application of this axiom is the *Gentile*. Right from the beginning of the letter Paul affirms rather boldly (τολμηρότερον; 15:15) the place of the Gentiles in God's economy. Then, Cosgrove's perception is largely correct:

> While Paul's attack remains inclusive of all throughout 1:18-2:16, his rhetorical strategy seems to draw the Jew into special focus. In 2:17-29 the Jew becomes the explicit and exclusive target. .....*From the standpoint of the Jewish auditor, there is nothing even-handed about Paul's rhetoric in Rom 1:18-2:29.* ... Paul's rhetorical construct of the Jew weakens the political position of the concrete Jewish auditor because *everything Paul says tends to reinforce the ethos of gentile Christians. And all in the name of divine impartiality.*[110]

Up to this point Cosgrove seems right, but his understanding of the reason for Paul's unevenness seems implausible. He understands that the background of Paul's assertion of God's impartiality is the unbalanced situation of 'church politics' at Rome.[111] He seems to go too far in suggesting that the Gentile Christians would have been encouraged to see Paul attacking the Jews, because they 'now enjoy a political reversal of their former situa-

---

109 Throughout Rom 1-2 Paul says that the Jews are disobedient and obstinate whilst the Gentiles are obedient and have faith; again he asserts that the Jews do not do good (2:17-29), whilst the (believing) Gentiles do good (1:14-16; 2:14-15, 26-27). Thus the blessing which 'everyone who does good' (2:10) can enjoy is portrayed primarily for the (believing) Gentiles. Cf. Gaston, *Paul*, 119-122.
110 Cosgrove, 'Rom 1:18-4:25', 622; emphases added.
111 *Pace* Cosgrove, 'Rom 1:18-4:25', 624, who asserts (p. 628):
Paul vindicates the self-understanding of the gentile majority and leaves the Jewish minority in a doubtful position. ... Paul first curries the favour of the majority of law-free gentile Christians at the expense of the Torah-faithful minority of Jews' (pp. 622, 623). He repeatedly maintains: 'The theological justification of all in Rom 3:21-31 is a political vindication of the gentile majority at Rome.

tion as Godfearers. The tables have turned.'[112] We have no evidence to suggest that Paul addresses them as a *'church politician'* who studies what pleases others and acts according to the situation. Later his tone of rebuke (2:17-29) seems to indicate him to be rather a *prophet to the Jews*[113] who has great sorrow and unceasing grief for the sins of the Jews (cf. 9:2).[114] Now he has an even better reason to rebuke them, for they persistently refuse to believe in Jesus, God's Messiah, and the message about him (9:1-4a; 11:14). Paul stands in line with the OT prophets (especially Jeremiah and Amos), John the Baptist, Jesus and Stephen, who often had to proclaim the danger of judgement to their own people. They all offer a *criticism from within* the covenant community.[115] On the other hand, Paul is *apostle to the Gentiles*, who not only preaches the gospel to them, but also provides a theological basis for the legitimacy of the salvation of the Gentiles, which is now available by faith apart from the law. Despite the theological emphasis on the theological axiom of divine impartiality, Paul's argument is consistently tilted (rhetorically) in favour of the Gentiles. We trace such a 'shape' in Paul's argument to his self-understanding in being the 'apostle to the *Gentiles*'.

---

112 Cosgrove, 'Rom 1:18-4:25', 624. See Chae, 'Paul's Apostolic Self-Awareness', 116-123, for our discussion on a different reconstruction of the composition of the Roman church.

113 K.O. Sandnes impressively argues in his monograph, *Paul—One of the Prophets?*, that Paul is to be considered as one of the prophets. We may add that Paul can be considered to be so from the prophets' tone of rebuke and their anguished spirit against the sins of the Jews, and also from their recall of Israel to covenant fidelity, the covenant given to Abraham as prototype and father of the faithful and of all nations.

114 Perhaps the best example of an OT prophet who resembles the Paul of 1:18-3:20 is Amos, who pronounces judgement on Judah (Amos 2:4-5) and on Israel (Amos 2:6-16). But it is to be noted that, unlike Paul in Romans, he previously announces judgement on Israel's Gentile neighbours in Amos 1:3-2:3, (though a much larger section is allocated to pronounce judgement on Israel according to their sins; Amos 2:6-9:10).

115 Dunn, *Romans* 2, 540, notes that Paul's debate is still within Judaism.

C. Critical Arguments about Jews and Affirmative Statements about Gentiles: 2:12-29

2:1-29 (especially 2:12-29) is considered to contain 'perhaps the most extensive and direct critique of Jews and Judaism in the letters of Paul'.[116] On the other hand, it is admitted that the same passage offers the most affirmative and favourable picture of the Gentiles: indeed this is portrayed 'in radical consistency'.[117] The nature of this argument has given rise to a diversity of interpretation. According to Räisänen, Paul's charge is 'a piece of propagandist denigration' based on an inaccurate understanding of contemporary Judaism.[118] Furthermore he asserts that the primary aim in Romans 2 is to prove that Jews are guilty, and that Paul's affirmative statements about Gentiles do not arise from a genuine interest in them but are intended to emphasise that Jews do not fulfil the law.[119] Sanders has a similar view. Noting that Paul's view on the law here is different from what he says elsewhere,[120] Sanders concludes that Paul's argument for universal sinfulness in 1:18-2:29 is internally inconsistent and a gross exaggeration, which stresses universal sinfulness in order to claim Christ's universal saviourhood.[121]

Bearing such contentions in mind, we will argue that Paul's 'bias towards the Gentiles' is *rhetorically* motivated to emphasise the outworking of divine impartiality in the blessing of the Gentiles. We will note that Paul consistently makes criticisms of Jews and affirmative statements about Gentiles in this section (2:12-29).[122] We will propose that his argument is shaped to secure the

---

116 Carras, 'Romans 2,1-29', 185; so also Sanders, *Jewish People*, 124.
117 Käsemann, *Romans*, 73.
118 Räisänen, *Paul*, 101.
119 Räisänen, *Paul*, 101.
120 Sanders, *Jewish People*, 132, deals with Romans 2 in an appendix, because for him Paul's view of the law here 'cannot be fitted into a category otherwise known from Paul's letters'.
121 Sanders, *Jewish People*, 125. See critical discussion in Carras, 'Romans 2,1-29', 185-207. Watson's thesis (*Paul*, 109-122) that Paul writes Romans 2 to persuade the Roman Jewish believers to abandon their ties with Jews, is also implausible.
122 See Bassler, *Impartiality*, 137-138, for taking 2:12-29 as a well-defined unit of argument linked with the words ἀνόμως—νόμος—περιτομή—ἀκροβυστία.

theological legitimacy of the salvation of the Gentiles on the one hand, and to establish Jewish sinfulness and thus to undermine Jewish complacency on the other.

The section 2:12-29 will be examined in three parts. First, we will examine the significant claims (though made in passing) such as 'Gentiles .... do by nature the things of the law' and 'Gentiles have the law written on their hearts' (2:12-16). These claims are extraordinary in the light of their original application to Jews alone (cf. Jer 31:33-37). Second, we will consider 2:17-24 where Paul's most negative critique and vigorous argument are made so as to establish Jewish sinfulness and to undermine their complacency. We shall critically evaluate Elliott's contention that this passage does not represent Paul's indictment of Jews but rather his exhortation to keep the law.[123] Paul's use of the verb ἱεροσυλεῖν and his quotation of Isa 52:5 seem to support our view as we will show. Finally, we will investigate the significance of Paul's statements in 2:25-29 about physical circumcision for Jews, and about a spiritual one for Gentiles, and the implications of Paul's application of the 'outward Jew' to ethnic Jews, and of the 'inward Jew' to Gentiles. The section 2:12-29 is a part of Paul's argument for the equality of Jew and Gentile, but again in this section Paul's self-awareness of being the apostle to the Gentiles has controlled the shape of the argument in favour of the Gentiles.

(a) An Affirmative Statement—'Gentiles Do the Law': 2:12-16

The sub-section (2:12-16) continues the theological axiom of divine impartiality highlighted in 2:6-11,[124] but in the light of the relation of this axiom to the law. Now for the first time in the letter, the law becomes a dominant issue in the discussion. Paul describes Jews as those 'in the law (ἐν νόμῳ)' or as 'the hearers of the law' (v. 13), and Gentiles as those 'without the law (ἀνόμως)' or, specifically, those 'who do not have the law' (v. 14).[125] The γάρ in 2:12 indicates that God's impartiality is related

---

123 Elliott, *Rhetoric*, 191-198.

124 Bassler, *Impartiality*, 139-140. The four occurrences of γάρ in 2:11-14 indicate that the argument of 2:11-16 serves to substantiate divine impartiality mentioned in 2:9-10 (and 2:14-16 is one long sentence in Greek).

125 The νόμος in 2:12, even without the definite article, undoubtedly indicates the Mosaic Law. So correctly Cranfield, *Romans* 1, 154; Lightfoot,

The Equality of Jew and Gentile in Sinfulness 111

to the concept of judgement, (sin rather than possession of the law being the issue). But the γάρ in 2:13 seems to indicate that Paul's rhetorical emphasis in 2:12 is in the second half of it: καὶ ὅσοι ἐν νόμῳ ἥμαρτον, διὰ νόμου κριθήσονται.[126] In 2:13 Paul continues his main point that mere possession of the law does not bring any advantage[127]—it must be obeyed. That faithful observers of the law will be justified is not a peculiar assertion in Judaism,[128] but Paul's assertion that Gentiles do the work of the law although they have not heard or received it, is unprecedented and highly significant.

2:14-15 is to be regarded as a parenthesis,[129] deliberately inserted with significance: it contains the first affirmative statement about Gentiles. Paul stresses that (some, i.e. believing) Gentiles[130]

Notes, 260; Shedd, *Romans*, 43; most recently, Fitzmyer, *Romans*, 305-306, 308. So also the renderings of TEV, NEB, JB, NASB, Moffatt, Phillips; cf. Käsemann, *Romans*, 62. See Sanday and Headlam, *Romans*, 58, for the distinction between νόμος and ὁ νόμος.

126 So rightly Cranfield, *Romans* 1, 153.

127 Dunn, *Romans* 1, 95; Ziesler, *Romans*, 86.

128 E.g. Deut 4:1, 5-6, 13-14; 30:11-14; 1 Macc 2:67; 13:48; 1QpHab 7:11; 12:4-5; 4QpPs37 2:14, 22; Philo, *Cong.*, 70; *Praem.* 79; Josephus, *Ant.* 20.44: Dunn, *Romans* 1, 45, 97. Parallels to Paul's remarks include the Prologue of Sirach: 'those who love learning should make even greater progress in living according to the law', and *m. Ab.* 1:17: 'and not the expounding [of the Law] is the chief thing but the doing [of it]'; cf. Jas 1:22-25.

129 Ziesler, *Romans*, 88, seems right to take it as a parenthesis, for 2:13 and 2:16 are connected with the same subject of judgement as well as the same future tense, while 2:14-15 are in the present tense. See Käsemann, *Romans*, 67, for a different view on 2:14-15 in connection with the future tense of 2:16. Those who consider that 2:16 was originally placed directly after 2:13, include Sanday and Headlam, *Romans*, 62; Dodd, *Romans*, 60, following Moffatt's translation (though there is no supporting MS authority for this transposition); similarly Kirk, *Romans*, 180.

130 The absence of the article before ἔθνη in 2:14 indicates that Paul does not refer to *all* Gentiles (*the* Gentiles) but to *some* (i.e. *Christian*) Gentiles, in the light of 2:26-29; 11:13 and 15:9: Cranfield, *Romans* 1, 155-156. So also König, 'Gentiles', 53-60; Bassler, *Impartiality*, 141-142. But those who do not interpret the term as *Christian* Gentiles but just Gentiles as such, include Dunn, *Romans* 1, 98; Sanders, *Jewish People*, 125-126; Käsemann, *Romans*, 73; Ziesler, *Romans*, 86; Fitzmyer, *Romans*, 310. Cf. Sanday and Headlam, *Romans*, 59. Paul certainly means believing Gentiles here, but since he does not explicitly contrast Jews and believing Gentiles in Romans 2 we embrace both aspects by using a bracket.

who 'by nature' do not have the law[131] fulfil the intention of the law.[132] The γάρ clause confirms v. 13b, and (believing) Gentiles are mentioned as a concrete example of those who do the work of the law (i.e. obey the law), and thus are declared righteous (2:13). Such an affirmative assertion about Gentiles serves, on the other hand, as a sharp attack on Jews.[133] What Paul says in this passage is not just that they are equal without distinction in keeping the 'law';[134] rather, he asserts that (at least some) Gentiles indeed *do* the work of the law (τὸ ἔργον τοῦ νόμου; cf. 2:26; 8:4)[135] even though they do not have the written law (cf. Philo, *Abr.* 275-276; *T. Jud.* 20:3-5; *2 Apoc. Bar.* 57:2), while Jews do not keep the law even though they have it and hear it.[136]

Here Paul highlights the fact that Gentiles are doing the divine intention of the law rather than that they are fulfilling the letter of the Torah as the Jews were doing.[137] When Gentiles do the things required by the law (τὰ τοῦ νόμου), what they do becomes a law

---

131 BAGD, 869; NASB; Fitzmyer, *Romans*, 309. The 'by nature (φύσει)' can be connected to the phrase 'Gentiles who *do not have* the law' (e.g. Cranfield, *Romans* 1, 156-157; Achtemeier, *Romans*, 45), or to the clause '[they] *do* the requirement of the law' (Käsemann, *Romans*, 63; Leenhardt, *Romans*, 83; Wilckens, *Römer* 1, 134; Dodd, *Romans*, 37; Dunn, *Romans* 1, 156-157; Fitzmyer, *Romans*, 310; KJV, NIV, NEB, RSV). The former seems more probable, because Gentiles are those who by nature, i.e. 'by virtue of their descent' (Caragounis, 'L'universalisme', 34 n. 62) do not have the law. Furthermore, it would be theologically untanable if φύσις is connected to the latter clause, because then the verse is to indicate that 'they [the Gentiles] are morally superior to the Jews, who need the law to tell them what is good and how to do it. Such inherent moral superiority of gentiles over Jews not only makes the chosen people morally inferior to all others but it also makes nonsense of Paul's argument' (Achtemeier, *Romans*, 45).

132 Käsemann, *Romans*, 63.

133 Käsemann, *Romans*, 62; Bassler, *Impartiality*, 143.

134 Cf. Bassler, *Impartiality*, 143.

135 The singular τὸ ἔργον τοῦ νόμου seems to denote 'the concrete act demanded by the law in a general sense' (Käsemann, *Romans*, 64. cf. Cranfield, *Romans* 1, 158) or the essential element required by the law, because it could hardly mean that Gentiles do the work of 'the Law in its entirety' (so correctly, Ziesler, *Romans*, 88).

136 The noun ἀκροατής suggests that the person only hears, and does not convey the sense of 'listening to', as ἀκούειν does.

137 Käsemann, *Romans*, 65.

for themselves.¹³⁸ The (believing) Gentiles do the most essential requirement of the law (τὸ ἔργον τοῦ νόμου), i.e. they demonstrate faith, while (unbelieving) Jews miss it even though they may keep many other commands of the law.¹³⁹ Paul asserts that τὸ ἔργον τοῦ νόμου is written on the hearts of the Gentiles.¹⁴⁰ According to Jer 31 (LXX 38):33, writing the law on the heart is promised by a divine oath (Jer 31:37) exclusively to 'all the descendants of Israel' (Jer 31:33, 36, 37) as a new covenant.¹⁴¹ But Paul significantly applies this promise to the Gentiles by deliberately echoing it, and suggests that the nature of this promise now includes those Gentiles on whose hearts τὸ ἔργον τοῦ νόμου is written: *'I will be their God, and they will be my people'* (Jer 31:33c; cf. 17:1).

For Jeremiah 'their' and 'they' refer to 'the house of Israel'. So also clearly for Isaiah (Isa 51:7; cf. Deut 6:6; 11:18; 30:14; 32:46; Ps 26:2; 37:31; 40:8; 119:11; Prov 3:3; Ezek 40:4).¹⁴² But Paul is different. As Hays correctly says, 'Paul's echo inverts the motif, turning it into something that the prophets had never envisioned: a warrant for speaking of uncircumcised Gentiles—Paul probably

---

138 Paul seems to argue that for the Gentiles *faith* has become their law and that trust in the Lord is what the law was originally intended for, and therefore is τὸ ἔργον τοῦ νόμου. Elsewhere in the letter Paul often mentions that the Gentiles obey the requirement of the law by faith (1:5; 15:18; 16:26).

139 The idea that 'the doers of the law will be declared righteous' is a familiar one in the NT (Matt 7:21, 24; 12:50; Luke 6:47; John 13:17; Jas 1:22, 25; 4:11; 1 John 2:17; Rev 22:15), and in the later rabbinic literature (Str-B 3, 84-88); cf. Bassler, *Impartiality*, 140, 258 n. 65. In the LXX the phrase οἱ ποιηταὶ τοῦ νόμου occurs only in 1 Macc 2:67, and there it refers only to the pious observers of the law; Mattathias exhorts his sons to punish the non-law-observing Jews *and* the Gentiles; and so what Paul says here is significant.

140 See Cranfield, *Romans* 1, 159; Käsemann, *Romans*, 64. According to Dunn, *Romans* 1, 100, the phrase 'the works (plural) of the law' always has a negative sense in Paul (3:20, 28; Gal 2:16; 3:2, 5, 10). Therefore he uses the singular (τὸ ἔργον τοῦ νόμου) in 2:15 to portray a commendable feature of the 'work of the law' that is 'in the heart' (see references there). He also notes that the 'heart' elsewhere denotes the 'inner person' or 'the real person' (8:27; 1 Cor 4:5; 14:25; 2 Cor 3:2-3; 5:12).

141 See Kuhr, 'Römer 2:14f', 252-261.

142 Hays, *Echoes*, 45, is surely correct to say that 'he [Isaiah] is speaking not of Gentiles but of Israel, urging them not to be discouraged by the contempt of the Gentiles'.

has Gentile Christians in mind—as God's people'.[143] For Paul the promise includes Gentiles, and so later he affirms that God is the God of Gentiles too (3:29) and that the word of God concerning Jews *and* Gentiles has not failed (9:6).[144] Paul's two-fold purpose in inserting this parenthesis becomes clear: it is (a) to stress that Gentiles do the essential work of the law as God initially intended; (b) at the same time, to undermine the complacency of the Jews who do not produce the 'work of the law' and yet boast about their exclusive possession of it.[145]

Paul says God is impartial concerning Jews and Gentiles, but, at least *in his presentation of his argument* in Romans, Paul does not seem impartial; rather, he is 'on the Gentile's side'.[146] Our position is well expressed by G.N. Davies in a more precise structuring of argument:[147]

12-13 Impartial judgment	(οὐ γὰρ ....ἀλλά)
	(countering Jewish presumption)
14-16 Gentiles: *do* the law	law on hearts
17-24 Jews: *break* the law	blaspheme God

---

143 Hays, *Echoes*, 45.

144 See *infra* Chapter 5.

145 Similarly Eckstein, *Syneidesis*, 152, as cited in Dunn, *Romans* 1, 99. The second reason for Kirk, *Romans*, 180, namely, to rule out a possible Gentile excuse that they did not know the law and hence should be exempted from judgement, seems unconvincing; so also *pace* Käsemann, *Romans*, 67, who asserts that a parenthesis is added to 'show nothing more than that the Gentile is not wholly without law and thus falls into self-contradiction'. Most unlikely is the view of Sanday and Headlam, *Romans*, 62: to show that Gentiles have 'a second inferior kind of law', the law of conscience.

146 This does not necessarily mean that Paul presents a different picture of Gentiles in 2:14-15 and in 1:18-32, 3:9-18, as Ziesler, *Romans*, 85, 87, asserts. The fact that Paul does not directly indict Gentiles in 1:18-32 by referring to them specifically (as he does in 2:17ff with respect to Jews, or as the author of Wisdom does with respect to the Gentiles), may indicate that he treats the sinfulness of Gentiles not as harshly as that of Jews. Ziesler's contention that 3:9ff is Paul's further indictment of Gentiles as well as of Jews, does not seem correct (see our discussion below p. 138 n. 249); cf. both Käsemann and Cranfield, for example, who more plausibly take 2:1-3:20 as a pronouncement of judgement on Jews.

147 Davies, *Faith*, 58; with our emphasis. This presentation is a plausible expansion of Bassler's (*Impartiality*, 139).

```
    25a Jews: do the law              circumcision of value
    25b  Jews: break the law          circumcision of no value
    26-27 Gentiles: do the law
          uncircumcision=circumcision
    28-29 Impartial blessing          (οὐ γὰρ ....ἀλλά)
                                      (countering Jewish presumption)
```

However, Davies' repeated summaries 'Gentiles: do the law' and 'Jews: break the law', expose the weakness of his own and Bassler's views claiming that here Paul attempts to emphasise the impartiality of God. In our opinion, Paul's presentation is rhetorically shaped and implies *more than divine impartiality* in 2:12-29: he presents the Gentiles affirmatively, and the Jews critically.

(b) A Critical Argument—'Jews Break the Law': 2:17-24

Paul's direct and explicit indictment of Jews appears in 2:17ff for the first time. He starts by accusing Jewish self-confidence and pride in six areas in 2:17-20:

if you[148]
1. [boastfully[149]] call yourself a Jew
2. rely on the law
3. boast in God
4. think you know his will
5. approve what is superior
6. are convinced of your own roles on the basis of
   your knowledge and truth gained from the law to be
       -a guide for the blind
       -a light for those who are in the dark
       -an instructor of the foolish
       -a teacher of infants

Paul does not make an explicit accusation with these 'descriptions', and to some extent they reflect a genuine accep-

---

148 Note the emphatic σύ.
149 Lightfoot, *Notes*, 261; Stowers, 'Dialogue', 715; Earle, *Word*, 146. Dunn, *Romans* 1, 109, also notes that Ἰουδαῖος connotes with pride its distinctive self-identity and firm commitment to the law. So also the Stoic or philosopher: see Stowers, *Diatribe*, 96. Cf. Bar 5:4: 'Your name will for ever be called by God.'

tance and appreciation of Israel's unique position and gifts (cf. 3:1-2; 9:3-5). But the context (2:1-5 and 2:21-29) clearly suggests that these elements are mentioned to lay the basis for a more specific and direct attack from 2:21 onwards.[150] Paul lists (not positively as Elliott asserts, but negatively) the items of 'the real self-estimation of his contemporary Jews',[151] (Isa 42:6-7, 19-20; Wis 18:4; Sir 37:19; *1 En.* 105:1; *Sib. Or.* 3:195; 1QS 3:13; 8:11-12; Josephus, *Apion*, 2.42; Philo, *Abr.*, 98). He condemns the ethnically exclusive and complacent[152] Jewish boast in God,[153] for the Jew does not live in accordance with his claim. The OT had already warned Jews of relying on such a false security (Deut 29:19-21; Jer 8:7-8; Mic 3:11).[154]

Paul likewise completely overturns such Jewish complacency and accuses them of hypocrisy (cf. Matt 23:13-33). Paul blames them not only for teaching (and judging) others by words, but also for doing the same evil things about which they are teaching (most probably) the Gentiles (2:21-23; cf. 2:1-3).[155] To under-

---

150 So also Thompson, 'Double Critique', 525.
151 Elliott, *Rhetoric*, 128.
152 Bultmann, *Theology* 1, 243; Dunn, *Romans* 1, 110.
153 Cf. the positive aspect of boasting in God: 'let him who boasts boast of this: that he understands and knows me, that I am the LORD...' (Jer 9:24), is quoted in 1 Cor 1:31; 2 Cor 10:17.
154 If a disobedient Jew 'thinks, "I will be safe, even though I persist in going my own way." ... The LORD will never be willing to forgive him; his wrath and zeal will burn against that man' (Deut 29:19-21). '... my people do not know the requirements of the LORD', [but they say], 'We are wise, for we have the law of the LORD' (Jer 8:7-8). 'Is not the LORD among us? No disaster will come upon us' (Mic 3:11).
155 For the emphasis on the Jew as the teacher of the law to the Gentiles, see Schnabel, *Law*, 233-234; McKnight, *Light*, 105; Zeller, *Juden*, 155-157. Dunn, *Romans* 1, 112, is right to see that such Jewish awareness of status remained as a superior sense of privilege rather than as a missionary responsibility toward the Gentiles. See also the Gospel writers' portrayal of Jesus' view of the Jewish religious leaders as blind guides, hypocrites and wicked teachers (Matt 15:14; 23:1-36, especially vv. 27-28). Although the (leaders of the) Jews called themselves the disciples of Moses (John 9:28; cf. 5:45), and sat in Moses' seat (Matt 23:2), Jesus charges them, 'Yet not one of you keeps the law' (John 7:19). Furthermore, he charges, 'Inside you [Pharisees] are full of greed and wickedness' (Luke 11:39), and 'you do not have the love of God in your hearts' (John 5:42), and that they loved darkness instead of light because their deeds were evil (John 3:19-21).

mine Jewish complacency (cf. Luke 18:9-14), Paul furthermore specifically accuses them of stealing, adultery, idolatry and dishonouring, indeed blaspheming God (2:21-24); items which would be considered the worst indictment any Jew could fear.[156]

Curiously Elliott argues that in this passage Paul does not accuse Jews alone; moreover, he asserts that here Paul portrays a bright picture of Jews in contrast to a dark one of Gentiles in 1:18-32.[157] He goes on to say that Paul's accusation in 2:17-29 does not mean to establish the verdict to include Jews as declared in 3:9; rather it functions as an exhortation to keep the Law.[158] Basically, Elliott has two points of argument, which we will examine below.

First, Paul's charge in 2:17-24 is not solely or primarily against Jews, since he has been arguing toward his conclusion that 'Jews and Gentiles alike are all under sin' (3:9).[159] Paul's purpose in 2:17-24 is, of course, not a 'radical demolition of Jewish privileges', as Elliott correctly perceives[160] (because he maintains Jewish privileges elsewhere: 1:16; 2:9-10; 3:1-2; 9:3-5; 11:17-32). But this does not mean that he cannot indict Jews for their obvious misbehaviour as the covenant people. Paul's conclusion, 'Jews and Gentiles alike are all under sin', also suggests that his argument has targeted both ethnic groups. But his more fundamental conclusion (substantiated by the important γάρ), 'We [Jews] are not any better at all [than Gentiles]', indicates that his

---

156 *Pace* Elliott, *Rhetoric*, 129: 'His [Paul's] purpose is not to pronounce a verdict, ... the second apostrophe in 2:17-24 is intended not so much to disqualify the claims of actual Jews.' But here Paul pronounces a verdict in the style of the diatribe; otherwise, there would be no point in the charge of blasphemy.

157 *Contra* Elliott, *Rhetoric*, 127-128, 130-131, 191-192.

158 Elliott, *Rhetoric*, 194.

159 A similar view has been expressed by Bornkamm and Fitzmyer. Bornkamm, 'Last Will', 26, contends, 'For Paul, the Jew represents man in general, and indeed man in his highest potential: the pious man who knows God's demands in the law but who has yet failed to meet God's claim and is lost in sin and death.' Fitzmyer, *Romans*, 296-297, 315, asserts that in 2:17-24 Paul declares that divine wrath 'will be manifested against the Jews *as well as the pagan* because of the way *the Jew* lives (2:17-24)' (with our emphases).

160 *Contra* Käsemann, *Romans*, 78, as objected to in Elliott, *Rhetoric*, 130. Cf. Beker, *Paul*, 80, 'Paul's aim ... is the demolition of Jewish pride in the Torah and the destruction of Jewish narcissistic self-elevation over the Gentiles.'

argument has been directed to establish this verdict. What Paul has written in 1:18-2:29 (especially 2:1-29) is not 'an *exhortation to keep the law*'[161] but a condemnatory *charge* (προητιασάμεθα:[162] 3:9) of their sinfulness for not keeping the law (2:23).[163]

Second, and more importantly, Elliott asserts that Paul's accusation of the Jew (that he steals, commits adultery, 'robs' temples and dishonours God) is to be considered as 'the "exceptional" case', because the evidence for such sins is minimal, and only 'exceptional' Jews were involved in such misbehaviour. Thus he affirms that what Paul says here is not an indictment against Jews in general nor against a pretentious Jewish teacher or leader who teaches others whilst he himself does not embody what he teaches.[164] Elliott's point is that even Käsemann, who applies these sins to the Jewish community, could provide only a few pieces of Rabbinical evidence which Billerbeck mentions in his *Kommentar*. But we should note that one of these pieces of evidence from the *Kommentar* is most telling. It is that Jochanan ben Zakkai, writing in the late 60s AD, laments the appalling increase of murder, adultery, sexual immorality and other evils among the Jews.[165] If Paul had such moral degradation among his contemporaries in mind, what he writes in 2:17-24 can be taken as an accusation based on historical fact. Since he appeals to the OT to justify his accusation ('καθὼς γέγραπται': 2:24), he almost certainly had in mind some examples in the OT. The prophetic condemnation could have not only provided him with examples, but also have led to the boldness necessary to speak against his people as the prophets had to the former generations. Jer 7:9-11, for example, offers a striking parallel:

---

161 *Pace* Elliott, *Rhetoric*, 194. He quotes Sanders, *Jewish People*, 129, to support his contention. Against Sanders we may say that Paul does not need to call his readers to 'repent and obey the law', because they are already Christians: Paul's point does not seem to be to exhort his readers to 'become better Jews on strictly non-Christian Jewish terms' (p. 129).

162 αἰτία means a charge or an accusation: see Zerwick and Grosvenor, *Analysis*, 465; BAGD, 26.

163 So also John portrays Jesus as saying: 'I have much to say in judgment of you' (John 8:25).

164 *Pace* Elliott, *Rhetoric*, 191-192. Käsemann, *Romans*, 69, also sees this passage as dealing with 'an exception as representative of the community'.

165 See Dodd, *Romans*, 64.

Will you steal and murder, commit adultery and perjury, burn incense to Baal and follow other gods you have not known, and then come and stand before me in this house, which bears my Name, and say, "We are safe"— safe to do all these detestable things? Has this house, which bears my Name, become a den of robbers to you? But I have been watching! declares the LORD (Jer 7:9-11).

This accusation was given not only to 'exceptional' Israelites who misbehaved but to 'all you people of Judah' (Jer 7:2). A similar inclusive or 'corporate' charge was also made elsewhere to all Israelites: 'There is only cursing, lying and murder, stealing and adultery' (Hos 4:2). We may confine ourselves to examining the simple accusation: 'ὁ βδελυσσόμενος τὰ εἴδωλα ἱεροσυλεῖς; (You who abhor idols, do you rob temples?, 2:22b)'. The verb ἱεροσυλεῖν means either 'to rob the temple'[166] or 'to commit sacrilege,'[167] that is, 'to *behave irreverently* toward the sanctuary'.[168] D.B. Garlington has offered strong arguments that ἱεροσυλεῖν can be taken in the weaker sense 'to profane the temple by inadequate (and so idolatrous) worship'. We may add at least two more pieces of evidence from the context. First, Paul has already made an accusation against the 'robber' (λῃστής) with κλέπτειν ('to steal') in 2:21, so it is unlikely he is simply repeating the idea of 'robbing' here.[169] Second, ἱεροσυλεῖν is more likely to be related to idolatry according to the description βδελυσσόμενος τὰ εἴδωλα ('detesting the idols') (v. 22b) rather than to 'temple-robbery'. Our understanding is based on the fact that Paul makes accusations by repeating the same verb used in the description. Therefore ἱεροσυλεῖν probably connotes another form of Israel's 'idolatry'[170] and is related to the temple.[171] Thus it may be para-

---

[166] Both Wilckens, *Römer* 1, 150, and Ziesler, *Romans*, 91, take it quite literally, while Barrett, *Romans*, 54-55, takes it figuratively. Some examples used with this meaning include Acts 19:37; 2 Macc 4:39, 42; 9:2; 13:6; Josephus, *Ant.* 17.163; cf. *Ant.* 18.3, 5.

[167] Cranfield, *Romans* 1, 169-170.

[168] *EDNT* 2, 179; so also BAGD, 373.

[169] λῃστής and κλέπτης are used as synonyms in contrast to ποιμήν (shepherd) in John 10:1 and 8; cf. 2 Cor 11:26.

[170] It is said that Jewish idolatry had disappeared in Paul's days: Cranfield, *Romans* 1, 169; Garlington, "ΙΕΡΟΣΥΛΕΙΝ', 142. This seems correct, otherwise Paul could have written, 'You who abhor idols, do you *worship* idols?'

phrased: 'You who abhor idols, do you profane the Temple, which bears the Name of the true and only God, by behaving irreverently and idolatrously towards it?'[172]

In this connection we may return to the passage from Jeremiah quoted above (Jer 7:9-11). There God says that the Temple has been turned into 'a den of robbers' (σπήλαιον λῃστῶν: LXX Jer 7:11). Further, the Temple has often been robbed by Gentiles or Jewish kings (2 Kgs 12:18; 18:16; 2 Chr 12:9; 16:2; 25:24; 28:21-25; 36:10). But in this passage there is no indication that the Israelites rob the Temple; rather, they are accused of devaluing its role and behaving irreverently towards it. They are falsely assured that the Temple and God will grant them security, even though they constantly worship Baal. For Jeremiah they are 'robbers of the Temple', because they misunderstood the fundamental purpose of the Temple and abused it in connection with their idolatrous sacrifices to Baal. In a figurative sense, for Jeremiah, they 'robbed' the original nature and intention of the Temple and used it for another purpose, not to worship the LORD but to provide a form of divine insurance. Such an attitude was 'irreverence toward God, and profanation of the Divine majesty (Ezek 36:23)'.[173]

In 2:21-22 Paul accuses the Jews of stealing, committing adultery and idolatry, and thus affirms that they are not 'doers of the law'[174] but rather 'breakers of the law'.[175] Such a portrayal is significant in the light of the fact that he has already said that the (believing) Gentiles are 'doers of the law' (2:14-15). Thus Paul declares, in conclusion, that the Jew boasts in the law and yet

---

[171] According to Garlington, "ΙΕΡΟΣΥΛΕΙΝ', 148, 'for Paul *the new idol is the Torah*! The 'sacrilege' in question is *Israel's idolatrous attachment to the law itself*' (his italics). However, his assertion does not seem to be in line with what Paul says elsewhere in Romans (3:31; 7:7, 12, 16; 9:4).

[172] *Apoc. Abr.* 25:1-6 also refers to the idolatrous profanation of the Jerusalem Temple *before* the destruction. According to the author, the idolatrous profanation of the Jerusalem Temple was one of the most important causes behind the destruction of Jerusalem: see Rubinkiewicz and Lunt, 'Apocalypse of Abraham', 685.

[173] Shedd, *Romans*, 55, who lists Luther, Calvin, Bengel and Hodge as maintaining this view.

[174] Fitzmyer, *Romans*, 315.

[175] The accusation that Jews have despised the law is not new (2 Chr 36:16; Ps 78:10; Isa 5:24; 30:9; Jer 6:9; 9:13; Hos 4:6; Amos 2:4; Mark 7:9).

The Equality of Jew and Gentile in Sinfulness   121

dishonours God by breaking the law itself as expressed in the Decalogue (2:23; cf. John 7:19: 'Yet not one of you keeps the law').[176] Rom 2:23 concludes 2:21b-22, and 2:24 scripturally backs up the accusation made in 2:21-23. Elliott seems to have missed the point of Paul's contrasting affirmative statements about Gentiles and critical ones about Jews, and implausibly maintains that in 2:17-24 Paul appeals to the Jews' accountability rather than to their culpability.[177]

Paul's characteristic indictment of Jews is once again stressed in the quotation of LXX Isa 52:5 in 2:24. His intention can be perceived from two observations. First, he radically modifies the context of Isa 52:5.[178] In Isaiah the context is one *of promise to and blessing of the Jews*. It may be paraphrased as follows:

My name is constantly blasphemed among the Gentiles (v. 5b), for my people have been taken away for nothing, and those who rule them mock (5a). Since you were sold for nothing, without money I will redeem you, O captive Daughter of Zion (3). So awake, O Zion, put on your garments of splendour, O Jerusalem. Rise up, sit enthroned (1a, 2a). The uncircumcised and defiled will not capture or rule you again (1b), and thus my people will know and honour my name (6a). You will burst into songs of joy together, for I have comforted you, and I have redeemed Jerusalem (9), and all the ends of the earth will see my salvation (10).

Thus, in Isaiah, God's name is blasphemed because his own people are in captivity among the Gentiles, who constantly mock them. In short, *the blasphemy is caused by Israel's Gentile oppressors*: '"because of your misfortunes"'[179] [i.e. caused by the Gentile enemies]. But Paul turns Isaiah's 'blasphemy among the

---

176 The γάρ of 2:24 seems to allow us to take 2:23 as a statement rather than a question (correctly Ziesler, *Romans*, 91; Sanday and Headlam, *Romans*, 54); so also in Nestle-Aland[26], UBS[3]; JB, NEB; *pace* KJV, RV, RSV, NIV, TEV, NASB, Moffatt, Lutherbibel.

177 *Pace* Elliott, *Rhetoric*, 196-197. We find Meyer's perception (*Romans* 1, 130) more convincing: 'in vv. 17-24 [Paul throws] a bright light of illumination on the culpability of the Jews in presence of the law'.

178 Although the LXX text of Isa 52:5 (which adds 'δι' ὑμᾶς' and 'ἐν τοῖς ἔθνεσιν' to the Hebrew text) is almost exactly quoted here (2:24) both in words and substance, the two *contexts* in which the texts appear are significantly different: Giblin, 'As It Is Written', 482-483, who notes Paul's application to a different context.

179 Moxnes, *Theology*, 60 n. 13. So also Cranfield, *Romans* 1, 171 n. 1.

nations' 'into its exact opposite'.[180] It has become a matter of God's name being blasphemed 'because of your *misbehaviour* in breaking the law' (2:23b),[181] and here is a link with Jesus' teaching.[182]

Our interpretation can be further supported from the fact that Paul quotes Isa 52:7 in 10:15 without changing the original context of blessing. If he cites Isa 52:7 according to its original context,[183] he must have known the context of Isa 52:5 as well. Then most probably the modification here in 2:24 has been made specifically to support his argument. Thus one cannot say that Paul has misread Isa 52:5, nor that his out-of-context reading of Isa 52:5 is only provisional.[184] It seems most probable that here Paul

---

180 Käsemann, *Romans*, 71. Paul could have appealed to the references which explain clearly that the Jews ended up in such a situation through their own disobedience to God's law (e.g. 2 Kgs 17:7-23; Dan 9:4-16). But the fact that he draws his reference from Isa 52 suggests more than merely the introduction of a wider context.

181 Thus Paul's appeal to LXX Isa 52:5 is not to affirm that *as in former days* the Jews' hypocrisy brings blasphemy to God among the Gentiles (2:24); cf. Fitzmyer, 'Use', 324; Lindars, *Apologetic*, 22.

182 According to the Gospels, Jesus made the same charge: Jews irreverently turned the Temple, a house of prayer, into a 'market place', and a 'den of robbers' (σπήλαιον λῃστῶν: Matt 21:12-13=Mark 11:15-17; Luke 19:45-46; John 2:14-16). The charge was made not only against the merchants in the Temple but more significantly against the religious leaders (cf. Mark 11:15-18), who misused the Temple for more 'important' purposes (e.g. accumulating wealth) than prayer and worship. See Jeremias, *Jerusalem*, 96-99, who has documented the shameless collection of wealth and 'the remarkable wealth of the priestly aristocracy' before AD 66. In addition to the regular income for their official duties, the high priests received a considerable portion of income from the sacrificial offerings and temple-related 'business'; cf. Matt 23:16-18; Luke 16:14. Like their forefathers, they also 'robbed' the Temple by using it for purposes other than worshipping God, purposes contrary to the will of the God who was worshipped there. Paul further says that greed is idolatry (Col 3:5, cf. Eph 5:5).

183 So also Hays, *Echoes*, 45, but his contention, 'the scripture quotation evokes, metaleptically, echoes of the promise that God, in vindicating his name, will also redeem Israel', is not convincing, because in the context of Rom 2:21-24 Paul does not allude to such a promise at all. Cf. Stanley, *Language*, 84-86, 134-141, who does not pay attention at all to the change of contexts.

184 *Pace* Hays, *Echoes*, 45-46. See Lincoln's objection, 'Wrath', 209 n. 36.

reconstructs the context with the deliberate intention of establishing Jewish sin in their breaking the law while being complacent about the Judgement.

The second observation is that Paul intensifies his attack on the Jews by adding the significant 'γάρ', which does not appear in the MT nor in the LXX. This, Paul's own and only addition right after his remark that Jews have broken the law, is probably intended to provide a crucial scriptural proof for his 'bitter indignation'. In this way Paul successfully 'transforms Isaiah's oracle of promise into [his own] word of reproach',[185] stressing that it is the Jews' own disobedience and inconsistency, and not their misfortune, that has brought blasphemy to God's name.[186] The phrase καθὼς γέγραπται is uniquely mentioned after the quotation[187] probably to stress the significance of the γάρ as well as to give a proper connection. Thus the quotation here serves well as the climax of the indictment of the Jews.[188]

(c) The Physical Circumcision of the Jews and the Spiritual Circumcision of the Gentiles: 2:25-29

Paul's reinterpretation of 'circumcision' and 'Jew' (2:25-29) offers a further critical picture of the Jews and an affirmative one of the Gentiles. Circumcision was given as the seal of God's eternal covenant with Israel (Gen 17:10-11; *Jub.* 15:9-11, 25-34; cf. 1 Macc 1:48, 60-61; 2 Macc 6:10); thus it was 'a seal of the

---

185 Hays, *Echoes*, 45. Meyer, *Romans* 1, 130, is surely right to say: 'He [Paul] applies the quotation in such a way that *he makes it his own* by the γάρ not found in the original or the LXX.'

186 Correctly Fitzmyer, *Romans*, 318. Ezek 36:21, 22 is much closer to Paul's point of emphasis that Israel's hypocritical wickedness is the cause for the profanation. It is possible that Paul has borrowed the ideas from Ezek 36, but it might not have a direct influence on 2:24 because the wording is quite different. So rightly Bassler, *Impartiality*, 263 n. 109. See also Cranfield, *Romans* 1, 171 n. 2.

187 This is the only place where Paul puts καθὼς γέγραπται after the quotation. Some have suggested that such a placement was to make a free quotation (e.g. Gore, *Romans* 1, 112; Sanday and Headlam, *Romans*, 67), or to disengage the sentence from its [original] context (Lightfoot, *Notes*, 263). But it seems more probable to link the quotation directly with the preceding charges that the Jews do steal, commit adultery, rob the temple and break the law.

188 Murray, *Romans* 1, 85.

righteousness' (4:11) and was believed to be 'a certain passport to salvation'.[189] It is also 'the single clearest distinguishing feature of the covenant people, the most obvious boundary line which divided Jew from Gentile'.[190] It is furthermore 'a visible badge of [Jewish] superiority' over the Gentiles.[191] On this fundamentally unquestionable item of Jewish complacency, Paul offers a radical reinterpretation. His initial remark, 'Circumcision has value [only] if you observe the law' (2:25a), would be conceded by Jews, especially in radical circles (like the Zealots and the Essenes), because it represented commitment to the whole law (Lev 18:5; Deut 30:16; cf. Gal 5:3; 1 Cor 7:19).[192] Paul does not deny the value of circumcision (note the μέν in 2:25; cf. 3:1-2),[193] but the 'γάρ' indicates that Paul's argument in 2:25-29 is a continuation of 2:21-24, and thus his greater stress is on 2:25b: 'if you are a transgressor of the Law, your circumcision has become uncircumcision' (NASB). Since he has already affirmed that the Jews do not keep the law (2:21-23), and does so again in 2:27 ('you ... are a law-breaker'), what he says here confirms this: 'Your circumcision has [already] become [practically] uncircumcision'.[194]

---

189 Barrett, *Romans*, 55; Fitzmyer, *Romans*, 320. According to *Jub.* 15:25-34, those with circumcision are 'children of the covenant', and others without it are 'children of destruction'.

190 Dunn, *Romans* 1, 120; McKnight, *Light*, 79-82.

191 Barrett, *Romans*, 55. Circumcision was often practised among the Gentiles as well (cf. Jer 9:25-26), and they often claimed their circumcision was as equally sacred as that of the Jews (see Hengel, *Judaism* 1, 262, 293). Nevertheless, Jewish understanding of their circumcision was fundamentally different from that of the Gentiles. For the forced circumcision of Gentiles in Palestine to protect Jewish privileges, see 1 Macc 2:46; Josephus, *Ant.* 13.257-258, 318-319; 15.253-254, and Hengel, *Zealots*, 197-200.

192 Already some rabbis and John the Baptist (Matt 3:7-9) had questioned whether apostate Jews would be saved despite their physical circumcision (cf. Dodd, *Romans*, 65). Hengel, *Judaism* 1, 307-308; 2, 204 n. 305, suggests that Paul's view of circumcision is not a 'betrayal of Judaism'.

193 Cranfield, *Romans* 1, 139, seems right to assert that what Paul writes in 2:25-29 is to be understood with reference to 3:1-4; 4:9-12 and 9:1-11:36. Here Paul does not totally deny the value of its covenantal character.

194 The perfect tense γέγονεν may even imply that the Jew's physical circumcision has no longer any advantage as a matter of fact (Meyer, *Romans* 1, 131; cf. Sanday and Headlam, *Romans*, 67). He is in the same state as if he had never been circumcised (cf. TEV, NEB). But with this remark Paul does not seem to allude to the 'reversed circumcision' of Maccabean times.

This is indeed a bold statement for Paul the Jew to make to his fellow Jews.[195] But his boldness goes even further in 2:26-29, not only by providing an opposing case but also by expressing the deeper intention of this argument about circumcision, that is, that *the law-abiding Gentile is the (true) circumcision* (Phil 3:3; cf. Col 2:11).[196] The law-breaking Jews have become uncircumcision, and thus ('οὖν' for a logical connection[197]) the law-keeping Gentiles are to be 'reckoned as a substitute or equivalent for'[198] the (true) circumcision. Paul seems to suggest that, since God will affirm them as the true circumcision at the Judgement on the basis of their *present* practice of the law, Jews should also regard them as such.[199]

Paul's assertion in 2:26 is certainly not accepted even by the most liberal contemporary Judaism.[200] But he presses his argument still further. He goes on to assert that the law-keeping Gentiles are not only equal members of God's people with the Jews but also that they will be in a position to condemn the law-breaking Jews,[201] because as Gentiles they fulfil the law whereas

---

195 Fitzmyer, *Romans*, 321.

196 Once again, since Paul has affirmed that Gentiles do by nature the things required by the law (2:14-15), the presuppositional 'if' carries little conditional force. Meyer, *Romans* 1, 131, says that Paul does not use two 'ἐάν's in v. 25 and 26 presuppositionally, but in the sense of the actual case. This seems correct in the light of his earlier statements in 2:14-15 ('when' [ὅταν], so 'not merely hypothetical': Barrett, *Romans*, 55-56), and 2:21-24 ('You dishonour and blaspheme God by breaking the law'); thus the 'ἐάν' does not carry a natural force of condition, but a general and 'diplomatic' connotation (so also Morris, *Romans*, 139). Rather, greater force is on the οὐχί (2:26b), which indicates that Paul expects an affirmative 'Yes'. The law-keeping Gentiles should be reckoned as the true circumcision. Cf. the present subjunctive φυλάσσῃ in v. 26, which connotes that the uncircumcised Gentiles habitually 'guard the commandments of God with a solicitous care lest they be broken' (Wuest, 'Romans', 50).

197 Barrett, *Romans*, 55.

198 Sanday and Headlam, *Romans*, 67.

199 Again, Jeremiah's oracle about 'circumcision of the heart' may be in view.

200 See Dunn, *Romans* 1, 121; Dodd, *Romans*, 66.

201 Both Jesus and Stephen are depicted as condemning Jews: 'Yet not one of you keeps the law' (John 7:19); 'You ... have not obeyed it [the law]' (Acts 7:53).

the physical circumcision do not (2:27; cf. Matt 12:41).[202] Earlier Paul has vigorously argued that it is illegitimate and hypocritical for Jews to judge and condemn Gentiles because they do the same things (2:1-3), but now he declares that it is totally legitimate for law-keeping Gentiles to condemn law-breaking Jews. Not only the emphatic position of κρινεῖ but also the γάρ in 2:27-28 support this understanding. Paul argues that having the written code and physical circumcision has little significance (cf. 1 Cor 7:18-19).

Paul supports his most radical and apparently 'blasphemous' assertion that the uncircumcised will condemn the circumcised with a well-accepted Jewish teaching on 'circumcision of heart' (note the important γάρ). No-one would dispute Paul's interpretation of the word 'Jew' in its true sense and proper content. But what is striking is to see him applying this true meaning of the term 'Jew' to *Gentiles*.[203] 'Not the one who is outwardly (*sc.* a Jew) is the (real) Jew, nor that which is outwardly in the body the (true) circumcision,'[204] 'but he who is inwardly a Jew [even though uncircumcised outwardly] (is the true Jew), and heart circumcision, in spirit, not in letter (is the true circumcision).'[205] It is striking to see that Paul puts the inward and truly 'authentic Jew'[206] (though they are uncircumcised by race[207]) on a much higher level than the merely professing Jew.[208] They received God's acceptance and praise (2:29; 15:7).[209] In other words, Paul applies extraordinarily positive remarks to the Gentiles. This can

---

202 Dodd, *Romans*, 66; Käsemann, *Romans*, 74-75; Dunn, *Romans* 1, 122. Cf. Sanders, *Palestinian Judaism*, 253-254, who notes that according to 1QpHab 5:3-6 the Jewish elect will judge and punish the Gentiles.

203 Similarly, Paul later redefines the (true) descendants of Abraham (4:1-25) and the true Israel (9:6-9).

204 Zerwick and Grosvenor, *Analysis*, 463-464. Similarly Gifford, followed by Sanday and Headlam, *Romans*, 68.

205 Wuest, 'Romans', 51.

206 Minear, *Obedience*, 51.

207 Meyer, *Romans* 1, 133.

208 Robertson in Wuest, 'Romans', 51. Ziesler may be right to note that Paul is 'cutting the Jews down to the Gentiles' size' (*Romans*, 92; cf. Dodd, *Romans*, 65), but Boylan, *Romans*, 45, seems even more persuasive when he says, '[The] Jews are sinners, and liable to God's wrath—not in a lesser, but in a greater degree than the Gentiles.'

209 Minear, *Obedience*, 51.

be noted from the way he applies Jer 9:22-26 (Deut 30:6) and Ezek 36:26 (Jer 31:33), which are often regarded as the background for the present passage:[210]

> "The days are coming," declares the LORD, "when I will punish all who are circumcised only in the flesh—Egypt, Judah, Edom, Ammon, Moab and all who live in the desert in distant places. For all these nations are really uncircumcised, and even the whole house of Israel is uncircumcised in heart." (Jer 9:25-26)

However, it is again to be noted that Paul radically changes the context and the nature of this prophecy. According to Jeremiah, God will judge all Israel, because 'the whole house of Israel is uncircumcised in heart', and this despite the fact that they have been exhorted to circumcise their hearts (Lev 26:40-41; Deut 10:16; 30:6). Paul seems to draw upon this for his point of argument that circumcision *in heart* (that is, a repentant, obedient, new and committed heart) is fundamentally more significant than circumcision *in the flesh*. So in 2:25-29 Paul does not say anything very different from what Jeremiah had written, as far as Jews were concerned. But in relation to the Gentiles Paul presents a quite different modification. According to Jeremiah, all the Gentiles will be punished as well, for even though some of them bear physical circumcision, it has nothing to do with a covenant with God. In Judaism the exhortation to have, or promise of, circumcised hearts is exclusively given to and for the Jews (Deut 10:16; 30:6; Jer 4:4; 31:33; Ezek 36:26; *Jub.* 1:23; cf. Acts 7:51; 1QS 5:5; 1QH 11:5; 18:20); it is nowhere considered possible for the Gentiles to receive this blessing of 'circumcision of the heart'. But Paul now roundly declares that it has also been given to the Gentiles: Gentiles too can and do bear the seal of the covenant since they are living out what the law requires, even to the point where they could condemn Jews who were merely physically circumcised (cf. Luke 11:31-32).

(d) Summary

Our investigation in this section (2:12-29) allows us to conclude that Paul intends not only to establish Jewish sinfulness in regard

---

210 Fitzmyer, *Romans*, 320, for Jer 9:25-26; Wilckens, *Römer* 1, 156; Ziesler, *Romans*, 93, for Ezek 36:26, etc..

to the law but also primarily to make comparatively extraordinary positive statements about the Gentiles. Paul's critique of Judaism is more radical and strident than one would expect even of Jews with strong remnant theologies.[211] He presents his critique in an *argument*. But in passing *statements* he highlights the possibility and the legitimacy of Gentile righteousness in a way most favourable to them. Paul's point is *not* to assert that the concepts of 'law', 'circumcision' and 'Jew' are no longer applicable to his own people, but to affirm that the typical and complacent Jews have obviously failed to live out the reality of such concepts, while (some) Gentiles were doing so. Thus the apostle to the Gentiles indirectly and implicitly offers a defence for the Gentiles, that their faith, their salvation, and their Christian life in the Jewish Messiah are legitimate, by indicating that they are the ones who truly keep the requirement of the law, and thus are legitimately to be called the 'true circumcision' and the 'true Jews'.

Thus although Räisänen is right to say that Paul's primary aim for Romans 2 is to prove that Jews are guilty law-breakers, he has certainly missed a crucial point in Paul's argument in saying that Paul has no real interest in the *Gentiles* in Romans 2.[212] Furthermore, when we understand Paul's way of presenting his argument, we can rightly disagree with Sanders' assertion that Paul's argument for universal sinfulness in 1:18-2:29 is a 'gross exaggeration' *without* 'an objective, or even [internally] consistent description of Jews and Gentiles.'[213] G.P. Carras seems more accurate in asserting that 'throughout Romans 2 it is the *Gentiles* who form an integral part of the discussion',[214] although their

---

211 Sanders, *Jewish People*, 148: 'the argument that Jews are "under sin" is much fuller in Romans than in Galatians'.
212 *Pace* Räisänen, *Paul*, 106.
213 *Pace* Sanders, *Jewish People*, 125.
214 Carras, 'Romans 2,1-29', 203. Watson, *Paul*, 112-113, 115, 217 n. 74, also notes Paul's interest in the Gentiles throughout the chapter, but his hypothesis that Paul tries to persuade the Christian Jews of Rome to separate themselves from the rest of the Jewish community and join the Gentile Christian community, is hardly convincing. Paul, who eagerly hopes for the salvation of his own people (10:1; 11:14), could hardly encourage Jewish believers to isolate themselves from non-believing Jews: see Carras, 'Romans 2,1-29', 187-188, for further criticism.

case is indirectly (and yet very positively) presented.²¹⁵

The questions in 3:1, especially with the concluding particle 'οὖν', are clear indications that Paul has argued in Romans 2 as if Jews had no advantage, and that there was no value in circumcision. These corrective remarks unmistakably indicate that he knows that his readers would logically (οὖν) assume so, because his negative argument about Jews has evidently been liable to give such an impression. It is also possible that Paul's positive description of the Gentiles has further puzzled Jewish readers about their own traditional advantages: 'What advantage, then, is there in being a Jew, or what value is there in circumcision [if Gentiles are as described in 2:12-29]?'.

3. A Further Scriptural Argument against Jewish Complacency: 3:1-20

We have seen above that in 2:12-29 Paul makes accusatory arguments about Jews and discriminatingly positive statements about Gentiles. The structure of his argument has led him to deal with his readers' inevitable question about whether he totally denies the traditional advantages of the Jews. In this section we shall argue that although Paul does acknowledge Jewish advantages ('Much in every way!'), the only cited Jewish privilege, τὰ λόγια τοῦ θεοῦ, is employed to launch a further scriptural argument that reaffirms Jewish sinfulness, and so potentially further undermines any Jewish complacency. The argument in 3:1-20 is heavily supported by the OT quotations. It is astonishing, however, to see how little weight most commentators give to this, the longest catena of citations (3:10-18) in all the Pauline corpus.²¹⁶ We shall show that this OT catena provides us with a crucial key to understanding the main point and intention of Paul's argument.

---

215 Then Bassler, *Impartiality*, 153, again misses the mark in saying that 2:12-29 'emphasizes the divine equality of Jews and Greeks before the divine tribunal'. See our view already expressed *supra*, pp. 103-108.

216 Both Bruce and Nygren offer virtually no explanation at all except the sources of the quotations. Ziesler, Leenhardt, Käsemann and Black give about one page of comment, while Gifford and Sanday and Headlam give two. Dunn and Cranfield use three and four pages respectively to expound the catena. Although length of exegesis alone is not the issue, the minimal treatment by many commentators is indeed telling.

We shall examine this section in three stages. First, we will discuss how the argument in 3:1-8 with the quotation from LXX Ps 50:6 in 3:4 has contributed to deny Jewish superiority over Gentiles in 3:9. Secondly, we will assess the scholarly discussion concerning the focal point of 3:1-20. In this connection we shall trace three views so as to determine whether in fact Paul attempts to establish *universal* sinfulness or more specifically *Jewish* depravity. The three positions are (a) the 'older consensus' prevailed approximately prior to the Holocaust, (b) the traditional view established since the Holocaust, and (c) the 'new perspectives' offered by the post-Sanders scholars. In so doing the objections to the traditional view raised by G.N. Davies and J.D.G. Dunn will be examined. Finally, we shall pay special attention to the catena itself in 3:10-18, and discuss the significance of Paul's modification of the texts and contexts in the course of his argument. We will then propose that in this section Paul argues on two levels just as he did in 1:18-32 and 2:1-29. On the *theological* level he reaffirms the universal and equal sinfulness of Jews and Gentiles, but on the *rhetorical* level he constructs the argument to confirm more specifically the sinfulness of the Jews, not only by the key statements in 3:9, 19-20, but also by modifying the texts and contexts of the OT passages cited here.

A. Scripture Affirms God's Judgement upon Unbelieving Jews as Legitimate: 3:1-8

S.K. Stowers rightly highlights two points: (1) 3:1-8 fits well in the whole argument of 1:18-3:20, and so it is not a digression.[217]

---

[217] Many scholars have taken this sub-section as a digression (Black, *Romans*, 62; Cranfield, *Romans* 1, 140) Perhaps the strongest words are from Dodd, *Romans*, 70-71: Since the argument of 3:1-8 is so 'feeble and obscure', 'the argument of the epistle would go much better if this whole section were omitted.' Surely both the πρῶτον and the μέν suggest that the other items are to follow. The fact then that they do not does suggest some form of digression. However, the content of the passage (see below) and the οὖν in 3:1 and 9 seem to indicate the opposite: see Stowers, 'Dialogue', 720. On the other hand, some scholars take 3:1-8 as the key for interpreting the whole epistle, since, they say, Paul develops later what he says here: Dahl, *Studies*, 80; Käsemann, *Romans*, 85; also forcefully advocated by Campbell, 'Romans III', 23.

(2) Paul is talking here about Jewish issues.[218] The τινες in 3:3 indicates that he is talking about a large number of *Jewish* unbelievers.[219] So far in Romans 2 Paul has alluded to the fact that it is the Jews who do not have faith. He affirms, however, that the Jews' lack of faith does not nullify God's faithfulness (ἡ πίστις τοῦ θεοῦ) towards the unbelieving Jews.[220] Paul quotes LXX Ps 50:6b almost exactly to prove this assertion. Although Paul cites only the second half of the verse, Jewish readers would know that it was about the terrible sins (adultery and then murder) committed by King David. There David acknowledged God's right to judge him.[221]

Here, not only does Paul remind his readers of God's faithfulness to David despite his sins (cf. 4:6-8, quoted from Ps 32:1-2) but also affirms God's every right to judge his own people, even David, when they are ἄπιστος (unbelieving rather than unfaithful),[222] and without nullifying his own faithfulness. Paul has just

---

[218] For other detailed discussions on the interpretation of Rom 3:1-8, see Hall, 'Romans 3.1-8', 183-197; Cosgrove, 'What If Some Have Not Believed', 90-105; Moxnes, *Theology*, 37-39, who focuses on the importance of 3:1-8.

[219] Paul uses τινες only three times in Romans (3:3, 8; 11:17), and its usage in 3:3 closely parallels that in 11:17: cf. 1 Cor 10:7, where the word clearly indicates (many) unbelieving Jews (Hall, 'Romans 3.1-8', 185-186). The τινες in 3:8 probably also refers to Paul's critics among Jews.

[220] Hays, 'Psalm 143', 111. It is to be noted that God's faithfulness is based on his covenant (Stuhlmacher, *Gerechtigkeit*, 86. Cf. Hays, 'Psalm 143', 111 n. 18, for discussion there.), and his covenant faithfulness is applied only to Jews, and not to Gentiles (Davies, *Faith*, 75; Meyer, *Romans* 1, 141). But Paul contends that since God is a righteous judge, his judgement of bringing wrath upon the unrighteous (whether they be Jews or Gentiles) does not make him unjust. Rather, man's unrighteousness brings out God's righteousness 'more clearly' (NIV).

[221] Davies, *Faith*, 76 n. 2, seems right to take κρίνεσθαι as middle rather than passive, because God is not judged (i.e. appealed) by David for his forthcoming judgements including the death of David's child: 2 Sam 12:7-14); rather, David humbly acknowledges God's right to judge him.

[222] Meyer, *Romans* 1, 140. So also the rendering of KJV, RV, NIV, NASB; but the less plausible rendering 'unfaithful' is adopted in RSV, TEV, NEB, JB, Phillips, Moffatt. David can be seen to be unfaithful to God rather than unbelieving towards God, but here Paul changes the perspective to unbelief for his purpose of indicting Jewish unbelief (9:27-33; 10:16-21; 11:20, 23). Cf. Davies, *Faith*, 78: 'God will always judge those who sin, including the covenant community.'

listed 'τὰ λόγια τοῦ θεοῦ' (i.e. the OT Scriptures[223]) as the most prominent privilege of the Jews. In the quotation, however, he applies the words of God as the means of proving God's righteousness in the light of Jewish unbelief (ἡ ἀπιστία αὐτῶν).[224] The quotation from LXX Ps 50:6 serves as the main evidence to prove that human (Jewish) sinfulness or unbelief does not nullify God's faithfulness. On the other hand, it also condemns the Jewish assumption that their lack of faith does not really matter, seeing that God is faithful to his covenant promises to his own people.

The inclusion of ὅπως ἄν in the citation indicates that it is God's judgement against sin that is to be vindicated. David does not justify his sins; the purpose clause with ὅπως ἄν[225] appears to imply that his sins were actually committed in order to highlight the righteous judgement of God.[226] Thus the Jewish interlocutor[227] could have misunderstood Paul and David's accounts, saying, '"If my falsehood enhances God's truthfulness and increases his glory, why am I still condemned as a sinner?" Why not say ... "Let us do evil that good may result"?' (3:7). Paul's opponents even slanderously accuse Paul of saying that very thing. Paul's simple answer is, 'Their [i.e. the unbelieving Jews'][228] condemnation is deserved'.[229] They have misunderstood 'God's righteousness' as 'God's faithfulness and kindness' to the Jews (cf. 2:4), which is ongoing despite their sinfulness or unbe-

---

223 Davies, *Faith*, 74, following Doeve, 'Some Notes', 111-123; Meyer, *Romans* 1, 139-140.

224 It is quite striking to note that Paul often appeals to the Old Testament Scriptures to condemn the persistent unbelief of the Jews (Davies, *Faith*, 74-75), rather than to defend or vindicate the Jewish position, as we will show in detail later on in Chapter 5 on Romans 9-11.

225 BAGD, 576-577; Zerwick and Grosvenor, *Analysis*, 464. This important phrase is totally omitted in NEB and TEV.

226 Cranfield, *Romans* 1, 182-183; Hall, 'Romans 3.1-8', 186-187.

227 *Pace* Stowers, 'Dialogue', 715. Cf. NIV and JB, which add the description of the speaker, though it is not in the original Greek.

228 So correctly Moo, *Romans* 1, 182.

229 Johnson, 'Studies', 337: 'The final word is directed to Jews particularly, as the context indicates. They thought they were excused from divine judgment and free to judge the Gentiles, but they overlooked the justice of God. Thus Paul has very skilfully returned to the charge with which he began the section on the sins of the Jews [2:1].'

lief.²³⁰ For Paul, however, God's righteousness, at least here (3:5), means his righteous judgement of what man has done: 'our unrighteousness' (3:5).²³¹ Paul notes that salvation requires two elements: God's faithfulness in keeping his promise *and* man's faithfulness in keeping 'the requirement of the law' (i.e. faith: 2:14-15, 25-29). In 1:18-3:20, however, Paul's primary exposition is about the latter element, namely, that humanity, and especially the Jews, have failed to live up to God's faithfulness.²³²

B. *Jewish Depravity as the Focus of Paul's Argument in 3:1-20*

In the light of the wording of 3:9,²³³ 3:1 can be paraphrased as 'What then? Do we Jews have any advantages over the Gentiles? Yes, much in every way.' However, what Paul says in 3:9 represents a different position: 'We Jews are not at all better than Gentiles,²³⁴ [even though we have the oracles of God].' In fact,

---

230 Paul seems to employ the terms about man's ἀπιστία–ἀδικία–ψεῦσμα almost as synonyms, and contrasts them with God's πίστις–δικαιοσύνη–ἀλήθεια; cf. Dunn, *Romans* 1, 135-136; Käsemann, *Romans*, 79: 'Paul identifies πίστις and δικαιοσύνη τοῦ θεοῦ by making them parallel'; Stuhlmacher, *Gerechtigkeit*, 86.

231 Hays, 'Psalm 143', 110-111.

232 Thus we find the suggestion by Moxnes unconvincing (*Theology*, 37-39). He notes that scholars have taken 3:1-8 seriously primarily due to the discussion of the phrase δικαιοσύνη θεοῦ, and affirms that this is the central issue in this passage. Surely 3:1-8 can provide us with a better understanding of 'the righteousness of God' (most notably, Hays, 'Psalm 143', 107-115), but it does not seem to be the central issue under discussion. It is primarily about the sinfulness and the unbelief of (Jewish) people, which is also the topic of 1:18-3:20.

233 The textual and linguistic difficulties in interpreting 3:9a are well known (see Metzger, *Textual Commentary*, 507-508). For Cranfield, *Romans* 1, 187-190, the text of both Nestle-Aland²⁷ and UBS³ (Τί οὖν; προεχόμεθα; οὐ πάντως) is, with 'little doubt', correct (p. 189).

234 Obviously Paul has not changed his mind. The difference arises from the essential difference between περισσόν (3:1) and προεχόμεθα (3:9). The Jews have many *advantages* (because of God's earlier choice and gifting) but no *superiority*. The much-discussed question, προεχόμεθα;, is not easy to translate with confidence. For the discussion of this important verb, see Cranfield, *Romans* 1, 187-191; Lightfoot, *Notes*, 266-267; Turner, *Insights*, 106-107; Synge, 'Meaning', 351, who gives a unique interpretation of this word; but cf. Stowers, 'Dialogue', 709-710. Almost all English translations (except, e.g. RV, NEB mg, NIV mg) and commentators (except, e.g. Kirk, *Romans*, 185;

Jews are once again condemned by the words of God (3:4) and will be proved as sinful as the Gentiles from the words of God quoted in 3:10-18. We will leave the examination of the catena itself to a later discussion, but will now investigate different views concerning Paul's focal point in the argument in 3:1-20: whether he attempts to establish *universal* sinfulness or more specifically *Jewish* depravity.

The universal character of the passage is obvious.[235] Most of the older commentators (approximately prior to the Second World War), however, agreed that in this passage Paul was primarily trying to prove the sinfulness of the Jews, although Gentile sinfulness was not excluded. We may call this the '*older* consensus'. Among others, A. Barnes makes the strongest remarks:

> The apostle is reasoning with Jews .... from their own Scriptures. .... The point to be proved was, that the Jews, in the matter of justification, had no advantage or preference over the Gentiles. ... *The point, then, is to prove the depravity of the Jews, not that of universal depravity*. The interpretation should be confined to the bearing of the passages on the *Jews*, and the quotations should *not* be adduced as directly proving the doctrine of universal depravity.[236]

Stowers, 'Dialogue', 719-720) render it as an active middle, and the context seems to suggest this.

Since the catena of 3:10-18 serves to confirm once again that Jews and Gentiles are equally sinful by stressing Jewish sinfulness (see our discussion below), it is natural to read 3:9a as denying any special Jewish superiority over the Gentiles. If it is taken as a passive ('Are we Jews at a disadvantage?') together with the answer ('Not at all!'), then the Scriptural catena (3:10-18) would serve to affirm Jewish advantages. But Paul does not do this here. However, one thing is clear: whether it is used as a middle (Are we [Jews] superior?), or a passive (Are we [Jews] excelled?), it indicates that in 3:1-8 Paul has spoken of the disadvantage of the Jews. The insertion of 'Jews' by most translations, such as RSV, NEB, TEV, Phillips, Moffatt, does not seem illegitimate; so correctly Ziesler, *Romans*, 101-102; but *pace* Synge, 'Meaning', 351; Meyer, *Romans* 1, 151; cf. Dahl, 'Romans 3:9', 184-204, who understands 'we' as 'Christians'; Moule, *Romans*, 83-84.

235 Hodge, *Romans*, 81-86; Barth, *Romans*, 84-91.

236 Barnes, *Romans*, 83, also 87; emphasis added. Others who hold the same position include Lightfoot, *Notes*, 269: 'This [3:19a] can mean only one thing. Those who are addressed in the Old Testament, are the people under the Old Testament dispensation, i.e. the Israelites. The Old Testament speaks to Jews, not to Gentiles, and therefore to *Jews* this severe language applies';

However, this older consensus was superseded by a new consensus among many post-Holocaust commentators, according to whom Paul's primary intention in 3:1(or 9)-20 was not specifically to stress the depravity of the Jews, but to establish the general and equal sinfulness of *all* humanity without exception.[237] We may call this understanding the 'traditional' view. This position is no doubt plausible, at least at first sight, because of the references in 3:9, 'Jews and Gentiles alike are all under sin', and in 3:19, 'every mouth may be silenced and the whole world held accountable to God'. The repeated πᾶς and οὐκ ἐστιν seem to confirm this interpretation. Nevertheless, this interpretation has undermined the force of expressions such as 'τοῖς ἐν τῷ νόμῳ' (3:19) and 'ἐξ ἔργων νόμου οὐ δικαιωθήσεται πᾶσα σάρξ' (3:20). And so more recently some post-Sanders scholars[238] have

---

Locke, *Paraphrase* 2, 507 n.19: 'The meaning of St Paul here is [t]hat the declarations of [G]od which he had cited out of the [O]ld [T]estament were spoken of the Jews who were under the dispensation of the [O]ld [T]estament'; Gifford, *Romans*, 87: 'the passages just quoted ... speak to the Jew in order that his mouth, as well as every other, may be stopped by the denunciation of his sin'; Shedd, *Romans*, 68: 'The apostle now proceeds (vv. 10-18), to prove his assertion that the Jews are hearers and doers of the Law, by quotations from the Old Testament'; Boylan, *Romans*, 33: 'It is to the Jews ... that Scriptural utterances about men's sinfulness immediately refer (3:9-20).'

So also Dodd, *Romans*, 72: 'The purport of the passages is the unrelieved sinfulness of men, and *Paul takes this to mean primarily the sinfulness of the Jews*, on the ground that whatever the Law says, it says to those who are inside the Law' (emphasis added). Similarly, Nygren, *Romans*, 141: Paul's quotation is to convince the Jews of universal sinfulness (that means primarily Jewish sinfulness) from their own Scriptures. In the light of what 3:19 says, Nygren correctly argues: '*[T]he passages cited refer specially to the Jew. The Scriptures convict them of sin*' (Nygren, *Romans*, 142; emphasis added). Gore, *Romans* 1, 123: 'It is thus an authoritative rebuke to Jewish self-complacency.' Beet, *Romans*, 104, is also correct to assert that Paul's intention for the collection of citations is 'to prove that the O.T. teaches that Jewish privileges do not in themselves save even from the lowest depths of sin'; Kirk, *Romans*, 185; Weiss, *Earliest Christianity* 1, 222-223; Griffith, *Romans*, 37; Hudson, *Pauline Epistles*, 68.

237 E.g. Cranfield, *Romans* 1, 191; Murray, *Romans* 1, 102, 106; Barrett, *Romans*, 69; Black, *Romans*, 64; Taylor, *Romans*, 30-31; Moo, *Romans* 1, 199ff; Stuhlmacher, *Römer*, 51-54; Morris, *Romans*, 162-172. So also Keck, 'Function', 146; Hays, *Echoes*, 50; Stanley, *Language*, 89.

238 Sanders himself, *Jewish People*, 82, denies that 3:19-20 refers to Gentiles.

questioned such a consensus on the basis of their hypothesis that in Romans 1-4 Paul is attacking Jewish complacency based on 'covenantal nomism'.

The objections to the 'traditional' view have been raised by, e.g. G.N. Davies and J.D.G. Dunn. They both argue that the reaffirmation of the *universal* sinfulness of all humanity is *not* Paul's main point in appealing to the OT Scriptures, but Davies and Ziesler go as far as to deny that Paul asserts universal sinfulness. According to Davies, Paul has not maintained that '*all* Jews and *all* Greeks, without exception' are sinful; indeed, Paul makes 'the distinction between the righteous and the wicked ... throughout 2.12-16 and 2.25-29'. He continues to assert in regard to Romans 2, 'Yet even here it is the Jew, "who relies upon the law and boasts of his relationship to God through the law", who is the focus of Paul's attack, and not every Jew in Israel'.[239] Furthermore, Paul implies that *some* (i.e. not *all*) Jews had unbelief (3:3). Davies then suggests, 'It would be strange reasoning indeed, if in 3.9 Paul now wished to include all people without exception, including those who were workers of good (2.10)'.[240] Thus he argues in regard to 3:10-18:

> There is no *a priori* warrant to see a universalization of the condemnation to all men. .... It is much more likely that Paul is using these texts to establish *what they originally implied*, that *there is no righteousness among the wicked*, be they Jew or Gentile.[241]

Davies rightly pays attention to the original contexts of the passages cited here. His attempt to understand the passage (3:10-18) within the context of 1:18-3:20 is also plausible. Davies has to face, however, at least three objections. Firstly, although it is true that Paul does not *explicitly* charge that *all* Gentiles and *all* Jews without exception are under sin in 1:18-3:8 (cf. 11:32), neither does he explicitly say that some individual Jews are 'righteous'. Paul's claim that he has already charged that 'Jews and Gentiles alike are all under sin' (3:9), is not only a summary of what he has said so far but also an assertion which he wishes to substantiate with the ample evidence of the OT. Paul's effort to emphasise

---

239 Davies, *Faith*, 95.
240 Davies, *Faith*, 95.
241 Davies, *Faith*, 93-94 (emphasis added); so also 90.

the fact that all without exception are under sin is indicated not only in the emphatic use of, but also in the additions of, 'οὐκ ἐστιν' to the original text (cf. 3:23; 5:12, 18).

Secondly, Davies' assertion that Paul's fundamental distinction of the groups, even in Romans 2 is between the righteous and the wicked, is not convincing; it is rather between Jew and Gentile (2:12-16, 25-29).[242] We also need to note that even in his use of the terms 'Jew' and 'Gentile' Paul restrains himself from giving further details about whether he is talking about unbelieving/unrighteous Jews, or believing/righteous Gentiles. Thus it seems perilous for Davies to build an argument upon the details which Paul hesitates to specify.

Thirdly, although Davies pays attention to the original contexts of the cited passages, he fails to note the fact that Paul considerably modifies the contexts for his own argument.[243] According to Davies, Paul does not really modify the original contexts to substantiate his argument. Rather he insists that Paul applies the original contexts exactly to his own argument 'to express their original design, as a description of the wicked'.[244] Indeed, the main reason for Davies examining the original contexts of the quoted Psalms appears to be to prove the existence of the righteous and the wicked.[245] He often ends the examination of the quotations once he has established that the original contexts embraced the righteous and the wicked. However, had Paul wanted to prove only this 'commonsense' idea 'that there is no

---

[242] Paul presents the universal sinfulness of humanity from the Jew–Gentile perspective. In 1:18-3:31 the term 'Ιουδαῖος occurs: four times in the pair of Ἕλλην/ἔθνη (2:9, 10; 3:9, 29), while ἔθνη alone occurs three times (2:14, 24; 3:29). Paul also uses 'ἡ περιτομή' and 'ἡ ἀκροβυστία' to refer to Jews and Gentiles (2:27; 3:30).

[243] Cf. Stanley, *Language*, 93, (despite his explanation in 360 n. 50) who repeatedly pays attention mainly to the variation of the texts, but pays minimal attention to the modification of the contexts. Also *pace* Leenhardt, *Romans*, 95, who asserts that Paul modifies the texts and contexts without considering whether the original texts apply to the sins of Jews or Gentiles.

[244] Davies, *Faith*, 96.

[245] This is somehow the concluding remark after examining the OT passages quoted (Davies, *Faith*, 84, 85, 86, 87, 88), and his statement 'this is not to imply that there is no one who is righteous in Israel' (p. 87), seems arbitrary.

righteousness among the *wicked*,[246] why would he have bothered to quote such a long catena?[247]

Furthermore, Davies ends up in denying Paul's theological axiom of the universal sinfulness of humanity. He argues that since 'none of the texts cited refers to the universal sinfulness of man', Paul could not possibly quote the OT passages to assert universal sinfulness here.[248] It is true that in citing these OT passages Paul intends more than to prove universal sinfulness, but it is unconvincing to undermine Paul's charge that all humanity without exception is under sin. Furthermore, Davies fails to note the context in which 3:1-20 is placed within Paul's overall argument of the equality of sinfulness between Jew and Gentile, yet with the deeper intention to establish *Jewish* sinfulness, as we shall show later. In short, Davies' assertion is based on the notion of the psalmist, but not of Paul.[249]

Dunn offers a more formidable argument. He argues that in 3:9-20 Paul aims not only to affirm the universal sinfulness of all

---

246 Davies, *Faith*, 93; the italic is his in p. 90, where he writes the same phrase. Lincoln, 'Wrath', 211 n. 41, plausibly objects to Davies on this point.

247 The fact that 3:10-18 is the longest chain of citation in the Pauline letters expresses Paul's firm intention to establish his point of argument through this catena.

248 *Pace* Davies, *Faith*, 89. This point is made to disprove the contention, advocated by, e.g. Cranfield and Murray, that Paul cites the catena of OT passages to assert the universality of human sinfulness. Davies suggests some references (e.g. Num 23:19; 1 Kgs 8:46; 2 Chr 6:36; Ps 143:2; Prov. 20:9; Eccl 7:20) which, he thinks, would fit better for Paul to assert universal sinfulness. However, 1 Kgs 8:46, 2 Chr 6:36; Ps 143:2 are primarily references to the Israelites ('your people'); Num 23:19 and Prov 20:9 are rather obscure for Davies' purpose; and his interpretation of Eccl 7:20 is not convincing.

249 A similar view has been put forward by Ziesler, *Romans*, 99-106. For Ziesler, Paul's concern is *with peoples*, for his 'aim is to show that as a people the Jews are under the power of sin, just as the Gentiles as peoples are' (p. 100). Ziesler's view may be challenged with the objections which we have made above against Davies. He has made one valid point, however, that Paul attempts to affirm that sin is *equally rampant among the Jews* as it is among the Gentiles, and consequently nominal Jews are no safer than unrighteous Gentiles. By forcefully establishing Jewish sinfulness (for 'this was really the main point which needed proving': Sanday and Headlam, *Romans*, 80; similarly, Ziesler, *Romans*, 104, who also notes this), Paul could now declare that 'every mouth' should be completely speechless, because 'the whole world [will be] held accountable to God' (3:19).

The Equality of Jew and Gentile in Sinfulness 139

humanity without exception, but more specifically to establish Jewish depravity (as equal to Gentile sinfulness). Paul's expression τοῖς ἐν τῷ νόμῳ (3:19) is a clear indication that the OT Scriptures, especially the quoted passages,[250] are directed to 'those who are under the law', i.e. to the *Jews*.[251] Paul asserts: 'by the works of the Law no flesh will be justified in His sight' (3:20: NASB; cf. 8:3; Gal 2:16, 21; 3:11; Acts 13:39), and Dunn is correct to highlight the significance of the added and emphasised phrase ἐξ ἔργων νόμου to LXX Ps 142:2.[252] He argues that Paul specifically adds this phrase to oppose Jewish covenantal and national righteousness, such as circumcision, festivals and *kashrut*.[253] Jews could excuse themselves by saying that the OT passages quoted referred to the Gentiles (according to their origi-

---

[250] Cranfield, *Romans* 1, 195; Black, *Romans*, 64; Ziesler, *Romans*, 104; Bruce, *Romans*, 99; Meyer, *Romans* 1, 158; Lightfoot, *Notes*, 269; Boylan, *Romans*, 53 n. 1; Locke, *Paraphrase* 1, 507; Meyer, *Romans* 1, 158; Barnes, *Romans*, 87. *Pace* Sanday and Headlam, *Romans*, 75, 79-80, for taking the phrase as the law of Moses. Cf. Moo, *Romans* 1, 207, who accepts both.

[251] Watson, *Paul*, 128-129, is right to note that the law is designated a Jewish possession in Rom 2-3, and also that the phrase τοῖς ἐν τῷ νόμῳ in 3:19 is closely connected with that ὅσοι ἐν νόμῳ in 2:12. Cranfield, *Romans* 1, 195, further notes that γινώσκουσιν ... νόμον λαλῶ of 7:1 also clearly refers to Jews. So also Barnes, *Romans*, 87; Taylor, *Romans*, 31; Lightfoot, *Notes*, 269; Sanders, *Jewish People*, 82.

[252] Whether this sentence is quoted from LXX Ps 142:2, with Paul's addition of ἐξ ἔργων νόμου, is debated: Silva, 'OT in Paul', 631. For the affirmative position, see Cranfield, *Romans* 1, 197; Ziesler, *Romans*, 104; Lightfoot, *Notes*, 270; Hays, *Echoes*, 51. Ellis, *Paul's Use*, 153, takes this as an allusion; cf. Stanley, *Language*, 99 n. 43.

[253] Dunn, 'New Perspective', 95-122 (also reprinted in 1990 with additional notes in *Jesus, Paul, and the Law*, 183-214); he maintains this view in his commentary, *Romans* 1, 159. The fact that Dunn excludes the moral call of the Sinai covenant from this term has left him open to much criticism, especially by Cranfield, '"Works"', 89-101, and Schreiner, '"Works"', 217-244. Cf. Moo, *Romans* 1, 212-218, for similar yet more sympathetic criticism. Dunn, 'Yet Once More', 99-117, eventually concedes that Paul in fact condemns both. He seems right to do so in the light of the fact that the quoted passages are largely accusations based on moral issues, and that 3:20c ('*for through the Law comes the [full] knowledge of sin*': NASB; cf. 4:15; 5:13, 20; 7:7) can make proper sense only if Paul speaks to the Jews who think that not only their covenantal nomism but also their upright moral life are grounds for their justification (cf. 2:17-24; ch. 7).

nal contexts, as we shall show below), and not to themselves.[254] Paul thus makes it clear by adding 3:19a that his intention for selecting and forming the catena is fundamentally to include 'those who are under the law' in his argument.[255] Since it is Jews, and not Gentiles, who assume or attempt to be declared righteous by observing the law, it seems most probable that the central issue for which Paul now draws a conclusion (in 3:20), is primarily the sinfulness of the Jews.

Nevertheless, the weakness of Dunn's argument lies in the fact that he interprets the passage from the perspective that Paul's aim is simply to strip the Jews of their nomistic complacency.[256] Although there is some truth in this, Dunn does not note the wider Jew-Gentile context nor Paul's deeper intention of undermining Jewish superiority in relation to Gentiles. In 1:18-4:25 Paul's overall concern is to establish the fundamental equality between Jews and Gentiles, by stressing the sinfulness of the Jews despite their having the law, and by affirming the salvation of the Gentiles apart from the law. Paul's argument in 1:18-4:25 is almost entirely woven together in the light of the new dimension of God's righteousness, which has been made available in Christ for Jews and Gentiles equally. Thus Paul's overall argument is related to both *unbelieving* Jews and *believing* Gentiles, and 3:1-20 can also be best interpreted from this perspective. Paul's argument is not simply shaped to deny Jewish national righteousness (cf. 3:1-2; 9:3-5; 10:1; 11:13-14), but more probably devised to affirm the equality of Gentiles with Jews. His self-awareness of his being apostle to the Gentiles seems to have led him to understate Jewish superiority over Gentiles ('We [Jews] are not at all any better than Gentiles', 3:9) rather than merely to strip the Jews of their nomistic complacency, or to expound Jewish soteriology (How can a complacent Jew be saved?). Our view may be substantiated as follows.

What Paul writes in 3:9 (together with 'καθὼς γέγραπται' in one Greek sentence) indicates that the following OT passages are ultimately employed to reinforce the statement he has just made, namely, that Jews are *not at all* any better than *Gentiles*. It would

---

254 Luther, *Romans*, 74; Nygren, *Romans*, 142; Meyer, *Romans* 1, 157.
255 Nygren, *Romans*, 142: 'That is, the passages cited specially refer to the Jews.'
256 Dunn, 'Romans: Analysis', 2853.

The Equality of Jew and Gentile in Sinfulness 141

then be reasonable for us to interpret the quotations from the perspective that with the catena Paul attempts to deny Jewish superiority (and we will show below that this is indeed the case). Furthermore, our view can offer an explanation for the so-called contradiction between Paul's assertion '...by the works of the Law no flesh will be justified in His sight' (3:20: NASB) and his earlier claim '...the doers of the Law will be justified' (2:13).[257] The two claims are not to be taken as contradicting each other: while the earlier claim in 2:13 is made in the course of affirmative claims for the Gentiles,[258] the later affirmation in 3:20 is made to assert the impossibility of the Jews being justified by keeping the law.[259] *Theologically* Paul establishes the universal sinfulness of Jews and Gentiles, but his argument is *rhetorically* shaped to undermine Jewish superiority in order to affirm the legitimacy of Gentile salvation.[260] However, the most significant evidence for our interpretation comes from the catena itself, which we now examine.

C. Scripture Affirms Jewish Depravity as Equal to Gentile Sinfulness: 3:9-18

Before we discuss Paul's argument in 3:9-20 as a whole, we need to examine a hypothesis which assumes that the catena is pre-Pauline, and thus that one should not stress its interpretation to grasp *Paul's* argument. Although this view has gained much

---

257 Some scholars have seen Paul's two remarks as contradictions. O'Neill, *Romans*, 51, 66-67, explains that this oddity is due to the work of a later scribe. For Davies and Ziesler, *Romans*, 85, one should not thus read Paul talking about the sinfulness of absolutely everyone but about that of all races, that 'Jews are just as much sinners as Gentiles'. We find both interpretations unconvincing: see *supra* pp. 136-138, 138 n. 249, and n. 262 below.

258 The important γάρ indicates that the assertion is made on the basis of the fact that 'Gentiles ... do ... the things of the Law ... they show [do] the work of the Law' (2:13-15: NASB).

259 Boylan, *Romans*, 54, is right to see no contradiction between 2:13 and 3:20, but his explanation that 2:13 refers to the Last Judgement while 3:20 speaks about obtaining salvation, is unconvincing.

260 Meyer, *Romans* 1, 160, has certainly perceived the point, although he has overstated the case in saying that 'according to the context, it [3:20a] is only with reference to the *Jews*'.

support,[261] it remains unconvincing.[262] First, in the light of 'considerable care and artistry'[263] in the areas of selection, modification and planned lay-out of the quotations within the context of 2:1-3:20, it seems natural to conclude that Paul was the original author/compiler.[264] Second, even if the catena had existed at any previous stage, it might have been no more than an indictment of Jewish apostates or Gentile oppressors of the Jews.[265] Paul's adoption of it, however, to indict *all*, Jews as well as Gentiles, is indeed significant, and should be regarded as original. We can conclude, then, that it was Paul's intention to portray humanity in a strikingly negative way by selecting and shaping this long

---

[261] Most notably, Vollmer, *Citate*, 40-41, who is followed by, according to Koch, *Schrift*, 180 n. 52, Luz, Vielhauer, Käsemann, Schlier, Wilckens, van der Minde and Keck. We may add Leenhardt, *Romans*, 96; Hays, 'Psalm 143', 112 n. 21; Fitzmyer, *Romans*, 334: 'It is hardly a composition of Paul.' But Dunn, *Romans* 1, 150, finds it unlikely.

[262] Another unconvincing post-Pauline hypothesis (minor view) is asserted by O'Neill, *Romans*, 66-67 (more than a half century before O'Neill, McNeile, *St. Paul*, 194 n. 1, briefly asserted the same point). O'Neill plausibly notes the modification of the original contexts. He infers, however, that if the readers turned to the original texts, they would accuse Paul of mishandling the contexts. Paul would eventually lose the argument, because the catena would actually weaken his case. Thus O'Neill asserts that Paul could not possibly have cited these verses in the original letter to the Romans.

However, if O'Neill is correct, one should say that hardly any of the OT quotations in Romans and in the Pauline corpus can be considered original to Paul, because almost all of them have either textual or contextual modifications. This may still be true even though the modification may not always lead away from the original sense to an opposite position. Secondly, Paul's method of quoting or interpreting the OT is not unusual in Judaism (Black, *Romans*, 64). Paul, the trained Jewish rabbi, often uses implicit or explicit midrashim: see, e.g. Ellis, *OT in Early Christianity*, 99; Kugel and Greer, *Early Biblical Interpretation*, 52-72. Thirdly, Paul himself indicates that his citation of the OT texts is to substantiate his charge in the course of expounding 'the gospel promised beforehand through his prophets in the Holy Scriptures' (1:2; 3:21); see Maccoby, *Paul*, 143-144, for different objections to O'Neill.

[263] Cranfield, *Romans* 1, 191; Dunn, 'Romans: Analysis', 2852.

[264] Koch, *Schrift*, 181, 183, has well argued that the quotations were composed by Paul himself some time before the dictation of the letter, and that the catena is carefully structured in order to bring out the point of argument. Maccoby, *Paul*, 144: 'the conclusion is that Paul himself is responsible for all the quotations.' So also Dunn, *Romans* 1, 150; cf. Leenhardt, *Romans*, 95.

[265] Lincoln, 'Wrath', 211.

catena as it now stands in 3:10-18. We will now concentrate on an examination of Paul's modification of the *contexts*, which seems more significant than the actual textual changes, for '[t]he real force of the above quotations lies not so much in the words as in the entire context', as J.A. Beet correctly says.[266]

3:10-12 is quoted from LXX Ps 13:1c-3a, with some alterations to the text.[267] Paul repeats οὐκ ἔστιν five times here. Although οὐκ ἔστιν ἕως ἑνός (LXX Ps 13:1c) is replaced by οὐδὲ εἷς, there is no change in meaning and emphasis. Furthermore, οὐκ is substituted for εἰ, and another οὐκ ἔστιν is added before ἐκζητῶν. All these alterations probably indicate Paul's determination to affirm the sinfulness of all humanity.[268] In this connection it is to be noted that Paul does not cite another 'favourite' phrase of his, οὐκ ἔστιν, namely, in the οὐκ ἔστιν θεός of LXX Ps 13:1a. If he is including Jews in the indictment of the catena, he could not possibly cite that phrase, because Jews would immediately reply that Paul's description is appropriate for Gentiles [i.e. 'atheists'] only.

What has often been overlooked is Paul's modification or interpretation of the context.[269] The pronoun 'they' in the Psalm refers to the 'fools' who say 'There is no God', and who neither seek God nor do good to please him. They themselves are the evildoers (οἱ ἐργαζόμενοι τὴν ἀνομίαν; LXX Ps 13:4) who devour 'my people' and frustrate the plans of the 'poor'. But 'the Lord restores the fortunes of *his people* to make Israel be glad' (LXX Ps 13:7). So, according to the psalmist, 'they' are most probably Gentile enemies[270] who not only rebel against God but

---

266 Beet, *Romans*, 104.

267 We will avoid detailed examination of Paul's textual modifications from the original (LXX) texts, for this study has already been done by Stanley, *Language*, 87-99.

268 The additions of the relative pronoun 'ὁ' seem to stress the point that he is talking about humanity. The substitution of δίκαιος for ποιῶν χρηστότητα (3:10; LXX Ps 13:1c) may be due to Paul's purpose in emphasising his overall argument about attaining righteousness (Cranfield, *Romans* 1, 192; Davies, *Faith*, 82; Lincoln, 'Wrath', 210-211; Stanley, *Language*, 90), but this should not be overstressed because Paul retains the same phrase ποιῶν χρηστότητα in 3:12b.

269 Most notably, Stanley, *Language*, 89-93.

270 So correctly Kissane, *Psalms* 1, 54; Briggs and Briggs, *Psalms* 1, 105; Mowinckel, *Psalms* 1, 220-221; Meyer, *Romans* 1, 157. But less likely Weiser,

also oppress his people Israel. On the other hand, we may need to allow some room for a 'remnant theology' here. With the phrases 'my people' and 'the company of the righteous' (Ps 14:4-5), the psalmist might have referred to God's *true* people. But it is important to note that Paul identifies the wicked 'they' with both Gentiles *and* Jews to substantiate his charge,[271] that 'Jews and Gentiles alike are all under sin' (3:9). Paul's purpose *here* in quoting this Psalm is not to prove that there are some Israelites who are faithful, as Davies contends, but to substantiate that *all* Jews and *all* Gentiles are under sin.[272] In so doing Paul does not distinguish the 'righteous' from the 'wicked' among the Jews.

The OT writers had often remarked that '[Israel] is a people without understanding' (Isa 27:11; 42:25; 48:8; Mic 4:12; cf. Jer 8:7; 9:3; John 15:21; 16:3). We also note that the wording and ideas of Jer 4:22 (MT rather than LXX; cf. Jer 5:21) are very close to Rom 3:10-13:

> "My people are fools; they do not know me.
> They are senseless children; they have no understanding.
> They are skilled in doing evil; they know not how to do good"
> (Jer 4:22).

Thus it is commensurate with the evidence for Paul to assert in Romans that Jews did not understand 'the righteousness that comes from God and sought to establish their own, they did not submit to God's righteousness' (10:3).[273] They still have the veil unlifted, and thus have no proper understanding of God's covenant (2 Cor 3:12-18). They mistakenly pursued righteousness as if it were by works, and so they stumbled over the 'stumbling-stone' (9:32). Paul expresses, furthermore, that Israel does not have

---

Psalms, 192, and Oesterley, *Psalms*, 278-279, who assert that the psalmist is accusing the wicked (priests) among the Israelites. Cf. NIV mg. of Ps 14:1, which suggests that the Hebrew word *fool* (נָבָל) denotes a 'morally deficient' one. There can be room for 'remnant theology', that, i.e. 'my people' refers to God's *true* people, the remnant of Israel, but the fool here seems more likely to refer to Gentiles.

271 *Pace* Stanley, *Language*, 90, 91, 92, for repeatedly saying that Paul's wording is not out of context (i.e. the LXX's); but so correctly Lightfoot, *Talmud* 4, 155-156.

272 *Pace* Davies, *Faith*, 82-84.

273 Cf. in Eph 4:18 similar spiritual darkness is applied to Gentiles.

The Equality of Jew and Gentile in Sinfulness 145

understanding, since the μή–question: 'μὴ 'Ισραὴλ οὐκ ἔγνω;' (10:19), requires a negative 'No' in reply.

In this first set of quotations, Paul is not merely quoting LXX Ps 13 but probably combining it with LXX Eccl 7:21, where universal sinfulness is clearly affirmed.[274] So he concludes that 'all have sinned' (3:23; 5:12; 11:32; Gal 3:22). Of course, the Jews knew that they had sinned (1 Kgs 8:47; 1 Chr 5:25; 2 Chr 30:7; Ezra 9:7; Ps 78:8, 57; 106:6; 143:2; Jer 3:25; 11:10; Ezek 20:18, etc.), but they thought they were different from the Gentiles who did not acknowledge the God of Israel. Paul, however, attempts to establish in 3:10-12 that the Jews are fundamentally as sinful as the Gentiles. It is significant to note that Paul applies the context of LXX Ps 13:1-3, where wicked Gentiles (and unfaithful Jews) are accused, to Jews as well as to Gentiles, and thus skilfully includes *all* Jews in his indictment as well. Then in this 'summary introduction to the entire citation',[275] Paul sets forth his agenda, which is to affirm universal sinfulness, but with the primary intention of establishing *Jewish* sinfulness.

3:13-14 is to be taken together. It is interesting to note that, in this unit, Paul combines three passages (LXX Ps 5:10; 139:4; 9:28) which all contain the terminology related to the oral organs: throat, tongue, lips and mouth. Paul quotes LXX Ps 5:10b exactly in 3:13a and LXX Ps 139:4 in 3:13b. But the context is again significantly modified. In Psalm 5 the psalmist contrasts the sinfulness and rebellion of the 'wicked' (Ps 5:4-10) with the privilege and protection of the 'righteous' (LXX Ps 5:11-12; 139:14). The identification of 'my enemies' (Ps 5:8) cannot be determined with certainty. But according to the Hebrew text the phrase seems to refer to the ungodly within Israel itself rather than to Gentiles.[276] However, it is to be noted that the Hebrew text 'thou dost cover *him* with favour' (Ps 5:12; RSV) has been

---

274 Cranfield, *Romans* 1, 192. *Contra* Davies, *Faith*, 89-90 n. 3. Cf. Stanley, *Language*, 88, who does not take note of it at all. Although 3:10 ('οὐκ ἔστιν δίκαιος οὐδὲ εἷς') is closer to LXX Eccl 7:21, as Dunn, *Romans* 1, 150, notes, the subsequent quote in 3:11-12 makes it clear that LXX Ps 13:1-3 is the primary source of the quotation here; cf. Fitzmyer, *Romans*, 335.

275 Stanley, *Language*, 90; so also Meyer, *Romans* 1, 155, who also lists Michaelis, Eckermann, Koppe, Köllner and Fritzsche. So also Haldane, *Romans*, 115; Black, *Romans*, 64..

276 Perowne, *Psalms* 1, 137; Oesterley, *Psalms*, 132; Anderson, *Psalms* 1, 81; Briggs and Briggs, *Psalms* 1, 40.

changed in the LXX to 'thou hast compassed *us* as with a shield of favour' (ὡς ὅπλῳ εὐδοκίας ἐστεφάνωσας ἡμᾶς).[277] Thus, according to the LXX, the psalmist seems to have embraced the pious Jews by modifying the singular 'him' to the plural 'ἡμᾶς'. Therefore, the 'enemies' in the LXX could possibly refer to Gentile evildoers,[278] and this seems even more likely when it is considered together with what is cited in the next verse. On the other hand, even if the LXX wording does not indicate Gentiles with the change, the text clearly says that there are the 'righteous' who trust in God and the 'wicked' who rebel against him. Quoting from such a context in the LXX, Paul significantly ignores the distinction between the righteous and the wicked among the Jews, and then applies the Psalm to both Gentiles *and* Jews to imply that 'there is no distinction ... between Jewish 'righteousness' and gentile 'unrighteous-ness' ... before God'.[279]

3:14 is quoted from LXX Ps 9:28 (MT 10:7). The wicked (ἀσεβής) in this Psalm are clearly equated with the nations (ἔθνη)[280] whose names are to be blotted out for ever and ever (LXX Ps 9:5, 15, 16, 17, 19, 20, 22, 24, 33, 35, 36), for they forget the Lord (LXX Ps 9:17), do not seek him, and are far away from his law (LXX Ps 9:24-25). On the contrary, Israel is described as those who know the name of the Lord and who seek and trust in him (LXX Ps 9:10). Although they are oppressed (LXX Ps 9:9, 38), afflicted (LXX Ps 9:12, 18, 37), needy (LXX Ps 9:18) and helpless (LXX Ps 9:32), they will be saved whereas the Gentiles are to perish forever (LXX Ps 9:36). In such a context, the psalmist clearly refers to the Gentiles with the expression 'whose mouth is full of cursing and bitterness'. It is striking,

---

277 Brenton's translation, *Septuagint*, 701.
278 Ringgren, *Faith*, 43-44. The strongest case is (exaggeratedly) asserted by Birkeland, *Evildoers*, 93: 'the evildoers in the Book of Psalms are *gentiles in all cases* when a definite collective body or its representatives are meant' (added emphasis).
279 Dunn, *Romans* 1, 150-151.
280 Kissane, *Psalms* 1, 36; Briggs and Briggs, *Psalms* 1, 77. However, Oesterley, *Psalms*, 145, understands: 'the ungodly sinners among the people', 'the wicked among his own people', although he notes that the wicked in Ps 9 (Pss. 9 and 10 are one Psalm in the LXX and the Vulgate) are 'foreign enemies' (p. 144).

however, to see Paul applying the phrase to refer to both Gentiles and Jews.[281]

The bodily organs mentioned in 3:13-14 may be represented by 'mouth', and in this connection it seems significant to see Paul's use of 'mouth' three times in 10:8-10 as a means for the oral confession of faith in Christ. Thus 3:13-14 seems more than simple 'description of the sinfulness of men's speech'.[282] Rather, it is possible, and even probable, that here Paul has deliberately selected these verses to describe especially those who persistently refuse to confess that Jesus is Lord and Christ, and those who verbally interrupt Christian missionary preaching. Jews were told not to let the word of God depart from their mouth (Jos 1:18; Isa 59:21), and for Paul the word of God is 'the word of faith we are proclaiming' (10:8). Paul also says that the Jews have cursing and bitterness instead of God's word of faith. It is significant in this connection that in Romans it is the Jews who are described by this category of unbelief, as we shall see later in our examination of Romans 9-11. According to the Psalms, Jews are to use throat, tongue, lips and mouth to declare God's righteousness and praise (Ps 35:28; 51:14-15; 63:3, 5; 119:171-172; 149:6; cf. Sir 39:15; 50:20). But now Paul portrays their oral organs as functioning in precisely the opposite way.[283]

3:15-17 is quoted from LXX Isa 59:7-8 with textual modifications.[284] Isa 59:7-8 is the prophet's charge against Judah's failure to stand up against evil (cf. Isa 59:2-3, 20-21).[285] There the accusation is directed to the unrighteous in Judah, but here Paul implies that Jews as a whole are the 'wicked'.[286] According to Dunn, it is no accident that Paul appeals to the passage which condemns the lack of righteousness among Jews, to affirm that

---

281 Dunn, *Romans* 1, 151.
282 Cranfield, *Romans* 1, 193.
283 Noting that the Jews are depicted as the real opponents in the present passage, Käsemann, *Romans*, 87, plausibly says that Paul may be describing Jewish hatred of the gospel from vv. 13ff. Cf. Cranfield's view, *Romans* 1, 193, 'the description of the sinfulness of men's speech', which does not seem sufficient. *Pace* Moo, *Romans* 1, 206, who suggests that 3:13-14 is not directly related to Paul's purpose.
284 See Stanley, *Language*, 95-98, for details.
285 Westermann, *Isaiah 40-66*, 347-348; Watts, *Isaiah 34-66*, 280; Cranfield, *Romans* 1, 193.
286 Moo, *Romans* 1, 206.

his contemporary fellow-Jews are as sinful as the Israel of the past.[287] The blood-shedding feet in 3:15 that are swift to harm the preachers of the gospel, are contrasted with the beautiful feet of those who bring the good news in 10:15. Together with what was said above about the oral organs, we may infer that the catena was composed from a soteriological and evangelistic perspective.[288]

3:18 is a verbatim quotation of LXX Ps 35:2 except for Paul's change of the singular 'αὐτοῦ' to the plural 'αὐτῶν'. This alteration is most probably in order to be in line with other plurals in the catena which embrace both Jews and Gentiles. We note again, however, the shift in the Pauline context. In the Psalm, those who have 'no fear of God before [their] eyes' (LXX Ps 35:2) are 'the wicked', who are contrasted with 'those who know you [God]' (LXX Ps 35:11). Paul now applies again the expression which designated the Gentiles[289] to both Gentiles and Jews.[290] Jews have been taught that 'the fear of the Lord is the beginning of knowledge' (Prov 1:7; cf. Gen 22:12; Exod 20:20; Deut 6:2; Job 23:15; Ps 34:4-22; 112:1; Prov 9:10; 15:33; Isa 33:6; 50:10; 59:19; Jer 32:39). Paul now successfully includes Jews in his accusation that they also have no fear of God, just like the Gentiles. There is no-one, even among the Jews, who fears God. Thus this quotation effectively serves as the conclusion and the climax of the catena.[291]

Our investigation of Paul's use of the quotations leads us to conclude that his significant modification of the contexts of the quoted passages indicates his strong intention to include *all Jews* in his indictment. According to the original contexts, the Jews, or the righteous Jews, were excluded from the accusations, but Paul includes them without exception ('οὐκ ἔστιν δίκαιος οὐδὲ εἷς', 'οὐκ ἔστιν ἕως ἑνός', 'πᾶν στόμα', 'πᾶς ὁ κόσμος' and 'πᾶσα σάρξ').[292]

---

287 Dunn, *Romans* 1, 151.
288 Cf. Käsemann, *Romans*, 87.
289 *Pace* Briggs and Briggs, *Psalms* 1, 315: 'the wicked here seem not to be enemies of the nation, but wicked men among the people'.
290 Dunn, *Romans* 1, 151; Meyer, *Romans* 1, 157.
291 Taylor, *Romans*, 31; Cranfield, *Romans* 1, 193; Davies, *Faith*, 88.
292 In this connection, Lagrange, *Romains*, 69 (as cited in Davies, *Faith*, 90 n. 2), seems right to say: 'Theodore of Mopsuestia had well remarked that Paul does not use these texts as a prophetic testimony, but as a testimony which harmonises with what he wants to prove.' So also Bruce, *Romans*, 97;

D. Summary

Thus far we have examined 3:1-20 with special reference to Paul's use of the OT in this section, and now we may draw some conclusions. The quotations are carefully selected to clarify his charge that both Jews and Gentiles alike are all under sin (3:9). Paul asserts the universality of sin, thus including every single individual Jew and Gentile. Moreover, his modification of the texts and contexts reveals his firm intention to include the Jews in his indictment. A more careful and sensitive reader may be able to perceive that Paul's argument is to be applied even more forcefully to the Jews, not only to 'unfaithful' Jews but also 'righteous' ones. Thus we may suggest that his primary argument in 3:9-20 is to affirm that the Jews as a whole are not any better than the Gentiles, as their Scriptures clearly show.[293] The Jews boasted in the law (2:1-3:20) and in the ancestry of Abraham (4:1-25), which thus made them distinct from the Gentiles. As far as God's salvation was concerned most Jews thought that the Gentiles were automatically excluded. But Paul tries to show that the OT writers, especially David, had ruled out such a distinction by using the strongest possible words about Israel/Gentiles.[294] It is significant to note that all six passages quoted from the Psalms are expressed as Davidic in the LXX. Thus Paul seems to imply that it is not merely the OT Scriptures but David himself (to whom the Messianic covenant had been given) who accuses Jews of not believing the Davidic Messiah Jesus.[295]

Most significant of all is the fact that *it is Paul himself who launches a direct attack on Jewish pride and self-sufficiency by*

Wilckens, *Römer* 1, 173. But Davies himself implausibly rejects this view. Although Paul writes 'as it is written,' he does not seem to be concerned with the literal sense of the original texts quoted. Thus Giblin, 'As It Is Written', 487, seems correct to say: 'Paul speaks as a theologian and the sense of Scripture which interests him is its theological intelligibility or meaning.' Cf. Edgar, 'Respect', 56-57, who notes the general contextual changes in Paul, but not the intention or the significance of such modifications.

293 Cf. Lightfoot, *Notes*, 267: 'Your Scriptures show that you are not exempt.'

294 Lightfoot, *Notes*, 269.

295 The only passage that is not quoted from the Psalms is Isa 59:7-8, but it also has a close connection with the Davidic psalms, as Westermann shows (*Isaiah 40-66*, 346-348).

modifying the original texts and contexts, and so gives the impression that David and the prophets of the OT applied the condemnation equally to Jews as to Gentiles. Paul's presentation of the argument is not shaped by anti-semitism, as is sometimes alleged, but by his apostolic self-consciousness. Paul the apostle to the Gentiles argues that in the Messianic era and community, Jews are not superior to Gentiles, just as David, the original recipient of the Messianic covenant, had foretold. This observation leads us to understand that in 3:9-20 Paul's *primary* aim[296] is once again to affirm the sinfulness of the *Jews*, this time from their own Scriptures. The first (πρῶτον) and the only-mentioned item of Jewish advantage (3:1-2) itself serves as 'an irrefutable proof of Jewish depravity'.[297]

4. Conclusion

In this chapter we have attempted to show that the *content* and the *presentation* of the soteriology are moulded by Paul's self-awareness as the apostle to the Gentiles. We have proposed that the content for which the apostle is arguing in 1:18-11:36 is the equality of Jew and Gentile (and this claim still awaits substantiation in our following chapters). In the present section 1:18-3:20 Paul attempts to establish the equality of Jews and Gentiles in sinfulness, but we have found that he specifically structures his argument in order to affirm the sinfulness of Jews in particular. The following are our findings concerning his argument in 1:18-3:20.

First, we have argued that in 1:18-32 Paul indicts both Gentiles *and* Jews. The inclusion of Jews in Paul's indictment is not based on some linguistic correspondence with the Genesis narratives (i.e. Paul charges *human* sinfulness in general, *therefore*, Jews are included). Rather, it is because Paul accuses 'them' by reflecting on the sinful history of Israel. Scholars have often contended that Paul indicts Jews of idolatry by alluding to Jewish history. But we have shown that not only idolatry but also (homo)sexual immor-

---

296 So also Luther, *Romans*, 74-75. Even though the expressions like πᾶν στόμα, πᾶς ὁ κόσμος and πᾶσα σάρξ certainly have the further connotation of including Gentiles as well, Jews are primarily intended (Cranfield, *Romans* 1, 196; *pace* Murray, *Romans* 1, 106).

297 Boylan, *Romans*, 53; also 33.

ality and refusal to retain the knowledge of God, all recall the sinful history of Israel. Paul charges Jews as seriously as Gentiles. By shaping the accusation of human sinfulness by reflecting Israel's history, Paul paves the way for the more direct attack on complacent Judaism from 2:1 onwards.

Secondly, we have shown that Paul's rebuke of complacency in 2:1-4 is in line with the rebuke against Jews in the Wisdom tradition, and in the OT prophetic tradition. Moreover, since the expressions σκληρότης and ἀμετανόητος (2:5) have a rich background in the OT in denoting the stubbornness of the Jews, it is most probable that Paul had Jews in mind with his indictment. The logical connector διό of 2:1 indicates that he develops a more direct accusation towards the Jews. The theological axiom of divine impartiality in judgement and salvation certainly establishes the equality of Jew and Gentile. But the axiom is rhetorically mentioned to develop his argument further. Paul stresses the axiom in order to affirm the sinfulness of, and thus the inevitable judgement upon the Jews, and in order to establish the legitimacy of the salvation of the Gentiles. In the presentation of the argument Paul himself does not remain impartial but is 'biassed towards the Gentiles'.

Thirdly, in 2:12-29 Paul constantly makes affirmative statements about Gentiles and critical arguments against Jews. He affirms that Gentiles do the requirement of the law (2:12-16), while Jews break the law (2:17-24). Furthermore, he makes statements about physical circumcision for Jews and a spiritual one for Gentiles, and applies the term 'outward Jew' to (the unbelieving) ethnic Jews and the term 'inward Jew' to (the believing) Gentiles. It is clear that Paul the apostle to the Gentiles structures his argument in this section (2:12-29) to secure the theological legitimacy of the Gentiles on the one hand, and to establish Jewish sinfulness (and thus to undermine Jewish complacency) on the other.

Finally, we have seen that although Paul affirms that Jews have advantages (3:1-2), his main argument in 3:1-20 is devoted to establishing that Jews are not any better than Gentiles (3:9). He cites some OT passages to support his argument. We have shown that Paul makes a direct accusation of Jewish pride and self-complacency by modifying the original texts and contexts.[298]

In conclusion, we have found that the apostle argues on two levels. On the *theological* level he affirms the universal and equal sinfulness of Jew and Gentile, but on the *rhetorical* level he argues to establish more specifically Jewish depravity. The verse 3:20 sums up the entire argument of 1:18-3:20, that is, of universal sinfulness, but it is rhetorically presented as an argument 'with a special reference to Jews'.[299] Gentile sinfulness is also stated (1:18-32), yet without specific focus upon it. It is the sinfulness of the Jews, however, that is argued and stressed in 1:18-3:20 (especially in 2:12-3:20), so that the Jews might not despise the Gentiles nor undermine their legitimate salvation in the Jewish Messiah Jesus. Paul's obvious bias towards the Gentiles suggests that his self-awareness as being the apostle to the Gentiles has influenced him to shape the argument in favour of the Gentiles. Paul's indictment of Jewish complacency required boldness and yet skilful diplomacy (cf. 15:14-15).[300] Paul establishes the equality of Jew and Gentile in this section (1:18-3:20) mainly by underlining the sinfulness of the Jews.

In the next section (3:21-4:25) he continues to affirm their equality, but this time their equality *in justification*, and with a more specific affirmation of *Gentile* justification, as we will see in the next chapter.

---

298 Tobin, 'Controversy', 298-318 argues that Paul's appeal to Jewish Scripture to establish the sinfulness of both Jews and Gentiles is to undermine Jewish attitude toward Gentiles.

299 Lincoln, 'Wrath', 212. So also Moo, *Romans* 1, 207-208.

300 Locke's observation (*Paraphrase* 2, 489) is acute: 'It cannot be sufficiently admired how skilfully to avoid offending those of his own nation St Paul here [i.e. 1:16-2:29] enters into an argument so unpleasing to the Jews as this of perswadeing them that the Gentiles had as good title to be taken in to be the people of god under the Messiah as they themselves which is the main designe of this Epistle.'

Chapter 3

The Equality of Jew and Gentile in Justification: 3:21-4:25

In Chapter 2, we have tried to demonstrate that in 1:18-3:20 Paul attempts to establish Jewish sinfulness within an overall theological assertion of the universal and equal sinfulness of both Jew and Gentile. There we have suggested that Paul unremittingly stresses Jewish sinfulness. By contrast, we observed that he makes quite affirmative remarks about the Gentiles; despite his appeal to the theological axiom of divine impartiality, Paul himself does not remain impartial, but is somewhat 'on the Gentiles' side'. We have traced this to Paul's self-awareness as apostle to the *Gentiles*.

In this chapter we will show that Paul continues his theme of the equality of Jew and Gentile in 3:21-4:25; but this time he stresses their equality *in justification*.[1] Paul's emphasis is espe-

---

1 We indicate that 1:18-4:25 constitutes one large argument by retaining our Chapter 2 title 'The Equality of Jew and Gentile' in Chapter 3, though more specific qualifications are added to both titles so as to highlight Paul's argument for each section. Those who regard Rom 1-4 as one unit include Cranfield and Moo. Compare Dunn and Sanday and Headlam, for whom 1:18-5:21 is a unit; for Stuhlmacher, 1:18-8:39; for Boylan, 1:18-11:36. Käsemann and Bruce implausibly divide 1:18-3:20 and 3:21-4:25 into two *independent* sections. Hays, 'Psalm 143', 115, has correctly pointed out that the connection and continuation of the argument before and after 3:21 should not be overlooked. This view is followed by Elliott, *Rhetoric*, 147; Dunn, 'Romans: Analysis', 2853. So also Cosgrove, 'Rom 1:18-4:25', 626, who gives three

cially directed to affirm the justification of the Gentiles theologically by excluding Jewish boasting and by explaining the sufficiency of faith from the case of Abraham. He recapitulates the issue of 'boasting' in the law and in God (2:17, 23) in order to deny the grounds of Jewish boasting, as we shall see. Paul also asserts, through his reinterpretation of Abraham's standing before God, that Jewish boasting in the Abrahamic ancestry is also excluded. We will also show that Paul's surprising retelling of the Abraham story is rhetorically designed to maximise his argument that Abraham is also the father of many nations (=Gentiles), and that Abraham's faith was honoured and the promise to him was given also for the sake of the Gentiles.

Our view will undermine the traditional view that Paul's primary aim in this section is to expound the doctrine of justification by faith or of the righteousness of God,[2] with the case of Abraham as a scriptural proof for 'justification *by faith*'.[3] However, K. Stendahl has challenged even such an apparent consensus. He argues that in 3:21-4:25 Paul's primary intention is not to expound the doctrine of justification by faith, but to explain the Jewish–Gentile relationship in the light of the new revelation of the righteousness of God. He emphatically repeats that Paul does not use the Jewish–Gentile situation as an example to explain justification by faith, but that Paul is fundamentally interested in explaining the relation between Jews and Gentiles.[4] Stendahl's

---

reasons: (a) the δέ of 3:21 indicates continuity, (b) the attempt to undermine Jewish boasting in 3:27ff corresponds to that in 2:17ff, (c) the defence of the Gentile position is evident in 2:1ff and 3:21ff. Nevertheless, with the 'Νυνὶ δέ' Paul signals a decisive new situation over against the earlier one described in 1:18-3:20: so Ziesler, *Romans*, 108; Dunn, *Romans* 1, 161, 164; Nygren, *Romans*, 144.

2 Black, *Romans*, 65; Elliott, *Rhetoric*, 146-152; Käsemann, *Romans*, 91-101; Stuhlmacher, *Römer*, 54; Davies, *Faith*, 104-112; Gifford, *Romans*, 88-94; Nygren, *Romans*, 144-147; Seifrid, *Justification*, 219-223; Cranfield, *Romans* 1, 199-218.

3 Typically, Käsemann, 'Abraham', 79; *idem*, *Romans*, 105; Bultmann, *Theology* 1, 280; objected to by Wright, 'Romans', 191: rather, with the Abraham story Paul explains that 'all this [3:21-31] has taken place precisely *in fulfillment of the covenant*'.

4 Stendahl, *Paul*, 2, goes on to argue, 'Paul's doctrine of justification by faith has its theological context in his reflection on the relation between Jews and Gentiles, and not within the problem of how *man* is to be saved...' (p. 26);

view has increasingly gained approval from other Pauline scholars.[5] However, Stendahl seems to have gone to the other extreme, because the case that Romans is arguing for the relation between Jew and Gentile need not mean (and does not mean) that Romans 3 is not an exposition of justification by faith. Furthermore, he does not perceive that the *relation* that Paul is arguing for, is precisely their *equality*. E.P. Sanders has briefly mentioned that Paul's argument here is primarily shaped by his desire to affirm the status of the (believing) Gentiles,[6] yet this remark requires substantiation.

We shall begin by discussing 3:21-26, and will note that the argument in this highly concentrated passage is also developed in order to affirm the equality of Jew and Gentile (3:22), and to undermine the ground for Jewish boasting of their superiority (3:27). We will then move on to focus on Paul's argument, which excludes Jewish boasting in their ethnic identity, in their possession of the law, in their special relationship with God and in their Abrahamic ancestry. We will examine N. Elliott's arguments here. It is striking to note that while Paul argues for the exclusion of these items of Jewish boasting, he applies these same items to the Gentiles. Finally, Paul's theological argument in 4:1-25 will be investigated. Paul formulates his argument in Romans 4 to establish that Abraham is also the father of many nations/Gentiles. We will show that Paul achieves this purpose by stressing the chronological sequence of the account of Abraham's faith, on the one hand, namely, Abraham was reckoned righteous *before* his obedience in being circumcised or in 'sacrificing' Isaac

---

followed by Kaylor, *Covenant Community*, 61-62. See Käsemann's critique on Stendahl in his 'Justification', 70-78, and Stendahl's response in *Paul*, 129-32.

5   Kaylor, *Covenant Community*, 51: '... the central purpose of Paul in this section [3:21-4:25], is to show that the new covenant in Christ binds Gentile, as well as Jew, to God.' So also Dunn, 'Romans: Analysis', 2853-54: 'Paul's concern here is more for what this means for the Jew and Gentile.' Donfried, 'Romans 3:21-28', 60: Paul writes this letter so as to deal with a concrete situation in the Roman church, 'namely, the relationship of Jewish and Gentile Christians to one another', and 'this was one of the burning issues in early Christianity as a whole'. So also Wright, 'Romans', 191; Ziesler, *Romans*, 120-121. But Elliott, *Rhetoric*, 161-163, rejects this view without interacting with Stendahl, but briefly with Hays, 'Abraham', 76-98, who maintains the same position as Stendahl.

6   Sanders, *Jewish People*, 34.

(4:1-12). But, on the other hand, he does the same thing by (deliberately) passing over the issue of the chronological sequence in 4:13-22. This crucial point has hardly been noted by exegetes. Our study will show the extent to which Paul's self-awareness as apostle to the Gentiles has influenced such shaping of the structure of his argument in this section (3:21-4:25).

1. The Equality in Justification by Faith: 3:21-26

The importance of 3:21-26 is often stressed,[7] and the general consensus is that this passage expounds the doctrine of the righteousness of God, as mentioned above. We propose to refocus this passage to determine not only its content but also Paul's intention in shaping his argument as presented here. For the first time since his thematic statement in 1:16-17, Paul begins to expound δικαιοσύνη θεοῦ/δικαιόω (3:21, 22, 25, 26) and πίστις/πιστεύειν (3:22, 25, 26, 27, 28, 30, 31), which become dominant themes in this section.[8] We will examine how Paul reinterprets the phrase 'the righteousness of God' by adding the emphatic 'apart from the law', and the significance of 3:22c-26 (one long sentence in Greek) as it establishes the corollary affirmation, 'There is no distinction [between Jew and Gentile]'. Our investigation will enable us to see that Paul's intention here is to affirm, theologically, the equality of Jew and Gentile by stressing the legitimacy of the justification of the believing Gentiles.

---

7   E.g. Cranfield, *Romans* 1, 199, designates 3:21-26 as 'the centre and heart of the whole of Rom 1.16b-15.13'; Campbell, 'Romans III', 23: 'the centre of Paul's theology in Romans'. For Käsemann, *Romans*, 91, 3:21-26 contains 'the thesis proper' of the Epistle. D.A. Campbell, who has recently produced a monograph on this short passage, *Rhetoric*, 11, takes it as the *crux interpretum* for the entire letter. Almost all exegetes would also agree with Käsemann, *Romans*, 92, however, that this sub-section is 'one of the most obscure and difficult [ones] in the whole epistle'. Such difficulties have led to disagreement on the interpretation of the passage itself. See Käsemann, Campbell, *Rhetoric*, 11-12, n. 3, for more references. The lengthy bibliography for this section in Fitzmyer's commentary shows the importance and complexity of the passage.

8   Except the appearances of ἡ πίστις τοῦ θεοῦ and θεοῦ δικαιοσύνη (3:3, 5), which Paul simply mentions to contrast '*our* unrighteousness' which is a focal point in 3:1-8.

A. The Righteousness of God apart from the Law

The Jews thought that the law was the means for righteousness and salvation (cf. 9:31-10:3), but now Paul declares that the righteousness of God has been revealed *apart from the law* (3:21-22).[9] This righteousness of God was already known or promised in the OT Scriptures of the Law and the Prophets.[10] Here Paul indicates that he will demonstrate this righteousness of God from the OT Scriptures,[11] because the gospel or this righteousness is consistent with the OT (cf. 1:2; 4:1-25; 9:25-33; 10:6-13; 16-21; 11:1-10, 26-29; 15:8-12).[12]

Syntactically the phrase 'χωρὶς νόμου' receives full emphasis. N.T. Wright explains why Paul stresses it: 'the law was given to Jews, whereas God's plan was and is to save a world-wide people: therefore *justification must be apart from the law, since otherwise God's purposes of salvation would be frustrated*'.[13] R.D. Kaylor independently offers a similar reason: since the Torah had been applied only to the Jews as the way through which they could become right with God, *it divided Gentiles from Jews*. But out of his major concern to establish the equality of Gentile and Jewish believers, Paul stresses the concept, 'apart from the law'.[14] Both Wright and Kaylor seem right in the light of Paul's following explanations that (a) this righteousness of God is

---

9 Note the emphatic position of χωρὶς νόμου; 4:6, 13-15. The expression χωρὶς νόμου may be synonymous with χωρὶς ἔργων νόμου (3:28) and with χωρὶς ἔργων (4:6; cf. 7:8, 9), and is then contrasted with ἐν τῷ νόμῳ and ἐξ ἔργων νόμου in 3:19-20 (Dunn, *Romans* 1, 165; Cranfield, *Romans* 1, 201). Cf. Dunn, *Romans* 1, 165: '"Without the law" ... means outside the national and religious parameters set by the law, without reference to the normal Jewish hallmarks'.

10 Only here does Paul use the phrase 'the Law and the Prophets' to denote the entire OT Scriptures (but cf. Matt 5:17; 7:12; 11:13; 22:40; Luke 16:16; [24:44]; John 1:45; Acts 13:15; 24:14; 26:22; 28:23; 2 Macc 15:9; *4 Macc* 18:10).

11 For Paul the OT still serves (the present participle μαρτυρουμένη) 'as a privileged preparation for this new disclosure of God's uprightness' (Fitzmyer, *Romans*, 344).

12 So also Cranfield, *Romans* 1, 202; Barrett, *Romans*, 70.

13 Wright, *Messiah*, 99, with his emphasis.

14 Kaylor, *Covenant Community*, 19, 61. Similarly Sanders, *Jewish People*, 33.

available 'not for Jews only but for all, ...*all who have faith*'[15] (3:22),[16] and that (b) Paul thus quickly declares his point first: 'for there is no distinction'.

Paul's point is then particularly made for the sake of the Gentiles. As apostle to the Gentiles he theologically explains that now Gentiles have also been brought into a right relationship with God because of Christ's faithful obedience unto death. '*For* there is no distinction,' claims Paul. Between Jews and Gentiles there is no difference in their sinfulness (1:18-3:20), and in their need (3:23), thus they are all included in the same method of justification (3:30).[17]

The γάρ in 3:22 introduces the theological ground for the availability of this righteousness to all who believe in Jesus Christ, regardless of their ethnic origins.[18] Here Paul does not attempt to argue the equality between Jew and Gentile; he simply declares that there is no difference between the two.[19] Since the OT clearly confirms the distinction between Jew and Gentile (Exod 8:23: 'I will make a distinction [LXX: διαστολή] between my people and your people'; cf. Exod 9:4, 6; 10:23; 11:7; 12:13, 23, 27), we should not assume that the believing Jews would know and accept this axiom without any difficulty. So Paul clarifies things further with another γάρ in 3:23: all, both Jew and Gentile,[20] have sinned (cf. *4 Ezra* 8:35), and fall short of God's glory.[21] Thus the universal and equal sinfulness of all humanity is

---

15 Barrett, *Romans*, 70: his emphasis.
16 For the textual issues see Metzger, *Textual Commentary*, 508.
17 Gifford, *Romans*, 89; Ziesler, *Romans*, 107; Shedd, *Romans*, 76.
18 Shedd, *Romans*, 76.
19 The abolition of distinctions between Jews and Gentiles does not necessarily include the abolition of Jewish privileges. See below pp. 225-227. So Cranfield, *Romans* 1, 203-204, who correctly rejects Michel's view, *Römer*, 1966[4], 105. Paul does not deny the privileges of the Jew (1:16; 3:2; 9:4-5; 11:17-18, 28-29), but he affirms that Jews have no real advantage over the Gentiles as far as obtaining this righteousness is concerned. It is to be noted that Paul's assertion of equality between Jew and Gentile is mainly related to his argument about inclusive soteriology.
20 Barrett, *Romans*, 70. For Ziesler, *Romans*, 109-110, 'all' does not denote every single individual, but 'all' Jews and Gentiles as nations are sinful. We have already discussed this in the section 3:1-20. See Fitzmyer, *Romans*, 346, for a more plausible view.
21 Dunn, *Romans* 1, 168, asserts that the phrase 'fall short of the glory of God' echoes Adam's story (cf. *Apoc. Moses*, 21:6; *Gen. R.* 12:5; *3 Apoc. Bar.*

the theological basis for Paul's declarations not only concerning the abolition of a distinction between Jew and Gentile, but also concerning the revelation of God's righteousness apart from the law. That is why Paul started his major argument by establishing this universal sinfulness,[22] and, as we have demonstrated earlier (1:18-3:20), he did this by stressing *Jewish* depravity.

B. *Justification by God's Grace and by Human Faith in Christ*

The long Greek sentence 3:22c-26 explains that the abolition of the distinction between Jew and Gentile is based not only on universal sinfulness but also on equal justification by God's grace, which has become available to all who have faith in Jesus. Paul writes about the latter basis in 3:24-26. There 3:24 is most emphasised,[23] and 3:25-26 is one single relative clause describing the 'Christ Jesus' of 3:24. The section 3:25-26 is constructed with the repeated purpose-clauses (εἰς ἔνδειξιν ....; πρὸς τὴν ἔνδειξιν ....; εἰς τὸ εἶναι αὐτὸν...);[24] and this structure indicates

---

4:16). But the present tense ὑστεροῦνται ('come short') seems to indicate that here Paul is not focusing on Adam's fall but on the present plight of humanity (Barrett, *Romans*, 71; Ziesler, *Romans*, 110; Fitzmyer, *Romans*, 347), in the sense of 'be deprived of'.

22 So Cranfield, *Romans* 1, 204, is correct to say that 3:23 sums up the whole argument of 1:18-3:20.

23 Barrett, *Romans*, 71: 3:24 is 'the heart of his [Paul's] gospel, as he expounds it in Romans'.

24 The compact composition without explanation in 3:24-26 has led many scholars to take it as a pre-Pauline formula: Käsemann, 'Römer 3,24-26', 96-100; *idem, Romans*, 92; Dunn, *Romans* 1, 163-164; Wilckens, *Römer* 1, 183-184; Ziesler, *Romans*, 110; *idem, Meaning*, 209-210; Fitzmyer, *Romans*, 342-343; Kertelge, *Rechtfertigung*, 48-62; Reumann, *Righteousness*, 36-38; Stuhlmacher, 'Römer 3,24-26', *passim*; Donfried, 'Romans 3:21-28', 64.

We disagree with the pre-Pauline hypothesis for the following reasons: The expression, 'being justified as a gift by his grace', is not found elsewhere in the NT apart from Paul (4:16; cf. Eph 2:8-9; Titus 2:11). No one can be sure whether phrases such as 'as a gift' (*pace* Ziesler, *Romans*, 111; Kertelge, *Rechtfertigung*, 48-62), 'by his grace' (*pace* Reumann, *Righteousness*, 36-37; Fitzmyer, *Romans*, 343), 'through faith' (3:25), or 'by his blood' are additions. The repeated words, 'freely', 'by his grace', and 'the demonstration of his righteousness' in 3:25 and 26, are emphatic expressions rather than unnecessary repetition (*pace* Fitzmyer, *Romans*, 342). Furthermore, since Paul uses

Paul's desire to stress God's purpose or intention (προέθετο)[25] to demonstrate his righteousness through the sacrifice of Christ Jesus. Whatever meaning the term ἱλαστήριον may carry, it is a soteriological term in a sacrificial metaphor:[26] Christ shed his blood when he was crucified so that all humanity might receive redemption. Paul declares that God, in his forbearance, demonstrates his righteousness through passing over the punishment due with respect to those sins committed previously. For Paul, God's generosity is now applied to both Jews and Gentiles.[27] In the atoning sacrifice of Christ, God has not only demonstrated his righteousness but also prepared the way to justify all those who have faith in Christ.

The brevity of 3:21-26 is well noted. According to J.D.G. Dunn the brevity indicates that Paul merely claims, and does not argue, that God has provided Jesus Christ as a ransom for all humanity 'under sin', and that this saving act of God is the fulfilment of his

---

cultic language in 12:1; 15:15-16, the assertion that he could not possibly use the term ἱλαστήριον, a cultic term, cannot stand (*pace* Ziesler, *Romans*, 110).

Others insist that it is Paul's own composition: e.g. Hultgren, *Gospel*, 60-64; Cranfield, *Romans* 1, 200 n. 1: 'It is very much more probable that these verses are Paul's own independent and careful composition reflecting his own preaching and thinking.' Cf. Fitzer, 'Der Ort der Versöhnung', 163-166, who sees them as post-Pauline.

25 Scholars are almost evenly divided on the meaning of the verb προέθετο. Those who opt for 'God set him forward publicly' include Pelagius, Sanday and Headlam, *Romans*, 87; Dunn, *Romans* 1, 170; Nygren, Michel, Barrett, Kuss. Others, who take 'God purposed Christ to be a ἱλαστήριον', include Lightfoot, *Notes*, 271; Cranfield, *Romans* 1, 209, who lists Origen, Ambrosiaster, Chrysostom, Lightfoot, Lagrange, Cambier, NEB, JB as following this view.

26 For recent discussion and bibliography, see Gundry-Volf, 'Expiation', 279-284; Fryer, 'Meaning', 99-116; Campbell, *Rhetoric*, 107-113. A good treatment of this term is in Morris, *Apostolic Preaching*, 144-213; *idem*, 'Meaning', 33-43; see also Deissmann, 'ἱλαστήριος', 193-212; Manson, 'ἱλαστήριον', 1-10.

27 Gager, *Origins*, 216, may be correct to say that with this expression Paul had Gentile sins in mind, since a very similar message is reported to have been given by Paul to the Gentiles (cf. Acts 14:16; 17:30). On the contrary, if Paul had Jewish sins in mind, it is probably because Paul has said that God has ανοχή towards Jews (2:4), rather than because 'the formula was first framed within Jewish Christianity' (Dunn, *Romans* 1, 173).

covenant promises to Israel.²⁸ What Paul argues, however, is that participation in this righteousness of God that comes through faith in Jesus Christ, is now available 'to all who believe' in his atoning blood.²⁹ This indicates that the focal point of Paul's argument in 3:21-26 is that both Jew and Gentile can be equally justified by God's grace and through exercising faith in Christ. The term πίστις/πιστεύειν has been emphasised throughout 3:21-26. It is striking to note that so far Paul has given the impression that only (believing) *Gentiles* have had this faith (cf. 2:14-15, 26-29), and explicitly confirms this in 9:30. Here we can detect Paul's apostolic self-consciousness structuring the argument in order to affirm the Gentile position.

We note that the primary addressees of this section are Jewish believers.³⁰ Even though they are believers they may still understand 'Christianity' from *Jewish* perspectives. If they shared the perspective of what is later written in *4Ezra*, for example, they would note that Paul's teaching was markedly different from their position since in that writing works and faith are made equal means of salvation: 'And every one that shall (then) be saved, and shall be able to escape on account of his *works or his faith* by which he has believed' (*4 Ezra* 9:7; cf. 6:5; 7:77; 8:33, 36). But even here '"faith" ... seems to mean the righteousness which comes from fidelity to the Law (or "fidelity to the OT religion")', as *4 Ezra* 5:1; 6:28; 7:34 show.³¹ In Judaism it is often believed that righteousness is the result of fidelity to the law (cf. *2 Apoc. Bar.* 54:21). Moreover, 'everyone' who 'shall see my salvation' (*4 Ezra* 9:8) is not every Jew and Gentile, but only 'every (righteous) Jew' who dwells 'in my land, and within the borders which I have sanctified for myself eternally' (*4 Ezra* 9:9).³² Furthermore, 'in the Old Testament the very phrase, "to justify the wicked", is constantly used of unjust judges (e.g. Isa. v. 23; Pro.

---

28 Dunn, *Romans* 1, 183. Wright, 'Romans', 190, also suggests that the brevity indicates that the exposition of the meaning of Jesus' death is not the main thrust of the letter.

29 Dunn, *Romans* 1, 164, 183; Howard, 'Romans 3:21-31', 223-233.

30 *Pace* Elliott, *Rhetoric, passim*; for our reasons see *infra* pp. 167-168 n. 60.

31 Charles, *Apocrypha* 2, 574.

32 See Longenecker, *Eschatology*, for a comparative study of *4 Ezra* and Romans 1-11.

xvii. 15; Exod. xxiii. 7)'.³³ Paul would have been considered radical enough if he had only claimed that God would justify the *Jewish* wicked without any works of the law, but the degree to which he has moved away from contemporary Judaism is seen in his assertion that God now justifies not only wicked Jews but also *Gentiles*, and most strikingly, apart from the law but by faith in Christ Jesus.

M. Black is correct to say that Paul's thesis of justification by faith is in antithesis to contemporary rabbinical Judaism.³⁴ Paul is doing 'a daring thing' in saying that God justifies the wicked,³⁵ and that his righteousness is extended to the Gentiles. Asserting Jewish sinfulness and wickedness, and their deserved wrath from God, requires boldness; pronouncing free justification of the Gentiles, and their equal participation in God's righteousness with the Jews, demands even greater courage. Here Paul's use of 'the Day of Atonement' imagery, and its application in a *universal* salvation is highly dramatic (cf. Isa 63:1-6). That Paul boldly structures his argument in order to affirm Gentile salvation cannot be disputed.

Furthermore, Paul's use of the phrase 'δικαιοσύνη τοῦ θεοῦ/αὐτοῦ' is also very different from the perception of traditional Judaism. In Judaism the phrase 'the righteousness of God'³⁶ includes his covenant faithfulness in saving the oppressed people of Israel by destroying their Gentile foes (e.g. Ps 5:5-11; 7:7-18; 50:6, 16-23; Isa 45:17; 46:13; 51:4-8; 63:1-7).³⁷ Thus some Jews would take it as their slogan when they set out to destroy the Gentiles (1QM 4:6).³⁸ According to Wright 'the covenant context [of the righteousness of God] remains fundamental',

---

33   Dodd, *Romans*, 76.
34   Black, *Romans*, 65.
35   Dodd, *Romans*, 76.
36   The precise meaning of this phrase has been much debated through the generations. Yet modern scholars still offer a diversity of interpretation: Wright, *Messiah*, 61, 71: '[God's] "covenant faithfulness"'; Watson, *Paul*, 131: 'his [God's] faithfulness in Christ to the covenant-promise of salvation'; Cranfield, *Romans* 1, 202: a righteous status before God; Ziesler, *Romans*, 108: God's saving activity. See also Manfred Brauch's helpful survey of the discussion among German scholars on the phrase 'the righteousness of God', in Sanders, *Palestinian Judaism*, 523-542.
37   Seifrid, *Justification*, 221.
38   Seifrid, *Justification*, 221 n. 171.

and so 'the righteousness of God, and of his people, can only be understood in terms of God's promises to, and continued dealings with, his people Israel'.[39]

However, Paul reinterprets the phrase 'the righteousness of God' and extends its blessing to Gentiles also: for Paul it is equally manifested to both Jews and Gentiles who are alike under the power of sin.[40] The qualifying remark, εἰς πάντας τοὺς πιστεύοντας, 'to [or, for] all those (who are) believing', states that the righteousness of God is manifested and offered equally on the sole basis of faith to all humanity without ethnic distinction. The wrath of God is being revealed (ἀποκαλύπτεται) to all those who are under sin (1:18; 3:19-20), but now the righteousness of God has been revealed (πεφανέρωται) to all those believing in Jesus (3:21-22).[41] Thus 3:21-22 recapitulates the thematic statement in 1:17. At first sight Paul merely seems to establish a *universal equality*. However, we can discern a deeper intention in the shaping of his argument: Paul has declared the revelation of God's wrath to include *Jews* in a scenario of universal sinfulness and judgement, but he now claims the manifestation of 'the righteousness of God' (which he reinterprets) in order to affirm theologically the blessing which the (believing) *Gentiles* now enjoy.

To sum up: The apostle boldly insists not only that the righteousness of God has been revealed *apart from the law*, but also that Jews and Gentiles are equal because there is no distinction in their sinfulness and in the means for salvation. It seems most probable then that it is Paul's self-awareness of being apostle to the Gentiles that has made him structure his argument in such a way that the salvific blessing for the Gentiles can be affirmed. Thus Stendahl seems correct to assert that only 'in the development of *this* concern he [Paul] used as one of his arguments the idea of justification by faith'.[42]

---

39 Wright, *Messiah*, 64-65.
40 So correctly Ziesler, *Romans*, 108.
41 The verbs φανερόω and ἀποκαλύπτω are synonyms (*TDNT* 9, 4; *EDNT* 3, 413-414; Cranfield, *Romans* 1, 202; Dunn, *Romans* 1, 165).
42 Stendahl, *Paul*, 3. Stendahl's assertions are made in conjunction with the entire letters of Romans and Galatians. He claims that Galatians is about Paul's 'defense of the rights and the freedom of *Gentile* converts' (*Paul*, 2). That Romans is 'about God's plan for the world and about how Paul's mission

2. Jewish Boasting is Excluded: 3:27-4:25

The concluding particle οὖν in 3:27 indicates either that Paul's argument in 3:21-26 logically affirms the exclusion of ἡ καύχησις, or that his argument there has been in order to arrive at this conclusion. The latter is to be preferred, however, from the facts that 3:21-26 does not contain a specific reference to *'the* boasting', and that the claim of 3:28 (which is expounded in 3:21-26) affirms the elimination of *'the* boasting'. The sub-section 3:27-31 is crucial in the course of the argument in Romans 1-4, because it not only sums up the argument from 2:17 (or 1:18[43]) onwards, but also forms a bridge to Romans 4,[44] where the implication of Abraham's justification is clearly expounded at great length. In this section we will mainly examine 3:27-31. After we have established why *the* boasting refers to *Jewish* boasting, we will discuss some specific areas in which Jews made their boast, namely, boasting in the law, in God and in their Abrahamic ancestry. Then we shall examine how Jews would have understood Paul's absolute exclusion of the grounds of their traditional boasting, and the reasons why Paul forcefully shapes his argument as written in this passage.

A. Human Boasting or Jewish Boasting?

The interpretation of 'ἡ καύχησις' has been a central issue for many exegetes of Romans, and recently Neil Elliott has revived the discussion by claiming that it does not refer to *Jewish* boasting, but to *human* boasting in general. He asserts that 'the Jew's accountability to God through the Torah has been made paradigmatic for *universal* human accountability to God (3.19-20)' so as to deny the boasting of '*any* human beings', thus the καύχησις of 3:27 does not specifically refer to Jewish boasting.[45] He also contends that Abraham's justification by faith and his fatherhood 'of us all' (4:16) are *premises* upon which Paul builds his argu-

---

to the Gentiles fits into this plan' (*Paul*, 27), also seems plausible. So also Dahl, *Studies*, 156. Pace Kim, *Origin*, 357.

43 Elliott, *Rhetoric*, 157.
44 Moxnes, *Theology*, 223-230, has the section title, 'Rom 3:27-31 as an introduction to chapter 4'.
45 Elliott, *Rhetoric*, 148, 152, 155, 214.

ment rather than *conclusions* which he attempts to reach through the argument. This challenge constitutes, as he admits, the heart of his 57-page-long excursus whose fundamental thesis is that Romans 1-4 is not a debate with Judaism but 'with a misunderstanding of Judaism that in his [Paul's] view threatens the righteousness of God'.[46] We will make a brief survey of other interpretations before we particularly address Elliott's contention.

R. Bultmann and E. Käsemann took 'the boasting (in the Law)' as the fundamental sin of the Jews; the absolute opposite to 'faith'. The declaration of the exclusion of this boasting is specifically directed against the religious *Jew* who assumes his self-righteousness in the law.[47] E.P. Sanders and H. Räisänen also maintain that here Paul argues against *Jewish* boasting. But since they assert contemporary Judaism did not seek 'justification' by works of the law,[48] Paul's accusation cannot be directed to the Jew's attitude, but to the Torah itself; and it is made only retrospectively with the intention of defending the legitimacy of a Gentile faith.[49] Developing Sanders' view, Dunn and J.A. Ziesler argue that Paul does not primarily oppose the claim of *individual* merit, but rather (a general) *Jewish* boasting of a 'national righteousness' in the possession of the law, and in an exclusive covenantal relationship with God.[50] Finally, J. Gager and L. Gaston assert that Paul does not present a polemic against Judaism, but merely attacks *Jewish* exclusive boasting in order to include Gentiles in God's salvation apart from the law.[51] Although these views may differ in details and emphases, that 3:27 is against

---

46 Elliott, *Rhetoric*, 149 n. 2. In fact, his entire book seems to aim to establish this thesis.

47 Bultmann, *Theology* 1, 242-243, 283; Käsemann, *Romans*, 102. So also Hübner, *Law*, 117-118.

48 This is also the opinion of a Jewish scholar Lapide: Lapide and Stuhlmacher, *Paul*, 37-39, and of Wright, *People*, 334-335, who endorses Sanders.

49 Sanders, *Jewish People*, 32-36, 46; Räisänen, *Paul*, 170-71.

50 Dunn, *Romans* 1, 185, 191; *idem*, *Jesus*, *Paul*, 222-225, objects to Sanders, *Jewish People*, 3; cf. Räisänen, *Paul*, 50, 69-71; Ziesler, *Romans*, 116-117.

51 Gager, *Origins*, 250-252; Gaston, *Paul*, 122-123.

Jewish boasting has become a traditional view,[52] against which, however, Elliott argues.

Following Sanders, Elliott maintains that the pursuit of righteousness by works of the Law is not predominant in early Judaism, and so Paul does not need to present a polemic against Judaism.[53] On the other hand, against Dunn and Gager, Elliott attempts to prove that 3:20 and 3:27 do not present a dispute over Jewish convictions. He asserts two points in his argument. First, since the phrase δικαιωθήσεται ἐξ ἔργων νόμου (3:20) is not found outside Paul, there is little ground to conclude that his readers will understand this declaration as a repudiation of Jewish convictions. After all, Elliott does not regard 3:21-4:25 as an argument directed primarily to the *Jewish* readers (in the Roman church), and thus the boasting in 3:27 does not refer to Jewish, but to human boasting in general. Second, the boasting in 3:27 does not specifically refer to Jewish boasting, because it is not in line with Paul's theological axiom of divine impartiality. Although 'boasting in God' and 'boasting in the law' in 2:17-23 clearly refer to Jewish boasting, these boasts are not *rejected* but *qualified*. Thus Jewish boasting in 2:17-23 cannot be direct evidence for Paul's exclusion of the boasting in 3:27.[54]

We do not find Elliott's hypothesis convincing, however. Firstly, he clearly understands 'the law' in 3:20 and 3:27 as the Mosaic Law. Boasting is excluded not διὰ νόμου ... τῶν ἔργων, but on the contrary (οὐχί, ἀλλὰ)[55], διὰ νόμου πίστεως as explained in 3:21-26. The righteousness of God is revealed χωρὶς νόμου (3:21), so justification is possible only χωρὶς ἔργων νόμου (3:28). If this is the case, then who can possibly assume that they are justified by works of the Mosaic Law if not the *Jews* who possess it? Elliott's assertion that 'the Jew's accountability to God through the Torah has been made paradigmatic for *univer-*

---

52 Haldane, *Romans*, 94-95; Meyer, *Romans* 1, 181-182; Schoeps, *Paul*, 205; Watson, *Paul*, 133; Moxnes, *Theology*, 40, 269; Wilckens, *Römer* 1, 244, 248; Howard, 'Romans 3:21-31', 232; Hübner, *Law*, 115, 117-118; Vincent in Wuest, 'Romans', 63; Black, *Romans*, 71; Barrett, *Romans*, 78; Käsemann, *Romans*, 102; Gifford, *Romans*, 94; Locke, *Paraphrase* 2, 509: even to the point of judging Gentiles; some say human boasting in general, others say Christian boasting (see Meyer, *Romans* 1, 181, for reference).

53 Elliott, *Rhetoric*, 207-208.

54 Elliott, *Rhetoric*, 214.

55 See Thompson, 'Double Critique', 520-531.

sal human accountability to God (3:19-20)' so as to deny the boasting of '*any* human beings',[56] seems highly improbable, because Paul establishes Gentile sinfulness apart from the law (cf. 1:18-32; 5:12-21). Although the expressions with universal connotation in 3:19 ('every mouth', 'all the world') do not confine 3:20 to the Jew alone, Elliott fails to perceive that 3:19-20 is primarily designed to undermine *Jewish* complacency.[57] So also does he fail to note that some of the Qumran texts (especially 4QMMT 104-118=4Q 394-399) indicate that the concept of 'justification by the works of the law' was familiar to some Jews.[58]

Secondly, the clear Jewish boasting in 2:17-20 is not mentioned merely to *qualify* Jewish boasting, but ultimately to prepare the ground for a direct attack on the Jews, and consequently the indictment is intensified ('You boast in the law': 2:17b, 23a → 'but you break the law': 2:23c, 25; 'you boast in God': 2:17c → 'you dishonour God and blaspheme his name': 2:23b-24). And also in 3:27 Paul claims that it is excluded. The rhetorical question in 2:23 clearly implies that Jews cannot and should not boast in the law and in God. Elliott does not mention the significance of the definite article (ἡ) before καύχησις, although it has been taken by many exegetes as an indisputable reference to the Jewish boasting mentioned previously in 2:17, 23.[59] No universal or human 'boasting', only a Jewish one, has been mentioned in 1:18-3:26. But that Paul continues to talk primarily to the Jews is evident here.[60]

---

56 Elliott, *Rhetoric*, 148, 152, 155.
57 *Pace* Elliott, *Rhetoric*, 214. See above pp. 129-150 for our earlier discussion on 3:1-20.
58 See Eisenman and Wise, *Dead Sea*, 180-220, putting 'Works Reckoned as Righteousness' as the title of the chapter that expounds 4QMMT. See also Martínez, *Dead Sea*, 84-85.
59 Sanders, *Jewish People*, 33, who also lists Wilckens, Räisänen. So also Dunn, *Romans* 1, 185; *idem*, *Jesus, Paul*, 222, 238; Conybeare and Howson, *Life*, 506; Gifford, *Romans*, 94; Boylan, *Romans*, 60.
60 *Pace* Elliott, *Rhetoric*, 205ff. His contention is based on his hypothesis that 1:18-4:25 is not a debate with Judaism. In opposition to this position, we need to highlight several elements which indicate the weakness of Elliott's view:
(1) Paul's polemical declaration that the righteousness of God has been revealed 'apart from the law' is most probably directed to those who assume a

Thirdly, Elliott does not note that Paul's rhetorical argument in Romans 1-4 is presented on two levels: on the surface he appears to deal with universal issues, but at a deeper level he directs his indictment especially towards the Jews. Thus Elliott exposes the weakness of his view when he asserts that applying the exclusion of boasting only to the Jews undermines Paul's theological axiom of divine impartiality and universal accountability at the Judgement. Paul's constant concern (at least in Romans 1-4) is to explain the issues within the context of the relationship between Jews and Gentiles, with the aim of undermining Jewish pride and boasting. As in the Corinthian church, boasting is an immense threat to unity in the Roman church.[61] So Paul opposes all boasting: against the judgemental attitude of the 'weak'/the 'strong' in general (14:1-15:7, cf. 12:16), and more specifically against the (foreseeable[62]) arrogance of the Gentile believers towards the Jews (11:17-24). Excluding the spirit of boasting and arrogance is, for Paul, the prerequisite for affirming equality and for pro-

---

righteousness by observing the law (cf. 3:20).

(2) His appeal to 'the Law and the Prophets' for witness is to authenticate 'the righteousness of God apart from the law' to those who acknowledge the authority of the OT, and, in general terms, it is Jews who are the ones who certainly do.

(3) The terms δικαιοσύνη θεοῦ, ἱλαστήριον and ἀπολύτρωσις carry strong Jewish atonement motifs, and the fact that Paul does not elucidate these complicated terms seems to indicate that he assumes that his (primary) addressees know their meanings, or that he is taking over, with redacted additions, a preformed (Jewish Christian) tradition.

(4) The exclusion of 'ἡ καύχησις' seems to have been asserted to undermine the Jewish boasting mentioned in 2:17, 23.

(5) That God is not the God of Jews only but of Gentiles too, is recalled most probably to correct a Jewish conviction that (despite the Shema) only the Jews have a special relationship with God.

(6) Whether 'faith' nullifies the law or not is primarily a Jewish concern.

(7) The phrase 'Abraham, our forefather according to flesh' (4:1) almost certainly indicates that Paul is talking to the Jewish readers (though 'honorary Jews' are not excluded).

Therefore these items are almost certainly directed to a Jewish readership. This consideration will enable us to interpret 3:21-4:25 from the perspective that here Paul is explaining his doctrine of justification to the *Jewish* believers (in Rome), with the implication that the justification of (believing) Gentiles can thus be theologically affirmed or even defended.

61 Moxnes, *Theology*, 272.
62 See *infra* pp. 220-221, 270-271.

moting unity. But in 1:18-4:25 Paul rejects primarily the national, religious, and ethical boasting of the Jews over and against Gentiles. He indicates that the Jews boast in their possession of the law, in their special and exclusive relationship with God, and in their Abrahamic ancestry. We will now turn to examine these areas of boasting in order to grasp the significance of the absolute exclusion of such boasting for the Jews and the implication of its exclusion for the Gentiles.

B. The Jewish Boasting in the Law

Dunn is probably correct to note that the order of the questions in 3:27 indicates that the boasting is related to the law.[63] That the question, 'Where then is *the* boasting?' refers back to Jewish pride in God and in the law (2:17, 23), is indicated by the second question, 'By what (kind of) law?'. The third question, 'Of works?', clarifies further that the boasting is related to the Torah.[64] Paul rhetorically and progressively confirms that the boasting on the basis of the works of the law was to be excluded. The Torah was given to Israel by God. Thus it was not wrong to possess it and to rely upon it, if they also observed it (cf. 2:25).[65] He also regarded positively the Gentiles' performance of the requirement of the law (2:14-15), i.e. the obedience of faith (9:30-10:8; 15:17-18). His indictment of the Jewish interlocutor in 2:21-24, however, indicates that Jews generally boasted of keeping the law too (as *2 Apocaypse of Baruch*, which is strongly Pharisaic in character, portrays).[66]

---

63 Dunn, *Romans* 1, 191-192.

64 Hübner, *Law*, 115; Rienecker and Rogers, *Linguistic Key*, 357; Dunn, *Romans* 1, 192.

65 According to the Gospel tradition, Jesus said that his disciples should do what the Pharisees *teach* but should not follow what they *do*, since they do the opposite of what they say (Matt 5:20; 23:3). The Pharisees boasted of living according to the law (Luke 18:11-12; cf. John 9:41), so they proudly declared to Jesus, 'We are disciples of Moses!' (John 9:28), which implies that they not merely possessed the law but actively followed the instructions of Moses (cf. *Yom.* 4a; see Str-B 2, 535); Beasley-Murray, *John*, 158; Schnackenburg, *John* 2, 251, 498 n. 38. However, Jesus did not endorse their claim that they kept the law (Matt 23).

66 E.g. *2 Apoc. Bar.* 43:1, 3; 44:7, 14; 46:4-6; 85:2-3 indicate Jewish self-complacency in ability to fulfil the law (cf. Phil 3:6). But such compla-

What Paul objects to is that not only do Jews not *do* the law (2:21-24), but they also boast against the *Gentiles* who do not have it (cf. *2 Apoc. Bar.* 77:3).[67] Paul then denounces their boasting in the possession of the law *without* corresponding works of the law, that is to say, '(an alleged) *fulfilment of the works of the Law*'.[68] Paul has already argued that the possession of the law without obedience to it cannot justify Jewish boasting, for whilst (believing) Gentiles *do* the law (2:14, 15, 26, 27), (unbelieving) Jews *break* it (2:17-24, 25b).[69] On the basis of performance of the law Jewish boasting over Gentiles is ruled out absolutely (3:27).

Furthermore, it is excluded by the place given to νόμος πίστεως. The aorist passive ἐξεκλείσθη, 'it *was* excluded', denotes that the main reason for the exclusion is related to what has been already accomplished by Christ as described in 3:25,[70] rather than to the *present* Jewish ill-performance of the law. 'By what *kind* of law?', asks Paul, and confirms that the boasting is excluded *not* through the Torah that requires works, but through 'the Torah, now fulfilled in faith'.[71] He stresses this with the

---

cency is in contrast to the self-depreciation of *4 Ezra* (see Charles, *Apocrypha* 2, 478); Ps 119 does not allow for 'boasting' about Torah fidelity either, while extolling Torah as a divine gift of light and life.

67 Cf. Haldane, *Romans*, 95. Although Hübner, *Law*, 113, seems incorrect to say that Jews do not boast in the *performance* of the law (for, he asserts, 'nothing is said about his being proud of having done the Law': cf. Luke 18:11-12), he is certainly right to stress that they boast in the *possession* of the law over the Gentiles who do not have it.

68 Hübner, *Law*, 113-114, 124; Bauernfeind, *TDNT* 1, 351.

69 *Supra* pp. 109-129.

70 Dunn, *Romans* 1, 185.

71 Wright, *Messiah*, 117: 'νόμος refers not to some abstract "principle", but to the Torah, now fulfilled in faith.' So also Cranfield, *Romans* 1, 219-220; Wilckens, *Römer* 1, 245; Friedrich, 'Gesetz', 415: 'The law of faith in Rom 3:27 is the [Mosaic] Law which testifies to righteousness by faith in Rom 3.21' (as cited in Hübner, *Law*, 115).

The interpretation of the νόμος in 3:27-28 as 'principle' also gains wide support: e.g. Sanders, *Jewish People*, 33; Zerwick and Grosvenor, *Analysis*, 466; Shedd, *Romans*, 85; Nygren, *Romans*, 162-163; Barrett, *Romans*, 79; NIV, REB, NAB, NJB, RSV. Recently Watson, *Paul*, 132, following Michel, Kuss and van Dülmen, has defended this view. This may be reasonable in Greek, but to Jewish readers, as we have established earlier (p. 168-169 n. 60), the νόμος

The Equality of Jew and Gentile in Justification 171

οὐχί, ἀλλὰ construction, which indicates a strong denial of the former with a strong alternative (cf. Luke 1:60; 12:51).[72] He further reinforces his argument (γάρ)[73] with a concluding remark, 'By faith [alone] a man (ἄνθρωπος: i.e. *all* humanity) is justified', and he further clarifies by adding, 'apart from the works of the law' (3:28).[74] The faith is the faith in Jesus Christ that brings the righteousness of God to *all* who believe, whether they be Jews or Gentiles (3:21-22). It is faith which believers exercise,[75] and Paul knows that some Gentiles are exercising such a faith (1:5; 9:30; 15:18; 16:26; cf. 2:14-15, 25-29), while most Jews pursue righteousness through keeping the law, and do 'not submit to God's [way to obtain] righteousness' (9:31; 10:2-3; 11:7). Later Paul openly describes the lack of faith of many Jews (Rom 9-11), but here in 3:21-31 he intends to establish the firm foundation of the significance of faith for this new era (νυνί: 3:21) in obtaining God's righteousness and man's justification. The argument by Paul, apostle to the Gentiles, concerning the law of faith apart from the works of the law clearly secures the sufficiency and the legitimacy of Gentile salvation obtained by faith alone and grace alone.

C. The Jewish Boasting in God

With the particle ἤ, 'or' (3:29) Paul reinforces his argument,[76] and this time he attempts to exclude Jewish boasting in God. The

---

would mean the Torah. However, Räisänen, '"Gesetz"', 101-117, sharply opposes Hübner's view that the νόμος here is to be identified with the Torah.

72 See Thompson, 'Double Critique', 528-530.

73 The γάρ is preferred to the οὖν in Nestle-Aland[27] and UBS[4]; see Metzger, *Textual Commentary*, 509.

74 This contention stands in contrast with Jewish belief (e.g. *2 Apoc. Bar.* 51:3, 7; *4 Ezra* 7:77).

75 Dunn, *Romans* 1, 186; *pace* Gaston, *Paul*, 172: 'the Torah of [God's] faithfulness'; Barth, *Romans*, 107, 110: 'God's faithfulness'.

76 The particle does not introduce 'an alternative hypothesis' (*pace* Sanday and Headlam, *Romans*, 96; Moo, *Romans* 1, 254), nor simply 'add[s] rhetorical questions' (*pace* BAGD, 342), 'in case what has just been asserted in ver. 28 might still be doubted' (Meyer, *Romans* 1, 183). Rather it introduces another set of questions to stress the same essential argument. The first set of questions (3:27) is substantiated by the γάρ in v. 28, and the second (v. 29) by the εἴπερ in v. 30; thus the argument in 3:27-30 is increasingly intensified.

rhetorical question, 'Is God the God of Jews only?,' indicates a Jewish claim over against the Gentiles of a special and exclusive relationship with God,[77] as was indeed the case in Judaism. The Jewish boast in God shown in the OT certainly affected views in Paul's day. We shall examine the Jewish boasting in God in order to assess the significance of Paul's argument that God is the God of the Gentiles too.

God had chosen Israel out of all the peoples (Deut 7:6) and made a covenant with them: 'I will take you as my own people, and I will be your God' (Exod 6:7); 'Before all your people I will do wonders never before done in any nation in all the world' (Exod 34:10). Thus Jews thought their boasting in God was perfectly legitimate (cf. Jer 9:23-24; Ps 34:2; 44:8), for they have the true God as their God, who is far beyond comparison with the gods of the Gentiles.[78] *Their boast in God is clearly over against the Gentiles.* 'All [Gentiles] who have raged against him will come to him and be put to shame. But in the Lord all the descendants of Israel will be found righteous and will exult' (Isa 45:24b-25; 41:16; 60:19; cf. 2 Kgs 21:12; Jer 23:2). 'He is your praise (LXX: καύχημα); he is your God' (Deut 10:21a); '...he will set you in praise (LXX: καύχημα), fame and honour high above all the nations' (Deut 26:19; cf. Deut 4:7-8; 28:1, 12-13, 43-44). Such a Jewish claim to be a people special to God was also abundantly expressed during the intertestamental period.[79]

The notion of the father-child relationship is especially stressed (*Pss. Sol.* 17:26-27). The arrival of the son of David would mean the end of Jewish association with Gentiles: 'the aliens and foreigners will no longer live near them. ... He will judge peoples and nations in the wisdom of his righteousness. And he will have Gentile nations serving him under his yoke' (*Pss. Sol.* 17:28-30).

---

77 Beet, *Romans*, 124: 'another ground of Jewish boasting' that God is the God of Jews only.

78 Haldane, *Romans*, 95.

79 E.g. God is the Father of Israel (Wis 2:16; *Jub.* 1:13, 24-25, 28; *Sib. Or.* 3:726), so he is called 'Lord our God' (more than a dozen times in Bar 1-2; *Pss. Sol.* 17:3), the 'saviour of Israel' (*3 Macc* 7:16), and the 'God of Israel' (Bar 3:1, 4). Thus God is the ground for their boasting (Sir 31:10; *Pss. Sol.* 17:1). For the Jews Israel is God's first born (Sir 36:12; *4 Ezra* 6:58; *Jub.* 2:20; *Pss. Sol.* 18:4), and God's own people (*Ass. Mos.* 1:12). The Gentile Assyrians may boast in their mighty weapons, but the Jews glory (καυχᾶσθαι) in the name of the Lord (Jdt 9:7; 10:8; Sir 50:20).

That God is the father of the Israelite nation is clearly known in the OT (e.g. Deut 14:1; 32:6; Isa 63:16; Jer 31:9). God has promised even the unfaithful northern kingdom of Israel that they will again be called 'the sons of the living God' (Hos 1:10), and this promise is claimed again in *Jub.* 1:24-25[80] (cf. Sir 4:10). Such references surely highlight the Jews' complacency in seeing themselves as distinct from the Gentiles; they 'possessed' the most powerful God (e.g. Bar 3:35; 4:4).[81] Thus E. Urbach's 'exaggeration' can be accepted: 'The belief common to all Jews at the beginning of the first century was that their God was the only God and their religion the only true religion.'[82]

Such a declaration in 3:29-30 is a radically bold assertion against the dominant conception of God in Judaism in Paul's day, as may plausibly be reconstructed, for example, from the remark made by R. Simeon ben Jochai of the second century AD: 'God spoke to the Israelites: I am God over all who come into the world, but my name have I associated only with you; I do not call myself the God of the nations of the world, but the God of Israel' (*Exod. R.* 29:4, the midrash on Exod 20:2).[83] Of course God's lordship over the whole universe had been claimed, as N.A. Dahl notes from Ps 50:7 and Exod 20:2.[84] However, the inclusion of Gentiles under God's lordship is not for their blessing but for God's judgement and eschatological rule over them (Zech 14:9),[85]

---

80 'I will be a father to them, and they will be sons to me. And they will all be called "sons of the living God." And every angel and spirit will know and acknowledge that they are my sons and I am their father in uprightness and righteousness' (*Jub.* 1:24-25).

81 Nickelsburg, *Jewish Literature*, 112.

82 Urbach, 'Self-Isolation', 273.

83 As cited in Dunn, *Romans* 1, 188; originally noted by Str-B 3, 185; followed by Käsemann, *Romans*, 103; Schoeps, *Paul*, 240; but see Dahl, *Studies*, 182-183, who points out that the assertion of *Exod. R.* 29:4 does not deny an axiomatic universalistic monotheism.

84 See Dahl, *Studies*, 183-184. We may add some more references, e.g. *1 En.* 84:2, where God is described as the 'King of kings and God of the whole world', and *Jub.* 15:31, which notes: 'there are many nations and many peoples, and all are His...'. The very next verse however affirms Israel's special relationship with God (*Jub.* 15:32; cf. Deut 32:8-9). The OT has already portrayed Yahweh as 'the Lord, the God of all mankind' (Jer 32:27), the 'King of the nations' (Jer 10:7), and the 'God of the spirits of all mankind' (Num 16:22; 26:17).

85 Similarly Dahl, *Studies*, 186.

and the Jewish claim of their own unique and exclusive relationship with God is certainly uncompromising.

It is striking indeed, then, to see Paul claiming, against such a background, that God is not the God of Jews only, but of Gentiles too.[86] This claim rests on the belief that Gentiles can also be God's people. Later in 9:25-26 Paul makes it explicit by quoting LXX Hos 2:1 and 23 that Gentiles who were not 'my people' are now called 'my people', and thus applies the promise to Israel in Hos 1:10 to the *Gentiles* solely (9:24-26).[87] But now here in 3:29-30 he confines himself to declaring that Gentiles too are included in the special relationship with God, which so far only Jews have claimed. For Paul the arrival of the Son of David does not mean the *end* of Jewish association with Gentiles; rather it is the *beginning* of the new and equal relationship between Jews and Gentiles in him. According to Judaism there was a clear distinction in the relationship of Jews and Gentiles vis-à-vis God, but Paul repeatedly denies this distinction (2:11; 3:22; 10:12; Gal 3:28; Col 3:11).[88]

It is universally recognised that here Paul uses the Shema, the fundamental Jewish confession, 'Hear, O Israel, the Lord our God is one Lord' (Deut 6:4; 2 Kgs 19:15; Isa 44:6; 45:6; cf. 1 Cor 8:4-6; 1 Tim 2:4-6), to overthrow the Jews' claims of their superiority and exclusive relationship with God, and to stress the equal belonging of the Gentiles to God.[89] Since God is one, and is the God of both Jews and Gentiles, he calls people 'not from among Jews

---

86 So correctly Grässer, *Alte Bund*, 256. *Pace* Fitzmyer, *Romans*, 365, for contending that here Paul is passing on the convictions already recognised by the psalmists and prophets. The wordings of LXX Ps 65:8, Εὐλογεῖτε ἔθνη τὸν Θεὸν ἡμῶν, 'Praise our God, O peoples', and LXX Ps 116:1, 'Praise the Lord, all you Gentiles, and sing praises to him, all you peoples,' may correspond with Paul's, but Fitzmyer does not note the contextual shift. Paul's modification must be regarded as significant and original. See our earlier discussion *supra* pp. 58-68.

87 See *infra* pp. 246-248, for further discussion. Paul quotes the Hosea passages to support his assertion that God's glory is also prepared for the Gentiles. Our qualification that the citation is 'solely' applied to the Gentiles, is based on the introductory remark in 9:27, 'But (δέ) *about Israel* Isaiah makes this proclamation' (REB); the quotation in 9:25-26 is about Gentiles. So also in 10:20-21.

88 Dahl, *Studies*, 186.

89 Beker, *Paul*, 82.

only, but also from among Gentiles' (9:24: NASB). He is the Lord of all, 'for there is no distinction between Jew and Greek' (10:12: NASB). Thus Gentiles can and do glorify God for his mercy (11:32; 15:9), because he welcomes, without any partiality, people from every nation (cf. Acts 10:34-35).

The grounds for Paul's own radical declaration that God is *equally* the God of the Gentiles, are emphatically demonstrated with very good reasons in 3:30. The particle εἴπερ[90] 'introduces a conditional clause which presents a new but decisive ground for the apodosis'.[91] Traditionally the notion of monotheism was understood as the basis for Paul's assertion that God is the God of Gentiles too. A. Nygren represents this view: 'As [i.e. Since indeed] there is only one God, so there is only one way of salvation for all mankind. There is no distinction here between Jew and Gentile.'[92]

R.W. Thompson has recently challenged this traditional view, saying, 'Monotheism alone was insufficient to lead to the idea of God's total lordship over the Gentiles.'[93] By rendering the relative pronoun ὅς as purely descriptive, he points out that Paul is not primarily stressing monotheism, but the fact that it is (one and) the *same* God who shall *justify* everyone by faith, and so he

---

90 This reading, rather than the more common variant ἐπείπερ, seems original: so Nestle-Aland[27]; UBS[4], Cranfield, *Romans* 1, 222 n. 2. 'Ἐπείπερ, 'since indeed', denotes 'known and unquestioned certainty' (Thayer, *Lexicon*, 229; cf. BAGD, 284; 'since' in NIV, NJB, NRSV, NASB). Cf. Shedd, *Romans*, 87: εἴπερ has a stronger meaning than ἐπείπερ, and 'introduces an assertion that is indisputable'. It connotes the condition that is in agreement with reality, with factual circumstances, i.e. 'since it is so'.

91 *EDNT*, 1, 393; so also Thayer, *Lexicon*, 172. *Pace* Lightfoot, *Notes*, 101, who asserts that εἴπερ introduces an assumption that is 'purely hypothetical and in itself seems to imply neither probability nor improbability'. Cf. Stowers, *Diatribe*, 166; Davies, *Faith*, 139; 'if' with a conditional force, NEB, RV, REB. The fact that there is only one God is an unquestioned certainty for Paul; thus even if εἴπερ is preferred as original, it is 'decisively attested in the place of ἐπείπερ' (Sanday and Headlam, *Romans*, 96).

92 Nygren, *Romans*, 166. So also Dunn, *Romans* 1, 188-189; Black, *Romans*, 71; Barrett, *Romans*, 80; Ziesler, *Romans*, 106. Similarly Beet, *Romans*, 124: 'If there be *one God*, and if He *will justify* all on the same terms, then is He the God of both Jews and Gentiles'; Ridderbos, *Paul*, 339.

93 Thompson, 'Inclusion', 546.

is certainly the God of Gentiles too.[94] Thus he renders 3:29c-30: "'Yes, of Gentiles also, since the God who will justify the circumcised by faith and the uncircumcised by faith is one'".[95] Paul makes a strong affirmation that *the God of Jews is equally the God of Gentiles* upon the basis *both* of the undeniable belief of monotheism *and* the assertion of justification by faith, which he has already established in 3:21-26, 28 and now uses to describe the monotheistic God. Paul's intention in stressing that both Jews and Gentiles have the same God, is to affirm that Gentiles have equal standing before God with Jews.[96]

Since the traditional division between Jews and Gentiles had been justified on a theological basis, Paul attempts to remove such a division by offering a new theological argument, employing 'God-language to create a new identity for a community consisting of Jewish and non-Jewish Christians'.[97] As he did in 2:11 (there is no partiality with God), again in 3:29-30 (there is only one God:[98] also 1 Cor 8:6; Gal 3:20), Paul uses the traditional Jewish expressions to argue against Jews (including Christian Jews).[99] He does not isolate himself from 'tradition' totally (cf. Gal 1:14).[100] Although he has destroyed his own building of

---

[94] Thompson, 'Inclusion', 546; the same point is made by Hays, 'Abraham', 84-85. This should be possible if we take εἷς to indicate not in the first place monotheism but sameness.

[95] Here Thompson's translation is not as original as he appears to claim: it is very similar to the translation of NASB, and to other descriptive renderings, including KJV, NIV, JB; cf. RSV, NEB, TEV.

[96] Cf. Grässer, *Alte Bund*, 257. The section 3:29c-30 is one sentence in Greek, so 3:30 may be divided (in translation or in interpretation) before the ναί, rather than before the εἴπερ, in which case the phrase ναὶ καὶ ἐθνῶν receives the strongest emphasis. Then we may render it, 'Since there is certainly one God who will justify the circumcision by faith and the uncircumcision through the same faith, he is surely the God of the Gentiles too'. Cf. Hays's rendering in 'Abraham', 84. Both Thompson and Hays stress that Paul does not merely repeat a common belief that God, being one, is the God of the Jews and of the Gentiles (Dahl, *Studies*, 189), but stresses that God justifies Gentiles in the same way as he does Jews.

[97] Moxnes, *Theology*, 14.

[98] See Dahl, 'The One God of Jews and Gentiles (Romans 3:29-30)', *Studies*, 178-191.

[99] Moxnes, *Theology*, 9; see *Theology*, 32-55 for Paul's special emphasis on 'God' in Rom 1-4, 9-11.

[100] Moxnes, *Theology*, 31.

Judaism, as a trained Jewish thinker, he erects a new one of Christian theology with the old bricks of Judaism.[101] 'Ironically, using a traditional belief that all Jews would agree upon, Paul has drawn a conclusion with which most Jews would disagree.'[102]

How could Paul have such a different understanding of monotheism? Dahl observes some fundamental differences between the traditional Jewish view and Paul's, and correctly concludes, 'Only if we understand the rabbinic doctrine of God on its own premises does it become clear in what sense Paul turns against it "with unheard of boldness"'.[103] However, Dahl does not even raise this important question. From Dahl's own references we can note that it is Paul's apostolic self-awareness concerning the Gentile mission that has resulted in such a departure. Dahl draws attention to the Midrash on the Psalm 93:1:

> "Who would not fear thee, O king of the nations"? The Holy One, blessed be he, said to Jeremiah: "You call me King of the nations? But am I not their (Israel's) king"? He said to Him: "Because thou hast called me prophet to the nations (Jer 1:5), I too call thee King of the nations."

The same understanding is expressed in *Exodus Rabba* 29:9:

> "I am YHWH your God" (Exod. 20:2): It is written: "The lion has roared, who will not fear"? (Amos 3:8). This explains what is written: "Who would not fear thee, O King of the nations? For this is thy due." The prophets said to Jeremiah: "What do you mean by saying King of the nations? All the other prophets call him King of Israel, and you call him King of the nations." He answered them: "I heard him say to me: 'I appointed you a prophet to the nations' (Jer. 1:5), and [that is why] I say: 'King of the nations'."[104]

The heart of the question of the prophets to Jeremiah is why he calls the God of Israel the King of the *nations*. In the first passage it is God who questions Jeremiah, and in the second one the many

---

101 I am indebted for this analogy to Professor Martin Hengel, who expressed it during our tutorial in Tübingen (25 April, 1992). M. Hooker, *Continuity*, 25, offers a similar analogy: 'the old water of Judaism has not been thrown away, but transformed into the wine of the gospel'.
102 Moxnes, *Theology*, 41.
103 Dahl, *Studies*, 188; the inner quotation is taken from Käsemann.
104 Both references are cited in Dahl, *Studies*, 185-186.

prophets ask him the same question, because Jeremiah is the only prophet who calls God the King of the *nations*. Jeremiah's answer clearly shows that it is his own self-consciousness of being called as *a prophet to the nations*. It seems most probable then that Paul's solemn declaration, 'Yes, God is certainly the God of Gentiles too', is also heavily linked to his own self-consciousness of being called to be an apostle to the Gentiles (11:13; 15:15-16; Gal 1:15-16; 2:7; cf. Acts 9:15; 22:21; 26:17-18; Eph 3:8-9; Col 1:23-2:5). It is then clear that Paul's consciousness had led him to shape the structure of his argument here.

Jeremiah was called to be a prophet *to* the nations (προφήτης εἰς ἔθνη) and appointed *over* the nations (ἐπὶ ἔθνη). His call was primarily to deliver the message of wrath to the nations (Jer 1:10); his message to the nations is full of woes and disasters, and it extends to many chapters (e.g. Jer 25:15, 29-32; chs. 46-51). In fact in the Book of Jeremiah he calls God the 'God of Israel' no fewer than thirty-five times, but never the 'God of the nations'! He makes it clear that the blessing of the nations is totally dependent upon Israel's obedience to God (Jer 4:1-2). Then he is *Israel's* prophet *to* the nations to bring them the message of *wrath* from the God of *Israel*.

Paul is, however, very different from Jeremiah, though he is also called 'to the nations' (λειτουργός ... εἰς τὰ ἔθνη: 15:15).[105] Above all, he is apostle *of* the Gentiles (ἀπόστολος τῶν ἐθνῶν). With the full consciousness of his vocation and with all possible emphatic construction, Paul declares, 'μὲν ... εἰμι ἐγὼ ἐθνῶν ἀπόστολος: *I am* indeed an apostle *of Gentiles*' (11:13). Again the ἐθνῶν is more emphasised than the ἀπόστολος. He *belongs to the nations*. He was called to be an apostle *to* the Gentiles, *of* the Gentiles and *for* the Gentiles. He is a Jewish apostle *for the nations* to bring them the message of *good news* from the God of Jews who *is also* the God of *Gentiles*. Paul may not be so unusual in believing that God had a universal purpose/rule,[106] but the way he establishes the place of the Gentiles is unprecedented. His self-understanding is much deeper and more radical than that of the prophets of the OT, even more pro-

---

[105] We may say that Paul declares 'the year of the Lord's favour' (cf. Isa 61:2a; Luke 4:19) whilst Jeremiah declared 'the day of vengeance of our God' (cf. Isa 61:2b).

[106] See Wright, *People*, 267-272.

found than that of Jeremiah, as far as their relation with Gentiles is concerned. Thus we suggest that it is his apostolic self-consciousness that has influenced the structuring of his argument for Gentile inclusion into God's salvific blessing (cf. 2:10; 15:8-9).[107]

D. The Jewish Boasting in Abraham

Having given the impression that he is saying that 'by this faith we cancel the Law',[108] Paul typically brings a balance by saying that the faith which excludes Jewish boasting in the law and in their special claim on God, does not nullify the Torah, but rather establishes it (3:31). This bold, at present unexpected claim, indicates that what Paul opposes is not the Torah itself, but the exclusivist Jewish complacency in the 'works of the law'.[109] For Paul 'faith is the true content of the law'.[110] He substantiates his remark by taking up the case of Abraham. On the other hand, the linguistic link of 'boasting'[111] indicates that he attempts to exclude Jewish pride in Abraham based on their exclusive ancestral covenant (cf. *Pss. Sol.* 18:4). Before we investigate Paul's argument in Romans 4, we shall briefly examine Jewish boasting in their Abrahamic ancestry so as to note the significance of including Gentiles in that same ancestry.

A Jewish Christian scholar, Jakób Jocz, remarks on the Jewish religious consciousness in connection with Abraham:

> To have Abraham as a father, to claim God's promises, to keep his Commandments, to belong to the commonwealth of the Chosen people were the *religious* prerogatives of the Jew. ..... To have been born a Jew had religious significance. Even the Jewish sinner was in a different posi-

---

107 Thompson, 'Inclusion', 543-546, plausibly asserts that 'the primary topic of Rom 3, 27-30 is the inclusion of the Gentiles', which also implies the exclusion of Jewish boasting. Howard, 'Romans 3:21-31', 232-233: 3:27-30 argues for 'one thing, i.e. the inclusion of the Gentiles'. See also Siker, *Disinheriting*, 185-198.
108 Dodd, *Romans*, 86.
109 So Dunn, *Romans* 1, 193-194.
110 Schoeps, *Paul*, 210.
111 Though the Greek is slightly different (καύχησις in 3:27 and καύχημα in 4:2), the terms have quite similar meaning; see BAGD, 426.

tion from the Gentiles: no Jew goes to Gehenna, as there is no Israelite without some good. Such notions had their root in the conviction that Israel stands in unique relationship to God. "God's love is primarily for Israel as a whole." Israel's election stands for eternity.[112]

Although the sectarian groups did not believe all Jews would be saved merely on the basis of their descent, Jews generally believed in their security in Abrahamic ancestry. According to the *Book of Jubilees*, for example, Jews are the children of God by virtue of their physical descent from Abraham, and especially from Jacob.[113] So Jews claimed to be the true descendants of Abraham (Luke 3:8; John 8:33, 39; cf. Acts 13:26; Isa 51:2; *4 Macc* 6:17, 22; 17:6; 18:1). Having Abraham as their father is especially important soteriologically for Jews (Isa 29:22; 41:8-10; Justin, *Dialogue*, 140), because they believed that, at the Judgement, 'Abraham will sit at the entrance to Gehenna (Gehinnom) and not let anyone from Israel who is circumcised go down there' (*Gen. R.* 48 (30a)).[114] It is also important for their national pride and hope for restoration (Isa 51:2-3; Ezek 33:24; Pr Azar 12). Dishonouring Abraham, thus, was an intolerable offence for the Jews (cf. John 8:53-59). 'We are Abraham's sons' was the religious slogan of the Jews against the oppressive Gentiles.[115] Paul alludes to the fact that (even Christian) Jews boast in being Jews (Hebrews/ Israelites) and in being descendants of Abraham, and so does Paul himself (2 Cor 11:21-22).[116] Paul himself was 'boastful' of his Jewish background (cf. Phil 3:4-6): in circumcision and in being a Jew, who took pride in the law as a son of Pharisees,[117] the most strict observers of the law.

---

112 Jocz, *Jewish People*, 305. See also Edersheim, *Life*, 271; Sadler, *Romans*, 29-30.

113 Charles, *Apocrypha* 2, 13 footnote. R. Shemaiah (c. 50 BC) claimed that Abraham's faith secured merit for his Jewish descendants (Davies, *Rabbinic Judaism*, 269).

114 As cited in Hübner, *Law*, 157 n. 70; see also Jocz, *Jewish People*, 305. Although *Genesis Rabba* is dated about 300 AD, the fact that the first century Jews took Abraham's bosom as a special and secure place of salvation is indicated in, e.g. Luke 16:22-31.

115 Lightfoot, *Galatians*, 163.

116 See Martin, *2 Corinthians*, 375.

117 Klausner, *Paul*, 450-451, infers that the emphatic expression, '*I am* a Pharisee, a son of Pharisees' (Acts 23:6) rather than 'the son of a Pharisee',

To the proud descendants of Abraham (4:1; 9:5), Paul turns to explain why Jews should not boast exclusively even in Abraham (cf. 1QS 2:9; Matt 3:9; Luke 3:8; John 8:33-39; Acts 7:51),[118] and asserts that Gentiles would share the same Abrahamic ancestry. Even more radically, later he openly introduces a notion that 'not all who are descended from Israel [i.e. Jacob] are Israel. Nor because they are his descendants are they all Abraham's children' (9:6-7). Rather he stresses that Abraham's faith through which he was reckoned righteous ultimately made him 'the father of many nations' (4:16-18), hence the blessedness of being justified by faith is also extended to the uncircumcised (4:4-9). Paul's argument in Romans 4 will include the (believing) Gentiles in the blessing of being Abraham's legitimate descendants, on the one hand, and will exclude Jewish boasting in their Abrahamic ancestry, on the other. Since Abraham was credited as righteous not by his works (of the law), he had nothing to boast of; and if Abraham had no grounds to boast of in his 'keeping of the law', how much less so, by implication, will his Jewish (Christian) descendants, who were also reckoned righteous not by works of the law but by faith?

To sum up: We have tried to elucidate Paul's structure of argument with regard to Jewish boasting. He shapes it to exclude Jewish boasting in the possession of the law, in the special relationship with God, and in the covenantal Abrahamic ancestry. On the other hand, he includes the Gentiles in the blessed lordship of God and into the promise given to Abraham. He again asserts the equality of Jew and Gentile. In so doing Paul radically departs from the Jewish understandings of his day, and has made some rather courageous assertions here. Such a perception and boldness derive from his apostolic self-awareness which seeks to affirm the place of the (believing) Gentiles.

3. Abraham the Father of Many Nations / Gentiles: 4:1-25

In this section we will examine the text of 4:1-25 with a special focus on Paul's theological argument that attempts to establish his

---

indicates that Paul's pride in a Pharisaic ancestry over generations is still legitimate (at least for Luke-Acts).
118 See Betz, "Άβραάμ', 2.

unique interpretation of Abraham. Paul lays emphasis on two verses: Gen 15:6 is the backbone of his argument in 4:2-12, and also, together with Gen 17:5, in 4:13-25.[119] Paul's argument in 4:1-12 is based on the chronological fact that Abraham was reckoned righteous *before* his obedience to being circumcised (4:10) or to 'sacrificing' Isaac. What seems most significant is that Paul asserts that this blessedness is *also for the uncircumcised* (4:9), and that Abraham believed *in order to become the father of all who believe without being circumcised* (4:11), as we shall show below. We will also attempt to demonstrate that the much-disputed 4:12 serves to sum up the Gentile emphasis of the argument.

The second part of the argument (4:13-25) is focused on the affirmation that Abraham is the father of many nations. Apart from the assertion that the promise was given *before* the law was instituted, in this section the chronology of Genesis becomes less important for Paul's argument. Here Paul asserts that what Abraham believed, and thus what actually brought him justification (Gen 15:6), was the *promise* that he would become the (spiritual) father of many nations (Gen 17:4-7). This does not seem to be consistent with the chronology of the Genesis narratives (see below). Paul claims further that against all hope Abraham believed the promise of Gen 15:5 in order to become the father of many nations (4:18). But here again Paul's descriptions of the quality of Abraham's faith and of the sequence of events seem incorrect. Philo's remark is more accurate: 'he [Abraham] had a doubt about the birth of Isaac' (*Mut.*, 177). According to 4:20-22 Abraham's faith was reckoned to him as righteousness (Gen 15:4-6) *because* he first believed the promise of the heir who would come from Sarah's dead womb and his own body of about a hundred years old (Gen 17:17-22). Unlike the first part of the argument (4:1-12) the chronology becomes far less important for Paul now; the force of the argument in the concluding part is not based on the logic of chronology but on its reverse.

Hardly any attention has been paid, however, to the exegetical significance of the fact that Paul passes over the issue of the chronological sequences in his argument in 4:13-22 in order to

---

119 See Robertson, 'Genesis 15:6', 262-264, who defends the historicity of Gen 15:6 against Wellhausen, *Prolegomena*, 318-319, von Rad, *Genesis*, 182, 190, and Clements, *Abraham*, 56-57.

affirm that Abraham is the father of many nations (=Gentiles). We will show that, for Paul, the ultimate purpose of the promise to Abraham was to make him the father of many nations, and furthermore, according to Paul, the ultimate reason for Abraham believing God in Gen 15:6 was for him to become the father of many nations (4:18). Our aim in this section is to examine Paul's intention in making such a considerable modification to the Genesis account, and to determine to what extent his argument here is shaped by his self-understanding as apostle to the Gentiles. This will be done with the intention of establishing the theological foundations for the legitimacy of Gentile salvation and of affirming that the blessedness which Abraham and David spoke of is also for the believing Gentiles, since they too are the *legitimate* descendants of Abraham, the father of many nations (=Gentiles).

A. Abraham's Justification and the Blessing of 'the Ungodly': 4:1-8

Paul continues the theme of 'boasting' in chapter 4, but as soon as he has introduced Gen 15:6 as a proof for the exclusion of any boasting in justification, he launches upon an exposition of the Genesis narratives. The understanding of E.H. Gifford, that the exclusion of Jewish boasting and the inclusion of Gentile salvation are further explained with the case of Abraham, seems more plausible than that of C.E.B. Cranfield, who maintains that this whole chapter is an exposition of 3:27.[120] The boasting is excluded because justification has not been earned by works, but it has been reckoned to those who simply believed in God, as the case of Abraham clearly demonstrates. Paul stresses not only the fact that Abraham was reckoned righteous, as Moxnes notes, but also Abraham's faith:[121] for Paul Abraham's faith is the sole basis for legitimising his status as righteous.[122]

---

120 Gifford, *Romans*, 98; *pace* Cranfield, *Romans* 1, 224.

121 Cf. Gifford, *Romans*, 100, may be right to say that in the quotation the verb 'believe' is most stressed. But in Paul's argument in the chapter both verbs, πιστεύω and λογίζομαι, are equally emphasised; see below, pp. 187-202.

122 Cf. Moxnes, *Theology*, 109, 129. Since Moxnes perceives that Paul's direct interest is the understanding of God (4:5, 17, 21, 24) rather than putting

After quoting Gen 15:6 Paul makes it into a general principle by connecting the μισθός: the justification reckoned by believing in God who himself is the 'reward' (μισθός: LXX Gen 15:1), and which is not to be reckoned as a deserved 'wage' (μισθός: 4:4) or debt but as gift and grace.[123] Paul's appeal to the account of David in 4:6-8 has often been understood as Paul's further elucidation of the fact that Abraham's righteousness was reckoned apart from works, by the sheer grace of God.[124] While such an understanding remains undeniable, Paul seems to have a deeper reason here: according to Paul, David talks about the blessedness of the man (ὁ μακαρισμός τοῦ ἀνθρώπου), and 'the man' here refers to 'the ungodly'. Paul affirms the fact that there is 'the ungodly' person whom God reckons righteous even though he only trusts in God. 'His' faith in 4:5 is not Abraham's faith, but 'the ungodly person's' faith. Here with the term ὁ ἀσεβής Paul seems to refer to ungodly humanity in a generic and general sense (cf. 5:6),[125] but more specifically he refers to 'the one who is

---

emphasis on 'faith' *per se* (p. 42), he tends to undermine the aspect of 'faith' which Paul stresses here. However, the fact that 'θεός' occurs only six times in Rom 4 whilst 'πίστις/πιστεύω' occurs fifteen times, suggests Moxnes' contention is not totally convincing. Furthermore, he bypasses 4:9-12, because any predication of God is not present in that passage. Thus he misses Paul's main assertion, 'This blessedness is also for the uncircumcised' (4:9), which Paul develops in the rest of the chapter. Paul's understanding of God in Romans is undoubtedly an important theme: he brings a new perspective on God. And Romans 4 can be considered as Paul's understanding of the God who justified Abraham in uncircumcision. One must note, however, that Paul's primary point of argument here is Abraham's being the father of many nations (i.e. of believing Gentiles), and that the blessedness of being credited righteous apart from works is, therefore, also promised to the Gentiles.

123 Both modification of the quotation to the present tense, 'his faith *is* reckoned as righteousness' (4:5), and the use of the present verbs in 4:4-6, seem to indicate that Paul already applies his argument to his contemporaries (so plausibly Robertson, 'Genesis 15:6', 271) rather than that he only begins the application in 4:23-25 (cf. Cranfield, *Romans* 1, 250).

124 E.g. Robertson, 'Genesis 15:6', 271-272.

125 So Gifford, *Romans*, 100. Here 'the ungodly' (ὁ ἀσεβής) does not seem to refer to Abraham (so also Nygren, *Romans*, 170; Watson, *Paul*, 139, 222 n. 70, but *pace* Hübner, *Law*, 121; Locke, *Paraphrase* 2, 513; Döllinger in Gifford, *Romans*, 100; Robertson, 'Genesis 15:6', 271: 'The beloved and idolized patriarch is the ungodly'), because identifying Abraham as an ἀσεβής is very un-Jewish (Fiedler, 'ἀσεβής', *EDNT* 1, 169; Pr Man 8). Although Abraham was portrayed as the type of proselytes in Judaism (Dunn, *Romans* 1,

outside the covenant, that is, outside the sphere of God's saving righteousness,'[126] i.e. the Gentiles.[127] But Paul certainly gives the impression that he refers to Abraham as ἀσεβής: Abraham was justified as a *Gentile* (ἐν ἀκροβυστίᾳ), and this is indeed one of the boldest points that Paul the Jew could possibly make.[128]

Paul implies that the ungodly *can* have and that some *do* have faith, and, moreover, that God will justify the *faithful* ungodly by reckoning his faith to him as righteousness. Nowhere in his epistles does Paul so stress the concept, 'it was reckoned to him as righteousness' as here in Romans.[129] The crucial verb λογίζομαι[130] connotes, like the Hebrew verb חשׁב in Gen 15:6, God's act of grace, i.e. 'God looked so graciously on the faith of Abraham'.[131] This suggests that Abraham 'had no actual righteousness, but was credited with that which he did not in himself possess'.[132] This also implies that Gentiles, who have neither their own actual righteousness nor covenant-righteousness, *can be* and *are to be nevertheless counted as righteous* when they exercise the faith which Abraham had while he was in uncircumcision.

---

205), neither Judaism nor Paul directly describes him as ungodly (Davies, *Faith*, 160). Cf. Ziesler, *Romans*, 125-126, and Sanday and Headlam, *Romans*, 101, who take the term as Paul's 'contemporary ungodly'.

126 Dunn, *Romans* 1, 205.

127 Paul uses the ἀσεβ- words only in Romans (1:18; 4:5; 5:6; 11:26), and highlights the concept that God justifies the ungodly, which is foreign to the OT and to pre-Pauline Jewish writings (e.g. Exod 23:7; Prov 17:15; 24:24; 28:4; Isa 5:23; CD 1:19, but cf. *4 Ezra* 8:33-40): so Käsemann, *Romans*, 111.

128 Similarly Cosgrove, 'Rom 1:18-4:25', 629, who goes too far, however, in saying that Paul asserts that Abraham is the father of the *believing* Jews who have the *Gentile* faith, and that he 'remains a gentile even after his circumcision'.

129 Paul quotes this clause in Gal 3:6, but it is not expounded in the argument there.

130 This is repeated eleven times in Rom 4 alone (4:3 twice, 5, 6, 8, 9, 10, 11, 22, 23, 24), and plays an important role in the interpretation of this chapter. See Bartsch, 'λογίζομαι', *EDNT* 2, 354-355. Out of 41 occurrences of the verb 'λογίζομαι' in the NT, 19 are found in Romans alone. There are only seven other NT occurrences outside the Pauline writings.

131 Boylan, *Romans*, 65.

132 Dodd, *Romans*, 90.

Probably following the exegetical principle of *gezerah shawah*, the second rule of the school of Hillel,[133] Paul appeals to David (LXX Ps 31:1-2) by emphasising the key verb λογίζεσθαι, although the Psalm contains no element of ἔργα to be quoted here,[134] or the terms 'faith' or 'righteousness'.[135] The quotation from the Psalm undoubtedly stresses that Abraham has found a blessing such as David describes here.[136] But according to the context of 4:5-9, Paul's primary intention is probably to support his own (radical) assertion that God justifies the ungodly and reckons his faith as righteousness. The God whom Abraham believed in Genesis 15 was the God who was faithful to his word of blessing, but here Paul introduces Abraham as though he believed the God who justifies the ungodly. Probably expecting an objection from Jews, he cites David by name[137] to establish 'the blessedness of *the* man', i.e. the ungodly, 'to whom God credits righteousness apart from the law' (4:6). Paul's intention in using ἀσεβής becomes clearer from the construction of 4:9, which

---

[133] Scholars are in agreement that here Paul follows this rule: e.g. Moxnes, *Theology*, 111. Dunn, 'Romans: Analysis', 2855; Lincoln, 'Wrath', 217. See Ellis, *OT in Early Christianity*, 87-91, for Hillel's rules of interpretation.

[134] Fitzmyer, *Romans*, 375; Elliott, *Rhetoric*, 161. The blessedness of forgiveness in David is preconditioned by confessing his transgression to Yahweh in true repentance without hiding nor deceiving (Ps 32:2, 3, 5). These may not be considered as 'works', but the fact that Paul does not quote LXX Ps 31:2b seems to suggest that Paul himself may have regarded 'honest confession' as a 'work' (see Stanley, *Language*, 101).

[135] Most translations render Ps 32:10 as 'he who *trusts* in the Lord' (e.g. NRSV, REB, NAB, NJB, NASB, Moffatt), but both the LXX (τὸν δὲ ἐλπίζοντα ἐπὶ Κύριον) and the MT (וְהַבּוֹטֵחַ בַּיהוָה) connote 'he who *hopes* in the Lord'.

[136] Gifford, *Romans*, 101, 102; Sanday and Headlam, *Romans*, 102.

[137] Together with Abraham and Moses, David is one of the most esteemed figures in first century Judaism (Guerra, 'Romans 4', 261, following Barrett, *First Adam*, 68). It seems significant that Paul especially introduces LXX Ps 31 with David's name: καὶ Δαυὶδ λέγει. The only other occasion with such an introduction in Romans is in 11:9-10, although no less than eleven quotations (cf. Ellis, *Paul's Use*, 150-151) are cited from Psalms attributed to David according to the LXX. Here Paul appeals to the authority of David (*pace* Dunn, *Romans* 1: 205, 'David is cited merely as author, not as a second example alongside Abraham'). Paul may have found it difficult to have Moses, the receiver of the Law for Israel, explicitly witness to his argument for justification by faith apart from the law. However, he indirectly indicates that Moses endorsed his point by using material from the First Book of *Moses*, implying that his interpretation is ultimately based on Moses' understanding.

stresses that this blessedness is also for *the uncircumcision*. With such an intention Paul may well have added the phrase, 'apart from works' (χωρὶς ἔργων: 4:6).

It is not clear according to Psalm 32 (LXX 31), however, whether or not David's point is to stress the blessedness of being forgiven *apart from works,* or to relate such a blessing to the ungodly, or to the Gentiles. In fact, David makes it clear that the blessedness is only for the godly (Ps 32:6), the righteous (Ps 32:11): 'the Lord's unfailing love surrounds the man who *trusts in* him' (Ps 32:10b). On the contrary, the ungodly (ἁμαρτωλός)[138] is destined to experience many woes (Ps 32:10a). So Cranfield seems right to say, 'it would be generally taken for granted by the Rabbis of Paul's day that the blessing pronounced in Ps. 32.1f. applied exclusively to Jews',[139] and so they often quoted the Psalm in connection with the Day of Atonement.[140] It is highly significant, then, to see Paul employing a psalm with such a context to support his assertion, 'God is the God who justifies the [Gentile] wicked (ἀσεβής)' (4:5). In effect Paul also reinterprets David: he was perceived as 'a man of Pious works' (4QMMT 31-118=4Q 397-399),[141] but Paul presents him as a man who upholds the blessedness of justification *apart from works* (4:6-8). It seems clear also that a main argument in 4:1-8 is to explain the application of such blessings not only to the περιτομή, to whom the promise of blessing was originally given (9:4), but also to the ἀκροβυστία, who have been 'excluded from citizenship in Israel and [are] foreigners to the covenants of promise, without hope and without God in the world' (Eph 2:12; cf. Gal 4:8; Col 2:21; 1 Thess 4:5).

B. *Abraham's Faith and his Fatherhood: 4:9-12*

Paul's intention of appealing to the case of Abraham is shown in 4:9-12. Since the μακαρισμός in 4:9 is related to the same noun in 4:6 and to its adjective in 4:7-8, God's declaration of bless-

---

138 In 5:6-8 Paul parallels ἀσεβής with ἁμαρτωλός as synonyms, and both are identified with the unbelieving state of Christians (so also 1 Tim 1:9; 1 Pet 4:18; cf. 2 Tim 2:16; Titus 2:12).
139 Cranfield, *Romans* 1, 234.
140 Str-B 3, 202-203.
141 As translated by Eisenman and Wise, *Dead Sea*, 200.

ing[142] for the uncircumcised is also emphasised through the citation of LXX Ps 31:1-2 as well as through the appeal to the case of Abraham. Certainly Paul's rhetorical question, 'Is this blessing then upon the circumcised, or upon the uncircumcised also?' (4:9a: NASB), acknowledges the blessing for both Jews and Gentiles. However, the absence of 'μόνον' in the first part and the particle ἤ attached to the second seem to indicate that Paul's emphasis is on the second.[143] Furthermore, Paul's immediate remark with the conjunction γάρ,[144] '[For] we have been saying that Abraham's faith was credited to him as righteousness' (4:9b), clearly indicates that his exposition of Gen 15:6 has been ultimately designed to establish the notion that this blessedness of justification and forgiveness is *also for the uncircumcision*. Paul seems to interrelate these two OT passages closely to make this point.

Paul now switches from the question *how* to *when* Abraham was reckoned as righteous, most probably to apply this blessing also to the Gentiles.[145] That Abraham was reckoned righteous *before* the institution of the rite of circumcision is a matter of first importance for Paul, and his words are emphatically constructed. Thus the blessedness mentioned in Psalm 32 is also for the uncircumcision, because Abraham was credited while he was yet uncircumcised just like any other Gentile believers. Uncircumcision did not disqualify Abraham from being counted as righteous, and so it is with the case of the Gentiles; as long as they have the faith that Abraham had, their justification is absolutely legitimate.[146] Unlike the exilic and the post-exilic prophets who pre-

---

142 Rienecker and Rogers, *Linguistic Key*, 357; Sanday and Headlam, *Romans*, 101.

143 This structure gives less emphasis to the first part than that in 3:29, 4:16 ('μόνον ... καί'). Most (modern) English translations (e.g. RSV, NIV, TEV, JB, Phillips, but not NASB, Moffatt) and commentators (Barrett, Cranfield, Fitzmyer, Käsemann, but not Dunn), add 'only', and miss this point.

144 The renderings of, e.g. NIV, RSV, NAB, REB, NRSV, ignore this important γάρ; but KJV and TEV correctly render it, cf. JB, NEB, Phillips, Moffatt.

145 Hays, *Echoes*, 56.

146 Since the Jewish believers are already circumcised, Paul's assertion here could effect a more practical implication for the Gentile believers. Thus, Ziesler, *Romans*, 128, is correct to note that Paul's stressing of the fact that Abraham was justified without having been circumcised, serves to establish the case for the Gentiles.

sented Abraham as the prototype of Israel,[147] Paul introduces him as that of the (Gentile) believer.[148] A central issue that can be drawn from the case of Abraham's justification is not simply related to the whole of humanity in general, but more specifically to the Gentiles.[149]

Paul's opponents might have asserted 'theologically' that since Abraham was circumcised *after* being counted righteous, and that the Gentiles who belonged to Abraham's household were also circumcised (cf. Gen 17:12-14), so must Gentile believers be circumcised *after* their justification as 'the seal of the covenant'.[150] But Paul does not deal with this issue; he does not use the phrase, 'the seal of the covenant', but 'the seal of righteousness', probably because the former could recall the rite of circumcision. Paul's argument is centred upon proving that the faith of the uncircumcised Gentile believers is soteriologically sufficient: the Gentile believers already have the seal of righteousness of faith (cf. 4:11).[151] So they do not need another seal, that of the old covenant. Paul takes up the *one* case of Abraham and generalises it as if it were *the* paradigm case.

Paul further asserts that there was a divine purpose in the case of Abraham, that he was justified *before* circumcision: 'The *purpose* was to make him the father of all who believe without being circumcised' (4:11: RSV). In fact, in v. 11 Paul makes two

---

147 See Fishbane, *Interpretation*, 374-376.

148 Betz, "Ἀβραάμ', 3.

149 So the assertion of Guerra, 'Romans 4', 260-261, that Paul relates Abraham's righteousness to all humanity, requires more specification and nuance.

150 Cf. Longenecker, "'Faith of Abraham'", 205.

151 I.e. by the Spirit: 8:9-11; 2 Cor 1:21-22; Eph 4:30: 'the seal of the Holy Spirit of the Promise' (Eph 1:13: NJB). Receiving the Holy Spirit was the clear evidence for the early church for confirming God's acceptance of the (believing) Gentiles. Peter's encounter with Cornelius was marked by such an incident (Acts 10:45-46). So it was in the case of the Galatian believers. Paul appeals to the experience of the receiving of the Spirit to persuade them that their righteousness was not based on the observance of the law (Gal 3:1-5), and to illustrate this assertion Paul turns to the case of Abraham from Gal 3:6 onwards. A study of the role of 'experience' in the formation or affirmation of 'theology' in the early church is an important subject, for which we cannot afford space in this present study.

constructions with εἰς followed by the accusative of the articular infinitive, and thus expresses the double divine purpose.[152]

'εἰς τὸ εἶναι αὐτὸν πατέρα πάντων τῶν πιστευόντων δι' ἀκροβυστίας,
εἰς τὸ λογισθῆναι [καὶ] αὐτοῖς [τὴν] δικαιοσύνην'
'in order for him *to become* the father of all who believe through
uncircumcision (i.e. without being circumcised),
also *in order* for righteousness *to be reckoned*[153] to them'

The phrase 'all those who believe through uncircumcision' refers to Gentile Christians, because Jews are already circumcised; then the αὐτοῖς also designates uncircumcised Gentile believers. Here Paul shows clearly that God intended, in the case of Abraham's justification *before* his circumcision, to justify Gentiles apart from circumcision on the sole condition of faith.[154] Ziesler is correct to note that Paul's bold assertion here is indeed a radical one from a Jewish point of view.[155] Paul's exposition of this doctrine is for the sake of Gentile believers, or we might say, in order to affirm (or defend) the legitimacy of Gentile salvation Paul has structured the argument in the way that it is spelled out here.

The same argument seems to have been further developed in 4:12, a verse which has received much scholarly attention.

καὶ πατέρα περιτομῆς τοῖς οὐκ ἐκ περιτομῆς μόνον ἀλλὰ καὶ τοῖς στοιχοῦσιν τοῖς ἴχνεσιν τῆς ἐν ἀκροβυστίᾳ πίστεως τοῦ πατρὸς ἡμῶν Ἀβραάμ (4:12).

The grammatical difficulties of this verse have caused the great majority of interpreters to misunderstand Paul's point. According

---

152 Dunn, *Romans* 1, 210; Hays, *Echoes*, 56. *Pace* Cranfield, *Romans* 1, 236-237, who takes the first εἰς τό as final, but the second as a mere consecutive.

153 The aorist passive infinitive indicates either purpose or actual result (Rienecker and Rogers, *Linguistic Key*, 357), but more probably it suggests the divine purpose (Turner, *Grammar* 3, 143; Sanday and Headlam, *Romans*, 107; Morris, *Romans*, 203 n. 46).

154 Dunn, *Romans* 1, 210: 'Paul argues that Gen 15:6 shows Abraham to be the father of the uncircumcised *in their uncircumcision*, so long as they have faith. It is precisely his own distinction between faith and works of the law which he finds validated by Gen 15:6.'

155 Ziesler, *Romans*, 128.

to the majority view, Paul affirms here that Abraham is the father not only of unbelieving Jews but also of believing Jews.[156] In other words, his fatherhood of the *Jews* is what Paul refers to here, and that of Gentiles is not included in this verse.[157] We will examine this view from the perspective of the context as well as of the syntax, and will support the alternative interpretation, with some new evidence, that both Jews and Gentiles are included in the Abrahamic ancestry.

The grammatical argument of the hypothesis of the majority scholars can be summed up as follows. Since the wording is τοῖς οὐκ .... μόνον (to those who not only ...), the first τοῖς embraces both '*not only of circumcision*' and '*but also those who walk in the footsteps of Abraham* ...'. If this verse referred to two groups (Jews and Gentiles), then the construction should have been οὐ τοῖς rather than τοῖς οὐ(κ).[158] Although the second τοῖς gives the impression that it is 'as if Paul meant to speak in this same verse of *two* different *classes* of individuals',[159] it is more probable, this view maintains, that the second τοῖς is either a careless insertion by Paul/Tertius or a mistake of a very early copyist misspelling the 'original' αὐτοῖς as the present τοῖς.[160] It must therefore be omitted,[161] because Paul certainly does not speak of two groups.[162]

Despite its strength, however, this hypothesis does not seem totally convincing. The unanimous textual agreement on the

---

156 Cf. Meyer's unconvincing interpretation that this first τοῖς covers both the Jewish Christians and the Pauline Jewish Christians (*Romans* 1, 203).

157 E.g. Käsemann, *Romans*, 116; Dunn, *Romans* 1, 210-212; Cranfield, *Romans* 1, 237; Shedd, *Romans*, 101; Moxnes, *Theology*, 112 n. 18.

158 Some have preferred the οὐ τοῖς construction, and applied the first τοῖς phrase to Jewish believers, and the second to Gentile believers: see Meyer, *Romans* 1, 203, for more advocates of this position.

159 As admitted by Godet, *Romans*, 174, though he does not accept this view.

160 Cranfield, *Romans* 1, 237; so also Dunn, *Romans* 1, 196. Earlier Gifford, *Romans*, 103; Sanday and Headlam, *Romans*, 108; Lagrange, *Romains*, 91; Boylan, *Romans*, 68. Such a proposal had been already denied by Lightfoot, *Notes*, 280, who noted a similar construction in Phil 1:29 (but cf. Meyer, *Romans* 1, 202-203).

161 Sanday and Headlam, *Romans*, 108; so also Meyer, *Romans* 1, 202, who lists no less than nineteen scholars of old whom he follows.

162 Sanday and Headlam, *Romans*, 108.

presence of the second τοῖς[163] suggests that there has been no attempt to omit or change the second τοῖς because of its 'awkwardness'.[164] It may seem unintelligible to some modern scholars, but it seems to have been taken as original by the earliest scribes. One cannot be certain whether the word order should be changed from 'τοῖς οὐκ' to 'οὐ τοῖς', or to ignore the second τοῖς as a careless insertion, or as a redundant repetition or a misspelling of 'αὐτοῖς'.[165] So we may turn to examine the *context* to determine whether 4:12 is speaking about one group, the Jews, or about two groups, Jews and Gentiles. The context has hardly been considered as a means to an intelligible solution. Godet appeals to the context but affirms that since Paul sufficiently described Gentile believers in v. 11b, it is difficult to see that in v. 12b Paul returns to speak about them again.[166] He appeals, however, to a context which is too narrow, and 4:12 may not simply repeat 4:11; rather it may well sum up or restate what Paul has been arguing. Moo plausibly takes a wider context, but his assertion, 'the context of Romans 4 focuses too much on the distinction between Jews and Gentiles', is hardly justifiable.[167]

We propose at least two contextual reasons to support the hypothesis that 4:12 refers to believing Jews and believing Gentiles.[168] First, it is highly unlikely that at this stage of the argument Paul would stress the Abrahamic fatherhood of unbelieving Jews, which he would deny elsewhere (9:6b-8; cf. 2:25-29). The section 4:10-12 is one long sentence in Greek, and its purpose is to establish that the blessedness mentioned in 4:6-8 is applicable to the uncircumcised also. Now the emphatic recurrence of 'ἐν τῇ ἀκροβυστίᾳ' in 4:12b, seems to sum up the argument related to

---

163 Cranfield, *Romans* 1, 237 n. 5.

164 Godet, *Romans*, 174, accepts the second τοῖς as original, but insists that it is 'not as a second parallel pronoun, but a simple definite article', 'the', as is the τοῖς in 4:24: τοῖς πιστεύουσιν (cf. Cranfield, *Romans* 1, 237). But the τοῖς in 4:24 is not a mere article; it also has the function of a pronoun, and so it is here.

165 Chrys C. Caragounis has drawn my attention to the fact that Chrysostom, for whom the language of the NT was his mother tongue, does not show any awareness of any problem with τοῖς οὐκ ἐκ περιτομῆς.

166 Godet, *Romans*, 174.

167 *Pace* Moo, *Romans* 1, 275.

168 The minority group of scholars who maintain this view include Cerfaux, Cambier, and Swetnam, 'Curious Crux', 110-115.

Gentile believers, that they are legitimate and authentic believers in the light of the fact that Abraham was reckoned righteous when he was in uncircumcision.

Moreover, Abraham is described as the father of circumcision (πατέρα περιτομῆς), not the father of *the* circumcision, as if referring to Jews.[169] Paul has already made it clear that the Gentiles' keeping of the requirements of the law should be regarded as true circumcision (2:26; cf. Phil 3:3). Our interpretation can be strengthened if R.B. Hays' rendering of 4:1 is correct: 'What then shall we say? Have we found Abraham to be our forefather according to the flesh?'. He continues, 'The answer demanded by this rhetorical question, as by other similar rhetorical questions in Romans (3:5, 6:1, 7:7, 9:14) is an emphatic negative.'[170] If Paul starts to deal with the case of Abraham with such an initial question, it seems hardly possible for him to assert that Abraham is the father of the unbelieving and the believing Jews (in other words, whether they believe or not), as most scholars insist. Furthermore, 4:14 clearly indicates that 'those who live by law' (οἱ ἐκ νόμου) are not Abraham's heirs: only those of faith are heirs whether they be Jews or Gentiles. Thus the pair of τοῖς in 4:12 is about believers, Jewish and Gentile Christians. 4:12 is then a bold statement, because Paul is here denying that Abraham is the father of unbelieving Jews.

Second, a similar thought pattern occurs in 4:16: 'οὐ τῷ ἐκ τοῦ νόμου μόνον ἀλλὰ καὶ τῷ ἐκ πίστεως Ἀβραάμ ὅς ἐστιν πατὴρ πάντων ἡμῶν'. The word order 'οὐ τῷ' clearly indicates that the ἀλλὰ καὶ τῷ ἐκ πίστεως Ἀβραάμ clause is only desig-

---

169 Jews claimed that only the children of Israel (Jacob) were the true circumcision, although Ishmael and Esau were also circumcised. Almost all modern translations incorrectly render this phrase: RSV, NRSV, REB, NAB, NJB, TEV, NIV, NEB, Moffatt, Lutherbibel; cf. KJV, NASB. Abraham circumcised Ishmael as well as Isaac, and Isaac circumcised both Esau and Jacob, but according to the Jews only Jacob's twelve tribes are *the* true circumcision.

170 Hays, *Echoes*, 54; already asserted in his earlier article, 'Abraham', 76-98. Unfortunately, Hays himself does not relate his translation to the interpretative issues of 4:12; rather he maintains 4:12b as referring to the believing Jews (*Echoes*, 56). For the translation of 4:1, Hays is followed by Wright, 'Romans', 191, yet their identification of 'we' is different. For Hays, 'we' refers to Jews (so also Haldane, *Romans*, 161; Lightfoot, *Notes*, 277; Lincoln, 'Wrath', 216; Beker, *Paul*, 78); for Wright, it means Christians (cf. Watson, *Paul*, 139: the Roman Jewish Christians).

nated for the believing Gentile. This phrase probably corresponds to the phrase 'τοῖς στοιχοῦσιν κτλ' (4:12b), and so the latter phrase probably refers to believing Gentiles.[171] Moreover, those who *can* walk in the footsteps of the faith that our father Abraham had *in uncircumcision* are Gentiles, because they believe while they are *in uncircumcision*, whilst Jews do so *in circumcision*. The emphatic position of 'ἐν ἀκροβυστίᾳ' (4:12) seems to suggest the state in which they believed.

In conclusion, having established Abraham's fatherhood of the uncircumcised in v. 11, Paul goes on in v. 12 to confirm that Abraham is the father of the *spiritual circumcision*, not only of those (believing Jews) who are of the circumcision, but also of those (believing Gentiles) who walk in the footsteps of the faith Abraham had while he was in uncircumcision. Jews believed that Abraham was the figure who differentiated Gentiles from themselves, but Paul argues that he is the one in whose ancestry Gentiles can also be included through faith.[172] Few Jews would have said that Abraham was the father of proselytes (cf. *Mechilta* 101a on Exod 22:21), but 'for Paul ... the order is almost reversed: he is the father of Gentiles who have faith more than of Israelites who do not'.[173] Michel seems to have gone too far in saying that Paul indicates that Abraham is the father of the uncircumcised than of the circumcised, but he has certainly perceived Paul's emphasis in the argument.[174] Paul does not merely affirm the inclusion of the Christian Gentiles in the Abrahamic ancestry; it has been his major concern in 4:1-12,[175] so he structures his argument to highlight this point. No one had ever emphasised Abraham's fatherhood of Gentiles as forcefully as Paul does here. Thus we affirm the originality of Paul's reinterpretation of Abraham;[176] and further it is our contention that Paul's position is most probably derived from his own apostolic self-consciousness, which seeks to establish a theological basis that can secure the legitimacy of

---

171 Swetnam, 'Curious Crux', 113, also notes this correspondence, but too easily assumes it.
172 Nygren, *Romans*, 175.
173 Ziesler, *Romans*, 129.
174 Michel, *Römer*, 104.
175 Hays, 'Abraham', 90-91.
176 *Pace* Leenhardt, *Romans*, 119; Ps 47:9 and Matt 8:11 are not exactly about Abraham's fatherhood of the Gentiles.

the justification of the Gentiles. By using chronological narrative sequences, Paul has logically argued to affirm his assertion (4:1-12); but he goes even further by (deliberately) reformulating chronology to achieve the same purpose, to which we turn next.

C. *The Promise and Abraham's Fatherhood of Many Nations / Gentiles: 4:13-25*

The motifs of the promise to Abraham, his faith and his fatherhood of many nations become prominent in the continuing argument in 4:13-22.[177] The presentation of Paul's argument will be examined against the background of the Genesis narratives in order to determine how far Paul departs from them to establish his own points in theological argument. We shall then attempt to demonstrate how Paul establishes especially Abraham's fatherhood of *many nations / Gentiles*. He relates God's promise, Abraham's faith and his fatherhood to the idea of Abraham being the father of many nations. The fact that in 4:13-25 Paul often overlooks or modifies the chronological account of Genesis reveals his intention in appealing to the case of Abraham. Just as Abraham was reckoned as righteous before his circumcision, the promise to him was given before the institution of the law. Thus it was not by the law[178] but 'through the righteousness that comes by faith' (διὰ δικαιοσύνης πίστεως).

The fulfilment of the promise to make Abraham the father of many nations is conditioned not by the law, because the law not only nullifies the promise but also brings about wrath (4:14-15; cf. 1:18; 5:13). Here again Paul makes an un-Jewish remark, for Jews understood the concept of promise to be based on the law; salvation and the security of their inheritance were perceived 'as

---

177 The term ἐπαγγελία / ἐπαγγέλλομαι occurs in 4:13, 14, 16, 20, 21, and πίστις / πιστεύειν in 4:13, 14, 16, 17, 18, 19, and πατήρ in 4:16, 17, 18. The latter two terms have already been used (πίστις/πιστεύειν occurs seven times in 4:3-12, and πατήρ three times in 4:11-12), but the motif of promise brings a new dimension to the argument.

178 Davies, *Faith*, 170, asserts that this νόμος is a reference to circumcision, but it is more probably to the Mosaic Law (cf. *Zad* 20:3: Abraham was circumcised on the day he knew the Mosaic Law), for Paul has already related the promise and the Law in Gal 3:15-18, and he often ignores chronology, as we will show below.

promised through the law' (2 Macc 2:17-18). But Paul directly denies such a contemporary concept.[179] Rather he insists that 'salvation' is conditioned by divine grace and by human faith, '*in order that* (εἰς τὸ εἶναι) the promise may be certain to all the descendants,[180] not only to those [Jews] who are of the Law, but also to those [Gentiles] who are of the faith of Abraham, who is the father of us all' (4:16, NASB). The construction of 'οὐ τῷ... μόνον, ἀλλὰ καὶ τῷ ...' clearly indicates two groups of Jews and Gentiles (cf. implicitly in v. 12), and that the emphasis of Paul's argument is that the promise includes believing Gentiles. He stresses the fact that God has chosen the way to reckon the ungodly as righteous through the means of human faith and divine grace, ultimately in order to include the Gentiles into Abrahamic righteousness and ancestry.

Paul argues that that is why the Gentile believers can also legitimately, in a theological sense, call Abraham, 'our father', not 'your father' as the proselytes were only allowed to call him (*Bikk.* 1:4).[181] For Paul this is what God meant when he said, 'I have made you a father of many nations' (Gen 17:5).[182] The change of Abram's name to Abraham is to reaffirm the promise of the great posterity among the nations. The change may not be

---

[179] So O'Neill, *Romans*, 83, takes 4:14-15 as a later gloss, for 'these verses clearly exclude Jews from the possibility of being heirs with Abraham' (p. 88). This view seems incorrect, but it certainly grasps the point that here Paul's wording upholds the Gentile position.

[180] The clause εἰς τὸ εἶναι κτλ ... is final (so Dunn, *Romans* 1, 216; Cranfield, *Romans* 1, 242; Oepke, *TDNT* 2, 430; Godet, *Romans*, 178; *pace* Käsemann, *Romans*, 121; Fitzmyer, *Romans*, 385), for Paul so constructs this as to convey a strong purpose (βέβαιος) with the emphasis on the phrase 'to *all* the descendants'.

[181] Lincoln, 'Wrath', 218; Davies, *Faith*, 148 n. 4.

[182] In Sir 44:19-21 Abraham was already seen as "the great father of many nations' ('Αβραὰμ μέγας πατὴρ πλήθους ἐθνῶν), and that 'the nations would be blessed through his posterity' was also perceived. But according to Jesus ben Sirach, Abraham's universal fatherhood is granted because he 'kept the law of the Most High ..., established the covenant in his flesh (i.e. circumcision), and when he was tested [to sacrifice Isaac] he was found faithful' (Sir 44:20). But for Paul Abraham's fatherhood was not given as a reward for what Abraham had done, but by God's grace in order to embrace both Jews and Gentiles. Abraham became the father of many nations not because of his deeds of obedience, but because of God's own decision: 'I have made you a father of many nations.'

so significant linguistically,[183] but Paul makes a crucial point in his argument out of this change. In fact the pun between Abraham (אַבְרָהָם) and *ab-hamon* (multitude: אַב-הֲמוֹן) stresses '*multitude*' rather than 'nations'. The new name Abraham means '"father of a multitude"' (cf. Heb 11:12),[184] but Paul stresses 'nations' and connotes that Abraham is the father of many *nations* (=Gentiles). Since Paul does not use ἔθνος/ἔθνη in the political or governmental sense of nation(s) in Romans, the phrase in 4:18 seems better translated as 'the father of many *Gentiles*'.[185] If von Rad is correct to say that the description 'the father of many nations' in Gen 17:5 may not fully include 'those who are outside God's covenant',[186] Paul's application and redefinition of Abraham's fatherhood become even more significant. The phrase 'the father of many nations' in 4:17, 18 is not a gloss[187] but takes the central part in Paul's argument,[188] which is in fact 'controlled by the conviction that God's promise to Abraham always had the nations as a whole in view (and not just Israel)'.[189] With the claim in 4:16-18 Paul defends the legitimacy of the Gentile believers from those Jewish believers who do not fully understand the place of the Gentile Christians.[190] He affirms that both Jewish and Gentile believers are equally Abraham's true descendants.

In 4:18-22 he turns to explain more specifically *how*, *what* and *why* Abraham believed. These three aspects constitute the argument in 4:18-22, and Paul seems to explain these with the special aim of affirming the theological points of the status and the legitimacy of Gentile salvation. First, he asserts that Abraham

---

183 Barrett, *Selected Documents*, 183; von Rad, *Genesis*, 199. But the changed names of both Abraham and Sarah are not unrelated to their parenthood of many nations (Gen 17:4-5, 15-16): 'Your name will be Abraham, *for* I have made you a father of many nations' (Gen 17:5).

184 Clifford and Murphy, 'Genesis', 22.

185 Barrett, *Romans*, 90: 'The LXX renders the word "nations" by the word which to Paul regularly means "Gentiles" (ἔθνη). Abraham is thus proved by Scripture itself to be the father of non-Jews'; so similarly Dunn, *Romans* 1, 217. Betz, "Ἀβραάμ', 3, does not fully convey Paul's point in taking the phrase to connote simply 'the father of all believers'.

186 von Rad, *Genesis*, 200.

187 *Contra* O'Neill, *Romans*, 88-89.

188 Dodd, *Romans*, 91.

189 Dunn, *Romans* 1, 216.

190 So correctly Watson, *Paul*, 141.

unwaveringly believed in hope against all hope (παρ' ἐλπίδα ἐπ' ἐλπίδι ἐπίστευσεν). Second, what Abraham believed was God's promise: 'So shall your offspring be' (4:18; Gen 15:5), but for Paul the phrase 'your offspring' means 'your offspring of many nations' (4:18). In other words, Paul insists that Abraham believed his descendants would be from many nations, i.e. he believed he would have many *Gentile* descendants. Third, Paul argues that Abraham believed *in order to become the father of many Gentiles*. We may note that these three assertions are not in accordance with the account in the Genesis narratives, but rather are significantly shaped to make Paul's own theological points. A comparative study will enable us to see his intention in the structure of his argument here.

Firstly, it is difficult to say that Abraham believed 'without weakening in his faith' (4:19). Despite God's promise of posterity in Gen 12:2, 7 and 13:16, Abraham had doubts and unbelief (Gen 15:1-3). Only after God's restatement of the promise (Gen 15:4-5) is it said that Abraham believed in him, for which God reckoned his faith as righteousness (Gen 15:6). Even after the covenant of circumcision, however, Abraham still did not fully believe God's promise about the heir from his own body: he laughed and doubted (Gen 17:17-18; so Philo maintains, *Mut.*, 177: 'he [Abraham] had a doubt about the birth of Isaac'). The faith that was reckoned to Abraham as righteousness is recorded in Gen 15:4-6. But here again it is difficult to assert that he believed *against all hope*, because according to the narrative of Genesis 16, both Abraham and Sarah knew that he could expect a child.[191]

The central 'problem' in Genesis 15 is Abraham's childlessness, as he confesses in 15:2-3. Yet Paul does not draw his argument from Genesis 15, but from Genesis 17 as he specifically mentions Abraham's age, ninety-nine. Then indeed Abraham realised that there was no hope of any possibility [of natural descendants] (Gen 17:17). But Paul reasons as if Abraham believed with full conviction (πληροφορηθείς) against all hope of possibility *already in Gen 15:6*,[192] and *therefore* (διό) this great

---

[191] *Pace* Robertson, 'Genesis 15:6', 261. Paul may only need to deal with the narrative to Gen 15:6, but it is striking to see him emphasising Gen 15:6 even by applying it 'out of context'.

[192] See Baldwin, *Genesis 12-50*, 51, for the typical mistake of interpreting Genesis through Paul's eyes.

faith was reckoned as righteousness (4:22).[193] In the earlier argument the correct chronology was the main point of the argument: he insisted that Abraham was reckoned righteous *before* circumcision. But here chronology plays no part in Paul's argument. He wishes to maximise the effect of Abraham's faith on the central 'problem' of his childlessness in Genesis 15. Such a device might not be unrelated to the Gentiles who eventually became Abraham's descendants 'beyond hope on hope: παρ' ἐλπίδα ἐπ' ἐλπίδι' (4:18, cf. Eph 2:12).[194]

Secondly, what Abraham believed in Gen 15:6 is God's promise that his own *physical* seed ('from your own body') would be as numerous as stars,[195] and *this* faith was reckoned as righteousness. That God's promise was concerned with Abraham's physical descendants becomes clearer when we note that the promise of the land was given to them: 'To your descendants I give this land....' (Gen 12:7; 15:18; 17:8; Exod 19:4-6). But Paul insists that the promise which Abraham believed: 'So shall your offspring be' (Gen 15:5), was firmly related to his fatherhood of many *spiritual* descendants including the Gentiles.[196] So he said in an earlier letter: 'If you [the Gentile believers in Galatia] belong to Christ, then you are Abraham's seed, and heirs according to the promise' (Gal 3:29).

---

193 Jews follow the chronology that there was a twenty-nine-year interval between Gen 15:6 and Gen 17:11: Str-B 3, 203; Black, *Romans*, 77; Leenhardt, *Romans*, 118; Morris, *Romans*, 202, n. 41. Cf. Boylan, *Romans*, 67; Wuest, 'Romans', 69: 14-year gap; Dunn, *Romans* 1, 208: 'several years'. See Maccoby, *Early Rabbinic Writings*, 220-225, who introduces *Seder 'Olam Rabbah* 1, which offers Abraham's chronology in much detail. Whatever 'gap' we may take, it is clear that Paul reverses the sequence of the events so as to make his point, unlike when he follows the logic of the time gap in Gal 3:15-18 and in Rom 4:10-11.

194 So rightly Giblin, '"As It Is Written"', 492-493. In Rom 4 pursuing theological meaning is, for Paul, far more vital than conveying the literal sense of the text because he is writing Romans from a theological viewpoint.

195 So also Mason, *Josephus*, 70. For Peter the unbelieving Jews are also clearly the descendants of Abraham (cf. Acts 3:12, 25). The singular noun σπέρμα in 4:13, 16, 18 (as in Gen 15:5) is a singular collective noun with a plural sense (Lightfoot, *Galatians*, 142, 152). Unlike in Gal 3:15ff, the term in a singular form here does not constitute a major point of argument.

196 Our interpretation is based on the fact that Paul uses the quotation from Gen 15:5e as scriptural proof for his assertion of Abraham's fatherhood of many nations/Gentiles.

Thirdly, Paul's interpretation of the reason why Abraham exercised such hope in that impossible situation was: 'εἰς τὸ γενέσθαι αὐτὸν πατέρα πολλῶν ἐθνῶν: *in order to become a father of many nations*' (4:18).[197] This point has indeed significant argumentative force, because according to the Genesis context it is difficult to say that it was *the* reason for or the content of his faith.[198] Although God's promise at the initial call: 'All peoples on earth will be blessed through you' (Gen 12:3b), includes 'many nations', it was only in Gen 17:4-6 that God gave Abraham a specific covenant for him to become a father of many nations, and his name was then changed accordingly.

Abraham believed that God would give him a son — *one* nation with as many descendants as the stars (Gen 15:4-6; and as interpreted in 2 Chr 27:23). Paul significantly interprets, however, that Abraham was conscious of his fatherhood of *many nations before* he believed as in Gen 15:6, and thus what he believed was that he would become the father of many nations. It is *that* faith, asserts Paul, which God honoured and so was reckoned to Abraham as righteousness. In other words, Abraham's faith that was reckoned to him as righteousness in Gen 15:6 was prompted *in order* for him *to become* the father of many nations (4:18-22).[199] Paul significantly relates Abraham's faith, which is the foundation of the existence of Israel, directly to 'many nations'. This indicates that Paul's ultimate argument in Romans 4 is aimed at affirming that God's promise and Abraham's faith are for all (Jewish and Gentile) descendants of Abraham (cf. 4:16).[200]

---

197 Perhaps the NASB conveys the best rendering of this purpose clause: 'in order that he might become a father of many nations'; so similarly, KJV, RV, RSV, Phillips; Dunn, *Romans* 1, 219; Godet, *Romans*, 181; *contra* Cranfield, *Romans* 1, 246.

198 See Davies, *Faith*, 163, for the importance of interpreting Paul's argument from 'a contextual reading of Genesis'; though he does not seem to pay sufficient attention to it. The absence of punctuation after ἐπίστευσεν may cause some to take the phrase 'εἰς τὸ γενέσθαι αὐτὸν πατέρα πολλῶν ἐθνῶν' as the content of Abraham's faith. Cf. Cranfield, *Romans* 1, 246, who suggests to put a comma after ἐπίστευσεν; but both Nestle-Aland[27] and UBS[4] do not put a punctuation mark there.

199 Dunn, *Romans* 1, 219, also notes this 'backward-connection', and the same logic in Philo, *Mut.*, 177-178.

200 Moxnes, *Theology*, 114.

The section 4:23-25 clearly demonstrates that Paul's exposition of the case of Abraham was intended to have a practical and contemporary application.[201] This shows that he has written about the case of Abraham in order to explain that if anyone, whether Jew or Gentile, believes in God who raised Jesus from the dead, one can also be sufficiently and legitimately credited as righteous, and thus have Abrahamic ancestry. Paul asserts that '[Gen 15:6] was written for the Christian believers'.[202] It seems significant that Paul compares the birth of Isaac with the resurrection of Jesus: both events are characterised by bringing life from impossible conditions.[203]

To sum up, Paul's interpretation of the case of Abraham is fundamentally based on a theological interest, rather than on a historical angle of facts or sequence.[204] Hays is thus correct to say, 'Paul's handling of the scriptural text [in Romans 4] is so idiosyncratic that misunderstanding is easily possible'.[205] Paul's argument is concentrated and woven together with a rather 'insignificant' verb, 'believe'. In Genesis, 15:6 is the only reference that indicates Abraham believed (אמן) in God.[206] Gen 15:6 does not seem to be so pivotal a verse for the author of Genesis. Rather it is Paul who uses this reference to maximise his theological argument; he implicitly highlights the point that Abraham's obedience was surely undergirded by his faith. Paul uses

---

201 Despite some elements that suggest the present verb μέλλει with the infinitive connotes the future, this does not seem to refer to the final judgement (*pace* Schlatter, Michel, Barrett, *Romans*, 92; Käsemann, *Romans*, 128) as much as to the present Christian life (see Cranfield, *Romans* 1, 250).
202 Baldwin, *Genesis 12-50*, 52.
203 Sanday and Headlam, *Romans*, 115.
204 Leenhardt, *Romans*, 125. Although one cannot say that Paul uses Abraham out of context, it seems true that Paul uses the Genesis narratives to score theological points.
205 Hays, *Echoes*, 54.
206 There are only three occurrences of Hebrew אמן (and also πιστεύειν in the LXX) in the whole of Genesis (Gen 15:6; 42:20; 45:26). Even in Gen 22 we do not find a reference that Abraham *believed* that God would raise Isaac from the dead. Despite the interpretation of the incident in connection with Abraham's *faith* (cf. Heb 11:17-19), that he did not withhold his only son suggests that he completely gave up Isaac in obedience to God's demand (Gen 22:16; cf. God gave up Jesus: Rom 8:32). According to Gen 22, then, it is because of his (*work of*) *obedience* (cf. Jas 2:20-23), rather than because of his *faith*, that the promise for the blessing of the nations is reaffirmed (Gen 22:18).

the history of Abraham to illustrate his theological assertions that Abraham's extraordinary faith is ultimately exercised not only to show an example of justification by faith, but more importantly to secure the legitimate entry of the Gentiles into the Abrahamic spiritual ancestry,[207] which would thus prepare his readers for the 'conflict with Judaising Christianity'.[208] In an earlier letter Paul had said, 'The Scripture foresaw that God would justify the Gentiles by faith, and announced the gospel in advance to Abraham: "All nations will be blessed through you"' (Gal 3:8). In Romans 4, very boldly and yet very carefully, Paul has provided the theological basis for what in Galatians is merely an assertion (Gal 3:8-9, 29).[209]

4. Conclusions

Now we may draw some conclusions from our findings above. First, just as in 1:18-3:20 Paul continues in this section to speak primarily to the (believing) Jews about equality between Jew and Gentile, only this time the emphasis is on their equality in justification. We have tried to demonstrate that Paul structures his argument in order to affirm that the Gentile believers are equally and legitimately included in the special relationship with God (3:29) and in Abrahamic ancestry. Paul repeatedly stresses that Gentile salvation gained by faith apart from works of the law is absolutely sufficient and legitimate (3:22, 28-29; 4:9, 16). As we have noted from an examination of 1:18-32,[210] Paul seems to operate a two-level argument: on one level he expounds the doctrine of justification in general terms, but on the other, as apostle to the Gentiles, he aims to affirm the legitimacy of Gentile salvation, and thereby the equality of Gentiles with Jews.

Second, both the revelation of a righteousness of God in Christ and apart from the law, and God's presentation of Christ as the ἱλαστήριον, signify not only the equality of all [Jews and Gen-

---

207 Cf. Moxnes, *Theology*, 9.
208 Jeremias, "Ἀβραάμ', 9.
209 The fact that the later Gentile believers in Rome did claim that '*Our father* Abraham .... attained righteousness and truth through faith' (*1 Clem.* 31:2), may indicate the success of Paul's argument; see Siker, 'Gentile Inclusion', 30-36.
210 *Supra* pp. 73-94, especially pp. 92-94.

tiles] who believe, but also the exclusion of Jewish boasting in the law, in their exclusive relationship with God and in the Abrahamic fatherhood. The affirmations that God is the God of the Gentiles too, and that Abraham is the father of the Gentiles too, are theologically constructed and vigorously asserted to vindicate the place of believing Gentiles in the new epoch. As we have suggested earlier, such perceptions are derived from Paul's self-awareness of being apostle to the Gentiles.

Third, Paul's interpretation of the Abraham story is uniquely surprising not only from the perspective of contemporary Judaism but also from that of other NT writers.[211] The different emphasis from Paul's own interpretation of the case of Abraham in Galatians 3 also indicates that here he presents the case apologetically to defend his theology (gospel) with respect to Gentiles' salvation and status.[212] Paul's interpretation of Abraham is based on his theological intentions: thus sometimes he lays emphasis on historical facts and chronology, and sometimes he regards them as being of little importance as long as they support his position in providing a theological basis for Gentile salvation apart from the

---

211 The LXX Gen 15:6 is quoted exactly in Rom 4:3, Gal 3:6 and in Jas 2:23, but Paul and James appeal to the quotation with very different intentions (see Longenecker, "'Faith of Abraham'", 203-212; Ellis, *Paul's Use*, 93-94; Dunn, *Romans* 1, 197; Eisenman and Wise, *Dead Sea*, 163). The author of Hebrews highlights three occasions in which Abraham particularly exercised his faith: (a) by faith Abraham left Ur for Canaan (Heb 11:8-10); (b) by faith he believed he would have a son through whom he would have many descendants (Heb 11:11-16); and (c) by faith he offered Isaac as a sacrifice (Heb 11:17-19). But Paul mentions only (b) in Rom 4; and even here there is a difference. Paul stresses that Abraham is the father of *many nations/Gentiles*, whilst the author of Hebrews points out that he is the father of *many (descendants)*: see Hahn, 'Genesis 15:6', 105 n. 61; Moxnes, *Theology*, 117-206, for the different interpretations of Abraham in and before the first century AD.

212 Paul's specific purpose in appealing to the case of Abraham in Rom 4 can be further detected from the differences between Rom 4 and Gal 3. According to Bruce, *Time*, 68-69, Paul makes two points in Romans which he does not make in Galatians. First, Abraham's faith was reckoned to him for righteousness while he was yet *uncircumcised*. Second, the change of Abram's name was connected with God's promise to make him the father of many nations (*Gentiles*). Yet it is these two points that comprise the core of Paul's argument in Rom 4. For comparative studies on Rom 4 and Gal 3, see Hübner, *Law*, 51-57; Boers, *Theology*, 74-104, especially 82-83; Calvert, 'Abraham', 2-8; Beker, *Paul*, 95-104, see also pp. 70-71.

law, and in affirming the equality of believing Jews and Gentiles under the lordship of God with a common Abrahamic ancestry. Paul does not misinterpret the Abraham story, but employs rhetorical force in order to maximise his argument that Jews and Gentiles are fundamentally equal.[213]

Finally, 1:18-4:25 is a debate with Judaism or an attempt to persuade Jewish believers who do not fully understand the implications of the gospel of Christ for their relation to Gentile believers. Theologically, Paul's argument provides the basis not only for the legitimacy of the salvation of Gentiles, but also for the equality of Jew and Gentile. Sociologically, it would serve to enhance the unity among Jewish and Gentile believers (e.g. in the Roman congregations) on the basis of their equality. Missiologically, it would prompt mission to the Gentile world (e.g. Spain). Paul's radical and bold arguments in this section (1:18-4:25) are presented on two levels, most probably in order to convey his theological assertions in a less offensive way to readers most of whom he has not yet met personally, and whose support for missionary work in the west would be vital. On the surface he appears to present the cases equally and generally, but at a deeper level he makes some critical arguments against Jews and affirmative statements about Gentiles (1:18-3:20).

In our present section (3:21-4:25) Paul argues for the inclusion of Gentiles in the Jewish privileges and the blessing of justification, but stresses the exclusion of Jewish boasting in their privileges. Above all, he contends for the equality of Jew and Gentile in sinfulness (1:18-3:20) and in justification (3:21-4:25).[214] In so doing Paul makes many bold assertions, as we have seen above. It is already apparent that Paul writes this letter rather boldly (cf. 15:15). We therefore conclude that Paul's self-awareness *as* apostle to the Gentiles has provided him with a new perception of being able to interpret theological issues from a Gentile perspective, and has influenced him in structuring his soteriological argument somewhat boldly for the sake of the Gentiles.

---

213 Gager, *Origins*, 218, accepted by Kaylor, *Covenant Community*, 183-184.

214 So correctly Sanders, *Jewish People*, 123: 'The basic theme of the first four chapters of Romans is that all can be saved equally on the basis of faith. The word "equally" emphasizes the equal opportunity of access on the part of the Gentiles.'

Paul continues the theme of justification in Romans 5-8, but discusses it on the basis of the fundamental equality between believing Jew and Gentile which he has just established in Romans 1-4. So there are no longer two groups (Jews and Gentiles) but one, 'we' (i.e. Christians). This section becomes less crucial for the purpose of our present study because it does not deal with Jew–Gentile issues. However, Paul resumes the inclusive soteriological argument in Romans 9-11, where he argues for the equality of Jew and Gentile, as he explains, most of all from the OT Scriptures, the phenomenon of the unbelief of Jews and the faith of Gentiles. We will examine these issues in detail in Chapter 5, after briefly summarising the argument of Romans 5-8 within the overall argument of the letter.

Chapter 4

The Equality of Jew and Gentile in the New Status: 5:1-8:39

In the previous two chapters we have tried to demonstrate that Paul expounds the equality of Jew and Gentile with regard to their sinfulness and justification, and that he substantiates his argument mainly by stressing Jewish sinfulness (1:18-3:20) and by affirming Gentile justification (3:21-4:25). We have maintained that such a 'biassed' structure in Paul's argument is shaped by his self-consciousness of his apostleship to the Gentiles. Later in Romans 9-11, as we will show in the next chapter, Paul continues the themes related to Jews and Gentiles with special reference to their equality in God's salvific plan. Since the primary focus of our present study rests on the aspect of *inclusive soteriology*, i.e. the Gentiles' inclusion in the salvific blessing promised to Israel,[1] and since the terms 'Jew/Gentile', 'Israelite/Greek' or 'the circumcised/the uncircumcised' do not appear in Romans 5-8 at all, we will examine the section rather briefly. The brevity of our treatment, however, may not be taken as a signal that this section is unimportant or does not contain the coherent theme of the equality of Jew and Gentile; we will show that the conclusion to be drawn is quite the reverse.

---

1 *Supra* p. 7 n. 30; cf. p. 158 n. 19.

Many commentators understand Romans 5-8 as describing the righteous life of the justified.[2] Very few scholars, however, perceive that Paul is dealing with issues concerning Israel and the Gentiles in this section, as N.T. Wright points out.[3] Jouett M. Bassler is a typical example: she excludes Romans 5-8 in examining divine impartiality because 'the question of Jews and Gentiles disappears in chapters 5-8'.[4] To be sure, Paul is not *arguing for* the equal status of Jew and Gentile on the surface, but he develops his argument in Romans 5-8 *on the basis of* this fundamental conclusion about their equality established in Romans 1-4.[5] Especially after affirming their equal status as true family members of Abraham (4:16), Paul begins to use the solidarity pronoun 'we' in 4:16, 17, 24-25, and throughout Romans 5-8. Jew and Gentile are one and together constitute 'the third race',[6] God's true people through Christ, who is thus called now *our* Lord Jesus Christ (4:24, 5:1, 11, 21; 6:23; 8:35).[7]

Whether Romans 5 belongs to the preceding chapters or to the following ones has been debated.[8] It is important to note, how-

---

2   E.g. Cranfield, Käsemann, Dodd, Boylan, Moo. Especially, for Nygren, Rom 5-8 expounds the theme of the letter (1:17): 'He who through faith is righteous shall live'– 'Free from the Wrath of God' (ch. 5), 'Free from Sin' (ch. 6), 'Free from the Law' (ch. 7) and 'Free from Death' (ch. 8).

3   Wright, *Messiah*, 134; a few recent exceptions include Kaylor, *Covenant Community*, 103; Beker, *Paul*, 86; Moo, *Romans* 1, 303: 'the concern for Jewish/Gentile relationships and the related topic of the Mosaic law ... is by no means dropped.' Wright, *Messiah*, 166, rightly asserts: 'Rom 5-8 is not about "Christ-mysticism", not "participation in Christ", not about Christian life or sanctification, not about anthropology, ...[but] that "Israel" is now a worldwide community.'

4   Bassler, *Impartiality*, 160; but Kaylor, *Covenant Community*, 103, is right to object to her view and to say that 'the question of Gentile and Jew is still reflected in chapters 5-8'.

5   In Romans 5-8 Paul treats Jewish and Gentile believers completely equally, putting into practice what he said 'theoretically' earlier on: 'There is no distinction between Jew and Gentile' (3:22; so again in 10:12).

6   Sanders, *Jewish People*, 171-178; Harnack, *Expansion*, 300-335.

7   It is noteworthy that the phrase, '*our* Lord Jesus Christ' or 'Christ Jesus *our* Lord' does not appear in 1:18-4:23, and 9:1-11:36, but only in the sections where Paul stresses the solidarity of Jew and Gentile (1:4, 7; 15:6, 30; 16:18, 20, 24).

8   Dunn, 'Romans: Analysis', 2855-56, asserts that since Rom 5 concludes the argument so far, Rom 1-5 must be regarded as a unit. Some linguis-

ever, that Paul does not make a clear-cut division when he moves from one major theme to another. What can be safely maintained is that, just as with other transitional passages, e.g. 3:21-26 and 9:30-33,[9] Paul uses 5:1-11[10] as both a conclusion to what has gone before (Rom 1-4) and as an introduction to what follows (Rom 5-8).[11] With the aorist participle δικαιωθέντες (5:1a and 9), Paul repeatedly confirms the justification of 'us', the Jewish and the Gentile believers, as a *fait accompli*, and moves on to develop the concept that this justification signifies their peace (or reconciliation) with God through Jesus Christ (5:1b, 10, 11: καταλλαγ- words). He affirms that since 'we' have been justified by faith in Christ, 'we' have peace with God, the hope of the glory of God, the love of God; and even much greater blessings (πολλῷ μᾶλλον) can be expected. The apostle explains in the subsequent passages how 'we' were reconciled to God through the death of his Son (5:10), and how 'we' can expect a greater blessing in Christ. Therefore 5:1-11 becomes the summary introduction to the entire argument of Romans 5-8.[12]

The main point of 5:1-11 is that 'we' have been reconciled to God through the death of his Son. Here Paul employs a concept of 'reconciliation' which was familiar to Jews and to those who knew Greek philosophy. Jews anticipated not only the covenantal reconciliation with God (2 Macc 7:32-3; cf. 2 Macc 1:5; 8:29), but also a cosmic reconciliation, which included God's ultimate victory over the power of Satan, the restoration of Israel, and 'all

---

tic and thematic connections between Rom 1-4 and 5 (p. 2856), and the aorist participle δικαιωθέντες together with the οὖν in 5:1, certainly support Dunn's contention. Fitzmyer's argument, 'Romans', 843-844, on the other hand, that Rom 5 belongs to the following chapters (so Rom 5-8 as a unit), is also weighty: (a) 5:1-11 is restated in 8:1-39; (b) the terms Jew/Gentile are completely absent in Rom 5-8, whilst they are dominant in Rom 1-4; (c) the concluding formula of 5:21 is very similar to that in 6:23; 7:24-25; 8:39; (d) Rom 1-4 is written in a juridical tone but 5-8 in an ethical tone (so also Moo, *Romans* 1, 301).

9   See *supra* pp. 156-163, and *infra* pp. 241-242.
10 The sub-division between 5:1-11 and 5:12-21 is universally recognised.
11 In 5:1-11 Paul introduces some new themes such as hope (5:2-5/8:20-25), suffering (5:3/8:18, 35-39), the Holy Spirit (5:5/8:9-27) and the love of God/Christ (5:5, 8/8:35, 39). See further in Dahl, *Studies*, 88-90.
12 So correctly Wright, 'Romans', 194-196.

the Gentiles' (πάντα τὰ ἔθνη) coming to worship the one true God (Tob 14:5-7; *Sib. Or.* 3:808; cf. Rom 16:20). Greeks were also familiar with the concept of cosmic reconciliation, i.e. the ultimate return of the cosmos to its original unity, as well as with that of human reconciliation in relationships.[13]

But for Paul reconciliation is fundamentally the restoration of peace through Christ's sacrifice in which God, at his own initiative, removed human trespasses and enabled himself to be reconciled to sinners (2 Cor 5:18-21).[14] 'When St. Paul says that God has given him the ministry of reconciliation, he means that he is a preacher of this peace. He ministers reconciliation to the world. His work [also] has no doubt a hortatory side.'[15] In 14:1-3 and 15:7 Paul makes it clear that God's/Christ's reception of 'us' is the fundamental reason for believers to accept/receive one another (cf. *1 Clem.* 49:6), and this admonition is given in the context of a concomitant and mutual acceptance among the Jewish and the Gentile believers (15:7-12). Most probably the exhortation is given primarily to the Jews because they, in general, used to despise the Gentiles and to separate themselves from them via the fence of the law 'to protect Israel from the impurity of the Gentiles'.[16] Paul's influence can be seen most explicitly in Ephesians 2:14-15, which indicates that Jesus has brought peace between Jews and Gentiles by destroying the dividing wall [of the law] through the cross.[17] The author stresses that the purpose of Christ's death 'was to create in himself one new man out of the two, thus making peace, and in this one body to reconcile both of them to God through the cross, by which he put to death their hostility. ..... For through him we both have access to the Father by one Spirit' (Eph 2:15-16, 18). Thus according to the author, the unity of the whole universe and a cosmic restoration and reconciliation (especially the unity of the church under the Lordship of Christ) is the ultimate purpose of God.

---

13   Keener, *Bible Background*, 423.
14   Martin, *2 Corinthians*, 146-147.
15   Denny as cited in Martin, *2 Corinthians*, 155.
16   Lincoln, *Ephesians*, 141: as symbolised in the Jerusalem Temple: Josephus, *Ant.* 15.11.5; *War*, 5.5.2.
17   Cf. Caragounis, *Mysterion*, 69-73, and also 136-146 on the συν- state of Gentiles and Jews.

The διὰ τοῦτο of 5:12 indicates that 5:12-21 will offer a further explanation of the assertion made in 5:1-11,[18] i.e. how 'we' were reconciled to God through the death of his Son, rather than summing up ('therefore') the argument of 5:1-11.[19] Paul thus offers a profound theological explanation (rather than quickly moving on to a practical admonition). Paul's overall intention is, no doubt, to affirm the overwhelming sufficiency of Christ's power to overcome all the consequences of Adam's disobedience ('how much more ...': 5:15, 17).[20] However, his reason for the shift to a universal focus seems deeper than that. An essential point which Paul has made in Romans 4 is that (believing) Gentiles equally have Abraham as their forefather; but in 5:12-21 he further affirms that all humanity, whether they be Jews or Gentiles, belong to the Adamic line.[21] Here Paul declares that Jew and Gentile are subsumed, without distinction, under the one man Adam the sinner, whose sin brought sin and death to all humanity (5:12, 16, 17, 18a).[22] Adam represents all of humanity in its solidarity in sinfulness,[23] and this clearly implies that Jews are equally as Adamic as Gentiles. Paul argues that Jews share with the Gentiles their forefather, Abraham, and also that they have joined the Adamic family of Gentile sinners (cf. Gal 2:15). Paul thus reaffirms with the figure of Adam the equality of Jew and Gentile in sinfulness, an equality which he has vigorously argued for in 1:18-3:20.

---

18 Commentators understand this διὰ τοῦτο with reference either to 5:9-11, or 5:1-11, or even 1:17-5:11 (Sanday and Headlam, *Romans*, 131, who themselves maintain that it covers 5:1-11). The identical theme of the reconciliation through Christ in 5:1, 9-11 allows us to maintain that it refers back to 5:1-11, and this indicates that 5:12-21 is the continuation of the discussion of 5:1-11 (Stuhlmacher, *Romans*, 83), rather than something added later as 'a theological excursus' (*pace* O'Neill, *Romans*, 96; similarly Luther: see. Beker, *Paul*, 84, for discusion), or 'ein erratischer Block' (*pace* Luz, *Geschichtsverständnis*, 193).

19 *Pace* Cranfield, *Romans* 1, 271; Fitzmyer, 'Romans', 845; but correctly O'Neill, *Romans*, 100.

20 Correctly Kaylor, *Covenant Community*, 106.

21 See Caragounis's article, 'Romans 5:15-16', 142-148, which fits well with our understanding here.

22 Beker, *Paul*, 83-85.

23 Ziesler, *Romans*, 144-145; Wedderburn, 'Adam', 423.

Then Paul quickly relates universal sinfulness to the law,[24] saying that it did not make any difference as far as the solution to the problem of sin and death was concerned. Rather it was intended to make the Jews more conscious of sin (5:13b; 7:7-8).[25] 'Torah, instead of lifting up Israel to a level above the rest of the human race, simply throws a bright spotlight on the fact that Israel, too, is "in Adam", is "fleshly", is "sold under sin".'[26] Certainly Paul does not make an affirmative statement in favour of the Jews. The function of the law is furthermore strikingly reinterpreted in 5:20-21, and is elaborated in 6:1-8:17,[27] as we will show below.

Paul also subsumes Jew and Gentile under another 'the-one-man' figure, Jesus Christ (5:15). Adam and Christ are compared in their capacity to represent all humanity in their solidarity, but the effects of such representation are sharply contrasted. The result of one act of righteousness has brought justification and life for all humanity (5:18; 1 Cor 15:22;[28] though not all have been justified, they are within the scope of Christ's accomplishment). Through Christ Jews and Gentiles can 'receive God's abundant provision of grace' (5:15, 17) and enter a new and righteous relationship with God. The distinctions made between Jew and Gentile through Abraham and the law are abolished in Christ. Paul asserts that if Adam's sinful act affected all humanity, then Christ's righteous act certainly affected them in much greater measure. Christ's obedience is more than enough to make righteous not only Jews, but also Gentiles who were thought to be outside God's salvific blessing. Paul's argument is structured to affirm the sufficiency and legitimacy of Gentile salvation in Christ. The analogy between Christ and Adam is then made not merely to add universal perspective, as Dahl points out,[29] but more fundamentally to affirm the equal status of Jew and Gentile: they are equal in Adam in their disobedience, sin, condemnation

---

24   He has not finished the Greek sentence of 5:12, yet mentions the law in 5:13-14.

25   So Wright, 'Romans', 198: 'Torah ... had been the divine instrument in confirming Israel under sin'; Kaylor, *Covenant Community*, 114-115.

26   Wright, 'Romans', 196.

27   Dahl, *Studies*, 91; Beker, *Paul*, 86.

28   Sanders, *Palestinian Judaism*, 473.

29   Dahl, *Studies*, 90-91.

and death; and equal also in Christ in obedience, atonement, forgiveness and life.[30]

The Jews might have wondered what was now the place of the law which had formerly divided them from the Gentiles. Paul recapitulates the issue of the law mentioned in 5:13-14, 20-21. He 'answers': 'The law was added so that the trespass might increase. ... [so as to increase] grace all the more' (5:20), and elaborates this point in 6:1-8:17. The thematic connection between 5:21 and 6:23 indicates that the conclusion of 5:12-21 is expounded in 6:1-23.[31] Then 'Paul here [in Romans 7] addresses another major divider between Jew and Gentile in his effort to bring the two together'.[32] The reason for the illustration from marriage in 7:1-5 is indicated in 7:6, and 7:7-25 expounds 7:6a, 'We have been released from the law'. The passage 8:1-17 elaborates 7:6b, 'We serve in the new way of the Spirit'. The theme of reconciliation / restoration is restated in 8:18-27, and 8:28-39 declares the basis for the assurance of God's election and of security in him. This brief survey suggests that 5:12-21 is the thematic passage within Romans 5-8. It sums up the arguments in 1:18-5:11: the equality of Jew and Gentile in the sin of Adam, and the equality of Jew and Gentile in the justification of Christ. Such a fundamental equality in justification enables Paul to claim that God glorified both Jews *and* Gentiles, and this is essentially because God foreknew, predestined and called both Jews and Gentiles on equal terms (8:28-30, 33), which Paul elaborates in Romans 9-11 (see the following chapter).

The section 6:1-14 explains the assertion made in 5:20, where Paul clarifies by differentiating increased grace *in spite of* increased sin from increasing sin *in order to* increase grace. The reason that believers should not go on sinning is the fact that they died to sin once and for all, as is symbolised by their baptism (6:2-4, 10, 11). Moreover, their 'old man' was crucified with Christ (6:6). So they have been freed from sin (6:7, 18, 22; cf. 8:2), and 'sin shall not be your master, because you [even the Jewish believers] are not under the law' (6:14, 15; cf. 2:12; 3:19;

---

30 Although the idea of Jew/Gentile is found implicit in the Adam-Christ typology, the corporate interpretation is a theme that permeates the whole letter (cf. 1:18-32; 5:12-21; 7:7-25).
31 So also Dunn, 'Romans: Analysis', 2861; Beker, *Paul*, 86.
32 Keener, *Bible Background*, 426.

7:6), and they are no longer slaves to sin (6:17-18). Although they should continue to keep away from sin in reality (6:12-13), believers, both Jewish and Gentile, have the new status that implies they cannot and should not continue to sin (6:13, 19).

This is also affirmed in 7:1-6. Just as a wife is released from the law of marriage after her husband's death, so also believers have died to the law (7:4). Thus Jewish believers 'have been released from the law' (7:6), and Gentile believers do not have any reason to be bound by the law. Although Paul solemnly denies that the law is sin, and states some positive aspects of the law (7:7, 12, 13, 14, 16; but 4:15), he confirms what he said earlier in 5:20: 'The law was added so that the trespass might increase' (cf. Gal 3:19). He implies that Jews under the law and the Gentiles without the law were not different in real terms.[33] Rather it was the Jews who had a greater sense of guilt (cf. 5:13b; 7:8, 13b). Paul's long discussion in 7:7-23 is to affirm the impotence of the law to bring salvation (8:3), and to stress that it was through Jesus Christ that both Jews and Gentiles were released from the law (7:24).

The law could not remove condemnation from 'us', but the law of the Spirit of life through Christ set 'us' free from the law of sin and death, and thus removed condemnation (8:1-2). Paul elaborates the life in the Spirit which he hinted of earlier: 'we serve in the new way of the Spirit' (5:5; 7:6). Paul puts believing Jews and Gentiles in one and the same category: 'those who are in Christ'. They have the same Spirit variously expressed as the Spirit of life/God/Christ (8:2, 9a, b, 14). This Spirit testifies that they are God's children, and in 8:12-30 Paul discusses who the children of God are, since this explanation will lay a foundation for his later argument in 9:7-13. The assurance of sonship enables believers to overcome sufferings, to anticipate future glory (8:18-27), and to be certain of the love of God (8:28-39).

To sum up: Paul expounds Romans 5-8 on the firm presupposition established in 1:18-4:25 that Jew and Gentile are fundamentally equal in their sinfulness and justification. This equality is unmistakably reaffirmed by the claim that they were all condemned to death due to their sin in Adam, and that they were all justified to new life by faith in Christ (5:12-21). No differentiation can be made even on the basis of the law, possession of

---

33 Kaylor, *Covenant Community*, 118-119.

which is the main division between the two groups, because it neither removes sin nor brings salvation. Only in and through Jesus Christ are justification, reconciliation, 'no-condemnation' and new status bestowed. God reconciled his enemies (5:9-11), both Jews and Gentiles, and justified them both by the same faith (5:1, 9a; 3:30). Thus there is no condemnation for them (8:1). Both were baptised into Christ and both received the Holy Spirit. They used to be slaves to sin (6:6, 17, 20; 7:5), but now 'have been set free from sin and have become slaves to righteousness' (6:6, 17, 18, 19, 22), through Christ and by the law of the Spirit of life (8:2). Both Jews and Gentiles have the Spirit of God/Christ in them, and are equally God's legitimate children (8:11, 14, 15, 16, 23). So they have become heirs of God with Christ (8:17).

What Paul has written in Romans 5-8 is again a very bold argument for a Jew to make. He has taken a courageous stand in expounding the place of the law, probably in order to equip his readers to resist any Judaisers who may soon be actively at work in Rome (cf. 16:17-20). Moreover, there could be nothing more offensive to (unbelieving) Jews than to insist that Gentiles have received the same privileges promised to Israel, and thus have fundamentally equal status with Jews themselves.[34] Paul's awareness of being the apostle to the Gentiles has led him to affirm the basic equality between Jew and Gentile and so treat them as one 'ethnic' group, 'we'. His apostolic self-awareness is expressed even further: their equality is not just because of Christ's work equally available to them, but more fundamentally because of God's salvific plan, in which he equally predestined and called Jew and Gentile (8:28-30, 33). Only when Paul could explain that God had indeed done so, could he firmly establish the equality of Jew and Gentile in this letter, and so make vital exhortations to promote their unity in the Roman community (Rom 12-16). Thus he undertakes the explication of their equality in the plan of God in Romans 9-11, to which we turn in the next chapter.

---

34 Correctly Locke, *Paraphrase* 2, 560; especially Howard, 'Romans 3:21-31', 223-233; Sanders, *Jewish People*, 33; Dunn, *Romans* 1, 191.

Chapter 5

The Equality of Jew and Gentile in the Plan of God: 9:1-11:36

Since the Holocaust and the founding of the state of Israel, Romans 9-11 has been at the centre of much scholarly attention,[1] especially in relation to Jewish-Christian dialogue.[2] F.C. Baur's perception that Romans 9-11 is 'the germ and the centre of the whole [epistle]', which contains the interpretative key for the entire epistle,[3] anticipated more recent discussion, and now this unit is generally taken as the climax of Paul's theological argument in Romans.[4] As a result there has been a substantial shift in the reformulations of Pauline theology and exegesis.[5] Perhaps the most important issue has related to the nature of these chapters: what is this section all about? Today most interpreters of Romans generally agree that the fundamental theological principle of Romans 9-11 is an affirmative exposition of *God's faithfulness to his promises to Israel* despite her failure to respond to the gospel.

---

1   Cf. Grässer, *Alte Bund*, 212-230.
2   See Wigoder, *Jewish–Christian Relations*. See Mussner's view described in Grässer, *Alte Bund*, 212, n. 1.
3   Baur, *Paul* 1, 315. So also notably Stendahl, *Paul*, 4, 28, 85, who regards Rom 1-8 as a preface (p. 29).
4   O'Neill, *Romans*, 145; Ziesler, *Romans*, 37, 39; Campbell, 'Freedom', 27-28; idem, 'Why?', 264-269; Beker, *Paul*, 87.
5   Haynes, 'Rediscovering', 70. See Grässer, *Alte Bund*, 259ff, for a critical examination of 'die hermeneutische Bedeutung des Holocaust' in the case of Heb 11.

According to this view Romans 9-11 fundamentally expounds the issues concerning *Israel*, especially their brighter future under God's providence.[6]

Such a move has certainly and rightly contributed to correct the undue 'biblical' presuppositions of anti-Judaism or anti-semitism, which were widely held in the pre-Holocaust era.[7] However, most post-Holocaust interpreters have moved too far in the other direction, and thus often advocate inadequate interpretations not only for this section, and for Romans generally, but also for a large part of Paul's theology. For them Paul's concern for the Gentiles is secondary and subordinate to that for the Jews. So B.W. Longenecker asserts that 'his [Paul's] point is not simply that Gentile Christians *cannot exist without* Israel but, even more, that Gentile Christians *cannot exist except within* Israel'.[8] Similarly, in Jewish–Christian dialogue, P. Stuhlmacher and P. Lapide have reached something like the same conclusion, one already expressed by J. Munck.[9] Concerning Paul's role as apostle to the Gentiles Stuhlmacher asserts, 'Paul conceived of himself as having been commissioned by Jesus as an apostle to the Gentiles *for Israel's sake*'.[10] Lapide similarly puts it, '... indeed it often appears as if the entire mission to the Gentiles is *only a roundabout way of saving all Israel*'.[11]

This position, however, does not take adequate account of Paul's affirmative statements about and argument for the Gentiles, and his largely critical portrayal of the Jews in these chap-

---

6   E.g. Stendahl, *Paul*, 3. See also *Paul*, 132 where he endorses Bornkamm, *Paul*, 95, who has contended that Rom 9-11 is primarily about the Jews, but objects to his reading the section as a polemic against Jews and their understanding of salvation. For Stendahl, Rom 9-11 is 'an apology for his [Paul's] mission in which he reflects on the mystery of God's dealings with *Israel*' (p. 132). So does he maintain in *Final Account*, 37.

7   See Ericksen, *Theologians Under Hitler*.

8   Longenecker, 'Different Answers', 113, with his emphasis.

9   Munck, *Paul*, 42-49: the Gentile mission is 'the shortest way' to bring salvation to Israel; Watson, *Paul*, 162. Cf. Fitzmyer, *Romans*, 541, 612. Note Stendahl, *Paul*, vi, who now thinks that Munck's view is rather a tour de force.

10 Stuhlmacher, in Lapide and Stuhlmacher, *Paul*, 25-30; the quotation is from p. 26 with added emphasis.

11 Lapide, in Lapide and Stuhlmacher, *Paul*, 44, emphasis added.

ters.¹² Furthermore, this common view undermines the theme of the fundamental equality of Jew and Gentile in the gospel, for which Paul so vigorously argues in Romans 1-4, and which he resumes in this section (cf. 10:11-13; 11:32).¹³ The true theme of Romans 9-11 is not just 'God and Israel', as J.D.G. Dunn contends,¹⁴ but God (and/or Christ), Israel *and* the Gentiles,¹⁵ or, to put it more precisely, the equality of Jew and Gentile in the plan of God.¹⁶ It is obvious that here Paul develops his argument in relation to both Jews and Gentiles. But his aim for this section, and indeed for the whole letter, is not to affirm that one ethnic group is superior to the other. That there is no difference between Jew and Gentile (3:22; 10:12, and 1:16; 2:9-10; 3:29; 4:16; cf. Gal 3:28; Col 3:11), is fundamental to the theological exposition and to the practical exhortation in Romans. He explains how both Jews and Gentiles are equal and mutually interdependent in God's outworking of salvation for all humanity. Our position coheres better with the earlier parts of Romans as well as with earlier Pauline letters (cf. 1 Thess 2:14-16; Gal 4:21-31). The explanation given by J.C. Beker and G. Wagner that Paul is now correcting what he has written earlier is (as we shall see) unlikely.¹⁷

Readers will soon notice that Paul's argument is substantially and distinctively woven together with numerous OT quotations.¹⁸

---

12 *Pace*, e.g. Wiefel, 'Jewish Community', 100-101, who asserts that Paul makes affirmative statements about Jews in Rom 9-11 (in order to prevent Christianity from turning into an anti-Jewish movement).

13 Wright's assumption (*Climax*, 234-236) that Paul is arguing for the equality of *Jews* with Gentiles by speaking on behalf of the Jews on the basis of the covenant faithfulness of God, is unconvincing; rather, he argues for the equality of the *Gentiles* with the Jews by speaking on behalf of the Gentiles, as we have seen in our previous chapters.

14 *Pace* Dunn, *Romans* 2, 520; Conzelmann and Lidermann, *Interpreting*, 193. Cf. Munck, *Paul*, 42; Barrett, 'Romans 9:30-10:21', 139, asserts that Paul's main concern in Rom 9-11 is with the Jews.

15 So correctly Dahl, *Studies*, 155.

16 Robinson, *Wrestling*, 109, plausibly asserts that 'the whole section [of Rom 9-11] is in effect the answer to the question in 3.9, which ever way it is translated: "Are we Jews any better off?" or "Are we Jews any worse off?" And the answer in either case is "No, not at all"'.

17 *Pace* Beker, 'Faithfulness', 16; Wagner, 'Future', 100-103; Noack, 'Current', 164; cf. Simpson, 'Future', 165-275; Getty, 'Covenants', 96.

18 Nearly 40 percent of Rom 9-11 is composed of the OT quotations (Guerra, 'Paul's Purpose', 226), and more than half of the OT citations in

The way Paul interprets the OT passages and applies them must therefore be taken into account if we are to understand this section. It is striking to note that when he cites OT passages concerning the Jews (ὑπὲρ τοῦ Ἰσραήλ; 9:27-29; 10:19, 21; 11:8-10), he chooses some of the most severely critical passages in the OT.[19] On the other hand, he applies to *Gentiles* some of the passages most affirmative of Israel. Dunn is certainly correct to affirm that Paul uses the OT as 'witness for Israel and accuser of Israel';[20] but Paul also employs it as an amicable testifier on behalf of the Gentiles. What is more, he never applies the OT to accuse Gentiles but rather to explain *Israel's* unbelief and the Gentiles' faith and inclusion in the true people of God.[21]

This leads us to consider how the thematic statement for Romans 9-11, 'It is not as though the word of God has failed' (9:6a), should be understood. Commentators correctly take this statement as the thesis for the entire section of Romans 9-11, but most of them designate 'the word of God' as God's promise or privileges given to *Israel*.[22] But in the light of the fact that Paul applies 'the word of God' to both Jews and Gentiles in the wider context of Romans 9-11, it seems better to understand Paul as saying that the plan or intention of God[23] as manifested in the Scriptures for both Israel *and the Gentiles*, has not failed. In fact, the reliability of God's word is questioned not just because many of the Israelites whose blessing is promised now experience God's 'rejection',[24]

Romans appear in Rom 9-11, and 66 percent of all Pauline quotations are found in Romans; that means more than one-third of the OT quotations in the authentic Pauline letters are cited in Rom 9-11. See also Ellis, *Paul's Use*, 98-103; Seifrid, 'Approach', 5.

19 Evans, '"True Prophecy"', 570.
20 Dunn, *Romans* 2, 520, following Michel.
21 Evans, '"True Prophecy"', 562-563.
22 Calvin, *Romans*, 197; Murray, *Romans* 2, 9; Barrett, *Romans*, 169; Käsemann, *Romans*, 261-262; Dahl, *Studies*, 143; Kümmel, 'Probleme', 20; Munck, *Christ*, 34; Campbell, 'Freedom', 28; Fitzmyer, *Romans*, 559. Dunn's addition to the sentence, 'the word of God (*to Israel*) has not failed', represents a common view: Dunn, 'Romans', 848, with our emphasis; idem, *Romans* 2, 539: 'God's specific word (=promise to Israel)', and the narrow context of 9:6 suggests that this view has some force.
23 Black, *Romans*, 130; Piper, *Justification*, 48-51; *pace* Käsemann, *Romans*, 262, for denying this.
24 Piper's perception (*Justification* 48-51) is not comprehensive enough.

but equally because many Gentiles, whose exclusion God has clearly declared, now enjoy God's salvific blessing. Although Paul considers τὰ λόγια τοῦ θεοῦ (3:2) as the most important (πρῶτον) advantage of the Jews, he has already used it critically to point out the equal sinfulness of Jews with Gentiles (3:10-18).[25] In Romans 9-11 Paul uses 'the word of God' to demonstrate Jewish unbelief and Gentile faith; for Paul it not only talks *about* the Gentiles but also speaks *for* them. Paul proves this through the OT quotations in Romans 9-11. Just as he has reinterpreted the concepts of circumcision, Jew, the Shema and the Abrahamic ancestry to affirm that believing Gentiles are included in these Jewish privileges, so does he here with the word of God in the OT by modifying its texts and contexts.

The purpose of this chapter is to propose a synthetical, not an antithetical, alternative interpretation to the view widely held today by highlighting the hypothesis that Paul, apostle to the *Gentiles*, argues for the equality of Jew and Gentile in the salvific plan of God by providing a Scriptural explanation of the phenomena of Israel's unbelief and the Gentiles' belief. Those who knew the OT would certainly acknowledge that Israel had a special place in God's plan,[26] but the apostle to the Gentiles boldly asserts that the Gentiles too have equal importance in God's purpose. Thus, once again, we will propose that Paul's apostolic self-awareness influences him to affirm the legitimacy and the sufficiency of the salvation of the Gentiles in Christ. We will show how Paul establishes (just as he did in Romans 1-4) the equality of Jew and Gentile in the salvific plan of God by drawing a largely critical picture of Israel's unbelief but an affirmative one of the Gentiles' faith; Paul's stress on the Gentiles has not received adequate attention in post-Holocaust interpretation.

With this preliminary understanding we will undertake an exegetical examination of the passages of the section. In the discussion of 9:1-29 we will propose that Romans 9 is Paul's implicit explanation that God had also predestined and called the Gentiles to be his beloved people according to his sovereign freedom and mercy. Our position denies both F. Watson's assertion that here Paul expounds the rejection of Jews,[27] and J. Piper's contention

---

25 See *supra* pp. 141-150 for our earlier discussion.
26 Cranfield, *Romans* 2, 446-447.
27 *Pace* Watson, *Paul*, 163-164.

that Romans 9 expounds God's justification for saving 'the "Israel" within Israel'.[28] We will then argue against those who contend that 9:30-10:21 stresses 'God's goodness towards Israel'.[29] Rather, we will suggest that Paul highlights the unbelief of Jews on the one hand, and both the universal principles of salvation and the Gentiles' positive response to the salvation message on the other. Our next passage is 11:1-36.[30] Paul continues to make sharply critical comments about Israel in 11:1-10, despite his solemn affirmation that God has not rejected ethnic Israel. In 11:11-16 Paul expects τὸ πλήρωμα of the Jews, but anticipates a greater blessing upon the Gentiles as the result of Israel's πλήρωμα. We will argue against the hypotheses (1) that Israel's hardening was a necessary step for God to save the Gentiles, and (2) that Paul's mission to the Gentiles was secondary to the ultimate aim to save the Jews through his apostolic ministry.

Paul's admonition concerning the olive tree (11:17-24) has greatly affected scholars' reconstruction of the constituency of the Roman church.[31] As a result, this passage is considered as indicating the purpose of the letter[32] and as significantly affecting the interpretation of the whole.[33] However, the passage does not necessarily suggest that the Gentile believers have already shown

---

28 Pace Piper, *Justification*, 218.

29 Pace Cranfield, *Romans* 2, 503, 541-542, for example.

30 It is difficult to make a sharp division between Rom 10 and 11:1-16 because both sections are thematically connected. In 11:1-16 Paul continues to make a harsh judgement upon Israel despite his solemn denial of the view that God has rejected ethnic Israel. 11:11-16 forms one unit syntactically but 11:13-32 is also one unit of Paul's specific address to the Gentile believers using second person pronouns. Thus 11:13-15 bridges two sections just as 9:30-33 does. Cf. Siegert, *Argumentation*, 148, who argues that Rom 10:1-11:32 is syntactically a single complex argument.

31 Sanday and Headlam, *Romans*, 324, infer that 11:13-24 provides conclusive evidence that the majority of the Roman church were Gentiles.

32 E.g. Elliott, *Rhetoric*, 291: 'Paul's goal is to avert the danger of Gentile-Christian boasting over Israel (cf. Rom 11.17-24); but this goal is manifest in the macro-structure of the whole letter, not only in the explicit apocalyptic admonition of Romans 11.' Lütgert in Käsemann, *Romans*, 305. Käsemann himself is of the opinion that 11:16-24 does not tell us much about the situation of the church in Rome.

33 E.g. Elliott; see the above note. For Schoeps, *Paul*, 235, 236, Romans 9-11 is an exhortation to the believing Gentiles in a situation where a Jewish minority was under the threat of complete Gentile domination.

arrogance towards the Jewish believers, nor that the Gentiles are a majority. We shall argue that 11:17-24 could well be a warning not to *become* arrogant (i.e. on the basis of what Paul has affirmatively written about the Gentiles in this letter). In 11:17-32 Paul certainly indicates the possibility of a brighter future for Israel, but we propose to interpret 11:25-32 in the light of Paul's entire argument in Romans 1-11, rather than to allow it to become the interpretative key for the whole section of Romans 9-11 (if not the entire letter!). It is crucial to note that Paul's mention of the 'mystery' of Israel's salvation (11:25b-26) is 'so that you [Gentile believers] may not be conceited' (11:25a). We will also attempt to show that the equality and the interdependence of Jew and Gentile in the salvific plan of God are portrayed in 11:25-32. We will attempt to qualify and substantiate the claim of some scholars that in Romans 11 Paul indicates the reversal of the salvation order from 'to the Jew first and also to the Gentile' (1:16) to '"to the Gentile first and also to the Jew" (11.25-26)'.[34] We will examine to what extent Paul's apostolic self-awareness has shaped his argument in Romans 9-11.

Before we discuss the main texts, however, it would be appropriate for us to examine briefly the connection between Romans 9-11 and the preceding chapters. The understanding of the connection has often determined the direction of the interpretation of Romans 9-11, or, conversely, the interpretation of Romans 9-11 has led to a search for a suitable connection to the preceding material.

1. The Connection between Romans 1-8 and 9-11

Few today would agree with C.H. Dodd that Romans 9-11 is mere digression.[35] Rather it is widely considered to be 'an integral part

---

34 Robinson, *Wrestling*, 110; this understanding has been also expressed by Dahl, *Studies*, 150; Kümmel, 'Probleme', 40-41; Käsemann, *Romans*, 274; Cranfield, *Romans* 2, 576.

35 *Pace* Dodd, *Romans*, 161; yet those who maintain this view include Bultmann, *Theology* 2, 132; Manson, *Studies*, 21; Beare, *St. Paul*, 103-104; Robinson, *Wrestling*, 108; and prior to Dodd, Sanday and Headlam, *Romans*, 225.

of the working out of the theme of the epistle'.[36] But the affirmation of a precise connection of these chapters to the rest of the letter is often made in the course of stressing the faithfulness of God to Israel in Romans 9-11. N.T. Wright, for example, asserts that it is now necessary for Paul to affirm that God will save Israel too, after having emphasised universal sinfulness, the world-wide family of Abraham and universal redemption in Christ (Rom 1-8).[37] F. Watson and C.K. Barrett contend that these chapters are needed in order to correct the charge or the impression that Paul neglects his own people.[38] These two explanations appear to endorse our interpretation of Romans 1-4, where Paul has offered a critical view of the Jews and an affirmative picture of the Gentiles. However, these views undermine the fact that (as we will show) Paul continues to draw a critical picture of Jews in 9:6-11:16.[39]

C.E.B. Cranfield, M. Barth and J.A. Ziesler offer another explanation for the connection of the two main sections (Rom 1-8 and 9-11). They argue that the affirmation of the faithfulness of God to Israel is essential to assure the Gentile believers that God is totally reliable as described in 8:35-39.[40] However, Paul's solemn warning to the Gentile believers that they could also be cut off (11:22) suggests that his exposition in Romans 9-11 does not assure them much in this regard. Since Paul has so strongly affirmed that they can rely on their security in God through Christ, he might not need to confirm it again in Romans 9-11. Rather, since the declaration in 8:31-39 depends on the assertions

---

36 Cranfield, *Romans* 2, 445. So also Davies, 'People', 13; Beasley-Murray, 'Righteousness', 438; Seifrid, 'Approach', 4; Hays, *Echoes*, 63; Barrett, 'Romans 9:30-10:21', 132; Wright, *Messiah*, 220, expresses this point aptly: 'Romans 1-8 create the problem to which 9-11 is the solution. ...1-8 is ultimately incomprehensible without 9-11, and vice versa.': also affirmatively cited in Dunn, *Romans* 2, 519.

37 Wright, *Messiah*, 220; idem, *Climax*, 232, raises the issue of the connection, but does not offer a clear alternative.

38 Watson, *Paul*, 161; Barrett, 'Gentile Mission', 69.

39 Cf. for Noack, 'Current', 163-166, Romans 9-11 emphasises the priority of the Jews, yet he admits that 9:1-11:10 does not contain the slightest solution for the salvation of the Jews.

40 Cranfield, *Romans* 2, 447; Barth, *People*, 30; Ziesler, *Romans*, 37. So also Beker, *Paul*, 91; idem, 'Faithfulness', 14; Piper, *Justification*, 19. Cf. Rese, 'Rettung', 423.

made in 8:28-30, he would have to expound those assertions in Romans 9-11.[41]

Among others, Cranfield plausibly notes the linguistic (1:5-7; 8:29-30, 33) and the thematic connection (1:1-4, 16-17) between Romans 1-8 and 9-11.[42] The theme of the epistle certainly requires an explanation of the implications of the gospel for the Jews (Israel), as Cranfield maintains.[43] However, it seems equally (if not more) important to observe that Paul is also explaining the gospel in relation to the *Gentiles*, who were thought to be excluded from God's salvific blessing and mercy. Cranfield is also certainly correct to observe the connection of thought between 8:28-33 and Romans 9-11, but it is not adequate to explain this connection exclusively in terms of the faithfulness of God towards Israel.

Paul has expressed the concepts that both the Jewish and the Gentile Christians 'have been called according to his purpose'; God [1] foreknew and [2] predestined them (8:28-29; cf. 1 Pet 1:2). And he repeats, 'those he predestined, he also [3] called; those he called, he also [4] justified; those he justified, he also [5] glorified' (8:30). Since God has chosen them, nothing will be able to separate them from the love of God (8:33, 39). Paul has vigorously argued that believers are justified (3:21-5:21; 8:30) and glorified (8:17, 18, 21, 30), regardless of their ethnic origins (cf. 1 Cor 1:2). In Romans 9-11 he turns to explain the first three verbs: how they are foreknown, predestined and called. Jewish believers would have no doubt that they were predestined and called by God.[44] When this assertion is applied to the (believing) Gentiles, however, a theological explanation is required. This issue becomes acute in the light of *Israel's* failure and the Gentiles' faith. How have so many Gentiles, who were considered to be outside God's call and saving purpose, come to faith and salvation (9:30-

---

41 Cf. Hays, *Echoes*, 63-64: Paul is dealing with the question whether or not Israel is included in Paul's 'us' whom nothing can separate from the love of God in Christ (8:39).

42 Cranfield, *Romans* 2, 445-447; Dunn, *Romans* 2, 541, also notes the strong linguistic connection of Rom 9-11 with Rom 4: 'ἐπαγγελία (4:13, 14, 16, 20; 9:4, 8, 9), λογίζεσθαι (4:3-6, 8-11, 22-24; 9:8), σπέρμα (4:13, 16, 18; 9:7-8)'.

43 Cranfield, *Romans* 2, 445.

44 E.g. Isa 44:1-2; 49:1; 65:12; 66:4; 1QM 3:2; 4:9-11; CD 4:4.

31)?⁴⁵ Such a phenomenon must be explained in connection with God's purpose of election (ἡ κατ' ἐκλογὴν πρόθεσις; 8:28 and 9:11), and Paul presents this explanation theologically from the OT Scriptures.⁴⁶ Effectively, his answer is that both Jewish rejection of the gospel and the call of the Gentiles into the people of God were already planned and indeed predicted in Scripture. The theme of 'calling' 'from among all the Gentiles' was already mentioned in the introduction of the letter (1:5-7), but until these chapters Paul has not elaborated this. The exposition of the calling of the Gentiles is important because it will lead to the explanation of the hardening/unbelief of the Jews which he briefly mentioned earlier (2:17-20; 3:3).⁴⁷

2. God's Freedom in Hardening Jews and Electing Gentiles: 9:1-29

J. Piper and F. Watson independently stress that in Romans 9 Paul firmly establishes God's consistent and sovereign activity of 'electing' from Scripture.⁴⁸ They arrive at substantially different conclusions, however, when they come to the chapter with the question, 'Whom did God elect?'. According to Watson, God 'elect[ed] Gentiles as children of Abraham and ... reject[ed] Jews'; for Piper, on the contrary, God elected 'the "saved" among [ethnic] Israel'.⁴⁹ However, we find Piper's view particularly one-sided and incomplete. Confining himself to examining 9:1-23, Piper does not pay adequate attention to the context of Romans 9-11, not even the immediate one of 9:1-33, whose main theme is related to both Jew *and* Gentile. Consequently, he does not sufficiently acknowledge the human responsibility of faith (9:30-33) nor God's freedom to elect Gentiles (9:22-26). Watson correctly

---

45 Baur, *Paul* 1, 315.
46 Guerra's entitling of the section Rom 9-11 as 'Paul's Scriptural Defence of His Gospel and Mission to the Gentiles' ('Purpose', 228), is highly plausible but rather incomplete, because Paul also uses the OT to explain the phenomenon of *Jewish* unbelief and their future.
47 Sanday and Headlam, *Romans*, 26; Schoeps, *Paul*, 236; Motyer, *Israel*, 30.
48 Both of them produced significant dissertations in the early 1980s, which were subsequently published in 1983 and 1986 respectively (Piper, *Justification*; Watson, *Paul*).
49 Watson, *Paul*, 163; Piper, *Justification*, 218.

The Equality of Jew and Gentile in the Plan of God 225

highlights Paul's intention to secure the legitimacy of the believing Gentiles, but unduly undermines the fact that 9:7-23 is fundamentally about Israel.

We shall show that Paul's aim in 9:1-29 is to affirm that Jews and Gentiles are equally called to be God's people. Since the election of the Jews was presupposed (cf. 9:3-5), he seeks primarily to establish God's election of the Gentiles, and he does this by stressing God's sovereign freedom in mercy. We have tried to demonstrate, in our examination of 2:6-11, that Paul establishes the theological axiom of divine impartiality, but there the passage suggests a deeper intention: to confirm that God's impartiality includes his judgement on Jews and election of Gentiles to blessing.[50] Paul uses the same tactic in presenting his argument here. His argument on 'the freedom of God' in 9:6-23 serves as a stepping stone from which to launch a more fundamental two-sided argument, as we have just suggested. Thus in Romans 9 Paul makes affirmative statements about the Gentiles and draws critical pictures of the Jews similar to the way in which he presented his argument in Romans 1-4.

A. *The Jewish Privileges (Shared by Gentiles): 9:1-5*

At the outset of the section Romans 9-11, Paul expresses his great sorrow and unceasing anguish, which has arisen from the fact that a great majority of Jews do not attain righteousness despite their zealous pursuit of it (9:31-33) and their exceptional preparation with many prerogatives (9:4-5). Paul's concern for his own people is certainly genuine, and his recognition of their privileges in this passage specifically conveys his loyalty to all Israelites.[51]

---

50 See *supra* pp. 103-108.
51 Piper's repeated assertion (*Justification*, 23-24, 45, 64) that Paul applies these privileges specifically to the *unbelieving* Israelites, is grammatically unconvincing. He incorrectly supposes that the antecedent of the relative pronoun οἵτινες is 'Paul's kinsmen *according to the flesh* who are *anathema, separated from Christ* (9:3)', namely, the unbelieving Jews. Rather, the antecedent is the clause 'τῶν ἀδελφῶν μου τῶν συγγενῶν μου κατὰ σάρκα', and here there is no specific indication that they are specifically *unbelievers*. Paul rather refers to the Jews in general, and so these privileges belong to the Jews generally. The clause ἀνάθεμα εἶναι αὐτὸς ἐγὼ ἀπὸ τοῦ Χριστοῦ does not refer to the Israelites but to Paul himself. The clause does not describe the

Watson remarks, 'The point of 9:6ff is to deny that Jewish people were *ever* elected for salvation; their privileges (9:4f) are in the sphere of σάρξ (9:8)'.[52] But this is far from the truth. Paul clearly presupposes the election of historical Israel.[53] Watson's further allocation of these privileges to being 'only in the flesh' by referring (implicitly) to Ishmael in 9:8, is a jump in logic. Neither does Paul say that these Jewish privileges are transferred to or continued in the church.[54] Paul *has* fundamental concern for his people.

What is striking, however, is the fact that he does not expound these privileges, whilst he has already applied these privileges to the believing Gentiles equally in Romans 1-8 and elsewhere. It is important to pay due attention to this point because 9:1-5 frames the topic for Romans 9-11 as a whole. Our summary below will show how Paul has been arguing for the Gentiles' inclusion in the privileges promised to Israel.

According to the OT these privileges were given exclusively to the Jews in contrast to the Gentiles: the concepts of 'sonship' (Exod 4:22; Deut 7:6; 14:1-2; Jer 31:9), 'glory' (Exod 13:21; Lev 9:6; 23:24, etc.), 'covenants' (Gen 17:2-4; Exod 34:27; Deut 4:13; 29:2-15; cf. Sir 44:12; Luke 1:72), 'the law-giving' (Deut 4:7-8, 32-34; Ps 147:19-20) and 'promises' (Deut 26:16-19; 28:1, 13; 33:29). But Paul has already included the (believing) Gentiles in these blessings. 'You [Jewish *and* Gentile believers] have received the Spirit of **sonship**' (8:15, 23), and to the Gentile-majority Galatian church, Paul writes that in Christ they have 'the full rights of sons' (Gal 4:5; cf. Eph 1:5).[55] To Gentiles he applies **glory** (2:10; 8:18; 2 Cor 4:17; cf. Col 1:27; 3:4), and has also indicated that the Gentile believers can take part in the new **covenant** as expressed in the Lord's Supper (1 Cor 11:25).[56] Paul has already condemned

---

ἀδελφοί, but expresses Paul's own desperate wish to become ἀνάθεμα for the sake of his unbelieving kinsfolk (cf. Exod 32:32).

52 Watson, *Paul*, 163, 227 n. 9. Dunn, *Romans* 2, 540, finds Watson's assertion astonishing.

53 So one does not need to wonder with Fitzmyer, *Romans*, 543, why Paul does not include 'election' as a Jewish prerogative here, but only in 11:28. Another term which can sum up these privileges is 'the love of God' (see Wright, *Messiah*, 139, 302 n. 37), and the terms 'election' and 'love' represent two sides of the same coin.

54 *Pace* Wright, *Messiah*, 139, 145, 148; Epp, 'Continuity', 80-90; Watson, *Paul*, 31.

55 See Scott, 'Adoption', 15-18, for a fuller account on this theme of sonship.

56 Cf. Campbell, 'Covenant', 179-182.

the Jews for not keeping the **law**, whilst believing Gentiles, though they do not have the law, do the requirements of the law by nature (2:14-15, 26; 8:4).

Paul's use of **worship** (λατρεία) here and in 12:1 indicates that believers (Jewish and Gentile) can offer reasonable acts of true worship.[57] The Gentile believers are also the children of **promise** (Gal 4:28), Abraham's offspring (4:16). Jesus' service is 'to confirm the promises made to the patriarchs so that the Gentiles may glorify God for his mercy' (15:8-9). The Gentile believers also have become the children of the **fathers**, and Paul has made it clear in ch. 4 as well as in Gal 3:29: 'If you belong to Christ, then you are Abraham's seed, and heirs according to the promise.' **Christ** is from Israel but Paul 'emphasises' the universal element of the Messiah: he is over all God blessed forever.[58] That God is also the God of Gentiles is clearly affirmed (3:29), and so the Christ is the Messiah for Jews and Gentiles.[59]

In the light of what he said in Romans 1-8, the scripture-based declaration 'For not all who are descended from Israel are Israel' (9:6b), suggests that while not all Israelites are enjoying the reality of these privileges,[60] many Gentiles are. He may imply: 'Some who are not descended from Israel are Israel.' By listing Jewish prerogatives Paul achieves two purposes: (1) he expresses his tie with his own people, and (2) he also sums up what he has written earlier about the blessing into which (the believing) Gentiles are included. Both Jews and Gentiles equally share these privileges, which previously were exclusively granted to the Jews.

B. *God's Freedom of Election: 9:6-23*

It is important to note that Paul does not elaborate the items of Jewish privileges but simply mentions them, just as he did with 'the words of God' in 3:2.[61] It is often asserted that the thematic statement, 'It is not as though God's word had failed' (9:6a), indicates that '[Paul's] primary aim is to demolish any assertion

---

57 Cf. Martin, 'Worship', 986-990.

58 For the discussion on the punctuation issues, see Cranfield, *Romans* 2, 464-470; Sanday and Headlam, *Romans*, 233-238; Barrett, 167-168. Here we follow UBS³, Nestle-Aland²⁷, Cranfield, Sanday and Headlam, Metzger, *Textual Commentary*, 520-523; Wright, *Climax*, 237.

59 Wright, *Climax*, 237.

60 Räisänen, *Jesus*, 30: 'Paul immediately in effect *denies* his fleshly kinsmen any of the said privileges.'

61 See our earlier comments in *supra* pp. 131-132.

that God has cast off Israel (cf. 11:1, 11)',[62] and to prove God's faithfulness to his promises to ethnic Israel as a whole (cf. 11:26-32) through Scripture. But the immediate basis for this thematic declaration is: 'For (γάρ) not all who are descended from Israel are Israel' (9:6b), which casts doubt on this position. Although such a remnant theology as in 9:6b itself was held in some Jewish circles,[63] it is indeed a bold statement for a Jew to make. This suggests that Paul intends to prove the notion that some/many who are descended from Israel [Jacob] do not belong to Messianic Israel.[64] Paul asserts that such a phenomenon is in accordance with the prediction in Scripture (e.g. 9:27-29; 10:21; 11:8-10), and does not impugn God's reliability. In 9:7-18 Paul opens his argument with Israel's own doctrine of election, but it is used, on the one hand, to criticise Israel's own unbelief (9:19), and on the other as a stepping stone to the assertion that God has total freedom to call and show mercy on whomever he wishes, including the Gentiles (9:22-26). An overview of the structure of Romans 9 will enable us to comprehend Paul's argument.

The Thesis for Romans 9-11: *God's word has not failed!* ---v. 6a

Proposition A: *Not all from Israel are Israel!* v. 6b-7a
    Aa. OT Proof (1)   v. 7b
    Ab. Interpretation   v. 8
    Ac. OT Proof (2)   v. 9
    Aa*. OT Proof (1)   v. 10
    Ab*. Interpretation   v. 11-12a
    Ac*. OT Proof (2)   v. 12b-13
Proposition B: *God is not unjust at all!* v. 14
    Ba. OT Proof (1)   v. 15
    Bb. Interpretation   v. 16
    Bc. OT Proof (2)   v. 17
Conclusion (1) for v. 6b-17 *God hardens or shows mercy on whomever he wants* (v. 18).

---

[62] Campbell, 'Freedom', 28.
[63] See Dunn, *Romans* 2, 539.
[64] The second 'Israel' refers to 'the true Israel' (Black, *Romans*, 131) rather than to 'an elect part of Israel' (Schoeps, *Paul*, 239), or to the church (Wright, *Messiah*, 193-197). See Dunn, *Romans* 2, 539-540, who objects to Schoeps and Wright's views.

Proposition C: *God cannot be blamed!*   v. 19-20a
    Ca. OT Proof (1)   v. 20b
    Cb. Interpretation   v. 21
    Cb*. Interpretation   v. 22-24
    Cc. OT Proof (2)   v. 25-29
Conclusion (2) for v. 6b-29 *Gentiles obtained righteousness, but Jews did not* (v. 30-31).
    2b. Interpretation   v. 32
    2a, 2c. OT Proof   v. 33[65]

A structural pattern is noticeable: each proposition is supported by an OT proof, then a pesher-style interpretative comment is made, which is also then reinforced by another OT proof. The three propositions above (A, B, C) and the OT proofs were nothing unusual for the Jews, and thus could be accepted without serious objection. The Jews might think that Paul is talking about the fate of the Gentiles, for if a Jew wrote on the subject of the divine 'election' as applied to the Gentiles (Ishmaelites, Edomites; cf. *Jub.* 16:17), his presentation would have been very similar to what Paul writes in 9:6-23. But if a Jew wanted to expound God's election of the *Jews*, he would have found other references from the OT and/or from the intertestamental literature. For example,

> For you are a people holy to the Lord your God. The Lord your God has chosen you out of all the peoples on the face of the earth to be his people, his treasured possession (Deut 7:6; and similarly Exod 6:7; Deut 14:2; 26:19; 1 Sam 12:22; Ps 135:4; Isa 41:8-9; *Pss. Sol.* 9:17-18; 14:3; *Jub.* 19:16; 22:9; *2 Apoc. Bar.* 48:20, 23; 77:3, etc.).

The puzzle expressed by the imaginary dialogue partner (9:19) indicates that he agrees (or Paul assumes that he would agree) with his explanation, yet he does not understand why Jews are

---

[65] Most commentators divide the units as 9:6-29 and 9:30-10:21, and since the phrase Τί οὖν ἐροῦμεν (9:30) indicates a new section, we follow this division. However, Paul does not make such a sharp break here. See Dahl, *Studies*, 143 n. 24; Siegert, *Argumentation*, 116, 119, 139, 148, who maintain a break between 9:33 and 10:1. The close connection between 9:6-29 and 9:30-33 is also noted by van Unnik and Barrett, in de Lorenzi, *Israelfrage*, 121-124. We may note the double function of 9:30-33: the conclusion of the previous section (9:6b-29) and the introduction of the following section (10:1-21).

blamed. But the argument in 9:20-23 is not an answer to this enquiry but rather a confirmation that the Jews are still blameworthy; they do not even have the right to talk back to God.

In the structure of the Proposition–OT Proof–Interpretation–OT Proof–Conclusion pattern, Paul's own interpretative remarks and conclusions are significantly helpful to detect the points of his argument. The first explanatory comment (Ab), 'it is not the natural children who are God's children, but it is the children of the promise who are regarded as (λογίζεται, as in ch. 4) Abraham's offspring' (9:8), indicates that Paul is primarily concerned with God's true children rather than Abraham's (ch. 4; 8:14-16). By mentioning the Isaac–Ishmael and the Jacob–Esau cases, Paul stresses one point: 'Racial descent is not enough: promise, or call, and (in the case of Abraham) faith are decisive.'[66] Paul has already said in the letter to the (predominantly Gentile) Galatians that they are, like Isaac, children of promise, and the Jews are, like Ishmael, children according to the flesh (Gal 4:28-29). So 'the children of promise' equates with 'the children of God' and with the second 'Israel' in 9:6b. For Paul, those who are in Christ Jesus are all children of God, seed of Abraham and heirs according to the promise, regardless of their ethnic origins (Gal 3:26-29). In fact, in Gal 3:26-29 Paul is primarily addressing Gentile believers. Paul states implicitly here in Romans what he wrote so explicitly in Galatians. The argument in Galatians seems purely exclusive, but the implicit argument in Romans indicates that Gentiles are included in God's election.

The second interpretation (Ab*) is added to make clear that the election between Jacob and Esau was predestined 'in order that God's purpose of election might stand' (9:11b). Dunn asserts that 'Paul uses this text [the Jacob-Esau episode] *against* Jacob (Israel)'![67] Paul's intent in 9:10-17, however, does not become apparent unless we understand whom Paul has in mind when he concludes in 9:18, 'Therefore God has mercy on whom he wants to have mercy, and he hardens whom he wants to harden.' Of course some Gentiles are shown mercy and others are hardened, and some Jews are shown mercy and others are hardened. But it is significant to note that, especially in Romans 9-11, Paul refers to the Gentiles as those who have been shown God's mercy and

---

66 Ziesler, *Romans*, 241.
67 Dunn, *Romans* 2, 545.

kindness (11:22, 30, 31; 15:9), but to the Jews as those who have been hardened (2:4f; 11:7, 17, 25; 2 Cor 3:14; 2 Thess 2:11; cf. John 12:40). Paul quotes Deut 29:4; Isa 29:10; LXX Ps 68:23f in 11:8-10, and Isa 1:9 in 9:29 probably to maximise Israel's hardness. But he does not mention the Gentiles' hardness (cf. Eph 4:17-19). That God's design is to show mercy to all in 11:32 implies that whilst Gentiles have *already* been shown mercy, Jews *will* be. Paul's designation becomes more significant when it is considered in the light of the OT; there it is the *Gentiles* whom God hardens (e.g. Exod 4:21; 7:3; 10:20, 27; 11:10; 14:4, 17; Deut 2:30; Josh 11:20), but the *Jews* who enjoy God's mercy.

These observations enable us to discern Paul's intent in 9:10-17. The climactic declaration of God's sovereign freedom of election in 9:15-17 is thus made to affirm that God is totally free to show mercy to the Gentiles, in order that his 'name might be proclaimed in all the earth' (9:17). LXX Exod 33:19b is quoted exactly in 9:15. Moses finds comfort in God's promise to accompany Israel and to make her a nation distinct from the Gentiles (Exod 33:16). From the same text Paul finds comfort in God's word that his mercy has been shown to the Gentiles.[68] Likewise, Paul applies the Pharaoh imagery to Israel.[69] As Pharaoh was hardened, so is (unbelieving) Israel. As Pharaoh was raised up (i.e. hardened) for a double purpose, so is part of Israel (1) to display God's power of deliverance, and (2) to proclaim his name throughout all the world.[70] Paul also implicitly equates the

---

68 Sanday and Headlam, *Romans*, 254, are correct to note that the emphasis in the original context was 'the certainty of the Divine grace for those whom God has selected'. But for Paul it is 'the independence and freedom of the Divine choice' (cf. Fitzmyer, *Romans*, 567). When the whole of Israel turned against God in the golden calf incident, God willed to show his mercy to Moses by revealing himself to him alone, but after hearing Moses' compelling plea (Exod 33:13b, 16; 34:9), he determined for Moses' sake to show compassion to Israel despite their idolatry (Exod 33:17; 34:10). Hanson, *Studies*, 157-158; Leenhardt, *Romans*, 253; and Campbell, 'Freedom', 30, assert that Paul maintains the original context of God's mercy towards Israel as in Exod 33:19, but do not note that Paul applies that mercy to the Gentiles.

69 Barrett, *Romans*, 174, 177; Boylan, *Romans*, 161.

70 Paul's citation of Exod 9:16 is textually modified perhaps in order to stress God's active role in the hardening of Pharaoh (see Stanley, *Language*, 106-109).

(unbelieving) Jews with Esau, the first son of Isaac,[71] and the (believing) Gentiles with Jacob.[72] Paul may have found justification for so doing because, in the context of Malachi, the Lord condemns the Jews for their blemished sacrifices and declares, 'My name will be great among the nations' (Mal 1:11a, d, 14).[73]

Paul's affirmation of God's absolutely sovereign freedom in 9:7-18 draws an anticipated objection: 'If God is totally free to favour or to harden those whom he wants, and furthermore even fulfils his purpose through hardened people (e.g. Pharaoh), and since no-one can resist his will, why does God still blame the hardened?'. Paul replies with the words in Isa 29:16 and 45:9.[74] Just as the clay can say nothing to the potter concerning what he has done to it, human beings are not allowed to talk back to God (9:20-21; cf. Job 1:22; 9:12; 33:13; 40:2). But Paul's reply does not really answer the interlocutor's protest,[75] but rather reaffirms God's right as the potter over the clay.[76] The potter–clay analogy in Isa 45:9 comes in the context of blessing to Israel,[77] and, according to Jewish theology, the irresistible freedom of God is applied to the destruction of the Gentiles: 'For who will say,

---

71 Hays, *Echoes*, 67. The Jews claimed that they were the 'first-born son' (Exod 4:22; Jer 31:9; Sir 36:12), and it is often (negatively) expressed in the NT (Matt 8:12; Luke 15:25-32).

72 Käsemann, *Romans*, 264, insists that the two quotes in 9:12-13 are taken out of context in the light of *4 Ezra* 3:16, quoting Mal 1:2-3, 'Thou didst set apart Israel for thyself, but Esau thou didst reject'. But Cranfield, *Romans* 2, 481, is correct: 'Paul's special interest in this quotation from Malachi was focused on its latter half (τὸν δὲ Ἠσαῦ ἐμίσησα); for his point was that the unbelief of the great majority of his Jewish contemporaries followed the pattern of this exclusion of Esau.'

73 In Mal 1:2 Jacob and Esau represent two ethnic groups, Jews and Gentiles (Gen 25:23); Ziesler, *Romans*, 241; Piper, *Justification*, 63.

74 UBS³, Ellis, *Paul's Use*; Käsemann, *Romans*, 269, and Stanley, *Language*, do not consider 9:20 a quotation, but Nestle-Aland²⁷ does.

75 Boylan, *Romans*, 160. Thus Dodd, *Romans*, 159, regard Paul's answer in 9:20-21 as 'the weakest point in the whole epistle'; but see Barrett, *Romans*, 175; Ziesler, *Romans*, 245-246.

76 God's right to mould Israel according to his own free will and Israel's total acceptance of whatever God does to them, are often described in a potter-clay imagery (Job 10:8-9; Isa 29:16, 45:9-13; 64:8; Jer 18:6-10; Wis 15:7; Sir 33:13).

77 See Käsemann, 269-270, for differences of Paul's context from that of Isa 45:9.

"What hast thou done?" Or who will resist thy judgment? Who will accuse thee for the destruction of nations which thou didst make?' (Wis 12:12). But for Paul God has total freedom to show grace to and/or to harden either Jews or Gentiles.[78]

Then the next interpretation (Cb*), expressed in one long sentence in Greek (9:22-24),[79] rhetorically reinforces the theme of God's sovereignty in handling human beings. Paul clearly identifies 'the vessels of mercy' with 'us', the Jewish and Gentile Christians. But the identification of 'the vessels of wrath' is debated. F.F. Bruce is of the opinion that since Gentiles were prepared for destruction according to the OT and God showed patience to them, the phrase refers to the Gentiles.[80] This interpretation then suggests that God had freedom to endure the vessels of wrath and to favour the Gentiles even though he had once prepared them for destruction to demonstrate his wrath and power.

But E.H. Gifford and E. Käsemann assert that the phrase refers to the mass of unbelieving Jews in Paul's day.[81] Dunn and N.A. Dahl go even further: 'Paul puts the non-believing Jews of his time on the same level not only with Ishmael and Esau, but also with Pharaoh and with Babylon (Jer. 50:25).'[82] This latter view is to be preferred for two reasons. First, it is in line with what Paul said earlier: 'because of your stubbornness and your unrepentant heart, you are storing up wrath against yourself' (2:4-5; cf. 1 Thess 2:14-16).[83] Second, throughout the argument in 9:7-22, Paul has presented his evidence symmetrically. In 9:22-24 he

---

78 Keener, *Bible Background*, 433.
79 Nestle-Aland[27] puts a question mark (;) at the end of v. 23, and starts a new paragraph from v. 24 by putting a capital letter Οὕς. UBS³ does the same except starting v. 24 as a new sentence. Many scholars also maintain the break between the verses: Käsemann, *Romans*, 271-272; Murray, *Romans* 2, 37; Gifford, *Romans*, 175; Dodd, *Romans*, 171-172; Fitzmyer, *Romans*, 564; Dunn, *Romans* 2, 570; Piper, *Justification*, 184-185. However, syntactically it is not plausible to break a sentence or paragraph between antecedent and relative pronoun. Moreover, it is inseparable thematically. It may be translated into a few sentences for a better understanding, but it is to be interpreted as a unit. So correctly Cranfield, *Romans* 2, 497-498; Barrett, *Romans*, 176-177.
80 Bruce, *Romans*, 191.
81 Gifford, *Romans*, 174; Käsemann, *Romans*, 270.
82 Dahl, *Studies*, 145; Dunn, *Romans* 2, 559.
83 See our earlier discussion in pp. 98-102.

juxtaposes 'the vessels of wrath' and 'the vessels of mercy', but since the latter are identified with Jewish and Gentile believers, the former are to be identified with Jewish and Gentile unbelievers, but especially Jewish, because unbelieving Gentiles are not focused upon in Romans 1-11. Paul's point then is that the Jews do not have any right to complain to God for hardening them and for showing mercy to the Gentiles.

C. *God's Election and its Application to Jews and Gentiles: 9:24-29*

After firmly establishing God's total freedom to choose whomsoever he wants, Paul now (9:24) introduces a change in the direction of Romans 9-11: he resumes the Jew-Gentile discussion more explicitly. M. Black is correct to say, 'The personal pronoun ["us"] brings a climax to the argument. God's purpose culminated in *us*, Jews *and* Gentiles.'[84] Paul affirms, with a grammatical emphasis (ἀλλὰ καὶ ἐξ ἐθνῶν) in 9:24, that God had prepared Gentiles beforehand as the vessels of mercy to declare the riches of his glory also to them. The inclusion of the Gentiles is probably 'the point up to which the argument has been leading',[85] rather than 'just a passing one in 9:24'.[86] The Hosea passages are affirmatively quoted in 9:25-26 to support the emphasised 'but also from the Gentiles' in 9:24.[87]

LXX Hos 2:25   καὶ ἀγαπήσω τὴν οὐκ ἠγαπημένην,
                 καὶ ἐρῶ τῷ οὐ λαῷ μου λαός μου εἶ σύ
LXX Hos 2:1b   καὶ ἔσται ἐν τῷ τόπῳ οὗ ἐρρέθη αὐτοῖς οὐ λαός
                 μου ὑμεῖς, κληθήσονται καὶ αὐτοὶ υἱοὶ θεοῦ ζῶντος

Rom 9:25-26   Καλέσω τὸν οὐ λαόν μου λαόν μου καὶ τὴν οὐκ
                 ἠγαπημένην ἠγαπημένην· 26 καὶ ἔσται ἐν τῷ τόπῳ
                 οὗ ἐρρέθη αὐτοῖς, Οὐ λαός μου ὑμεῖς, ἐκεῖ
                 κληθήσονται υἱοὶ θεοῦ ζῶντος.

---

84   Black, *Romans*, 135, with his emphases.
85   Ziesler, *Romans*, 248.
86   *Pace* Motyer, *Israel*, 76.
87   *Pace* Sanday and Headlam, *Romans*, 263, for taking the citation in 9:25-26 as an appendix to the main argument in 9:6-24, though they acknowledge it is cited 'to prove the calling of the Gentiles' (p. 264).

The Equality of Jew and Gentile in the Plan of God 235

Three features of these quotations are important for our present concern. First, the fact that the description in 9:27-28 is exclusively about Israel (as the introductory remark, Ἡσαΐας δὲ κράζει ὑπὲρ τοῦ Ἰσραήλ, indicates), suggests that Paul applies 9:25-26 (only) to believing Gentiles.[88] This is probably why Paul does not quote LXX Hos 2:1a: 'καὶ ἦν ὁ ἀριθμὸς <u>τῶν υἱῶν Ἰσραὴλ</u> ὡς ἡ ἄμμος τῆς θαλάσσης ....'. The τὰ ἔθνη of 9:24 is identified with the phrase οὐ λαόν μου,[89] and again with λαόν μου in 9:25.[90]

Second, Paul creatively modifies the texts.[91] He reverses the order of LXX Hos 2:25a and b, and substitutes καλέσω for ἐρῶ, thus making καλέσω the first word of the catena. Furthermore, by omitting the verb of the (now) second clause (ἀγαπήσω), he allows καλέσω to be the main verb for the whole verse. This is most probably to link it with the preceding ἐκάλεσεν ἡμᾶς of 9:24, and with the following κληθήσονται of 9:26, which is retained in the verbatim citation from LXX Hos 2:1b. This observation leads us to suggest that by emphasising the 'calling' Paul presents these quotations 'as a prophecy of Yahweh's coming election of the Gentiles'.[92] It is significant for Paul to assert that God also called (ἐκάλεσεν) some among the Gentiles, with the same verb that described God's election of Isaac (κληθήσεται: 9:7) and the general principle of God's election (καλοῦντος: 9:12). Gentiles are also the κλητοὶ Ἰησοῦ Χριστοῦ, the ἀγαπητοὶ θεοῦ and the κλητοὶ ἁγίοις (1:6-7), because God called (ἐκάλεσεν) them (8:30).

Third, there is a significant modification of the context. It is striking to see Paul accentuating the idea that the Gentiles had been legitimately called by God from a passage whose original

---

88 Weiss, *Earliest Christianity* 2, 662; Barrett, *Romans*, 191; Ellis, *Paul's Use*, 94; Fitzmyer, *Romans*, 573. See Battle, 'Paul's Use', 119, where reasons for taking the quotation as referring to the believing Gentiles are well summarised, though Battle himself does not opt for this view.

89 Stanley, *Language*, 110 n. 79.

90 Pace Barth, *People*, 11, who says that the λαός in 9:25-26 refers to the entire Christian community of Jews and Gentiles.

91 Käsemann, *Romans*, 274; Dunn, *Romans* 2, 570 and Stanley, *Language*, 112, are right to see that Paul himself combined the quotation to fit to the argument here as well as to affirm the assertion made in 9:6a.

92 Stanley, *Language*, 112; see especially pp. 109-113, for an examination on the changes of the text; also Cranfield, *Romans* 2, 498-501.

context says nothing about the calling of the Gentiles: rather, it is the promise of the restoration of the northern kingdom of *Israel*.[93] The apostle surprisingly applies this promise to the calling and the inclusion of the Gentiles among God's legitimate people and the beloved children of the living God.[94] Paul simply asserts that God has declared his intention to call Gentiles to be among his own beloved people through the prophet Hosea, and Hays is not off the mark in saying that this is Paul's 'hermeneutical coup' executed smoothly yet boldly.[95]

So far in 9:6-23 Paul has provided the scriptural evidence to explain why not all who are descended from Israel are Israel (9:6b). But now he includes Gentiles among those who are called and elected by God's mercy and compassion, not only as Paul maintained in 9:15-24, but more fundamentally as he declared in 8:29-30, 33. If 9:24-26 serves as the climax of the argument in Romans 9, as Black maintains,[96] then our understanding that the immediate connection between Romans 1-8 and 9-11 is the elucidation of the Gentiles' legitimate status as predestined and called by God, can stand.

The fact that Gentiles obtained righteousness (9:30) enabled Paul, on the one hand, to present the quotation concerning the Gentiles affirmatively. On the other hand, the fact that (the majority of) Israel did not attain righteousness despite their zealous pursuit, allows him to present LXX Isa 10:22-23 as a critique of Israel in 9:27-29.[97] Isa 10:22-23 was originally rather an oracle of

---

93 Cranfield, *Romans* 2, 499; Gifford, *Romans*, 175; Ziesler, *Romans*, 244, 248; Bruce, *Romans*, 196; Sanday and Headlam, *Romans*, 264; Fitzmyer, *Romans*, 573.

94 So Siegert, *Argumentation*, 139, infers that such a subtle change of the referent would certainly raise an objection from the (unbelieving) Jews.

95 Hays, *Echoes*, 66-67. *Pace* Battle, 'Paul's Use', 115-129, for understanding that Paul literally adopts the original context of the Hosea prophecy, and for stressing that Paul quotes this passage 'to prove the temporary but very real nature of Israel's period of unbelief and disenfranchisement prior to her final restoration' (p. 127); but this interpretation undermines the flow of Paul's argument in Rom 9-11, dealing with issues related to Jews and Gentiles.

96 Black, *Romans*, 135.

97 More than a third of the thirty OT citations in Rom 9-11 are made from Isaiah. Such heavy dependence indicates that it is the most influential OT book on Paul's theology of the relationship of Jew and Gentile in Christ. See

The Equality of Jew and Gentile in the Plan of God 237

comfort after the Lord's anger against Israel had been so vigorously announced in Isa 9:8-10:4. Leading up to it, God's judgement on Assyria is pronounced in Isa 10:5-19, with the implication that the liberation of Israel is near. Our present passage, Isa 10:22-23, appears in the middle of God's promise of the return of the remnant and of the ultimate destruction of the oppressors (Isa 10:20-34).[98] For Isaiah the return of the remnant was a reason for joy, and so pain and grief were overtaken by joy and gladness (LXX Isa 35:10; 51:11). But it is not so with Paul. He is anxious because a great number of Jews do not experience salvation; he is full of pain and grief because *only*[99] a remnant is being saved (9:1-2, 28).

Paul's point is not that the preservation of the remnant is the manifestation of God's mercy.[100] If that were so he would not confess to such grave anguish (9:1-2; 10:1). Rather he expresses his sorrow in this quotation that (only) a remnant out of a great number is to be saved and, in contrast, the present state of Israel is almost equated with that of Sodom and Gomorrah.[101]

We have mentioned above that in 9:25-26 Paul avoids the words from LXX Hos 2:1a because he wishes to apply the rest of the verse to Gentiles rather than to Israel. But in 9:27-28, he uses these very words about Israel from LXX Hos 2:1a to introduce his citation of *Isaiah*.

Isa 10:22 καὶ ἐὰν γένηται <u>ὁ λαὸς</u> Ἰσραὴλ ὡς ἡ ἄμμος τῆς θαλάσσης
Hos 2:1a καὶ ἦν ὁ ἀριθμὸς <u>τῶν υἱῶν</u> Ἰσραὴλ ὡς ἡ ἄμμος τῆς θαλάσσης
Rom 9:27 Ἐὰν ᾖ ὁ ἀριθμὸς <u>τῶν υἱῶν</u> Ἰσραὴλ ὡς ἡ ἄμμος τῆς θαλάσσης

D-A. Koch plausibly construes that since Paul has paralleled the λαός with the υἱοὶ θεοῦ ζῶντος, and applied the latter to the Gentiles in 9:25-26, Paul now avoids any reference to Israel as

---

Oss' dissertation, 'Paul's Use of Isaiah', *idem*, 'Note', 105-112; Dinter, 'Prophet Isaiah', 48-52; Hays, *Echoes*, 162.

98 *Pace* Ziesler, *Romans*, 249.

99 The addition of this adverb in some Bible versions (e.g. NRSV, NEB, NJB, NIV, TEV, NAB, Lutherbibel), is a reasonable interpretation.

100 *Pace* Cranfield, *Romans* 2, 502; Fitzmyer, *Romans*, 575.

101 Lübking in Dunn, *Romans* 2, 574; Gifford, *Romans*, 176. Thus Käsemann, *Romans*, 275, following Michel, correctly notes that the judgement on Israel's unbelief is so darkly portrayed that the force of the phrase οὐ μόνον ἐξ Ἰουδαίων in 9:24 is almost lost.

λαὸς θεοῦ ζῶντος.[102] Furthermore, we note that Paul's use of the λόγος in the quotation in 9:28 is also significantly modified from that of the original text in Isa 10:23. The λόγος in Isaiah 10:23 is God's word about the destruction of the whole land (cf. Isa 28:22) for the sake of the deliverance of Israel's remnant. But in Romans it appears to concern God's decision to bring quick destruction on unbelieving Jews.[103] Paul affirms that Isaiah clearly prophesied that only the remnant (a minority of Israelites[104]) would be saved (cf. 9:6b). He reinforces his argument with the verbatim citation and the identical context of Isa 1:9, where God's graciousness in leaving the remnant is highlighted and contrasted with the rebellious unbelief of the Israelites (cf. the pointed comparison with Sodom and Gomorrah). Thus Hays does not seem totally correct in asserting that Paul uses his scriptural quotations to affirm that both Gentiles *and* Jews have been equally 'called'.[105] Rather 9:27-29 is an affirmation of what he has written in 9:6b, 'Not all who are descended from Israel are Israel'. For Paul the call of Gentiles and the rejection of Jews are already predicted in the OT, and that is why (γάρ) God's word has not failed (9:6a), despite the phenomenon of Jewish unbelief and Gentile faith.

D. Summary

The purpose of 9:6-29 is primarily to elucidate the assertion that 'not all who descended from Israel are Israel'. The passage explains that the phenomenon of Jewish unbelief should not be surprising because God did not elect all the Jews (as the cases of Isaac–Ishmael and of Jacob–Esau clearly show). On the other hand, the phenomenon of Gentile belief should not be considered strange either, because God has total freedom to show mercy to them just as Moses (9:15; Exod 33:19) and Hosea (LXX 2:1, 25) had prophesied; so in this case also God's word has not failed, but

---

[102] Koch, *Schrift*, 167-168. Stanley, *Language*, 115, considers Koch's explanation as attractive. *Pace* Lindars, *Apologetic*, 243, for denying the citation in 9:25-28 as Paul's (conscious) conflation.

[103] Cf. Boylan, *Romans*, 163.

[104] *Pace* Black, *Romans*, 135, for taking the remnant here as the Christian Church, the true Israel. Paul clearly indicates that this citation concerns *ethnic* Israel (9:27a).

[105] *Pace* Hays, *Echoes*, 68.

rather come to unexpected fulfilment. Paul argues that God, who had called Israel in his own sovereignty, willed to have mercy on Gentiles and to call them to be his own beloved people, although they were once 'Not-my people'. Such a focus in his argument is endorsed by 9:30-33: Some Gentiles have obtained righteousness, but many Jews have not, despite their zealous pursuit of it. Thus what he argues in 9:6-29 establishes the basis for his further assertion concerning the unbelief of the Jews and the obedience of the Gentiles in the subsequent argument (9:30-10:21). It becomes apparent in 9:6-29 that Paul undermines the exclusive doctrine of Jewish election[106] and stresses a doctrine of Gentile election also, thereby affirming the equality of Jew and Gentile in God's plan of election. The reason for Paul's great sorrow and unceasing anguish (9:1-3; 10:1) is because (unbelieving) Israel awaits God's judgement in the condition of being like Sodom and Gomorrah. Israel falls under God's λόγος of *judgement*, and in this too his λόγος does not fail.

3. The Universal Salvific Principles and Israel's Unbelief: 9:30-10:21

It has been thought that a major difficulty for the interpretation of Paul's argument in 9:30-10:21 is its 'inconsistency' with the preceding and the following chapters. In 9:6-29 Paul has vindicated God's justice in exercising his sovereign freedom of election. But in the very next section (9:30-10:21) Paul seems to blame Israel for their own unbelief. Furthermore, in Romans 11 it has been generally assumed that Paul portrays God's plan for the ultimate future salvation of 'all' Israel. 9:30-10:21 appears then to be inconsistent with other sections. For Augustine and Calvin this section continues to expound the sovereignty of God: although the unbelief of the Jews is dealt with, it is not intended to stress human responsibility.[107] Paul's primary aim for Augustine and Calvin is rather to defend the legitimacy of the apostolic missionary work among the Gentiles. W. Sanday and A.C. Headlam disagree with this view. They assert that although reference to the

---

106 Dunn, 'Romans', 848: 'The main point of the discussion, as becomes steadily more apparent, is not to dictate a doctrine of predestination but to undermine Israel's own doctrine of predestination.'

107 Cf. Sanday and Headlam, *Romans*, 301.

Gentiles is clearly made, the defence of missionary work is not Paul's main point of discussion, because 'all the leading sentences are concerned not with the defence of any "calling", but with fixing the guilt of those [Jews] rejected'.[108]

We will suggest that the two positions above are not to be considered as 'either/or' but as 'both/and'. Paul certainly portrays Israel's unbelief as their responsibility,[109] and also explains the missionary principles for the salvation of Jew and Gentile. But Paul says more; he also makes affirmative remarks about the Gentiles' belief in 9:30-10:21. This aspect has not received adequate scholarly attention. Barrett seems to be a typical example: 'His [Paul's] main concern in Chapters 9-11 is with the Jews, but in 9.30 he takes up again the calling of the Gentiles, not so much for their own sake (they immediately fall out of consideration) as to establish certain terminology and terms of reference.'[110] We shall show that Paul has not set aside the Gentiles from consideration; rather we will argue that he introduces universal salvific principles in order to defend the legitimacy of the salvation of the Gentiles. Our position will also question Cranfield's assertion that Paul's primary focus is 'not on Israel's sin but on God's goodness towards Israel'.[111]

We shall argue that Paul continues to expound the equality of Jew and Gentile in the plan of God, especially his plan for the universal salvation of humanity and the means of bringing about that salvation. Paul declares, 'There is no difference between Jew and Gentile' in God's salvific means and strategy. Paul has vigorously argued that justification can be obtained by faith (alone) in 3:21-4:25, but only now does he explicitly explain what 'by faith' denotes (10:6-13) and how one can exercise 'faith' for salvation (10:14-17). On the basis of the salvific means which God has established in his plan to save humanity, the apostle to the Gentiles confirms that Gentile believers have correctly followed God's way of salvation, whilst many Jews have failed to do so, seeking rather their own righteousness.

---

108 Sanday and Headlam, *Romans*, 301.
109 Kümmel, *Introduction*, 307; Davidson and Martin, 'Romans', 1035.
110 Barrett, 'Romans 9:30-10:21', 139.
111 Cranfield, *Romans* 2, 503, 541-542.

A. Faith in Christ, the Means for Salvation: 9:30-10:13

Paul explicitly declares, for the first time, that it is Gentiles, not Jews, who obtained righteousness. 9:32-10:21 provides a necessary elaboration of this striking statement in 9:30-31 that Israel pursued τὴν τοῦ θεοῦ δικαιοσύνην but they did not know its true nature, and so did not submit themselves to it (10:3). It also explains why and how Gentiles could obtain it even without pursuing it (cf. 2:14).[112] God's means for salvation is Christ, but people must respond in faith, that is, by believing in their hearts and confessing with their mouths that Jesus is Lord. Some Gentiles have trusted in Christ in response to the gospel message they have heard,[113] but many Jews insisted on their own way because they thought it could be attained by works (ὡς ἐξ ἔργων),[114] as the 'as if' indicates.[115] This means that Jews understood the scope of righteousness too narrowly (as if it applied to Jews only),[116] and misunderstood the means for righteousness (as if it was by works of the law).[117]

---

112 Cranfield, *Romans* 2, 506-507, surveys different interpretations, and he himself takes this 'righteousness' as 'justification'. See also Ziesler, *Romans*, 251-252. It is important to note for an adequate interpretation of Romans that even though there are believing Jews, unbelieving Jews, believing Gentiles and unbelieving Gentiles, Paul is talking about the *unbelieving* Jews and the *believing* Gentiles, and generalises them as Jews and Gentiles in Romans; especially in 9:30 Paul does not say '*the* Gentiles' as if to denote *all* Gentiles (so Sanday and Headlam, *Romans*, 279; Barrett, *Romans*, 179).

113 The citation of Isa 28:16 in 9:33b is added to Isa 8:14 most probably to offer a scriptural exhortation to 'trust in him'. The original passage (Isa 28:16) is about the precious cornerstone in a positive sense, and Paul maintains the positive aspect for 'the one who trusts in him' (i.e. a Gentile according to 9:30). But by conflating it with Isa 8:14 (where the stumbling stone is Yahweh himself) Paul presents the citation in Rom 9:33 in negative terms especially for Jews (1 Cor 1:23; 3:11); so Stanley, *Language*, 120; Fitzmyer, *Romans*, 579. Thus Israel's privileges listed in 9:4-5 prove to be nothing in practice in the matter of the means of salvation (Watson, *Paul*, 164).

114 See Ziesler, *Romans*, 252-253, for a survey of the discussion on the phrase νόμον δικαιοσύνης.

115 E.g. Cranfield, *Romans* 2, 509-510. Sanders, *Palestinian Judaism*, *passim*, offers a fundamental objection to this view; he is now followed by Ziesler, *Romans*, 252-254; Wilckens, *Römer* 2, 213; Räisänen, *Paul*, 174-175.

116 Ziesler, *Romans*, 254.

117 This remark may shed light on some previous passages concerning who Paul primarily had in mind when he (implicitly) talked about 'faith' and

In fact God's righteousness has already been made known in Christ apart from the law (3:21-22). For Paul, Christ has been provided as the better and proper way through whom humanity can obtain God's righteousness, and so the soteriological function of the law has been brought to an end (10:4; cf. 3:21; 6:14).[118] The γάρ in 10:5 indicates that Paul turns to the OT passages in 10:5-8 to substantiate his assertion made in 10:4. By appealing to Lev 18:5 and Deut 30:11-14 Paul asserts that Moses had already talked about ἡ ἐκ πίστεως δικαιοσύνη,[119] and that this was the 'righteousness from God [which] comes through faith in Jesus Christ' (3:22). From Deut 30:11-14 Paul highlights two points: the *nearness* of the word, and the important function of the *heart and soul* in salvation.[120] First, Paul replaces the 'law' (the means for obedience to the Lord and attaining his righteousness) with 'Christ', through his interpretative comments in a characteristically thrice-repeated τοῦτ' ἔστιν.[121] This introduction of Christ here prepares Paul's argument from 10:9 onwards. His identification of the word [of the law] in Deut 30:14 with 'the word of faith we are proclaiming' (10:8), introduced by the third τοῦτ' ἔστιν, aims to achieve the most decisive effect.[122] Paul affirms that the

---

'works'. For example, those who pursue righteousness by observing the works of the law in 3:20 are mainly Jews; and the one who does not work but trusts God in 4:5 is a Gentile.

118 Longenecker, *Paul*, 144-153; Morris, *Romans*, 380. For the discussion on this crucial verse, see Cranfield, *Romans* 2, 515-520; Ziesler, *Romans*, 257-258; Fitzmyer, *Romans*, 584-585. Cf. *pace* Stendahl, *Paul*, *passim*, who insists that Christ is the end of the law for righteousness for those (Gentiles) who believe in Christ, but not so with the Jews; so similarly Mussner, as the title of his essay shows: '"Christus, des Gesetzes Ende zur Gerechtigkeit für jeden, der glaubt" (Röm 10,4)', in *Paulus*, 31-44.

119 See Dunn, '"Righteousness"', 216-228.

120 Cf. Suggs, 'Word is Near You', 289-312.

121 The use of Deut 30:12-14 in Bar 3:29-30 is well noted (e.g. by Ziesler, *Romans*, 260; Fitzmyer, *Romans*, 588), where the 'law' is identified with 'wisdom'.

122 So correctly Hays, *Echoes*, 80; Black, *Romans*, 139. The question, ἀλλὰ τί λέγει; (10:8a) and the content of it (10:8b) indicate that Paul has appealed to Deut 30:12-14 to stress the nearness of the word which Paul and others proclaim. Paul says that ἡ τοῦ θεοῦ δικαιοσύνη (10:3) is to be obtained by ἡ δικαιοσύνη ἐκ πίστεως (9:30), which is prompted by τὸ ῥῆμα τῆς πίστεως (10:8), which is in fact τὸ ῥῆμα Χριστοῦ, the word about Christ (10:17).

word of faith about Christ which they are proclaiming is not beyond their reach.

Second, Paul's version of the prerequisite for salvation is explicitly mentioned: 'If you confess with your mouth, "Jesus is Lord"[123] (cf. 1 Cor 8:5-6; Phil 2:11; Acts 2:36) and believe in your heart that God raised him from the dead, you will be saved' (10:9). He rephrases Moses' expression, 'in your mouth and in your heart' (Deut 30:14) as '*confess* with your mouth and *believe* in your heart' (10:9). The verse 10:10 is Paul's tautology reaffirming what he has just written in v. 9. The argument in 10:5-10 not only intensifies Israel's unbelief[124] but also prepares a launching pad for the universality of salvation. Paul quotes two OT verses to highlight a universal application with 'whoever (πᾶς)': one to stress 'believe' (10:11), and the other 'confess (call)' (10:13). LXX Isa 28:16 is cited again in 10:11, but this time Paul communicates more than he did in 9:33. (a) The ἐπ' αὐτῷ is now identified with 'in Christ'. (b) The πᾶς is deliberately added in an emphatic position, and it clearly indicates that this principle also applies to the Gentiles.[125] Thus Paul declares that between Jews and Gentiles there is no distinction (10:12; 3:22). Their equality is the basis (γάρ) for the universality of salvation; and their equality is fundamentally rooted in the universality of the Lordship of Jesus ('the same Lord [Jesus] is the Lord of all': 10:12; cf. Acts 10:36).[126]

LXX Joel 3:5 (EV 2:32) is cited, as the conclusion of the argument of 10:1-13,[127] so as to highlight the universality of salvation. Although Paul quotes the verse exactly from the LXX, he dramatically modifies the context in order to indicate that Gen-

---

123 In Romans the expression '(our) Lord Jesus (Christ)' as a title occurs no less than fourteen times, but κύριος Ἰησοῦς in 10:9 is used as the content of Christian confession (so also 1 Cor 12:3; cf. 2 Cor 4:5).

124 Just as the word [of the law] was as near as to be in one's mouth and in one's heart, so near also is the word of faith which has been preached. But Israel did not pay proper attention to it, nor did they exercise faith by believing 'with all their heart' to obtain τὴν τοῦ θεοῦ δικαιοσύνην, even though they were clearly told. Cf. pp. 145-147 above.

125 Siegert, *Argumentation*, 151; Barrett, *Romans*, 202.

126 Sanders, *Jewish People*, 40-41. Cf. earlier in 3:29, where Paul asserted that God is the God of all, i.e. of Jews and Gentiles, and now applies the same idea to Jesus the Lord.

127 Sanday and Headlam, *Romans*, 292.

tiles can also be saved by calling upon the name of the Lord. The πᾶς in LXX Joel 3:5 clearly refers to *'every Jew'* who will be saved by calling upon the Lord when the Lord offers deliverance on Mount Zion and in Jerusalem [i.e. on the day of the Lord]. There the Lord is comforting *his people, Israel* (EV Joel 2:18, 23, 26, 27). There it is to the Jews that salvation is promised, but for the Gentiles a severe *judgement is pronounced*: 'There [at the very place where God brings deliverance to the Jews, 2:32b] I will enter into judgment against them [i.e. *all nations*]' (Joel 3:1-2, 3-16). Joel then closes his prophecy by once again declaring blessings for the Jews (Joel 3:17-21). It is striking to note that Paul finds a quotation from a passage where the salvation of the Jews and the judgement of the Gentiles are so clearly contrasted, and yet uses it to affirm his doctrine of the soteriological equality of Jew and Gentile. He interprets these OT texts and presents them in order to affirm that God has included the Gentiles in his plan of salvific blessing, a blessing which was almost exclusively promised to Israel according to the OT.[128]

B. *The Missionary Principle and Israel's Unbelief: 10:14-21*

After establishing the fundamental means of salvation in God's plan, Paul now rhetorically explains the missionary principle applicable to both Jew and Gentile (10:14-17, in continuation of 10:9-13). At the same time Paul criticises unbelieving Jews for not following this principle despite the fact that they had a far better chance to do so. Verses 9:30 and 10:20 indicate that, nevertheless, *Gentiles* have adopted this principle and obtained the righteousness which God intended to offer humanity in Christ. Paul's use of the OT passages in 10:18-21 will be examined, and his critical judgement of the Jews and affirmative description of the Gentiles will once again be highlighted.

What is crucial to note is that in 10:14-18 Paul simultaneously presents *both* the Jewish failure to respond to the preached gospel message *and* the universal missionary principle for salvation.[129] In Romans those who do not accept the good news are the unbe-

---

[128] According to Acts 2:17-21, Peter also quotes Joel 2:28-32. But his reluctance to go to the Gentiles in the case of Cornelius (Acts 10:9-28) indicates that the πᾶς in Acts 2:17, 21, 39 does not really include Gentiles.

[129] Cf. Dunn, *Romans* 2, 620; Munck, *Christ*, 91-92.

lieving Jews.[130] Since those who understood 'our message' were the Jews (10:19), those who certainly heard it were also Jews (10:18; LXX Ps 18:5).[131] Yet they did not accept the message, nor did they believe it (10:16), because of their own obstinacy and disobedience to the gospel (10:21).[132] Thus the unspecified 'they' in 10:16-18 most probably refers to the Jews, and for Paul their excuses for unbelief are completely excluded.[133] The references related to the general missionary principle are, however, made to cover both Jew and Gentile (10:14-15, 17). Especially the term 'they' in 10:14 certainly refers to the πᾶς in v. 13, which covers both Jew and Gentile. Paul explains Jewish unbelief and the universal missionary principle at the same time in this passage. That is probably why he does not designate the pronoun more precisely.

Paul stresses the necessity or the importance of the preaching of the gospel to Jews and Gentiles by quoting LXX Isa 52:7 in 10:15 (cf. 1 Cor 9:16).[134] To be saved they must call upon the name of the Lord as they believe the message that they hear being preached by those who have been sent. The 'good news' in the original text of Isa 52:7 refers to the message of the restoration of Israel,[135] but for Paul it is the good news about Jesus Christ. Paul does not quote Isa 52:7c ('who proclaim salvation, who say to Zion, "Your God reigns!"'), most probably (or even certainly) because this shortened quotation fits his universalising application. Paul's appeal to Isa 52:7 is 'another case where Paul con-

---

130 So correctly Sanday and Headlam, *Romans*, 298; see *supra* p. 241 n. 112. NIV's addition of 'the Israelites' to 10:16 might not be totally illegitimate. To be sure Paul can refer to the fact that not all who hear the gospel believe it, whether Jews or Gentiles. It is still probable that he has unbelieving Jews in mind, especially in view of the fact that Paul uses the verb ὑπακούω, with which he describes the response of the Gentiles to the gospel (15:18; 16:26).

131 In the original context of LXX Ps 18:1-5, 'their voice' is the voice of the heavens and skies, but for Paul it is the voice of the preachers of the gospel. Thus he affirms that the gospel has been preached to the whole world, especially 'to the Jew first' (Gifford, *Romans*, 188-189).

132 Those references about the negative response to the gospel are progressively identified with that of the Jews (10:16, 18 in relation to the following 10:19, 21; so, clearly, in 9:31-10:3).

133 Käsemann, *Romans*, 295-296.

134 See Stanley, *Language*, 134-141, for textual modifications.

135 Westermann, *Isaiah 40-66*, 251.

sciously sees the [or his] apostolic mission as one of sharing and completing that of the Messiah'.[136]

The critical portrayal of the Jewish response to the gospel and the affirmative one of the Gentile are characteristically contrasted in 10:19-21. LXX Deut 32:21 is quoted, with the substitution of 'you' for 'them'.[137] The original passage is about God's pronouncement of judgement on the Israelites who angered him with their detestable idolatry (Deut 32:5, 16f, 21). Paul seems to anticipate two functions from this citation: first, it highlights the unbelief of the Jews (not idolatry as in Deut 32:21); second, it implies the belief of the Gentiles. At this point Stanley is correct:

> In verse 19, the focus of Paul's argument shifts from the universal availability of the message of salvation (10.5-18) to the contrasting response of Jews and Gentiles to the gospel message (10.19-11.36). The quotation in Rom 10:19b thus occupies a key place in the structure of Rom 10-11.[138]

In the concluding section of the chapter Paul divides LXX Isa 65:1-2, and most strikingly applies them to contrast the positive response of the Gentiles to the gospel and the negative one of the Jews:

LXX Isa 65:1   ἐμφανὴς ἐγενόμην τοῖς ἐμὲ μὴ ζητοῦσιν εὑρέθην τοῖς ἐμὲ μὴ ἐπερωτῶσιν εἶπα ἰδού εἰμι τῷ ἔθνει οἳ οὐκ ἐκάλεσάν μου τὸ ὄνομα

Rom 10:20   Εὑρέθην [ἐν] τοῖς ἐμὲ μὴ ζητοῦσιν, ἐμφανὴς ἐγενόμην τοῖς ἐμὲ μὴ ἐπερωτῶσιν.

The reason why Paul reverses the order of Isa 65:1a and b by swapping the verbs, has been hardly recognised.[139] But his reason

---

136 Dunn, *Romans* 2, 622. So similarly Käsemann, *Romans*, 296; Wright, *Messiah*, 178.

137 This change most probably serves to apply the quotation more directly to Israel, which has been just specifically introduced in 10:19 (*pace* Stanley, *Language*, 143, for insisting that the change is only stylistic without any significance).

138 Stanley, *Language*, 143.

139 Koch, *Schrift*, 50-51, argues that there is no reason to assume that Paul has reversed the clauses to establish his argument. For him the modifica-

The Equality of Jew and Gentile in the Plan of God   247

for the change is discernible and significant.¹⁴⁰ By placing the verb εὑρέθην at the beginning of the quotation, Paul seems to stress God's passiveness in 'being found'. The LXX as well as the Hebrew text imply that God revealed himself first, then was found, but for Paul, God was found first 'by those who did not seek me' previously (i.e. Gentiles: ἔθνη τὰ μὴ διώκοντα, 9:30). Our view can be strengthened by observing that Paul does not quote LXX Isa 65:1b, which stresses God's active role in revealing himself to those who did not seek him: εἶπα ἰδού εἰμι τῷ ἔθνει οἳ οὐκ ἐκάλεσάν μου τὸ ὄνομα. At the same time he perhaps omits this part because it could be taken to imply the Gentiles did *not* call on his name, while he himself has just emphasised the importance of 'calling on the name of the Lord' for salvation. Thus Paul contrasts Gentile obedience¹⁴¹ with the disobedience and obstinacy of the unbelieving Jews.

According to the original passage, Isa 65:1-2 is a prophecy that God would restore Israel even though they did not seek him. Both verses refer to apostate Israel. But Paul develops the contrast within the two verses and remarkably applies 65:1 to the Gentiles.¹⁴² He therefore even implies that Gentiles somehow sought God, and so God revealed himself to them. On the other hand, 65:2 is specifically applied to Israel, but in being taken apart from 65:1, it portrays a critical picture of Israel as a disobedient and obstinate people. In the light of such modifications Paul introduces the citation with the remark, Ἡσαΐας δὲ ἀποτολμᾷ καὶ

---

tion is rather a representation of textual development: Paul is following the 'original' LXX text, which is adopted by a later scribe as the present LXX text to match the Hebrew text. But he does not provide the evidence that the 'original' LXX text *was* identical with Paul's order. Stanley, *Language*, 144-145, follows this view (although he thinks it is speculative), because it suits his position to attribute the change to someone other than Paul. He objects to the interpretation that Paul reversed the order to bring about a greater emphasis on the 'seeking/finding' theme (advocated by Kautzsch, *Veteris*, 46; Vollmer, *Citate*, 43 n. 1; Michel, *Paulus*, 77, according to Stanley, *Language*, 145 n. 207), because he sees that the LXX text could have served the same purpose without much difference.

140 Despite the fact that one might argue that Paul swaps the verbs because they are interchangeable in this example of Semitic parallelism.

141 Paul's insertion of ἐν ('among') before τοῖς in 10:20a may suggest that not all Gentiles have found him; Stanley, *Language*, 145-146.

142 Sanday and Headlam, *Romans*, 300.

λέγει. Paul says Isaiah spoke very boldly when he said this, but it is in fact Paul himself who speaks so by shaping the quotation as if Isaiah had spoken 'very boldly'.[143] Such a bold contrast is probably related to Paul's apostolic self-awareness in wishing to affirm the legitimacy of the salvation of the Gentiles.

Cranfield suggests that in Romans 10 Paul concentrates more particularly on the issue of Israel (except 10:11f, 18ff) as he brings out not only the rejection of Israel[144] but also God's mercy towards Israel. He then puts more emphasis on the latter: 'it [Rom 10] focuses attention not on Israel's sin but on God's goodness towards Israel'.[145] Such an emphasis is based on 10:21 alone, and our argument above exposes the weakness of such a contention. Furthermore, Paul's transposing of the phrase ὅλην τὴν ἡμέραν to the beginning of the sentence, is to emphasise the persistent apostasy of the Jews[146] as well as the constant love of God towards them. The responses of the rebellious Jews and the receptive Gentiles towards the words of Christ preached by the messengers are clearly contrasted in 10:20-21.[147] The question in 11:1, 'Did God reject his people?', is further a clear indication that Paul has portrayed the Jews rather negatively in Romans 10, especially in v. 21, even to the point where his readers might suspect that God has indeed rejected the Jews.

C. Summary

The main aim of 9:30-10:21, then, is not merely to present an argument about 'Israel's failure' in contrast to 'God's sovereignty' in 9:6-29. Paul explains two things together—Israel's unbelief and the Gentiles' belief—at the same time and without contradiction. This is clear from the introductory and concluding sections: Israel did not obtain righteousness despite their zealous

---

143 See *supra* pp. 33-35.

144 Cranfield, *Romans* 2, 504-505.

145 *Pace* Cranfield, *Romans* 2, 503: 'the statement of Israel's disobedience is strictly incidental' (p. 541), is also rightly opposed by Dunn, *Romans* 2, 627.

146 So correctly, Fitzmyer, *Romans*, 600.

147 Fitzmyer, *Romans*, 600, is correct to note that 10:21 is 'Paul's scathing indictment of Israel. It is surpassed in his letters only by what he says in 1 Thess 2:14-16'.

pursuit of it. Paul explains that it was because they did not know the righteousness that comes from God that they sought to establish their own righteousness by works of the law. Furthermore, even though they heard 'the word of faith' from authorised preachers of the gospel and understood it, they did not believe their message. Thus they did not call upon the name of the Lord, although God had patiently stretched out his hands towards them. They remained disobedient and obstinate. Paul does not say or even imply that Israel does not believe because she 'has been set aside in favour of another nation',[148] or that 'Israel's guilt grows precisely out of its predestination'[149] (we will discuss these views in the next section). Paul makes it clear that the Jewish rejection, despite God's patience and mercy, is their own choice, and therefore their own responsibility.

On the other hand, Paul declares (for the first time explicitly in the letter) that Gentiles have obtained righteousness, the δικαιοσύνην ... τὴν ἐκ πίστεως (9:30; cf. 2:13f; 3:30). This is what Moses had already spoken about: ἡ ... ἐκ πίστεως δικαιοσύνη (10:6). This is the 'righteousness from God [which] comes *through faith* in Jesus Christ' (3:22). Paul asserts that righteousness was intended to be obtained by faith from as early as the days of Abraham (cf. Rom 4) and Moses (10:5-8). Thus the righteousness that Gentiles have obtained by faith in response to the gospel message they have heard, is totally legitimate. It is Gentiles who have followed the way God prepared for the justification of all humanity. Paul's apostolic desire to establish the fundamentally theological apology for the election and the legitimacy of the salvation of the Gentiles has largely influenced the shape of the argument in this section. He also lays the fundamental principles for missionary work: preachers must be sent and proclaim the message, hearers must believe in their heart and confess with their mouth that 'Jesus is Lord', calling on the name of the Lord. This principle applies to all, 'for there is no difference [between Jew and Gentile]' (10:12); God had planned an equal means of salvation for Jew and Gentile. Jews are to follow the way which Gentiles have exercised in obtaining the righteousness which God

---

148 *Pace* Ziesler, *Romans*, 267, who presents God's plan *and* Israel's rejection as the reasons for Israel's failure.
149 *Pace* Käsemann, *Romans*, 297.

intended for humanity: there is no *Sonderweg* for Jews[150] (as we will further demonstrate below).

4. The Messiah's Rejection: A Reversal of Priority in Mission: 11:1-36

More than any other chapter in the section, Romans 11 has been thought to deal most with the issue of the hope of the redemption of Israel.[151] Special attention has been paid to Paul's declarations that 'God has not cast off his people'[152] (11:1, 11), and that πᾶς Ἰσραὴλ σωθήσεται (11:26a).[153] For those scholars who interpret Romans 9-10 as focusing on Israel, especially on God's goodness towards it,[154] this chapter provides a confirmation of their view.[155] However, for those who understand Romans 9-10 to be either a legitimisation of the Gentiles or an explanation of the failure of Israel, it brings perplexity. Watson expresses such puzzlement by insisting that Paul, ironically, is inconsistent in arguing for the consistency of God in the section, because throughout chapter 11, according to Watson, 'Paul reverts to the old view of the people of God which he had previously rejected'.[156] R.D. Kaylor also notes that Romans 11 holds 'apparently contradictory lines of thought' from Romans 9-10, and adds that scholars find great difficulty in agreeing how to hold these lines together.[157]

In this section we will attempt to demonstrate that Paul presents the argument in Romans 11 in a way that coheres well with his belief in the equality of Jew and Gentile in the plan of God. He achieves this by stressing the unbelief of Israel and the faith of

---

150 Cf. Schreiner, 'Israel's Failure', 220.

151 E.g. Sanders, *Jesus*, 336: '... the hope for the redemption of Israel is implied throughout Rom 11 in particular and is precisely enunciated in 11:26.'

152 Cranfield's title, *Romans* 2, 542, for the entire chapter.

153 This verse is often regarded as centre or summary of Rom 9-11: cf. Sänger, 'Rettung', 115.

154 Most notably Cranfield, *Romans* 2, 503, 541-542; cf. our previous discussion on Rom 10.

155 E.g. Wagner, 'Future', 77-112.

156 Watson, *Paul*, 168, but finds the answer to the problem in the hypothesis concerning the social function of Romans.

157 Kaylor, *Covenant Community*, 162; so also Kümmel, 'Probleme', 32; Räisänen, 'Römer 9-11: Analyse', 2892; Becker, *Paul*, 457-458.

the Gentiles just as he did in Romans 9-10. In Romans 11 Paul explains why the main thrust of the mission has been reversed from 'to the Jew first, and also to the Gentile' to 'to the Gentile 'first' and also to the Jew', just as J.A.T. Robinson, Cranfield, Käsemann and E. Brunner have contended.[158]

None of the above-mentioned scholars, however, develops these highly suggestive remarks,[159] and their brief comments require clarification. Nonetheless, they certainly seem to have grasped Paul's main point of argument. Thus their terms 'reversal' and 'detour' need to be qualified and their claims require substantiation. To be sure Paul does not explicitly say that God reversed the *salvation order* from "Ἰουδαίῳ τε πρῶτον καὶ Ἕλληνι' to "Ἕλληνι τε πρῶτον καὶ Ἰουδαίῳ', nor does he suggest that 'God's promise of salvation is taken from Israel and given to the Gentiles'.[160] Salvation certainly came to the Jews *first*, and so the salvation order remains 'to the Jew first'. What is reversed is the *priority* of soteriological direction in mission, because the reversal is related to the salvation of τὸ πλήρωμα τῶν ἐθνῶν and that of πᾶς Ἰσραήλ. Thus the question of primacy is not the issue here but rather the sequence of the salvation of the 'fullness'/'all' of both ethnic groups. Paul suggests that God has determined to save τὸ πλήρωμα τῶν ἐθνῶν *before* he saves πᾶς Ἰσραήλ. Similarly the term 'detour' should not imply that the route to the salvation of the Jews was completely blocked

---

158 Thus our usage of this seemingly blunt phrase is not entirely original. Robinson, *Wrestling*, 110: 'The order of theology was "to the Jew first and also to the Greek" (1.16); the order of history has turned out to be "to the Gentile first and also to the Jew" (11.25-26).' Cranfield, *Romans* 2, 576: 'The οὕτως indicates an inversion of the order in which salvation is actually offered to men according to 1.16.' (Both Robinson and Cranfield independently made this important claim in 1979; see also Dahl's brief comment in his 1972 article, 'The Future of Israel', now reprinted in *Studies*, 137-158; see especially pp. 150 and iv). Käsemann, *Romans*, 274, who also points out that the fact that 'the Ἰουδαίῳ πρῶτον of 1:16 is paradoxically reversed', is not usually noted. Much earlier (1938) Brunner, *Romans*, 95, very briefly indicated that the mission had been *detoured* to the Gentiles due to the Jewish rejection of the Messiah

159 Robinson does not discuss this issue at all even in his exposition of 11:25-32. Cranfield insists that Rom 9-11 is fundamentally about God's faithfulness to Israel, and thus does not note the significance of his own finding of this inversion.

160 Correctly Dahl, *Studies*, 150.

so that a bypass towards the Gentiles can now be opened, because some Jews were still turning to Christian faith in Paul's day. What Paul clearly indicates is that the *priority* in mission is now predominantly 'to the Gentiles' as the result of the Jewish rejection of the Messiah. He must thus explain the new emphasis on the Gentiles.

Furthermore, we will attempt to demonstrate that Paul puts more emphasis on the Gentiles than on the Jews in his argument in Romans 11 (just as he does in Romans 9-10, and indeed in almost the entire letter). We shall examine to what extent this reversal can be traced to Paul's self-awareness as apostle to the Gentiles.[161] It is true that Paul portrays a brighter picture of Israel in Romans 11 than anywhere in his other letters. It is also to be noted, however, that he still maintains a rather critical position towards unbelieving Israel. We shall show how he carefully prepares the ground for his argument that the main thrust of the missionary endeavour has been reversed or redirected to the Gentiles (11:25-26).

By offering explanation from Scripture Paul continues to establish his thesis in Romans 9-11: 'It is not as though God's word had failed' (9:6a). Our study will focus on four sections. In the first section of 11:1-10, we shall argue that despite the declaration that God did not reject his people (11:1), Paul confirms the hardening of the 'rest' in 11:1-10. Here we shall argue that Israel's hardening is due to their own choice in rejecting the gospel rather than to the divine initiative in the salvific plan (although God was not taken by surprise: see below). This issue will be more specifically examined in our discussion of 11:11-16. Wright's hypothesis that Israel's hardening is a vital prerequisite for the salvation of the Gentiles will be critically examined.

It is also important to note that 11:17-24 is especially given as an admonition to Gentile believers. It is commonly accepted that the illustration of the olive tree indicates that the Gentile believers in Rome had already been arrogant towards the Jews.[162] We shall propose that this is not necessarily so; the warning might have been given in order to prevent them from becoming so, because of what Paul had written so far in the letter. The affirmative re-

---

161 Cf. Kümmel, 'Probleme', 40-41.
162 See *infra* p. 270 n. 239, and many others who maintain the Gentile-majority hypothesis concerning the constituency of the Roman church.

marks made about the Jews are to be understood from this perspective. The final section is 11:25-32 (36), which, we suggest, must be understood in the light of what has been written in the previous chapters (Rom 1-11), rather than by (for example) taking 11:26a as the interpretative key for these three chapters, or even the entire letter. Here Paul indicates the reversal of the main outworking of salvation, and thus establishes the soteriological equality of Jew and Gentile in the plan of God, so as to prepare the foundation for the socio-practical exhortations in the rest of the letter (chs. 12-16).

A. *Israel's Hardening: 11:1-10*

The reader of Romans 9-10 might conclude that God had indeed rejected the Jews. Paul himself sees the need to bring a balance to his presentation thus far.[163] Accordingly he reaffirms one of the well-known covenantal themes that God has not rejected Israel (e.g. Deut 31:6; Ps 37:28; 94:14; Isa 44:21; 46:4; 49:15; 54:10). However, he does not say that Israel will be safe simply because God did not reject them. Rather he confirms the existence of two groups within Israel: ἡ ἐκλογή and οἱ λοιποί (cf. 9:6b). We shall argue that Paul continually passes a critical judgement on unbelieving Jews, affirming that they are hardened, not because of God's predestining initiative in bringing salvation to the Gentiles, but as the result of their own refusal of the grace manifested in Christ. We shall examine the passive verb ἐπωρώθησαν as to whether it means a divine hardening or rather refers to God's judgement upon those who refused him. We will also show that Paul uses the OT passages, including the Elijah incident, to confirm his assertions concerning the unbelief of the λοιποί. Thus 9:30-11:10 indicates that Israel's unbelief is the reason why the priority in mission has switched to the Gentiles.

We note at least three indications of the fact that Paul condemns Israel's unbelief. First, in Paul's description of the Elijah incident. He writes that Elijah *pleaded* to God *against* Israel (ἐντυγχάνει τῷ θεῷ κατὰ τοῦ Ἰσραήλ). This phrase indicates not only Paul's interpretation (because both the Hebrew and the

---

[163] A solemn denial of such impression is not only anticipated by the μή-question but also stressed by the reinforced statements (μὴ γένοιτο, ὃν προέγνω) in 11:1-2.

LXX texts simply report that Elijah '*said*'), but also his intention of making a special point with this unique phrase (because it is never used elsewhere in Scripture outside Romans).[164] However, similar phrases (ἐντυγχαν- ... κατά) in apocryphal and pseudepigraphical writings (1 Macc 8:32, 11:25, cf. 10:61, 63, *1 En.* 9:3) help us understand Paul's intent. They imply a complaint and accusation *against* Israel,[165] being 'an indictment of evildoers and a plea that God take action against them'.[166] Paul seems to identify himself with Elijah under similar circumstances (cf. 1 Kgs 19:10),[167] and expresses the distress caused him by the national rebellion against God's Messiah (and indeed by the threats against his own person: 2 Cor 11:22-25). It seems significant that Paul implies that the unbelieving Jews should be compared with those who worshipped Baal. His distress, however, is surely greater than that of the author of 1 Kings, and even perhaps than that of Elijah himself, because most of his contemporary fellow-Jews had not simply apostatised but had rejected and crucified God's Messiah.

Second, Paul affirms again that the majority of the Jews did not obtain grace for salvation (9:31f; 10:2f), but only the elect remnant (λεῖμμα κατ' ἐκλογήν: 11:5, and ἡ ἐκλογή: 11:7). The rest [of Israel] were hardened (οἱ δὲ λοιποὶ ἐπωρώθησαν).[168] The passive verb ἐπωρώθησαν causes some difficulties for exegetes. Barrett may be correct in saying, 'It seems impossible here to distinguish between "hardened because disobedient" and "disobedient because hardened"; the two processes are concurrent.'[169] Nevertheless, it seems vital to understand this as far as is possible, because it directs the interpretation of the whole chapter

---

164 See Rom 8:26, 34, where Paul combines ἐντυγχάω with ὑπέρ (so also Heb 7:25), and Acts 25:24, where the same verb connotes 'to plead against', but without the κατά.

165 Sanday and Headlam, *Romans*, 311; Murray, *Romans* 2, 68; Cranfield, *Romans* 2, 546; Fitzmyer, *Romans*, 602. Cf. Käsemann, *Romans*, 300.

166 Morris, *Romans*, 399 n. 8; so also Black, *Romans*, 141.

167 Morris, *Romans*, 400.

168 The rendering of the NEB, 'nonelect', is not clear. Morris's view, *Romans*, 403, that it contains both Jews and Gentiles, is incorrect, but Dodd's, *Romans*, 185, 'the rest of Israel' (so Käsemann, *Romans*, 301; Fitzmyer, *Romans*, 606) seems most probable, because in 11:1-10 Paul is only talking about ethnic Israel.

169 Barrett, *Romans*, 210.

as well as of 11:1-10. Cranfield argues that the passive verb ἐπωρώθησαν does not mean that they hardened themselves but refers to a divine hardening.[170] The idea of a divine hardening is certainly not uncommon in the NT (e.g. Matt 13:13-15/Mark 4:12/Luke 8:10; John 12:40; Acts 28:26; 2 Cor 3:14; Eph 4:18). But here the context and Paul's wording seem to suggest that 'it is best to take this verb as a genuine passive and to assume that the act of hardening is God's judgment upon these people who have refused him'.[171] In 11:11 Paul uses an active verb (ἔπταισαν), which suggests that the Jews themselves have stumbled.

Similar is the case of ἡ ἀποβολὴ αὐτῶν (11:15). Along with many other scholars,[172] Cranfield takes God as the subject of the active verbs, and asserts that ἡ ἀποβολὴ αὐτῶν 'must mean their temporary casting away by God', while ἡ πρόσλημψις means 'God's final acceptance of what is now unbelieving Israel'.[173] However, Cranfield introduces a note which conflicts with what he says elsewhere when he asserts, 'The ἀποβολή of the Jews by God ... is ... identical with ... their rejection of the Messiah.'[174] He seems to contradict himself by asserting God's rejection of the Jews after having so forcefully argued that God did not reject his people in his interpretation of 11:1-10. Paul is not here blaming God for rejecting the Jews, but indirectly blaming the Jews for their unbelief and rejection of the Messiah. Paul asserts that they 'stumbled' (11:11), 'slipped away' (11:11, 12), 'were defeated' (11:12) and 'were broken off' because of their own unbelief (11:17, 19, 20, 23) rather than because of God's divine action. Paul argues that it is their unbelief that caused God to act against

---

170 Cranfield, *Romans* 2, 549; Stuhlmacher, *Romans*, 162-165. Earlier Black, *Romans*, 142, suggested that the passive voice is used to avoid the use of the divine name, which is however the real subject of the hardening.

171 Newman and Nida, *Romans*, 212; also Sanday and Headlam, *Romans*, 314; Brunner, *Romans*, 94. Cf. Wright, *Climax*, 247, who points out that according to Jewish apocalyptic thought '"hardening" is what happens when people refuse the grace and patience of God'.

172 E.g. Black, *Romans*, 144; Newman and Nida, *Romans*, 217-218; Dunn, *Romans* 2, 657-658; so also Wilckens, Davies, Morris.

173 Cranfield, *Romans* 2, 562. But πρόσλημψις does not mean 'final acceptance', but merely 'acceptance' (*EDNT* 3, 175; BAGD, 717).

174 Cranfield, *Romans* 2, 562. Cf. Dunn, *Romans* 2, 657-658, who says that the rejection is a 'divine action' by divine initiative 'without diminishing the culpability of human trespass'.

them: 'Because of their unbelief, they were broken off. ... God did not spare the natural branches' (11:20-21).[175]

Third, Paul finds the explanation from the Scriptures, where their hardening has already been 'foreshadowed':

LXX Isa 29:10 ὅτι πεπότικεν ὑμᾶς κύριος <u>πνεύματι κατανύξεως</u> καὶ καμμύσει τοὺς ὀφθαλμοὺς αὐτῶν καὶ τῶν προφητῶν αὐτῶν καὶ τῶν ἀρχόντων αὐτῶν οἱ ὁρῶντες τὰ κρυπτά.

LXX Deut 29:3 καὶ οὐκ ἔδωκεν κύριος ὁ θεὸς ὑμῖν καρδίαν εἰδέναι καὶ ὀφθαλμοὺς βλέπειν καὶ ὦτα ἀκούειν ἕως τῆς ἡμέρας ταύτης.

Rom 11:8 Ἔδωκεν αὐτοῖς ὁ θεὸς πνεῦμα κατανύξεως, ὀφθαλμοὺς τοῦ μὴ βλέπειν καὶ ὦτα τοῦ μὴ ἀκούειν, ἕως τῆς σήμερον ἡμέρας.

Paul first quotes LXX Deut 29:3 (EV 29:4) and Isa 29:10 (with some textual modifications[176]) to strengthen his argument about the unbelief of Israel. The modification of the context seems even

---

175 Even if we take the subject as God, one still cannot say that their hardening is totally God's responsibility. Sanday and Headlam, *Romans*, 313, are correct at this point: 'They have not failed because they have been hardened, but they have been hardened because they have failed' (cf. *'for this reason* God gave them up': 1:24, 26, 28). The classic case of Pharaoh's hardening is the product of both God's work and Pharaoh's own response (Exod 4:21; 7:22-23; 8:15, 32; 10:1, 27). Paul excludes the notion that God has totally or finally rejected the Jews (v. 1), but repeats the established fact that they themselves have rejected God's Messiah and the message about him, and thus have rejected God himself; cf. Dinter, 'Prophet Isaiah', 49.

176 (1) The subject of hardening is changed from 'the Lord' to 'God', possibly due to Paul's concern to avoid the impression that it is 'the Lord Jesus' who hardens. (2) The positive verb ἔδωκεν substitutes the negative οὐκ ἔδωκεν, but such a replacement does not necessarily bring a clearer thought of divine hardening (*pace* Cranfield, *Romans* 2, 549). (3) The indirect object 'you' is replaced by 'them' to explain that it is Israel who is hardened. (4) The construction, ἕως τῆς ἡμέρας ταύτης is rephrased as ἕως τῆς σήμερον ἡμέρας, and is transposed to the end of the sentence in order to emphasise the continuing attitude of Israel and to accuse the *present generation*. See Stanley, *Language*, 158-163, for a more detailed comparison.

more significant. 'The context of this verse in Deuteronomy is a *gracious one*, speaking of God's goodness to His people',[177] but Paul uses it to accuse Israel of their unbelief caused by their spiritual insensibility (cf. Acts 7:51). Deut 29:2-3 says, 'Your eyes *have seen* all that the Lord did in Egypt ... With your own eyes you saw those great [things]'. And v. 4 continues, 'But to this day the Lord has not given you a mind that understands or eyes that see or ears that hear. But ... the Lord is making a covenant with you this day' (Deut 29:10, 12, 15). Thus what Deut 29:4 actually says is, 'You have seen but *did not understand or see the significance* of those wonderful deeds of God. It has been kept secret *up to this day*. But *today* he reveals why he did so, and *from today* you will see it by entering into a covenant with God'. Thus, in Deuteronomy 29, the repeated phrase 'this day/today' (Deut 29:4, 10, 12, 15) marks a positive turning point. Nevertheless, for Paul *until the present day* Israel still 'cannot perceive or comprehend'[178] the significance of God's great work revealed in Jesus, despite the fact that they had heard and understood (10:18, 19).

Furthermore, David (LXX Ps 68:23-24: MT 69:22-23) is called as a witness (καὶ Δαυὶδ λέγει):[179]

LXX Ps 68:23-24	γενηθήτω ἡ τράπεζα αὐτῶν ἐνώπιον αὐτῶν εἰς παγίδα καὶ εἰς ἀνταπόδοσιν καὶ εἰς σκάνδαλον 24 σκοτισθήτωσαν οἱ ὀφθαλμοὶ αὐτῶν τοῦ μὴ βλέπειν καὶ τὸν νῶτον αὐτῶν διὰ παντὸς σύγκαμψον
Rom 11:9-10	Γενηθήτω ἡ τράπεζα αὐτῶν εἰς παγίδα καὶ εἰς θήραν καὶ εἰς σκάνδαλον καὶ εἰς ἀνταπόδομα αὐτοῖς, 10 σκοτισθήτωσαν οἱ ὀφθαλμοὶ αὐτῶν τοῦ μὴ βλέπειν, καὶ τὸν νῶτον αὐτῶν διὰ παντὸς σύγκαμψον.

---

[177] Cranfield, Rom 2, 549; *pace* Black, *Romans*, 142, who sees Deut 29:4 as 'a condemnation of Israel'.

[178] Newman and Nida, *Romans*, 213.

[179] This may indicate the greater importance of David as a witness (see 4:6-8, Acts 2:25, 34, 4:25) rather than the phrase, 'as it is written [in the Psalms]' (3:4, 10-18, 8:36, Acts 1:20), or a quotation without mentioning David or the Psalms.

In the original passage David expresses his distress and anger, and even calls down curses upon his unspecified 'enemies' within Israel (cf. Ps 69:7-12, 27-28) who seek to destroy him (Ps 69:4, 18, 19). He asks God to pour out his wrath on them forever. If a passage from such a context is 'deliberately adopted'[180] and directly applied to Israel, the unbelieving majority of Israel is clearly and strikingly identified with David's enemy against whom a severe imprecation and accusation has been made.[181] Paul seems to quote this to add to the intensity of his accusation against Israel. Paul's quote indicates that 'their table' (ἡ τράπεζα αὐτῶν), that is, (probably) their religious works (cf. 11:6, 9:31f),[182] has become a snare. The intensity is clearly shown in Paul's modification of the verse. The phrase ἐνώπιον αὐτῶν is omitted, but αὐτοῖς is added at the end of the verse to suggest that 'the snare and the trap are something they are going to be caught in themselves'.[183] The addition of the καὶ εἰς θήραν simply repeats the same meaning of εἰς παγίδα, and thus intensifies Paul's accusation.

11:10 is quoted exactly from LXX Ps 68:24. However, following Gaugler, F.J. Leenhardt asserts that since Paul's argument implies only temporary punishment, his exact quotation, including διὰ παντός, is a mistake.[184] For the same reason, Cranfield suggests rendering it as 'continually' rather than as 'for ever', which is, for him, 'surely mistaken'.[185] We propose that the phrase is not only to be included in the citation but is also to be rendered as 'for ever'. According to the original context, 'continually' is not what David means, because his enemies are not yet trapped or blind. David's fervent wish is not for them to

---

180 Liddon, *Romans*, 202; also cited in Murray, *Romans* 2, 74 n. 16. It seems to be a unique quotation, for Ps 69:22-23 is only quoted here in the NT, while the Psalm is often cited especially as a testimony to the passion of Christ (Ps 69:4 in John 15:25; v. 9 in John 2:17; Rom 15:3; v. 21 in Matt 27:34, 48//Mark 15:23, 36//Luke 23:36//John 19:29; v. 25 in Acts 1:20).

181 So also Cranfield, *Romans* 2, 551.

182 See Cranfield, *Romans* 2, 551-552, for different interpretations of the τράπεζα.

183 Newman and Nida, *Romans*, 213.

184 *Pace* Leenhardt, *Romans*, 280 n. 2, 4, who says, 'Paul is certainly quoting from memory' and that this shows that 'he [Paul] is not concerned with the detail of the quotation'.

185 Cranfield, *Romans* 2, 552.

The Equality of Jew and Gentile in the Plan of God 259

be continually blind, but rather to become 'incurably blind' (11:10, JB), i.e. forever. For Paul, the majority of Israel has already been hardened (11:7), so 'continually' could also be acceptable. Therefore, including διὰ παντός in the quotation is not to be regarded as Paul's mistake, but rather his deliberate application of this to the spiritual insensibility of Israel as if in answer to David's prayer. It is also to be noted that Paul deals with the issue of whether Israel stumbled so as to fall beyond recovery (v. 11) in order to counter such an impression received by his inclusion of the expression 'for ever'. The question in 11:11, 'Did they stumble so as to fall beyond recovery?', indicates that 11:1-10 has not offered the affirmative answer to the problem mentioned in 11:1a.[186] Rather it reaffirms the fact that, as we have maintained, the unbelieving Jews[187] indeed stumbled (cf. 9:32) even to the point, one might suspect, of falling beyond recovery.

B. *God's Outworking of the Salvation for Gentiles and Jews: 11:11-16*

Paul corrects the impression that the λοιποί have stumbled beyond recovery. It is to be noted, however, that he neither provides the basis for such a strong denial, nor carries on the argument as to why they have not fallen in a complete and final sense.[188] He simply mentions it,[189] and so confirms their slipping away (παράπτωμα) as a *fait accompli*. Then he quickly relates the Jewish sin of unbelief to the issue of the salvation of the Gentiles.

---

186 So correctly Käsemann, *Romans*, 304.

187 Cranfield's wording ('the unbelievers', *Romans* 2, 554) is precise, and is to be preferred to the renderings of TEV and JB ('the Jews') because the subject of ἔπταισαν is the λοιποί of 11:7, that is, those Jews who have rejected the gospel.

188 In contrast with the recoverable πταίω, the biblical πίπτω (LXX Isa 24:20; Heb 4:11; Pss. Sol. 3:13) implies a final destruction (Black, *Romans*, 143), 'an irrevocable fall' (Cranfield, *Romans* 2, 555), a 'total collapse' (Ziesler, *Romans*, 273), or 'fall utterly and permanently' (Murray, *Romans* 2, 75 n. 18). Cf. NEB: 'complete downfall', JB: 'fallen for ever'.

189 As we have observed above (pp. 130-133, 225-227), Paul does not argue for Israel. This observation leads us to assume that Paul's primary interest in Romans is not to emphasise the privileged position of the Jews (though it is presupposed and not denied), but to argue for the salvation and the place of the Gentiles in the plan of God.

But was Israel's παράπτωμα a necessary prerequisite for God in order to bring the blessing of salvation to the Gentiles? We shall argue that this is not what Paul says here; rather, Paul's point is that God shifted his salvific blessing 'to the Gentile "first"' as the result of Israel's rejection of the gospel of the Messiah. We shall show that Paul expects Israel's πλήρωμα, but furthermore, anticipates that it would bring a far greater blessing to the Gentiles than they enjoy now (11:12, 15). He stresses his apostleship to the Gentiles so as to justify his bold remarks on behalf of the Gentiles. We shall also attempt to expose the weakness of the hypothesis that Paul's ministry among the Gentiles is only secondary to his ultimate goal of saving his own people.

(a) Is Israel's Stumbling a Necessary Part in God's Plan?

While some commentators take τὸ παράπτωμα in an etymological sense in line with the metaphor of stumbling,[190] or a false step,[191] Cranfield understands this word in line with other references (Acts 8:1ff, 13:45-48, 18:6, 28:24-28) as denoting 'the sin committed by the λοιποί in rejecting the Gospel'.[192] Whatever meaning is taken it should be noted that the λοιποί of the Jews are blamed with the much stronger charge of the παράπτωμα than a mere 'stumble'. Although the unbelieving Jews have not yet fallen beyond a 'missionary hope for Israel',[193] Paul makes it clear that they have committed the sin of unbelief.

However, the statement, ἀλλὰ τῷ αὐτῶν παραπτώματι ἡ σωτηρία τοῖς ἔθνεσιν, εἰς τὸ παραζηλῶσαι αὐτούς, has been much debated among scholars. For Stendahl and Leenhardt God modified his plan of salvation *after* Israel's fall to extend it to the Gentiles, so that both Jews and Gentiles could be saved.[194] Taking the τῷ αὐτῶν παραπτώματι as an instrumental dative, Wright also maintains the same position that God intended to save the world through the Jewish rejection of the Messiah and

---

190 Barrett, *Romans*, 213, Murray, *Romans* 2, 76.
191 Ziesler, *Romans*, 274.
192 Cranfield, *Romans* 2, 555-556. Dunn, *Romans* 2, 653, admits the sense of 'false step', but accepts Cranfield's view, adding that the transgression of the Jews is not only in rejecting the gospel message (so also, Newman and Nida, *Romans*, 215), but also the Christ (cf. 5:9-10; 1 Cor 1:18).
193 Motyer, *Israel*, 138.
194 Stendahl, *Paul*, 28; Leenhardt, *Romans*, 21, 251, 281-282.

The Equality of Jew and Gentile in the Plan of God   261

his gospel. Wright's objection, however, to the former view is, in fact, that Israel's fall was not a cause for God to change his plan, but was a *necessary* prerequisite of God's salvific plan.[195] Thus he asserts, '*Only so can he save Gentiles at all, and only so can Jewish salvation* (which is still on offer) *be by grace alone.* ... [The rejection of Jesus] is her tragedy and her glory', and is not 'an unfortunate historical accident'.[196] Some have endorsed this position,[197] but we find it unconvincing for the following three reasons: First, this defence of God may imply the consequence of placing the responsibility of Israel's rejection of the Messiah and the gospel upon God himself (though Wright does not assert this explicitly).[198] Second, Paul himself does not see it in terms of

---

195 Wright, *Messiah*, 308 n. 21; Watson, *Paul*, 169: 'Israel's failure was needed in order to make room for Gentiles.'

196 Wright, *Messiah*, 173, 308 n. 21, emphasis added. He repeatedly stresses this point: 'Her [Israel's] "fall" is ... a sign of a great, though terrible, privilege' (p. 199); and in his later work, *Climax*, 240, 247-248; *idem*, 'Romans', 193-194: 'the divine intention from the beginning [was] that Israel according to the flesh should be cast away in order that the world might be redeemed.'

197 E.g. Dunn, *Romans* 2, 653-654, 667-668.

198 According to this interpretation Israel's fall can be defended as an inevitable fate, since no one can resist God's will (indeed, Rese, 'Rettung', 425, asserts that Israel's hardening is not their own fault). But in Rom 11 Paul does not specify God as the agent of hardening (so correctly, Davidson and Martin, 'Romans', 1038). Although Paul *may* imply God as the agent with the terms ἀποβολή (11:15), ἐφείσατο (11:21), and the (divine) passives ἐξεκλάσθησαν (11:17) and ἐνεκεντρίσθης (11:24), he still maintains that the Jews are to be blamed (11:20, 23; cf. 9:19-20). Asking the question whether Israel has fallen according to God's original plan to save the world through her fall, or whether God changed his plan to include the Gentiles after her fall, is something akin to asking whether it was the chicken or the egg which came first; both conclusions may have good grounds.

But the former question is inappropriate here. What is important is to discern from whose perspective Paul is arguing here. Since human beings can only see *after* the event, from their perspective salvation has come to the Gentiles as a consequence of the Jewish rejection. From God's perspective, though, knowing beforehand that the Jews would reject their Messiah, he might have used their foreseeable rejection as the instrument of his extension of salvation beyond the Jews. So God planned to save both Jews and Gentiles (cf. John 3:16-17; 1 Tim 2:4), but his original plan was 'for the Jew first and also for the Gentile', or 'through Jewish obedience to Gentile obedience', as is the pattern in the OT. But Israel has failed in that function. For Paul, therefore,

'fate' or 'tragedy'.[199] Third, Paul's point is that Israel's παράπτωμα/ἥττημα was very much *second* best even in God's plan; the best scenario is their πλήρωμα (11:12),[200] as we will show below.

(b) Israel's Loss and the Gentiles' Riches

In 11:12 Paul restates the theological and missiological fact that the Jewish transgression of unbelief and their refusal of the gospel[201] have brought the fullness of the salvific blessing (9:23; 10:12) to the world (and to the Gentiles in particular). He furthermore insists that the obedience of the full number of the Jews (τὸ πλήρωμα αὐτῶν)[202] will 'bring an even vaster increase of wealth *to the world*'.[203] J. Murray expresses it more clearly: 'The

---

God has used Israel's rejection as the opportunity to divert the main thrust in mission: he has turned to the Gentiles preferentially with the blessing of the gospel. Paul here does not seem to see the event from God's perspective, but from a human and historical point of view (Fitzmyer, *Romans*, 611). That is why he never rationalises Israel's unbelief, but accuses them for it: 'they are broken off because of [their own] unbelief' (11:20).

199 So correctly Betz, 'Israels Mission', 56.

200 Wright appears to admit this in his later article, 'Romans', 195-196: 'Israel's obedience/faithfulness should have been the means of undoing the problem of Adam, of humanity as a whole (2.17-24, 3.2f.)'. Wagner, 'Future', 96, is wrong to say that God's plan to bless Gentiles in Gen 12:3; 17:4 is through Israel's rebellion and disobedience; it was rather through their obedience and blessing.

201 Some take ἥττημα quantitatively in relation to πλήρωμα and understand it as 'loss' (most notably Barrett), but most commentators (including Knox, Gaugler, Sanday and Headlam, Leenhardt, Murray, Cranfield) comprehend it as qualitative, a 'defeat' or 'degeneration'. However, Dunn, *Romans* 2, 654, seems right to say that the word is chosen to be in parallel with παράπτωμα as a literary device (words ending in -μα rather than for its precise meaning), and so also for the later πλήρωμα. With ἥττημα, according to Dunn, Paul expresses Israel's plight by their refusal of the gospel (9:31-33; 10:21; 11:7).

202 The phrase τὸ πλήρωμα αὐτῶν certainly implies *Israel's* 'fullness'. The πλήρωμα has been interpreted in many ways: 'full strength' in numbers (Barrett, *Romans*, 214); 'full inclusion' (Black, *Romans*, 143); 'the majority of Israelites' (Ziesler, *Romans*, 274-275); unquestionably 'the fulness of Israel as a people' (Murray, *Romans* 2, 78); the full inclusion of the 'rest' with the remnant, i.e. all Israel (Wagner, 'Future', 92). See also TEV, Goodspeed, Moffatt, for their understanding of a quantitative fullness.

203 Black, *Romans*, 143, with added emphasis. So also Fitzmyer, *Romans*, 611: 'Paul hints at the untold benefits *for the world* [i.e. *Gentiles*]' (added emphasis); Stuhlmacher, *Romans*, 167. Cf. Donaldson, 'Riches', 81-98.

argument of the apostle is not ... the restoration of Israel; it is the blessing accruing *to the Gentiles* from Israel's "fullness".'[204] It can then be said that it is for the *Gentiles' interest* that he craves the salvation of the Jews.[205] Even if Israel's failure was a necessary component, the apostle to the Gentiles can still say that it was for the sake of the Gentiles that God allowed Israel to stumble. So much so is he the apostle to the Gentiles![206] His primary concern is to affirm the blessing of the Gentiles as expressed in 11:12 and 15 (see below).

The extremely emphatic declaration of his apostleship to the Gentiles in 11:13 ('Ὑμῖν δὲ λέγω τοῖς ἔθνεσιν. ἐφ' ὅσον μὲν οὖν εἰμι ἐγὼ ἐθνῶν ἀπόστολος, ...) is made to elucidate why he makes such a bold and affirmative statement on behalf of the Gentiles. The emphatic composition is significant. By adding ὑμῖν to τοῖς ἔθνεσιν and placing it at the beginning of the sentence, Paul emphasises that what has been said (γάρ[207]), and what will be said are specifically written '*to you, the Gentiles*'. However, in the light of Paul's indication that he longs for the salvation of the Jews for the greater riches of the Gentiles, the emphatic dative ὑμῖν can be taken as '*for* you'. The affirmative particle μέν further strengthens the already emphasised εἰμι ἐγώ. Then Paul designates himself as ἐθνῶν ἀπόστολος, whose word-order clearly shows that the stress is on the ἐθνῶν.[208] Furthermore, he adds οὖν[209] to summarise[210] and relate what has been

---

204 Murray, *Romans* 2, 79; the second emphasis is added; similarly, Käsemann, *Romans*, 306.

205 So correctly, Motyer, *Israel*, 138.

206 Here again Paul seems to reverse the Jewish expectation of Gentile blessing, which depends on the eschatological pilgrimage to Zion of Gentile proselytes. See Dunn, *Romans* 2, 655. The pre-Pauline references include Ps 22:27; Isa 2:2-3; 45:22-23; 56:6-8; 60:2, 5; 66:23; Mic 4:2; Zeph 3:9; Zech 2:11; 8:20-22; Tob 13:11; 14:6-7; *Pss. Sol.* 17:34; *Sib. Or.* 3:710-720, 772-775; *T. Zub.* 9:8; *T. Benj.* 9:2; cf. Matt 8:1; Mark 11:17; Luke 13:29.

207 As in D F G Ψ 33 𝔐, and adopted in TBS, but δέ in UBS³ and Nestle-Aland²⁷.

208 Paul puts ἀπόστολος first in similar expressions: 'ἀπόστολος Ἰησοῦ Χριστοῦ' (1 Cor 1:1, Eph 1:1, cf. 2 Tim 1:1).

209 The οὖν is not included in the TBS, but in UBS³ and Nestle-Aland²⁷.

210 Dunn, *Romans* 2, 655. Cf. Cranfield's interpretation of μὲν οὖν in line with μενοῦνγε (9:20, 10:18, Phil 3:8) is unconvincing: see Dunn, *Romans* 2, 655-656.

said to an emphatic expression of his apostleship to the Gentiles. Finally, the emphatic position of τὴν διακονίαν μου expresses 'the zealous pursuit of the Gentile ministry'.[211] In such a way, Paul's Gentile apostleship, his duty to the Gentiles (15:16), and his desire to communicate this position are given a most emphatic literary expression.[212] Paul saw the need to explain why he has made such affirmative remarks about the Gentiles before he says the same thing again in 11:15: Paul answers, '[Because] I am indeed an apostle of the Gentiles'.

A chiastic structure of 11:12 and 15 is noticeable: both stress that Jewish fullness and acceptance will bring a much greater blessing to the world/the Gentiles. Then the carefully structured 11:13-14 is inserted in between the verses[213] to affirm that it is his apostolic ministry for the Gentiles that enables him to expect much greater blessing for them.

---

211 Murray, *Romans* 2, 80 n. 24. *Pace* KJV's rendering as an 'office'. The emphatic position of τὴν διακονίαν, and thus Paul's concern for his role, and the absence of the definite article in the designation ἐθνῶν ἀπόστολος, suggest that Paul understands his apostleship as a function rather than as an 'office'; see Dunn, *Romans* 2, 656. Apostleship as an 'office' seems restricted to the Twelve (Acts 1:20). Since Paul never speaks of his apostleship as temporary, 'inasmuch as' or 'since' is to be preferred to TEV's rendering 'as long as' for the meaning of the ἐφ' ὅσον (Cranfield, *Romans* 2, 559; Newman and Nida, *Romans*, 217; Dunn, *Romans* 2, 655).

212 One may argue that such an emphatic expression indicates Paul's intention to establish his authority for the severe warnings to the Gentile Christians that come in 11:17-22. Indeed he warns the Gentiles (11:18, 20, 22). However, Paul's words in 11:17-22 are not only to warn Gentile believers but also to explain their relationship to the Jews with the exhortation not to follow their example of unbelief. In this passage Paul praises the Gentiles for (unlike the hardened Jews) standing by faith and for receiving God's kindness; see below.

213 Robinson, *Wrestling*, 128. The continuation of the thought of 11:12 in 11:15 has led some to comprehend 11:13-14 as a parenthesis (e.g. Sanday and Headlam, *Romans*, 325; Cranfield, *Romans* 2, 558-559; but not so Ellison, *Mystery*, 85). For Dunn, *Romans* 2, 652, it is an 'apparent digression'. If the introduction of the theme on Paul's apostleship and ministry can be regarded as a parenthesis, it is only the parenthesis of reinforcement or clarification rather than that of digression, because the γάρ of 11:13 (which is related to 11:12) and of 11:15 (related to 11:13f rather than 11:12; *pace* Cranfield, *Romans* 2, 561) do not seem to identify it as a digression in its structure.

v. 12 εἰ δὲ τὸ παράπτωμα αὐτῶν πλοῦτος
κόσμου καὶ τὸ ἥττημα αὐτῶν πλοῦτος
ἐθνῶν,   πόσῳ μᾶλλον τὸ πλήρωμα αὐτῶν.
              [μᾶλλον πλοῦτος κόσμου/ἐθνῶν]

v. 15 εἰ γὰρ ἡ ἀποβολὴ αὐτῶν καταλλαγὴ
κόσμου,   τίς ἡ πρόσλημψις εἰ μὴ ζωὴ ἐκ νεκρῶν;
              [μᾶλλον ζωὴ ἐκ νεκρῶν κόσμου]
v. 13 Ὑμῖν δὲ [γὰρ] λέγω τοῖς ἔθνεσιν.
ἐφ᾽ ὅσον μὲν οὖν εἰμι ἐγὼ ἐθνῶν ἀπόστολος, τὴν διακονίαν μου
δοξάζω,
v. 14 εἴ πως παραζηλώσω μου τὴν σάρκα καὶ σώσω τινὰς ἐξ αὐτῶν.

Nevertheless, most scholars implausibly assert that Paul's ministry to the Gentiles had only a *secondary* purpose, mainly on the basis of 11:14: εἴ πως παραζηλώσω μου τὴν σάρκα καὶ σώσω τινὰς ἐξ αὐτῶν. Watson, for example, underlines, 'The ultimate purpose of Paul's mission is thus not the salvation of Gentiles but the salvation of Jews.'[214] Of course, Paul anticipates the effect of his ministry for the Jews and their salvation as well. But he does not state that the salvation of the Jews is the ultimate aim of his work among the Gentiles. Rather, this majority view seems unconvincing. It is not plausible to relate 11:13c to v. 14 so directly and exclusively. The phrase τὴν διακονίαν μου δοξάζω is rather related to 11:13b as the principal clause of the sentence in 11:13b-c. To be sure, the phrase can belong either to the preceding clause or to the following one, as TBS and UBS³/Nestle-Aland²⁷ respectively punctuate.[215] But the phrase seems to be

---

214 Watson, *Paul*, 169. But this assertion apears to contradict Watson's own thesis that Paul exhorts the Jewish believers in Rome to separate themselves from the Jewish community and join the Pauline or Gentile congregation. How could Paul say so, and why should Jewish believers separate themselves from the community, if Paul's ultimate goal is the salvation of the Jews and not of the Gentiles? So also Johnson, 'Jews', 120: 'Paul magnifies his ministry to the Gentiles for the very purpose of serving Israel's salvation (11:13-14)'; Leenhardt, *Romans*, 283: '... the final aim of Paul's ministry to the Gentiles is the conversion of Israel itself'; and Motyer, *Israel*, 139, 'So even though his activity was directed towards Gentiles, his strategy focused on Israel'; Fitzmyer, *Romans*, 612, 541, also insists, 'Although Paul's ministry primarily concerns itself with the salvation of Gentiles, he insists that there is a deeper motivation in his mission: the salvation of Israel.'

215 Most English translations and commentators follow the punctuation of the latter (RSV, NRSV, NIV, NEB, NAB, NASB, Moffatt; Dunn, Cranfield, Fitz-

connected to 11:13b rather than to 11:14, if the following points are considered:

First, after such a strong affirmation of his apostolic function in 11:13a-b, the expression with somewhat indefinite nuance εἴ πως ('if somehow') seems strange,[216] if it is to be connected to the following clause. If that were the case a more definitive composition (e.g. εἰς τὸ παραζηλῶσαι, as used in v. 11) could be expected. Second, the context of this chapter makes it preferable to connect the phrase τὴν διακονίαν μου δοξάζω to v. 13b: when Paul magnifies his ministry among the Gentiles, Jews can be provoked to jealousy (11:11), and when the πλήρωμα of the Gentiles comes in, 'so "all" Israel will be saved' (11:25-26). He declares that his glory lies with his work among the Gentiles, as 15:17-18 most clearly indicates (cf. 2 Cor 9:12-13). Thus Ziesler's paraphrase seems accurate: 'I make the most of the significance of the Gentile mission, which is my particular concern.'[217] Paul's usage of the aorist subjunctives (as most commentators take παραζηλώσω and σώσω to be) also indicates that provoking the unbelieving Jews to jealousy and thus saving some of them (τινὰς ἐξ αὐτῶν) is his desired and additional expectation rather than '"the true aim of his Gentile mission"'.[218] Paul's apostolic ministry is directly related to the Gentiles as their apostle; it is also indirectly connected to the conversion of the Jews 'precisely in virtue of the Gentile mission'.[219]

Paul seems to add 11:13 to explain why (γάρ) he makes such a remarkable statement concerning the Gentiles' blessings, and 11:14 to assure his (Jewish) readers that even though he magnifies his ministry among the Gentiles he is not indifferent about the salvation of the Jews, who are even described as μου τὴν σάρκα. But he does not say that the ultimate purpose of the Gentile mission is primarily the salvation of the Jews. Rather, he

---

myer, Barrett, Käsemann), but KJV and TEV the former. JB's rendering has been changed in NJB from the former punctuation to the latter one.

216 Whether the παραζηλώσω is taken as the aorist subjunctive or the future indicative, the phrase εἴ πως παραζηλώσω certainly carries an indefinite connotation (BAGD, 220; cf. 1:10; Phil 3:11).

217 Ziesler, *Romans*, 275.

218 So rightly Dunn, *Romans* 2, 656. So also Dodd, *Romans*, 187, who notes that it does not seem to be '[Paul's] motive to missionary work'.

219 Käsemann, *Romans*, 307; Brunner, *Romans*, 95; Sänger, 'Rettung', 110; *pace* Rese, 'Rettung', 428.

The Equality of Jew and Gentile in the Plan of God 267

repeats his earlier formula (11:12), thus implying that the salvation of the Jews, prompted subsequently by the believing Gentiles, would increase the blessing of the Gentiles.[220] In that sense the γάρ of 11:15 is vital: not because it provides 'the theological reasons for giving Israel strategic priority in Christian mission',[221] but because it explains 'why he is so keen to provoke Israel to salvation'.[222] The reason why Paul hopes for the salvation of some of Israel, is because their acceptance will certainly bring a greater blessing to the Gentiles (or rather to *all* believers).

This crucial verse (11:15) requires a detailed examination of at least two issues: (a) the identification of the unspecified subject of the verse, and (b) the meaning of the phrase, ζωὴ ἐκ νεκρῶν. Since we have already discussed the first issue,[223] here we will devote ourselves to the second. The meaning of the ζωὴ ἐκ νεκρῶν can be taken either literally or figuratively. The former interpretation, which has received wide support from the majority of scholars,[224] understands it as a reference to the general resurrection, 'the climax of the eschatological drama of salvation'.[225] The traditional 'Reformed' figurative interpretation, however, still receives much support.[226] Murray forcefully supports the figurative interpretation, seeing it is a reference to 'an unprecedented quickening for the world'.[227] Irrespective of the exegetical

---

220 See *supra* pp. 260-265 on our discussion of 11:11-12.
221 *Pace* Motyer, *Israel*, 140.
222 Dunn, *Romans* 2, 657.
223 *Supra* pp. 253-259.
224 Modern scholars who maintain this view include Black, *Romans*, 144; Davies, *Jewish and Pauline Studies*, 133; Munck, *Christ*, 126-127; Sanday and Headlam, *Romans*, 325f; Motyer, *Israel*, 140; Cranfield, *Romans* 2, 562-563; Dunn, *Romans* 2, 658; Barrett, *Romans*, 199-200, and Lagrange, Lietzmann, Schrenk, Michel, etc..
225 Black, *Romans*, 144. So also Käsemann, *Romans*, 307. For Dunn, *Romans* 2, 658, the idea of the eschatological force is beyond dispute; but see Sanday and Headlam, *Romans*, 325-326, who reject its eschatological timing, although they relate it to resurrection.
226 Most notably Murray, *Romans* 2, 82-84. Morris, *Romans*, 411, Newman and Nida, *Romans*, 218, and Calvin, Godet, Gaugler.
227 Murray, *Romans* 2, 84; so also Fitzmyer, *Romans*, 613; Dahl, *Studies*, 154: Paul 'stresses ... the enrichment of the whole world'.

details here,[228] the fact that the context is about conversion and salvation, and not about the final resurrection,[229] persuades us to prefer the figurative interpretation. Ziesler's own alternative interpretation, which takes the phrase as a reference to 'the restoration of Israel',[230] is not convincing, for Paul is not talking about the blessing of the Jews as the result of their acceptance of the Messiah and his gospel (though that is assumed) but about the spiritual 'vivification that would come *to the whole world* from the conversion of the mass of Israel'.[231] Thus we may note the strong possibility that Paul asserts, in line with his argument in 11:12, that if (it were actually happening) the Jewish rejection of the gospel has brought the reconciliation of the world, then 'life from the dead', that is, 'the greatest blessing imaginable',[232] would accrue to the Gentiles if (the full number of) the Jews accepted Jesus as the Messiah.

Such extraordinary remarks in favour of the Gentiles (11:12, 15) have led Paul to make two other comments, one with the optimistic expectation of a Jewish acceptance in view of the irrevocable election on account of the ancestors (11:16), and a second in the form of a solemn admonition to Gentiles believers not to become conceited (11:17-24). What is written in 11:17-24 appears to undermine the remark of 11:16b, 'if the root is holy, so are the branches'. This seems to indicate that the main point of the (unsubstantiated) statement in 11:16 is to bring balance after making such an affirmative declaration about the Gentiles in 11:15. Paul seems to use the holy 'firstfruits' and 'root' identically,[233] and probably refers to the patriarchs.[234] However, since

---

228 See Murray, *Romans* 2, 82-84, for his argument: see Morris, *Romans*, 411 n. 69, in support of Murray. See also Cranfield's argument (*Romans* 2, 562-563) against Murray; cf. Motyer, *Israel*, 140.

229 So correctly, Fitzmyer, *Romans*, 613.

230 *Pace* Ziesler, *Romans*, 276-277. So also Leenhardt, *Romans*, 285 n. 1, who asserts that whether the phrase is interpreted literally or figuratively, it applies 'the idea of Resurrection to the people of Israel'.

231 Murray, *Romans* 2, 84, with added emphasis. Similarly Dodd, *Romans*, 187.

232 Newman and Nida, *Romans*, 218, and affirmatively quoted by Morris, *Romans*, 410.

233 But Ziesler, *Romans*, 277, notes that although Paul equates the terms the argument is different, for Paul does not say that the first offering frees the rest for secular use.

The Equality of Jew and Gentile in the Plan of God 269

Paul has already rejected nationalism in 9:6-13 (cf. 4:12, 22-24), a clarification is necessary. Ziesler's suggestion, for example, is highly improbable: 'if the Fathers belonged to God, so do their descendants, despite the fact that in the meantime most of them have rejected their place in the divine strategy'.[235] Similarly we should reject Black's assertion, 'Israel, as a whole, is consecrated through the patriarchs.'[236] These conclusions are negated by 11:17a, 20, 21: despite growing from the root *some* branches have been cut off. Paul's argument thus far does not hint that 'the unbelieving majority of the Jews are hallowed by their relation to the patriarchs'.[237] Paul indeed sees the potentiality in the remnant and in the promise to the ancestors, but this does not make him relax, but rather agonise, because he knows that such a potentiality will be fully implemented only on the firm condition that the unbelieving Jews do not persist in unbelief (v. 23). The οἱ κλάδοι provides a literary connection to the next section of admonition.

---

234 There has been much debate, however, in attempting to identify what Paul means by the 'root'. At least three options are suggested: (a) the patriarchs, especially Abraham, (b) the contemporary Jewish Christians as the remnant, (c) Jesus Christ (1 Cor 15:20, 23). Despite the heavy support of the Church Fathers and the lengthy argument in its favour by Barth (*Dogmatics* 2, 285ff) and Hanson, *Studies*, 104-125, especially p. 117, (c) barely fits the context. (b) seems plausible because the ῥίζα is often paralleled with the λεῖμμα (Dunn, *Romans* 2, 657-658. So also in 2 Kgs 19:30; Isa 37:31; Sir 47:22; 1 Esdr 8:75, 84-86), and the Jewish Christian remnant (Barrett, *Romans*, 216; Dodd, *Romans*, 187-188; Leenhardt, *Romans*, 286; Bruce, *Romans*, 217; Dunn, *Romans* 2, 659) is the hope for the rest of Israel ('lump' and 'branches'), and for the greater blessing of the world. However, since the Jewish remnant Christians are clearly described as the branches in the following passage (11:17-24), and in 11:16 the root is not identical with the branches, the root does not seem to denote the Jewish remnant. So the 'first fruits'/the 'root' as indicating (a) seems most plausible, especially in connection with the reference in 11:28 and Jer 11:16-17; *1 En.* 93:5. Those who uphold this view include Calvin, Cranfield, *Romans* 2, 565; Sanday and Headlam, *Romans*, 326; Käsemann, *Romans*, 308; Morris, *Romans*, 411-412; Newman and Nida, *Romans*, 219; Guerra, 'Paul's Purpose', 235; Sänger, 'Rettung', 118: 'Die Wurzel ist vielmehr Gottes Verheißung an die Väter, insbesondere Abraham – oder Gott selbst.' Cf. Ziesler, *Romans*, 277-278, who accepts both (a) and (b) for the interpretation of 'firstfruit', but takes only (a) for 'root'.

235 Ziesler, *Romans*, 278.
236 Black, *Romans*, 144.
237 *Pace* Cranfield, *Romans* 2, 564-565; similarly Dodd, *Romans*, 188-189.

C. An Admonition to Gentile Believers: 11:17-24

The first function of this passage is quite straightforward. Paul warns the Gentile believers in Rome not to be arrogant over 'those branches' (the Jews[238]) on account of their being grafted into the place where those branches had been broken off (11:17, 19f), for they (the Gentiles) are supported by the Jewish 'root' (11:17, 18). Furthermore, those branches can be readily grafted back in again (11:23, 24), whilst Gentile believers could possibly be cut off (11:21, 22). Paul, however, communicates more than this. He repeatedly affirms that some Jews are broken off (11:17, 19, 20, 21) because of their own persistent unbelief (11:20, 23). Thus Paul alludes to the fact that they can be grafted back in only when they believe.

This passage has often been taken as indicating the situation of the Roman church, and thus a key to interpreting the letter, and of Romans 9-11 in particular. H.J. Schoeps represents the majority view that Romans 9-11 is an exhortation to the Gentiles in a situation where a Jewish Christian minority was striving against the threat of complete suppression by Gentile believers.[239] This may be true, but other factors must be also considered before this view can be upheld. Although Paul warns the Gentile believers, it is not absolutely clear whether that warning is given because they have already been arrogant or because Paul anticipates they might become so on the basis of what he has written in this letter, especially in Romans 1-4 and 9-11. We propose that the latter is perhaps the stronger possibility.[240]

In 11:18 Paul writes, 'Do not boast over those branches' (μὴ κατακαυχῶ τῶν κλάδων). Paul frequently uses the present middle imperative with negative μή 'to forbid what one is already

---

[238] Wright, *Climax*, 248, may be right to point out that here Paul's admonition is particularly directed to the Gentile Christians' attitude towards *unbelieving* Jews since he refers to branches broken off. There is no reason, however, to exclude believing Jews, about whom the Gentiles should not be arrogant (cf. Dahl, *Studies*, 151).

[239] Schoeps, *Paul*, 235-236. So also Martin, 'Romans', 903; Wagner, 'Future', 98; Käsemann, *Romans*, 305; Beker, 'Faithfulness', 16; Lincoln, 'Abraham', 168; Sandnes, *Paul*, 148; Schrenk, 'Missionsdokument', 85.

[240] Stendahl, *Final Account*, 34, 37, opts the former: 'Paul considers the Gentiles to be potentially and actually conceited in their attitude toward Israel' (p. 34).

The Equality of Jew and Gentile in the Plan of God 271

doing', but it is equally used in the inchoative sense.²⁴¹ Paul employs five other usages of μή + the present middle imperative in Romans (6:12; 11:20[cf. NRSV]; 12:14, 16; 13:14), and there is no sure evidence that he commands the Roman believers to stop the actions in progress; it is equally possible that he exhorts them not to commence such actions. Neither does the entire context of the letter suggest clearly that Gentile Christians have become arrogant. According to 2:17, 23; 3:27, it is the Jews who boast over the Gentiles; the verb here, καυχάομαι, belongs to the same word-group as κατακαυχάομαι (11:18). The fact that the Gentile believers in Galatia and Antioch were so quickly persuaded by the 'brothers' from Jerusalem, may indicate their respect or dependence upon the Jewish believers, rather than their arrogance towards the Jews occasioned by their majority. Paul's warning seems to have been based not merely on 11:11-12,²⁴² but also on his affirmative description of the Gentiles in Romans 1-11, given that the present passage appears in the concluding part of the entire theological and doctrinal section.

Certainly the Gentiles would discover from what Paul had written affirmatively about themselves (as we have seen above) their position had been much strengthened. They would see that the apostle is 'on their side' by his determined advocacy of their position in Christ. They also see that Paul is almost unremittingly critical of the Jews. If they do not understand Paul's intention for presenting the content and the structure of his argument in such a way, they could misunderstand Paul and become arrogant. Paul himself recognises this danger and hence gives his admonition.²⁴³ Paul's remark, 'You ... have been grafted in among others [i.e. Jewish believers] and now share in the nourishing sap from the olive root' (11:17), indicates that he speaks about Gentiles' inclusion, and not replacement, as an analogy of complete unity and equality.

---

241 Robertson, *Grammar*, 890; Rienecker and Rogers, *Linguistic Key*, 373.

242 *Pace* Sanday and Headlam, *Romans*, 327; although their view is more plausible than others', it is not comprehensive enough.

243 The admonition in 11:17-24 thus provides a basis for a more general exhortation later: 'I say to every one of you: Do not think of yourself more highly than you ought to' (12:3); 'Do not be conceited' (12:16); and 'Do not judge .... or look down on your brother' (14:10).

D. The Mystery of the Interdependence and Equality of Jew and Gentile: 11:25-32

This passage contains undoubtedly the most affirmative description of Israel in the authentic Pauline letters. And so it is commonly understood that although unbelieving Jews were broken off so that Gentiles might be grafted in, the Jews will certainly and readily be grafted back in again. The Gentiles should not boast over the Jews, because the hardening of the latter has brought the benefit of the Gentiles (11:31), and, what is more, their hardening is only temporal, i.e. until the fullness of the Gentiles has come in. Then eventually 'all Israel will be saved', because God's call of Israel is irrevocable. Thus, according to this view, God's salvific blessing will ultimately be granted to 'all' Israel; even Paul's own ministry among the Gentiles as their apostle is fundamentally for the sake of Israel,[244] and Paul firmly maintains the principle of 'to the Jew first'. Some scholars, like Mussner, Gaston and Stendahl, have even taken this passage to indicate that Israel will be saved *without* believing the gospel of Christ. Although their *Sonderweg* hypothesis itself has hardly received much support, a strong consensus has been reached on the point that here Paul is indicating the primacy of Israel in the salvific plan of God.

In this section we will examine how well this (common) view is grounded. First, it is largely based on the assertions 'all Israel will be saved' (11:26a) and '[God's] call of Israel is irrevocable' (11:29). But we must note that these declarations are not expounded systematically (even though one would expect some explanations if the superiority of the Jews were to be asserted especially after such a critical portrayal of the Jews). Second, this interpretation does not take sufficient account of the critical comments (although made in passing) about the Jews in this passage itself. Third, and most importantly, it does not pay adequate attention to Paul's affirmation of the Gentiles. Thus we shall argue that in this section as well Paul affirms that Jew and Gentile are not only fundamentally equal, but also inseparably interdependent in the salvific plan of God. Paul hints that the precedence of the mission has been reversed from 'for the Jew

---

[244] Scott, 'Restoration', 799-805; Campbell, 'Israel', 445.

The Equality of Jew and Gentile in the Plan of God 273

first' to 'for the Gentile first': especially after the full number of the Gentiles has come in will 'all' Israel be saved (11:25-26).

Paul's aim here is not to raise Israel above the Gentiles and to deny the principle of 'the equality of Jew and Gentile', which he has vigorously argued all along. Rather, in this concluding part of his exposition, he affirms the fundamental equality of both ethnic groups. Just as the affirmative presentation of the Gentile position in Christ in the previous chapters necessitates a warning to the Gentile believers, the darker picture of the Jews there now understandably requires some brighter colours here. Paul bursts into joy and admiration for God's merciful plan and outworking based on God's equal dealing with Jew and Gentile for their salvation in Christ (11:33-36).

(a) The Possible Gentile Arrogance and the Mystery

It is now well acknowledged that the Jews believed that 'all' Israel would be saved (Jer 31:34; Isa 45:17: 'Israel will be saved by the Lord with an everlasting salvation'; *Sanh.* 10:1: 'All Israelites have a share in the world to come'). According to their understanding the expression πᾶς 'Ισραήλ referred to the nation as a whole, without necessarily including every individual Israelite.[245] Even the 'all Israel' in *Sanh.* 10:1 clearly excludes some Israelites from this 'all'.[246] So, it is contended, Paul's announcement of their ultimate salvation does not itself really constitute a 'mystery'.[247] Thus scholars tend to argue that the mystery is about the *manner* of Israel's salvation rather than about their ultimate and individual salvation in itself.[248] So Siegert asserts that the 'mystery' is that Israel 'should be saved *in this way*; i.e. as a

---

245 Barrett, Käsemann, Cranfield, Dunn; Dahl, *Studies*, 153; Hahn, *Mission*, 106-107 n. 1. See Cranfield, *Romans* 2, 576-577, where he sums up four different interpretations of 'all Israel'. That the phrase indicates all the elect of ethnic Israel and Gentiles, i.e. the messianic people of God, has been recently defended by Wright, *Climax*, 249-251; cf. Motyer, *Israel*, 156-157.

246 See the list of those who are excluded from 'all Israel', which extends for two pages in Danby's *Mishnah*, 397-399. See Osborne, 'Romans 11:26a', 290, who also contends that Paul's πᾶς 'Ισραήλ has its background in the use of the term in 1 and 2 Chronicles, where it occurs no less than 34 times. There the term connotes the (large) majority of Israel.

247 Siegert, *Argumentation*, 173.

248 Dahl, *Studies*, 152-154; Sanders, *Jewish People*, 205 n. 85; Wright, *Climax*, 249; Siegert, *Argumentation*, 173; Wagner, 'Future', 95-96.

temporary instrument for the purpose of the inclusion of the full number of the Gentiles. Thus Paul tries to base it on something new'.[249]

Wright also takes the οὕτως as 'thus' or 'in this manner'. But he asserts that the πᾶς Ἰσραήλ does not refer to *national* Israel nor even to *Jewish* believers, but to *all* messianic believers. What the Gentiles 'enter' in 11:25 is 'Israel'. Jews who have been hardened until the fullness of the Gentiles are accomplished, will not *then* be added to this messianic Israel (according to Wright); the hardening is *until* judgement comes on them. He strongly argues that Paul does not hint at 'a large-scale, last minute salvation of the Jews'; the way of salvation for Jews is through 'the process of "jealousy", and consequent faith'.[250]

However, we do not find Wright's contention entirely convincing. Firstly, since Paul's main aim for disclosing the 'mystery' is to restrain Gentiles from being arrogant in the light of the present hardening of Jews, it seems probable that he would indicate a brighter future for *national* Israel. The πᾶς Ἰσραήλ is contrasted to the Ἰσραήλ .... ἀπὸ μέρους of 11:25, so one can anticipate a greater scale of salvation. Also, according to 11:26b, the Redeemer's task is to banish impiety from *Jacob*. Secondly, the ἄχρις of 11:25 certainly implies the sequence of time, and the οὕτως of 11:26 does not totally rule out such a meaning. Thirdly, it is not convincing that we should take the 'Israel' of 11:26a as the 'spiritual' Israel, when 'Israel' (11:25), 'Jacob' (11:27) and 'they' (11:28-32) clearly refer to *national* Israel, as Wright admits. Finally, the salvation of Jews is not only through 'jealousy' but also as a result of God's mercy to the Gentiles (11:31). Wright is certainly correct to oppose the *Sonderweg* interpretation and also the unreasonable contention by, e.g. Mussner, Gaston and Stendahl of the primacy of national Israel, but Wright seems to have gone too far in undermining the 'mystery' concerning the salvific future of ethnic Israel.

The salvation of πᾶς Ἰσραήλ, after the full number[251] of the Gentiles has come in, is supported by the quotations from Isa

---

249 Siegert, *Argumentation*, 173: my translation.

250 Wright, *Climax*, 246-251: the quotations are from p. 251 and p. 250, respectively. Cf. Bell, *Provoked to Jealousy* (1994).

251 It is not easy to interpret the πλήρωμα of 11:25. Some have taken it in a qualitative sense in the light of πλήρωμα of the Jews in 11:12 (Munck,

59:20-21; 27:9. The quotations, however, do not seem to stress the πᾶς but the prediction of the salvation of Israel in general. However, a greater scale of national Israel's conversion to Christ is predicted. The deliverer will come to turn away Israel's ungodliness and to take away their sins. The active verbs in the citation seem to stress the divine initiative in Israel's salvation. Some caution is necessary, however, on at least two points. First, one must not assert, with Sanders, that God has *intentionally* hardened Israel, so that Israel will be saved in an unexpected way which God has planned, after the full number of the Gentiles has come in.[252] As we have already seen above, Paul never rationalises Israel's hardening, nor does he say that God *intentionally* hardened Israel.[253] Second, Paul's description of a temporal sequence in the salvation of Gentiles and Israel does not necessarily indicate that 'Israel's salvation will not happen earlier. But then [i.e. at the Parousia] it will happen'.[254] Paul speaks of the salvation of πᾶς 'Ισραήλ as a future event,[255] but this does not preclude that (some) Jews are already experiencing salvation. The νῦν (11:30, 31) indicates that their salvation is not just a future eschatological

---

Christ, 134: 'the full dissemination of the gospel to the Gentiles'; Osborne, 'Romans 11:26a', 289: until the Gentiles would be fully blessed), but there is no firm evidence for this interpretation. Dunn, *Romans* 2, 654-655, suggests that Paul uses πλήρωμα to match other -μα words in v. 12. It probably carries a quantitative connotation: 'when far more or the full number of Jews believe in Christ...'. The πλήρωμα in 11:25 seems to suggest a quantitative interpretation (Cranfield, *Romans* 2, 576; Fitzmyer, *Romans*, 622; Murray, *Romans* 2, 93; cf. Dunn, *Romans* 2, 680), especially in connection with the 'ἀπὸ μέρους', which indicates that some portion of the Jews are hardened rather than that Jews are hardened to a certain degree; cf. *supra* pp. 24-25.

252 *Pace* Sanders, *Jewish People*, 193-194. His further assertion that Israel will be saved through the result of the Gentile mission, not of the Jewish mission led by Peter, seems unbalanced.

253 One may argue that God *intentionally* hardened Pharaoh (cf. 9:17-18) *for the sake of* Israel, and this analogy can be applied to Israel's hardening: if God intentionally hardened Israel it is *for the sake of* the Gentiles. Thus even if one maintains that God hardened Israel, the point of argument is not that Israel can be excused, but that God had a special plan for the Gentiles.

254 *Pace* Wagner, 'Future', 96.

255 Becker, *Paul*, 471, asserts that the prophetic future verbs in 11:26b-27 are to be understood as referring to the present time. This is correct in the cases of 9:25-28, 33; 10:6, 13, 19. But not so with 11:26-27, because the quotation is made to support the still future verb σωθήσεται of 11:26a.

last-minute event, but can happen 'now'. If this were not so, Paul's desire to provoke Israel to jealousy and to save some of them through his own present ministry (11:14; 1 Cor 9:16, 19-23) would barely make sense.[256] The difference is that the future event he anticipates is to be on a much greater scale; a great number of Jews will turn to Christ in faith.

These positive assertions concerning the future of Israel, however, do not indicate his (inconsistent) intent to elevate Israel to a position of salvific or historical superiority. He continues to make critical comments about Israel: Israel's hardening and disobedience are once again recalled (11:25, 30-31), and their hardening, stumbling, transgression, loss, rejection and unbelief are for the first time viewed as Israel's fundamental sin (11:27).[257] Furthermore, Paul says that the (unbelieving) Jews are God's[258] 'enemies' as far as the gospel is concerned (11:28). This designation explains why Paul has portrayed such a dark picture of Israel throughout Romans 1-4; 9-11. Although he declares that the Jews are beloved on account of the patriarchs, it is important to note that he does not expound the blessedness of God's election of Israel in this letter. Rather, 'Paul makes it abundantly clear that there is no covenant membership, and consequently no salvation, for those who simply rest on their ancestral privilege.'[259]

(b) Paul's Restraint from Advocating the Jewish Primacy

On the other hand, Paul still portrays the affirmative remarks about the Gentiles even in this 'pro-Israel' passage, and we may detect at least three areas which indicate that Paul's intention here is not to advocate the primacy of the Jews in the salvific plan of God. First, Paul indicates that God will save 'all' Israel after the full number of the Gentiles has come in. He began to expound the gospel by saying that 'it is the power of God for the salvation of everyone who believes, Ἰουδαίῳ τε πρῶτον καὶ Ἕλληνι' (1:16). But in the concluding section he makes it clear that the priority of the mission is reversed to make the Gentile first, and when the full number of the Gentiles are saved, a more substantial

---

[256] So similarly Dahl, *Studies*, 153.
[257] Stanley, *Language*, 169.
[258] So Black, *Romans*, 148; NEB, TEV, RSV, JB. The term ἐχθροί is a strong designation for unbelievers (cf. 5:10; Col 1:21-22).
[259] Wright, *Climax*, 246.

salvation of 'all' Israel will follow, as we suggested earlier. This may indicate that Paul has been arguing all along to establish the claim that Gentiles are now the primary beneficiary in the salvific plan of God. This could be an apology for why his apostolic ministry is so much devoted to the Gentiles; it hastens Israel's ultimate salvation.260 It could also be advice for the missionary strategy which the Roman community was to follow as Paul anticipates their involvement and support for the mission to Spain;261 the present is the time to concentrate on the Gentile mission (cf. Matt 24:14//Mark 13:10).

In this connection it is significant to see Paul reversing the order of the Jewish understanding of the 'fullness of time'. That God works according to his timetable was a common Jewish belief. The harvest of Israel's reward is also not until 'the number of those like yourselves [i.e. the righteous] is completed; for he has weighed the age in the balance' (2 Esdr [=*4 Ezra*] 4:35-36: RSV). According to Jewish thinking, the fullness of time is set for the final salvation of Israel, and the relation of this timetable with the salvation of the Gentiles is not clearly expressed. In an earlier generation, Tobit also knew that God had predetermined the time, and so he prophesies to his son, on his deathbed, that Israel will completely rebuild Jerusalem and the Temple after returning from all over the world, according to the time pre-set by God. Only when 'the times of the fulfilment shall come', 'then the nations in the whole world (πάντα τὰ ἔθνη) will all be converted and worship God in truth'. Then both Israel and the Gentiles will praise God (Tob 14:5-7: NRSV). For Tobit, Israel will experience God's salvation first, and then the Gentiles. Paul also affirms that the gospel is for the Jew first, but as far as the conversion of the 'fullness' of them is concerned, Paul indicates that the order is reversed: when the time for the full number of the Gentiles is completed, then 'all' Israel will enter God's full blessing. 'They [the Gentiles] are now the ones who are favoured.'262 The reversal of the primary beneficiary of the salvific blessing was a real problem for a Jew, and such an assertion was a bold one for Paul the Jew to make. Kümmel is right to say that Paul solves this problem by thinking through his own theological position as the

---

260 Fitzmyer, *Romans*, 622.
261 Guerra, 'Paul's Purpose', 237.
262 Brunner, *Romans*, 96.

missionary apostle to the Gentiles.²⁶³ We contend that his apostolic self-awareness has influenced his theological formulation, and his missionary experience certainly has confirmed his conviction.²⁶⁴

Second, Paul seems to restrain himself from asserting the national primacy of Israel by making the deliberate substitution of ἐκ Σιών for the ἕνεκεν Σιών of the original LXX Isa 59:20.²⁶⁵ This change probably indicates that he undermines the notion that the Deliverer comes on the sole and special behalf of the Jews. The LXX text has already modified the original Hebrew text with a more nationalistic connotation: not merely the Redeemer will 'come *to* Zion (לְצִיּוֹן)', but will 'come *for the sake of* Zion (ἕνεκεν Σιών). But for Paul he is coming *from* Zion (ἐκ Σιών). The ἐκ Σιών indicates more than the origin of the Deliverer, or the place of Christ's resurrection,²⁶⁶ or that the Messiah comes *out of* Zion (i.e. David's city) and brings salvation *to* Israel.²⁶⁷ Paul seems to indicate also that the Redeemer comes *from* Zion (thus Israel will benefit first, of course) and goes *out for others outside* Israel. Paul regards Zion as a centrifugal point rather than as a centripetal centre, because the Redeemer who is from Zion is already working among the Gentiles. Sanders then is incorrect to say that this quotation 'has nothing to do with the Gentile mis-

---

263 Kümmel, 'Probleme', 41.

264 Getty, 'Paul', 457, is correct to say that 'Paul identified himself as the Apostle to the Gentiles and it was primarily the Gentile mission that shaped Paul's message'. 'Paul is motivated in his argumentation by his missionary experience as Apostle to the Gentiles' (p. 462). So also Munck, *Paul*, 67: 'All Paul's work as a thinker arises from his missionary activity, and its object is missionary work. ... His theology arises from his work as apostle and directly serves that work.' Dahl, *Studies*, 86: 'The inner unity of Paul's mission and theology is nowhere more obvious than in Rom. 9-11.'

265 Cf. Hvalvik, '"Sonderweg"', 93-95, who is of the opinion that the alteration would be pre-Pauline (following Koch), and thus the change does not reflect Paul's intention; but Dunn, *Romans* 2, 682, asserts that Paul deliberately modified the preposition. This change, however, seems deliberate and significant when we note that Paul adopts ἕνεκεν in 8:36 in the citation of LXX Ps 43:23, where the ἕνεκα is original. Hvalvik, '"Sonderweg"', 94, also finds Schaller's suggestion (ἐκ is a corruption of εἰς [?]) attractive, but there is no textual evidence to support this hypothesis: cf. Dunn, *Romans* 2, 682.

266 Fitzmyer, *Romans*, 625.

267 Black, *Romans*, 148.

sion'.[268] Although Paul predicts a greater salvific event for the Jews, he does not want to suggest that Jews have a salvific primacy. The fact that he does not continue to quote Isa 59:21b, where God assures that his words spoken to Israel will never fail throughout the generations, seems to support further our view that this is probably why he changes the preposition.[269]

Third, the apostle to the Gentiles also demonstrates that Jew and Gentile are equal *and* interdependent. Just as Gentiles were at one time disobedient to God (11:30a), Israel has now become disobedient (11:31a); they were equally bound to disobedience (11:32a). On the other hand, just as Gentiles have now received mercy (11:30b), Jews will also be shown mercy (11:31b). The salvation of Jews and of Gentiles is paradoxically interdependent: Gentiles have received mercy as a result of Israel's disobedience, and Israel will receive mercy as a result of God's mercy to the Gentiles (cf. 11:12, 15). Here Paul affirms that God's mercy has already been shown to the Gentiles, but the salvation of 'all' Jews remains a future event (though Jewish salvation in the present time is not excluded). Now Israel's salvation is interdependent with God's mercy to the Gentiles (note the emphatic-position of τῷ ὑμετέρῳ ἐλέει): one may even say that Israel has become a debtor to the Gentiles. They equally benefit each other. Furthermore, just as πᾶς 'Ισραήλ, i.e. Israel's fullness (τὸ πλήρωμα αὐτῶν; 11:12) will be saved, τὸ πλήρωμα τῶν ἐθνῶν will be saved as well (11:25-26). So Paul confirms in 11:32 what he has written earlier: both Jew and Gentile are equal in sinfulness (1:18-3:20), which he now rephrases as: 'all men are disobedient'; and both Jew and Gentile are equal in justification (3:21-4:25), because God shows mercy to all.[270] The new factor that he adds in Romans 9-11 is that *they are made equal in the plan of God*: 'For God has shut up (συνέκλεισεν) all in disobedience that he might show mercy to all' (11:32: NASB). Earlier he wrote: 'The Scripture has shut up (συνέκλεισεν) all men under sin, that the promise *by faith in Jesus Christ* might be given to those who believe' (Gal 3:22: NASB).

---

268 Sanders, *Jewish People*, 194.
269 Cf. De Waard, *Comparative Study*, 11-13, who asserts that there is no significant 'evidence of a "hermeneutical purpose"'.
270 So Brunner, *Romans*, 98; Sanders, *Jewish People*, 195.

(c) Salvation by Faith in Christ, not by a Sonderweg

It is clear then that Paul does not suggest a *Sonderweg* for the salvation of the Jews. Paul does not perceive the Jesus movement as only a Gentile movement, as Stendahl asserts, nor does he hint that God has prepared a *Sonderweg* for the salvation of all Israel that they should be saved apart from faith in Christ.[271] The fact that the term 'Christ' does not occur in 10:18-11:36 does not necessarily indicate that God himself will save Israel as her Deliverer apart from Christ,[272] because Paul has already declared, 'This righteousness from God comes through faith in Jesus Christ to all who believe. There is no difference [between Jew and Gentile]' (3:22). Mussner contends that God saves all Israel through Christ, but implausibly maintains, 'The *parousia* Christ saves all Israel without a preceding "conversion" of the Jews to the gospel. God saves Israel by a "special path".'[273] Even though Mussner and Stendahl differ slightly from each other, both of them agree that there is a *Sonderweg* for ethnic Israel: Israel will be saved at the Parousia without believing in the gospel message.

Their hypotheses have been criticised by many,[274] and so we do not need to offer similar criticism here. But we reaffirm that promoting a *Sonderweg* for Israel largely reflects post-Holocaust

---

[271] *Pace* Stendahl, *Paul*, 4, 132; Gaston, *Paul*, 92-99, 139-150; Lapide, *Paul*, 51; Gager, *Origins*, 251-252, 261-64. In *Final Account*, x, 7, Stendahl denies that he has held 'two ways of salvation'. Yet he maintains that Israel will be saved not by accepting Jesus but by God's special mercy (pp. 38-40); and so he does not encourage Christian witness to the Jews (pp. 33-34, 40).

[272] Cf. Stendahl, *Paul*, 4. Fitzmyer, *Romans*, 624, is correct to point out that the Deliverer in 11:26 denotes Christ as 1 Thess 1:10 indicates.

[273] Mussner, *Tractate*, 34; idem, 'Ganz Israel', 250-253. Mussner has consistently maintained that all Israel will be saved by a '*Sonderweg*' in a later work ('Heil', 210): 'Meine These lautet: "Ganz Israel" wird auf einem "Sonderweg" gerettet werden und zwar im Zusammenhang der Parusie, unter Berufung auf Röm 11,26b. ... Das bedeutet: Die Rettung ganz Israels erfolgt durch den Parusiechristus selbst, da man den "Retter aus Sion" am besten mit diesem identifiziert.' Then, for Mussner, Israel will be saved by *sola gratia*, but not by *sola fide* in Christ; see Sänger, 'Rettung', 103-105.

[274] Most obviously by Wright, *Climax*, 246-251, and Grässer, *Alte Bund*, 212-230. Also by Sanders, *Jewish People*, 194; idem, 'Attitude', 175-187; Hafemann, 'Salvation', 38-58; Hvalvik, '"Sonderweg"', 87-107; Hahn, *Mission*, 106-107 n. 1; Dahl, *Studies*, 153; Fitzmyer, *Romans*, 620; Becker, *Paul*, 470-472; Dunn, *Romans* 2, 683; Sänger, 'Rettung', 99-119.

The Equality of Jew and Gentile in the Plan of God 281

sensitivity, and that within the argument of Romans this is simply implausible,[275] because Paul strives to establish a fundamental equality between Jew and Gentile throughout Romans 1-11. Hahn has put this clearly:

> It would be un-Pauline to expect this Israel to be saved at the end of the ages through its mere presence and its physical descent from Abraham. It is rejected simply because it has not believed. Thus the offer of salvation will be again made to Israel, which will again be faced with a decision about belief, and as a believing Israel will attain salvation.[276]

Paul has maintained all along that salvation is granted equally to Jews and Gentiles as they have faith in Jesus Christ (1:16; 3:22; 4:11-16; 5:1; 10:9-13). The unbelieving Jews are broken off because of their unbelief, and thus they will be readily grafted in again on only one condition: 'if they do not persist in unbelief' (11:23). Paul has already made it clear that 'God ... will justify the circumcised by faith [in Christ]' (3:30). 'All' Israel will be saved by a special mercy, yet it is in the same manner in which the remnant was saved. This means 'mercy has faith [in Christ] as its condition'.[277] Paul seems to use πᾶς Ἰσραήλ in the sense of πᾶς in 1:16; 9:33; 10:11, 13. Thus what Paul means in 11:26a is most probably 'all *believing* Israel will be saved' (πᾶς Ἰσραὴλ [ὁ πιστεύων ἐπ᾽ αὐτῷ] σωθήσεται).[278] One may reject this because it is so obvious, and is thus not a 'mystery'.[279] But there is no need to stress the 'mystery' if it really is about the well-known assumption of the salvation of 'all' Israel.[280] It is already revealed in the OT from which Paul quotes, and when he quotes the OT passages elsewhere he does not say that he is revealing a mystery. The phrase καὶ οὕτως denotes the way in which the Gentiles

---

275 So Hvalvik, '"Sonderweg"', 89. For Kümmel, the *Sonderweg* interpretation is 'a highly dangerous misinterpretation of the text' (my translation), as affirmatively cited in Grässer, *Alte Bund*, 229. But Rese, 'Rettung', 430, implausibly sees a possibility of *Sonderweg* for the unbelieving Jews.

276 Hahn, *Mission*, 107.

277 So correctly Sanders, *Jewish People*, 196; Käsemann, *Romans*, 302.

278 This position is the same as that 'all *elect* Israel will be saved', but we prefer 'all *believing* Israel' in the light of Paul's consistent stress on believing/faith. Our emphasis on 'believing' is the conditional factor (*if* any Israelite *believe*, he/she will be saved).

279 Cranfield, *Romans* 2, 576-577; Godet, *Romans*, 411.

280 Cf. Sänger, 'Rettung', 112-115.

have come in, i.e. 'in the manner of faith'. If we take Paul himself as an example, '"Israel will come to faith in the same way as Paul himself!" i.e. through a personal encounter with the exalted Christ'.[281]

E. Summary

In Romans 11 Paul continues to discuss the issue of the equality of Jew and Gentile in the plan of God, and in so doing he indicates Israel's unbelief and the Gentiles' belief. Despite his affirmation that God did not reject Israel, Paul does not issue an assured 'blank cheque' that Israel, as a whole, will be safe and saved simply by conveying the covenant assurance that God does not reject all of his people.[282] Neither does he say that Israel's unbelief is due to God's initiative in hardening them. The unbelieving Jews *are* hardened, not because of God's predestining initiative or saving purpose for all humanity but as the result of their own refusal of the grace manifested in Christ. Knowing that 'at all times God's faithfulness to his covenant promises has been expressed as much through the covenant curses as the covenant

---

281 Dunn, *Romans* 2, 683; the inner citation is affirmatively quoted from Hofius, 'Evangelium', 319-320. So correctly Sanders, *Jewish People*, 196: 'The simplest reading of 11:13-36 seems to be this: the only way to enter the body of those who will be saved is by faith in Christ.'

282 It is to be noted that God's assurance of not rejecting his people is usually preconditioned. Lev 26:40-42 says that '*if* they [Israel] will confess their sins and ... , *then* ... I will remember my covenant with Jacob, ... Isaac, ... Abraham'. But when they reject God's law, 'they will pay for their sins' (Lev 26:43). Although God says, 'I will not reject them ... so as to destroy them *completely*' (Lev 26:44), a punishment in such a case for the majority, or at least for some of the Israelites, is clearly indicated. Furthermore, the wider context of 1 Sam 12:22 ('For the sake of his great name the Lord will not destroy his people') also unambiguously shows that Israel may experience God's anger (1 Sam 12:16-18). Samuel solemnly warns, 'Yet *if* you persist in doing evil, both you and your king will be swept away' (1 Sam 12:25). Both Paul and his readers, who knew the basics of the covenant, would have hardly missed such contexts. For Paul, the majority of Israel has persisted in doing evil by rejecting God's Messiah, and so deserves to 'be swept away'. Paul cannot help but weep for his people (Motyer, *Israel*, 134), though he finds a comfort from the mysterious covenant relationship between Israel's stumble, which is not beyond recovery, and the Gentiles' blessing (11:11-26).

The Equality of Jew and Gentile in the Plan of God 283

blessings',[283] Paul argues that there is only a remnant chosen by grace. The general picture in 11:1-10 is not optimistic for Israel, but rather intense and pessimistic, because for Paul Israel's 'stumbling' has been so total and catastrophic (though it is not beyond recovery).

In 11:11-16 Paul affirms that the Jews have not stumbled so as to fall completely, and also hints that Jewish 'fullness' and 'acceptance' (τὸ πλήρωμα αὐτῶν and ἡ πρόσλημψις [αὐτῶν]) are expected. However, he continually confirms the stumbling, transgression, unbelief and rejection of Jews as a *fait accompli*. Paul does not say that a Jewish fall was a necessary step for God to direct the salvific blessing to the Gentiles. Rather, after the occasion of the Jewish rejection,[284] God determined the salvific blessing to come upon the Gentiles as the primary beneficiary. This does not mean that God changed his salvific plan in this way only after Israel's fall; the Gentiles were chosen and called, according to Paul, as early as when the Jews were first elected, but the Gentiles' election remained hidden for generations (cf. 16:25-26; Col 1:25-27). Paul expects a far greater blessing upon the Gentiles when Israel experiences the fullness of the blessing of the gospel. Paul's apostolic ministry is undoubtedly related to Israel, but that does not mean that his apostolic commission is ultimately given for the sake of Israel, as is often assumed.[285] Rather he glorifies his ministry for the Gentiles, and it may be partly for their benefit that he craves the salvation of the Jews.

In 11:17-24 Paul warns the Gentile believers not to become arrogant towards the Jews (after discovering their theologically strengthened new position in God through Christ), because they are indebted to the Jews, and also because the 'broken-off branches' can be readily grafted back into their own olive tree. Paul repeatedly confirms, however, that the unbelieving Jews have been cut off from the olive tree, Israel (11:17, 19, 20, 21, 22), and thus explains why not all who are descended from Israel are Israel (cf. 9:6b). It is striking to see Paul so openly drawing the darkest picture of unbelieving Israel's spiritual condition. On

---

283 Motyer, *Israel*, 133.
284 So correctly Betz, 'Israels Mission', 56.
285 *Pace* Scott, 'Restoration', 799: For Scott, the gospel which Paul was commissioned to preach was 'the good news of Israel's restoration'. Cf. Campbell, 'Israel', 445; Kim, *Origin*, 97.

the contrary, he affirms that believing Gentiles have been certainly grafted in 'among others and now [equally] share in the nourishing sap from the olive root' (11:17b). Paul stresses the importance of 'faith': some Jews were cut off because of their unbelief, but they will be grafted in again if they do not persist in unbelief; some Gentiles have been grafted in by faith (11:20).

Paul continues his admonition to Gentile believers in 11:25-32 by disclosing the 'mystery', which is often understood as the salvation of 'all' Israel. However, the aim of this passage is not to establish the primacy of the Jews over the Gentiles. Rather, Paul declares that Israel will experience hardening until the full number of the Gentiles comes in to God's salvific blessing. Here he hints that the main concentration of mission has been reversed to: 'to the Gentile first'. Despite the indication of a substantial future conversion among the Jews, Paul still makes critical remarks about Jewish unbelief. He does not say that every individual Jew will be saved on account of God's faithfulness to the promise to the patriarchs; rather, he declares that all Israel [who do not persist in unbelief] will be saved, and this understanding is in line with what he has said in Romans 1-11. Paul does not suggest a salvific *Sonderweg* for Israel.[286]

Paul modifies his prepositional phrase from ἕνεκεν Σιών to ἐκ Σιών, which seems to indicate that Paul's concern is not to advocate the primacy of Israel. We have suggested, rather, that Paul indicates that the Redeemer comes *from* Zion (thus the Israelites will benefit, of course) and goes *out for those outside* Israel. Paul also portrays that Jew and Gentile are interdependent in the outworking of God's salvific plan: just as the blessing of salvation has first come to the Gentiles as the result of Jewish disobedience, so now Israel will experience that blessing as the result of God's mercy shown to the Gentiles. Jew and Gentile are fundamentally equal in sinfulness and disobedience, and also in justification and in receiving God's mercy. Even in this 'pro-Israel' passage the apostle to the Gentiles offers a theological explanation for the equality and the interdependence of Jew and Gentile in the salvific plan of God.

---

286 So correctly, Sänger, 'Rettung', 116: neither Jew nor Gentile has a higher position as far as salvation is concerned.

5. Conclusion

In this final chapter of our study we have attempted to establish that in Romans 9-11 Paul affirms the equality of Jew and Gentile in the salvific plan of God. Our understanding of Romans 9-11 is, we claim, coherent with the earlier parts of the letter: he has been arguing for the fundamental equality of Jew and Gentile in sinfulness (1:18-3:20), in justification (3:21-4:25), in the new status (Rom 5-8), and now in the plan of God (Rom 9-11). What is written in Romans 1-4 is sufficient to affirm their equality, and so in Romans 5-8 Paul no longer distinguishes (believing) Jews and Gentiles as two groups; they are one, as signalled by the common pronoun 'we' (see Chapter 4). In the course of expounding Romans 5-8, Paul seems to see the need to prepare for his conclusions that Gentiles also receive God's sonship and glory (8:9-17) and that they were predestined and called (8:28-30, 33). Romans 9-11 coheres well with the previous chapters, and we have shown the weakness of those views which fail to perceive this and so offer unconvincing interpretations of Romans 9-11.

In Romans 9-11 Paul largely answers the questions raised by believing Jews, such as: Why have a great majority of Jews, God's chosen people, not believed in Jesus, Israel's Messiah? How is one to explain that so many Gentiles, thought to be outside God's election, were turning to Christ?[287] Paul provides his answer largely from the OT Scriptures. Post-Holocaust scholarship has tended to interpret Romans 9-11 as Paul's great affirmation of God's faithfulness to ethnic Israel. But we have demonstrated that Paul seeks to establish the fundamental equality of Gentiles with Jews in the light of the Christ event. In so doing Paul is unremittingly critical of the unbelieving Jews, not only in Romans 9-10 but also in Romans 11, while by contrast he is largely affirmative of the Gentiles (as in Romans 1-4; see Chapters 2 and 3). Paul's aim is not to elevate one ethnic group above the other, but the apostle to the Gentiles certainly seems to be biassed towards the Gentiles in his rhetoric. His critical portrayal of Jews attempts to undermine their complacency, and his affirmative picture of Gentiles is to establish their new status and legitimacy in Christ. He thus intends to bring balance and equality so that both groups will humble themselves and respect one another in love (Rom 12-16).

---

287 Similarly Baur, *Paul* 1, 315.

In 9:1-29 Paul carefully argues that Gentiles too were predestined, elected and called to be God's beloved people. This should not be a surprise because God has total freedom to show mercy on whomever he wants. The unbelief of many Jews is also 'understandable', 'for not all who are descended from Israel are Israel' (9:6b), and also because God has a sovereign right to harden whomever he wants. The apostle declares that it is the Gentiles who have obtained righteousness, but, despite their sincere pursuit of righteousness and the nearness of the word of faith, Israel has failed to attain righteousness and salvation because they sought to establish their own way (9:30-10:3). Paul insists that God's plan has always been to save humanity through the means of faith, and affirms that believing Gentiles have adopted the right way. Therefore, implies Paul, their salvation is totally legitimate; it is granted according to the original salvific means (i.e. faith) in God's plan.

We have also tried to demonstrate that Paul's use of the OT in these chapters also indicates that the apostle is 'on the Gentiles' side'. When he quotes the OT texts concerning the Jews, he selects some of the most sharply critical (9:27-29; 10:19, 21; 11:8-10), while, by contrast, he uses some of the most affirmative OT passages concerning the Jews, but now applied to Gentiles (9:25-26; 10:11, 13, 20). Then with the thematic statement, 'It is not as though the word of God has failed' (9:6a), Paul maintains that just as Israel's unbelief was anticipated by God's word (i.e. the OT), so also was the salvific blessing which the Gentiles now enjoy. He uses the OT to accuse unbelieving Israel and to affirm the salvific legitimacy of the Gentiles. Paul creatively modifies the texts and/or contexts of the quotations to achieve the latter purpose, and this endeavour demonstrates his deliberate attempt to secure for the believing Gentiles their status as the true people of God.

We have also argued that Romans 11 is not only coherent with Romans 9-10, but also with Romans 1-8. Despite some affirmative remarks about the Jews, Paul does not argue to establish them further. Rather, he continues to make sharply critical statements about Jews, and so confirms that they are hardened and cut off (11:7, 17, 19, 20, 21, 25); that they have rejected God's Messiah (11:15); that they have persisted in unbelief (11:20, 23, 30), and have experienced transgression, loss and God's sternness (11:12, 22) to the point of becoming God's enemies (11:28). The brightest remark concerning Israel in the entire authentic Pauline

The Equality of Jew and Gentile in the Plan of God 287

epistles, is, allegedly, a short statement, 'καὶ οὕτως πᾶς 'Ισραὴλ σωθήσεται' (11:26a). But even here Paul confirms that because of Israel's rejection of the Messiah the mission thrust has been reversed. If the salvific blessing was 'to the Jew first and also to the Gentile' (1:16), it has effectively become 'to the Gentile first and also to the Jew'. As far as the salvation of πᾶς 'Ισραὴλ and τὸ πλήρωμα τῶν ἐθνῶν is concerned, the Gentiles are the primary beneficiaries. Paul's argument in 9:1-11:24 provides the theological background of this reversal. Moreover it implies that the timing of the salvation of 'all' Israel is closely related to the salvation of the full number of the Gentiles. With this implication Paul legitimises the mission to the Gentiles and exhorts his readers to participate in it.

It is our contention that 11:17-24 is a warning lest Gentiles should *become* arrogant (on the basis of what he has written in this letter). There is no evidence that he is aware that Gentiles at Rome have already become so with respect to the Jewish 'minority'. Indeed, the fact that Paul constantly makes critical statements about the Jews and affirmative ones about Gentiles seems to suggest that it was the *Jews* who were (spiritually) arrogant towards the Gentiles, and not *vice versa*. Here Paul maintains that since unbelieving Jews were cut off from the olive tree because of their unbelief, they will be readily grafted in again whenever they do not persist in unbelief (11:20, 23-24). Thus there cannot be any *Sonderweg* for Israel; Israel will be saved by faith in Christ in the same manner (καὶ οὕτως) in which both τὸ πλήρωμα τῶν ἐθνῶν and the Jewish remnant were saved (i.e. by faith in Jesus Christ).

We have sought to highlight Paul's affirmation of Gentiles in Romans 9-11 because this has not received adequate attention among Pauline scholars. Whether Paul writes affirmatively or critically he does not intend to exalt one ethnic group above the other,[288] but the apostle to the Gentiles seems to evince a certain 'bias' towards the Gentiles in his rhetoric. For Paul, advocating

---

288 Although the prophecies quoted in 9:25-26; 10:20 are certainly about the Gentiles in the light of the contrasted citation specifically about Israel (see *supra* pp. 234-238, 244-248), Paul does not specifically indicate their being applied to the Gentiles. So he omits 'Gentiles' in 11:12, 15, where the clear chiastic structure certainly suggests a greater blessing for the Gentiles. This may indicate that as long as the context is clear enough Paul attempts to avoid objections from his Jewish readers, or possibly that he does not want to elevate Gentiles too much lest they become arrogant.

the equality of Jew and Gentile is vital not only for Christian unity but also for defending the church against any (future) judaising attack which may seek to undermine the law-free gospel.

Romans 9-11 is the climax of Paul's argument concerning the equality of Jew and Gentile, and it is our contention that his self-consciousness of being the apostle to the Gentiles has shaped the argument. He affirms that God's word has not failed, because God has been faithful to both Israel and to the Gentiles according to his word. With this section of Romans 9-11 Paul ends his theological *Lehrteil*, and so we close this present study. But on the firm basis of what he has written in Romans 1-11, Paul is now ready to move on to make the practical exhortations for unity and love (Rom 12-16).[289] He is conscious of his apostleship to the Gentiles as he begins to give his exhortation to the Jews and the Gentiles in the Roman church: 'For by the grace given me (i.e. apostleship to the Gentiles: cf. 1:5; 15:15-16) I say to every one of you' (12:3).[290]

---

[289] So rightly Wilckens, *Römer* 3, 84-85, 106. Cf. The author of Ephesians also stresses the theological unity of Jewish and Gentile believers in Christ (Eph 1-3), on the basis of which he then exhorts them for unity in practical Christian life (Eph 4-6): see Turner, 'Mission', 138-166.

[290] Paul's first admonition in Rom 12-16 is that they should not be conceited (12:3b), but rather 'honour one another above yourselves' (12:10). They must not be proud, nor be conceited (12:16). Instead Paul stresses brotherly love (12:10; 13:9-10; 14:19), so as to be able to live in harmony with one another (12:16). They are to maintain unity as one body, in which each member belongs to all the others (12:5). They are not to judge nor despise their fellow-believers (14:1, 10, 13), because God has accepted them all (14:3c). Paul exhorts them, as the apostle to the Gentiles, to maintain perfect unity on the basis of their equality and interdependence.

Conclusions

We have paid special attention to the fact that in Romans Paul insistently claims that he is 'apostle to the Gentiles' (1:5; 11:13; 15:16). If he is so conscious of that title or role, we asked, how did that consciousness relate to his theology? In fact, Paul explicitly states that he has written somewhat boldly on some points on the basis of the grace God gave him, knowing that he has the priestly duty of proclaiming the gospel of God, so that Gentiles might become an offering acceptable to God (15:15-16). The *Gentile*-focussed statement is also made in 1:1-17 and 11:13-32. From these passages we have noted that Paul indicates an undeniable link between his self-understanding of being apostle to the *Gentiles* and what he has written (i.e. his theology) in this letter. Our particular concern in this study, therefore, has been to investigate the influence of Paul's self-awareness of being apostle to the Gentiles in the content and the structure of his soteriological argument in Romans, and we have noted that he argues in favour of the Gentiles.

To be sure Paul often says affirmatively about Jews in Romans concerning Jewish privileges (1:16; 3:1-2; 9:4-5) and their special relationship with Christ (1:3; 9:5; 15:8), and recognises the law as holy and spiritual (7:12, 14, 16). He also expresses his fundamental concern for his own people, and anticipates the conversion of the greater number of Jews through faith in Christ Jesus (9:1-3; 10:1; 11:14, 26-32). He has certainly made a departure from his earlier position expressed in other letters.[1] Nevertheless, it is

---

1   Elsewhere Paul insists that the Jews have no special advantages over the Gentiles (cf. 1 Cor 1:23; Gal 3:28), and that the law cursed Christ and

crucial to note that in Romans Paul does not mention such affirmative remarks so as to establish the primacy of the Jews as the main point of his argument, as often alleged in the past. He does not expound them, but simply assumes or mentions them. We are aware that the implied assumptions cannot be undermined, but our main attention has been paid to what Paul primarily argues for in the letter.

Now it is time to conclude this investigation as we summarise our findings and expound their significance. Our conclusions will be drawn as we answer three questions: (1) What is the main subject matter for which Paul is arguing? (2) How does Paul structure his argument to establish the main theme? (3) Why has Paul written in the way he has?

1. *The main subject matter of Paul's soteriological argument in Romans is the fundamental equality of Jew and Gentile in Christ.* He indicates this theme in the thematic statement that the gospel brings salvation to *everyone* who believes in Christ Jesus, to the Jew first and also equally to the Gentile. He declares that the gospel is intended equally for both Jew and Gentile. In 1:18-3:20 Paul argues that Jew and Gentile are equally sinful, and so both are in equal need of salvation, and that 'faith in Christ' is the only and equal means for salvation for Jews and Gentiles (3:30). As far as judgement and salvation are concerned, God does not show favouritism on the basis of ethnic origin (2:6-11). Despite some Jewish advantages (3:1-2; 9:3-5), Paul clearly declares that 'we [Jews] are not any better [than Gentiles]' (3:9). The catena of OT quotations confirms that both Jews and Gentiles are indeed sinful without exception.

Paul affirms once again that the righteousness of God that comes through faith in Christ is available to all who believe without ethnic distinction (3:22). God is not merely the God of Jews, but the God of Gentiles too (3:29). The blessedness of being reckoned righteous is not only for the circumcised but also for the uncircumcised (4:9). Abraham's faith and his being reckoned righteous are examples for Jews and Gentiles to follow. Most of all Abraham is the father of Jews and of 'those [Gentiles]

---

imprisoned humanity (cf. Gal 3:13, 23), and that he is willing to break with his past that was 'in the flesh' (Phil 3:11), and that Jews deserve God's wrath and judgement (1 Thess 2:14-16).

who are of the faith of Abraham' (4:16). He is the father of the Jews, and equally he is the father of many nations (=Gentiles).

Having established the equality of Jews and Gentiles in their sinfulness and in justification, Paul treats them as 'one' in Christ in Romans 5-8. He embraces them in the pronoun 'we', and explains how they equally have a new status and a new life in Christ. As they are equal in Adam (i.e. sinfulness), so they are in Christ. Both Jews and Gentiles fell into sinfulness in their ancestor Adam before they were even divided into two groups (cf. 1:18-32: 5:12-21), so they are fundamentally equally sinful. But Christ the second Adam makes many righteous, whether they be Jews or Gentiles (5:12-21). More fundamentally, Paul argues that God predestined, called, justified and glorified 'those who love him' regardless their ethnic origins (8:28-30).

Paul argues this further in Romans 9-11. Although Romans 1-8 can be directly connected to Romans 12-15 (with a seemingly logical flow), Paul writes Romans 9-11 in order to establish the equality of Jew and Gentile on the firmest ground possible by expounding their equality in the salvific plan of God. He affirms that God deals with Jews and Gentiles equally according to his salvific plan for humanity. He has sovereign freedom to harden or to show mercy on either of them. He has the total right to make them the objects of his wrath or of his mercy. As long as anyone believes in Christ 'there is no difference between Jew and Gentile' (10:12), because Christ is the Lord of all who call upon his name. Paul also declares that both Jews and Gentiles have equally heard the same message (10:16-19). Since 'faith in Christ' is the sole means for salvation (from a human perspective), those who believe in Christ are qualified to remain in or to be grafted into the olive tree. Jews can be cut off if they do not believe, but Gentiles can be grafted in if they believe. The unbelieving Jews will be grafted in if they do not persist in unbelief, but the believing Gentiles will be broken off if they cease to believe (11:17-24). God has bound Jews and Gentiles over to disobedience so that he may have mercy on them all (11:32). Paul's fundamental argument in the main body of the letter is that God treats Jews and Gentiles equally. Paul also asserts that Christ's service is equally applicable to Jews and Gentiles (15:8-9a), and that the OT predicted that Jews and Gentiles would have equal access to God and worship him jointly (15:9b-12; 16:25-27).

The above summary leads us to conclude two points. First, in opposition to Käsemann and S. Kim, Paul's most important theological concern throughout the letter is not to argue for the doctrine of justification by grace and faith, but to establish the inclusion of the Gentiles in equal terms with Jews into God's salvific blessing. Only in the course of arguing for the latter theme does Paul refer to the justification by faith apart from the law.[2] The 'centre of gravity' of Romans is Paul's affirmation of Gentile salvation (on equal terms with Jews), although most scholars do not perceive that to be the precise focus of the letter (but rather an important sub-theme). One may say that since the equality of Jew and Gentile is an *implication* of the gospel, it is to be said that what Paul argues in Romans is the gospel, which is the prior point. However, we would still want to put it the other way round: what Paul exounds in the letter is not the gospel itself, but its implication with respect to the equal relation of Jew and Gentile in Christ. Paul's insistence on the equality of Jew and Gentile is not derived from sociological explanation, but is based on his theological conviction in the gospel of Christ Jesus.

Second, against many post-Holocaust interpreters of Romans, we conclude that Paul does not argue for the primacy of the Jews but for the equality of Jew and Gentile. During the last half century, most interpreters of Romans have unduly interpreted the letter from the perspective gained from the atrocity of the Holocaust incidents. Thus they have often asserted that Romans assures the primacy of the Jews and the brightest future (or a salvific *Sonderweg*) for Israel, because, they contend, Paul understood himself 'as an apostle to the Gentiles *for the sake of Israel*',[3] and whose 'entire mission to the Gentiles is only a roundabout way of saving all Israel'.[4] So it is contended that Paul has written this letter in order to correct an 'anti-semitism' among the Gentile believers in Rome. Our study has demonstrated that these views find little basis in the text. We should not allow the contemporary sense of guilt for the Holocaust (though, of course, we should never discount the extent of its wickedness) to influence our

---

2   *Pace* Käsemann, 'Justification', 60-78; Kim, *Origin*, 357; see *supra* pp. 2-3 n. 10.
3   Stuhlmacher, in Lapide and Stuhlmacher, *Paul*, 26, with added emphasis.
4   Lapide, in Lapide and Stuhlmacher, *Paul*, 44.

exegesis of an ancient text as is Romans. This point will become clearer when we note the way Paul structures his argument, to which we now turn.

2. *In order to affirm the equality of Jew and Gentile in Christ, Paul boldly structures his argument affirmatively concerning the Gentiles and critically concerning the Jews.* Paul affirms the equality of Jew and Gentile in sinfulness in 1:18-3:20, but he argues to establish the sinfulness of Jews in particular. In 1:18-32 Paul indicts the unidentified 'them' by reflecting the sinful history of *Israel* in the areas of idolatry, (homo)sexual immorality, refusal to retain the knowledge of God. This indicates that Paul is assimilating *Jews* into his indictment (understood as directed towards Gentiles), and so paves the way for the more direct attack on them from 2:1 onwards.

Moreover, it is very important to note that Paul's rhetorical insistence on the theological axiom of divine impartiality is not stressed as the goal towards which Paul leads his argument. It is rather employed as a stepping stone from which he develops it further. He affirms the inevitable judgement upon the (unbelieving) Jews and establishes the legitimate inclusion of the (believing) Gentiles in God's salvific blessing. It is clear that Paul himself does not remain impartial, but structures the argument in favour of the Gentiles.

Paul's 'biased' structure in his argument towards the Gentiles is even more apparent in 2:12-29. There he repeatedly argues that it is Gentiles who do the requirement of the law (2:14-16, 26-27) whereas Jews break the law (2:17-24, 25b). His affirmative presentation of the Gentiles is maximised when he strikingly presents the (believing) Gentiles to be the true circumcision and the 'inward Jews' (2:25-29). Yet he asserts that the circumcision of the (unbelieving) Jews has no value at all, for it is only physical and outward circumcision. Paul's argument is shaped to affirm the place of the Gentiles in Christ; he asserts that they are the ones who truly keep the requirement of the law, and thus are legitimately to be regarded as the 'true circumcision' and (the) 'true Jews'. Räisänen is certainly right to say that Paul's primary aim in Romans 2 is to affirm that Jews are guilty law-breakers, but he has missed a crucial point in Paul's argument in saying that Paul has no real interest in the Gentiles in this chapter.[5]

---

5   *Pace* Räisänen, *Paul*, 106.

In 3:1-20 Paul launches a further scriptural argument. He quotes many OT passages (3:10-18) in order to justify his claim that Jews are not any better than Gentiles (cf. 3:9). Here again he structures his argument on two levels. On the *theological* level he reaffirms the universal and equal sinfulness of Jews and Gentiles, but on the *rhetorical* level he constructs the argument to confirm more specifically the sinfulness of the Jews by modifying the texts and contexts of the OT quotations cited there. It is Paul himself who presents OT passages as if they condemned Jewish sinfulness. He structures his argument towards the conclusion, 'Therefore, no-one [particularly 'no Jew'] will be declared righteous in his sight by observing the law' (3:20).

In 3:21-4:25 Paul continues with his theme of the equality of Jew and Gentile, but this time he argues mainly to establish *the legitimacy of the justification of Gentiles*. In this section Paul continues to undermine Jewish boasting in their possession of and keeping the law, in their special relationship with God and in their pride in having Abraham as their ancestor. On the other hand, Paul vigorously affirms the inclusion of the (believing) Gentiles into these traditional Jewish privileges. He has already asserted that Gentiles 'do' the fundamental requirement of the law (2:14-15, 26-27). Now he argues that God is the God of the Gentiles too, not only because he is the only God but more significantly because he justifies Gentiles too (3:29-30). We have shown that such an understanding comes from Paul's self-awareness of being (the) apostle to the *Gentiles*.

Paul has a particular concern to establish that Abraham is also the father of many nations (=Gentiles). His interpretation of the Abraham story is unique and surprising not only from the perspective of contemporary Judaism but also from that of other NT writers. Paul's interpretation here is different from his own earlier presentation in Galatians 3. His overriding concern in this 'surprising' reinterpretation is to provide a theological basis for Gentile salvation apart from the law and by faith alone. To make this point he makes a strong appeal to historical facts and chronology: Abraham believed in God *before* he did any 'work' for him to be reckoned righteous. Paul asserts that what Abraham believed was the *promise* that he would have many descendants from many nations, and so the reason why he believed was in order to become the father of many nations (=Gentiles). This point has indeed significant rhetorical force, and here he regards chronology as being of little importance. We have argued that Paul's reinterpretation of the Abraham story in Romans is derived from his apostolic self-awareness, which seeks to establish a theological basis that can secure the legitimacy of the justification of the Gentiles gained by believing in Christ.

In Romans 9 Paul argues for God's total freedom either to harden or to show mercy on those whom he wants. Upon this theological assertion, the apostle claims that Gentiles too were predestined and called to be God's people, and their inclusion is divinely intended so that they could become, from God's perspective, 'my beloved one', 'my people' and 'sons of the living God' (9:25-26). So the phenomenon of Gentile salvation should not take us by surprise. He also argues that the unbelief of many Jews is according to the word of God (i.e. the intention of God) 'for (γάρ) not all who are descended from Israel are Israel. Nor because they are his descendants are they all Abraham's children' (9:6b-7a). He further declares that it is the Gentiles who have obtained righteousness, but Israel have failed to attain it despite their sincere pursuit of it (9:30-10:3), because they are a disobedient people (10:21).

Just as he did in Romans 1-4, Paul makes critical remarks about Jews and affirmative ones about Gentiles in Romans 9-10; and this tendency continues in Romans 11. He confirms that Jews are hardened and cut off (11:7, 17, 19, 20, 21, 25); they have rejected God's Messiah (11:15); they have persisted in unbelief (11:20, 23, 30) and they have experienced transgression and loss (11:12, 22), even to the point of becoming God's enemies (11:28). We have argued that Paul's warning in 11:17-24 does not provide any concrete evidence that the Gentile believers in Rome had already become arrogant towards the Jews. Rather, it seems more probable that Paul's exhortation to the Gentiles is directed to avoid any arrogant misunderstanding on their part of what he has written in this letter. He structures his argument so affirmatively about Gentiles and so critically about Jews, but with the aim of establishing the equality of Jew and Gentile, not to provide Gentiles with reasons for becoming conceited.

The short statement, καὶ οὕτως πᾶς 'Ισραὴλ σωθήσεται (11:26a) certainly conveys the brightest remark concerning Israel in the Pauline letters, but it is to be noted that this is claimed without substantial argument. The fact that he does not elaborate this (important) verse indicates that the exposition of the brighter future of Israel has not been Paul's overriding concern in this letter. With this phrase he does not suggest a salvific *Sonderweg* for Jews. The only condition for Jews to be grafted back into the olive tree is 'if they do not persist in unbelief' (11:23). The apostle affirms that 'salvation has come to the Gentiles' (11:11), namely, believing Gentiles are grafted into the olive tree (11:17-24). The full number of the Gentiles will be saved *before* 'all' Israel will be. Here Paul boldly suggests the reversal of the priority in mission: 'to the Gentile first and [then] to the Jew'. Furthermore he asserts that Jews and Gentiles are interdependent, and it is now for Jews to be dependent upon Gentiles (11:31).

The striking feature that we discovered is that Paul selects the most critical OT passages (or modifies more positive ones into negative ones) when he applies them with respect to the Jews, and the most affirmative ones (or modifies critical into positive ones) to the Gentiles. In fact, he often chooses OT passages which are most affirmative of Israel, yet modifies their texts and/or contexts so as to be affirmative of the Gentiles (as well). For example, the text of 10:13 is one of the few citations quoted verbatim from the LXX Joel 3:5. But the context is dramatically changed by Paul. The πᾶς in LXX Joel 3:5 clearly refers to 'every Jew' who will be saved by calling upon the name of the Lord, because for the Gentiles a severe judgement is pronounced (EV Joel 3:1-16). It is striking indeed to note that Paul selects this quotation from a passage where the salvation of Jews and the judgement of Gentiles are so obviously contrasted, and yet uses it to argue for the inclusion of the Gentiles into God's salvific plan and for the equality of Jew and Gentile! He frequently uses the OT as an accuser of Israel, and as an amicable testifier on behalf of the Gentiles. In Romans 9-11, in particular, he never uses the OT to accuse Gentiles but rather to explain Israel's unbelief and the Gentiles' faith and inclusion in the true people of God. Paul's endeavour demonstrates his deliberate attempt to secure for the believing Gentiles the status of the true people of God.

Now it is absolutely clear that the apostle evinces a substantial 'bias' towards the Gentiles in the presentation of his rhetoric. On the one hand, he argues that Jewish boasting in the possession of the law, their special relationship with God and their Abrahamic ancestry, are excluded, but on the other hand, he argues that Gentiles are also included in these items. Paul admits that he has written the letter 'rather boldly' (15:15), and most probably with this adverb he means that he needed boldness to present his argument affirmatively regarding the Gentiles while critically regarding the Jews. Finally, then, we need to ask why Paul has written in the way he has.

3. *It is Paul's self-awareness of being apostle to the Gentiles in God's salvific plan for all humanity that has led him to structure his argument in favour of Gentiles as he affirms their equality with Jews in the people of God.* As we have shown in Chapter 1 Paul expresses, right at the beginning, that this letter springs from his apostolic self-awareness (1:1-15), and reaffirms, towards the end, that he has written under his apostolic consciousness of being apostle to the Gentiles (15:15-16). With such introductory and concluding remarks Paul clearly testifies that he has written the way he has in order to fulfil his apostolic calling to the Gentiles (15:16) — which can mean only that his inclusive soteriology flows primarily from his self-awareness as apostle to the Gentiles. In other words, he has written Romans *as* apostle to the *Gentiles*. Paul also says that some of his theological and practical admonitions are made knowing that God has given him a special grace to be apostle to the Gentiles (11:13; 12:3). Therefore we found justification in interpreting the main body of the letter (1:16-15:13) from the perspective that his apostolic self-understanding has significantly influenced the content and the structure of his soteriological argument.

Paul is fully aware of his role that as apostle to the Gentiles he is not only called to preach the gospel (1:1-5, 16-17; 10:9-15; 16:25-27; 1 Cor 9:6; 15:3-8; Gal 1:15-16) but also under obligation to affirm or defend the legitimacy of the salvation of the Gentiles and of mission to the Gentiles by providing the theological basis for them. He is also fully conscious of himself as a debtor to the Gentiles, and as one whose aim in life is to live and work *for the sake of the Gentiles*.

We propose to interpret Paul's phrase 'τὸ εὐαγγέλιόν μου' (2:16; 16:25) from this perspective. Although Paul does not insist with this phrase that he has a message peculiar to himself,[6] his

---

6   Keck, *Paul*, 34-35; so also Cranfield, *Romans* 1, 163. Elsewhere he makes it clear that he has preached the same gospel as others have preached (cf. 1 Cor 15:3-8; Gal 2:7), and so it is often described as 'our gospel' (2 Cor 4:3; 1 Thess 1:5; 2 Thess 2:14). It is the gospel of [i.e. about] Christ (2 Cor

phrase seems to denote more than 'simply the gospel which he preached together with other Christian preachers'.[7] The expression 'τὸ εὐαγγέλιόν μου' occurs nowhere else in the Pauline letters except for the two occurrences in Romans (2:16; 16:25; cf. 2 Tim 2:8), and very similarly in Gal 2:2: 'the gospel that I preach among the Gentiles' (i.e. '*my* gospel'). He uses this phrase when he is conscious of his role as the chief defender of the gospel of uncircumcision (τὸ εὐαγγέλιον τῆς ἀκροβυστίας; Gal 2:7).[8] Paul writes in 16:25: 'Now to him [God] who is able to establish you by *my gospel* and the proclamation of Jesus Christ ... be glory for ever through Jesus Christ!' (16:25-27).[9] It seems highly significant that Paul writes 'my gospel *and* the proclamation of Jesus Christ' as two distinct elements. Here Paul differentiates 'my gospel' from 'the proclamation of Jesus Christ'. Thus, with this expression, he probably does not mean the gospel of Christ that

---

2:12; 2 Thess 1:8), and at the same time the gospel of God (1:1; 15:16; 2 Cor 11:7; 1 Thess 2:2, 8, 9; cf. 1 Pet 4:17).

7   Cranfield, *Romans* 1, 163; so also Keck, *Paul*, 34-35; so similarly Locke, *Paraphrase* 2, 499, 'as I make known in my preaching the gospel [as in Acts 17]'.

8   Fourteen years after the Damascus experience he went to Jerusalem to set before the Jerusalem apostles 'the gospel that *I* preach among the Gentiles' 'so that the truth of the gospel might remain with you [the Gentiles]' (Gal 2:2, 5). Although Barnabas and Titus were with him ('*we* did not give in to them for a moment': Gal 2:5), Paul insists as if the Jerusalem apostles recognised him *alone* as having been entrusted with the gospel of uncircumcision and with apostleship to the Gentiles (Gal 2:8)—'they saw that *I* had been entrusted with the task of preaching the gospel to the Gentiles .... as an apostle to the Gentiles'; 'they recognised the grace given to *me*'; 'they agreed that *we* should go to the Gentiles' (Gal 2:7-9). According to Rom 16:21 Timothy was with Paul, but uniquely he does not include Timothy as a co-sender of the letter, and also insists on '*my* gospel': cf. Paul and Timothy as co-senders (2 Cor 1:1) and so '*our* gospel' in 2 Cor 4:3; so also in 1 Thess 1:1 and 1:5; in 2 Thess 1:1 and 2:14.

9   The original location of 16:25-27 varies according the some ancient texts: the passage appears after 14:23 or after 15:33, or in both places, or is not included in the letter at all; see Metzger, *Textual Commentary*, 533-536, 540; Keck, *Paul*, 17. The authorship of this doxology has been debated, but arguments against Pauline authorship (cf. Dunn, *Romans* 2, 912-913) do not seem totally convincing: see Sanday and Headlam, *Romans*, 432-436; Bruce, *Romans*, 281-282. Fitzmyer, *Romans*, 753, is correct to say, 'Even if not authentically Pauline or originally part of Romans, it forms a fitting conclusion to the letter'.

he preached together with other preachers. It may rather mean the implication of the gospel he expounds *as apostle to the Gentiles*. This gospel is the truth of the gospel that should remain with the Gentiles (cf. Gal 2:5).

In this connection it is also highly significant that only in Romans and Galatians does Paul stress the fact that he is himself apostle to the Gentiles (11:13: εἰμι ἐγὼ ἐθνῶν ἀπόστολος; 15:16: λειτουργὸν Χριστοῦ Ἰησοῦ εἰς τὰ ἔθνη; Gal 2:7-9). The expression 'my gospel' is closely related to the awareness of his own apostleship to the Gentiles, which has led him to emphasise 'the evenhandedness of God in treating Jews and Gentiles exactly alike'.[10] It is the gospel expounded 'according to the revelation of the mystery hidden for long ages past, but now revealed and made known through the prophetic writings by the command of the eternal God, so that *all nations* (πάντα τὰ ἔθνη = all *Gentiles*) might believe and obey him' (16:25-26). It is the gospel expounded by Paul *as* apostle *for* the Gentiles.[11] Paul works out his role as a minister of Christ to the Gentiles in explaining his theology by writing Romans as well as by carrying out his missionary work. Thus if anything can be distinguished as *Paul's* gospel, it is probably 'his personal way of announcing the good news',[12] and more specifically his way of *defending* the gospel of God (1:1; 15:16; 2 Cor 2:12; 1 Thess 2:8-9) with a special reference to the fact that '*all* the Gentiles (τὰ ἔθνη)'[13] can become joint-heirs and

---

10 Ziesler, *Romans*, 88; so also Dunn, *Romans* 1, 103.

11 A corresponding idea is expressed in Eph 3:1-9. According to the author of Ephesians Paul is 'the prisoner of Christ Jesus *for the sake of you Gentiles*' (ὑπὲρ ὑμῶν τῶν ἐθνῶν': Eph 3:1), and 'the mystery [of Christ is] made known to [Paul] by revelation' (Eph 3:3). 'This mystery is [specifically] that the Gentiles are to be (εἶναι) joint-heirs [with the Jews] and joint-[members of the] body and joint-partakers of [God's] promise in Christ through the gospel' (Eph 3:6; this paraphrased translation is mine). The thrice-repeated prefix συν- indicates that 'the Gentiles are an essential constituent of this new entity [i.e. the Church]' (Lincoln, *Ephesians*, 180; see also Turner, 'Mission', 145-146). Although this mystery has been revealed to other apostles and prophets (Eph 3:5), it is to Paul that God's special grace is given to preach this mystery to the Gentiles (1:1, 5; 15:15-16; Gal 1:15; 2:7-9; cf. Eph 3:7-9; Acts 9:15).

12 Fitzmyer, *Romans*, 754.

13 Barth, *Ephesians 1-3*, 336-37. For the fact that Paul has been entrusted with the gospel for 'all the Gentiles', see 1:5; 15:16; Gal 1:16; 2:7, 9.

joint-partakers with believing Jews in God's salvific blessing (cf. Eph 3:6).

The above summary-conclusion directs us towards our thesis statement: *Paul's self-awareness of being apostle to the Gentiles has significantly influenced the shape, the content and the structure of his inclusive soteriological argument in Romans. As apostle to the Gentiles he boldly presents the theological argument in favour of the Gentiles in his attempt to affirm the legitimacy of Gentile salvation by establishing the equality of Jew and Gentile in Christ.*

'Romans is [arguably] Paul's most important letter as well as the most significant theological document of Christendom,'[14] containing his most mature and deepest theological ideas.[15] It is thus often said that 'different ways of reading Romans usually reflect different understandings of Paul's whole theology',[16] and that historically it is true that 'a fresh reading of Romans has itself generated a new way of reading Paul as a whole'.[17] Our study suggests that this letter should be reread.[18] Much of the modern interpretation of Romans has been dictated by the apologetic stance of a guilty conscience arising out of a misplaced understanding of the past, i.e. the Holocaust. Now we propose to reread this Paul's most important letter from his Gentile apostolic perspective, through which he understands his role, Christ's service,

---

14 Conzelmann and Lindemann, *Interpreting*, 192. Luther, *Luther's Works*, 35.365: 'This epistle [Romans] is really the chief part of the New Testament, and truly the purest gospel'. See Stortz, 'Romans and Reform', 369, who briefly examines the place of Romans in Christian history, and observes that Romans has been a platform for reform in Christian history by listing no less than seventeen great reformers who have written commentaries on Romans. See also Godsey, 'Interpretation', 3-16; Deidun, 'Romans', 601.

15 Cf. Käsemann, *Romans*, 390: 'The letter ... presents an almost complete summary of Paul's theology.'

16 Wright, 'Romans', 184.

17 Wright, 'Romans', 184. For example, Stendahl, *Paul*, vi: 'The most important shift in my position centers in my more recent understanding of Paul's Epistle to the Romans.'

18 Stowers's recent study *A Rereading of Romans* (1994) also urges us to reread Romans. However, his assertion that the central theme here is not salvation from sin, but psychological self-mastery not available from the Jewish law, is unconvincing.

the OT, the story of Abraham and the effect of Adam's fall. This letter contains a summary of Paul's missionary convictions gained from his missionary work among Jews and Gentiles.[19] We have proposed to take 15:14-21 as the best interpretative key to the meaning of the letter. Paul has written this letter not only as apostle *to* the Gentiles (εἰς τὰ ἔθνη; 15:16) but also as apostle *of* the Gentiles (ἐθνῶν ἀπόστολος; 11:13). Thus Paul is portrayed as apostle *for* the Gentiles (ὑπερ ... τῶν ἐθνῶν; Eph 3:1) by the deutro-Pauline author of Ephesians. He has written Romans in favour of the Gentiles in order to affirm the legitimacy and the sufficiency of their salvation, and to establish that they are equally included in God's salvific blessing and promise. He was not primarily apostle to the Gentiles for the sake of *Israel*, but rather was apostle to the Gentiles for the sake of the *Gentiles*.

The greatest merit of Paul as apostle to/of/for the Gentiles was not his extensive missionary endeavour, undoubtedly great though this was (cf. 15:19-21; 1 Cor 15:10; 2 Cor 11:23), but rather his theological establishing of the salvation of Gentiles apart from keeping the Jewish law, and thus of their equality with Jews in the salvific plan of God. This is his lasting contribution to the Gentile world, even to this day.

---

[19] Schrenk, 'Missionsdokument', 83.

Appendix

Further Notes on Paul's Apostolic Self-Awareness and his 'My Gospel'

In the main text of our study, we have sought to demonstrate that Paul's self-awareness of being apostle to the Gentiles has significantly influenced the shape, the content and the structure of his inclusive soteriological argument in Romans. However, his apostolic self-awareness and the gospel we refer to here are presented with a different emphasis from what he initially perceived at the Damascus Christophany and later preached, for example, in Galatia. So we need to clarify what exactly we mean by the phrases 'Paul's apostolic self-awareness' and his 'my gospel'. We will elucidate their precise meanings as we interact with S. Kim. According to Kim, '[Paul's] gospel and apostleship are grounded *solely* in the Christophany on the Damascus road and that he understands himself *solely* in the light of it'.[1] Thus, Paul's Damascus Christophany experience is, for Kim, the origin and therefore the interpretative key for Paul's theology.[2] Kim asserts that Paul's soteriology and Christology were formed at the time of his Christophany experience, or, 'certainly, at latest .... on the eve of

---

1 Kim, *Origin*, 61, with added emphases. Kim qualifies this by admitting development in Paul's understanding of his call (pp. 60-61), but this reservation does not seem to have much significance, for he devotes himself to arguing that there and then (at the Christophany on the Damascus road) Paul received the call and he fully knew it was for the Gentile mission (pp. 58-66).

2 Kim, *Origin, passim*.

his world-wide missionary journey'.³ Since Paul was fully conscious of his call to apostleship to the Gentiles, and of the gospel as the law-free gospel, he (almost) immediately moved out for Gentile mission.⁴ Thus, for Kim, Pauline theology becomes a theological exposition of the Damascus road experience.

Kim is certainly right to suggest that the *origin* of the *substance* of Paul's gospel can be located at the Damascus Christophany, but he fails to explain the context within which Paul's gospel has been proclaimed and the perspective through which Pauline theology has been shaped and expressed in his letters. Kim undermines the significance of subsequent revelations (ἀποκάλυψεις: 2 Cor 12:1; cf. Acts 13:1-3; 16:6-10; 22:17-21), of the contribution of Paul's (new) study of the OT, and of his missionary experience among Jews and Gentiles, which took place during the period between his conversion-call and the times of writing the epistles. For Kim this 'middle period' is not important, because Paul has received the totality of his gospel at the Damascus Christophany.⁵ Kim might argue that the study of the factors that enabled Paul to mould, arrange and develop his fundamental principles, and to present what is now in his letters, does not belong to his immediate concern for the particular research referred to here.⁶ But the *consequence* of his methodologi-

---

3   Kim, *Origin*, 335.

4   Kim, *Origin*, 271: it is 'abundantly clear that Paul perceived the revelation of the Son of God on the Damascus road as the revelation of God's righteousness apart from the law (Rom 3.21) *immediately*', and he made 'his *immediate* response to God's call to the Gentile mission' (emphases added).

5   This is also the view of Kim's teacher, F.F. Bruce, *Paul: Apostle*, 188: 'Paul's Damascus-road experience ... contained within itself the totality of his apostolic message. But that totality was, naturally, not grasped by him in all its detail immediately.' So does Kim reserve some room for the development of Paul's theological ideas (*Origin*, 335), but, perhaps apart from eschatology, such reservation would either serve to weaken his own conclusion or does not bear much significance for him. But this reservation contradicts his earlier remarks (see the above note 4). Thus Dunn, 'Light', 259, does not seem to have misread Kim; but cf. Newman, *Glory-Christology*, 179.

6   I am grateful to Professor S. Kim for reading one of my essays (which is not included in this book) and commenting in detail. He wrote me, 'I do not object that Paul's understanding of his Gentile apostleship [and his theology] developed. .... But in my book [i.e. *Origin*] I was not concerned to demonstrate the *stages of development* in Paul's apostolic self-understanding or his theology, but to prove the *origin* of them' (his emphases). However, Kim does not

cal approach indeed does minimise the possibility that the content and the structure of Paul's soteriological argument has been influenced by, for example, his missionary experience, his conflict with judaisers and his apostolic self-consciousness in response to such circumstances. For Kim, the content and the presentation of Paul's self-understanding and of his gospel in the letters are much the same as that which he originally received at the Christophany.

Kim thus vigorously argues that 'the fundamental fact [is] that the gospel—the law-free gospel—which Paul defends in Gal. is *precisely* the gospel which he already preached in his initial mission to Galatia (Gal 1.11). *Precisely* the gospel which Paul preached in Galatia is under attack'.[7] Kim's assertion would have more weight if he had demonstrated that the law-free gospel written in Galatians is precisely what he preached to them, and is precisely what he had received at the Damascus Christophany. But using material written about two decades or so later to assert that it was precisely what he had received at the Christophany without allowing some room for 'development', is methodologically unsound. Yes, Paul received his apostleship and the gospel at the Damascus Christophany, but one cannot be certain that what is written in the letters in their *content* and *presentation* is precisely what he received at the Christophany. For example, the Abraham story is presented with different emphases (and from different perspectives) in Galatians and in Romans. A further example is Paul's interpretation of Adam in 1 Corinthians and Romans.

Similarly, Kim does not consider the possibility that the same gospel can be presented with a different emphasis and shape of argument. Paul preached the 'gospel' during his initial missionary work in Galatia, but it is highly improbable that he emphatically presented the content of the law-free gospel in quite the way we read it in Galatians.[8] This does not mean, of course, that he preached a law-observant gospel to them. Rather, we mean that during his initial missionary work there, Paul preached the gospel, the message of the death and the resurrection of Jesus Christ. He

---

allow Paul's theological development after he left for his first missionary journey (*Origin*, 335).

7   Kim, *Origin*, 271 (added emphases); similarly in p. 272.
8   Cf. Stuhlmacher, 'Purpose', 242.

explicitly reminds the Corinthians that 'what I received [at the Damascus Christophany, according to Kim][9] I passed on to you [during my missionary work] as of first importance' (1 Cor 15:3) was clearly the message about the death and the resurrection of Christ (1 Cor 15:3-8). What Paul reminds the Galatians of, namely, that 'before your very eyes Jesus Christ was clearly portrayed as crucified' (Gal 3:1b), indicates that he also preached the death and the resurrection of Christ.

Paul probably did not stress the implications of the gospel in relation to the Jewish law during that time.[10] If Paul had already taught them very clearly the precise or even substantial content of what he wrote in the letter (as Kim repeatedly asserts), then the Galatians would not have been persuaded by the judaisers so quickly (cf. Gal 1:6). They would have noticed the difference between Paul's teaching and the judaisers', and most probably doubted the validity of what the agitators said. It is most unlikely that what is written in Galatians is 'precisely' what he preached in his initial mission. Hardly any missionary would repeat his/her missionary preaching almost word for word in a follow-up letter.[11] But if Paul did so he would have used the *'reminder-formula'*—"Didn't I tell you ....?". Indeed Paul often uses this reminder-formula in his letters.[12] The fact that Paul does not use this formula, except in appealing to their *experience* of the Spirit when they first believed in Christ (Gal 3:1-5; cf Gal 4:13-16; 5:19-21), indicates that he did not clearly teach the gospel together with its implication with the law. His remark in Gal 3:1b (just quoted above) indicates that the gospel Paul preached there earlier was the gospel of the cross and the resurrection of Christ.

---

9   Kim, *Origin*, 69-70, 275.

10   Paul the missionary perhaps did not see the need to do so to a Gentile audience who knew almost nothing about the Jewish law. Would any missionary emphatically explain to a group of new converts whether or not they should keep the Jewish law if he/she saw no need to keep that law?

11   So correctly, Stanton, *Jesus*, 113; cf. Dodd, *Apostolic Preaching*, 11-12.

12   E.g. 'I already gave you a warning when I was with you' (2 Cor 13:2); 'In fact when we were with you, we kept telling you that we would be persecuted' (1 Thess 3:4); 'We do not need to write to you, for you know very well that the day of the Lord will come like a thief in the night' (1 Thess 5:1-2); 'Don't you remember that when I was with you I used to tell you these things' (2 Thess 2:5); similarly, 1 Thess 4:6b, 11; 2 Thess 2:15; 3:6, 10.

People responded to that gospel by faith and received the Holy Spirit (Gal 3:1-5).

When judaisers later tried to force the Galatians to keep the Jewish law, the new believers accepted their teaching probably without even questioning it (cf. Gal 1:6; 'so quickly'), because they were not theologically prepared to analyse and reject it. Paul then saw the urgent need to defend the gospel by explaining the *implications* of the gospel which he had preached earlier, i.e. the sufficiency and legitimacy of Gentile salvation by faith alone apart from the law. *Paul's emphasis on the content of the gospel in the letter to the Galatians is differently shaped from what he preached during his initial missionary work there.*[13] He has the same gospel, but explains it with different emphases; earlier he had preached 'justification *by believing in the death and resurrection of Christ*', but now in the letter he stresses 'justification by faith *apart from the law*'. The content and the structure of Paul's soteriology in the text of Galatians is shaped by the need to defend the legitimacy of Gentile salvation, acquired by faith alone in response to the gospel message about the death and the resurrection of Jesus Christ. Romans is written in very similar circumstances.[14]

By the time he writes the letters (especially Galatians and Romans) Paul is fully aware of God's call for him to be apostle to the Gentiles, and thus he is keenly conscious of his apostolic obligation as apostle to the *Gentiles*.[15] His obligation does not merely constitute preaching to them, but more importantly involves affirming and defending the theological legitimacy of Gentile salvation whenever it is threatened.[16] His defence of his

---

13 Stanton, *Jesus*, 113: 'the emphases of the epistles were not those of Paul's missionary preaching'. For the reconstruction of Paul's missionary preaching by employing the reminder formular, see my 'From Preaching the Gospel to Expounding its Implications: Rediscovering Paul's Missionary Preaching and its Development', which has been presented at Paul Seminar, British New Testament Conference, Aberdeen (13 September, 1996).

14 See Chae, 'Paul's Apostolic Self-Awareness', 116-137.

15 The risen Christ called Paul on the Damascus road; then he progressively unfolded the content of his call (cf. Acts 9:3-19//22:6-16//26:12-23; 22:17-21; 13:1-3; 16:6-10; 18:9-10; 23:11), and Paul's understanding of his task and capacity as apostle to the Gentiles was accordingly developed; so similarly Hengel, *Earliest Christianity*, 88; Bornkamm, *Paul*, 49.

16 Knox, 'Romans 15:14-33', 1-11.

Gentile apostleship in Galatians and Romans is made in order to defend the place of (believing) Gentiles in Christ. Paul therefore presents his argument (i.e. theology) *as* apostle to the Gentiles. *Paul's self-awareness of being apostle to the Gentiles in Romans (and in Galatians) is not merely his awareness of his call to preach the gospel to the Gentiles, but more fundamentally his awareness that he is the one who should theologically affirm and defend the legitimacy of Gentile salvation gained apart from the law. It is this latter self-awareness that has led Paul to shape the content and the structure of his soteriological argument in Romans.* This self-consciousness must have become particularly acute in the light of the predictable threat of judaising agitators in Rome and the foreseeable threat to his own life in Jerusalem. Likewise, with the phrase 'my gospel', Paul does not merely refer to the message of the death and resurrection of Christ (cf. Gal 1:15-16).[17] More fundamentally, he refers to the *implication* of the work of Christ with respect to the equal standing of Jew and Gentile in God's salvific plan, namely, to the gospel that he preaches *as* apostle to the *Gentiles*.

---

17 See *supra* pp. 297-299.

Abbreviations

ABD	D.N. Freedman *et al* (eds.), *The Anchor Bible Dictionary* (6 Vols., New York: Doubleday, 1992).
AnBib	The Anchor Bible
ANRW	W. Hasse (ed.), *Aufstig und Niedergang der Römischen Welt*, Geschichte und Kultur Roms im Spiegel der Neueren Forschung, Teil II: Principat, 25.4 (Berlin/New York: W. de Gruyter, 1987).
BAGD	W. Bauer, W.F. Arndt, F.W. Gingrich and F.W. Danker, *A Greek–English Lexicon of the New Testament and Other Early Christian Literature* (Chicago/London: University of Chicago Press, [1958^5] 1979).
BBR	*Bulletin for Biblical Research*
BDF	F. Blass, A. Debrunner and R.W. Funk, *A Greek Grammar of the New Testament*
Bib	*Biblica*
BibNot	*Biblische Notizen*
BibSac	*Bibliotheca Sacra*
BJRL	*Bulletin of the John Rylands University Library of Manchester*
BTB	*Biblical Theology Bulletin*
CBQ	*Catholic Biblical Quarterly*
DPL	G.F. Hawthorne, R.P. Martin and D.G. Reid (eds.), *Dictionary of Paul and his Letters* (Downers Grove/Leicester: IVP, 1993.)
EDNT	H. Balz and G. Schneider (eds.), *Exegetical Dictionary of the New Testament* (3 Vols., Grand Rapids: Eerdmans, [1978-80] 1990).

EKK	Evangelisch-katholischer Kommentar zum Neuen Testament
EB	*Encyclopaedia Britannica* (32 Vols., Chicago *et al*: 1975^{15} reprinted 1992).
ET	English translation
EV	English versions
EvQ	*Evangelical Quarterly*
ExAud	*Exod Auditu*
ExpT	*Expository Times*
FRLANT	Forschungen zur Religion und Literatur des Alten und Neuen Testaments
GTJ	*Grace Theological Journal*
HTR	*Harvard Theological Review*
IBD	*The Illustrated Bible Dictionary*
ICC	International Critical Commentary
Interp	*Interpretation*
ITQ	*Irish Theological Quarterly*
JB	The Jerusalem Bible
JBL	*Journal of Biblical Literature*
JETS	*Journal of Evangelical Theological Society*
JRE	*Journal of Religious Ethics*
JSNT	*Journal for the Study of the New Testament*
JSNTS	Journal for the Study of the New Testament Supplement Series
JThSAf	*Journal of Theology for South Africa*
JTS	*Journal of Theological Studies*
KD	*Kerygma und Dogma*
KJV	King James Version
Lutherbibel	Die Bibel nach der Übersetzung Martin Luthers
MNTC	The Moffatt New Testament Commentary
Moffatt	The Bible: A New Translation, trans. J. Moffatt
MT	Masoretic text
NAB	The New American Bible
NASB	The New American Standard Bible
NCB	The New Century Bible
NCBC	The New Century Bible Commentary
NEB	The New English Bible
Neot	*Neotestamentica*
Nestle–Aland	Nestle–Aland *Novum Testamentum Graece*
NICOT	The New International Commentary on the Old Testament
NIV	New International Version

NJB	The New Jerusalem Bible
NovT	*Novum Testamentum*
NRSV	New Revised Standard Version
NTS	*New Testament Studies*
OBS	The Oxford Bible Series
Phillips	*The New Testament in Modern English*, trans. J.B. Phillips
REB	The Revised English Bible
RefR	*Reformed Review*
RevBib	*Revue biblique*
RevExp	*Review and Expositor*
RHPR	*Revue d'Histoire et de Philosophie Religieuses*
Romans Debate	K.P. Donfried (ed.), *The Romans Debate*, Revised and Expanded Edition (Peabody: Hendrickson, [1977] 1991^2).
RSV	Revised Standard Version
RTR	*Reformed Theological Review*
RV	Revised Version
SBL	Society of Biblical Literature
SBLDS	SBL Dissertation Series
SBT	Studies in Biblical Theology
SNovT	Supplements to Novum Testamentum
SNTSMS	Society for NT Studies Monograph Series
Str-B	H. Strack and P. Billerbeck, *Kommentar zum Neuen Testament aus Talmud und Midrasch* (6 Vols., Munich: Beck, 1926-1963).
StTh	*Studia Theologica*
TBS	Η ΚΑΙΝΗ ΔΙΑΘΗΚΗ, The Trinitarian Bible Society
TDNT	G. Kittel and G. Friedrich (eds.), *Theological Dictionary of the New Testament*
TEV	Today's English Version
ThLZ	*Theologische Literaturzeitung*
ThZ	*Theologische Zeitschrift*
TNTC	Tyndale New Testament Commentary
TOTC	Tyndale Old Testament Commentary
TPINTC	TPI New Testament Commemtaries
trans.	translated by
TriJ	*Trinity Journal*
UBS^3	*The Greek New Testament*, United Bible Societies
USQR	*Union Seminary Quarterly Review*
VigChr	*Vigiliae Christianae*
VoxEvang	*Vox Evangelica*

W&W	*Word & World*
WBC	Word Biblical Commentary
WEC	The Wycliffe Exegetical Commentary
WTJ	*Westminster Theological Journal*
WUNT	Wissenschaftliche Untersuchungen zum Neuen Testament
ZNW	*Zeitschrift für die neutestamentliche Wissenschaft*
ZTK	*Zeitschrift für Theologie und Kirche*

Bibliography

I. Sources

A. The Bible

Nestle–Aland *Novum Testamentum Graece* 27th edition (Stuttgart: Deutsche Bibelgesellschaft, [1898] 1993).

Aland, K., Black, M., Martini, M., Metzger, B.M. and Wikgren, A. (eds.), *The Greek New Testament*, 3rd edition (New York: United Bible Societies, [1966, 1968, 1975] 1983).

Η ΚΑΙΝΗ ΔΙΑΘΗΚΗ *The Greek Text Underlying the English Authorised Version of 1611* (London: The Trinitarian Bible Society, n.d.).

Elliger, K. and Rudolph, W. (eds.), *Biblia Hebraica Stuttgartensia* (Stuttgart: Deutsche Bibelgesellschaft, [1967, 1977] 1990).

Rahlfs, A. (ed.), *Septuaginta* (Stuttgart: Deutsche Bibelgesellschaft, 1935).

Brenton, L.C.L., *The Septuagint with Apocrypha: Greek and English* (Peabody: Hendrickson, [1851] 1986).

Stern, D.H., *Jewish New Testament: A Translation of the New Testament that expresses its Jewishness* (Jerusalem: Jewish New Testament Publications, [1979, 1989, 1990] 1991).

Eight Translation New Testament: King James Version, The Living Bible, Phillips Modern English, Revised Standard Version, Today's English Version, New International Version, Jerusalem Bible, New English Bible (Wheaton: Tyndale House Publishers, 1974).

The Complete Parallel Bible with Apocryphal / Deuterocanonical Books: New Revised Standard Version, Revised English Bible, New American Bible, New Jerusalem Bible (Oxford/New York: Oxford University Press, 1993).

The Apocrypha of the Old Testament, Revised Standard Version (London *et al*: Nelson, 1957).
The Holy Bible, Revised Version (Oxford/London: The British Foreign Bible Society, 1884).
The Holy Bible, New International Version Reference Edition (London/Sydney/Auckland/Toronto: International Bible Society/Hodder & Stoughton, [1973, 1978, 1984] 1986).
Moffatt, J., *The Bible: A New Translation* (London: Hodder & Stoughton, [1924, 1926] 1935).
New American Standard Bible (La Habra: The Lockman Foundation, [1960, 1962, 1963, 1968, 1971, 1972, 1973, 1975] 1977).
Die Bibel nach der Übersetzung Martin Luthers (Stuttgart: Deutsche Bibelgesellschaft, 1985).

B. Jewish and Christian Sources

Charles, R.H. (ed.), *The Apocrypha and Pseudepigrapha of the Old Testament in English* (2 Vols., Oxford: Clarendon Press, [1913] 1963).
Charlesworth, J.H. (ed.), *The Old Testament Pseudepigrapha* (2 Vols., New York/London/Toronto/Sydney/Auckland: Doubleday, 1983).
Danby, H. (ed.), *The Mishnah: Translated from the Hebrew with Introduction and Brief Explanatory Notes* (Oxford: Oxford University Press, 1933).
Eisenmann, R. and Wise, M., *The Dead Sea Scrolls Uncovered: The First Complete Translation and Interpretation of 50 Key Documents Withheld for Over 35 Years* (Shaftesbury/Rockport/Brisbane: Element, 1992).
Josephus, *The Works of Flavius Josephus*, trans. W. Whiston (4 Vols., Grand Rapids: Baker, 1974).
Lightfoot, J.B., Harmer, J.R., (eds. and translators) and Holmes, M.W. (ed. and Reviser), *The Apostolic Fathers: Greek Texts and English Translations of Their Writings* (Grand Rapids: Baker, [1891] 1992^2).
Martínez, F.G., *The Dead Sea Scrolls Translated: The Qumran Texts in English*, trans. W.G.E. Watson (Leiden: E.J. Brill, [1992] 1994).
Neusner, J. (ed.), *The Mishnah: A New Translation* (New Haven/London: Yale University Press, 1988).
Philo, *The Works of Philo Complete and Unabridged in one Volume*, New Updated Edition, trans. C.D. Yonge (Peabody: Hendrickson, 1993).

Schneemelcher, W. (ed.), *New Testament Apocrypha*, Revised edition, trans. and ed. R.MaL. Wilson (2 Vols., Cambridge: James Clarke & Co.; Louisville: Westminster/John Knox Press, [1904, 1968^4, 1990] 1991).

Vermes, G. (ed.), *The Dead Sea Scrolls in English* (Sheffield: JSOT Press, [1962, 1975] 1987^3).

II. Reference Works

A Concordance to the Apocryphal/Deuterocanonical Books of the Revised Standard Version (Grand Rapids, Eerdmans; London: Collins, 1983).

Balz, H. and Schneider, G. (eds.), *Exegetical Dictionary of the New Testament* (3 Vols., Grand Rapids: Eerdmans, [1978-80] 1990).

____, *Exegetisches Wörterbuch zum Neuen Testament* (2 Vols., Stuttgart: Verlag W. Kohlhammer, 1978-1980).

Bauer, W., *A Greek–English Lexicon of the New Testament and Other Early Christian Literature*, revised and augmented by W.F. Arndt, F.W. Gingrich and F.W. Danker (Chicago/London: University of Chicago Press, [1958^5] 1979).

Blass, F. and Debrunner, A., *A Greek Grammar of the New Testament and Other Early Christian Literature*, trans. and revised by R.W. Funk (Chicago/London: University of Chicago Press, [1896, 1954^9, 1959^{10}] 1961).

Darton, M. (ed.), *Modern Concordance to the New Testament* Based on the French *Concordance de la Bible, Nouveau Testament* produced under the aegis of the *Association de la Concordance française de la Bible* (London: Darton, Longman & Todd, 1976).

Hatch, E. and Redpath, H.A., *A Concordance to the Septuagint and the Other Greek Versions of the Old Testament (Including the Apocryphal Books) in Three Volumes* (3 Vols., Grand Rapids: Baker, [1897] 1987).

Kittel, G. and Friedrich, G. (eds.), *Theological Dictionary of the New Testament*, trans. and ed. by G.W. Bromiley (10 Vols., Grand Rapids: Eerdmans, [1932] 1963).

Liddell, H.G. and Scott, R., *An Intermediate Greek–English Lexicon* (Oxford: Clarendon Press, 1900).

Moulton, J.H., *A Grammar of New Testament Greek* (4 Vols. [Vol. 2: Moulton, J.H., and Howard, W.F.; Vols. 3-4: Moulton, J.H., and Turner, N.], Edinburgh: T&T Clark, [1906-1976] reprinted 1988).

Porter, S.E., *Idioms of the Greek New Testament* (Sheffield: JSOT Press, [1992] 1994²).
Rienecker, F., *A Linguistic Key to the Greek New Testament*, trnas. and ed. by C.L. Rogers, Jr. (Grand Rapids: Regency Reference Library/Zondervan, [1970, 1976] 1980).
Robertson, A.T., *A Grammar of the Greek New Testament in the Light of Historical Research* (Nashville: Broadman Press, [1914, 1915, 1923⁴] 1934).
Smith, G.A., *A Manual Greek Lexicon of the New Testament* (Edinburgh: T&T Clark, 1937³).
Thayer, J.H., *The New Thayer's Greek–English Lexicon of the New Testament* (Peabody: Hendrickson, [1885, 1889] 1981).
Zerwick, M. and Grosvenor, M., *A Grammatical Analysis of the Greek New Testament*, Unabridged, revised edition in one volume (Rome: Biblical Institute Press, [1966³] 1981).

III. Secondary Literature

Achtemeier, P.J., *Romans: Interpretation, A Bible Commentary for Teaching and Preaching* (Atlanta: John Knox Press, 1985).
Albright, W.F., and Mann, C.S., *Matthew: Introduction, Translation and Notes*, AnBib 26 (New York/London/Toronto/Sydney/Auckland: Doubleday, 1971).
Allen, L.C., 'The Old Testament in Romans I-VIII', *VoxEvan* 3 (1964), 6-41.
Anderson, A.A., *The Book of Psalms*, NCBC (2 Vols., London: Oliphants, 1972).
Aus, R. D., 'Paul's Travel Plans to Spain and the "Full number of the Gentiles" of Rom 11:25', *NovT* 21 (1979), 232-262.
Baab, O.J., 'Homosexuality', *IBD* 2, 639.
Baldwin, J.G., *The Message of Genesis 12-50 From Abraham to Joseph*, The Bible Speaks Today Series (Leicester: IVP, 1986).
Barnes, A., *Notes, Explanatory and Practical, on the Epistle to the Romans*, revised by S. Green (London: B.L. Green, [1834, 1835⁵] 1851).
Barnett, P.W., 'Apostle', *DPL*, 45-51.
Barrett, C.K., *The New Testament Background: Selected Documents* (London: SPCK, 1957).
____, *The Epistle to the Romans* (London: A&C Black, [1957] 1991²).
____, *From First Adam to Last: A Study in Pauline Theology* (London: A&C Black, 1962).

_____, 'I am Not Ashamed of the Gospel', in D.G.B. Franzoni (ed.), *Foi et Salut selon S. Paul (Épître aux Romains 1,16)*, Analecta Biblica Investigationes Scientificae in Res Biblicas 42 (Rome: Institut Biblique Pontifical, 1970), 19-50.

_____, 'Romans 9.30-10.21: Fall and Responsibility of Israel', *Essays on Paul* (London: SPCK, 1982), 132-153.

_____, 'The Gentile Mission As an Eschatological Phenomenon', in W.H. Gloer (ed.), *Eschatology and the New Testament: Essays in Honor of George Raymond Beasley-Murray* (Peabody: Hendrickson, 1988), 65-75.

_____, 'Paulus als Missionar und Theologe', in M. Hengel and U. Heckel (eds.), *Paulus und das antike Judentum*, Tübingen-Durham Symposium im Gedenken an den 50. Todestag Adolf Schlatters (Tübingen: J.C.B. Mohr [Paul Siebeck], 1991), 1-15.

Barth, K., *The Epistle to the Romans*, trans. E.C. Hoskyns (Oxford (London/New York: Oxford University Press, [1918, 1928^6] 1933, reprinted 1968).

_____, *Church Dogmatics*, trans. G.W. Bromiley (12 Vols., Edinburgh: T&T Clark, 1956).

Barth, M., *Ephesians 1-3: Introduction, Translation, and Commentary*, AnBib 34 (New York/London/Toronto/Sydney/Aukland: Doubleday, 1974).

_____, *The People of God* (Sheffield: JSOT Press, 1983).

Bartsch, H.W., 'Die historische Situation des Römerbriefs' in F.L. Cross (ed.), *Studia Evangelica* IV, TU 102, 1968, 281-291.

_____, 'Die Empfänger des Römerbriefes', *StTh* 25 (1971), 81-89.

Bassler, J.M., *Divine Impartiality: Paul and a Theological Axiom* (Chico: Scholars Press, 1982).

Battle, Jr., J.A., 'Paul's Use of the Old Testament in Romans 9:25-26', *GTJ* 2 (1981), 115-129.

Bauernfeind, O., 'ἀναπαύω, ἀνάπαυσις, ἐπαναπαύω', *TDNT* 1, 350-351.

Baur, F.C., *Paul The Apostle of Jesus Christ, His Life and Work, His Epistles and His Doctrine: A Contribution to a Critical History of Primitive Christianity* (2 Vols., London/Edinburgh: Williams and Norgate, [1845] 1876^2).

Beardslee, W.A., *Human Achievement and Divine Vocation in the Message of Paul*, SBT 31 (Naperville: A.R. Allenson, Inc., 1961).

Beare, F.W., *St Paul and his Letters* (London: A&C Black, 1962).

_____, *The Gospel According to Matthew: Translation, Introduction and Commentary* (Peabody: Hendrickson, 1981).

Beasley-Murray, G.R., 'The righteousness of God in the History of Israel and the Nations: Romans 9-11', *RevExp* 73 (1976), 437-450.
___, *John*, WBC 36 (Waco: Word Books, 1987).
Becker, J., *Paul: Apostle to the Gentiles*, trans. O.C. Dean, Jr. (Louisville: Westminster/John Knox Press, [1989] 1993).
Beet, J.A., *A Commentary on St. Paul's Epistle to the Romans* (London: Hodder & Stoughton, 1902).
Beker, J.C., *Paul the Apostle: The Triumph of God in Life and Thought* (Philadelphia: Fortress, 1980).
___, 'The Faithfulness of God and the Priority of Israel in Paul's Letter to the Romans' *HTR* 79 (1986), 10-16.
Bell, R., *Provoked to Jealousy: The Origin & Purpose of the Jealousy Motif in Romans 9-11*, WUNT 2.63 (Tübingen: J.C.B. Mohr [Paul Siebeck], 1994).
Best, E., 'The Revelation to Evangelize the Gentiles', *JTS* 35 (1984), 1-30.
___, 'Paul's Apostolic Authority—?', *JSNT* 27 (1986), 3-25.
___, *Paul and His Converts* (Edinburgh: T&T Clark, 1988).
Betz, O., ''Αβραάμ', *EDNT* 1, 2-4.
___, 'Israels Mission an der Welt – unsere Mission an Israel', in H. Kremers and E. Lubahn (eds.), *Mission an Israel in heilsgeschichtlicher Sicht* (Neukirchener, 1985).
Birkeland, H., *The Evildoers in the Book of Psalms* (Oslo: Dybwad, 1965).
Black, M., *Romans*, NCBC (Grand Rapids: Eerdmans; London: Marshall, Morgan & Scott, 1973).
Boccaccini, G., *Middle Judaism: Jewish Thought 300 B.C.E. to 200 C.E.* (Minneapolis: Fortress, 1991).
Boers, H., *Theology out of the Ghetto: A New Testament Exegetical Study concerning Exclusiveness* (Leiden: E.J. Brill, 1971).
Bornkamm, G., 'The Letter to the Romans as Paul's Last Will and Testament', reprinted in *Romans Debate*, 16-28.
___, *Paul*, trans. D.M.G. Stalker (London: Hodder & Stoughton, [1969] 1985).
Bowers, W.P., 'Fulfilling the Gospel: The Scope of the Pauline Mission', *JETS* 30 (1987), 185-198.
___, 'Mission', in *DPL*, 1993, 608-619.
Boylan, M.P., *St. Paul's Epistle to the Romans: Translation and Commentary* (Dublin: M.H. Gill and Son Ltd., 1947).
Briggs, C.A. and Briggs, E.G., *A Critical and Exegetical Commentary on the Book of Psalms*, ICC (Edinburgh: T&T Clark, 1906-07).

Bruce, F.F., *The Epistle of Paul to the Romans*, TNTC (London: Tyndale Press, 1963).
____, *Paul: Apostle of the Heart Set Free* (Grand Rapids: Eerdmans, 1977).
____, *The Time is Fulfilled: Five Aspects of the Fulfilment of the Old Testament in the New* (Exeter: Paternoster, 1978).
Brunner, E., *The Letter to the Romans: A Commentary*, (Philadelphia: Westminster Press, [1938, 1956] 1959).
____, *The Christian Doctrine of God: Dogmatics*, trans. O. Wyon (Vol. 1, Philadelphia: Westminster Press, 1949).
Bultmann, R., 'Glossen im Röm', *ThLZ* 72 (1947), 197-202.
____, *Theology of the New Testament*, trans. K. Grobel (Vol. 1, London: SCM, [1948] 1952).
Calvert, N.C., 'Abraham', *DPL*, 1-9.
Calvin, J., *Commentaries on the Epistle of Paul the Apostle to the Romans* (Grand Rapids: Eerdmans, [1540] reprinted 1947).
Campbell, D.A., *The Rhetoric of Righteousness in Romans 3.21-26*, JSNTS 65 (Sheffield: Sheffield Academic Press, 1992).
Campbell, W.S., 'Why did Paul Write Romans?', *ExpT* 85 (1973-74), 264-269.
____, 'Romans III as a Key to the Structure and Thought of the Letter', *NovT* 23 (1981), 22-40.
____, 'The Freedom and Faithfulness of God in Relation to Israel', *JSNT* 13 (1981), 27-45.
____, 'Did Paul Advocate Separation from the Synagogue?', in *Paul's Gospel in an Intercultural Context: Jew and Gentile in the Letter to the Romans* (Frankfurt et al: Peter Lang, 1992), 122-131.
____, *Paul's Gospel in an Intercultural Context: Jew and Gentile in the Letter to the Romans* (Frankfurt et al: Peter Lang, 1992).
____, 'Covenant and New Covenant', *DPL*, 179-183.
____, 'Israel', *DPL*, 441-446.
Canales, I.J., 'Paul's Accusers in Romans 3:8 and 6:1', *EvQ* 57 (1985), 237-245.
Caragounis, C.C., *The Ephesian Mysterion: Meaning and Content* (Lund: Gleeup, 1977).
____, 'Romans 5:15-16 in the Context of 5:12-21: Contrast or Comparason?', *NTS* 31 (1985), 142-148.
____, 'L'universalisme Moderne: Perspectives bibliques sur la révélation de Dieu', *Hokhma* 45 (1990), 17-45.
____, 'The Biblical Attitude to Homosexuality', 1-20, Unpublished article written in 1992.

Carras, G.P., 'Romans 2,1-29: A Dialogue on Jewish Ideals', *Bib* 73 (1992), 183-207.
Chae, D.J.-S., 'Paul's Apostolic Self-Awareness and the Occasion and Purpose of Romans', in A. Billington, T. Lane and M. Turner (eds.), *Mission and Meaning: Essays Presented to P. Cotterell* (Carlisle: Paternoster, 1995), 116-137.

____, 'From Preaching the Gospel to Expounding its Implications: Rediscovering Paul's Missionary Preaching and its Development', unpublished paper presented at Paul Seminar, British New Testament Conference, Aberdeen (13 Sept., 1996).

Chance, J.B., *Jerusalem, the Temple, and the New Age in Luke–Acts* (Macon, Georgia: Mercer, 1988).

Clements, R.E., *Abraham and David: Genesis 15 and its Meaning for Israelite Tradition*, SBT 2.5 (London: SCM, 1967).

Clifford, R.J., and Murphy, R.E., 'Genesis', in R.E. Brown, J.A. Fitzmyer and R.E. Murphy (eds.), *The New Jerome Biblical Commentary* (Eaglewood cliffs, NJ: Prentice Hall, [1968] 1990^2), 8-43.

Cole, A., *Exodus: An Introduction and Commentary*, TOTC (Leicester: IVP, 1973).

Conybeare, W.J. and Howson, J.S., *The Life and Epistles of St. Paul* (Grand Rapids: Eerdmans, [1862] reprinted 1989).

Conzelmann, H. and Lindemann, A., *Interpreting the New Testament: An Introduction to the Principles and Methods on N.T. Exegesis*, trans. S.S. Schatzmann (Peabody: Hendrickson, [1985^8] 1988).

Cosgrove, C.H., 'What If Some Have not Believed? The Occasion and Thrust of Romans 3:1-8', *ZNW* 78 (1987), 90-105.

____, 'The Justification of the Other: An Interpretation of Rom 1:18-4:25', *SBL 1992 Seminar Papers* (Atlanta: Scholars Press, 1992), 613-634.

Cotterell, P. and Turner, M., *Linguistics & Biblical Interpretation* (London: SPCK, 1989).

Craigie, P.C., *The Book of Deuteronomy*, NICOT (Grand Rapids: Eerdmans, 1976).

Cranfield, C.E.B., *The Epistle to the Romans*, ICC (2 Vols., Edinburgh: T&T Clark, 1975).

____, '"The Works of the Law" in the Epistle to the Romans', *JSNT* 43 (1991), 89-101.

Craus, H.-J., *Psalms*, trans. H.C. Oswald (2 Vols., Minneapolis: Augsburg, [1961, 1978] 1989).

Cullmann, O., 'Le caractère eschatologique du devoir missionnaire et de la conscience apostolique de Saint Paul. Étude sur le κατέχον

(–ων) de II Thess. 2, 6-7', *RHPR* 16 (1936), 210-245; the German translation of this article, 'Der eschatologische Charakter des Missionsauftrages und des apostolischen Selbstbewusstseins bei Paulus', appears in his *Vorträge und Aufsätze. 1925-62* (Tübingen: Mohr; Zurich: Zwingli, 1966), 305-336.

____, 'Eschatology and Missions in the New Testament', trans. O. Wyon, reprinted in G.H. Anderson (ed.), *The Theology of the Christian Mission* (London: SCM, [1956] 1961), 42-54.

____, *Salvation in History* (London: SCM, [1965] 1967).

Cundall, A.E., *Judges*, TOTC (Leicester: IVP, 1968).

Dahl, N.A., 'The Future of Israel', *Studies in Paul: Theology for the Early Christian Mission* (Minneapolis: Augsburg, 1977), 137-158.

____, 'The Missionary Theology in the Epistle to the Romans' (1956), reprinted in his *Studies in Paul: Theology for the Early Christian Mission* (Minneapolis: Augsburg, 1977), 70-94.

____, 'The One God of Jews and Gentiles (Romans 3:29-30)', *Studies in Paul: Theology for the Early Christian Mission* (Minneapolis: Augsburg, 1977), 178-191.

____, *Studies in Paul: Theology for the Early Christian Mission* (Minneapolis: Augsburg, 1977).

____, 'Romans 3:9: Text and Meaning', in M. Hooker and S.G. Wilson (eds.), *Paul and Paulinism: Essays in Honour of C.K. Barrett* (London: SPCK, 1982), 184-204.

Davidson, F. and Martin, R.P., 'Romans', in D. Guthrie, J.A. Motyer (eds.), *The New Bible Commentary* (Leicester: IVP, [1953] revised 1970), 1012-1048.

Davies, G.H., *Exodus*, Torch Bible Paperbacks (London: SCM, 1967).

Davies, G.N., *Faith and Obedience in Romans: A Study in Romans 1-4*, JSNTS 39 (Sheffield: JSOT Press, 1990).

Davies, W.D., *Paul and Rabbinic Judaism: Some Rabbinic Elements in Pauline Theology* (London: SPCK, [1948] 1955).

____, 'Paul and the Gentiles: A Suggestion Concerning Romans 11:13-24', in *Jewish and Pauline Studies* (Philadelphia: Fortress, 1984), 153-163. Originally published as 'Romans 11:13-24. A Suggestion', in *Melanges offerts à Marcel Simon. Paganisme, Judaïsme, Christianisme*, Editions E. (Paris: de Boccard, 1978), 131-144.

____, 'Paul and the People of Israel', in *Jewish and Pauline Studies* (Philadelphia: Fortress, 1984), 123-152. Originally published in *NTS* 24 (1978), 4-39.

____, *Jewish and Pauline Studies* (Philadelphia: Fortress, 1984).

Deidun, T.J., 'Romans', in R.J. Coggins and J.L. Houlden (eds.), *A Dictionary of Biblical Interpretation* (London: SCM, 1990), 601-604.

Deissmann, A., 'ἱλαστήριος und ἱλαστήριον. Eine lexikalische Studie', *ZNW* 4 (1903), 193-212.

———, *Paul: A Study in Social and Religious History*, trans. W.E. Wilson (New York: Harper & Brothers Publishers, [1912, 1927²] reprinted 1957).

Delitzsch, F., *Biblical Commentary on the Prophecies of Isaiah*, Clark's Foreign Theological Library New Series 44, trans. S.R. Driver (2 Vols., Edinburgh: T&T Clark, 1890).

Dinter, Paul E., 'Paul and the Prophet Isaiah', *BTB* 13 (1983), 48-52.

Dodd, C.H., *The Epistle of Paul to the Romans*, MNTC (London: Collins, [1932] 1959).

———, *The Apostolic Preaching and its Developments* (London: Hodder & Stoughton, 1936, reset 1972).

Doeve, J.W., 'Some Notes with Reference to τὰ λόγια τοῦ θεοῦ in Romans 3.2', in J.N. Sevenster & W.C. van Unnik (eds.), *Studia Paulina in honorem Johannis de Zwaan Septuagenarii* (Haarlem: De Erven F. Bohn, 1953), 111-123.

Donaldson, T.L., '"Riches for the Gentiles" (Rom 11:12): Israel's Rejection and Paul's Gentile Mission', *JBL* 112 (1993), 81-98.

Donfried, K.P., 'Romans 3:21-28', *Interp* 34 (1980), 59-64.

Dover, K.J., *Greek Homosexuality* (Cambridge: Harvard University Press, 1978).

Dunn, J.D.G., *Jesus and the Spirit: A Study of the Religious and Charismatic Experience of Jesus and the First Christians as Reflected in the New Testament* (London: SCM, 1975).

———, *Christology in the Making: An Inquiry into the Origins of the Doctrine of the Incarnation* (London: SCM, [1980] 1989²).

———, '"A Light to the Gentiles": The Significance of the Damascus Road Christophany for Paul', in L. Hurst and N.T. Wright (eds.), *The Glory of Christ in the New Testament* (Oxford: Clarendon Press, 1987), 251-266.

———, 'Paul's Epistle to the Romans: An Analysis of Structure and Argument', *ANRW* 2.25.4, 2842-2890.

———, '"Righteousness from the Law" and "Righteousness from Faith": Paul's Interpretation of Scripture in Romans 10:1-10', in G.F. Hawthorne with O. Betz (eds.), *Tradition and Interpretation in the New Testament: Essays in Honor of E.E. Ellis* (Grand Rapids: Eerdmans; Tübingen: J.C.B. Mohr [Paul Siebeck], 1987), 216-228.

____, 'The New Perspective on Paul', *BJRL* 65 (1983), 95-122.
____, *Romans*, WBC 38A-B (2 Vols., Dallas: Word Books, 1988).
____, 'The New Perspective on Paul', reprinted with Additional Notes in *Jesus, Paul and the Law* (London: SPCK, 1990), 183-214.
____, *Jesus, Paul and the Law* (London: SPCK, 1990).
____, 'Yet Once More – "The Works of the Law"', *JSNT* 46 (1992), 99-117.
____, 'Romans, Letter to the', *DPL*, 838-850.
Earle, R., *Word Meanings in the New Testament* One-Volume Edition (Grand Rapids: Baker, [1974, 1977, 1980, 1982] 1989).
Eckstein, H.-J., *Der Begriff Syneidesis bei Paulus*, WUNT 2.10 (Tübingen: J.C.B. Mohr, 1983).
Edersheim, A., *The Life and Times of Jesus the Messiah* (Peabody: Hendrickson, [1883, 1886^3] reprinted n.d.).
Edgar, S.L., 'Respect for the Context of Quotations from the Old Testament', *NTS* 9 (1962-63), 55-62.
Eisenman, R. and Wise, M., *The Dead Sea Scroll Uncovered: The First Complete Translation and Interpretation of 50 Key Documents Withheld for Over 35 Years* (Shaftesbury, Dorset; Rockport, Massachusetts; Brisbane, Queensland: Element Books, 1992).
Elliott, N., *The Rhetoric of Romans: Argumentatative Constraint and Strategy and Paul's Dialogue with Judaism*, JSNTS 45 (Sheffield: JSOT Press, 1990).
Ellis, E.E., *Paul's Use of the Old Testament* (Grand Rapids: Baker, 1957).
____, *The Old Testament in Early Christianity: Canon and Interpretation in the Light of Modern Research*, WUNT 54 (Tübingen, J.C.B. Mohr [Paul Siebeck], 1991).
Ellison, H.L., *The Mystery of Israel: An Exposition of Romans 9-11* (Exeter: Paternoster, [1966] 1976^3).
Epp, E.J., 'Jewish–Gentile Continuity in Paul: Torah and/or Faith (Romans 9:1-5)', *HTR* 79 (1986), 80-90.
Ericksen, R.P., *Theologians Under Hitler* (New Haven: Yale University Press, 1985).
Evans, C.A., 'Paul and the Hermeneutics of "True Prophecy": A Study of Romans 9-11', *Bib* 65 (1984), 560-570.
Ferguson, E., *Backgrounds of Early Christianity* (Grand Rapids: Eerdmans, 1987).
Fiedler, P., 'ἀσεβής', *EDNT* 1, 168-169.
Field, D.H., 'Homosexuality', *IBD* 2, 657.
Fischer, J.A., 'Pauline Literary Forms and Thought Patterns', *CBQ* 39 (1977), 209-223.

Fishbane, M., *Biblical Interpretation in Ancient Israel* (Oxford: Clarendon Press, 1985).
Fitzer, G., 'Der Ort der Versöhnung nach Paulus: Zu der Frage des "Sühnopfers Jesu"', *ThZ* 22 (1966), 161-183.
Fitzer, G., 'πορνεία', *EDNT* 3, 137-139.
Fitzmyer, J.A., 'The Use of Explicit Old Testament Quotations in Qumran Literature and the New Testament', *NTS* 7 (1960-61), 297-333.
_____, 'The Letter to the Romans', in R.E. Brown, J.A. Fitzmyer and R.E. Murphy (eds.), *The New Jerome Biblical Commentary* (Eaglewood Cliffs: Prentice Hall, [1968] 1990²), 830-868.
_____, *Romans: A New Translation with Introduction and Commentary*, AnBib 33, New York (London/Toronto/Sydney/Auckland: Doubleday, 1993).
France, R.T., 'The Formula Quotations of Matthew 2 and the Problem of Communications', *NTS* 27 (1980-81), 233-251.
_____, *The Gospel According to Matthew: An Introduction and Commentary* (Leicester: IVP, 1985).
Fridrichen, A., 'The Apostle and his Messege', *Uppsala Universitets Aarsskrift* (1947.3), 1-23.
Friedrich, G., 'Das Gesetz des Glaubens Röm 3,27', *ThZ* 10 (1954), 401-417.
Fryer, N.S.L., 'The Meaning and Translation of *Hilasterion* in Romans 3:25', *EvQ* 59 (1987), 99-116.
Gager, J.G., *The Origins of Anti-Semitism: Attitudes toward Judaism in Pagan and Christian Antiquity* (Oxford/New York: Oxford University Press, 1983).
Gardiner, F., *The Old and New Testaments in Their Mutual Relations* (New York: James Port, 1885).
Garlington, D.B., 'ΙΕΡΟΣΥΛΕΙΝ and the Idolatry of Israel (Romans 2.22)', *NTS* 36 (1990), 142-151.
Gaston, L., *Paul and the Torah* (Vancouver: University of British Columbia Press, 1987).
Gempf, C., 'Athens, Paul at', *DPL*, 51-54.
Getty, M.A., 'Paul on the Covenants and the Future of Israel', *BTB* 17 (1987), 92-99.
_____, 'Paul and the Salvation of Israel: A Perspective on Romans 9-11', *CBQ* 50 (1988), 456-469.
Giblin, C.H., '"As It Is Written ..." A Basic Problem in Noematics', *CBQ* 20 (1958), 477-498.
Gifford, E.H., *The Epistle of St. Paul to the Romans with Notes and Introduction* (London: John Murray, 1886).

Godet, F., *Commentary on St. Paul's Epistle to the Romans*, trans. A. Cusin (2 Vols., Edinburgh: T&T Clark [1883] 1892).

Godsey, John, 'The Interpretation of Romans in the History of Christian Faith', *Interp* 34 (1980), 3-16.

Gore, C., *St. Paul's Epistle to the Romans: A Practical Exposition* (2 Vols., London: John Murphy, 1902).

Grässer, E., *Der Alte Bund im Neun: Exegetische Studien zur Israelfrage im Neuen Testament* (Tübingen: J.C.B. Mohr [Paul Siebeck], 1985).

Grayston, K., '"Not Ashamed of the Gospel". Romans 1,16a and the Structure of the Epistle', in F.L. Cross (ed.), *Studia Evangelica II* (Berlin: Akademie-Verlag, 1964), 569-573.

Griffith, G.O., *St. Paul's Gospel to the Romans* (Oxford: Blackwell, 1949).

Guerra, A.J., 'Romans 4 as Apologetic Theology', *HTR* 81 (1988), 251-270.

____, 'Romans: Paul's Purpose and Audience with Special Attention to Romans 9-11', *RevBib* 97 (1990), 219-237.

Gundry-Volf, J.M., 'Expiation, Propitiation, Mercy Seat', *DPL*, 279-284.

Gunther, J. J., *St. Paul's Opponents and Their Background: A Study of Apocalyptic and Jewish Sectarian Teachings*, SNovT 35 (Leiden: E.J. Brill, 1973).

Guthrie, D., *New Testament Introduction* (Leicester: IVP, 1970).

Hafemann, S., 'The Salvation of Israel in Romans 11:25-32: A Response to Krister Stendahl', *ExAud* 4 (1988), 38-58.

____, 'Paul and His Interpreters' in *DPL*, 666-679.

Hahn, F., *Mission in the New Testament*, trans. F. Clark (London: SCM, [1963] 1965).

Haldane, R., *An Exposition of the Epistle to the Romans* (MacDrill, Florida: MacDonald Publishing Co., n.d., cf. 1958).

Hall, D.R., 'Romans 3.1-8 Reconsidered', *NTS* 29 (1983), 183-197.

Hall, W.S., *Paul as a Christian Prophet in His Interpretation of the Old Testament in Romans 9-11* (Ann Arbor: University Microfilms International, 1982).

Hanson, A.T., *Studies in Paul's Technique and Theology* (London: SPCK, 1974).

____, *The Paradox of the Cross in the Thought of St. Paul*, JSNTS 17 (Sheffield: Sheffield Academic Press, 1987).

Harnack, A., *The Expansion of Christianity* (London: Williams & Norgate, [1904] 1958^5).

Haynes, S., '"Rediscovering the Real Paul": Theology and Exegesis in Romans 9-11', *ExAud* 4 (1988), 70-84.
Hays, R.B., 'Psalm 143 and the Logic of Romans 3', *JBL* 99 (1980), 107-115.
___, '"Have We Found Abraham to Be Our Forefather according to the Flesh?": A Reconsideration of Rom 4:1', *NovT* 27 (1985), 76-98.
___, 'Relations Natural and Unnatural: A Response to John Boswell's Exegesis of Romans 1', *JRE* 14 (1986), 184-215.
___, *Echoes of Scripture in the Letters of Paul* (New Haven/London: Yale University Press, 1989).
___, 'Christ Prays the Psalm: Paul's Use of an Early Christian Exegetical Convention', in A.J. Malherbe and W.A. Meeks (eds.), *The Future of Christology: Essays in Honor of L.E. Keck* (Minneapolis: Fortress, 1993), 122-136.
___, 'On the Rebound: A Response to Critiques of *Echoes of Scripture in the Letters of Paul*', in C.A. Evans and J.A. Sanders (eds.), *Paul and the Scriptures of Israel*, JSNTS 83 (Sheffield, JSOT Press, 1993), 70-96.
Hengel, M., *The Zealots: Investigations into the Jewish Freedom Movement in the Period from Herod I until 70 A.D.*, trans. D. Smith (Edinburgh: T&T Clark, [1961, 1976] 1989).
___, *Judaism and Hellenism: Studies in their Encounter in Palestine during the Early Hellenistic Period*, trans. J. Bowden (2 Vols., London: SCM, [1973^2] 1974).
___, *Between Jesus and Paul: Studies in the Earliest History of Christianity*, trans. J. Bowden (London: SCM, 1983.)
___, *Earliest Christianity* (London: SCM, 1986).
___, *The Pre-Christian Paul*, trans. J. Bowden (London: SCM; Philadelphia: Trinity International Press, 1991).
Henry, P., *New Directions in New Testament Study* (Philadelphia: Westminster, 1979; London: SCM, 1980).
Hill, G., *The Discovery Bible* (Chicago: Moody Press, 1987).
Hodge, C., *A Commentary on Romans*, (Edinburgh/Carlisle: Banner of Truth, [1835, 1864, 1972] reprinted 1975).
Hofius, O., 'Das Evangelium und Israel: Erwägungen zu Römer 9-11', *ZTK* 83 (1986), 297-324.
Holter, K., 'A Note on the Old Testament Background of Rom 1,23-27', *BibNot* 69 (1993), 21-23.
Holtz, T., 'Zum Selbstverständnis des Apostels Paulus', *ThLZ* 91 (1966), 321-330.
Hooker, M., 'Adam in Romans 1', *NTS* 6 (1959-60), 297-306.

———, 'A Further Note on Romans 1', *NTS* 13 (1966-67), 181-183.
———, *Continuity and Discontinuity: Early Christianity in its Jewish Setting* (London: Epworth Press, 1986).
Howard, G., 'Romans 3:21-31 and the Inclusion of the Gentiles', *HTR* 63 (1970), 223-233.
Hübner, H., *Law in Paul's Thought*, trans. J.C.G. Greig (Edinburgh: T&T Clark, [1978] 1984).
Hultgren, A., *Paul's Gospel and Mission: The Outlooks from His Letter to the Romans* (Philadelphia: Fortress, 1985).
Hudson, J.T., *The Pauline Epistles and Their Meaning and Message* (London: James Clarke & Co., 1958).
Hunter, A.M., *Paul and His Predecessors* (London: SCM, [1940] 1961²).
Hvalvik, R.A., '"To the Jew First and also to the Greek": The Meaning of Romans 1:16b', *Mishkan* 10 (1989), 1-8.
———, '"SONDERWEG" for Israel: A Critical Examination of a Current Interpretation of Romans 11.25-27', *JSNT* 38 (1990) 87-107.
Hyldahl, N., 'A Reminiscence of the Old Testament at Romans i. 23', *NTS* 2 (1955-56), 285-288.
Jeremias, J., ''Αβραάμ', *TDNT* 1, 8-9.
———, *Jesus' Promise to the Nations*, trans. S.H. Hooke (London: SCM, [1956] 1958).
———, *Jerusalem in the Times of Jesus: An Investigation into Economic and Social Conditions during the New Testament Period*, trans. F.H. & C.H. Cave (London: SCM, [1962, 1967] 1969).
Jervell, J., 'The Letter to Jerusalem', reprinted in *Romans Debate* 53-64.
Jervis, L.Ann, *The Purpose of Romans: A Comparative Letter Structure Investigation*, JSNTS 55 (Sheffield: JSOT Press, 1991).
Jewett, R., 'Major Impulses in the Theological Interpretation of Romans Since Barth', *Interp* 34 (1980), 17-31.
———, 'Romans as an Ambassadorial Letter', *Interp* 36 (1982), 5-20.
———, 'Ecumenical Theology for the Sake of Mission: Romans 1-17 + 15:14-16:24', *SBL 1992 Seminar Papers* (Atlanta: Scholars Press, 1992), 598-612.
Jocz, J., *The Jewish People and Jesus Christ: A Study in the Relationship between the Jewish People and Jesus Christ* (London: SPCK, 1949).
Johnson, E.E., 'Jews and Christians in the New Testament: John, Matthew, and Paul', *RefR* 42 (1988), 113-128.
Johnson, S.L., 'Studies in Romans', *BibSac* 130 (1973), 329-337.

Kähler, M., *Schriften zur Christologie und Mission* (Munich: Chr. Kaiser Verlag, [1908] 1971).
Kaiser, Jr., W.C., *The Uses of the Old Testament in the New* (Chicago: Moody Press, 1985).
Karris, R.J., 'The Occasion of Romans: A Response to Prof. Donfried', reprinted in *Romans Debate*, 65-84.
Käsemann, E., 'Zum Verständnis von Römer 3, 24-26', in *Exegetische Versuche und Besinnungen* I (Göttingen: Vandenhoeck & Ruprecht, 1960), 96-100.
———, 'Justification and Salvation History in the Epistle to the Romans', *Perspectives on Paul* (London: SCM, 1971), 60-78.
———, 'The Faith of Abraham in Romans 4', *Perspectives on Paul* (London: SCM, 1971), 79-101.
———, *Perspectives on Paul* (London: SCM, 1971).
———, *Commentary on Romans* trans. and ed. by G.W. Bromiley (London: SCM, [1973], 1980).
Kautzsch, E., *De Veteris Testamenti locis a Paulo Apostolo allegatis* (Leipzig: Metzger und Wittig, 1869).
Kaylor, R.D., *Paul's Covenant Community: Jew and Gentile in Romans* (Atlanta: John Knox Press, 1988).
Keck, L.E., 'The Function of Rom 3:10-18; Observations and Suggestions', in J. Jervell and W.A. Meeks (eds.), *Studies in Honor of N.A. Dahl* (Oslo: Universitetsforlaget, 1977), 141-157.
———, 'Romans 1:18-23', *Interp* 40 (1986), 402-406.
———, *Paul and His Letters: Revised and Enlarged* (Philadelphia: Fortress, [1979] 1988^2).
Keener, C.S., *The IVP Bible Background Commentary, New Testament* (Downers Grove, Ill.: IVP, 1993).
Kennedy, H.A.A., 'St. Paul's Apostolic Consciousness and the Interpretation of the Epistles', *ExpT* 27 (1915-16), 8-13.
Kertelge, K., *"Rechtfertigung" bei Paulus: Studien zur Struktur und zum Bedeutungsgehalt des paulinischen Rechtfertigungsbegriffs* (Münster: Aschendorff, [1967] 1971^2).
Kettunen, M., *Der Abfassungszweck des Römerbriefs*, Annales Academiae scientarum Fennicae: dissertations humanarum literterum 18 (Helsinki: Suomalainen Tiedeakatemia, 1979).
Kim, S., *The Origin of Paul's Gospel* (Grand Rapids: Eerdmans, [1981] 1984^2).
Kirk, K.E., *The Epistle to the Romans with Introduction and Commentary* (Oxford: Clarendon Press, 1937).
Kissane, E.J., *The Book of Psalms* (2 Vols., Dublin: Richview, 1953).
Kitchen, K.A., 'Calf, Golden', *IBD* 1, 225-226.

Klausner, J., *From Jesus to Paul*, trans. W. Stinespring (New York: Menorah, [1939, 1943] reprinted 1979).
Klein, G., 'Paul's Purpose in Writing the Epistle to the Romans', reprinted in *Romans Debate*, 29-43.
Knox, J., 'The Epistle to the Romans', in *Interpreter's Bible* Vol. 9 (Nashville: Abingdon, 1954).
____, 'Romans 15:14-33 and Paul's Conception of his Apostolic Mission', *JBL* 83 (1964), 1-11.
Koch, D.-A., *Die Schrift als Zeuge des Evangeliums* (Tübingen: J.C.B. Mohr [Paul Siebeck], 1986).
König, A., 'Gentiles or Gentile Christians? On the meaning of Rom. 2:12-16', *JThSAf* 15 (1976), 53-60.
Kugel, J.L. and Greer, R.A., *Early Biblical Interpretation*, Library of Early Christianity (Philadelphia: Westminster Press, 1986).
Kuhr, F., 'Römer 2:14f. und die Verheissung bei Jeremia 31:31ff.', *ZNW* 55 (1964), 243-261.
Kümmel, W.G., *Theology of the New Testament*, trans. J.E. Steely (London: SCM, [1972] 1974).
____, *Introduction to the New Testament* (London: SCM, revised 1975).
____, 'Die Probleme von Römer 9-11 in der gegenwärtigen Forschungslage', in L. de Lorenzi (ed.), *Die Israelfrage nach Römer 9-11* (Rome, 1977, 14-33).
Lacey, D.R. de, 'Gentiles', *DPL*, 335-339.
Lagrange, M.-J., *Saint Paul: Epître aux Romains* (Paris: J. Gabalda, [1915, 1922] 1950^6).
Lapide, P. and Stuhlmacher, P., *Paul Rabbi and Apostle*, trans. L.W. Denef (Minneapolis: Augsburg, [1981] 1984).
Leenhardt, F.J., *The Epistle to the Romans: A Commentary*, trans. H. Knight (London: Lutterworth Press, [1957] 1961).
Liddon, H.P., *Explanatory Analysis of St. Paul's Epistle to the Romans* (London: Longmans, Green, & Co., [1876] 1899^4).
Lietzmann, H., *An die Römer*, HNT 8 (Tübingen: J.C.B. Mohr, [1933] reprinted 1971).
Lightfoot, J.B., *A Commentary on the New Testament from the Talmud and Hebraica* (4 Vols., Peabody: Hendrickson, [1859] reprinted 1989).
____, *Saint Paul's Epistle to the Galatians* (London: Macmillan, 1865).
____, *Notes on Epistle of St. Paul from Unpublished Commentaries* (London/New York: MacMillan, 1895).
Lincoln, A.T., *Ephesians*, WBC 42 (Dallas: Word Books, 1990).

____, 'Abraham Goes to Rome: Paul's Treatment of Abraham in Romans 4', in M.J. Wilkins and T. Paige (eds.), *Worship, Theology and Ministry in the Early Church: Essays in Honor of R.P. Martin* (Sheffield: JSOT Press,1992), 163-179.

____, 'From Wrath to Justification: Tradition, Gospel and Audience in the Theology of Romans 1:18-4:25', *SBL 1993 Seminar Papers* (Chico: Scholars Press, 1993), 194-226.

Lindars, B., *New Testament Apologetic* (London: SCM, 1961).

Locke, J., *A Paraphrase and Notes on the Epistles of St Paul*, The Clarendon Edition of the Works of John Locke, edited with an Introduction by A.W. Wainwright (2 Vols., Oxford: Clarendon Press, 1987).

Longenecker, B.W., 'Different Answers to Different Issues: Israel, the Gentiles and Salvation History in Romans 9-11', *JSNT* 36 (1989), 95-123.

____, *Eschatology and the Covenant: A Comparison of 4 Ezra and Romans 1-11*, JSNTS 57 (Sheffield: Sheffield Academic Press, 1991).

Longenecker, R.N., *Paul the Apostle of Liberty* (New York: Harper and Row, 1964).

____, 'The "Faith of Abraham" Theme in Paul, James and Hebrews: A Study in the Circumstantial Nature of New Testament Teaching', *JETS* 20 (1977), 203-212.

Lorenzi, L.de (ed.), *Die Israelfrage nach Röm 9-11*, Monographische Reihe von Benedictina, Biblisch-ökumenische Abteilung 3 (Rom: Abtei von St. Paul vor den Mauern, 1977).

Luther, M., *Commentary on Romans* (Grand Rapids: Kregel, [1954] 1976).

____, *Luther's Works Vol. 35, Word and Sacrament I*, ed. And trans. Bachmann (Philadelphia: Muhlenberg, 1960).

Luz, U., *Das Geschichtsverständnis des Paulus* (München: Kaiser Verlag, 1968).

Maccoby, H., *Early Rabbinic Writings*, Cambridge Commentaries on Writings of the Jewish and Christian World 200 BC to AD 200 Vol. 3 (Cambridge: Cambridge University Press, 1988).

____, *Paul and Hellenism* (London: SCM; Philadelphia: Trinity Press International, 1991).

Manson, T.W., "ΙΛΑΣΤΗΡΙΟΝ', *JTS* 46 (1945), 1-10.

____, *Studies in the Gospels and Epistles*, ed. by M. Black (London: Westminster Press, 1962).

Manson, W., 'Notes on the Argument of Romans (Chapters 1-8)', in A.J.B. Higgins (ed.), *New Testament Essays Studies in Memory of*

T.W. Manson (Manchester: Manchester University Press, 1959), 150-164.
Marshall, I.H., *The Acts of the Apostles: An Introduction and Commentary*, TNTC (Leicester: IVP, 1984).
Martin, R.P., *Reconciliation: A Study of Paul's Theology* (London: Marshall, Morgan & Scott, 1981).
____, 'Romans, Letter to the', in W.H. Gentz (ed.), *The Dictionary of the Bible and Religion* (Nashville, Abingdon, 1986), 902-903.
____, 'Worship', *DPL*, 982-991.
____, *2 Corinthians*, WBC 40 (Waco: Word Books, 1986).
Marxsen, W., *Introduction to the New Testament* (Philadelphia: Fortress, 1968).
Mason, S., *Josephus and the New Testament* (Peabody: Hendrickson, 1992).
McKnight, S., *A Light Among the Gentiles: Jewish Missionary Activity in the Second Temple Period* (Minneapolis: Fortress, 1991).
McNeile, A.H., *St. Paul: His Life, Letters, and Christian Doctrine* (Cambridge: Cambridge University Press, 1920).
Metzger, B.M., *A Textual Commentary on the Greek New Testament* (London/New York: UBS, [1971] 1975).
Meyer, H.A.W., *The Epistle to the Romans*, trans. J.C. Moore, Critical and Exegetical Commentary on the New Testament, Part IV (2 Vols., Edinburgh: T&T Clark, 1876).
Michel, O., *Paulus und seine Bibel* (Gütersloh: C. Bertelsmann, 1929; reprinted Darmstadt: Wissenschaftliche Buchgesellschaft, 1972).
____, *Der Brief an die Römer* (Göttingen: Vandenhoeck & Ruprecht, $1966^{13}, 1978^{14}$).
Milne, D.J.W., 'Genesis in the Letter to the Romans', *RTR* 39 (1980), 10-18.
Minear, P.S., *The Obedience of Faith: The Purposes of Paul in the Epistle to the Romans*, SBT 2.19 (London: SCM, 1971).
Moiser, J., 'Rethinking Romans 12-15', *NTS* 36 (1990), 571-582.
Moo, D., *Romans 1-8*, WEC (Chicago: Moody Press, 1991).
Morris, L., 'The Meaning of ἱλαστήριον in Romans iii.25', *NTS* 2 (1955-56), 33-43.
____, *The Apostolic Preaching of the Cross: A Study of the Significance of Some New Testament Terms* (Grand Rapids: Eerdmans, [1955, 1960] 1965^3 reprinted 1988).
____, *The Epistle to the Romans* (Grand Rapids: Eerdmans; Leicester: IVP, 1988).
Motyer, S., *Israel in the Plan of God: Light on Today's Debate* (Leicester: IVP, 1989).

Moule, H.C.G., *The Epistle to the Romans* (Fort Washington: Christian Literature Crusade, [1928] 1975).
Mowinckel, S., *The Psalms in Israel's Worship* (Oxford: Blackwell, 1962).
Moxnes, H., *Theology in Conflict: Studies in Paul's Understanding of God in Romans*, SNovT 53 (Leiden: E.J. Brill, 1980).
Müller, P., 'Grundlinien paulinischer Theologie (Röm 15:14-33)', *KD* 35 (1989), 212-235.
Munck, J., *Paul and the Salvation of Mankind*, trans. F. Clarke (Atlanta: John Knox Press, [1954] 1959).
____, *Christ and Israel: An Interpretation of Romans 9-11* (Philadelphia: Fortress, 1967).
Murray, J., *The Epistle to the Romans: The English Text with Introduction, Exposition and Notes* (2 Vols., Grand Rapids: Eerdmans, [1959, 1965, 1968] reprinted 1987).
Mussner, '"Christus, des Gesetzes Ende zur Gerechtigkeit für jeden, der glaubt" (Röm 10,4)', in *Paulus–Apostat oder Apostel* (Regensburg: Pustet, 1977), 31-44.
____, '"Ganz Israel wird gerettet werden" (Röm 11,26): Versuch einer Auslegung', *Kairos* 18 (1976), 241-255.
____, 'Heil für Alle: Der Grundgedanke des Römerbriefs', *Kairos* 23 (1981), 207-214.
____, *Tractate on the Jews: The Significance of Judaism for Christian Faith* (London: SPCK; Philadelphia: Fortress, 1984).
Newman, B.M. and Nida, E.A., *A Translator's Handbook on Paul's Letter to the Romans*, Helps for Translators 14 (London: UBS, 1973).
Newman, C.C., *Paul's Glory-Christology: Tradition and Rhetoric*, SNovT 69 (Leiden: E.J. Brill, 1992).
Nickelsburg, G.W.E., *Jewish Literature between the Bible and the Mishnah: A Historical and Literary Introduction* (London: SCM, 1981).
Noack, B., 'Current and Backwater in the Epistle to the Romans', *StTh* 19 (1965), 155-166.
North, C.R., *Isaiah 40-55*, Torch Bible Paperbacks (London: SCM, [1952] 1964).
Nygren, A., *Commentary on Romans*, trans. C.C. Rasmussen (Philadelphia: Fortress, [1944, 1949, 1972] reprinted 1988).
O'Brien, P.T., *Introductory Thanksgivings in the Letters of Paul*, SNovT 49 (Leiden: E.J. Brill, 1977).
Oepke, A., 'εἰς', *TDNT* 2, 420-434.

O'Neill, J. C., *Paul's Letter to the Romans* (Harmondsworth: Penguin, 1975).
Oesterley, W.O.E., *The Psalms: Translated with Text-Critical and Exegetical Notes* (London: SPCK, 1959).
Olson, Stanley N., 'Romans 5-8 as Pastoral Theology', *W&W* 4 (1986), 390-397.
Osborne, W.L., 'The Old Testament Background of Paul's "All Israel" in Romans 11:26a', *Asia J Theology* 2 (1988), 282-293.
Oss, D.A., 'A Note on Paul's Use of Isaiah', *BBR* 2 (1992), 105-112.
____, 'Paul's Use of Isaiah and Its Place in His Theology with Special Reference to Romans 9-11', PhD dissertation, Westminster Theological Seminary, 1992.
Oswalt, J.N., 'Golden Calves and the "Bull of Jacob": The Impact on Israel of Its Religious Environment', in A. Gileadi (ed.), *Israel's Apostasy and Restoration: Essays in Honor of R.K. Harrison* (Grand Rapids: Baker, 1988), 9-18.
Parker, T.H.L., *Commentaries on Romans 1532-1542* (Edinburgh: T&T Clark, 1986).
Perowne, J.J.S., *The Book of Psalms: A New Translation with Introductions and Notes Explanatory and Critical*, Vol. 1 (London: G. Bell & Sons, [1864, 1878^4] 1892^8).
Pfeiffer, R.H., *History of New Testament Times with an Introduction to the Apocrypha* (New York: Harper, 1949).
Piper, J., *The Justification of God: An Exegetical & Theological Study of Romans 9:1-23* (Grand Rapids: Baker, [1983] 1993^2).
Plevnik, J., 'The Center of Pauline Theology', *CBQ* 51 (1989), 461-478.
Pohlenz, M., 'Paulus und die Stoa', *ZNW* 42 (1949), 69-104.
Rad, G. von, *Genesis: A Commentary*, trans. J.H. Marks (London: SCM, [1961, 1972^9] rev. ed. 1972).
Räisänen, H., *Paul and the Law* (Tübingen: J.C.B. Mohr, 1983).
____, 'Römer 9-11: Analyse eines geistigen Ringens', *ANRW* 2.25.4, 2891-2939.
____, *Jesus, Paul and Torah: Collected Essays*, trans. D.E. Orton (Sheffield: Sheffield Academic Press, 1992).
Rese, M., 'Die Rettung der Juden nach Römer 11', in A. Vanhoye (ed.), *L'Apôtre Paul: Personnalité, style et conception du ministère* (Louvain: Leuven University, 1986), 422-430.
Reumann, J., *Righteousness in the New Testament* (Philadelphia: Fortress, 1982).
Ridderbos, H., *Paul: Outline of His Theology*, trans. J.R. de Witt (London: SPCK, [1966, 1975] 1977).

Ringgren, H., *The Faith of the Psalmists* (London: SCM, 1963).
Robertson, O.P., 'Genesis 15:6: New Covenant Expositions of an Old Covenant Text', *WTJ* 42 (1979-80), 259-289.
Robinson, D.W.B., 'The Priesthood of Paul in the Gospel of Hope', in R. Banks (ed.), *Reconciliation and Hope: New Testament Essays on Atonement and Eschatology Presented to L.L. Morris on his 60th Birthday* (Grand Rapids: Eerdmans, 1974), 231-245.
Robinson, J.A.T., *Wrestling with Romans* (London: SCM, 1979).
Rubinkiewicz, R. and Lunt, H.G., 'The Apocalypse of Abraham', in J.H. Charlesworth (ed.), *The Old Testament Pseudepigrapha Apocalyptic Literature & Testaments* (New York/London/Toronto/Sydney/Auckland: Doubleday, 1983), 689-705.
Sadler, M.F., *The Epistle to the Romans with Notes Critical and Practical* (London: G. Bell and Sons, 1910).
Sanday, W. and Headlam, A.C., *The Epistle to the Romans*, ICC (Edinburgh: T&T Clark [1895, 1902^5] reprinted 1968).
Sanders, E.P., *Paul and Palestinian Judaism: A Comparison of Patterns of Religion* (London: SCM, 1977).
___, 'Paul's Attitude Toward the Jewish People', *USQR* 33 (1978), 175-187.
___, *Paul, the Law and Jewish People* (London: SCM, 1983).
___, *Jesus and Judaism* (London: SCM, 1985).
Sandnes, K.O., *Paul – One of the Prophets? A Contribution to the Apostle's Self-Understanding*, WUNT 2.43 (Tübingen: J.C.B. Mohr [Paul Siebeck], 1991).
Sänger, D., 'Rettung der Heiden und Erwählung Israels: Einige vorläufige Erwägungen zu Römer 11,25-27', *KD* 32 (1986), 99-119.
Schlatter, A., *The Church in the New Testament Period* (London: SPCK, [1926] 1955).
___, *Gottes Gerechtigkeit: Ein Kommentar zum Römerbrief* (Stuttgart: Calwer, 1952^2).
Schlier, H., *Der Römerbrief* (Freiburg/Basel/Wien: Herder, 1977).
Schmeller, T., *Paulus und die 'Diatribe': Eine vergleichende Stilinterpretation* (Münster: Aschendorff, 1987).
Schmithals, W., *Paul and James*, trans. D.M. Barton (London: SCM, 1965).
Schnabel, E.J., *Law and Wisdom from Ben Sira to Paul*, WUNT 2.16 (Tübingen: J.C.B. Mohr [Paul Siebeck], 1985).
Schnackenburg, R., *The Gospel According to St. John* (3 Vols., New York: Cross Road, 1990).

Schoeps, H.J., *Paul: The Theology of the Apostle in the Light of Jewish Religious History*, trans. H. Knight (London: Lutterworth Press, [1959] 1961).
Schreiner, T.R., '"Works of Law" in Paul', *NovT* 33 (1991), 217-244.
____, 'Israel's Failure to Attain Righteousness in Romans 9:30-10:3', *TriJ* 12 (1991), 209-220.
Schrenk, G., 'Der Römerbrief als Missionsdocument', reprinted in his *Studien zu Paulus* (Zürich: Zwingli-Verlag, [1933] 1954), 81-106.
Schweitzer, A., *The Mysticism of Paul the Apostle* (London: Black, [1931] 1953^2).
____, *Paul and His Interperters: A Critical History*, trans. W. Montgomery (London: Adam and Charles Black, 1912).
Scott, J.M., 'Adoption, Sonship', *DPL*, 15-18.
____, 'Restoration of Israel', *DPL*, 796-805.
Seifrid, M.A., 'Paul's Approach to the Old Testament in Rom 10:6-8', *TriJ* 6 (1985), 3-37.
____, *Justification by Faith: The Origin and Development of a Central Pauline Theme* (Leiden/New York/Köln: E.J. Brill; 1992).
Shedd, W.G.T., *A Critical and Doctrinal Commentary on the Epistle of St. Paul to the Romans* (Grand Rapids: Zondervan, [1879] 1967).
Siegert, F., *Argumentation bei Paulus: gezeigt an Röm 9-11* (Tübingen: J.C.B. Mohr [Paul Siebeck], 1985).
Siker, J.S., 'From Gentile Inclusion to Jewish Exclusion: Abraham in Early Christian Controversy with Jews', *BTB* 19 (1989), 30-36.
____, *Disinheriting the Jews: Abraham in Christian Controversy* (Lousville: Westminster/John Knox Press, 1991).
Silva, M., 'Old Testament in Paul', *DPL*, 630-642.
Simpson, John W., Jr., 'The Future of Non-Christian Jews: 1 Thessalonians 2:15-16 and Romans 9-11', PhD Dissertation, Fuller Theological Seminary, 1988.
Sinclair, S.G., *Jesus Christ According to Paul: The Christologies of Paul's Undisputed Epistles and the Christology of Paul* (Berkeley, California: Bibal Press, 1988).
Stamm, J.J. and Andrew, M.E., *The Ten Commandments in Recent Research*, STB 2.2, trans. M.E. Andrew (London: SCM, [1962] 1967^2).
Stanley, C.D., *Paul and the Language of Scripture: Citation Technique in the Pauline Epistles and Contemporary Literature*, SNTSMS 74 (Cambridge: Cambridge University Press, 1992).
Stanton, G.N., *Jesus of Nazareth in New Testament Preaching* (Cambridge: Cambridge University Press, 1974).

Stendahl, K., *Paul Among Jews and Gentiles and Other Essays* (Philadelphia: Fortress, 1976).

___, *Final Account: Paul's Letter to the Romans* (Minneapolis: Fortress Press, [1993] 1995).

Stevens, George B., *The Pauline Theology: A Study of the Origin and Correlation of the Doctrinal Teachings of the Apostle Paul* (New York: Charles Scribner's Sons, [1892] 1903^2).

Stortz, Martha E., 'Romans and Reform', *W&W* 6 (1986), 369-372.

Stowers, S.K., *The Diatribe and Paul's Letter to the Romans*, SBLDS 57 (Chico: Scholars Press, 1981).

___, 'Paul's Dialogue with a Fellow Jew in Romans 3:1-9', *CBQ* 46 (1984), 707-722.

___, *A Rereading of Romans: Justice, Jews and Gentiles* (New Haven/London: Yale University Press, 1994).

Stuart, M., *A Commentary on the Epistle to the Romans with a Translation and Various Excurses* (London: William Tegg, [1832], 1865^6).

Stuhlmacher, P., *Gerechtigkeit Gottes bei Paulus*, FRLANT 87 (Göttingen: Vandenhoeck & Ruprecht, 1975).

___, 'The Purpose of Romans', reprinted in *Romans Debate*, 231-244.

___, 'Zur neueren Exegese von Röm 3,24-26', in E.E. Ellis and E. Grässer (eds.), *Jesus und Paulus* (Göttingen, Vandenhoeck & Ruprecht, 1975); reprinted in *Versöhnung, Gesetz und Gerechtigkeit* (Göttingen: Vandenhoeck & Ruprecht, 1981), 117-135; trans., 'Recent Exegesis on Rom 3:24-26', *Reconciliation, Law, and Righteousness: Essays in Biblical Theology* (Philadelphia: Fortress, [1981] 1986).

___, *Der Brief an die Römer* (Göttingen: Vandenhoeck & Ruprecht, 1989).

___, *Paul's Letter to the Romans A Commentary*, trans. S.J. Hafemann (Louisville: Westminster/John Knox Press, [1989] 1994).

Suggs, M.J., '"The Word is Near You": Romans 10:6-10 within the Purpose of the Letter', in W.R. Farmer, C.F.D. Moule, R.R. Niebuhr (eds.), *Christian History and Interpretation* (Cambridge: Cambridge University Press, 1967), 289-313.

Swetnam, J., 'The Curious Crux at Romans 4,12', *Bib* 61 (1980), 110-115.

Synge, F.C., 'The Meaning of προεχόμεθα in Romans 3.9', *ExpT* 81 (1970), 351.

Taylor, V., *The Epistle to the Romans* (London: Epworth Press, 1955).

Thompson, J.A., *Deuteronomy: An Introduction and Commentary* (Leicester: IVP, 1974).

Thompson, R.W., 'Paul's Double Critique of Jewish Boasting: A Study of Rom 3:27 in its Context', *Bib* 67 (1986), 520-531.

___, 'The Inclusion of the Gentiles in Rom 3:27-30', *Bib* 69 (1988), 543-546.

Tidball, D.J., 'Social Setting of Mission Churches', *DPL*, 883-892.

Tobin, T.H., 'Controversy and Continuity in Romans 1:18-3:20', *CBQ* 55 (1993), 298-318.

Toit, A.B. du, 'Die Kirche als doxologische Gemeinschaft im Römerbrief', *Neot* 27 (1993), 69-77.

Toorn, K. van der, 'Cultic Prostitution', *ABD* 5, 510-513.

Turner, M.M.B., 'Mission and Meaning in Terms of "Unity" in Ephesians', in A. Billington, T. Lane and M. Turner (eds.), *Mission and Meaning: Essays Presented to P. Cotterell* (Carlisle: Paternoster, 1995), 138-166.

Turner, N., *Grammatical Insights into the New Testament* (Edinburgh: T&T Clark, 1965).

Urbach, E.E., 'Self-Isolation or Self-Affirmation in Judaism in the First Three Centuries: Theory and Practice', in E.P. Sanders (ed.), *Jewish and Christian Self-Definition* 2: Aspects of Judaism in the Graeco-Roman Period (London: SCM, 1981), 269-298.

Vaughan, C.J., *St. Paul's Epistle to the Romans with Notes* (London: MacMillan, [1859] 1880^5).

Vollmer, H.A., *Die alttestamentlichen Citate bei Paulus* (Freiburg: Mohr, 1895).

Waard, J. de, *A Comparative Study of the Old Testament Text in the Dead Sea Scrolls and in the New Testament*, Studies on the Texts of the Desert of Judah 4 (Leiden: E.J. Brill, 1965).

Wagner, G., 'The Future of Israel: Reflection on Romans 9-11', in W.H. Gloer (ed.), *Eschatology and the New Testament: Essays in Honor of George Raymond Beasley-Murray* (Peabody: Hendrickson, 1988), 77-112.

Watson, F., *Paul, Judaism and the Gentiles: A Sociological Approach* (Cambridge: Cambridge University Press, 1986).

Watts, J.D.W., *Isaiah*, WBC 24 (2 Vols., Waco: Word Books, 1985).

Wedderburn, A.J.M., 'Purpose and Occasion of Romans Again', reprinted in *Romans Debate*, 195-202.

___, 'Adam in Paul's Letter to the Romans', *Studia Biblica 1978, III. Papers on Paul and Other New Testament Authors*, Sixth International Congress on Biblical Studies, JSNTS 3 (Sheffield: JSOT Press, 1980), 413-430.

___, *The Reasons for Romans* (Edinburgh: T&T Clark, 1988).

Weiser, A., *The Psalms* (London: SCM, 1962).

Weiss, J., *Earliest Christianity: A History of the Period A.D. 30-150* trans. F.C. Grant (vol. 1) and P.S. Kramer (vol. 2) (New York: Harper, [1937] 1959).
Wellhausen, J., *Prolegomena to the History of Ancient Israel* (New York: World Publishing Co., 1961).
Westermann, C., *Isaiah 40-66 A Commentary*, trans. M.G. Stalker (London: SCM, [1966] 1969).
Wiefel, W., 'The Jewish Community in Ancient Rome and the Origins of Roman Christianity', reprinted in *Romans Debate*, 85-101.
Wigoder, G., *Jewish-Christian Relations since the Second World War* (Manchester/New York: Manchester University Press, 1988).
Wilckens, U., *Der Brief an die Römer* EKK 6.1-3 (3 Vols., Einsiedeln: Benzieger; Neukirchen-Vluyn: Neukirchen-Verlag, 1978, 1980, 1982).
Winston, D., *The Wisdom of Solomon: A New Translation with Introduction and Commentary*, AnBib 43 (New York/London/Toronto/Sydney/Auckland: Doubleday, 1979).
Wright, D.F., 'Homosexuals or Prostitutes? The Meaning of Ἀρσενοκοῖται (1 Cor 6:9; 1 Tim 1:10)', *VigChr* 38 (1984), 125-153.
___, 'Homosexuality', in *DPL*, 413-415.
Wright, N. T., *The Messiah and the People of God: A Study in Pauline Theology with Particular Reference to the Argument of the Epistle to the Romans*, PhD Dissertation, Oxford University, 1980.
___, *The Climax of the Covenant: Christ and the Law in Pauline Theology* (Edinburgh: T&T Clark, 1991).
___, 'Romans and the Theology of Paul', *SBL 1992 Seminar Papers* (Atlanta: Scholars Press, 1992), 184-213.
___, *The New Testament and the People of God* (London: SPCK, 1992).
Wuellner, W., 'Paul's Rhetoric of Argumentation in Romans: An Alternative to the Donfried-Karris Debate Over Romans', reprinted in *Romans Debate*, 128-146.
Wuest, K.S., 'Romans in the Greek New Testament', *Wuest's Word Studies from the Greek New Testament for the English Reader*, Vol. 1: Mark, Romans, Galatians, Ephesians and Colossians (Grand Rapids: Eerdmans, [1955] 1973).
Young, J.B. de, 'The Meaning of "Nature" in Romans 1 and Its Implications for Biblical Proscriptions of Homosexual Behavior', reprinted in J.I. Packer (ed.), *The Best in Theology*, Vol 4 (Carol Stream, Ill.: Christianity Today, Inc., 1990), 85-97; originally in *JETS* 31 (1988), 429-441.

Zeller, D., *Juden und Heiden in der Mission des Paulus: Studien zum Römerbrief* (Stuttgart: Katholisches Bibelwerk, [1973] 1976²).

Zerwick, M., *Biblical Greek Illustrated by Examples*, English Edition Adopted from the Latin Edition (Rome: J. Smith, 1963).

Ziesler, J., *Pauline Christianity*, OBS (Oxford: Oxford University Press, 1983).

———, *Paul's Letter to the Romans* TPINTC (London: SCM; Philadelphia: Trinity Press International, 1989).

Index of Passages

I. OLD TESTAMENT*
*The mark (S) indicates "Septuagint text".

Genesis

1	82
1-3	74, 78, 79n
1:20ff	76
1:20-26	77
1:20-30	78
1:21	77
1:24	77
1:25	77
1:26	76, 77, 79n
1:26ff	74
1:27	77
1:28	77
1:30	77, 78
3	78
12:2	198
12:3	200, 262n
12:7	198, 199
13:13	85n
13:16	198
15	198
15:1(S)	184
15:2-3	198
15:4-5	198
15:4-6	182, 198, 200
15:5	198, 199, 199n
15:6	182, 182n, 183, 184, 184n, 185, 188, 190n, 198, 198n, 199,199n, 200, 201, 201n
15:6(S)	203n
15:16	90
15:18	199
16	198
17	198
17:2-4	226
17:4	262n
17:4-5	197n
17:4-6	200
17:4-7	182
17:5	182, 196, 197, 197n
17:8	199
17:10-11	123
17:12-14	189
17:15-16	197n
17:17-18	198
17:17-22	182
19:5	84, 84n
19:7	86n
22	201n
22:12	148
22:16	201n
22:18	201n
25:23	232n
26:8	84n
34:7	85n, 86n
42:20	201n
45:26	201n

Exodus

3:14	34
4:21	231, 256n
4:22	226, 232n
6:7	172, 229
7:3	231
7:22-23	256n
8:15	256n
8:23	158
8:32	256n
9:4	158
9:6	231n
9:16(S)	58
10:1	256n
10:20	231
10:23	158
10:27	231, 256n
11:7	158
11:10	231
12:13	158
12:23	158
12:27	158
13:21	226
14:4	231
14:7	231
19:4-6	199
19:5	100
20:2	173, 177
20:3-6	80, 92
20:4	81
20:6	60
20:20	148
20:23	81
22:21	194
23:3	105n
23:7	162, 185n
23:31	90n
32:1-4	81
32:4-8	80n
32:6	84n, 86
32:9	101
32:18-25	80n
32:32	226n
32:35	80n
33:13	231n
33:16	231, 231n
33:17	231n
33:19	231n, 238
33:19(S)	231
33:20	89n

34:9	231n	4:7-8	172, 226	28:43-44	172
34:10	172, 231n	4:12	89n	29	257
34:14	81	4:13	226	29:2-3	257
34:17	81	4:13-14	111n	29:2-15	226
34:27	226	4:15-18	74, 75, 76, 78, 80, 81, 93	29:3(S)	256
				29:4	231, 257, 257n
Leviticus		4:15-18(S)	80n	29:10	257
9:6	226	4:16	76	29:12	257
18	85, 86	4:23	81	29:15	257
18:5	124, 242	4:32-34	226	29:18-19	101, 101n
18:21	81n	5:10	60	29:19-21	116
18:22	85	6:2	148	30:2	41
19:4	81	6:4	174	30:6	127
19:15	105n	6:6	113	30:11-14	111n, 242
20	86	7:6	44, 172, 229	30:12-14	242n
20:13	85	7:8	105n	30:14	113, 242, 243
23:24	226	7:14	105n	30:16	124
26:1	81	7:25	81	31:6	253
26:9	105n	9:16	80n	31:27	101
26:25	90	9:21	80n	32	61
26:40-41	127	9:27	101	32:5	100, 246
26:40-42	282n	9:29	100	32:6	173
26:43	282n	10:14-22	105n	32:8-9	173n
26:44	282n	10:15	105n	32:15-18	81
		10:16	101, 127	32:16f	246
Numbers		10:17	105n	32:21	246
16:22	173n	10:21	172	32:21(S)	246
21:2	90n	11:16	81	32:35	61
21:3	90n	11:18	113	32:41	61
21:34	90n	12:31	81n	32:43	61
23:19	138n	14:1	173	32:43(S)	61
25	84	14:2	100, 229	32:46	113
25:1-3	81	18:10	81n	33:29	226
25:1-13	84	19:12	90n	37:27	101
26:17	173n	21:20	101		
		23:15	90n	**Joshua**	
Deuteronomy		23:17	85	1:18	147
1:8	90n	23:18	85	2:14	90n
1:17	105n	24:17	105n	2:24	90n
1:43	101	26:16-19	226	7:7	90n
2:24	90n	26:17	41	11:20	231
2:30	231	26:19	100, 172, 229		
4	82	27:15	81	**Judges**	
4:1	111n	28:1	172, 226	1:4	90n
4:5-6	111n	28:12-13	172	2:10-15	90
4:6-8	100	28:13	226	3:7	81

Index of Passages

3:10	90n	16:3	81	30:8	101
3:28	90n	17:7-23	122	36:10	120
6:1	90	17:12-17	81	36:11-14	101
6:13	90n	17:15	88	36:16	120n
13:1	90	17:16-20	80n		
16:23-24	90n	17:37(S)	88	**Ezra**	
19-21	84	18:30(S)	90n	9:7	145
19:22	84, 84n	19:10(S)	90n		
19:22ff	84	19:15	174	**Nehemiah**	
19:23	85, 86, 86n	19:30	269n	9:16-18	101
20:6	85n	21:6	81	9:18	80n
20:27-28	84	21:12	172	9:26	101
		21:14-15(S)	90		
1 Samuel/ 1 Kingdoms		21:21	81	**Job**	
2:22	85	23:7	85, 86	1:22	232
8:7	101	23:10	81	5:9	89n
8:19	101	23:13	82n	9:12	232
12:16-18	282n	23:14	85	10:8-9	232n
12:22	100, 229, 282n			11:7-9	89n
12:25	282n	**1 Chronicles**		13:8	105n
14:10(S)	90n	5:25	145	13:10	105n
14:12(S)	90n	10:13-14	87	23:15	148
17:47(S)	90n			32:20-21	105n
23:4(S)	90n	**2 Chronicles**		33:13	232
28:18-19(S)	90	6:23	103n	34:11	103n
		6:36	138n	34:17-19	105n
2 Samuel/ 2 Kingdoms		10:29	80n	40:2	232
12:7-14	131n	11:14-15	80n		
13:12	85n	12:9	120	**Psalms**	
22:1(S)	60	13:8	80n	2:8-9	65
22:50(S)	59	13:16	90n	5	145
		15:16	85	5:4-10	145
1 Kings/ 3 Kingdoms		16:2	120	5:5-11	162
8:46	138n	16:8	90n	5:10(S)	145
8:47	145	19:7	105n	5:11-12(S)	145
12:26-33	80n	24:19	101	5:12	145
12:32-33	81	24:24	90	7:7-18	162
14:16(S)	90	25:14	81	9	146n
14:24	85	25:20	90	9:5(S)	146
15:12	85	25:24	120	9:9(S)	146
16:31-33	81	27:23	200	9:12(S)	146
19:10	254	28:1-5	90	9:15(S)	146
22:46	85	28:2-4	81	9:16(S)	146
		28:21-25	120	9:17(S)	146
2 Kings/ 4 Kingdoms		30:7	90, 145	9:18(S)	146
3:18(S)	90n	30:7-8	91	9:19(S)	146

Psalms (Cont'd)		32:6	187	77:62(S)	91n
9:20(S)	146	32:8-9	101	78	91
9:22(S)	146	32:10	186n, 187	78:8	101, 145
9:24(S)	146	32:11	187	78:10	120n
9:24-25(S)	146	34:2	172	78:32	101
9:28(S)	145	34:4-22	148	78:57	145
9:33(S)	146	35:2(S)	148	78:65-72	92
9:35(S)	146	35:11(S)	148	79:6	101n
9:36(S)	146	35:28	147	81:11-14	81
9:37(S)	146	37:28	253	82:1-4	105n
9:38(S)	146	37:31	113	86:9	65
10	146n	40:8	113	93:1	177
10:7	146	43:23(S)	278n	94:14	253
13(S)	145, 146	44:8	172	95:8	101
13:1(S)	143, 143n	47	62n	97:1	61n
13:1-3(S)	143, 145	47:9	194n	100	62n, 78
13:4(S)	143	50:6	162	105(S)	84
13:7(S)	143	50:6(S)	130, 131, 132	105:20(S)	74, 75, 76, 76n,
14:1	144n	50:7	173		79, 79n, 80n, 82
14:4-5	144	50:16-23	162	105:34-41(S)	90
16:3	44	51:14-15	147	106	79, 79n, 80, 82, 93
17	58n	60:1-12	43	106:6	145
17:1(S)	60	60:5	43	106:15	80
17:38f(S)	60	62:12	102n, 103n	106:16-22	80
17:42(S)	60	63:3	147	106:19	80
17:45-49(S)	60	63:5	147	106:19-20	80n
17:49f(S)	60	65:8(S)	174n	106:20	75, 78, 79, 79n
17:50(S)	59, 59n, 60	67:3	61n	106:23	80
17:51(S)	60	67:4	61n	106:26	80
17:52(S)	61	67:5	61n	106:26-27	80
18:1-5(S)	245n	68:23f(S)	231, 257	106:28-31	84
18:5(S)	245	68:24(S)	258	106:30	84
19	87	69:4	258, 258n	106:34-41	90
22:27	65, 263n	69:7-12	258	106:37-39	81
22:27-29	62n	69:9	258n	106:40	80
26:2	113	69:18	258	108:1-13	43
28:4	103n	69:19	258	110:1	65
29:11	100	69:21	258n	110:5-6	101n
31(S)	187	69:22-23	257, 258n	112:1	148
31:1-2(S)	186, 188	69:25	258n	113:2-3	62n
31:2(S)	186n	69:27-28	258	115:4-8	75n
32	187, 188	72:8-9	65	116:1(S)	62, 174n
32:1f	187	72:11-19	62n	116:2(S)	63
32:2	186n	77:48(S)	91n	117:1	62
32:3	186n	77:50(S)	91n	119:11	113
32:5	186n	77:56-62(S)	91	119:171-172	147

Index of Passages

135:4	229	10:10-11	81	44:1-2	226
135:15-18	75n	10:20-34	237	44:6	174
139:4(S)	145	10:22	237	44:9-20	75n
139:14(S)	145	10:22(S)	237	44:21	253
142:2(S)	139	10:22-23	236, 237	45:6	174
143:2	138n, 145	10:22-23(S)	236, 237	45:9	232
146:9	105n	10:23	238	45:9-13	232n
147:19-20	87, 87n, 226	11(S)	64	45:17	162, 273
149:6	147	11:10(S)	64	45:22-23	263n
		11:11-12	64	45:24-25	172
Proverbs		11:13	64	46:4	253
1:7	148	11:16	64	46:13	162
3:3	113	12:1-2	64	48:4	101
9:10	148	24:5	101n	48:8	101n, 144
10:6	87	24:20	101n	49:1	226
11:18-19	87	24:20(S)	259n	49:1-8	39
15:33	148	27:9	275	49:5	30
17:15	161f, 185n	27:11	144	49:6	40, 65
20:9	138n	28:12	101	49:15	253
24:12	102n, 103n	28:15	88n	50:10	148
24:24	185n	28:16	241n	51:2-3	180
28:4	185n	28:16(S)	244	51:4-8	162
28:14	101	28:22	238	51:7	113
28:21	105n	29:10	231	51:11(S)	237
29:1	101	29:10(S)	256	52	122n
		29:13	88n	52:5	110, 121, 121n, 122, 122n
Ecclesiastes		29:16	232, 232n		
3:11	89n	29:22	180	52:5(S)	121
7:20	138n	30:1	101n	52:7	122, 245
7:21(S)	145, 145n	30:9	101n, 120n	52:7(S)	245
		30:15	101	52:15	30
Isaiah		33:6	148	52:15(S)	30
1:2	101n	35:10(S)	237	54:10	253
1:4	101n	37:31	269n	56:6-7	65
1:5	101	40-55	64	56:6-8	263n
1:9	238	40:18-20	75n	57:4	101n
1:23	101n	41:6-7	75n	59:2-3	147
2:2-3	263n	41:8-9	229	59:7-8	147, 149n
2:2-4	64	41:8-10	180	59:13	101
4:3	44	41:16	172	59:19	148
5:23	161, 185n	42:6-7	116	59:20(S)	278
5:24	120n	42:8	81	59:20-21	147, 275
8:4	241n	42:18-25	101	59:21	279
9:2	65	42:19-20	116	60:2	263n
9:8-10:4	237	42:25	144	60:3	65
10:5-19	237	43:3ff	92	60:19	172

60:21	100	8:7-8	116, 116n	16:1-52	91
61:2	178n	9:3	88n, 144	16:8	86
63:1-6	162	9:6	88n	16:18-42	90, 91
63:1-7	162	9:13	120n	16:20-22	81
63:16	173	9:13-14	101	16:39	91
64:8	232n	9:15-16	81	18:4	87
65:1	33, 33n, 247	9:22-26	127	18:20	87, 103n
65:1(S)	33, 246	9:23-24	172	20:18	145
65:1-2	33, 34n, 37, 69, 247	9:24	116n	20:23-26	81
		9:25	106n	20:24-25	88
65:1-2(S)	34, 246	9:25-26	124n, 127	23:10	86
65:2	33, 33n, 34, 35, 101n, 247	10:2-5	75n	23:11-21	91
		10:7	173n	23:18	86
		10:14-15	75n	24:3	101n
65:2(S)	33	10:25	101n	33:8-9	87
65:12	226	11:10	145	33:24	180
66:4	226	11:13	82n	36:21	123
66:22	101n	11:16-17	269n	36:22	123
66:23	263n	13:25	88n	36:23	120
		17:1	113	36:26	127, 127n
Jeremiah		17:10	103n	40:4	113
1:5	30, 177	18:6	232n		
1:10	178	19:5	81	**Daniel**	
2	80	23:2	172	5:4	75n
2:5	78, 82, 88	25:15	178	5:23	75n
2:8	82	25:29-32	178	7:14	65
2:11	75, 78, 82, 93	31:9	173n, 226, 232n	9:4-16	122
2:11(S)	80n, 82	31:33	113, 127		
2:17	82	31:33-37	110	**Hosea**	
2:19	82	31:34	273	1:10	173, 174
2:28	82n	31:36	113	2:1(S)	174, 235, 237, 238
3:25	145	31:37	113	2:9-13	86
4:1-2	178	32:33	101	2:23(S)	174
4:4	127	32:27	173n	2:25(S)	235, 238
4:22	144	32:39	148	4:1	88n
5:3	101	35:17	101	4:2	119
5:3	101	38:33(S)	113	4:6	120n
5:5	87, 87n	44:15-19	81	4:13-14	85
5:21	144	44:16	101	4:14	85n
6:9	120n	44-51	178	4:16	101
6:30	90	50:25	233	5:4	88n
7:2	119			7:14	101
7:9-11	118, 119, 120			8:4-6	80n
7:29	90	**Ezekiel**		9:9	85
7:31	81	8	81	10:9	85
8:7	144	8:14	85	13:2	80n

Index of Passages

Joel			Malachi			24:14	277
2:18		244	1:2-3		232n	24:22	26n
2:23		244	1:6		101n	25:17	98n
2:26		244	1:11		232	27:34	258n
2:27		244	1:14		232		
2:28-32		244	2:2		101	**Mark**	
2:32		244	2:9		106n	2:27	26n
2:32-3:21		50	3:5		101n	3:5	101n
3:1-2		244				4:12	255
3:1-16		295				6:26	26n
3:3-16		244	**II. NEW TESTAMENT**			7:9	120n
3:5(S)	244, 245, 296					7:21-22	83n
3:17-21		244	**Matthew**			7:69	88n
			3:7-9		124n	11:15-17	122n
Amos			3:7-10		102n	11:15-18	122n
1:3-2:3		108n	3:9	102n, 181		12:21	98n
2:4		120n	3:10		102n	13:10	277
2:4-5	88n, 108n		5:17		157n	14:31	98n
2:6-16		108n	5:20		169n	15:23	258n
2:6-9:10		108n	7:12		157n	15:36	258n
3:2		100n	7:19		102n		
3:8		177	7:21		113n	**Luke**	
5:25-27		91	7:24		113n	1:60	171
			8:11		194n	1:72	226
Micah			8:11-12		102n	3:8	180, 181
3:11		116n	8:12		232n	3:9	102n
4:2		263n	10:1		29n	4:19	178n
5:3		90	11:13		157n	6:47	113n
6:16		91	12:41		126	8:10	255
			12:50		113n	8:31-41	102n
Habakkuk			13:13-15		255	11:31-32	127
2:4		41n	13:15		101n	11:39	116n
2:18-19		75n	15:7-9		88n	12:51	171
			15:14		116n	15:25-32	232n
Zephaniah			19:8		101n	16:14	122n
3:9		263n	20:5		98n	16:16	157n
			21:12-13		122n	16:22-31	180n
Haggai			21:28-30		98n	18:9-14	117
1:12		101n	21:36		98n	18:11-12	169n, 170n
			23		169n	19:45-46	122n
Zechariah			23:1-36		116n	20:31	98n
2:11		263n	23:2		116n	22:20	98n
7:11		101	23:3		169n	23:36	258n
7:12		101	23:13-33		116	24:27	42n
8:20-22		263n	23:16-18		122n	24:44-46	42n
14:9		174	23:27-28		116n	24:47	42n

John		10:9-28	244n	28:23	157n
1:45	157n	10:34	104	28:24-28	260
2:14-16	122n	10:34-35	105n, 175	28:26	255
2:17	258n	10:36	243		
3:16-17	261n	10:45-46	189n	**Romans**	
3:19-21	116n	11:9	105n	1	78, 79n, 81, 82,
4:22	49	13:1-3	303		83n, 85n, 92
5:42	116n	13:15	157n	1-2	103, 107n
5:45	116n	13:26	180	1-4	2, 2n, 6, 17, 36,
7:19	116n, 121, 125n	13:45-48	260		136, 153n, 164, 165,
8:33	180	13:47	40		168, 176n, 205, 207,
8:33-39	181	13:49	139		208n, 217, 219, 222,
8:39	180	14:16	94n, 160n		270, 276, 285, 295
8:53-59	180	14:27	41	1-5	2n
9:28	116n, 169n	15:1ff	15n	1-8	2n, 18n, 221, 222,
10:1	119n	15:3-4	41		222n, 223, 236, 286
10:8	119n	15:12	41	1-11	3, 12, 17, 161n,
11:42	26n	16:6-10	303, 306n		221, 234, 253,
12:30	26n	17	87n		271, 281, 284, 288
12:37-43	101n	17:30	94n, 160n	1:1	31, 40, 45, 49,
12:40	231, 255	18:2	26n		298n, 299, 299n
13:17	113n	18:6	260	1:1-2	40
15:21	144	18:9-10	306n	1:1-4	223
15:25	258n	19:9	101n	1:1-5	36n, 70n, 297
19:29	258n	19:21	15	1:1-7	39, 42n
20:31	23n	19:37	119n	1:1-15	7, 13, 16, 17,
		20:22-25	15		20, 38, 46,
Acts		20:31	97n		69, 70, 297
1:20	257n, 258n, 264n	21	8	1:1-17	38n, 68, 69,
2:17	244n	21:4-14	15		70, 289
2:17-21	244n	21:19-20	41	1:1-4:25	23n
2:25	257n	22:3	40n	1:2	13, 41n, 42n, 58,
2:34	257n	22:6-16	306n		59n, 67, 142n, 157
2:36	243	22:17-21	26, 303, 306n	1:2-3	4
2:39	49, 244n	22:21	178	1:2-5	42
3:12	199n	23:6	40n, 180n	1:3	289
3:25	199n	23:11	306n	1:5	1, 25, 27, 29, 31,
4:25	257n	24:14	157n		40, 41, 42n, 45, 48n,
7:41	80n	25:24	254n		49, 68, 106n, 113n,
7:42	91	26:5	40n		171, 288, 289, 299n
7:51	101n, 127,	26:12-23	306n	1:5-6	29
	181, 257	26:16f	26	1:5-7	223, 224
7:53	125n	26:16-20	1	1:6-7	235
8:1ff	260	26:22	157n	1:7	43, 46
9:3-9	306n	27:25	97n	1:8	22, 49
9:15	1, 26, 178, 299n	28:2	26n	1:8-13	15

Index of Passages

Romans (Cont'd)

1:8-15	39, 44
1:9	25, 43, 44, 49
1:10	266n
1:11	23, 36n
1:12	49
1:14	26, 44
1:14-15	15, 28, 37, 45
1:14-16	107n
1:15	36, 47, 49
1:15-16	39
1:16	4, 6, 32, 35, 35n, 37, 47, 48, 48n, 49, 50, 52, 69, 83, 105, 106, 117, 158n, 217, 251n, 276, 281, 289
1:16-17	5, 13, 17, 20, 21, 35, 37, 39, 41n, 46, 46n, 49, 50, 51, 66, 69, 70, 223, 297
1:16-2:11	103, 104, 106
1:16-2:29	104, 152
1:16-15:13	25, 38, 39, 67, 70, 156n, 297
1:17	49, 207n
1:17-5:11	210n
1:18	79, 87, 93n, 163, 164, 185n, 195
1:18-23	99n
1:18-25	81
1:18-32	72, 73, 74, 75n, 78, 80n, 82, 88, 89, 90, 92, 93n, 94, 94n, 95, 95n, 96, 97, 97n, 98, 99, 99n, 114n, 117, 130, 150, 152, 167, 202, 212n, 291, 293
1:18-2:5	95
1:18-2:16	107
1:18-2:29	104n, 107, 109, 118, 128
1:18-3:8	136
1:18-3:20	17, 72, 108n, 130, 133, 133n, 136, 150, 152, 153, 153n, 154n, 158, 159, 159n, 202, 204, 206, 210, 279, 285, 290, 293
1:18-3:31	137n
1:18-4:23	207n
1:18-4:25	45n, 72, 99n, 104n, 108n, 140, 153n, 167n, 213
1:18-5:11	212
1:18-5:21	153n
1:18-8:39	153n
1:18-11:36	25, 150, 153n
1:18-15:13	25, 38, 66
1:19-20	87, 89
1:19-21	88
1:19-23	87
1:19-32	102n
1:20	27n, 105n
1:21	87, 88, 89, 96
1:21-23	79
1:22	28n
1:23	74, 76, 76n, 77, 78, 79n, 80, 82
1:23ff	79n
1:23-25	74, 82, 90
1:23-28	79
1:24	79, 79n, 87, 89, 90, 91, 91n, 96, 256n
1:25	79, 79n
1:26	79, 79n, 89, 91n, 96, 256n
1:26-27	90
1:27	86
1:28	79n, 89, 91n, 96, 256n
1:28-32	98n
1:29	88n,
1:29-31	82, 83n
1:32	87, 88, 89, 98n
1:32-2:3	82
2	82, 94n, 109, 109n, 111n, 128, 129, 131, 293
2-3	139n
2-4	57, 105
2:1	72, 73, 82, 86, 94, 94n, 95, 96, 97, 98n, 99, 103, 105n, 132n, 151, 293
2:1ff	93n, 94n, 95, 97, 98, 98n, 154n
2:1-3	82, 116, 126
2:1-4	99, 151
2:1-5	97n, 102, 116
2:1-11	73, 96
2:1-16	95, 96, 97, 98, 99
2:1-29	74, 93, 97n, 104n, 109, 109n, 118, 128n, 130
2:1-3:20	73, 73n, 89, 94, 94n, 114n, 142, 149
2:2	100n
2:3	100n
2:4	102n, 132, 160n
2:4f	231, 233
2:5	101, 101n, 151
2:6	18, 102n, 103, 105
2:6-11	4, 95, 103, 104n, 110, 290
2:7	106
2:8	102
2:8-9	106
2:9	102, 137n, 137n
2:9-10	47, 52, 105, 110n, 117, 217
2:9-11	5
2:10	93n, 107n, 137n, 179, 226
2:11	6, 48, 48n, 103, 104n, 105n, 106, 106n, 174, 176
2:11-14	110n
2:11-16	110n
2:12	94n, 110, 110n, 111, 139n, 212
2:12-13	114
2:12-16	105n, 110, 136, 137, 151
2:12-27	95

Romans (Cont'd)

2:12-29	73, 109, 109n, 110, 127, 129, 129n, 151, 293		122n, 123n, 137n	3:9ff	104n
		2:25	27n, 94n, 115, 124, 125n, 169, 293	3:9-18	114n, 141
2:12-3:20	152			3:9-20	135n, 138, 141, 149, 150
2:13	18, 110, 111, 111n, 112, 141, 141n	2:25-29	110, 123, 124, 124n, 127, 133, 136, 171, 192, 293	3:10	143n, 145n
				3:10-12	143, 145
2:13f	249	2:26	94n, 112, 125, 125n, 170, 193, 227	3:10-13	144
2:13-15	141n			3:10-18	129, 130, 134, 134n, 135n, 136, 138n, 143, 219, 257n, 294
2:14	4, 57, 89, 94n, 110, 137n, 170, 241				
		2:26-27	107n, 115, 293, 294		
2:14-15	107n, 111, 111n, 114n, 120, 125n, 133, 161, 169, 171, 209, 227, 294			3:11-12	145n
		2:26-29	111n, 125, 161	3:12	48n, 106n, 143n
		2:27	124, 126, 170	3:13	145
		2:27-28	126	3:13ff	147n
2:14-16	110n, 114, 293	2:28-29	115	3:13-14	145, 147, 147n
2:15	102, 113n, 170	2:29	102, 126		
2:16	9n, 36n, 105n, 111n	3	19n, 130n	3:14	146
2:17	4, 94n, 96, 98n, 154, 164, 167, 168n, 169, 271	3-4	3n, 42, 59n	3:15	148
		3:1	129, 133n	3:15-17	32n, 147
		3:1-2	4, 48, 73, 87, 88, 116, 117, 140, 150, 151, 289, 290	3:18	148
2:17ff	114n, 115, 154n			3:19	48n, 106n, 135, 135n, 138n, 139, 139n, 167, 212
2:17-20	88, 115, 167, 224	3:1-4	124n		
		3:1-8	48n, 130, 130n, 131n, 133n, 134n, 156n	3:19-20	94n, 130, 135n, 157n, 163, 164, 167
2:17-23	166				
2:17-24	110, 114, 115, 117, 117n, 118, 121, 139n, 151, 170, 262n, 293			3:20	48n, 106n, 113n, 135, 139, 140, 141, 141n, 152, 166, 167, 168n, 242n, 294
		3:1-20	73, 129, 130, 134, 135, 138, 140, 149, 151, 158n, 294		
		3:2	88, 158n, 219, 227		
2:17-29	107, 107n, 108, 117	3:2f	262n	3:21	13, 142n, 154n, 156, 166, 170n, 171, 242, 303n
		3:3	131, 131n, 136, 156n, 224		
2:19-20	88				
2:21	116, 119	3:3-8	48	3:21ff	154n
2:21-22	82, 120, 121	3:4	130, 134, 257n	3:21-22	43, 157, 163, 242
2:21-23	116, 121, 124	3:5	133, 156n, 193		
2:21-24	88, 122n, 125n, 169, 170	3:7	132	3:21-26	7n, 48, 155, 156, 156n, 160, 161, 164, 176, 208
		3:8	131n		
2:21-29	116	3:9	5, 6, 48, 48n, 92, 94n, 104, 104n, 105, 106n, 117, 118, 130, 130n, 133, 133n, 134n, 135, 136,140, 144, 149, 151, 217n, 290, 294	3:21-28	155n, 159n
2:22	86, 119			3:21-31	50, 107n, 161n, 166n, 171, 179n
2:23	4, 118, 121, 121n, 122, 154, 167, 168n, 169, 271				
				3:21-4:25	17, 72, 152, 153, 153n, 154, 155n, 156, 166,
2:23-24	167				
2:24	32n, 42, 118, 121, 121n, 122,				

Index of Passages

Romans (Cont'd)
204, 206, 241, 279, 285, 294
3:21-5:21   223n
3:22   5, 6, 48, 48n, 50, 104, 105, 106, 106n, 155, 156, 158, 174, 202, 207n, 217, 243, 280, 281, 290
3:22-26   156, 159
3:23   48n, 106n, 137, 145, 158, 159n
3:24   159, 159n
3:24-26   159n
3:25   26n, 94n, 156, 159n, 170
3:25-26   159
3:26   27n, 156, 159n, 167
3:27   4, 155, 156, 164, 165, 166, 167, 170, 170n, 171n, 179n, 183, 271
3:27ff   154n
3:27-30   171n, 179n
3:27-31   48n, 106n, 164, 164n
3:28   36, 38, 113n, 156, 157n, 166, 171, 171n
3:28-29   202
3:29   114, 137n, 171, 171n, 188n, 202, 217, 227, 243n, 290
3:29-30   4, 5, 57, 104, 173, 174, 176, 176n, 294
3:30   38, 137n, 156, 158, 171n, 176n, 214, 249, 281, 290
3:31   18, 120n, 156, 179
4   52, 155, 164, 179, 184n, 186n, 201, 202, 203n, 223n, 227, 249
4:1   168n, 181, 193n

4:1-8   183
4:1-12   156, 182, 194, 195
4:1-25   4, 126n, 149, 155, 157, 181
4:2   179n
4:2-12   182
4:3   185n, 203n
4:3-6   223n
4:3-12   195n
4:4-6   184n
4:4-9   181
4:5   183n, 184, 184n, 185n, 187, 187n, 242n
4:5-9   186
4:6   157n, 185n, 186, 187
4:6-8   131, 184, 187, 192, 257n
4:7-8   32n, 187
4:8   185n
4:8-11   223n
4:9   43, 104, 182, 184n, 185n, 186, 187, 188, 202, 290
4:9-12   124n, 184n, 187
4:10   182, 185n
4:10-12   192
4:11   27n, 48n, 54, 106n, 124, 182, 185n, 189, 192, 194
4:11-12   195n
4:11-16   281
4:12   48n, 53, 54, 106n, 182, 190, 192, 193, 193n, 194, 196, 269
4:12ff   24
4:13   54, 195n, 199n, 223n
4:13ff   199n
4:13-16   57
4:13-22   156, 182, 195
4:13-25   182, 195
4:14   195n, 223n
4:14-15   195, 196
4:15   94n, 139n, 213

4:16   5, 6, 27n, 48n, 53, 54, 104, 106n, 164, 188n, 195n, 196, 199n, 200, 202, 207, 217, 223n, 227, 291
4:16-17   58
4:16-18   57, 181, 197
4:16-22   43
4:17   54, 183n, 195n, 197, 207
4:18   53, 182, 183, 195n, 197, 198, 199, 199n, 200
4:18-22   197, 200
4:19   24, 195n, 198
4:20   223n
4:21   183n
4:22   96, 185n, 199
4:22-24   53, 223n, 269
4:23   185n
4:23-25   184n, 201
4:24   183n, 185n, 192n, 207
4:24-25   7n, 207
4:25   26n
5   207n, 208n
5-8   2, 2n, 17, 43, 205, 206, 207, 207n, 208, 208n, 212, 213, 285, 291
5:1   207, 208, 210n, 214, 281
5:1-11   208, 208n, 210, 210n
5:1-8:39   206
5:2-5   208n
5:3   208n
5:5   208n, 213
5:6   185n, 187n
5:6-8   187n
5:8   7n
5:9   214
5:9-10   260n
5:9-11   210n, 214
5:10   208, 276n

350   Paul as Apostle to the Gentiles

Romans (Cont'd)

5:11	29n, 207, 208
5:12	48n, 106n, 137, 145, 210, 211n
5:12-21	5, 58, 68, 79, 167, 208n, 210, 210n, 212, 212n, 213, 291
5:12-11:36	23n
5:13	94n, 139n, 195, 211, 213
5:13-14	211n, 212
5:15	210, 211, 211
5:15-16	210n
5:16	210
5:17	210, 211
5:18	48n, 106n, 137, 210, 211
5:20	94n, 139n, 212, 213
5:20-21	211, 212
5:21	207, 208n
6	207n
6-8	2n
6:1	193
6:1-14	212
6:1-23	212
6:1-8:17	212
6:2-4	212
6:4	7n
6:5	27n
6:6	212, 214
6:7	212
6:10	212
6:11	212
6:12	271
6:12-13	213
6:13	213
6:14	212, 242
6:15	212
6:17	22, 43n, 214
6:17-18	213
6:18	212, 214
6:19	213, 214
6:20	214
6:22	212, 214
6:23	207, 208n
7	139n, 207n, 212
7:1	139n
7:1-5	212
7:1-6	213
7:4	213
7:5	214
7:6	212, 213
7:7	88, 94n, 120n, 139n, 193, 213
7:7-8	211
7:7-23	213
7:7-25	212, 212n
7:8	157n, 213
7:9	157n
7:12	18, 120n, 213, 289
7:13	27n, 213, 213
7:14	18, 213, 289
7:16	18, 120n, 213, 289
7:24-25	208n
8	207n
8:1	214
8:1-2	213
8:1-17	212
8:1-39	208n
8:2	212, 213, 214
8:3	139, 213
8:4	112, 227
8:9	24, 213
8:9-17	285
8:9-27	208n
8:11	214
8:12-30	213
8:14	213, 214
8:14-16	230
8:15	214, 226
8:16	214
8:17	214, 223n
8:18	208n, 223n, 226
8:18-27	212, 213
8:20-25	208n
8:21	223n
8:22	98
8:22-25	65
8:23	214, 226
8:23-25	98
8:26	98, 98n, 254n
8:26-27	98
8:27	113n
8:28	224
8:28-29	223n
8:28-30	212, 214, 285, 291
8:28-39	212, 213
8:29	27n
8:29-30	223n, 236
8:30	223n, 235, 285
8:31-39	222
8:32	48n, 106n
8:33	43, 212, 214, 223, 223n, 236
8:34	7n, 254n
8:35	207, 208n
8:35-39	208n, 222
8:36	257n
8:39	208n, 223n
9	53, 219, 220, 224, 225, 228, 236, 295
9-10	3n, 250, 251, 285, 294
9-11	2, 2n, 3, 6, 9n, 17, 18n, 36, 42, 43, 52, 57, 59n, 64, 68n, 105, 132n, 147, 171, 176n, 205, 206, 212, 214, 215, 216, 216n, 217, 217n, 218, 218n, 219, 220n, 221, 222, 222n, 224, 224n, 225, 230, 234, 236, 236n, 240, 250n, 251n, 270, 276, 278n, 279, 285, 287, 288, 291, 296
9:1-2	237
9:1-3	239, 289
9:1-4	108
9:1-5	225, 226
9:1-23	224
9:1-29	219, 224, 225, 286
9:1-33	224
9:1-11:10	222n

Index of Passages

Romans (Cont'd)
9:1-11:24	287
9:1-11:36	124n, 207n, 215
9:2	108
9:3	225n
9:3-5	4, 117, 140, 225, 290
9:4	54, 120n, 187, 223n
9:4-5	4, 48, 88, 158n, 225, 226, 289
9:5	4, 181, 289
9:6	13, 53, 114, 218, 218n, 227, 228, 230, 235n, 236, 238, 252, 253, 283, 286
9:6ff	226
9:6-7	181, 228, 295
9:6-8	192
9:6-9	126n
9:6-13	269
9:6-17	228
9:6-23	225, 227, 229, 236
9:6-24	234n
9:6-29	229, 229n, 238, 239, 248
9:6-11:16	222
9:7	228, 235
9:7-8	223n
9:7-18	228, 232
9:7-22	233
9:7-23	225
9:8	54, 223n, 226, 228, 230
9:9	223n, 228
9:10	228
9:10-17	230, 231
9:11	224, 230
9:11-12	228
9:12	235
9:12-13	232n
9:13-14	228
9:14	193, 228
9:14-18	104n
9:15	32n, 228, 231, 238
9:15-17	231
9:15-23	57n
9:15-24	236
9:16	228
9:17	41, 58, 228, 231
9:17-18	275n
9:18	101, 228, 230
9:19	228, 229
9:19-20	261n
9:20	229, 263n
9:20-21	232, 232n
9:20-23	230
9:21	229
9:22-24	229, 233
9:22-26	224, 228
9:23	233n, 262
9:24	48n, 106n, 175, 233n, 234, 235, 237n
9:24-26	57, 174, 236
9:24-29	234
9:25	61n, 235
9:25-26	4, 50, 174, 174n, 234, 234n, 235n, 237, 286, 287n, 295
9:25-28	238n, 275n
9:25-29	229
9:25-33	157
9:27	174n, 237, 238n
9:27-28	32n, 235, 237
9:27-29	4, 50, 218,228, 236, 238, 286
9:27-33	131n
9:28	237, 238
9:29	32n
9:30	4, 34, 38, 41, 50, 57, 93n, 161, 171, 236, 240, 241n, 242n, 244, 247, 249
9:30-31	223, 229, 241
9:30-33	224, 229n, 239
9:30-10:3	295
9:30-10:13	241
9:30-10:21	220, 229n, 239, 240, 240n, 248
9:31	101, 171
9:31f	254, 258
9:31-33	4, 38, 50, 225, 262n
9:31-10:3	157, 245n
9:32	38, 144, 229, 259
9:32-10:21	241
9:33	32n, 229, 229n, 241n, 275n, 281
10	33, 220n, 248
10-11	246
10:1	128n, 140, 237, 239, 289
10:1-13	243
10:1-21	229n
10:1-11:32	220n
10:2-3	171, 254
10:3	101, 144, 241, 242n
10:4	48n, 106n, 242, 242n
10:5	32n
10:5-8	242, 249
10:5-18	246,
10:6	249, 275n
10:6-13	157, 240
10:8	147, 242, 242n
10:8-10	147
10:9	242, 243, 243n
10:9-13	6, 244, 281
10:10	18, 243
10:11	32n, 48n, 64, 106n, 243, 281, 286
10:11ff	248
10:11-12	35
10:11-13	5, 36, 41f, 217
10:12	5, 6, 48, 48n, 50, 104, 106n, 174, 175, 207n, 217, 243, 249, 262, 291
10:13	48n, 64, 106n, 243, 245,275n, 281, 286, 296
10:14	245
10:14-15	245
10:14-17	240, 244
10:14-18	244
10:14-21	244

352   Paul as Apostle to the Gentiles

Romans (Cont'd)

10:15	32n, 148, 245		231, 286		287, 291, 296
10:16	32n, 245, 245n	11:9-10	186n, 257	11:17-25	52
10:16-18	245	11:10	258, 259	11:17-32	117, 221
10:16-19	291	11:11	4, 228, 250, 255,	11:18	270, 271
10:16-21	131n, 157		259, 266, 296	11:19	32n, 255, 270,
10:17	242n	11:11-12	267n, 271		283, 286, 295
10:17-19	88	11:11-15	57	11:19-20	4
10:18	245n, 263n	11:11-16	220, 220n,	11:20	4, 38, 50, 131n,
10:18ff	248		259, 283		255, 261n, 262n,
10:18-19	4, 88	11:11-24	252		264n, 269, 270,
10:18-21	244	11:11-26	282n		283, 284, 286,
10:18-11:36	280	11:12	255, 260, 262,		295
10:19	32n, 218, 245,		263, 264, 264n,	11:20-21	101, 256
	245n, 246, 246n,		265, 267, 268,	11:21	261n, 269, 270,
	275n, 286		274n, 275n, 279,		283, 286, 296
10:19-21	246		287, 287n, 295	11:22	4, 222, 231,
10:19-11:36	246	11:13	1, 8, 28, 29,		264n, 270, 283,
10:20	4, 32n, 32,		40, 70, 111n,		287, 295
	35, 38, 50, 57,		178, 263, 265, 266,	11:23	101, 131n,
	93n, 244, 246,		289, 297, 299, 301		255, 261n, 269,
	247n, 286, 287n	11:13-14	140, 264,		270, 286, 296
10:20a	33n		264n, 265n	11:23-24	287
10:20-21	30, 33, 46,	11:13-15	220n	11:24	261n, 270
	69, 174n, 248	11:13-24	220n	11:25	24, 57, 101,
10:21	4, 32n, 33n, 38,	11:13-32	7, 220n,		231, 274, 274n,
	50, 61, 88, 101, 218,		252, 289		275n, 286, 295
	228, 245, 245n, 248,	11:13-36	282n	11:25-26	221, 251n,
	248n, 262n, 286, 295	11:14	108, 128n, 265,		252, 266, 273, 279
11	221, 239, 250, 261n,		266, 276, 289	11:25-32	221, 251n,
	282, 285, 286, 295	11:15	260, 261n, 263,		253, 272, 284
11:1	4, 228, 248, 250,		264, 264n, 265,	11:26	185n, 250,
	252, 256n, 259		267, 268, 279,		250n, 253, 272,
11:1-2	253n		286, 287n, 295		274, 275n, 280n,
11:1-10	157, 220, 252,	11:16	203n, 268		281, 287, 295
	253, 254n, 255, 259	11:16-24	220n	11:26-27	32n, 275n
11:1-16	220n	11:17	4, 131n, 231,	11:26-29	4, 157
11:1-36	220		255, 261n, 269,	11:26-32	4, 58n, 228, 289
11:5	254		270, 271, 283,	11:27	274, 276
11:6	258		284, 286, 295	11:28	4, 26n, 48, 226n,
11:7	50, 101, 171, 231,	11:17ff	24		269n, 276, 287, 295
	254, 259, 259n,	11:17-18	158n	11:28-29	158n
	262n, 286, 295	11:17-19	203n	11:28-32	274
11:7-10	4, 38, 101	11:17-22	264n	11:29	272
11:8	32n, 256	11:17-24	168, 220,	11:30	231, 275,
11:8-10	218, 228,		220n, 221, 268,		279, 286, 295
			269n, 270, 271n,	11:30-31	276

Index of Passages

Romans (Cont'd)		14:17	18		26n, 35, 35n, 106, 107, 178, 204, 296
11:30-32	5, 57n	14:19	288n		
11:31	57n, 231, 272, 274, 275, 279, 296	14:23	298n	15:15-16	7, 17, 19, 20, 23, 26, 29n, 40n, 43, 44, 68, 70n, 160n, 178, 288, 289, 297, 299n
		15:1	24		
		15:1-13	51, 93n		
11:32	48n, 57n,	15:3	258n		
11:34-35	32n, 64, 91n, 92n, 106n, 136, 145, 175, 217, 231, 279, 291	15:4-6	65		
		15:5-7	52	15:15-21	25
		15:6	207n	15:16	1, 25, 27n, 29, 40, 43, 46, 65, 264, 289, 298n, 297, 299, 301
11:33-36	273	15:7	21n, 56, 67, 96, 126, 209		
12-15	291				
12-16	2, 2n, 214, 253, 286, 288, 288n	15:7-8	97n, 266		
		15:7-12	5, 18, 56, 209	15:16-21	1
12:1	25, 44, 160n	15:7-13	13, 17, 20, 39, 50, 51, 52, 67, 68n, 69, 70	15:17	29,
12:1-3	17			15:17-18	37, 38, 169
12:1-21	23n			15:17-20	28
12:1-15:7	17	15:8	4, 51, 52n, 53, 55, 56, 57, 57n, 289	15:17-21	26, 68
12:1-15:13	24, 25, 65			15:18	29, 29n, 32, 35, 41, 113n, 171, 245n
12:3	7, 24, 26n, 40n, 70, 70n, 271n, 288, 297				
		15:8-9	21, 21n, 51, 52, 53, 57, 57n, 59, 59n, 62, 67, 227, 291	15:18-19	28n
12:5	43n			15:19	1, 30
12:6	168			15:19-20	30
12:9-15:13	22n	15:8-12	69, 157	15:19-21	1, 301
12:10	288n	15:8-13	23n	15:21	30, 31, 32n, 37, 46
12:12	65	15:9	41 52, 53, 55, 56, 57, 57n, 58n, 59, 60, 63, 67, 111n, 175	15:22	96
12:14	271			15:22-33	39
12:16	271, 271n, 288n			15:24	24
12:21	271			15:30	207n
13:3ff	24	15:9-12	21, 21n, 51, 52, 58, 59n, 60, 66, 67, 93n, 291	15:31	15n
13:5	96			15:33	23n, 298n
13:8-10	23n			16:9	22
13:9-10	288n	15:10	61, 67	16:17-20	16, 214
14	24, 68n	15:11	48n, 62, 106n	16:18	207n
14-16	2n	15:12	32n, 64, 65	16:19	43n
14:1	288n	15:13	21n, 65, 65	16:20	207n, 209
14:1-3	209	15:13-33	38n	16:21	298n
14:1-15:4	23n, 52	15:14	22, 22n	16:21-23	23n
14:1-15:7	168	15:14-15	21, 43n, 152	16:24	207n
14:1-15:13	18n, 23n	15:14-21	13, 16, 17, 19, 20, 21, 37, 38, 39, 46, 59, 68, 69, 70, 301	16:25	10n, 36n, 66, 297, 298, 298n
14:3	288n				
14:5-7	23n			16:25-26	13, 283, 299
14:10	271n, 288n			16:25-27	291, 297, 298
14:11	32n	15:14-21(33)	21, 38, 69	16:26	41, 113n, 171, 245n
14:13	288n	15:14-33	7, 19		
14:14-32	23n	15:15	5, 22n, 23n, 24,		

1 Corinthains		14:13	96	10:8	36n
1:1	263n	14:25	113n	10:8-10	36n
1:2	44, 223	14:26	36n	10:10	36n
1:5-7	22n	15:1-5	15	9:12-13	266
1:18	260	15:3	305	10:15	29
1:22-24	48n, 106n	15:3-8	7n, 297, 297n, 305	10:15-17	28n
1:23	241n, 289n	15:3-11	36	10:17	116n
1:30	27n	15:8-9	26n	11:7	298n
1:31	116n	15:10	1, 27n, 28,	11:21	23, 29n
3:5	30n		29n, 30, 301	11:21-22	180
3:6	28	15:20	269n	11:22-25	254
3:9	30n	15:22	211	11:23	1, 28, 301
3:10	27, 40n	15:23	269n	11:23-33	29n
3:11	241n	15:37	27n	11:26	119n
4:5	28, 113n	21:20-26	15	11:30	29n
5:9	23n			12:1	303
5:11	23n	**2 Corinthians**		12:7	96
6:9	85n	1:1	298n	12:10	96
7:18-19	126	1:12-14	29	12:19	36n
7:19	124	1:20	96	13:2	305n
8:4-6	174	1:20-21	54-55	13:10	36n
8:5-6	243	1:21-22	189n		
8:6	176	2:3	23n	**Galatians**	
8:9	27n	2:4	23n	1:1-2	70n
9:1-2	26n	2:8	96	1:4	58n
9:1-18	28	2:9	23n	1:6	10n, 305, 306
9:2	1, 28, 37	2:12	298n, 299	1:11	304
9:6	297	2:14-16	30n	1:11-16	70n
9:16	245, 276	3:2-3	113n	1:12	36
9:19-23	1, 276	3:6	30n	1:14	176
9:20	27n	3:12-18	144	1:15	30, 299n
9:22	27n	3:14	231, 255	1:15-16	9n, 26, 26n,
10:6	27n	4:3	297n, 298n		29, 40, 40n, 68,
10:7-8	84n	4:5	243n		178, 297, 307
10:32	106n	4:13	96, 97n	1:16	1, 299n
11:25	98n, 226	4:17	226	2-3	3n
12-14	22n	5:9	96	2:1-5	15
12:3	96, 243n	5:12	113n	2:1-9	70n
12:13	48n, 106n	5:18-21	209	2:1-12	15
13:1	27n	5:20	30n	2:2	298, 298n
13:2	22n	5:21	27n	2:2-5	15
13:10	36n	6:1	30n	2:5	298n, 299
14:3	36n	6:14	27n	2:7	178, 297n, 298, 299n
14:5	36n	6:17	96, 97n	2:7-9	1, 28, 29, 40,
14:6	8	7:8-12	23n, 24n		298n, 299, 299n
14:12	36n	9:5	40n	2:7-10	15n

Index of Passages

2:8	298n	5:19-21	305	3:4-8	4
2:8-9	1	5:22	66	3:4-6	180
2:9	27n, 40n	6:11	23n	3:6	169n
2:14	11	6:11-18	23n	3:8	263n
2:14-16	48n, 106n	6:15	48n, 106n	3:11	266n, 290n
2:15	210			4:19	102
2:16	113n, 139	**Ephesians**			
2:21	139	1-3	288n	**Colossians**	
3	203n, 294	1:1	263n	1:2	44
3:1	305	1:5	226	1:12	44
3:1-5	11n, 26,	1:7	102	1:21-22	276n
	28, 68,	1:9	66n	1:22	44
	189n, 305, 306	1:12	27n	1:23	30n
3:2	113n	1:13	189n	1:23-2:5	178
3:3	27n	2:7	102	1:24-29	28
3:5	113n	2:8-9	159	1:25-26	66
3:6	189n, 203n	2:11	97n	1:25-27	1, 283
3:8	42, 202	2:12	66, 187, 199	1:27	66, 226
3:8-9	202	2:12-13	89n	2:11	125
3:10	113n	2:15-16	209	2:21	187
3:11	139	2:18	209	3:4	226
3:13	4, 290n	3:1	299n, 301	3:5	122n
3:14	58n	3:3	299n	3:11	5, 48, 48n,
3:15ff	199n	3:1-9	299n		106n, 174, 217
3:15-18	199n	3:1-13	1		
3:16	61n	3:5	299n	**1 Thessalonians**	
3:19	94n, 213	3:6	299n, 300	1:1	298n
3:20	176	3:6-9	66n	1:5	297n, 298n
3:22	145, 279	3:7-9	299n	1:9	89n
3:22-23	92n	3:8	27n	1:10	280n
3:23	290n	3:8-9	178	2:2	298n
3:26-29	48n, 106n, 230	4:8	61n	2:8	298n
3:28	5, 48, 174,	4:17-19	93, 231	2:8-9	299
	217, 289n	4:18	255	2:9	298n
3:29	199, 202, 227	4:30	189n	2:14-16	217, 248, 290n
4:5	226	5:5	122n	2:15	4
4:8	187	5:14	61n	2:19-20	28n
4:8-9	89n			3:4	305n
4:13-16	305	**Philippians**		3:6-9	28n
4:21-31	221	1:1	43n	4:5	89n, 187
4:28	227	1:5-19	28n	4:6	305n
4:28-29	230	1:23	27n	4:7-8	65
4:31	96	1:25	66	4:11	305n
5:3	124	1:29	29n, 191n	5:1-2	305n
5:5	65	2:11	243	5:11	96, 97n
5:6	48n, 106n	3:3	125, 193		

2 Thessalonians		James		9:7	172n
1:1	298n	1:22	113n	10:8	172n
1:8	298n	1:25	113n		
2:5	305n	2:20-23	201n	**Wisdom**	
2:6-7	8	2:23	203n	2:12	100n
2:11	231	4:11	113n	2:13	100n
2:13	66			2:16	83, 100n, 172n
2:14	297n, 298n	**1 Peter**		2:18	100n
2:15	305n	4:17	298n	3:9	100n, 106
3:6	305n	4:18	187n	3:9-10	100, 100n
3:10	305n			3:10	100n
		1 John		4:12	83
		2:17	113n	4:15	106
1 Timothy				5:15-16	100, 100n, 106, 106n
1:9	187n	**3 John**			
1:10	85n	9	23n	6:7	106n
1:13	94n			11-15	99
2:4	261n	**Jude**		11:9-10	100, 100n
2:4-6	174	7	86n	11:9-11	106n
2:7	1			12-15	74, 99
2:9	98n	**Revelation**		12:12	233
3:8	98n	12:11	26n	12:22	99, 99n, 100n, 106n
3:11	98n	13:14	26n		
5:25	98n	22:15	113n	12:18	99n
				12:20-21	99n
2 Timothy				12:27	100n
1:1	263n	**III. APOCRYPHA**		13:1	88
2:8	36n, 298			14:12-31	75
		1 Esdras		14:23-26	83n
Titus		1:53-57	91	14:26	84
2:3	98n	6:15-16	91	14:31-15:2	106
2:6	98n	8:75	269n	15:1-6	75n
2:11	159	8:75-78	91	15:1ff	102n
		8:84-86	269n	15:2	100
Philemon				15:2a	99
8	96	**2 Esdras**		15:7	232n
19	23n	4:30	78	16:1-2	106
		4:35-36	277	16:2	100n
Hebrews				16:4-5	100n
4:11	259n	**Tobit**		16:16	100n
7:25	254n	13:11	65, 263n	16:26	100n
11	215n	14:5-7	209, 277	17:2	100n
11:8-10	203n	14:6-7	65, 263n	18:1	100n
11:11-16	203n			18:2	100n
11:12	197	**Judith**		18:4	116
11:17-19	201n, 203n	8:18	75n	18:5	100n

18:7-8	100n	10:63	254	84:2	173n
18:9	44	11:25	254	93:5	269n
18:25	100n	13:48	111n	105:1	116
19:1	100n				
19:2	100n	**2 Maccabees**		*4 Ezra*	
19:22	100n, 106	2:17-18	196	3:16	232n
		4:39	119n	4:1-11	89n
Sirach		4:42	119n	4:23	91
3:21-23	89n	6:10	123	4:30	78
4:10	173	9:2	119n	4:35-36	277
31:10	172n	13:6	119n	4:38	92
33:13	232n	15:9	157n	5:1	161
35:12	106n			5:28-30	91
36:12	172n, 232n			6:5	161
36:1-17	34			6:28	161
37:19	116	**IV. PSEUDEPIGRAPHA**		6:58	172n
39:15	147			7:34	161
43:31	89n	*Apoc. Abraham*		7:77	161, 171n
44:12	226	25:1-6	120n	8:33	161
44:19-21	196n			8:33-40	185n
44:20	196n	*Apoc. Moses*		8:35	158
47:22	269n	21:6	158n	8:36	161
50:20	147, 172n			9:7	161
		2 Apoc. Baruch		9:8	161
Baruch		43:1	169n	9:9	161
1-2	172n	43:3	169n	10:14	78
3:1	172n	44:7	169n		
3:2	172n	44:14	169n	*Jubilees*	
3:29-30	242n	46:4-6	169n	1:11	81
3:35	173	48:20	229	1:13	172n
4:4	173	48:23	229	1:23	127
5:4	115n	51:3	171n	1:24-25	172n, 173, 173n
		51:7	171n	1:28	172n
Prayer of Azaria		54:21	161	2:20	172n
12	180	57:2	112	5:15-16	106n
		77:3	170, 229	11:4-6	75n
Prayer of Manasseh		78:3	43n	11:16-17	75n
8	184n	85:2-3	169n	12:3-5	75n
				15:9-11	123
1 Maccabees		*3 Apoc. Baruch*		15:25-34	123
1:48	123	4:16	158n	15:31	173n
1:60-61	123			15:32	173n
2:46	124n	*1 Enoch*		16:17	229
2:67	111n, 113n	9:3	254	19:16	229
8:32	254	19:1	75n	20:8	75n
10:61	254	46:7	75n	21:4	106n

21:5	75n	3:195	116	*Exodus Rabba*		
22:9	229	3:279	75n	29:4		173, 173n
22:16	34	3:605-606	75n	29:9		177
22:17	75n	3:710-720	263n			
22:20f	34	3:722-723	75n	*Seder 'Olam Rabba*		
30:16	106n	3:726	172n	1		199n
32:19	34	3:763f	88			
33:18	106n	3:772-775	263n	*Zadokite Work,*		
35:14	34	3:808	209	*Fragments of a*		
		4:6-23	75n	20:3		195n
4 Maccabees		5:356	75n			
6:17	180	5:403	75n	Mechilta on Exodus		
6:22	180			22:21		194
17:6	180	*T. Judah*				
18:1	180	14-15	83	*VI. QUMRAN*		
18:10	157n	20:3-5	112	*LITERATURE*		
Psalms of Solomon		*T. Zubulon*		**CD**		
1:18	106n	9:8	263n	1:19		185n
2:15	86			4:4		223n
2:18	106n	*T. Naphtali*				
2:19	105n	10	75n	**1QH**		
3:13	259n			11:5		127
7:5-9	106n	*T. Benjamin*		18:20		127
8:8-12	86	9:2	263n			
8:14	106n			**1QM**		
8:32	92			3:2		226
8:35	92	*V. RABBINIC*		4:6		162
9:17	229	*LITERATURE*		4:9-11		226
9:18	106n					
10:3	92	Mishnah				
10:8	106n	*Bikkurim*		**1QS**		
11:9	106n	1:4	196	2		101n
12:7	106n			2:9		181
13:5-9	92	*Yoma*		3:13		116
14:3	229	4a	169n	5:5		127
17:1	172n					
17:3	172n	*Sanhedrin*		**1QpHab**		
17:26-27	172	10:1	273	5.3-6		126n
17:28-30	172	*Aboth*		7:11		111n
17:35-36	65	1:17	111n	12.4-5		111n
Sibylline Oracles		Midrash Rabba		**4QpPs37**		
2:29-39	75n	*Genesis Rabba*		2:14		111n
2:73	85	12:5	158n	2:15		111n
3:8-26	88	48 (30a)	180			

Index of Passages

4QMMT
31-118	187
104-118	167

VII. ANCIENT WRITINGS

Josephus
Jewish Antiquities
13.257-258	124n
13.318-319	124n
15.253-254	124n
17.163	119n
18.3	119n
18.5	119n
20.44	111n

Against Apion
2.33-35	75n
2.38	83n
2.42	116

Jewish War
7.346	89n

Philo
De Congressu Eruditionis gratia
70	111n

De Praemiis et Poenis
79	111n

De Abrahamo
98	116
275-276	112

De Somniis
1.88-91	84

De Decalogo
61-63	89n

De Somniis
1.88-91	84

De Specialibus Legibus
1.13-27	89n
4.181	100

De Mutatione Nominum
177	182, 198
177-178	200n

De Vita Contemplativa
5-10	89n

1 Clement
31:2	202n
49:6	209

Justin
Dialogue with Trypho
140	180

Index of Authors

Achtemeier, P.J., 112
Albright, W.F., 101, 102
Allen, L.C., 31
Anderson, A.A., 60, 62, 63, 145
Andrew, M.E., 80, 81

Baab, O.J., 84, 86
Baldwin, J.G., 198, 201
Barnes, A., 134, 139
Barnett, P.W., 2
Barrett, C.K., 10, 26, 46, 47, 49, 54, 56, 59, 68, 73, 74, 78, 97, 99, 119, 124, 125, 135, 157, 158, 159, 160, 166, 170, 175, 186, 188, 197, 201, 217, 218, 222, 227, 229, 231, 232, 233, 235, 240, 241, 243, 254, 260, 262, 266, 267, 269, 273
Barth, K., 23, 28, 46, 103, 134, 171, 269
Barth, M., 222, 235, 299
Bartsch, H.W., 43, 45, 74, 97, 185,
Bassler, J.M., 96, 99, 102, 103, 104, 105, 106, 109, 110, 111, 112, 113, 114, 115, 123, 129, 207
Battle, Jr., J.A., 235, 236
Bauernfeind, O., 170
Baur, F.C., 2, 18, 51, 215, 224, 285
Beardslee, W.A., 1
Beare, F.W., 102, 221
Beasley-Murray, G.R., 169, 222
Becker, J., 9, 250, 275, 280
Beet, J.A., 135, 143, 172, 175
Beker, J.C., 48, 93, 117, 174, 193, 203, 207, 210, 211, 212, 215, 217, 222, 270
Bell, R., 274
Best, E., 1, 93
Betz, O., 181, 189, 197, 262, 283
Billerbeck, P., 34, 113, 169, 173, 187, 199
Birkeland, H., 146
Black, M., 22, 29, 30, 46, 47, 73, 74, 97, 103, 129, 130, 135, 139, 142, 145, 154, 162, 166, 175, 199, 218, 228, 234, 236, 238, 242, 254, 255, 257, 259, 262, 267, 269, 276, 278
Boccaccini, G., 102
Boers, H., 203
Bornkamm, G., 3, 16, 73, 117, 216, 306
Bowers, W.P., 8, 12, 28
Boylan, M.P., 61, 73, 126, 135, 139, 141, 150, 153, 167, 185, 191, 199, 207, 231, 232, 238
Brenton, L.C.L., 146
Briggs, C.A., 143, 145, 146, 148
Briggs, E.G., 143, 145, 146, 148
Bruce, F.F., 129, 139, 148, 153, 203, 233, 236, 269, 298, 303
Brunner, E., 87, 251, 255, 266, 277, 279
Bultmann, R., 28, 29, 49, 96, 99, 116, 154, 165, 221

Calvert, N.C., 203
Calvin, J., 61, 120, 218, 239, 267, 269
Campbell, D.A., 156, 160
Campbell, W.S., 18, 19, 130, 215,

218, 226, 228, 231, 272, 283
Caragounis, C.C., 9, 83, 101, 112, 192, 209, 210
Carras, G.P., 94, 97, 104, 109, 128
Chae, D.J.-S., 4, 14, 44, 48, 108, 306
Chance, J.B., 65
Charles, R.H., 106, 161, 170, 180
Clements, R.E., 182
Clifford, R.J., 197
Cole, A., 84
Conybeare, W.J., 167
Conzelmann, H., 217, 300
Cosgrove, C.H., 45, 99, 104, 106, 107, 108, 131, 153, 185
Cotterell, P., 14, 25
Craigie, P.C., 61, 85
Cranfield, C.E.B., 2, 22, 24, 26, 27, 28, 29, 31, 34, 35, 40, 43, 44, 45, 46, 47, 49, 50, 53, 54, 59, 60, 62, 65, 67, 68, 89, 95, 97, 99, 102, 103, 110, 111, 112, 113, 114, 119, 121, 123, 124, 129, 130, 132, 133, 135, 138, 139, 142, 143, 145, 147, 148, 150, 153, 154, 156, 157, 158, 159, 160, 162, 163, 170, 175, 183, 184, 187, 188, 190, 191, 192, 196, 200, 201, 207, 210, 219, 220, 221, 222, 223, 227, 232, 233, 235, 236, 237, 240, 241, 242, 248, 250, 251, 254, 255, 256, 257, 258, 259, 260, 262, 263, 264, 265, 267, 268, 269, 273, 275, 281, 297, 298
Craus, H.-J., 60, 63
Cullmann, O., 7, 8, 11
Cundall, A.E., 85

Dahl, N.A., 11, 35, 47, 103, 130, 134, 164, 173, 174, 176, 177, 208, 211, 217, 218, 221, 229, 233, 251, 267, 270, 273, 276, 278, 280

Danby, H., 273
Davidson, F., 240, 261
Davies, G.H., 84
Davies, G.N., 41, 99, 104, 114, 131, 132, 136, 137, 138, 143, 144, 145, 148, 154, 175, 185, 195, 196, 200
Davies, W.D., 9, 115, 130, 141, 180, 222, 255, 267
Deidun, T.J., 2, 300
Deissmann, A., 7, 160
Delitzsch, F., 31
Dinter, P.E., 32, 237, 256
Dodd, C.H., 34, 48, 73, 111, 112, 118, 124, 125, 126, 130, 135, 162, 179, 185, 197, 207, 221, 232, 233, 254, 266, 268, 269, 305
Doeve, J.W., 132
Donaldson, T.L., 262
Donfried, K.P., 155, 159
Dover, K.J., 83
Dunn, J.D.G., 1, 2, 22, 24, 25, 26, 27, 29, 31, 34, 35, 39, 40, 41, 44, 45, 46, 47, 49, 50, 54, 57, 59, 60, 61, 62, 65, 66, 68, 74, 78, 92, 99, 102, 103, 108, 111, 112, 113, 114, 115, 116, 124, 125, 126, 129, 130, 133, 136, 138, 139, 140, 142, 145, 146, 147, 148, 153, 155, 157, 158, 159, 160, 161, 163, 165, 166, 167, 169, 170, 171, 173, 175, 179, 184, 185, 186, 188, 190, 191, 196, 197, 199, 200, 203, 207, 212, 214, 217, 218, 222, 223, 226, 228, 230, 233, 235, 237, 239, 242, 244, 246, 248, 255, 260, 261, 262, 263, 264, 265, 266, 267, 269, 273, 275, 278, 280, 282, 298, 299, 303

Earle, R., 115
Eckstein, H.-J., 114
Edersheim, A., 180

Edgar, S.L.,	149	Giblin, C.H.,	41, 121, 149, 199
Eisenman, R.,	167, 187, 203, 323	Gifford, E.H.,	22, 56, 73, 126, 129, 135, 154, 158, 166, 167, 183, 184, 186, 191, 233, 236, 237, 245
Elliott, N.,	19, 75, 94, 95, 96, 97, 98, 99, 100, 104, 105, 110, 116, 117, 118, 121, 153, 154, 155, 161, 164, 165, 166, 167, 168, 186, 220	Godet, F.,	45, 53, 56, 191, 192, 196, 200, 267, 281
Ellis, E.E.,	13, 31, 37, 42, 59, 139, 142, 186, 203, 218, 232, 235	Godsey, J.,	2, 300
		Gore, C.,	123, 135
		Grässer, E.,	174, 176, 215, 280, 281
Ellison, H.L.,	264	Grayston, K.,	35
Epp, E.J.,	226	Greer, R.A.,	142
Ericksen, R.P.,	216	Griffith, G.O.,	135
Evans, C.A.,	218	Grosvenor, M.,	60, 118, 126, 132, 170
		Guerra, A.J.,	186, 189, 217, 224, 269, 277
Ferguson, E.,	83		
Fiedler, P.,	184	Guthrie, D.,	73
Field, D.H.,	85		
Fischer, J.A.,	96		
Fishbane, M.,	189	Hafemann, S.,	19, 280
Fitzer, G.,	85, 86, 160	Hahn, F.,	19, 203, 273, 280, 281
Fitzer, G.,	85, 86, 160		
Fitzmyer, J.A.,	2, 75, 76, 80, 83, 93, 101, 111, 112, 117, 120, 122, 123, 124, 125, 127, 142, 145, 156, 157, 158, 159, 174, 186, 188, 196, 208, 210, 216, 218, 226, 231, 233, 235, 236, 237, 241, 242, 248, 254, 262, 265, 267, 268, 275, 277, 278, 280, 298, 299	Haldane, R.,	145, 166, 170, 172, 193
		Hall, D.R.,	131, 132, 319
		Hall, W.S.,	9
		Hanson, A.T.,	58, 231, 269
		Harnack, A.,	207
		Hatch, E.,	90
		Haynes, S.,	215
France, R.T.,	67, 102	Hays, R.B.,	31, 32, 37, 53, 58, 59, 68, 94, 113, 114, 122, 123, 131, 133, 135, 139, 142, 153, 155, 176, 188, 190, 193, 194, 201, 222, 223, 232, 236, 237, 238, 242
Fridrichen, A.,	9		
Friedrich, G.,	170		
Fryer, N.S.L.,	160		
Gager, J.G.,	45, 160, 165, 166, 204	Headlam, A.C.,	22, 24, 26, 29, 51, 52, 54, 58, 59, 62, 67, 73, 74, 75, 95, 96, 97, 111, 114, 121, 123, 124, 125, 126, 129, 138, 139, 153, 160, 171, 175, 185, 186, 188, 190, 191, 201, 210, 220, 221, 224, 227, 231, 234, 236, 239, 240, 241, 243, 245,
Gardiner, F.,	13		
Garlington, D.B.,	74, 78, 119, 120		
Gaston, L.,	99, 107, 165, 171, 272, 274, 280		
Gempf, C.,	87		
Getty, M.A.,	217, 278		

247, 254, 255, 256, 262, 264, 267, 269, 271, 298
Hengel, M., 11, 14, 30, 40, 65, 124, 177, 306
Henry, P., 10
Hill, G., 44
Hodge, C., 54, 120, 134
Hofius, O., 282
Holter, K., 76
Holtz, T., 9
Hooker, M., 74, 78, 79, 99, 177
Howard, G., 161, 166, 179, 214
Howard, W.F., 33
Howson, J.S., 167
Hübner, H., 165, 166, 169, 171, 180, 184, 203
Hudson, J.T., 98, 135
Hultgren, A., 160
Hunter, A.M., 13
Hvalvik, R.A., 49, 278, 280, 281
Hyldahl, N., 74, 76, 77, 78, 79, 99

Jeremias, J., 58, 122, 202
Jervell, J., 28
Jervis, L.A., 7, 40
Jewett, R., 2, 12, 45, 47, 51, 94
Jocz, J., 179, 180
Johnson, E.E., 265
Johnson, S.L., 132

Kähler, M., 9, 10
Kaiser, Jr., W.C., 13
Käsemann, E., 2, 22, 23, 24, 25, 27, 28, 29, 31, 41, 43, 46, 46, 61, 62, 66, 73, 75, 76, 77, 93, 96, 97, 98, 106, 109, 111, 112, 113, 114, 117, 118, 122, 126, 129, 130, 133, 142, 147, 148, 153, 154, 155, 156, 159, 165, 166, 173, 177, 185, 188, 191, 196, 201, 207, 218, 220, 221, 232, 233, 235, 237, 245, 246, 249, 251, 254, 259, 263, 266, 267, 269, 270, 273, 281, 291, 300
Kautzsch, E., 247
Kaylor, R.D., 6, 48, 155, 157, 204, 207, 210, 211, 213, 250
Keck, L.E., 52, 99, 135, 142, 297, 298
Keener, C.S., 209, 212, 233
Kennedy, H.A.A., 9
Kertelge, K., 159
Kettunen, M., 19
Kim, S., 1, 2, 3, 9, 26, 164, 283, 291, 302, 303, 304, 305
Kirk, K.E., 111, 114, 133, 135
Kissane, E.J., 143, 146
Kitchen, K.A., 80
Klausner, J., 180
Klein, G., 19, 23, 38, 43
Knox, J., 45, 262, 306
Koch, D.-A., 142, 237, 238, 246, 278
König, A., 111
Kugel, J.L., 142
Kuhr, F., 113
Kümmel, W.G., 11, 47, 218, 221, 240, 250, 252, 277, 278, 281,

Lacey, D.R. de, 1
Lagrange, M.-J., 97, 148, 160, 191, 267
Lapide, P., 3, 16, 165, 216, 280, 292
Leenhardt, F.J., 97, 112, 129, 137, 142, 194, 199, 201, 231, 258, 260, 262, 265, 268, 269
Liddell, H.G., 29
Liddon, H.P., 31, 55, 56, 73, 258
Lietzmann, H., 56, 95, 96, 103, 267
Lightfoot, J.B., 40, 41, 43, 73, 74, 88, 97, 110, 115, 123, 133, 134, 139, 144, 149, 160, 175, 180, 191, 193, 199
Lincoln, A.T., 88, 94, 122, 138, 142, 143, 152, 186, 193, 196, 209, 270, 299

Lindars, B., 122, 238
Locke, J., 135, 139, 152, 166, 184, 214, 298
Longenecker, B.W., 161, 216
Longenecker, R.N., 189, 203
Lorenzi, L. de, 229
Lunt, H.G., 120
Luther, M., 60, 61, 120, 140, 150, 191, 210, 300
Luz, U., 142, 210

Maccoby, H., 142, 199
Mann, C.S., 101, 102
Manson, T.W., 160, 221
Manson, W., 10
Marshall, I.H., 49
Martin, R.P., 19, 63, 177, 180, 209, 227, 240, 261, 270
Martinez, F.G., 167
Marxsen, W., 73
Mason, S., 199
McKnight, S., 116, 124
McNeile, A.H., 142
Metzger, B.M., 133, 158, 171, 227, 298
Meyer, H.A.W., 1, 40, 46, 48, 73, 95, 96, 121, 123, 124, 125, 126, 131, 132, 134, 139, 140, 141, 143, 145, 148, 166, 171, 191
Michel, O., 96, 99, 158, 160, 170, 194, 201, 218, 237, 247, 267
Milne, D.J.W., 78
Minear, P.S., 2, 29, 38, 45, 92, 93, 126
Moiser, J., 56
Moo, D., 2, 78, 103, 132, 135, 139, 147, 152, 153, 171, 192, 207, 208
Morris, L., 27, 45, 57, 60, 65, 125, 135, 160, 190, 199, 242, 254, 255, 267, 268, 269
Motyer, S., 224, 234, 260, 263, 265, 267, 268, 273, 282, 283
Moule, H.C.G., 134

Moulton, J.H., 23, 26, 27, 33, 66
Mowinckel, S., 143
Moxnes, H., 52, 97, 121, 131, 133, 164, 166, 168, 176, 177, 183, 186, 191, 200, 202, 203
Müller, P., 19, 26, 30, 40, 44
Munck, J., 2, 8, 9, 10, 16, 27, 40, 216, 217, 218, 244, 267, 274, 278
Murphy, R.E., 197, 319, 324, 325
Murray, J., 22, 24, 27, 42, 45, 49, 65, 68, 73, 123, 135, 138, 150, 218, 233, 254, 258, 259, 260, 262, 263, 264, 267, 268, 275
Mussner, 49, 215, 242, 272, 274, 280

Neusner, J., 314
Newman, B.M., 24, 40, 73, 255, 257, 258, 260, 264, 267, 268, 269
Newman, C.C., 303
Nickelsburg, G.W.E., 173, 333
Nida, E.A., 24, 40, 73, 255, 257, 258, 260, 264, 267, 268, 269
Noack, B., 3, 217, 222
North, C.R., 31
Nygren, A., 46, 73, 96, 97, 99, 129, 135, 140, 154, 160, 170, 175, 184, 194, 207

O'Brien, P.T., 22, 66
Oepke, A., 196
Oesterley, W.O.E., 88, 144, 145, 146
O'Neill, J.C., 141, 142, 196, 197, 210, 215
Osborne, W.L., 273, 275
Oss, D.A., 32, 236
Oswalt, J.N., 80

Parker, T.H.L., 73
Perowne, J.J.S., 145

Index of Authors

Pfeiffer, R.H., 75
Piper, J., 104, 105, 218, 219, 220, 222, 224, 225, 232, 233
Plevnik, J., 19
Pohlenz, M., 103

Rad, G. von, 81, 182, 197
Räisänen, H., 103, 109, 128, 165, 167, 171, 227, 241, 250, 293
Redpath, H.A., 90
Rese, M., 222, 261, 266, 281
Reumann, J., 159
Ridderbos, H., 175
Rienecker, F., 33, 169, 188, 190, 271
Ringgren, H., 146
Robertson, A.T., 22, 23, 26, 27, 29, 271
Robertson, O.P., 126, 182, 184, 198
Robinson, D.W.B., 24,
Robinson, J.A.T., 217, 221, 251, 264
Rogers, C., 33, 169, 188, 190, 271
Rubinkiewicz, R., 120

Sadler, M.F., 180
Sanday, W., 22, 24, 26, 29, 51, 52, 54, 58, 59, 62, 67, 73, 74, 75, 95, 96, 97, 111, 114, 121, 123, 124, 125, 126, 129, 138, 139, 153, 160, 171, 175, 185, 186, 188, 190, 191, 201, 210, 220, 221, 224, 227, 231, 234, 236, 239, 240, 241, 243, 245, 247, 254, 255, 256, 262, 264, 267, 269, 271, 298
Sanders, E.P., 5, 6, 10, 11, 12, 49, 50, 65, 80, 103, 109, 111, 118, 126, 128, 130, 135, 139, 155, 157, 162, 165, 166, 167, 170, 204, 207, 211, 214, 241, 243, 250, 273, 275, 278, 279, 280, 281, 282
Sandnes, K.O., 2, 8, 9, 108, 270

Sänger, D., 250, 266, 269, 280, 281, 284
Schlatter, A., 13, 97, 201
Schlier, H., 60, 96, 142
Schmeller, T., 96
Schmithals, W., 23
Schnabel, E.J., 116
Schnackenburg, R., 169
Schoeps, H.J., 166, 173, 179, 220, 224, 228, 270
Schreiner, T.R., 139, 250
Schrenk, G., 12, 267, 270, 301
Schweitzer, A., 2, 7, 8
Scott, J.M., 226, 272, 283
Scott, R., 29
Seifrid, M.A., 2, 16, 24, 25, 35, 49, 154, 162, 218, 222
Shedd, W.G.T., 22, 96, 111, 120, 135, 158, 170, 175, 191
Siegert, F., 220, 229, 236, 243, 273, 274
Siker, J.S., 179, 202
Silva, M., 139
Simpson, J.W., 217
Sinclair, S.G., 3, 5, 47
Stamm, J.J., 80, 81
Stanley, C.D., 14, 33, 59, 63, 122, 135, 137, 139, 143, 144, 145, 147, 186, 231, 232, 235, 238, 241, 245, 246, 247, 256, 276
Stanton, G.N., 305, 306
Stendahl, K., 2, 3, 5, 9, 10, 16, 18, 49, 154, 155, 163, 215, 216, 242, 260, 270, 272, 274, 280, 300
Stern, D.H., 47
Stevens, G.B., 9
Stortz, M.E., 300
Stowers, S.K., 30, 97, 115, 130, 132, 133, 175, 300
Strack, H., 34, 113, 169, 173, 187, 199
Stuart, M., 53, 56, 67, 337
Stuhlmacher, P., 2, 3, 16, 131, 133, 135, 153, 154, 159, 165, 210, 216, 255, 262, 292, 304

Suggs, M.J.,	242	Wellhausen, J.,	182
Swetnam, J.,	192, 194	Westermann, C.,	31, 147, 149, 245
Synge, F.C.,	133, 134	Wiefel, W.,	3, 16, 217
		Wigoder, G.,	215
Taylor, V.,	135, 139, 148	Wilckens, U.,	24, 26, 29, 46, 51, 53, 62, 65, 97, 103, 112, 119, 127, 142, 149, 159, 166, 167, 170, 241, 255, 288
Thayer, J.H.,	44, 175		
Thompson, J.A.,	85		
Thompson, R.W.,	116, 166, 171, 175, 176, 179		
		Winston, D.,	100
Tidball, D.J.,	7	Wise, M.,	167, 187, 203
Tobin, T.H.,	152	Wright, D.F.,	83, 85
Toit, A.B. du,	93	Wright, N.T.,	3, 18, 25, 47, 51, 68, 75, 154, 155, 157, 161, 162, 163, 165, 170, 178, 193, 207, 208, 211, 217, 222, 226, 227, 228, 246, 252, 255, 260, 261, 262, 270, 273, 274, 276, 280, 300
Toorn, K. van der	84		
Turner, M.M.B.,	25, 288, 299		
Turner, N.,	14, 23, 26, 27, 66, 133, 190		
		Wuellner, W.,	23
Urbach, E.E.,	173	Wuest, K.S.,	125, 126, 166, 199
Vaughan, C.J.,	55		
Vermes, G.,	101	Young, J.B. de,	83
Vollmer, H.A.,	142, 247		
		Zeller, D.,	73, 116
Waard, J. de,	279	Zerwick, M.,	22, 60, 118, 126, 132, 170
Wagner, G.,	217, 250, 262, 270, 273, 275		
		Ziesler, J.,	26, 29, 30, 40, 42, 45, 46, 49, 52, 68, 73, 103, 111, 112, 114, 119, 121, 126, 127, 129, 134, 136, 138, 139, 141, 154, 155, 158, 159, 162, 163, 165, 175, 185, 188, 190, 194, 210, 215, 222, 230, 232, 234, 236, 237, 241, 242, 249, 259, 260, 262, 266, 268, 269, 299
Watson, F.,	2, 18, 19, 22, 43, 97, 109, 128, 139, 162, 166, 170, 184, 193, 197, 216, 219, 222, 224, 226, 241, 250, 261, 265		
Watts, J.D.W.,	147		
Wedderburn, A.J.M.,	19, 23, 65, 74, 78, 99, 210		
Weiser, A.,	143		
Weiss, J.,	99, 135, 235		

Index of Subjects

Abraham 4, 43, 53, 68, 149, 154, 154n3, 164, 168n7, 211, 227, 230, 249, 281, 301
   faith of 43, 55, 154, 155, 180n113, 181-186, 184n123, 187-202, 200n198), 201n206, 203n211, 290, 291, 294
   father of circumcised 193
   father of many nations 53, 154, 155, 181-183, 187-202, 196n182, 199n196, 204, 291, 294
   father of uncircumcised 189, 190, 190n154, 191, 194, 194n176
   Jews descended from 155, 169, 191, 203, 290, 294, 296
   Jewish boasting in 179-181
   justification of 164, 183-187, 184n122, 189, 290
   justified by faith 154, 164
   name changed from Abram 196
   obedience of 155, 201, 201n206
   righteousness of 183, 184, 188, 189n149, 195, 196, 198-200
   unbelief of 198
   world-wide family of 222
Adam 4, 78-80, 80n22, 158n21, 210-213, 262n200, 291, 301, 304
Adam-Christ typology 212n30
Adultery 84, 86n43, 92, 117-120, 123n187, 131
Anti-Semitism 3, 6, 16, 150, 216, 217n12, 292
Arrogance (*see also* Boasting) 168, 221, 252, 270, 270n238, 271, 273, 274, 283, 287, 295,
Assyria 172n79, 237
Atonement 7n30, 61, 168n60, 212
Augustine 239

Baal (*see also* Worship)
   worship of 82, 119, 120, 254
Babylon 75n6, 233
Baptism 212, 214
Blasphemy 117n156, 123
   of Gentiles 121
   of Jews 117, 122n181, 212, 167
Blessedness (*see also* Blessing; Gentiles; Salvation)
   35, 42, 181-184, 184n122, 186-188, 186n134, 192, 196n182, 200, 227, 275n251, 276, 290
Blessing 163, 186-188, 218-220, 223, 227, 244, 260, 263, 263n206, 264, 266-268, 277, 282n282, 283, 284, 287, 287n287
Boasting (*see also* Arrogance) 166n52, 170n66
   of Gentiles 220n32, 270, 272
   of Jews 4, 116n153, 154, 154n1, 155, 164-181, 165n50, 168n60, 172nn77-79, 179n107, 183, 203, 204, 294, 296
   of Paul 28n46

Calvin 61n194, 120n173, 239
Child-sacrifice 81, 81n26, 90
Christianity 3, 11, 13, 22, 52, 99, 135, 142, 155, 160, 161, 186, 202, 217, 235
Christophany 1, 302, 303, 304, 305, 322
Church (of God) 10, 28n44, 55, 61, 66, 226, 228n64, 238n104, 288
   in Corinth 168
   in Galatia 226
   in Jerusalem 15, 98, 298n8,
   in Rome 15, 16, 22n9, 25, 30,

43nn104-105, 70n229, 94n61, 107, 108n112, 155n5, 166, 168, 204, 220, 220nn31-32, 252, 252n162, 270, 271, 287, 288
unity of 209, 288
Circumcision 51, 115, 124, 128, 129, 139, 182, 188-190, 193, 194, 195n178, 198
  as seal of covenant 123, 124, 124n189, 196n182, 198
  believing Gentiles included in 125, 128
  guarantee of salvation 124, 124n189, 192
  Jewish 123, 124, 180, 282n282, 290
  negated by disobedience 124, 127
  of Abraham 155, 185n128, 190, 193, 195
  of the heart 102, 125n199, 127
  physical 110, 123, 124, 124nn192-194, 126, 127, 149, 151, 293
  practised by Gentiles 124n191
  refers to Jews 51, 176n96, 191, 193
  spiritual 110, 123, 126, 194
  true 124-126, 125n196, 128, 193n169, 293
Condemnation
  in Adam 213
  of Gentile towards Jew 125, 126, 126n202, 127
  of Jew towards Gentile 82, 126
  Paul's 74, 83, 87, 88, 94n61, 116, 136, 253, 294
  prophetic 88n49, 118, 150
  removal of 213, 214
  towards Jews 80, 82, 88, 97n72, 118, 125n201, 132, 132n224, 134, 147, 232, 253, 257n177, 294
Covenant 41, 92, 108, 124n193, 127, 131n220, 144, 155n4, 5, 161, 162, 162n36, 165, 172, 185, 187, 189, 198, 226, 257, 282
  conditioned 282n282
  leading to Jewish complacency 73, 99, 117, 124n189, 165, 179, 181
  Messianic 149, 150

  moral call of 108n113, 139n253
  new 30n52, 113, 155n5, 226
  seal of covenant 189, 198 (*see also* Circumcision)
  Sinai 139n253
  with Abraham 54, 108n113, 196n182, 200
  with Israel 60-62, 100, 107, 123, 124, 217n13, 253
Covenantal Nomism 73, 100n86, 136, 139, 139n253, 185, 208, 282
Creation 75-80
  God revealed in 87, 93, 98

David 32n65, 40n89, 43, 60, 65, 131, 131nn221-222, 132, 149, 149n295, 150, 172, 174, 183, 184, 186, 186n137, 187, 257, 258, 259, 278
Day of Atonement 162, 187
Death 84, 85, 87, 209, 210, 211, 213
  of Christ 16, 41, 42, 42n102, 158, 161n28, 208, 209, 304-307
  of Paul 16n56
Decalogue, the 80, 81, 121
Diaspora 61
Disobedience (*see also* Israel) 211, 247, 254, 279, 291, 295
  of Gentiles 279
  of humanity 91n56, 92n57, 211, 284, 291
  of Jews 34, 35, 41, 80, 90, 92n57, 101, 102, 107n109, 123, 240n145, 245, 247, 249, 262n200, 276, 279, 284, 295

Election 43, 44, 180, 212, 224-230, 226n53, 234-236, 238, 239, 249, 281n278,
  of Gentiles 104n99, 224, 225, 230, 235, 236, 239, 283, 286
  of Israel 180, 224-229, 239, 268, 276, 283
Elijah 253, 254
Equality
  of Jew and Gentile, 2, 4, 5, 6, 9, 12,

Index of Subjects

16, 17, 36, 47, 50, 70, 71, 72, 94, 104, 106, 110, 150, 151, 152, 153, 155, 156, 158n19, 181, 204, 205, 206, 210, 212, 214, 217, 219, 239, 240, 244, 250, 253, 273, 282, 285, 288, 289, 290, 292, 293, 294, 295, 296, 300
Esau 193n169, 230, 232-234, 232nn72-73, 238
Eschatology 30n5, 62
Essenes 124

Faith (*see also* Abraham; Justification) 11n45, 38, 53, 66, 68, 155, 159, 168n6, 170, 179, 184-186, 190n154, 193, 194, 243n124, 252, 282, 306
  as requirement of law 113n138, 133
  demonstration of 113
  Gentile 4, 29, 34, 35, 38, 41, 42, 107n109, 113, 128, 165, 171, 185n128, 189, 190, 218, 219, 223, 238, 250, 296, 306
  in Christ 36, 36n77, 42, 105, 147, 159-163, 171, 208, 213, 242, 249, 279-282, 282n281, 287, 290, 291, 296
  Jewish lack of 131, 132, 147, 171
  necessary for salvation 36, 38, 41, 42, 50, 163, 171, 175, 176, 176n96, 230, 240-244, 284, 286, 287, 290, 291
  obedience of 40-42, 45, 169
  oral confession of 147
  reckoned as righteousness 185, 186, 188, 195, 207n2
  word of 147, 242, 243, 243n124, 249, 286
Fear of God 148, 177
Festivals 139
Forgiveness 186n134, 188, 212
Freedom
  of Gentile converts 163n42
  of God 219, 224-234, 231n68, 238, 239, 286, 291, 295

Gehenna 180
Gentile Mission (*see also* Paul: mission to Gentiles) 9, 11-13, 12n49, 69, 47, 177, 216n9, 266, 275n252, 277, 278, 278n264, 302n1, 303
Gentiles (*see also* Faith; Justification; Righteousness; Salvation)
  as children of Abraham 187-199, 199n196, 210, 224, 227, 294
  as those who do not have the law 110, 112, 112n131, 227
  believing 36, 58, 62, 63, 111, 111n130, 113, 137, 140, 155, 156, 161, 163, 181, 183, 184n122, 188, 188n146, 189, 190, 192-194, 196-199, 201, 203, 210, 219, 220n33, 225-227, 230, 232, 235, 235n88, 241n112, 246, 252, 267, 270, 271, 284, 286, 291, 293, 295, 296
  believing Gentiles as children of God/promise 213, 214, 227, 230, 236
  believing Gentiles as true circumcision 125, 125n196, 128, 193 (*see also* Circumcision)
  belonging equally to God 174-176
  bias towards 95, 103, 108, 109, 114, 129, 204, 285, 288, 293, 296
  blessing of 109, 260, 262-264, 266-268, 275n251
  calling of 37, 54, 174, 175, 212, 214, 219, 223-225, 234n87, 238, 285, 286, 294, 295
  faith of 4, 35, 128, 185, 189, 204, 218, 233, 238, 250, 251, 296, (*see also* Faith)
  hope of 31, 64-66, 106n105
  justified by faith 17, 20, 29, 37, 42, 156, 162, 188, 190, 202, 205, 249, 293, 294, 306 (*see also* Faith; Justification)
  law-free 107n111

legitimacy of salvation/ justification of 5, 15, 20, 32, 37, 41n96, 51, 68, 69, 104, 108, 110, 151, 156, 194, 204, 240, 248, 249, 294, 295, 297
obedience of 29, 32, 40, 45, 112-115, 149, 239, 247
referred as uncircumcision 89, 176n96, 187, 188, 298, 298n8
righteousness of 128 (*see also* Righteousness)
salvation of 5, 10, 11, 12, 15, 20, 21, 28, 31, 32, 73, 110, 128, 197, 252, 253, 277 (*see also* Salvation)

Glory 4, 47, 67, 82, 106, 107, 132, 158, 172n79, 174n87, 208, 213, 226, 234, 261, 266, 285, 291, 298

God
as Creator 87-89, 93
faithfulness of 131-133, 162, 162n36, 171n75, 215, 217n13, 222, 223, 228, 282, 285, 288
freedom of (*see* Freedom of God)
grace of 17. 26, 27, 27n37, 34, 44, 45, 159, 161, 184, 196n182, 211 (*see also* Grace)
impartiality of 4, 73, 95, 103, 103n95, 104, 104n100, 105, 105nn102-105, 106, 106n105, 107-109, 109n122, 110, 114, 138, 149, 151, 153, 155, 166, 168, 176, 225, 293
judgement of 4, 73, 73n3, 81, 100, 103, 103n93, 105, 107, 108n114, 130, 133, 141n259, 149, 253, 255, 290, 293, 296
kindness of 100, 101n87
King of the nations 177, 178
love of 116n155, 208, 208n11, 223, 223n41, 226n53, 248
mercy of 52-57, 57n171, 60, 62, 63, 99n82, 102, 104n99, 106, 223, 225, 228, 230, 231, 231n68, 233-239, 248, 249, 274, 279, 280n271, 281, 284, 286, 290, 291, 294, 295
patience of 34, 100, 233, 249, 255n171
plan of 215-288, 291
power of 35, 47, 69, 87, 231, 233, 276
promises of 3, 7n30, 42, 45, 51-58, 61, 63, 68, 90, 122n183, 133, 163, 173, 174, 179, 195, 197-200, 203n212, 218, 231, 237, 251, 299n11, 301 (*see also* Promise)
righteousness of 18, 23n16, 35, 49, 131n220, 132, 133, 133n232, 140, 144, 147, 154-157, 159-166, 162n36, 167-168n60, 171, 202, 242, 290, 303n4
salvific blessing of 7n30, 34n69, 20, 32, 34, 35, 46, 50, 51, 64, 67, 107, 163, 179, 206, 211, 219, 223, 244, 260, 262, 272, 277, 283, 284, 286, 292, 293, 300, 301 (*see also* Blessing)
salvific plan of 17, 70, 206, 214, 219, 221, 252, 261, 272, 276, 277, 283-285, 291, 296, 297, 301, 307
saviour of Israel 172n79
self-revelation of 34, 86, 87, 87n44, 89, 93
universal lordship of 173, 175
wrath of 4, 73n3, 93n60, 107, 116n154, 117n159, 131n220, 126n208, 162, 163, 178, 207n2, 233, 258, 289n1, 291

Golden calf (*see also* Idolatry) 80, 80n22, 23, 84, 84n34, 231n68

Gomorrah 237-239

Gospel (*see also* Paul) 1, 41n90, 42, 42n102, 203, 215, 246, 283, 288, 297, 298, 298nn7-8, 299, 302, 304, 306
consistent with the OT 67, 157
conversion of Jews to 280
expounded in Romans 23, 159n23, 292, 298, 299, 300n14

Index of Subjects

implication of 70, 223, 292, 299, 305, 306
intended for both Jews and Gentiles 31, 35-37, 41, 47, 66n220, 217, 245, 245n130, 289, 290
law-free 8n31, 16, 288, 303, 304
of God/Christ 7, 19, 29, 40, 41, 45, 46, 63, 204, 260, 272, 289, 292, 297n6, 298
Paul set apart for 29, 40, 297, 298n8, 299n13
Paul's consciousness to preach 15, 16, 26, 36, 37, 44-47, 289, 297-299, 302, 303, 307
power of God for salvation 35, 47, 68, 69, 276
preached first to Jews 48, 245nn131-132, 277, 283n285
preached to Gentiles 8n37, 11n47, 15, 29, 31, 44-46, 63, 108, 298n8, 305
promised through the prophets 13, 40-42, 40n89, 58, 67, 142n262, 202
rejected by Jews 3, 3n10, 48, 69, 92n57, 147, 147n283, 215, 224, 245, 245n132, 246, 252, 259n187, 260-262, 260n192, 262n198, 262n201, 268, 276
relation with law 70
response of Gentiles to 41, 241, 245n130, 246, 249, 306
truth of 15, 36, 298n8

Gospels 58n176, 102n91, 122n182, 169n65

Grace 40, 45, 159, 159n24, 161, 184, 212, 233, 253, 254, 255n171, 282

Grief 108, 237

Guilt 86, 96, 109, 128, 213, 240, 249, 292, 293, 300

Holocaust 130, 215, 215n5, 216, 292, 300
post-Holocaust (*see* Theology: post-Holocaust)
pre-Holocaust 216

Homosexuality
connected with pagan practices 85, 86, 86n42,
evidenced in the tribe of Benjamin 84, 84n36, 85nn37-39, 86n43
found in Jewish society 84, 85, 86, 90, 149, 293
of Gentiles 83, 83nn29-32, 84, 84n33, 90, 98
practised in Greek society 83, 83nn29-32, 84, 84n33

Hope 31, 34, 64-66, 65n214, 92, 106n105, 180, 182, 187, 198-200, 208n11, 250, 250n151, 260, 269n234

Hosea 82, 85, 174n87, 234, 236, 236n95, 238

Humanity
failed to acknowledge God 86, 89n52, 133
salvation of 49n131, 249

Idolatry
condemned in Jew and Gentile 74, 75, 75n7, 78, 86, 88, 88n50, 98n73
Gentile 75, 82, 83, 90, 98
Jewish 76, 76n10, 80-82, 84n35, 90-92, 117-119, 119n170, 120, 120n172, 149, 246, 293
Moses' warning against 80
seen as prostitution 91

Immorality—sexual (*see also* prostitution)
associated with worship of golden calf 84 (*see also* Golden calf)
practised by gentiles 84, 90, 98
practised by Jews 74, 82, 83, 84n35, 86, 90, 92, 98, 118, 149, 293

Interdependence of Jew and Gentile 217, 221, 272, 279, 284, 288n290, 296

Isaac 102n91, 155, 182, 193n169, 196n182, 198, 201, 201n206, 203n211, 230, 232, 235, 238,

282n282
Isaiah
  book of 30, 32, 37, 39, 121, 237
  Paul's favourite prophet 31
  Prophet 31-37, 40, 64, 69, 100, 113, 123, 237, 238, 248
Ishmael 193n169, 226, 229, 230, 233
Israel (*see also* Jews; Judaism)
  disobedience of (*see* Disobedience)
  failure of 3, 80, 86, 89, 128, 147, 215, 223, 240, 244, 248, 249n148, 250, 256n175, 261n195, 263, 286, 295
  fall of 80n22, 101n89, 239, 259, 260, 261, 261n196, 283
  future of 216, 221, 239, 274-276, 279, 284, 292, 296
  given over to sinfulness 89, 93
  hardening of 24, 101, 101n88, 220, 224, 231, 252, 253-259, 256n175, 261n198, 264n212, 275, 275nn251-253, 276, 282, 284, 286, 295
  lacking understanding 144, 145
  modern state of 215
  not rejected by God 220, 220n30, 250, 253, 282, 282n282
  rebellion of 80
  redemption of 250
  rejecting God's grace 34
  restoration of 32, 143, 180, 208, 236, 236n95, 245, 247, 263, 268, 283n285
  salvation of 33, 61, 62, 221, 222, 222n39, 239, 265n214, 266, 267, 272, 273, 275, 275n252, 276, 277, 279, 280n271, 273, 281, 281n278, 282, 284, 292
  sinful history of 72, 74, 80, 93, 150, 151, 293
  stubbornness of 81, 101, 101n87, 151
  true 126n203, 228, 228n64, 238n104
  unbelief of 4, 101, 218, 228, 238-240, 243, 244-248, 250, 253, 257, 258, 260, 282, 286

Jacob 40, 87n45, 102n91, 180, 181, 193n169, 228, 230, 232, 238, 274
Jealousy 91, 266, 274, 276
Jeremiah 82, 108, 113, 120, 125n199, 127, 177-179, 178n105
Jerusalem 3n15, 15, 15n55, 16, 16n56, 23n16, 28n46, 40n88, 91, 120n172, 121, 244, 271, 277, 307,
Jesus Christ
  compared to Adam 211, 291
  cross of 7n30, 209, 305
  death of (*see* Death: of Christ)
  lordship of 207, 209, 241, 243, 291
  Messiahship of 10n40, 41, 42, 58, 67, 108, 149, 152, 227, 285 (*see also* Messiah)
  ministry of 51, 52, 56, 58
  obedience to death 158
  Redeemer 284
  resurrection of 7n30, 16, 41, 42, 42nn101-102, 201, 278, 304-307
  Saviourhood of 109
  service of 51-54, 57-59, 62
  special relationship to Jews 4, 289
Jews (*see also* Israel; Judaism)
  advantages of 48, 48n128, 49, 129, 133, 133n234, 149, 150, 151, 219, 289n1, 290
  as children of Abraham 181, 295
  as children of God 180, 214, 173, 173n80
  as covenant people 117, 124n189
  as hearers of the law 110
  believing 46, 50, 62, 68, 69, 158, 161, 185n128, 188, 191-194, 193n170, 201, 202, 204, 213, 241, 270n238, 271, 281, 285, 299, 300
  boasting of 155, 203 (*see also* Boasting)
  chastised by God 92
  complacency of 5, 34, 73, 94, 95,

Index of Subjects

99-102, 101n91, 102n91, 110, 114, 116, 117, 128-130, 136, 140, 169n66, 173, 179
covenantal privileges of 99
critical attitude to Gentiles 65, 100, 116, 126, 172
depravity of 133-135, 139, 141, 152, 159
disobedience of (*see also* Disobedience: of Jews) 34, 109, 114-117, 116n155, 117n160, 149, 168, 169
exclusive relationship to God 4, 203
failure to retain knowledge of God 86-92 (*see also* Knowledge)
given over to sinfulness 89-92
God's blessing of 218
hardening of 24, 101, 101n88, 224, 230, 231, 234, 272, 274, 275n251, 286, 295 (*see also* Israel: hardening of)
hypocrisy of 82, 116, 116n155, 122n181, 123n186, 126
pride of 115-117, 116n155, 117n160, 149, 168, 169
primacy of 4-6, 47, 51, 251, 276-280, 284, 292
priority of 3, 46-48, 52, 67
privileges of 4, 47, 48, 104, 117, 129, 132, 135n234, 158n19, 204, 214, 219, 226, 227, 227n60, 289, 294
rebellion of 80, 101, 254, 262n200
rejection of 37, 218, 238, 249, 283
salvation of (*see* Salvation: of Jews)
superiority of 44, 50, 112n131, 130, 134n234, 140, 141, 155, 174, 272, 274,
unbelief of 5, 15, 24, 35, 36, 48, 51, 63, 88, 108, 113, 131, 132, 136, 137, 140, 147, 191-193, 204, 220, 224, 224n46, 232, 233, 238, 239, 244-246, 245n130, 247, 253, 255, 256, 259, 262, 269, 270, 272, 276, 282-285, 287, 291, 295, 296

unfaithfulness of 51
Joy 31, 65, 66, 66n217, 121, 237, 273
Judaism (*see also* Jews) 11, 102n91, 161, 162, 164, 166, 167n60, 172, 173, 177, 177n101, 184n125, 186n137, 204, 294
criticised by Paul 72, 75, 83, 94, 94n61, 95, 100n86, 109, 128, 151, 165
influence on Paul 19n3
Paul's departure from 14, 106n106, 124n192, 125, 142n262, 162, 173, 174, 203
soteriology in 111, 161, 162, 165, 166
view of Gentiles in 44, 127
Judaisers 15, 214, 304-307
Judgement (*see also* God: judgement of) 5, 79, 81, 100, 103, 105, 111, 111n129, 123, 125, 132, 133, 141n259, 168, 180, 201n201, 233, 237
against the Gentiles 31, 108, 114, 244, 296
against Israel 4, 73, 81, 102n91, 105, 106n105, 107, 108n114, 114n146, 118n163, 151, 220n30, 225, 237n101, 239, 244, 246, 253, 289n1, 293
universal 130, 131n220, 163, 168
Justification (*see also* Justification by faith; Righteousness) 134, 152, 165, 204, 205, 208, 211, 214, 223, 241n112, 249
apart from law/works 7n30, 36, 108, 139, 141, 157, 162, 166, 171, 183, 186n137, 187, 202, 306
by grace 68, 159, 159n24, 161, 184, 261, 292
by law in Judaism 111, 165-167, 242n117
equality of Jew and Gentile in 17, 72, 134, 153, 159, 161, 202, 204, 208, 212, 213, 279, 285, 290, 291
of Abraham 164, 182, 185, 189, 202

of Gentiles 152, 154, 156, 162, 187, 188, 190, 204, 294, 295
of the ungodly 185, 185n127, 186, 196
universality of 42, 158, 211, 249

Justification by faith 2n9, 3n10, 10, 18, 36, 154, 155, 162, 163, 171, 175, 176, 184, 240, 292, 294
as theme of Romans 2, 18, 155
doctrine of 10, 103, 154, 154n4, 162, 202, 292

Knowledge
of God available to Jews 74, 87, 87n45, 89, 148
of God possessed by Gentiles 89
of God refused by Gentiles 88, 93, 94
of God refused by Jews 79, 86-93, 149, 151, 293
of God through creation 86, 87, 87n44, 89n52, 93

Law (*see also* Requirement of the law; Torah; Works of the law) 70, 85, 88, 110, 110n125, 157, 161, 165, 167, 168n6, 193, 195, 207n2, 211-214, 241-243, 242n117, 118, 243n124, 289, 305
as a fence between Jew and Gentile 209
bringing knowledge of sin 139n253
causing division between Jew and Gentile 157, 209
Gentiles not having 89, 110, 111, 114n145, 170, 213
given to the Jews 55, 74, 87, 87n45, 88, 88n47, 93, 110, 114, 140, 157, 166, 293, 294
giving of 182, 226
in Judaism 161, 166
Jewish boasting in 4, 120, 136, 149, 164, 169-171, 170n67, 179, 294
Jewish breaking of 4, 74, 109, 112, 113n139, 114, 115, 117, 117n159, 120-124, 120n175, 122n180, 126, 149, 151, 167, 170, 227, 293
Jews as teachers of 116n155
kept by believing Gentiles 102, 110-114, 113n138, 125, 125n196, 127, 141n258, 149, 151, 169, 170, 193, 227, 293, 294
no transgression without 94n61
obedience to 111-115, 111n128, 113n138, 139
of faith 170n71
of the Spirit 214
Paul's view of 10, 11
possession of 111, 139n251, 170, 170n67
relationship to salvation 139, 141, 157, 196, 213, 242, 305
written on hearts of believing Gentiles, 102, 110, 113, 113n140

Lord's Supper 226

Love 223n41, 226n53, 116n155, 208n11
brotherly 285, 288, 288n290
of God 43, 63, 180, 187, 208, 213, 223, 248

Mercy (*see* God: mercy of)

Messiah (*see also* Jesus Christ)
acceptance by Jews 268
hope of the Gentiles 65
Jewish 128, 152, 278, 285
rejected by Jews 250, 251n158, 252, 254, 255, 256n175, 260, 261, 261n198, 282n282, 286, 287, 295
ruler over the nations 64, 65
universal messiahship 42n101, 152n300, 227

Mission 94n61, 250-253, 277, 295, 304
Paul's work in 3, 9-12, 11n48, 163n42, 216n6, 220, 246, 265
theology of 9-10n40, 12n49, 30
to Gentiles 13, 15, 28, 34n73, 69, 177, 204, 216, 216n9, 253, 266, 277, 278n264, 287, 292, 297, 302n1

Index of Subjects

thrust reversed 250-253, 251n158, 276, 284, 287
Missionary principle 240, 244, 245
Monotheism 173n83, 175, 175n91, 176, 176n94, 177
Moses 32n65, 34, 40n89, 61, 80, 100, 116n155, 139n250, 169n65, 186n137, 231, 231n68, 238, 242, 243, 249
Murder 88n47, 118, 119, 131
Mystery 8, 66, 66-67n220, 216n6, 221, 272-274, 281, 284, 299, 299n11

Obedience (*see also* Disobedience) 127, 169, 182, 201n206, 212, 242, 247, 261n198
   of Christ 211
   of Israel 178, 261n198, 262, 262n200
Old Testament
   Paul's use of 13, 30-32, 39, 40, 42, 43, 51, 58, 60, 61, 63-65, 136, 138, 139, 142n262, 143, 145, 146, 148, 149, 178, 218, 253, 281, 286, 293-296
   textually and/or contextually modified in Paul 13, 14, 14n51, 30, 32, 35, 59, 59n185, 61, 63, 64, 66, 67, 121, 122, 127, 130, 137, 137n243, 142, 142n262, 143, 143n267, 145, 146-152, 174n86, 183, 184n123, 195, 219, 231n70, 235, 238, 243, 245n134, 246-247n139, 256, 258, 260, 278, 278n265, 284, 286, 294, 295
Olive tree 220, 252, 283, 287, 291, 295

Parousia 7n31, 275, 280
Patriarch 1n3, 9n37, 268, 269, 276
Paul (*see also* Gospel)
   apostolic calling of 1, 9, 10, 12, 28-31, 36, 39, 40, 45, 58, 68-70, 178, 283, 297, 303, 303n4, 304, 306
   appearance of Christ to 1, 26n34, 302-305, 302n1, 303n4
   as apostle to the Gentiles 1, 6, 8, 16, 28, 68, 70, 153, 156, 158, 183, 202, 204, 216, 252, 278n264, 297, 299, 300, 301, 306, 307
   as prophet to the Jews 8, 108, 108n113
   biassed towards Gentiles 5, 151, 206, 285, 293
   boldness of 19, 22-28, 32-37, 36n77, 44, 46, 48, 68, 69, 71, 83, 94, 106, 107, 118, 125, 142, 162, 163, 177, 181, 190, 204, 214, 228, 248, 260, 277, 289, 297
   defender of gospel for Gentiles 5, 10, 12, 15, 16, 190, 197, 203, 239, 240, 297-299, 304, 306, 307
   mission to Gentiles 9, 11-13, 12n49, 15, 26, 28-31, 43, 69, 177, 260, 264-266, 272, 278n264, 283, 284, 303, 303n4 (*see also* Gentile mission)
   missionary work of 7n31, 10, 15, 26n34, 29-31, 43, 70, 204, 266n218, 278n264, 299, 301, 304, 305, 306
   'my gospel' of 9n40, 36n78, 298, 298n8, 299, 302, 303, 307
   obligation to Gentiles 44, 45, 69
   priestly ministry of 7, 16, 25, 31, 44, 46, 289
   primary concern of 5, 48, 69, 263
   self-awareness/ self-consciuosness of being apostle to the Gentiles 2, 6-12, 15-17, 20, 21, 25, 26, 30, 32, 38, 46, 68-70, 72, 73, 93, 103, 108, 110, 140, 150, 152, 153, 156, 161, 163, 177-183, 194, 203, 204, 206, 214, 219, 221, 248, 252, 278, 288, 289, 295, 297, 300, 302, 303n6, 304, 306, 307
   sorrow of 108, 225, 227, 239
   theology of 9-12, 19, 25, 29, 30
Peace (*see also* Reconciliation) 4, 47, 66, 101n89, 106, 107, 208, 209

People of God 6n25, 273n245, 297
  believing Gentiles to be included in 4, 5, 10, 21, 66, 67, 152n300, 218, 224, 286, 289
  Israel as 44, 250
Pharaoh 101, 110n88, 231-233, 231n70, 256n175, 275n253
Pharisees 40n84, 102n91, 116n155, 169, 169n65, 180, 180n117
Praise 60-64, 126, 147, 172, 174n86
  of Gentiles of God 56, 60n191, 61-63, 61n194, 277
Predestination 223, 236, 249, 253, 286, 291, 296
Priority
  in mission 250-253, 267, 276, 296
  of Jews 3, 3n15, 46, 47, 47n124, 48, 48-49n130, 50-52, 67 93n60, 222n39 (see also Jews)
Proclamation 31, 42n101, 174
  of Christ as the gospel 42n101, 46, 298
Promise (see also Promise: of God) 31, 34n73, 40-43, 52-54, 65-68, 107, 113, 114, 121, 123, 127, 132, 154, 160, 161, 162n36, 181-183, 184n122, 187, 189n151, 195, 196, 198, 199, 201n206, 206, 214, 215, 218, 218n22, 226-228, 230, 236, 244, 269, 279, 282, 284, 294
Prophecy 30-34, 40, 61, 65, 127, 235, 236n95, 244, 247
Proselytes 184n125, 194, 196, 263n206
Prostitution
  cultic 85, 86, 91 (see also Immorality)
Punishment 79, 80, 99n83, 106n105, 160, 258, 282n282

Qumran 75n7, 101n89, 167

Ransom 160
Reconciliation (see also Peace) 106n105, 208-210, 210n18, 212, 214, 268

Redemption 66, 160, 222, 250, 250n151
Reformation, the 2
Relationship
  between Jew and Gentile 106n105, 154, 155, 155n5, 168, 174, 207n3, 263n97, 264n212
  between Jews and God 4, 136, 155, 165, 168n60, 169, 172, 172n79, 174, 180, 181, 203, 211, 289, 294
  of Gentiles with God 158, 174, 202, 211
  of Jesus to Jews 2, 289
Remnant 144n270, 228, 237, 238, 238n104, 254, 262n202, 269, 269n234, 281 283, 287 (see also Theology: remnant)
Requirement of the law (see also Law) 112n131, 113, 113n138, 128, 133, 151, 169, 293, 294
Restoration
  cosmic 209, 212
  of Israel (see also Israel: restoration of)
Resurrection (see also Jesus Christ: resurrection of) 62, 267, 267n225, 268, 268n230
Revelation
  general 87
  in creation 87-89, 87n44, 89n52
  to Jews 87, 88
Righteousness (see also Abraham; God: righteousness of; Justification) 136, 146, 161, 189, 214, 225, 241n112, 242n117, 118, 248,
  apart from law 156, 157, 167, 168n60, 189n151, 202, 242, 303n4
  available to Jew and Gentile by faith 140, 158, 161, 163, 171, 244, 244n118, 249, 280, 286, 290
  by works 166, 171, 240, 241, 242n117, 249
  Gentile 128, 158n19, 162, 236, 239, 241, 244, 249, 286, 294

Index of Subjects

Jewish 139, 140, 144, 146, 147, 149, 165, 225
national 165
not possible by works 144, 165, 286

Romans, letter to the
as an ambassadorial letter 93-94n61
expounds justification by faith/righteousness of God? 2, 18, 49, 156
importance of 300, 300nn15-18
interpretative key for 2, 2n9, 13, 16, 18, 18-19n3, 20, 21, 38, 39, 70, 215, 221, 253, 301, 302
occasion and purpose of 14-16
soteriological argument in 2, 7, 9, 12, 17, 20, 69, 70, 204, 205, 289, 297, 300, 302, 304, 307
subject matter of 2, 2n9, 5, 18, 20, 21, 38, 41, 51, 68, 292, 300n18
written boldly 5, 7, 22, 107, 162, 163, 202, 204, 236, 289, 293, 295, 296, 300

Rome 15, 16, 19, 25, 36, 39, 43, 45-47, 107, 108n112, 252, 270, 287, 288, 295

Sacrifice
of Abraham 196n182
of Christ 160, 209
of Christians 25, 44, 203n211
to Baal 82, 120

Salvation (*see also* Justification; Righteousness) 103-105, 104n99, 197, 141n259, 161, 163, 195, 214, 217, 223, 237, 240, 242, 243, 253, 254, 277
by faith 7n30, 12, 20, 41, 50, 108, 140, 171, 196, 202, 240-244, 280-282, 282n281, 287, 292, 301, 306
by grace 196, 261
for Jews and Gentiles alike 10, 69, 240, 251, 259-269, 273, 276, 279, 281, 290
fulfilment of prophecy 65, 67
God's purpose of 157
legitimacy of Gentile 3n10, 15, 20, 21, 28, 31, 32, 35, 37, 41n96, 51, 57, 59n181, 60-69, 73, 104, 108, 110, 140, 151, 162, 165, 171, 183, 190, 197, 202, 204, 211, 219, 226, 240, 244, 248-253, 259-261, 261n198, 265, 265n214, 275, 277, 286, 292, 294, 295, 296, 300, 301, 306
of Jews 33, 35, 49n132, 50, 61-64, 128n214, 140, 222n39, 239, 244, 251, 263, 265, 265n214, 266, 267, 274, 275, 277, 280-284, 287, 289
refused by Jews 3n10, 240

Sanctification 43, 207n3
Sarah 182, 197n183, 198
Servant of Yahweh 31
Shema 168n60, 174, 219
Sin (*see also* Sinfulness) 42, 78, 85n37, 86, 117n159, 163, 165, 207n2, 210, 211-214
Christian freed from 212
of Adam 78, 210, 212
of Jew and Gentile 86, 117, 149, 152n298, 212
universality of 42, 110

Sinfulness (*see also* Sin) 94, 97
Gentile 73, 74, 83, 93n61, 96, 98, 99, 114n146, 134, 139, 141, 152, 167
Israel given over to 89-92, 90n54, 55, 91n56
Jewish 17, 72-74, 82, 85, 92, 93, 95, 97n69, 102n92, 105, 110, 118, 123, 127, 129, 130, 132-135, 133n232, 134n234, 135n236, 138, 138n249, 140, 145, 149-155, 162, 165, 240, 248, 259, 260, 276, 294
Jews and Gentiles equal in 17, 72-152, 141n257, 155, 204-206, 210, 213, 219, 279, 284, 285, 290, 291, 293, 294
universal 72, 83, 93, 94, 104n100, 109, 117, 128, 130, 134-138, 135n236, 137n242, 138n248,

141-143, 145, 149-153, 158, 158n20, 159, 163, 210, 211, 222
Sodom 83n29, 85n37, 85n41, 237-239
Sonderweg for Jews 49n132, 250, 272, 274, 280, 280n273, 281n275, 284, 287, 292, 296
Sonship
  of believers 213, 214, 226, 226n55, 285, 295
Soteriology
  inclusive 68, 206, 297
  Jewish 140
  Paul's 9, 11n45, 150, 302, 306
Status 8n31, 102n92, 116n155, 162n36, 183, 197, 203, 236, 286, 291, 296
  of Jew and Gentile 17, 43, 155, 205-214, 285
Suffering 42n101, 208n11, 213

Temple 26n32, 60n189, 80n23, 85, 118-120, 120n172, 122n182, 123n187, 209n15, 277
Theology
  post-Holocaust 3, 6, 16, 130, 135, 216, 219, 280-282, 285, 292
  remnant 95, 128, 144, 144n270, 228
Timothy 298n8
Torah (*see also* Law) 112, 117n160, 120n171, 157, 164-166, 165n50, 169-171, 170nn66,71, 171n71, 179, 211, 211n25
  fulfilled in faith 170, 170n71
Tübingen School 8

Uncircumcision 115, 124, 187, 188, 190, 190n154, 194, 290, 298, 298n8
  Abraham justified in 184n122, 185, 188, 193, 194, 203n212
  Jews uncircumcised in heart 125, 127
  the uncircumcised as referring to Gentiles 43, 89, 121, 126, 181, 182, 187-190, 192, 194, 290
Ungodly (*see also* Justification) 100n83, 145, 146n280, 184-187, 184n125, 196
Unity 68, 168, 209, 214, 288, 288n289
Universality (*see also* Justification; Sin; Sinfulness) 31, 32n65, 38, 42, 64, 74, 88n47, 138n248, 149, 243

Word (*see also* Faith: word of)
  of God 42, 53, 66, 67, 87, 114, 147, 218, 218n22, 219, 238, 242, 242n122, 286, 295
Works of the Law (*see also* Law) 139, 141, 162, 165-167, 169-171, 179, 181, 202, 241, 242n117, 249
Worship 19, 32, 59, 60, 60n189, 76, 77, 120, 122n182, 209, 227, 274, 277, 291
  idol worship 80, 80nn22-23, 119, 119n170, 120, 254

Zealots 124
Zion 32, 121, 244, 245, 263n206, 278, 284

www.ingramcontent.com/pod-product-compliance
Lightning Source LLC
Chambersburg PA
CBHW071438300426
44114CB00013B/1487